MORMONISM

MORMONISM

A HISTORICAL ENCYCLOPEDIA

W. Paul Reeve and Ardis E. Parshall, Editors

 ABC-CLIO

Santa Barbara, California • Denver, Colorado • Oxford, England

Library of Congress Cataloging-in-Publication Data

Mormonism : a historical encyclopedia / W. Paul Reeve and Ardis E. Parshall, editors.
    p. cm.
  Includes bibliographical references and index.
  ISBN 978-1-59884-107-7 (alk. paper) — ISBN 978-1-59884-108-4 (ebook)
1. Church of Jesus Christ of Latter-Day Saints—History—Encyclopedias. 2. Mormon
Church—History—Encyclopedias. 3. Church of Jesus Christ of Latter-Day Saints—
Biography—Encyclopedias. 4. Mormon Church—Biography—Encyclopedias.
I. Reeve, W. Paul. II. Parshall, Ardis E.
  BX8605.5.M67   2010
  289.3—dc22   2010014518

ISBN: 978-1-59884-107-7
EISBN: 978-1-59884-108-4

14   13   12   11   10   1   2   3   4   5

This book is also available on the World Wide Web as an eBook.
Visit www.abc-clio.com for details.

ABC-CLIO, LLC
130 Cremona Drive, P.O. Box 1911
Santa Barbara, California 93116-1911

This book is printed on acid-free paper ∞

Manufactured in the United States of America

CONTENTS

PREFACE AND ACKNOWLEDGMENTS

From its small beginnings in 1830 in upstate New York to its emergence as an international Church with a presence across the globe in the 21st century, Mormonism has always been a multifaceted living, evolving, faith. The challenge inherent in organizing a single-volume encyclopedia such as this is to capture the contours, nuances, subtleties, complexities, and dynamic aspects of Mormonism, plot change and continuity over time, and provide the reader a strong sense of Mormonism's place in an ever-shifting historical context. We agonized over what to include, what to exclude, and how best to ensure adequate coverage while simultaneously avoiding excessive overlap. Readers will no doubt question the inclusion of some entries and the exclusion of others. This encyclopedia does not pretend to cover all things Mormon and maintains as its focus Mormon history, not doctrine. The reader will of necessity find that aspects of Mormon doctrine and theology infuse this volume, partly because history and theology are tightly intertwined for Mormons but also because a basic understanding of Mormon doctrines is essential to understanding Mormon history. Nonetheless, all entries maintain a historical focus.

With a limited number of biographies, events, and issues allowed, we struggled to decide what to include but ultimately settled upon the entries found herein. Our selections were driven by an effort to best represent as many aspects of Mormonism to the reader as possible. The six era entries cover the span of Mormon history in broad chronological overviews, giving the reader a history of Mormonism from Joseph Smith Jr.'s First Vision, in 1820, to its international reach in the 21st century. Event entries focus upon prominent aspects of Mormon history for which a reader might consult an encyclopedia in the first place.

The biography section was perhaps the most difficult. The prophet-presidents of Mormonism were obvious choices but made gender balance impossible and prevented the inclusion of other deserving individuals. Ultimately, the people we selected (apart from the Church presidents) all represent one or more aspects of Mormonism that are much broader than the individuals themselves. Aurelia Spencer Rogers and LaVern Watts Parmley, for example, are both included for their roles in founding and then shaping the Primary (children's organization) of the Church. Patty Bartlett Sessions represents common (yet uncommon) pioneer Mormon women; Mormon intellectuals (Brigham H. Roberts, James E. Talmage), humanitarians (Lowell L. Bennion), Relief Society leaders (Emma Hale Smith, Eliza R. Snow, Barbara Bradshaw Smith, Emmeline B. Wells, Belle Smith Spafford, Amy Brown Lyman), and historians (Juanita Brooks and Leonard James Arrington) are also represented through biographies.

Issue essays, perhaps the most exciting aspect of this volume, address prevalent themes in Mormon history. They provide historical context and trace change and continuity over time. Essays on Mormonism and women, Mormonism and blacks, local worship, Mormonism and Native Americans, Mormon scripture, genealogy and family history, Church organization and government, Mormonism and secular government, Mormonism and men, Mormonism and family history, and Mormonism and violence are only some of the themes tackled in this section. These essays not only offer readers introductory overviews of their topics but make suggestions for further reading and provocative arguments in their own right. Finally, short sidebar entries on such topics as the Mormon Tabernacle Choir, Brigham Young University, the Extermination Order, and the beloved Mormon hymn "Come, Come Ye Saints" pepper the encyclopedia with fascinating tidbits. The bulk of these unattributed sidebars are the work of Ardis E. Parshall, but Matthew Grow and Blair Hodges also contributed.

Some of the most well respected names in Mormon scholarship are represented here, including Jan Shipps, James B. Allen, Thomas Alexander, Armand Mauss, Kathryn Daynes, Ben Bennion, Richard Turley, Levi Peterson, Lavina Fielding Anderson, Gary Bergera, Mary Lythgoe Bradford, David Knowlton, Jessie Embry, Margaret Blair Young, and Darius Gray. Their reputations speak for themselves, and their contributions here add immeasurably to the quality of this volume. Readers will also find entries by a variety of young, bright, up-and-coming scholars who represent the rising generation of Mormon intellectuals, a clear indication of the field's vitality.

We acknowledge the effort of more than 50 contributors, without whom this volume would not exist.

—*W. Paul Reeve and*
Ardis E. Parshall

Seeking a place where they could practice their religion in peace, the Mormons moved as a body several times from 1830 to 1847.

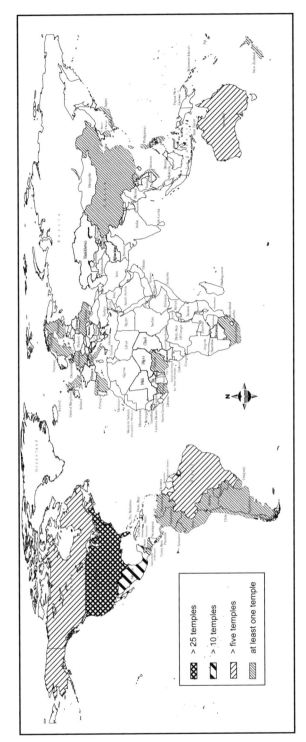

One indication that Mormonism has become a religion with a global reach at the beginning of the 21st century is the location of its temples. Each temple represents the church's maturity, both in numbers and practice in a given region.

Legend:
- > 25 temples
- > 10 temples
- > five temples
- at least one temple

MORMONISM IN HISTORICAL CONTEXT: AN INTRODUCTION

When Paul Reeve talked with me about writing this introductory essay, he unintentionally reminded me of my advancing age. He asked me to look back over my "long experience" in dealing with the history of Mormonism and reflect on what I have learned. His phrase "long experience" sobered me, but the assignment delighted me, for it would give me chance to comment, however briefly, on two of my favorite themes: (1) change, and (2) the relationship between the Church and what was going on around it—how its historical context affected what happened in the Church and vice versa. Volumes could, and should, be written on all of this, but there is room here to barely touch a few highlights.

When the Church was organized, on April 6, 1830, the chief differences between Mormons and other Christians were Mormons' belief in the Book of Mormon, their acceptance of Joseph Smith as God's prophet, and their belief that God's true priesthood had been restored through Joseph Smith, making their nascent Church the only "true" Church on earth. Such differences were substantial, and, as change occurred over the years, they became even more substantial.

Many changes took place before the death of Joseph Smith. One was simply the Church's name, which migrated from the Church of Christ (though sometimes called the Church of Jesus Christ) when it was founded to the Church of the Latter-day Saints in 1834 to the Church of Jesus Christ of Latter-day Saints in 1838. There were also changes in Church doctrine and practice, mostly the result of the founding prophet's progressive revelations and teachings. The Church's organizational structure was likewise altered. These changes were not necessarily contradictions of earlier doctrines and practices but simply the unfolding of new concepts and structure.

After Joseph Smith's death and the Church's move to the Great Basin, the changes continued. Before the end of the century, both priesthood organization and local administrative structure were transformed. The "gathering," the practice of urging converts to emigrate from Europe and elsewhere to be with the body of the Saints in Utah, came to an end as Saints were advised to stay in their own countries and build up "Zion" there. Various unusual practices, such as baptism for health, were abandoned. Most significant, however, was the practice of plural marriage, which began with Joseph Smith but officially ended with the issuance of the "Manifesto" in 1890.

In the 20th century, changes came at a seemingly increasing pace. Many were the result of sheer growth in numbers and the dramatic explosion of worldwide membership in the second half of the century, though some were also related to Mormonism's response to and interaction with its broader environment. They included numerous organizational and administrative adjustments, elimination of some programs and the addition of others, changes in missionary policies and methods, and, most important, the opening of the priesthood to men of black African ancestry.

During all this time, the history of the Church was inevitably affected by the world around it, especially its American context. Traditional Church histories, especially those written before 1950, have sometimes recognized this, but often that recognition has been perfunctory, not going far enough to provide readers with a real appreciation of how much and how often the American context helped mold the course of Mormon history.

The relationship between American history and the story of Mormonism seems evident on every hand. Nothing could be more American than the ancestry of the Church's founder, Joseph Smith. He was a sixth-generation New Englander on his father's side and fifth-generation on his mother's. His grandparents were avid supporters of the American Revolution, and he grew up in a religious home steeped in Puritan values.

The Smith family's move to western New York, in 1816, was part of an early American westward movement: the transplanting of thousands of New Englanders to that same area in search of better economic opportunity. The Smiths were simply moving with the tide as they settled in the place where young Joseph would have his early religious experiences and organize the Church.

The founding episode in Mormon history was Joseph Smith's grand epiphany; in response to deep concerns for his own spiritual well-being, he received a vision of the Father and the Son. The catalyst for this experience was the intense revivalism that spread across America as part of the Second Great Awakening. With some important exceptions, his experience had similarities to those of other young men and women of the time who became "convicted of their sins," sought divine mercy and forgiveness, and told of dramatic religious experiences in which, some said, they received redemption and a manifestation of Jesus Christ. Joseph's experience is covered in more detail in the first essay in this volume, "Foundation: 1820–1830."

Early America was the seedbed for a variety of new religious movements. Some, including the Disciples of Christ, or Campbellites, were Christian primitivists, looking forward to the reestablishment of the primitive Christian Church. This was one of Mormonism's attractions. Its claim to be *the* restoration of the ancient Church of Christ appealed to many who felt that the Churches they knew did not fully comport with that of the New Testament. The rapid growth of Mormonism was strongly influenced by this historic context, especially after a primitivist Campbellite minister, Sidney Rigdon, and most of his congregation joined the Church in Ohio.

The Book of Mormon, an account of certain inhabitants of ancient America who were visited by Jesus Christ himself, also fit an American pattern. The main group of people in the book were Israelites and were among the ancestors of the American Indians. The Book of Mormon was, at least in part, directed toward persuading the Indians of this and converting them to Christ. But the idea that the Indians were descended from the tribes of Israel was not new in America. Among the popular books that made this claim were Elias Boudinot's *A Star in the West,* published in 1816, and Ethan Smith's *View of the Hebrews,* first published in 1823 and appearing in a second edition in 1825. Thus, the Book of Mormon's claim that the Indians were descended from the Hebrews would have fit a perspective already held by many Americans. So would other aspects of the Book of Mormon, for several of its doctrinal pronouncements seemed to deal with, or answer, some of the controversial religious issues of the day. In addition, the most powerful of all its messages concerned the divinity and atoning sacrifice of Jesus Christ. In that sense, the Book of Mormon fit well into Christian orthodoxy. Significantly, it was the Book of Mormon, not the story of Joseph Smith's First Vision (which was not even in print until the 1840s), that persuaded the earliest converts.

The early westward movement of the Church was directly influenced by American primitivism, American Indian policy, and the Mormon counterpart of efforts by many American clergymen to convert the Indians to Christianity. Less than a year after the organization of the Church, four missionaries were sent to work among Native Americans located west of Missouri. They were there because of a tragic American Indian policy that forcefully relocated many eastern tribes west of Missouri and Arkansas. One of the missionaries, Parley P. Pratt, was a former member of the primitivist Disciples of Christ. On the way to Missouri, the missionaries passed through Mentor, Ohio, where Pratt was instrumental in converting his former pastor, Sidney Rigdon, along with many members of his congregation. Rigdon, in turn, traveled to Palmyra, New York, and helped persuade Joseph Smith to relocate, along with his followers, to Ohio. Meanwhile, the four missionaries went on to western Missouri. Largely unsuccessful in the mission to the Indians, partly because of opposition from Christian missionaries already there, they converted a few people in Jackson County and began to prepare the way for the arrival of Joseph Smith. He had been told in a revelation that this area would be another gathering place for the Saints and, eventually, the location of Zion, or the New Jerusalem. Before long, thousands of Mormons would gather in both Ohio and Missouri.

Other developments in early Mormonism fit nicely into its American setting. The United Order was the Mormon counterpart of the numerous communal experiments that characterized the period. The "Word of Wisdom," revealed to Joseph Smith in 1833, required, among other things, abstinence from "hot drinks" (interpreted as tea and coffee), alcohol, and tobacco. It no doubt struck a familiar note to most Mormons, for, at the time, there were thousands of local temperance societies in America, including one in Kirtland, Ohio, where the Prophet lived. Other kinds of health reform were also popular. Joseph Smith must have been familiar with them and pondered them before he prayed about the matter and received his revelation.

Serious internal dissent among the Mormons, as well as persecution in this era, also reflected the larger American scene. In Ohio, the failure of the Mormon banking enterprise was related to the nationwide panic of 1837. The result was economic distress for Joseph and many of his followers and the onset of such bitter dissent among the Kirtland Saints that Joseph was forced to leave. At the same time, violent persecution dogged the Saints in Missouri and soon drove them from the state. One factor in that persecution was the unfounded fear in Missouri, a slave state, that Mormons were abolitionists. Later, the Mormons were driven from Nauvoo, Illinois. Though more intense and consequential than the harassment practiced against others, the persecution of the Mormons was not unprecedented in America. Particularly in the mid-1830s, riots, vigilante terrorism, and other forms of violent hostility involved persecution of Catholics, Masons, Mormons, and various immigrant groups who were charged by nativists with anti-American activities and, in the case of Irish Catholics, political loyalty to the Pope instead of to America. Even the persecution of the Mormons had a semi-nativist element, as they were accused of being treasonously subservient to Joseph Smith and his political kingdom rather than loyal to America.

Their constant harassment and their eventual expulsion from the nation itself in 1846 caused some Mormons in mid-century to express disgust with the American government and to rejoice at the idea of its eventual demise and the consequent establishment of the Kingdom of God on Earth with Christ at its head. Despite such rumblings, however, Latter-day Saints considered themselves true Americans in the most positive sense. Like most of their contemporaries, they revered the U.S. Constitution as God-given. Joseph Smith called it a "glorious standard" and a "heavenly banner" (Smith, *History* 3:304) and one of his revelations declared that the Lord himself had "established the Constitution of this land, by the hands of wise men whom I raised up unto this very purpose" (Doctrine and Covenants 101:80).

Some of Joseph Smith's concerns were related to the constitutional question of states' rights, one of the most complex and controversial political issues of the day. In 1832–1833, the United States came close to civil war after South Carolina exercised its presumed right to nullify a law of Congress by nullifying the hated tariff acts of 1828 and 1832 and refusing to allow federal tariffs to be collected within its borders. Convinced that no state had such a right under the Constitution, President Andrew Jackson was ready to send troops into South Carolina to enforce the law, until the problem was solved by a compromise tariff. Joseph Smith, meanwhile, kept his own eye on the controversy and supported Jackson's actions. Like Jackson, he had little sympathy for the right South Carolina claimed under the doctrine of states' rights. It was in this context that, in December 1832, he received a revelation known as his "Prophecy on War." Clearly based on what was happening in South Carolina, it foretold the eventual outbreak of civil war and is still cited by Mormons as evidence of Joseph's prophetic prowess.

However, states' rights went deeper than the tariff controversy. During the Missouri persecutions, the Mormons twice requested President Jackson to send federal troops to help them regain their property. Jackson refused both times, on the grounds that the Constitution gave the government no authority to intervene in such internal affairs except at the request of the state legislature or the governor. No such request was forthcoming from Missouri, and the Mormons were eventually expelled from the state. This resulted in Joseph Smith's trip to Washington, D.C., in 1840, during which he asked President Martin Van Buren as well as a congressional committee for heavy financial compensation. He was turned down, not only because the Mormons were unpopular but also because of possible constitutional issues with respect even to that kind of help. The matter continued to fester with the Prophet, so much so that in 1843 he declared with disgust that "The State rights doctrines are what feed mobs. They are a dead carcass—a stink, and they shall ascend up as a stink offering in the nose of the Almighty" (Smith, *History* 6:95). Despite his adulation of the Constitution, he finally realized that in this case it would not work for him.

The following year, Joseph Smith decided to run for the office of president of the United States, but only after writing five leading candidates and asking what their course of action toward the Mormons would be if they were elected. Only three replied, one refusing to state a position, another with a terse comment that he did not see what power the president had over such matters, and the third, John C. Calhoun, repeating what he had told Joseph Smith in Washington in 1840, that "the case does not come within the jurisdiction of the Federal Government, which is one of limited and specific powers" (Smith, *History* 6:155–156).

The Mormon prophet felt that he had no choice but to present himself as a candidate. His campaign began in mid-May 1844. His political tract, carried around the country by hundreds of missionaries, dealt with all the major issues of the day: governmental reform, economic reform, the creation of a national bank, prison reform, slavery, westward expansion, and states' rights. On that issue he called for a constitutional amendment that would give the president "full power to send an army to suppress mobs, and the States authority to repugn that relic of folly which makes it necessary for the governor of a state to make the demand of the President for troops, in case of invasion or rebellion" (Smith, *History* 6:206). In some respects, his proposal foreshadowed the Fourteenth Amendment, which prohibited any state from depriving anyone of "life, liberty, or property, without due process of law; nor deny to any person within its jurisdiction the equal protection of the laws." By implication, the national government could intervene to enforce these provisions.

Joseph Smith probably knew that he had no chance to win the election. Rather, his campaign was an effort to show Americans that he was truly a part of their political mainstream. However, he was murdered just five weeks after his campaign began.

As the Mormons left Nauvoo, in 1846, and then pushed on to the Great Basin, in 1847, they became part of the vast westward movement already taking place. They had carefully studied maps of the Great Basin published earlier by John C. Fremont. They followed already well-known routes to the West, including the Oregon Trail from Iowa to Fort Bridger and then the trail blazed into the Salt Lake Valley in 1846 by the ill-fated Donner Party. In addition, in 1846 the U.S. War with Mexico began, and 500 Saints joined the Army of the West that was on its way to secure for the United States the Mexican territory known as California. That territory included the Great Basin. Thus, the American westward movement, the Oregon Trail, the War with Mexico, the explorations of John C. Fremont, and the knowledge of the Great Basin obtained from mountain men such as Jim Bridger all influenced the course of Mormon history.

At the same time, in a kind of symbiotic relationship, the Mormons had an impact on American history. Members of the Mormon Battalion blazed the trail from Santa Fe to San Diego and constituted the occupation forces in San Diego. After they were mustered out, some members of the unit went to work for John Sutter and were the actual discoverers of gold at Sutter's mill. The gold rush that followed was stimulated, in part, by Sam Brannan, a Mormon who arrived in California by ship, refused to go back to the Salt Lake Valley, and settled in San Francisco. It was his newspaper that got the word about gold out to the rest of the nation. During the gold rush of 1849, the Mormons in Salt Lake City both helped and profited from the gold seekers. They helped by selling much-needed supplies and fresh horses to the hard-pressed California-bound migrants. They profited by charging inflated prices for things the gold seekers needed and by obtaining at depressed prices various items that the gold seekers wanted to unload in order to hasten their journey.

The Mormon experience influenced and was influenced by its American context in other ways. The tens of thousands of immigrants who came to the Territory of Utah were a distinctive part of the massive European immigration that helped build America and settled much of the West. The Mormon settlements in the Great Basin filled in a region that otherwise might not have been effectively settled for decades. The Mormons were there to provide riders for the Pony Express, and they provided the labor to construct a major portion of the Central Pacific's share of the transcontinental railroad, which met up with the Union Pacific in the Territory of Utah in 1869. Mormon polygamy became part of the American scene as it attracted wide attention and led to all kinds of social commentary, legislative battles, and legal decisions that are still in force. As Sarah Barringer Gordon has observed, "the conflict over polygamy became the preoccupation of novelists, journalists, political cartoonists, and newspaper editors, clerics, lecturers, lobbyists, woman's rights activists, political theorists, missionaries, state and national politicians, criminal defendants and their families, constitutional and criminal defense lawyers, federal and territorial officials, presidents, and Supreme Court justices." In the end, she demonstrated, "the contours of the law of church and state in America, as well as the limits of local sovereignty, were forever changed by the battle over polygamy" (Gordon, *The Mormon Question* 1, 238).

As the Mormons entered the 20th century, much was changing for them, including their relationship with the rest of America. Polygamy was discontinued, Utah had been admitted as a state, and there was a kind of political reconciliation with the nation. The old territorial political parties, one dominated by the Church and the other by those unfriendly to the Church, had been abandoned, and, at the urging of Church leaders, the Mormons had somewhat unevenly divided themselves between the two national parties. Economically, they were moving away from the various communal and cooperative enterprises promoted by the Church in the 19th century and aligning more fully with American capitalism.

The Mormons also took more interest in American politics and often demonstrated that, in contrast to their position in the 19th century, they were no longer always politically unified. During the national controversy over the League of Nations, some General Authorities publicly opposed it, while other leaders, including the president of the Church, publicly supported it. In the 1930s, Church leaders strongly urged Utahns (who were still mostly Mormons) to reject the 21st Amendment, which repealed prohibition. To their chagrin, however, Utah became the 33rd, and deciding, state to vote for the amendment.

Mormon leaders refused to endorse particular parties or candidates, but at times they took a proactive stance on public issues that they considered to be issues of morality. One of the most controversial was the proposed Equal Rights Amendment to the U.S. Constitution. An official statement, issued by the First Presidency in October 1976, recognized the need to remedy the injustices faced by American women before the law but opposed the ERA as the means to reach that objective. Mormons were still divided, but Church influence had a great deal to do with the defeat of the amendment in Utah. It also helped in other states, including Florida, Virginia, and Illinois, where Latter-day Saints worked effectively with other groups to defeat it.

On other public issues, Church leaders opposed legalized abortion and gambling, called for stronger measures against child abuse, urged parental control of sex education, and exhorted members to become involved in efforts to stop the spread of pornography. They also opposed gay marriage. In 2008, the Church was instrumental in defeating California's Proposition 8, which would have legalized gay marriage in that state. It was both commended and criticized for its actions, but the point here is simply that this is another example of how in modern times the Church was affected by, and often affected in return, what was happening in the broader society.

One result of the gradual reconciliation between the Mormons and America at the beginning of the 20th century was that several Mormons became prominent in American economics and politics. These included industrialist David Eccles, his son Marriner Eccles, Senator Reed Smoot (a Mormon apostle), Elbert D. Thomas, James H. Moyle, Edgar B. Brossard, and J. Reuben Clark Jr. The activities of such people did not mean that the Mormons immediately became popular, but at least Mormons' national image gradually became more positive and Mormons began to play important roles in the progress of American history. As the century progressed, such contributions became more frequent. Mormons from various states were regularly elected to Congress. A Mormon apostle, Ezra Taft Benson, served as secretary of agriculture under President Dwight D. Eisenhower. Mormons were appointed to other cabinet positions, the federal judiciary, ambassadorial posts, and positions at all levels of the national government. In addition, young Mormons who had served as missionaries in foreign countries were heavily recruited, because of their linguistic skills, by various government agencies dealing with national security and international affairs.

At the same time, the Church itself continued to be affected by what was going on around it. World War I presented a new kind of dilemma, for this was the first time that substantial numbers of Mormons fought on both sides of such a conflict. The Church's response to this perplexity came in a statement by the president of the Church in April 1917. Encouraging American Saints not to think ill of their German counterparts, he declared that "their leaders are to blame, not the people. Those who embrace the gospel are innocent of these things and they ought to be respected by the Latter-day Saints everywhere" (as quoted in Allen and Leonard, *Story of the Latter-day Saints* 493). World War II led to the founding of the Church's servicemen's program. After the war, Church leaders took a political stance against the proposed idea of universal military training. In the 1930s, the exigencies of the Great Depression led to the founding of what is now the Church's highly acclaimed welfare program.

The Church was also unavoidably influenced by the intellectual secularism of the world around it, particularly when secular learning and religious faith appeared to clash. One of the most knotty issues was the theory of organic evolution, which, by the early 20th century, was causing burning controversy within many faiths. In November 1909, the First Presidency responded by publishing a statement entitled "The Origin of Man." Though it reaffirmed certain basic doctrines, including the idea that Adam was "the first man," the question of how Adam and Eve were created was not discussed. A later statement mentioned several possibilities but strongly cautioned Church members that these were "questions not fully answered in the revealed word of God" (as quoted in Allen and Leonard, *Story of the Latter-day Saints* 487). In effect, Church leaders stood on safe ground by straddling this secular challenge, a policy that still continues.

Among the countless changes in the patterns of American life in the 20th century was the profound alteration in the role of women. In traditional Mormonism, as in America, the husband was the "head of the house" as well as the bread winner, and women stayed home to care for the house and children. However, after World War II, two-income families became commonplace, partly out of need but also because many married women also longed for and found great personal enrichment as they made a variety of professional contributions. Like their counterparts in the broader society, Mormon women became more deeply involved in business, law, medicine, and all the other professions, and the proportion of women involved in higher education, including graduate schools, jumped dramatically. Church leaders continued to stress traditional values, but they also began more frequently to emphasize the broader concept of parenthood, which included more serious consideration of the role of fathers.

Church leaders placed heavy emphasis on the idea that, even though the husband was the titular head of the house, he was not the boss. Husband and wife were to share responsibility and decision making equally. In these and many other ways, the attitude toward women at the end of the 20th century and the role of women in the Church were very different from those that prevailed a century earlier.

In the second half of the 20th century, the Church experienced unprecedented numerical growth, saw rapid expansion outside North America, and adopted numerous administrative and program changes. As individuals, however, the Saints faced new challenges that could hardly be solved by structural and procedural changes alone. Traditional moral and ethical teachings were challenged by new and seemingly more alluring enticements that affected the spiritual wellbeing of everyone, especially youth. These included rampant sexual permissiveness, changing ethical values, drug abuse, and pornography. The continuing challenge for the Church was to see that such enticements did not divert its youth in wrong directions. In addition, as the Church grew more rapidly than ever before in Asia, Latin America, and Africa, as well as among the diverse cultural and ethnic groups in the United States itself, many long-time Saints were forced to reexamine traditional attitudes toward other races and cultures. Could traditional white, American-born, Wasatch Front Latter-day Saints fully and sincerely accept those of other races and cultures, including blacks, as brothers and sisters in the fullest sense? To what degree, if any, must the Church adapt its policies in order to ensure that people of all cultures felt fully accepted? Or, as some people asked, what traditional LDS policies, practices, and teachings were essential to the gospel, and which ones were merely convenient and subject to change? Such questions are still being answered, but, in 1971, Elder Bruce R. McConkie, then a member of the First Quorum of the Seventy, anticipated some aspects of the future. He reminded American Mormons that in New Testament times even the apostles found it difficult to take the gospel to the gentile nations and then applied the lesson to the modern Church. "There are going to be some struggles and some difficulties, some prejudices, and some uncertainties along the way," he foretold, but he called upon the American Saints to rise above their biases, as the apostles of old rose above theirs. Other peoples, he said, "have a different background than we have, which is of no moment to the Lord [!] . . . It is no different to have different social customs than it is to have different languages. . . . And the Lord knows all languages" (as quoted in Allen and Leonard, *The Story of the Latter-day Saints* 559–560).

In that spirit, Church leaders emphasized the vision of an international, worldwide Church in which people of all nations, races, and cultures could act as brothers and sisters in the truest sense of Christ's teachings. A major step in that direction was President Spencer W. Kimball's revelation in June 1978. Prior to that time, men of black African descent could not hold the priesthood, and, therefore, neither they nor their wives and families could enjoy all the blessings of the Church, including temple activity. The new revelation immediately opened the priesthood to all worthy male

Latter-day Saints, regardless of race. This was the pivotal event of the 20th century. It brought the Church even more fully into the American mainstream and made it possible for the Church to expand its missionary force into black Africa. Whereas there were no members in the West African nations in 1950, there were more than 146,000 members and two temples there in 2008. But the revelation was pivotal not just because faithful black Church members could now enjoy everything the Church had to offer or because it opened the way for dramatic Church growth in Africa; it was important because of what it did to build closer bonds of love and brotherhood within the Church and across racial barriers.

The dramatic worldwide growth of Mormonism after 1950 is illustrated by a few statistics. Between 1950 and 2008, Church membership grew from about 1.1 million to more than 13.5 million. In 1950, there were 180 organized stakes (the basic unit of Church organization, usually consisting of 5 to10 wards, or congregations), about 47 percent of them in Utah. In 2008, there were 2,849 organized stakes, 49 percent of them outside the United States. In 1950, the Church was organized in fewer than 50 nations or territories, but by the end of 2008 it was present in around 170. In 1950, some 7.7 percent of the population of the Church lived outside the United States and Canada, but by 2008 this figure had changed to nearly 50 percent. During that same period the Church's full-time missionary force jumped from fewer than 6,000 to nearly 53,000. In 1950, most missionaries received minimal training as they spent 10 days or so in a mission home in Salt Lake City. In 2008, they received intensive language and missionary training in 15 missionary training centers around the world. In 1950, the Church operated 8 temples, all but one located in the United States; in 2008, there were 129 in operation, more than half of which were outside the United States.

At least in part, America was a catalyst for the international spread of Mormonism, for the American presence actually paved the way for missionaries in some areas. World War II brought American military personnel into the Philippines. Among them were Mormons, who conducted the first Mormon meetings and paved the way for missionaries. Likewise, during the Korean War, it did not take the Mormon service- men long to organize, begin to hold meetings, and, in some cases, privately engage in missionary work. The result was the baptism of a few military buddies but also the baptism of the first Korean members. In Italy, an American Latter-day Saint working for Lockheed in Torino was asked to serve as the Church's servicemen's coordina- tor in the area and to serve as "district president." He and other Americans who were asked to work with him became the nucleus of the Church in Italy as they assisted in fellowshipping new converts made by the missionaries just assigned to that country. In other countries, also, including Japan, it was the American presence that helped open the way for American Mormons to begin their missionary work.

Another outside force that had a vast effect on the Church and its programs was technological development. In the 19th century, the perfection of the steamship and the completion of the transcontinental railroad changed the operation of the Church's immigration program. Beginning in the 1950s, the jet airplane changed the nature of travel, eventually resulting in the Church establishing its own travel department. As new developments in communication came along, the Church harnessed the telegraph, then the telephone, then radio, then television, and then the computer and the Internet to enhance its communication with its burgeoning worldwide membership. The computer and the Internet also affected the Church's record-keeping program (including financial records) and completely changed the way Church members went about one of their most pressing responsibilities, family history and genealogical research.

Inevitably, television and the Internet brought undesirable things, such as pornography, requiring Church leaders to add a new dimension to their preaching—continual and forceful warnings against letting such things into the home and/or tampering with them in any way. At the same time, leaders welcomed new technology as a blessing from the Lord because of the positive things it could do for the burgeoning Church. In 1950, the full impact of technology would have been almost impossible for the people of today's younger generation to imagine.

Over the years, the Church has changed in many ways, and so has the way its history has been presented. Beginning around 1950, Mormon as well as non-Mormon scholars asked new questions, approached topics seldom if ever dealt with in earlier histories, and integrated Mormon history more fully with the broader American scene. Some saw Mormonism as something more significant than just a new religious movement of the early 19th century. Rather, they saw it as having consequences for American history or as providing valuable insight into some broad historical theme.

The result was a stunning rise in the total number of books, articles, theses, and dissertations dealing with Church history. A glance at the remarkable online bibliography found at http://mormonhistory.byu.edu illustrates the point. This bibliography attempts to list and index all books, articles, theses, and dissertations on Mormon history produced since the founding of the Church. As of mid-July 2009, it listed 856 items produced in the 19th century, 2,347 items from 1900 to 1950, 13,240 from 1951 to 2000, and 2,666 items from 2001 to mid-July 2009. If that pace keeps up, nearly 15,000 titles will be produced between the years 2001 and 2050. It seems likely, however, that the pace will accelerate. The scholarly *Journal of Mormon History,* for example, was founded in 1974 and struggled to obtain enough funding as well as enough scholarly articles to produce one volume a year, but by 2009 it was issuing four volumes a year and the editors had a plethora of articles from which to choose. In addition, articles on Mormon history continued to appear with increasing frequency in other scholarly journals, including prominent national journals.

There is no space here to itemize the books and articles that have attempted to integrate Mormon history with its historical context, but a few of the most prominent examples, listed chronologically, may suffice. One of the first scholars to integrate early Mormon history with an important aspect of the American scene was Whitney R. Cross, who included a chapter on the Mormons in his *The Burned-Over District: The Social and Intellectual History of Enthusiastic Religion in Western New York* (Ithaca, NY: Cornell University Press, 1950). The University of Utah's William Mulder quipped, in a 1957 article, "The Mormons and American History," that Mormonism "is as native to the United States as Indian corn and the buffalo nickel" (Mulder, "Mormons in American History," 60). Mulder's contributions also included studies of Mormon immigration in their broader context. Thomas F. O'Dea's *The Mormons* (Chicago: University of Chicago Press, 1957) was a sociological study of Mormon origins and values. Beginning with his 1960 Yale Ph.D. dissertation, "The Development of Mormon Communitarianism, 1826–1845," Mario De Pillis studied Mormon communitarianism in its larger context. Milton V. Backman placed Mormonism in the context of American religion in general with his 1965 book *American Religions and the Rise of Mormonism* (Salt Lake City, UT: Deseret Book). A prominent American history textbook, first published in 1977, included a section titled "Mormonism as a Test Case" within a chapter on the nature of and limits on dissent in the period 1820–1860 (Bailyn et al., *The Great Republic,* 532–541). In 1980, Timothy L. Smith published an article titled "The Book of Mormon in a Biblical Culture" (*Journal of Mormon History* 7 [1980], 3–21), which showed that the Book of Mormon appealed to Americans because of its strong biblical overtones and, in fact, its literal support of the Bible. Klaus J. Hansen's *Mormonism and the American Experience* (Chicago: University of Chicago Press, 1981) argued that, by the end of the 19th century, Mormonism had transformed itself from a radical, idiosyncratic movement into a pillar of modern Americanism. Mormon polygamy was placed in context by Lawrence Foster in two major books, *Religion and Sexuality: Three American Communal Experiments in the Nineteenth Century* (New York: Oxford University Press, 1981) and *Women, Family, and Utopia: Communal Experiments of the Shakers, the Oneida Community, and the Mormons.* (Syracuse, NY: Syracuse University Press, 1991). In 1985, Jan Shipps published *Mormonism: The Story of a New Religious Tradition* (Urbana: University of Illinois Press). Widely hailed as one of the most brilliant books yet written on the Church, it not only shed new light on Mormon history itself but also explored in depth the way the Church fit into, or contrasted with, the American religious tradition. In his important 1989 book *The Democratization of American Christianity* (New Haven, CT: Yale University Press), Nathan O. Hatch spent several pages describing Mormonism as one of the appealing mass movements of the early republic. In 2002, Sarah Barringer Gordon looked at the antipolygamy movement in the 19th century not just as a concerted attack on the Mormons but, more important for American history, as a milestone in legislative and judicial history. Her book *The Mormon Question: Polygamy and Political Conflict in Nineteenth-Century America* (Chapel Hill: University of North Carolina Press) received well-deserved kudos as a pivotal event in both Mormon history and American legal history. In 2004, Teryl Givens published

The Latter-day Saint Experience in America (Westport, CT: Greenwood Press), in which he dealt extensively with the American context. Chapter 5 of this work considered the Mormon engagement with political and social issues in modern America. Two years later, Givens published his especially remarkable *People of Paradox: A History of Mormon Culture* (New York: Oxford University Press), which moved in important new directions as he went into more depth, viewing Mormon culture and religious thought in the context of the broader American and world scenes. In 2009, Givens, along with Reid L. Neilson, edited *Joseph Smith: Reappraisals after Two Centuries* (New York: Oxford University), which included important essays by 15 scholars (some Mormon and some non-Mormon), several of which also placed Mormonism in a larger context.

Mormonism in its American historical context has been considered with increasing frequency at scholarly conventions and in various scholarly journals. Of particular importance are the Tanner Lectures, presented at the annual meeting of the Mormon History Association. Since 1980, each year a well-known non-Mormon scholar whose specialty is not Mormon history has been invited to spend a year studying Mormon history and then to present a lecture from the perspective of his or her own specialty. The results have been both fascinating and important, and most have been published in *The Journal of Mormon History.* The first 21 lectures are now available in book form in *The Mormon History Association's Tanner Lectures: The First Twenty Years,* edited by Dean L. May and Reid L. Neilson (Urbana: University of Illinois Press, 2006). The initial Tanner lecture, Gordon Wood's "Evangelical America and Early Mormonism," effectively set the tone for looking at the American context. Mormonism, Wood said, was "born at a peculiar moment in the history of the United States, and it bears the marks of that birth. Only the culture of early nineteenth-century evangelical America could have produced it. And through it we can begin to understand the complicated nature of that culture" (Wood, "Evangelical America" 386).

The challenge now is to deal effectively with an even broader picture: Mormonism in its worldwide context. Numerous books and articles have presented the history of the Church, or part of it, in various countries, and some have done a fine job of placing it in the historic context of those countries. We look forward to more and, eventually, to a scholarly synthesis of the story of Mormonism not just as an American religion but also as a world religion and how world events have helped shape its history.

The Church will continue to face a multitude of challenges as what happens in America and the world continues to impinge upon it. But when I look back upon my "long years" of experience with Mormon history, as Paul Reeve so delicately asked me to do, I see some remarkable things. I have seen the Church change in many ways. I have also seen the nature of Church history change for the good. Historians of Mormonism, whether Church members or not, meet on common ground as they continue to ask new questions, share new insights into the past, and recognize the importance of historic context in what they write. Just as I am optimistic about the future of the

Church, I am optimistic about the future of its history. The fact that this book is published by a major American press, one not connected with the Church, only feeds that optimism.

—James B. Allen

References

Allen, James B., and Glen M. Leonard. *The Story of the Latter-day Saints,* 2nd ed. Salt Lake City, UT: Deseret Book, 1992.

Bailyn, Bernard, et al. *The Great Republic.* Lexington, MA: D. C. Heath, 1977.

Doctrine and Covenants of the Church of Jesus Christ of Latter-day Saints. Salt Lake City, UT: The Church of Latter-day Saints, 1981.

Gordon, Sarah Barringer. *The Mormon Question: Polygamy and Political Conflict in Nineteenth-Century America.* Chapel Hill: University of North Carolina Press, 2002.

Mulder, William. "The Mormons in American History." *Utah Historical Quarterly* 27 (January 1959): 59–77.

Smith, Joseph, Jr. *History of the Church of Jesus Christ of Latter-day Saints.* 6 vols. Ed. B. H. Roberts. Salt Lake City, UT: The Church of Jesus Christ of Latter-day Saints, 1973.

Wood, Gordon S. "Evangelical America and Early Mormonism." *New York History* 61 (October 1980): 359–386.

Eras

Foundation: 1820–1830

Joseph Smith Jr., founder of the Church of Jesus Christ of Latter-day Saints, could not help being affected as a youth by the religious fervor of the Second Great Awakening. Beginning about 1790 and lasting for around 50 years, the Awakening manifested itself in many ways. In some cases, there were intense revivals in which people received visions and Pentecostal-like experiences and conversions. So prevalent was the Awakening in western New York that the area was dubbed the Burned-Over District. During one 12-month period beginning in 1819, revivals took place in at least 10 towns within 20 miles of the Smith home in Palmyra.

Around the age of 12, Joseph Smith became concerned for the welfare of his soul and took to studying the scriptures. He attended revivals and was influenced by them, though he did not succumb to the animated shouting, jumping, and loss of consciousness that some experienced. He later told a friend that, in attending a revival meeting with his mother and sister, he "wanted to feel & shout like the rest" but was unable to do so (Jesse, *Accounts* 25). He soon found himself concerned not only about his personal salvation but about which of the contending Churches, if any, was right. Sometime in the spring of 1820, he determined to follow the biblical admonition "If any of you lack wisdom, let him ask of God, that giveth to all men liberally, and upbraideth not, and it shall be given him" (James 1:5). He retired to a grove of trees near his family's log home and began to pray. Almost immediately, he was nearly overcome by some force that seemed intent on destroying him, but, after he struggled and prayed inwardly, the darkness left, and he beheld an astonishing vision. In a shaft of light, he saw the Father and the Son, both of whom spoke to him. He was told, among other things, that his sins had been forgiven, that he should join none of the Churches of the day, for their doctrines were incorrect, and that at some future time the "fullness of the gospel" would be made known to him. After the vision ended, he wrote later, "my soul was filled with love and for many days I could rejoice with great Joy and the Lord was with me but [I] could find none that would believe the heavenly vision" (Jessee, *Accounts* 7).

It was not uncommon in that religious climate for men and women to report such spiritual experiences, including visions of Christ. Smith, however, received ridicule rather than praise. Accordingly, he soon stopped telling the story, confiding in only a few friends and family members. Twelve years later, he wrote an account of the vision, but he did not prepare a version for publication until 1838.

For three years after the vision, he experienced no further heavenly manifestations. Meanwhile, according to Smith's own account, "I frequently fell into many foolish errors, and displayed the weakness of youth, and the foibles of human nature; which, I am sorry to say, led me into divers temptations." He was guilty not of any "great or malignant sins" but, rather, too much levity and joviality "not consistent with that character which ought to be maintained by one who was called of God as I had been" (Smith, *History* 1:9).

The turning point came three years later. On the night of September 23, 1823, he went to bed and began to pray for forgiveness of his sins as well as for information about his standing before the Lord. Suddenly the room filled with light, and a personage calling himself Moroni appeared. Moroni said that God had a work for Smith to do and then described an ancient record, written on plates of gold and hidden in a hillside not far from the Smith family home. It contained a history of some of America's ancient inhabitants, including the record of a visit to them by the resurrected Jesus Christ. The angel showed Smith in vision where the plates were buried and cautioned that he should show them to no one. Then the angel vanished, only to reappear twice more that night. The angel repeated the same message, adding the caution that Joseph must avoid the temptation to use the plates to acquire wealth.

The next morning, after telling his father, Smith went to the hill (now known as the Hill Cumorah) and found the buried plates, hidden in a stone box, but he was unable to retrieve them. Moroni appeared, chastened him for thoughts of personal gain, and told him that he must return to that spot each year for four years, at which times Moroni would meet and instruct him.

During the next four years, Smith continued to work on his father's farm, as well as other places. He developed a reputation as a village "seer" for his unusual powers of discernment. He possessed a small, smooth, egg-shaped stone, obtained from a well, that he called a seerstone, and he sometimes used it to help friends find buried objects. In the religious and social milieu of the time, many respectable people believed in the use of divining rods and in stone gazing in the search for lost articles and buried treasures. To some people, Smith's early involvement in such folk magic seemed only natural, giving credence in their minds to his story of buried golden plates. By 1827, however, when he finally received the plates, Joseph had abandoned such activity.

During these years, Smith also made many friends who would later prove valuable to the Church he would found. Among them was the family of Joseph Knight Sr., who lived in Colesville, Broome County, New York. Another was Josiah Stowell, who lived in Bainbridge. While working for Stowell, Joseph boarded at the home of Isaac Hale, where he met and fell in love with Isaac's daughter, Emma. However, when the two decided to get married, her parents refused to consent. Emma was 22 years of age, old enough to do as she pleased. The young couple eloped and were married by a justice of the peace on January 18, 1827. They then returned

The Hill Cumorah, near Joseph Smith's Palmyra, New York, home, where he reported finding the plates from which the Book of Mormon was translated. (Courtesy of the Church History Library, The Church of Jesus Christ of Latter-day Saints.)

to Palmyra, where they lived in the Smiths' new frame home and Joseph worked the farm with his father.

In September, the time arrived for Joseph to receive the buried record. Both Josiah Stowell and Joseph Knight Sr. came to visit the Smiths on September 20, and on the morning of September 22 Joseph borrowed Knight's horse and wagon. Taking Emma with him, he drove to the hill where he had met Moroni each year for the past four years. This time Moroni gave him the plates, with a warning not to be neglectful or careless with them or he would be "cut off." He also received a curious instrument called the Urim and Thummim, consisting of "two stones in silver bows" that could be fastened to a breastplate and used in translating the ancient record.

It is not clear exactly how Joseph Smith used the Urim and Thummim or what else may have helped in the translation process, for he left no firsthand account. Various associates left their own descriptions, sometimes slightly conflicting, of the process, but Joseph Smith wrote only that "Through the medium of the Urim and Thummim I translated the record by the gift and power of God" (Smith, *History* 4:537). However, he could not translate all of the record, for a third of it, for some unknown reason, was sealed.

It quickly became known that Smith had, or claimed to have, the golden plates. As a result, he became the target of ridicule and plots to get the plates. Preserving them from thieves and beginning translation was not easy. Former friends and others who thought of the plates as a source of wealth devised various schemes to steal them. Smith often changed their hiding place, sometimes just before the arrival of a mob.

It was not just potential thieves that delayed the translation process. Smith had to earn a living, and he could ill afford to take time away from work. However, he and Emma finally decided to move to Harmony, Pennsylvania, where they could live on property owned by Emma's father and translate in relative peace. Help arrived in the person of Martin Harris, a prosperous farmer in the area, who gave Smith $50 to pay his debts before leaving Palmyra.

In Harmony, Smith finally had time to translate, but the work was slow. As Richard Bushman observed, Smith had to learn the translation process, a challenge that took time (Bushman, *Joseph Smith* 63). In February 1828, Martin Harris arrived, expecting to help with the translation, but Smith soon sent him on a special mission. He was to take a transcript of several characters from the gold plates to a linguist and to attempt to obtain some kind of certification that the characters were genuine and that the translation was authentic. Harris took the transcript to Charles Anthon, a professor of classical studies at Columbia University, in New York. What Anthon actually said about the transcript is not clear, but when Harris returned he was more certain than ever that the plates were authentic. He then went to work helping with the translation, serving as scribe as Joseph dictated.

Something Anthon said to Harris had a significant impact on the way Mormons came to view the Book of Mormon. According to Harris, Anthon signed a paper confirming the authenticity of the characters and their translation but then asked where Smith got the plates. When Harris reported that they came from an angel, Anthon tore up the certificate, saying there was no such thing as ministering angels. He told Harris to bring the plates to him and that he would translate them. Harris replied that the plates could not be shown and that part of the record was sealed. Anthon rejoined, "I cannot read a sealed book." Joseph Smith saw this story as a fulfillment of a biblical prophecy recorded in Isaiah: "And the vision of all is become unto you as the words of a book that is sealed, which men deliver to one that is learned, saying, Read this, I pray thee: and he saith, I cannot; for it is sealed: And the book is delivered to him that is not learned [i.e., Joseph Smith], saying, Read this, I pray thee: and he saith, I am not learned" (Isaiah 29:11–12). Mormons have since used this passage as biblical evidence of the authenticity of the Book of Mormon.

By June 14, 1828, Harris had recorded 116 translated manuscript pages, but then tragedy struck. Convinced that if he showed the manuscript to his unbelieving wife she would change her mind, Harris repeatedly pressured Smith to let him take it home. Smith finally relented, extracting a promise that Harris would show it to five specified people. The next day, June 15, Emma nearly died in childbirth, losing her baby boy in the process. Smith spent the next two weeks caring for Emma but also worrying about the manuscript. Smith went to Palmyra, where he confronted Harris, who sadly confessed that he had shown it to more people than was authorized and that it had disappeared. What happened to the manuscript may never be known, but the loss so shocked Smith that he felt condemned. A revelation chastised him for allowing it to leave his possession; for a time, he lost the power to translate, and the plates were taken from him. The result was a time of anguish and soul-searching, which ultimately strengthened Smith in his resolve to be more careful and more faithful.

The plates and the ability to translate were restored later that summer. However, Smith was told in a revelation that those who took the 116 pages planned to prove Smith a fraud by altering the words of the manuscript. If Smith retranslated and the new manuscript did not agree with the old, his detractors would expose him as a charlatan. Nevertheless, there was an out. The plates actually contained two parallel records. One was a first-person account by the original recordkeeper, an ancient American prophet named Nephi, and a few others. The other was an abridgement by Mormon, the last in a string of recordkeeper/historians of a larger record covering the same period. Joseph had translated from the abridgement, but now he was told to translate from the first-person record. When he began again, Joseph picked up his translation where he had stopped in the abridgement, then, when finished, went back and translated from the first-person account.

The translation, with Emma assisting, proceeded only slowly and intermittently. Then, on April 5, 1829, Oliver Cowdery arrived. This young schoolteacher had boarded at the Smith Sr. home in Palmyra and had become intrigued with what he heard about Joseph. After earnest prayer, he became convinced that Joseph's story was true and insisted on going to Harmony with Joseph's brother Samuel. Cowdery proved a godsend. Two days later, he began transcribing, and, by the end of June, a period of less than 60 days, Smith had translated virtually all of the Book of Mormon.

This two-month period was an exhilarating time, for new revelation and spiritual experiences seemed to pour from heaven as Smith and Cowdery worked. One of the most important events occurred on May 15, when the two men came to a Book of Mormon passage dealing with baptism. They wondered who had the authority to baptize, and they decided to retire to a spot on the banks of the Susquehanna River and pray. What ensued would form the foundation of the Mormon claim to legitimate authority from God to perform baptism and other priesthood ordinances. Smith and Cowdery reported that, as they prayed, a heavenly personage appeared who said that he was John the Baptist, a resurrected being, the same who had baptized Jesus Christ. He announced that his purpose was to restore the long-lost Aaronic Priesthood. He laid his hands upon Smith and Cowdery and conferred upon them that priesthood, which, he said, "holds the keys of the ministering of angels, and of the gospel of repentance, and of baptism by immersion for the remission of sins" (Doctrine and Covenants 13:1). He then instructed them to baptize each other.

The importance of this event, and the later bestowal of the higher or Melchizedek Priesthood authority by Peter, James, and John, cannot be overemphasized when it comes to understanding both the distinctiveness and the spread of early Mormonism. For some converts, it fit beautifully with their quest for a restoration of the "ancient order of things," as expressed by Alexander Campbell, founder of the Disciples of Christ. Scholars have called these people Christian primitivists, for they looked forward to the reestablishment of the primitive Church of Christ. For many converts, the Mormon claim to authentic priesthood authority, traceable directly to God himself, fulfilled what they were looking for. As one non-Mormon historian put it, "Indeed, the origin and whole doctrinal development of Mormonism under the Prophet may be characterized as a pragmatically successful quest for religious authority, a quest that he shared with many other anxious rural Americans of his time, class, and place" (De Pillis, *Quest* 88).

One believer was David Whitmer, who in June moved Smith and Cowdery to his father's home in Fayette, New York, where they completed the translation. Shortly thereafter, Cowdery, David Whitmer, and Martin Harris were told that they would be allowed to see the plates, fulfilling a promise in the Book of Mormon itself that certain witnesses would be given that privilege. These three, along with Joseph Smith, knelt in prayer in the woods near Fayette. Each prayed twice, but with no effect, until Martin Harris withdrew, thinking he might be to blame. The others then knelt again, whereupon, as Smith later related, "we beheld a light above us in the air, of exceeding brightness; and behold, an angel stood before us. In his hands he held the plates which we had been praying for these to have a view of. He turned over the leaves one by one, so that we could see them, and discern the engravings thereon distinctly." They also heard a voice from out of the bright light above them, saying, "These plates have been revealed by the power of God, and they have been translated by the power of God. The translation of them which you have seen is correct, and I command you to bear record of what you now see and hear." Smith then looked for Harris, finding him engaged in fervent prayer. Harris asked Smith to pray with him, which he did, and ultimately the same vision opened and Harris cried out in ecstasy, "Tis enough; tis enough; mine eyes have beheld; mine eyes have beheld." He then jumped up, shouted "Hosanna," and blessed God (Smith, *History* 1:54–55).

The solemn testimony of the three witnesses was placed in the front of the first edition of the Book of Mormon and of every edition thereafter. The Book of Mormon also carries the testimony of eight additional witnesses to whom Smith showed the plates. For Smith, these events were tremendously important, for now he was no longer the only witness. "I feel as if I was relieved of a burden which was almost too heavy for me to bear," he told his mother, "and it rejoices my soul, that I am no longer to be entirely alone in the world" (Smith, *History of Joseph Smith* 154).

The next task was publication, and again Martin Harris was called upon to help. E. B. Grandin, a Palmyra publisher, accepted the job, but only after Harris agreed to pay $3,000 for the work and mortgaged his farm as security. Grandin printed 5,000 copies, but the book was not a commercial success. True to his word, Harris gave up his mortgaged farm to pay the bill.

With publication of the Book of Mormon secured, on April 6, 1830, perhaps 50 believers, some of whom had been baptized, met in the home of Peter Whitmer Sr. for the purpose of organizing a church. They voted to accept Joseph Smith and Oliver Cowdery as their teachers, after which the two ordained each other as elders in the Church. They then blessed and passed to the group the emblems of the sacrament of the Lord's Supper, bread and wine, after which they laid hands on many present, bestowing upon them the gift of the Holy Ghost and confirming them as members. They also ordained some men to various priesthood offices, and that evening several more people were baptized, including Smith's parents. The new organization was called the Church of Christ. It adopted its current name eight years later.

At a conference on June 9, in Fayette, Smith presented a new revelation. Now published, with a few additions, as Section 20 of the Doctrine and Covenants, this revelation became known as the "Articles and Covenants of the Church of Christ." Among other things, it listed the duties of various priesthood offices, the responsibilities of members, the prayers to be used in performing baptisms and in administering the sacrament of the Lord's Supper, and instructions on how to deal with transgressors. Though many additions have been made to Church organization and doctrine since then, this revelation stands as an important constitution for the Church.

Within two months, formal missionary calls were issued, the first going to Samuel Smith, Joseph's brother. He returned from his short-term mission saddened and discouraged by his lack of success, not realizing that a copy of the Book of Mormon that he left behind would eventually fall into the hands of several people who subsequently joined the Church, including Brigham Young.

As the Church slowly grew, it also met opposition, including threats of mob violence. The reasons for these reactions are not entirely clear, but the Mormon insistence on an exclusive priesthood authority as well as a "gold bible" no doubt contributed. Joseph was arrested twice during the summer on charges of disorderly conduct, but he was quickly acquitted.

A revelation given the day the Church was organized identified Joseph Smith as a "seer," a translator, and a prophet. It also instructed members of the Church that they should "give heed unto all his words and commandments which he shall give unto you as he receiveth them. . . . For his word ye shall receive as if from mine own mouth" (Doctrine and Covenants 21:4–5). Nevertheless, a few members challenged the wording of one of his revelations, and Hiram Page claimed to receive revelations for the Church through the use of a personal seerstone. This resulted in still another revelation, addressed to Oliver Cowdery. It read, in part: "Verily, verily I say unto thee that no one shall be appointed to receive commandments and revelations in this church excepting my servant Joseph Smith." Others could speak and write by way of wisdom, but not by way of commandment. "And thou shalt not command him who is at thy head, and at the head of the church" (Doctrine and Covenants 28:2, 4–6). Thus, as a result of early internal dissent, Smith established a precedent for his role as prophet and president as well as for that of his successors in the prophetic office.

In the same revelation that outlined a stronger sense of Smith's mission, Smith reported new information that would hold lasting importance for his fledgling Church. Cowdery was commanded to "go unto the Lamanites [i.e., the American Indians] and preach my gospel unto them." He was then told that "no man knoweth where the city of Zion shall be built, but it shall be given hereafter. Behold, I say unto you that it shall be on the borders by the Lamanites" (Doctrine and Covenants 28:8–9). Those two verses were filled with portents for the future. The state of Missouri was "on the borders by the Lamanites." Beginning in the 1820s, the federal government forced many eastern Native American tribes to remove to what was soon dubbed the "permanent Indian frontier," beyond the 95th meridian. Western Missouri was thus "on the borders by the Lamanites." The Book of Mormon instilled a special interest in early Mormons in preaching to the Indians, and Oliver Cowdery had long wondered when this would begin. The revelation thus directed him and others to Jackson County, Missouri, as missionaries. Then, in July 1831, Smith visited Jackson County and in another revelation designated it as a land of promise for the Mormons, the place where they would build their city of Zion, with Independence as its "center place" (Doctrine and Covenants 57:3–4). This set the stage for one of the most important and most tragic eras in Mormon history.

Peter Whitmer Jr., Parley P. Pratt, and Ziba Peterson were called to accompany Cowdery on his mission to the Indians. The four set out in mid-October, spent time with two tribes along the way, and soon arrived in Mentor, Ohio. They made no converts among the Indians, but something else happened that had far-reaching implications. Before his conversion to Mormonism, Parley P. Pratt was a disciple of Sidney Rigdon, pastor of a congregation in Mentor. Rigdon, who had been associated earlier with Alexander Campbell, believed strongly in trying to establish the "ancient gospel" based on New Testament principles. Pratt had been converted to Mormonism while on a mission to New York, and now he was back, hoping to convert his former pastor. He left a copy of the Book of Mormon with Rigdon, and, when he returned about two weeks later, he found that Rigdon not only had read it but had received a personal witness to its truthfulness. After his baptism, in mid-November, Rigdon moved to nearby Hyrum, where a small branch of the Church was formed.

In addition to Rigdon's baptism, the stop in Ohio was auspicious in other ways. Before leaving for Missouri, the missionaries baptized about 130 people, many of them, like Rigdon, former Campbellites. As for Rigdon, he would not be happy until he met Smith for himself. In December, he went to New York, taking with him

Edward Partridge, who was not yet converted and who wanted to learn something about the character of Joseph Smith. They met Smith at Waterloo, where Partridge became convinced and was baptized. Less than a year later, Partridge became the first bishop in the Church.

Rigdon's background and religious charisma prepared him for an even greater role, at least in the near future. Smith reported a revelation directed to Rigdon that said, in part. "I have looked upon thee and thy works. I have heard thy prayers and prepared thee for a greater work." Most of what he had been teaching was correct, though one important thing was lacking. "Thou didst baptize with water unto repentance, but they received not the Holy Ghost." Now, through him, converts would also receive the Holy Ghost "by the laying on of hands, even as the apostles of old." The fullness of the gospel had been sent forth through Joseph, "and in weakness have I blessed him," but now Rigdon was assigned to "watch over him that his faith fail not," to write for him as he received revelation, and to "preach my gospel and call on the holy prophets to prove his words" (Doctrine and Covenants 35:3–6, 17, 19, 23). Almost immediately, Rigdon began to assist Joseph in his revision (or, as Joseph and the Mormons called it, inspired "translation") of the Bible, and, in 1833, he was designated by revelation as a "spokesman" for Joseph (Doctrine and Covenants 100:9). He later became first counselor in the presidency of the Church.

Meanwhile, the four missionaries went on to Missouri, taking with them an Ohio convert, Frederick G. Williams. Arriving in mid-December, three of them spent several days in Indian Territory, until other Christian missionaries complained and federal agents ordered them to leave. Back in Jackson County, the missionaries baptized several converts, and all but Parley P. Pratt remained there until after Smith arrived six months later.

In New York, the Church continued to grow only slowly and was plagued with persecution. It may have been Rigdon who helped open Smith's eyes to the possibility that things would be better in Ohio, especially because the Church was growing much more rapidly there. In any case, a revelation through Smith told him to go to Ohio. In addition, the whole Church in New York was told to move. Near the end of January 1831, Joseph and Emma Smith, Sidney Rigdon, and Edward Partridge were on their way; they arrived in Kirtland, Ohio, early in February. There was some disgruntlement among the New York Mormons at the prospect of leaving their homes, but eventually, in the spring of 1831, most packed up their goods and left. Traveling in groups, they went via the Erie Canal to Buffalo, along Lake Erie by steamer or sloop to Fairport, Ohio, and then a short distance overland to Kirtland. This was the first of several Mormon migrations that would end only after the Saints found relative peace and safety in the Rocky Mountains of the Far West.

The foundation years 1820–1830 set important precedents for the future in terms of doctrine, practice, organization, and administrative procedures. Though the Mormons of 1830 believed that Joseph had received direct instruction from God, the

Joseph Smith's vision of the Father and the Son has inspired Mormon folk and fine artists of many cultures. (Courtesy of the Church History Museum, The Church of Jesus Christ of Latter-day Saints.)

story of his first vision was unknown to them. By the end of the century, that vision was well established in Mormon minds as *the* founding event and the beginning of the restoration of the ancient gospel. In contrast, the story of the Book of Mormon was well known, and the book itself was used by missionaries as the means for introducing Joseph Smith and the gospel of Christ. The reality of both the First Vision and the Book of Mormon became, for Mormons, the ultimate test of the veracity of the Church itself.

By the end of 1830, certain other basic practices and beliefs were established. Members believed that they belonged to the divinely restored Church of Christ, which held the priesthood or authority to act in the name of God. Joseph Smith and Oliver Cowdery were designated as the first and second elders of the Church, but they were also apostles, and the Mormons anticipated the imminent establishment of a permanent quorum of 12 apostles. Church organization would expand over the years, but by this time the duties of various priesthood officers had been outlined. Joseph Smith, as prophet and president, was clearly in charge, but the priesthood was strictly a lay priesthood. Both the Bible and the Book of Mormon were accepted as scripture. In addition, the principle of continuing revelation was well established, and Joseph Smith's revelations were accepted as if they were scripture. Certain basic doctrines were recognized as essentials of the new faith. They included faith, repentance, baptism by immersion for the remission of sins, the laying on of hands for the gift of the Holy Ghost, spiritual gifts, and the sacrament of the Lord's Supper. Further, the Mormons believed strongly in the fall of Adam and the atonement of Jesus Christ. They also believed that the millennium was coming soon, a time when Christ would reign on Earth for a thousand years, and that the gospel had been restored through Joseph Smith in preparation for that event. All this became the unchanging foundation for a more elaborate development of doctrine and practice in later years.

—*James B. Allen*

See also: Book of Mormon; Church Organization and Government; First Vision; Mormonism as Restoration; Organization of the Church; Rigdon, Sidney; Smith, Emma Hale; Smith, Joseph Jr.; Smith Family; Witnesses to the Book of Mormon.

References

Allen, James B., and Glen M. Leonard. *The Story of the Latter-day Saints,* 2nd ed. Salt Lake City, UT: Deseret Book, 1992.

Bushman, Richard L. *Joseph Smith: Rough Stone Rolling: A Cultural Biography of Mormonism's Founder.* New York: Knopf, 2005.

Bushman, Richard L. *Joseph Smith and the Beginnings of Mormonism.* Urbana: University of Illinois Press, 1984.

De Pillis, Mario S. "The Quest for Religious Authority and the Rise of Mormonism." *Dialogue: A Journal of Mormon Thought* 1 (Spring 1966): 68–88.

Doctrine and Covenants of the Church of Jesus Christ of Latter-day Saints. Salt Lake City, UT: The Church of Jesus Christ of Latter-day Saints, 1981.

Jessee, Dean C. "The Earliest Documented Accounts of Joseph Smith's First Vision." In *Opening the Heavens: Accounts of Divine Manifestations.* Ed. John W. Welch, 1–33. Provo, UT, and Salt Lake City, UT: BYU Press and Deseret Book, 2005.

Smith, Joseph, Jr. *History of the Church of Jesus Christ of Latter-day Saints.* 6 vols. Ed. B.H. Roberts. Salt Lake City, UT: The Church of Jesus Christ of Latter-day Saints, 1973.

Smith, Lucy Mack. *History of Joseph Smith by His Mother, Lucy Mack Smith.* Ed. Preston Nibley. Salt Lake City, UT: Bookcraft, 1958.

Development: 1831–1844

The period 1831–1844 witnessed the most peripatetic era in LDS history, with the Church as a whole moving from New York to establish settlements in Ohio and Missouri and, eventually, in Illinois. Organizationally and doctrinally, the governing priesthood structure of the Church was elaborated and expanded, and the teachings of Joseph Smith Jr. grew increasingly innovative. Mormonism during this period also spread overseas, with missions to Great Britain and Scandinavia yielding thousands of converts that made their way to Mormon settlements in the United States. Mormons also engaged actively with American culture during this era: they published multiple newspapers and chartered a city in Illinois, and Joseph Smith ran for president of the United States. The period ends with the murder of Mormonism's founding prophet, Joseph Smith, in June 1844.

From 1831 until 1838, the Church was gathered into two general regions—Kirtland, Ohio, and various settlements in Missouri. From 1839 until 1844, the Church concentrated its membership in Nauvoo, Illinois, and some smaller surrounding communities. This essay deals first with Kirtland, moves on to discuss the events in Missouri, and concludes with a broad survey of the major and significantly more complex events that transpired at Nauvoo between 1839 and June 1844, with the murder of Joseph Smith.

Kirtland, Ohio, 1831–1838

In the fall of 1830, Joseph Smith organized a mission to various Native American tribes, who were referred to as "Lamanites" because of the Mormon belief that they were descendants of Book of Mormon Lamanites. The missionaries met with the Catteraugus tribe near Buffalo, New York, and presented them with a copy of the Book of Mormon. Farther west, in Kansas Territory, the group spent some time with the Delaware Indians before eventually making their way back to the main body of the Church. Although the "Lamanite mission" was not successful in bringing large numbers of Native American converts into the Church, it was on this mission that Mormon missionaries first visited and won converts in Kirtland, Ohio. Kirtland and its immediate environs already boasted a significant religious presence. Methodists, Congregationalists, and Baptists had established congregations in the area before the arrival of the first Mormon missionaries, in November 1830. Sidney Rigdon, a local Campbellite preacher who, along with many of his congregants, had broken with Alexander Campbell over a variety of issues, converted to Mormonism in 1830 and influenced many of his flock to follow suit. Joseph Smith was so impressed by the number of converts won to his cause in such short order that he visited Kirtland early in 1831. By the time of Smith's arrival, more than 100 people from the area had accepted membership in the Mormon Church, prompting Smith to move the headquarters there later that year. The Mormon population in Kirtland continued to grow steadily, reaching its zenith of 2,500 persons, which represented about two-thirds of the total population of the town, in 1837.

The Church's hierarchical model became more elaborate during its time in Kirtland. In addition to the First Presidency, the office of Bishop (and later, Presiding Bishopric) was established in 1831, the office of Patriarch of the Church came into existence in December 1833, and a Quorum of the Twelve Apostles and a Quorum of the Seventy were established in February 1835. As the Church continued to grow, the membership was divided into "stakes of Zion," each overseen by a stake presidency. Beginning in 1834, each stake also housed a 12-man "high council" to settle disputes among Church members. Later, during the Nauvoo period, Joseph Smith would break stakes into even smaller geographical units called wards. Although the First Quorum of Seventy would undergo augmentation and eventual circumscription during the Nauvoo period and later and the office of Presiding Patriarch was effectively dissolved in 1979, the other offices and quorums established at Kirtland in the 1830s have remained constant elements of the Mormon hierarchical landscape.

While in Kirtland, Smith continued to record revelations that addressed a wide range of practical and theological issues. On the basis of these revelations, Smith introduced a plan of communitarian living known as the Law of Consecration and Stewardship, which existed in Ohio and Missouri from 1832 to 1834. Under this system, participants agreed to consecrate all of their possessions and property to a Church agent, who would decide how much the family or individual needed in order to carry on with its work and who would give back that much property and personal goods as a stewardship. The excess was redistributed among members of the Church in need. Whatever surplus was earned would be returned to the Church for redistribution in perpetuity. The system was short lived and of limited success and resulted in the Church's involvement in costly lawsuits filed by members who left the Church and sought to regain their consecrated lands and possessions. Nevertheless, the Mormon approach to a communitarian standard is notable because it relied upon an unusual alloy consisting of private individuals actively engaged with the growing market economy and a more traditional communitarian impulse of economic redistribution.

During this period, the Church also established extra-ecclesiastical bodes that served a wide range of functions. In 1831, Smith established a "literary firm" to handle the publication of a book of Smith's revelations and other materials. The following year, he established the United Firm, which, in addition to administering the law of consecration, was to unite all Church business interests under one banner in what one historian calls the Church's "first master plan of business and finance" (Parkin, *Joseph Smith* 3). Like many such activities during this period, the United Firm had branches in Ohio (Newel K. Whitney and Company) and Missouri (Gilbert, Whitney and Company).

A somewhat more problematic economic venture was undertaken in January 1837. The Mormons in Ohio were land-rich and cash-poor and Church leaders, in debt to eastern banks, found themselves in something of a credit crisis. The state of Ohio turned down the Mormon proposal for a bank charter, something Smith had hoped would allow the Church to bring in liquid assets. In response, Smith launched the "Kirtland Safety Society Anti-Banking Company." Backed by a small amount of specie, the society quickly circulated $100,000 worth of bank notes. Unfortunately, the faltering economic environment of 1837 merged with an unexpected run on the bank's specie reserves from note holders and led to the eventual collapse of the society, in November 1837. Although devastating financially, the collapse of the bank also contributed to a growing sense of disillusionment with Smith and Mormonism among some high-ranking Church officials. In late 1837, bitter dissension cleaved the Mormon leadership structure, leading to the excommunication of nearly one-third of the Church's general officers and the loss of at least 10 percent of general Church membership in the Kirtland area (Backman, *Heavens Resound* 328). Fearing for his life and the safety of his family, Joseph Smith and other Church members who had remained loyal during this time fled Kirtland in January 1838 for the relative protection of the Mormon settlements in Missouri.

For all of the difficulties that transpired in Kirtland, the Church's stay there also resulted in the introduction of important ritual and theological elements of Mormonism. The dedication of the Kirtland temple in 1836, with its accompanying notion of temples as centers for divine endowment, and Joseph Smith's vision of the structure of heaven, which he called "three degrees of glory" proved to be important and persistent ideas throughout the history of Mormonism. The Mormon code of health, known as the "Word of Wisdom," which provided Mormonism with what would become the important boundary markers of abstention from coffee, tea, tobacco, and alcohol, came into being at Kirtland in 1833. Nearly one-third of the revelations recorded in the current edition of the LDS Church's Doctrine and Covenants were received at Kirtland, many of them first published in the Church's Ohio newspaper, the *Messenger and Advocate*.

Missouri, 1833–1839

Joseph Smith taught that Kirtland would only be a temporary stopping place for the Mormons. Their final destiny was in the West, on the Missouri frontier. One of the most turbulent passages in Mormon history occurred during the Church's attempts at community building in Missouri between 1831 and 1839. While Joseph Smith resided at Kirtland, a large number of Mormons occupied settlements in Missouri along what was then the western frontier of the United States. Responding to a revelation that Smith recorded in 1831 designating the area near Independence, Missouri, as the "center place" of Zion, Mormons began purchasing property and settling in nearby Kaw township. Smith projected an important eschatological role for this center place: it would be the site of Christ's triumphant Second Advent, which many Mormons understood to be imminent. By 1833, about 1,200 Mormons had settled in the area, and they began to publish a Church newspaper, the *Evening and the Morning Star*. More important, they carried with them their ideas about communalism, the law of consecration, and stewardship. While this law was actually a failure, stories about the negative impact such a practice might have on the local economy soon spread. Similar concerns surfaced with regard to Mormon political power and the threat of Mormon bloc voting, even though no political party had been formed by the Mormons. Intensifying these issues was the fear on the part of the Missourians that the Mormons would bring an active antislavery agenda to bear in the region.

The apocalyptic rhetoric of the Mormons and the fear on the part of local Missourians that the Mormons would exert undue political and economic power in the area led to tension almost immediately. Local Protestant ministers undertook a door-to-door campaign against the Mormons in the summer of 1833, and citizens of

Jackson County held impassioned meetings designed to address the Mormon threat. The result of these efforts was the publication of a letter from several hundred Jackson County citizens to Missouri governor Daniel Dunklin. The letter complained in general terms about the "fanatics" and "knaves" that had been plaguing the region for the past two years with their pretenses to divine revelation that "openly blaspheme the most high God" (Smith, *History* 1:375).

A close reading of the letter reveals that, in addition to the general doctrinal issues, there were two major foci of concern for the non-Mormons in Jackson County. One was that the Mormons "would corrupt our blacks and instigate them to bloodsheds." The other was the Mormon assertion that "God hath given them this county of land, and that sooner or later they must and will have possession of our lands for an inheritance" (Smith, *History* 1:375–376). Mormon resistance to threats in Missouri continued throughout 1833. In that year, however, the citizens of Jackson County made it abundantly clear that the proposed city of Zion would not be built in Independence. In the summer of 1833, a group of Missourians destroyed the Mormon printing press, vandalized a Mormon store, and brutalized several Church leaders. In the aftermath of the violence, the local group informed the Mormons that their only course of action was to leave the area. Half of the Mormons were to leave by the end of the year, the other half by April 1834. When the Mormons appeared unmoved by the intimidation, violence escalated. On October 31, Mormon settlements were attacked just west of the Big Blue River. These attacks lasted for more than a week as homes were ransacked and razed and men, women, and children were beaten. The attacks climaxed on November 4, when two Missourians and one Mormon were killed. In December, the Mormons fled north and found temporary refuge in Clay County.

Although they had hastily abandoned their lands and homes in Jackson County, the Mormons still sought compensation for their losses. In May 1834, Joseph Smith led an armed contingent of more than 200 Mormons, mostly men but including some women and children, on a journey of more than 1,000 miles, from Kirtland, Ohio, to Jackson County. The purpose of this expedition, known as "Zion's Camp," was to reclaim the lands seized by the Missouri militia the previous year. By the time Smith and his small but very well armed band reached the area around Jackson County, in June, their presence was already expected, and they met with stiff resistance. Bloodshed was avoided by a fortuitous and vicious thunderstorm that caused a rising river to serve as a buffer between the Mormons and the Missourians dispatched to meet them. Almost immediately following this, many of the members of Zion's Camp fell violently ill with cholera, and Joseph Smith disbanded the group. Smith interpreted the outbreak, which eventually killed more than 10 people, as evidence of God's displeasure with contention and disharmony in the ranks. Despite the failure of Zion's Camp to achieve its stated goal of reclaiming the lost property in Jackson County, it proved to be an important event in the history of the Church. When Joseph Smith began organizing the Church hierarchy into quorums in 1835, the vast majority of those chosen to fill the positions of leadership in the Church were those who had proven their loyalty to Smith during the arduous and grueling Zion's Camp experience.

With the exception of the Zion's Camp episode, the Mormons in Missouri lived in relative peace for two years in Clay County, but, in 1836, local residents began holding meetings with the aim of forcing the Mormons to withdraw and to stop any further influx of Mormons from the east. Wishing to avoid the sort of violence visited upon them in Jackson County, the Mormons agreed to leave Clay County, and they began to settle in Caldwell County, farther north, in the fall of 1836. Caldwell County was created by the state legislature for the specific purpose of accommodating Mormon settlement. The county seat, Far West, became a major center of Mormon activity, and, by the time the Mormons left the area, in 1838, Far West was the largest city in the area, with an estimated population of around 4,000. Radiating out from Far West were nearly a dozen smaller Mormon settlements. Daviess County, bordering Caldwell on the north, was also friendly toward the Mormons, and by the summer of 1838 the Mormons had established a settlement there that they called Adam-ondi-Ahman and which Joseph Smith associated with important eschatological themes involving the return of Jesus Christ and other former prophets.

The turbulent Mormon sojourn in Missouri reached a violent climax in the summer and fall of 1838. During the so-called Mormon War of 1838, the Latter-day Saint settlements in Missouri came under attack from a variety of groups, including local vigilantes and the state militia. Two Mormons, including apostle David Patten, were killed on October 24 during the Battle of Crooked River. The Haun's Mill Massacre, which occurred on October 30, 1838, was the bloodiest single event of the Mormon War. On that day, 200 Missourians attacked a group of Mormon settlers on Shoal Creek, killing 17 and wounding 14. Governor Lilburn W. Boggs gave the attacks on Mormon settlements a tacit stamp of approval when he issued an "extermination order" decreeing that all Mormons must be either driven from the borders of the state or exterminated. It was during this time that the infamous "Danites" emerged as a secret extra-ecclesiastical society that engaged in the defense of Mormon settlements, particularly in Daviess County. The Danites also turned their attention to former members of the Church and those that the Danite leadership believed to be insufficiently dedicated to the cause of the Church. The Danites engaged in intimidation of disaffected Church members and apparently attempted to interfere with an election to bring about an outcome favorable to the Mormons. Despite all of their efforts to stave off the Missourians, the Mormons formally surrendered at Far West in November and were forced to surrender all property to the state militia. More than 10,000 Mormons found themselves homeless in the early winter months of 1839.

Compounding the Mormon predicament was the incarceration of six Church leaders, including Joseph and Hyrum Smith, in Liberty Jail in Clay County. The Mormons were being held on charges stemming from the Mormon War, which the

Missouri government blamed entirely on the Latter-day Saints. From December 1838 until April 1839, the Smith brothers languished in the cramped and freezing jail. Nothing came of the charges, and the Mormons were allowed to escape and rejoin the main body of the Mormons, who had managed, under the leadership of apostle Brigham Young, to find a temporary refuge in Quincy, Illinois. Ten thousand Mormons found hospitable treatment at the hands of the citizens of Quincy, and, by the summer of 1839, Joseph Smith was out of jail and had found a place in which he could gather all of the dispersed Mormons.

Nauvoo, 1839–1844

In Nauvoo, Smith introduced an ambitious new agenda that encompassed theological innovations, social experimentation, and political ambition. In the years between 1839, when the Mormons arrived, and 1844, when Smith was murdered, he introduced polygamy, eternal marriage, the temple endowment, and the secret Council of Fifty, and he ran for president of the United States. The Church also continued its tradition of newspaper publishing with the religiously oriented *Times and Seasons,* which published in serialized form what would later become the *Book of Abraham,* the more politically inclined *Mormon Wasp,* and the *Nauvoo Neighbor.*

Shortly after leaving Liberty Jail, Joseph Smith arranged to purchase 18,000 acres of land in Hancock County, Illinois, and Lee County, Iowa, for $50,000. On the Illinois side of the Mississippi River, there existed a small town called Commerce, which the Mormons purchased and made the focal point of their new settlement effort. Joseph Smith rechristened the town Nauvoo, which Smith suggested was a Hebrew name denoting a place of rest or refreshing. In the wake of the violent Missouri years, Smith was determined to create as much legal protection as possible for the Mormons in Illinois. To that end, he secured a city charter that granted sweeping powers to Nauvoo as an incorporated city. The Illinois legislature had granted a spate of charters to various municipalities in the state in the years immediately preceding the Mormons' arrival in Nauvoo. All of these charters contained much of the same language and provided for many of the same offices and government organizations. The Nauvoo charter differed in that it allowed for the creation of a militia, the Nauvoo Legion, which would one day become second only to the U.S. Army in size. Although the Nauvoo charter was similar to those in other cities, because Church leaders also held the most prominent government positions, the situation quickly came to be viewed by outsiders as a quasi-theocracy. Joseph Smith did not deny his efforts to merge civil and ecclesiastical government, although he demonstrated his Jacksonian roots with his preference for the term "theodemocracy." The charter ceded to Smith all legal and police authority, which meant that he was ensconced behind a barrier of religio-legal power unheard of in American history. As one historian put it, Nauvoo became a "state within a state" (Kimball, "Nauvoo Charter" 67). With the powerful

The Mormons built the city of Nauvoo, Illinois, on the bank of the Mississippi River, beginning in 1841, and abandoned it five years later. So many of its comfortable and substantial brick homes remained standing that some parts of the city could be restored to their 1840s state in the mid-20th century. (Courtesy of the Church History Library, The Church of Jesus Christ of Latter-day Saints.)

Nauvoo charter providing a measure of independence for the Mormons, Smith moved forward with what he believed were his God-given mandates. In January 1841, Smith announced that a temple would be built in Nauvoo. It was within the context of temple building that Smith introduced some of his most unusual theological ideas, including baptism for the dead and the sealing of families together for eternity.

During the Nauvoo period, Smith developed at least three important groups that served as loci of power within the community. The first consisted of the general authorities of the Church, which consisted of the Church's official hierarchy that had been part of the governing structure since the 1830s. The second group was the "quorum of the anointed," which began in May 1842 and consisted of men and, beginning in 1843, women who had been initiated into the new rituals known collectively as the endowment. It was in the context of the anointed quorum that Smith began to teach and practice the principle of plural marriage. The third group, and the last to be established, was the Council of Fifty. Smith organized this secret council in 1844 in the hope that it would provide the foundation for the government of the Kingdom of God after Christ's Second Coming. Although this organization has received a great deal of attention from historians, during Smith's lifetime the Council of Fifty had little impact on Mormon life. When Smith ran for president, in 1844, however, he drew on members of the Council to actively campaign for him throughout the eastern portions of the United States. These three foci of power were not discrete; most of the apostles, for example, were also members of the anointed quorum and the Council of Fifty, but the existence of three different groups, each with a focus on either the hierarchical, theological, or political elements of Mormonism, bear witness to the increasing complexity of Joseph Smith's movement as it progressed in the 1840s.

The accumulation and organization of Mormon power in the 1840s has led to speculation about Joseph Smith's motives. Some observers argue that he was attempting to build an empire, while others suggest that he sought to create a refuge from the chaotic pluralistic nature of Jacksonian America. There is little debate, however, that Smith continued to believe that he carried a mandate from heaven to build the Kingdom of God on Earth and that this belief led him to take bold and socially transgressive steps. The most famous Mormon practice in the 19th century was, of course, plural marriage. It was in the crucible of Nauvoo that Smith first introduced this doctrine and practice.

Although Joseph Smith had considered polygamy to be a necessary part of the restoration of the true faith since the early 1830s, it was not until he was ensconced in the relative safety of Nauvoo that he began introducing other men to the idea of taking additional wives. Historians face a daunting task when trying to reconstruct the nature and extent of polygamy as practiced during Joseph Smith's lifetime owing to the paucity of archival sources addressing the matter. Smith worked hard to keep his teachings and practices on the subject secret, and it is not clear how many wives Smith himself married before his death, although scholarly estimations range from a dozen to more than 30.

It is difficult to address Smith's thoughts on the matter of polygamy, because he left very little for historians to consider. An early and persistent interpretation is that Smith simply fashioned a religious justification for adultery and called it a revelation. Others have argued that polygamy performed the social chore of caring for women living in a society with unequal sex ratios. More nuanced readings have suggested that Smith was obsessed with the idea of ever-expanding kinship groups and that the practice of plural marriage served to expand geometrically such familial webs.

What is clear is that Smith was a practicing polygamist and that he urged the practice on his closest associates as a solemn religious obligation. Many of these men, most notably Brigham Young, reported abhorrence at the prospect of taking a step so sharply contrary to traditional family arrangements. Despite initial misgivings, approximately 30 families were involved with plural marriage before Smith's death. It must be borne in mind that, during the Nauvoo period, polygamy was a rite reserved for a small number of Latter-day Saints. The vast majority of Mormons in Nauvoo and surrounding communities were new converts, many from Europe, who were largely unaware of the practice and for whom it played no part in daily or religious life. It is worth noting that, while approximately 100 persons were initiated into the anointed quorum before Smith's death, the overall Mormon population of Nauvoo and the surrounding settlements was around 14,000 in 1844. Between 1840 and 1844, nearly 4,000 English converts arrived. All of this underscores the division in Nauvoo between the three hierarchical, theological, and political elites and the overwhelming majority of Mormons new to the faith and even to the nation.

While plural marriage was being taught and practiced among Smith's inner circle, the Church was also active in far more obvious challenges to the status quo, this time in the realm of politics. By 1844, Mormons had already been involved on some level with American political culture for more than a decade. During the 1830s, Mormons held elective office side by side with men of other faiths in the Kirtland, Ohio, area. The Church also published two politically oriented newspapers, the *Northern Times,* in Ohio, and the *Upper Missouri Advertiser,* in Missouri. In addition,

Mormons filled the majority of local governmental posts in Nauvoo. In February 1844, however, Mormon engagement with the American political scene took on an entirely new cast when Smith announced his candidacy for the presidency of the United States. Eschewing affiliation with either the Whigs or the Democrats, Smith put forth a mixed platform calling for the abolition of slavery by 1850, the reduction of the U.S. Congress by half, and a general amnesty for all convicts incarcerated in state prisons except those convicted of murder. Still incensed over the governmental treatment of Mormons in Missouri, Smith also included language that would provide a federal mandate for intervention in mob violence at the state level. Smith also came out in favor of a national bank. Very little came of this campaign, because electioneers were out spreading the word of Smith's political views in the summer of 1844 when word reached them of his murder. The impetus behind the presidential bid is significant, however, in that it provides another window in Joseph Smith's ever-expanding views of the role of his restored faith in the history of the world. Mormonism in the 1840s was not another sect content to gather sheep. Rather, it was Joseph Smith's ambition to "revolutionize the world" and he was taking concrete steps to that end.

Joseph Smith's powerful position in Nauvoo religious and political life and his willingness to transgress societal norms when they conflicted with his grand religious

Whistling and Whittling Brigade

Following the 1844 murder of Joseph Smith and the revocation of the Nauvoo city charter, which ended Mormon control of local courts and required the disbanding of the Nauvoo Legion, the Saints in and around Nauvoo felt increasingly vulnerable to dissenters and resentful neighbors. They turned to novel forms of self-protection, the most colorful of which was the "Whistling and Whittling Brigade."

Folklore depicts the members of this brigade as children and young teens who would surround a suspicious outsider, neither making overtly threatening moves nor engaging him in conversation but merely whistling cheerfully and whittling on sticks with their pocket knives. In this romanticized version, the children were too small to hit, too many to chase away, and too watchful to evade. Frustrated ne'er-do-wells would abandon their schemes and leave town.

In reality, the "boys" of the Brigade were older teens and young adults; their "pocket knives" were enormous Bowie knives; their sticks were whittled into sharply pointed weapons; their cheerful nonengagement was unmistakable hostility and sometimes took the form of pressing close to a stranger and "accidentally" prodding him with their knives and sticks. Such intimidation was effective if not pretty and usually resulted in undesirables hastily leaving the city.

vision proved dangerous. In 1843, a familiar pattern emerged within Mormon society at Nauvoo. As had happened in Kirtland and in Missouri during the preceding decade, Joseph Smith faced a serious problem stemming from internal dissent at Nauvoo. A few of Smith's close associates could not bring themselves to accept Smith's teachings regarding plural marriage and, believing that Smith was a fallen prophet, left Mormonism and started a rival church. Led by former First Presidency Councilor William Law, this group purchased a printing press and established a newspaper to expose what they believed to be Smith's abuses of ecclesiastical and political power. The *Nauvoo Expositor* published only one issue, in June 1844, but it would prove a decisive moment in Mormon history. Smith, enraged by the betrayal and the exposure of plural marriage, held a meeting of the city council at which he decreed that the press that printed the *Expositor,* together with all available copies of the newspaper, should be destroyed. Smith's aggressive and impulsive act against the *Expositor* had immediate consequences. Most significant, a warrant was issued for Smith's arrest. Initially, Smith sought refuge across the Mississippi River in Iowa. Unable to leave his followers alone in such straits for long, Smith returned to Nauvoo on June 23 and headed for Carthage, the Hancock County seat, the next day. While he was being held over for trial at Carthage, a mob with blackened faces stormed the jail. Joseph Smith attempted to fight off his assailants with a small handgun, but there was no hope of escape. Smith's brother Hyrum leaned against the door in a vain attempt to keep the armed group at bay when a slug blasted through the door, striking him in the face. Joseph headed for the window and reached it just as the mob burst through the door and emptied four slugs into his body. Smith fell from the second story window into the midst of the whooping crowd below. Among the Mormons, reactions to the murders ranged from disbelief to devastation.

Smith's death signaled the end of a period of LDS history in which remarkable growth and development ran concurrent with times of violence and conflict. Smith left behind as his legacy the development of the Church he achieved in the 1830s and 1840s, a period in which he managed to create a fully articulated religious tradition with an elaborate hierarchy, a sophisticated theology, and a dedicated and sizable core of believers. In the years since 1831, the Church had grown to more than 15,000 members, had survived violent clashes with vigilantes and militia, and had managed to build a thriving city in which members were able, for a time, to develop and practice their religious faith in relative peace.

—Stephen C. Taysom

See also: Church Organization and Government; Haun's Mill Massacre; Martyrdom of Joseph and Hyrum Smith; Missouri War; Mormon Scripture; Mormonism and Blacks; Mormonism and Economics; Mormonism and Native Americans; Mormonism and Secular Government; Mormonism and Violence; Nauvoo Legion; Polygamy; Smith, Joseph Jr.; Word of Wisdom; Zion's Camp.

References

Backman, Milton V. *The Heavens Resound: History of the Latter-day Saints in Ohio, 1830–1838.* Salt Lake City, UT: Deseret Book, 1983.

Baugh, Alexander L. *A Call to Arms: The 1838 Mormon Defense of Northern Missouri.* Provo, UT: BYU Studies, 2000.

Bushman, Richard L. *Joseph Smith: Rough Stone Rolling: A Cultural Biography of Mormonism's Founder.* New York: Knopf, 2005.

Compton, Todd. *In Sacred Loneliness: The Plural Wives of Joseph Smith.* Salt Lake City, UT: Signature Books, 1997.

Hansen, Klaus J. *Quest for Empire: The Political Kingdom of God and the Council of Fifty in Mormon History.* Lansing: Michigan State University Press, 1967.

Hill, Marvin S. *Quest for Refuge: The Mormon Flight from American Pluralism.* Salt Lake City, UT: Signature Books, 1989.

Kimball, James L., Jr. "The Nauvoo Charter: A Reinterpretation." *Journal of Illinois State Historical Society* 54 (Spring 1971): 66–78.

LeSueur, Stephen C. *The 1838 Mormon War in Missouri.* Columbia: University of Missouri Press, 1987.

Parkin, Max H. "Joseph Smith and the United Firm." *Brigham Young University Studies* 46, no. 3 (2007): 1–73.

Smith, Joseph Jr. *History of the Church.* Ed. B. H. Roberts. Salt Lake City, UT: Deseret Book, 1973.

Exodus and Settlement: 1845–1869

The years from 1845 to 1869 saw the Mormons forced to leave their city-state on the Mississippi and found a new kingdom in the Rocky Mountains. Accomplishing this feat required transplanting tens of thousands of emigrants from Europe and the eastern United States to the new western homeland and the creation of settlements, a government, social structures, and an economy where no such Anglo-American civilization had previously existed. Along the way, the Saints struggled with weather, geography, and the allocation of basic resources and clashed with both the American nation they had left and the Indians among whom they settled. Situated as they were on the main highway across North America, the Mormons were never as isolated as they or their antagonists might have wished, and, with the completion of the transcontinental railroad in 1869, its final spike driven deep in Mormon territory, all pretense of isolation ended.

After his martyrdom, the matter of a successor to Joseph Smith was the first question facing the Latter-day Saints. A number of aspirants made their claims in public and private venues in the summer of 1844. Several claimants succeeded in gaining followers, and some of the variant churches formed at that time have survived into the 21st century.

The bulk of Church members accepted the leadership of the Quorum of the Twelve Apostles with Brigham Young as president of that quorum. Under his direction, a general epistle was circulated throughout the Church, reassuring members that the Church would survive, calling on members abroad to gather at Nauvoo, directing missionary work to continue, and promising that the temple at Nauvoo would be completed.

Although the Mormons planned to continue as they had been living, outside forces soon made that goal first difficult and ultimately untenable. In January 1845, the state legislature revoked both the Nauvoo city charter and the charter of the Nauvoo Legion, leaving the Saints at Nauvoo without a city organization, courts, or protection by either police or militia. Vigilante action against Mormons and their property in outlying areas increased, and in October 1845 Brigham Young announced that the Saints would leave Nauvoo in the spring and relocate in the Rocky Mountains.

The Mormons rushed to complete this temple at Nauvoo, Illinois, before fleeing to the West in 1846 (Courtesy of the Church History Library, The Church of Jesus Christ of Latter-day Saints.)

As the Saints built wagons and stockpiled supplies, continued harassment led to an exodus earlier than planned, with the first companies leaving Nauvoo on February 4, 1846. Some 600 sick or poor Saints who stayed in Nauvoo as late as September fled after a violent battle, including cannonading of the Saints' homes, and the evacuation was complete.

The Saints were strung out across the width of Iowa for most of 1846, with advance companies establishing semipermanent settlements at Garden Grove and Mount Pisgah to benefit the Saints in the rear, many of whom had to be helped forward by wagons and provisions sent back to them. By that fall, 4,000 of the emigrants had settled into Winter Quarters (now Florence, Nebraska) in a camp consisting of brick houses, cabins, dugouts, and tents, with some 8,000 scattered in smaller settlements in Iowa. Hundreds of Saints died that winter in the primitive wilderness conditions.

In the spring of 1847, Brigham Young led a company consisting of 143 hand-picked men, with 3 women and 2 children, across the plains, reaching the Salt Lake Valley late in July. Other, larger companies, organized according to the plan established by Brigham Young, arrived later that summer and wintered over in the

Valley, while Young returned to Winter Quarters to lead another company, his last, across the plains in 1848.

An elaborate system to facilitate immigration to Utah developed over the next two decades. Many Saints paid their own travel costs; others were aided by the Perpetual Emigrating Fund, a revolving fund that lent aid to the needy with the understanding that they would repay the loan once they reached Utah, making those funds available to additional emigrants. Between 1856 and 1860, 10 companies of Saints, largely Europeans, walked across the plains pulling their belongings and provisions on handcarts. Beginning in 1862, the Saints employed the down-and-back system of sending teams and wagons from Utah to pick up emigrants on the frontier. As the railroad progressed westward, the point for outfitting Mormon companies also shifted, until the need for wagon travel ceased with the completion of the railroad in 1869.

At each stage of the journey—from Liverpool, England, where most European Saints embarked for North America, to New Orleans or New York or Philadelphia, where they landed, to the outfitting points at Winter Quarters, St. Louis, Mormon Grove (near Atchison, Kansas), Iowa City, Iowa, or points farther west, as the circumstances of each year's emigration demanded—Mormon emigration agents were stationed. These agents arranged for ship passage, train fare, and the purchase of cattle, wagons, and provisions. They dealt with bureaucracies and protected the emigrants from the fraud and theft that plagued other emigrants. At the western end of the journey, emigrants were hosted temporarily at camps in Salt Lake City until they could be met by friends or directed to new settlements according to community need.

Some emigrants reached the Salt Lake Valley through other means. In 1846, following Mormon pleas for work assignments from the U.S. government to help finance their move, 500 Mormon men were recruited by the U.S. Army for service in the U.S. War with Mexico. This Mormon Battalion, accompanied by some wives and children, mustered at Fort Leavenworth, Kansas, and marched across the continent through Arizona and New Mexico, encountering no hostile action, and arrived in San Diego in January 1847, helping to secure California for the United States. Some Battalion members were present at the discovery of gold at Sutter's Mill, touching off the gold rush. From there, most traveled eastward to join the Saints at Salt Lake or farther east to pick up their families in Nebraska before returning to Utah. On the same day in 1846 that the first companies left Nauvoo, a shipload of Saints aboard the *Brooklyn* under the leadership of Sam Brannan left New York harbor and sailed around the southern tip of South America and up the west coast, landing at what is now San Francisco. While Brannan himself eventually left the Church, most of the *Brooklyn*'s passengers made their way to Utah. As missionary work progressed in the Pacific, especially in Australia, more converts arrived on the west coast and trekked eastward to Utah.

One of the first acts of the members of the 1847 vanguard company after reaching the Salt Lake Valley was to rebaptize one another; virtually all other Mormons of this period repeated the act of baptism upon their arrival in the Valley. This symbolic act of recommital set the tone for Mormon settlement of the Great Basin. The settlers were a people apart from the larger American community and owed loyalty to the Kingdom of God as much as to any earthly government. The towns and temples they would build, the culture they would create, the industry they would foster were intentionally distinct and apart from the mainstream, no matter how alike they might be on the surface.

The first government established in the Valley was a purely ecclesiastical one in both form and substance. By 1849, after the early 1848 signing of the Treaty of Guadalupe Hidalgo, which transferred ownership of the new Mormon homeland from Mexico to the United States, and with sufficient population in the Valley to support a more formal government, the Mormons petitioned Congress to be admitted to the Union as the State of Deseret, with Brigham Young as governor. Instead, Congress created the Territory of Utah, an act signed by President Millard Fillmore on September 9, 1850. Filmore named Brigham Young governor and appointed additional prominent Mormons to other offices; non-Mormons from outside the new Territory were also appointed to office.

The territorial government began operating in April 1851, although the non-Mormon federal officers, including the territorial secretary and two of the three

---

State of Deseret

When Mormons in the Salt Lake Valley petitioned for U.S. statehood or, alternatively, for territorial status, in 1849, they designated their settlement as the State of Deseret. (*Deseret* is a word meaning "honeybee" in the Book of Mormon.) For reasons of its own, the U.S. Congress turned down that proposed name and chose "Utah," derived from the Ute tribe, one of the major Native American peoples in the Great Basin, as the name for the Territory created in 1850.

As relations with the national government deteriorated in the 1850s, Mormons' desire for self-rule under full statehood became more and more urgent. From 1862 until 1870, the General Assembly of the State of Deseret met in annual session as a sort of dress rehearsal for that statehood. The General Assembly made appointments and passed laws—completely without governmental authority and with no power of enforcement—in preparation for governing Deseret once statehood was won. This "ghost government" was a source of hostility between the Mormons and federally appointed territorial officers throughout the territorial period.

While it failed to win acceptance as a state name, "Deseret" remains an affectionate designation for Utah among many Mormons with ties to their pioneer heritage.

court justices, did not arrive in Utah until later that summer. The newly arrived federal officers found a functioning government but almost from the first moment were embroiled in clashes with the local residents. Secretary Broughton Harris was angered that Young had arranged for the 1850 census (taken in Utah in 1851), which Harris claimed was his responsibility; because of this and other perceived irregularities, Harris refused to release any of the federal funds sent with him from Congress to help the new Territory with its lawful expenses. Chief Justice Lemuel Brandebury quickly found himself on the fringes of Utah society rather than at its center as he had expected, not only because he did not understand the culture of his new neighbors but because he apparently was an awkward man who did not meet community norms for cleanliness and behavior.

It was Associate Justice Perry E. Brocchus, however, who most clashed with the people of Utah. Invited to speak at the Mormon General Conference held soon after his arrival, he seized the opportunity to chastise them for offenses as disparate as not yet having contributed a stone to the Washington Monument, then under construction, and treason for having made statements that recently deceased former president Zachary Taylor was damned and in hell. Having become aware of the Mormon practice of polygamy—which was not formally announced to the public until the following year—Brocchus compared Mormon women to prostitutes and called for their return to virtue. The Mormon audience became so upset by this comparison that Brigham Young called a recess for participants to get control of their tempers. Brocchus would later claim that, had Young not taken control at that moment, his (Brocchus's) life would have been in danger from a Mormon mob.

The accumulation of social and political slights, conscious and unconscious, culminating in the near-riot following Brocchus's speech, caused the non-Mormon federal officers to leave Utah in the fall of 1851. Once they reached the Mississippi River, these "runaway officials" began to give newspaper interviews, eventually followed by an excessively negative report to Congress on conditions in Utah. These reports, coupled with complaints by overland emigrants of mistreatment while passing through Utah to California (some legitimate, some not), created a climate of mistrust between Utah and the rest of the nation that would endure throughout the territorial period.

Almost as soon as the Saints reached the Salt Lake Valley, exploring parties were sent out to search for natural resources to sustain an economy that was otherwise fully dependent upon freighting supplies across the continent and to seek out sites for future settlements. New colonies within a few miles of Salt Lake City were established in the fall of 1847; more ambitious colonies farther afield were established at Provo and Manti (1849), at San Bernardino (now California) and Parowan (1851), and at many other sites. In 1854 and 1855, concern for religious proselytizing among the Native Americans sent missions to such disparate places as Elk Mountain (near today's Moab), Las Vegas, Carson Valley (now Nevada), Fort Supply (in today's Wyoming), and Fort Limhi (now Idaho).

These missions to the Indians continued a complicated relationship between Mormon and Native American that would grow more complex throughout this period. On the one hand, the Mormons felt a religious obligation to the Indians that caused them to seek treaties, adopt Indian children (including children rescued from the intertribal slave trade), marry Indian wives, and attempt to improve Native lives by teaching agriculture and providing tools. On the other hand, Mormon settlements were planted along streams and in fertile valleys where Natives had traditionally gathered their food, and resentment grew on the one side because of perceived invasion and on the other because of perceived thefts. A series of small but bloody wars ensued: the Provo War in 1850; the Tintic War in 1850–1851; and the Walker War in 1853–1854; these were followed by the Black Hawk War of the 1860s, the most widespread and expensive (to both sides) of these clashes.

Although the Mormons had sought solitude in the wilderness, they soon found their community to be the natural stopping point for a vast continental migration. Sometimes this worked to the Mormons' advantage. Following the discovery of gold in California, thousands of men heading to the gold fields passed through Salt Lake City. When they lightened their loads for the mountainous travel ahead or traded little-used items for more critical foodstuffs and fresher animals, the Mormons benefited from the abandoned or low-priced goods. Coming as it did during a period of extreme poverty among the Mormons, this gold rush trade helped the community survive. In other cases, the transcontinental traffic was a source of trouble: Travelers stranded at Salt Lake City for the winter pretended to convert to Mormonism, some even marrying wives and fathering children, only to abandon their families in the spring. Some travelers felt they had been cheated in the sale of their surplus goods; some undoubtedly were overcharged for tolls on the roads and bridges; others, well treated in Utah, joined in the general anti-Mormon prejudice on both coasts and spread exaggerated tales, even outright falsehoods, about their treatment by the Mormons.

By far the greatest source of friction for the Mormons came with the typically poor quality of federal officers appointed in Washington to govern in Utah. The "runaway officials" of 1851 were only the first among many. Throughout the territorial period, Utahns, like others in western territories, complained that federal appointees did not fulfill their duties, were more interested in private money-making ventures than in governing, or were hostile to the social structure of those among whom they lived. Mail service—the chief connection between Mormons in Utah and family and business interests in the east—was poor; service was understandably interrupted in the winter, but even in good weather Utah could count on neither regular delivery of the mail nor the condition of mail received—mail bags were routinely left at way stations or dumped in mountain streams, magazines and newspapers were pilfered, and private letters were opened and read along the way. The Nauvoo Legion, Utah's territorial militia, was not supplied with weaponry as required by law but was furnished instead with ancient and outdated muskets from federal arsenals. No federal land office was established in Utah during its first 20 years of settlement, meaning that Mormons could neither hold legal title to their lands nor be assured that they would receive the benefit of improvements made. When the first judges returned to Washington, in 1851, Utah was left without functioning courts; to meet the need, the Utah legislature expanded the powers of the probate courts, whose judges were appointed by territorial authority, to include civil and criminal powers ordinarily vested in the federal courts. This competing court system was another source of misunderstanding between Mormons and their appointed leaders and generated additional hostility in Washington, where it was wrongly reported that the probate judges were bishops and the probate courts were controlled by the Church.

The Mormon Reformation of 1856–1857, in part a reaction to increasing contact between Mormons and non-Mormons, added to the mix of hostility and resentment on both sides. Beginning with a call by Church leaders for increased observation of the faith, the Reformation brought the rebaptism of believers, a stricter attention to religious duty, and an increase in the number of plural marriages among the faithful. Religious fervor and the level of rhetoric in sermons, rising in some cases to a call for the shedding of blood of the unfaithful, however, contributed to a climate of unease and even fear in some quarters. Backsliders and those who had left the Church began leaving the Territory, heading west to California or east to their former homes. Some of these travelers, attempting to leave with unpaid debts, were halted by posses, legally deputized in response to lawful complaints filed by creditors, and sufficient goods, including in some cases wagons and livestock, were seized to settle debts in Utah. These seizures—but not usually the lawful grounds behind them—were reported with great indignation to the national press, together with lurid tales of polygamy, terror on the part of those who opposed the Church, allegations of Mormon involvement in Indian depredations (including the 1853 murder of Captain John W. Gunnison and a party of the U.S. Corps of Topographical Engineers), and an unfortunate handful of indisputably violent actions against either travelers or apostates, combined to raise the level of hostility in the United States toward the Mormons, creating a view of the Church as one vast criminal enterprise.

Mormons chafed under the failures of the territorial system, complained that they were treated worse than the British had treated the American colonists, and resented the salacious tales told about them by travelers, federal appointees, and even scandalmongers who had never set foot in Utah. Relations between Utah and Washington had deteriorated so badly that when the Utah legislature met in late 1856, it drafted a petition for statehood, supported by memorials signed by Mormon citizens, that went beyond the usual form of such documents. Rather than a humble petition for admission as a state, the Mormon petition demanded statehood and said, in effect, that if statehood were denied, Utahns would feel themselves under no obligation to obey officers and laws forced upon them from outside.

When combined with exaggerated reports of conditions in Utah reaching him on every hand, the petition and memorial were interpreted by newly inaugurated president James Buchanan as a declaration of war on the part of the Mormons. One of his first major acts of office was to create an Expedition for Utah, a 2,500-soldier army escort for an as-yet-unnamed successor to Brigham Young as governor, with orders to install the successor and to take any other steps necessary to subdue rebellion and enforce federal law in Utah.

Brigham Young responded to news of the approaching army in September 1857 by considering it a hostile force, successor to the mobs, some of them uniformed, that had driven the Mormons from Missouri and Illinois. Martial law was declared in Utah, and the Nauvoo Legion was put on a war footing. Although there were no pitched battles between the federal army and the Mormon legionnaires, the Mormons fought a delaying war by harassing the federal troops at every turn; such harassment, greatly augmented by losses to military livestock, essential for the movement of supplies and troops, caused by weather and poor military organization in the early months of the Utah War, succeeded in forcing the army to go into winter quarters at Fort Bridger.

The infamous Mountain Meadows Massacre, perpetrated by Mormon settlers in the southern part of the Territory and resulting in the deaths of an estimated 120 California-bound Arkansas travelers, was caused in part by war hysteria, in part by years of growing hostility between Mormons and non-Mormons, and was the worst loss of life during the Utah War. While there were no pitched battles between the Utah Expedition and the Nauvoo Legion, there is no doubt that both sides were mentally and rhetorically prepared for an all-out shooting war in the spring of 1858. But other considerations brought an end to the Utah War before that point. Congressional inquiry and media outcry in the east prevented an increase in the army that would have been necessary to guarantee military success and caused Buchanan to send a peace commission to Utah. Brigham Young's attitude toward a military presence in Utah softened, in large measure due to negotiations brokered by Thomas Kane, a non-Mormon Pennsylvania lawyer and longtime friend to the Mormons, who traveled to Utah at his own expense and shuttled between the Mormon capital at Salt Lake City and the military camp at Fort Bridger, convincing Alfred Cumming, Buchanan's appointee as governor of Utah, to enter the Salt Lake Valley without a military escort and assume his duties there. The active phase of the Utah War ended in late June with the peaceful march through a Salt Lake City evacuated of virtually all civilians to establish quarters well south of the city at Camp Floyd and the return to the northern Utah settlements of the Mormons who had evacuated to the central part of the Territory.

While a nominal peace returned with the end of the Utah War, hostilities between Mormons and non-Mormons remained simmering just beneath the surface throughout the 1860s and beyond. Camp Floyd was closed in 1861, its soldiers marching east to take up roles in either the Union or the Confederate armies. The army returned to Utah in 1862, however, when Abraham Lincoln, not entirely trusting the professed loyalties of the Mormons, stationed California Volunteers under Patrick Edward Connor at a new military installation, Camp Douglas, on the high ground above Salt Lake City.

General Connor and former governor Young (still president of the Church and as firmly in charge of religious and social affairs in Utah as he had ever been, although no longer holding a role in civil government) never met, yet they were at odds with each other throughout the 1860s. Young had long counseled his people to concentrate on agriculture, to become self-sufficient through home industry, and to shun the lust for wealth and the immoralities that so often accompanied mining in the west. Connor, on the other hand, heavily promoted mining, both for his own advancement and in an attempt to dilute Mormon influence by encouraging an influx of non-Mormons into the area. Although the Mormon region was a mineral treasury and a mining industry was established during this period, the Mormons managed, by and large, to remain aloof from it; when gold and silver were found in the Tushar Mountains along the Sevier River, for instance, Mormons immediately took up all available agricultural land in the area in an effort to control the number of outside miners who could be supported at the mineral camps. When reportedly enormous deposits of silver were found west of the Mormon town of Panaca, the state of Nevada annexed the region. Although Panaca remained a Mormon town, the Mormons largely evacuated their settlements along the Muddy River farther south, which also fell within the district transferred to Nevada. Unrecognized at the time was that this reduction of Utah's borders would soon become a central tactic in the attempt to legislate Mormonism out of existence by reducing its geographic and political presence to a mere shadow of its former self.

Another massacre, rivaling Mountain Meadows in the number of its dead and in its treachery and wantonness, occurred just north of the Utah border in what was then Washington Territory, in January 1863. The Bear River Massacre had Mormon ties in that, in the months preceding the massacre, Mormon settlers in Cache Valley had protested repeated Indian incursions into their fields and herds and had requested protection from the California Volunteers at Camp Douglas. Troops led by Connor and assisted by Mormon guides attacked the Shoshone village on Bear River in the early morning of January 29. Even after the few Indian men in camp had been killed, Connor's frenzied soldiers hunted down and murdered fleeing women and children. Fourteen soldiers were killed, while a disputed number (in the hundreds) of Shoshones died. The wounded troops were given shelter in a Mormon meetinghouse before they returned to Camp Douglas. (Ironically, most of the Shoshone survivors of the massacre eventually became Mormons themselves, settling in the Indian town of Washakie on the Utah side of the state line.)

Beyond their mixed involvement with and hostility to the California Volunteers, Utah and the Mormons otherwise played little role in the Civil War. Two small units formed exclusively of Mormons served 90-day enlistments guarding the telegraph lines east and west of Salt Lake City, and individual Mormons living in various eastern states served in the armies with units from their states. The primary Mormon attitude toward the Civil War was an expectation that the bloody battles of that war were merely the opening scenes of the final wars of eschatological prophecy, and Mormons in Utah, for the most part, simply watched and waited for events to develop.

Nor did they become disturbed by (or submit to) the first national law passed with an aim to ending the Mormon practice of plural marriage: The Morrill Act, passed in 1862, made bigamy a crime in the territories. But, because of the lack of any funds provided by Congress to implement the terms of the Act and the far more pressing concerns of the Civil War, added to the geographical distance that still impeded the arrival in Utah of any but the most determined of non-Mormon authorities and immigrants, that law quickly became a dead letter.

Like the Morrill Act, which hinted of things to come, another event of 1862, relatively minor at the time, was a forerunner of major challenges in the 1870s and beyond. A small number of breakaway Mormons led by Joseph Morris formed a community in the Ogden area. A schism within that breakaway group occurred, and the two sides of the schism took up arms against each other, resulting in the holding of unlawful prisoners. A territorial posse sent to establish order was fired upon; the posse fired back; and the deaths on both sides are remembered as the "Morrisite rebellion." Although of only slight impact within Mormondom, the rebellion would be followed by more serious challenges later.

As the decade of the 1860s progressed, a major topic of interest was the approaching transcontinental railroad. While the national press predicted that the railroad would bring the end of Mormonism along with the end of isolation, the Mormon press anticipated a new spurt of Mormon vitality as the rails made it easier for Mormon converts to gather to Zion, along with the easier and cheaper importation of the materials needed to build the intermountain empire. Which side was right would be known only after the railroad was completed by the driving of the Golden Spike at Promontory Point, deep within Mormon territory, in May 1869.

—*Ardis E. Parshall*

As this era began with the construction of a temple at Nauvoo, it closed with construction of the iconic Salt Lake Tabernacle in the late 1860s. (Courtesy of the Church History Library, The Church of Jesus Christ of Latter-day Saints.)

See also: Black Hawk War; Colonization; Divergent Churches; Exodus from Nauvoo; Handcart Migration; Immigration; Martyrdom of Joseph and Hyrum Smith; Mormon Battalion; Mormonism and Economics; Mormonism and Native Americans; Mormonism and Secular Government; Mormonism and Violence; Mormonism and Women; Mountain Meadows Massacre; Nauvoo Legion; Pioneering; Polygamy; Pratt, Orson and Parley P.; Reformation; Seagulls and Crickets; Sessions, Patty Bartlett; Utah War;Young, Brigham.

References

Alexander, Thomas G. *Utah, the Right Place: The Official Centennial History.* Salt Lake City, UT: Gibbs Smith, 1995.

Allen, James B., and Glen M. Leonard. *The Story of the Latter-day Saints,* rev. ed. Salt Lake City, UT: Deseret Book, 1992.

Arrington, Leonard J. *Great Basin Kingdom: An Economic History of the Latter-day Saints, 1830–1900.* Cambridge, MA: Harvard University Press, 1958.

Arrington, Leonard J., and Davis Bitton. *The Mormon Experience: A History of the Latter-day Saints.* New York: Knopf, 1979.

Bagley, Will. *Blood of the Prophets: Brigham Young and the Mountain Meadows Massacre.* Norman: University of Oklahoma Press, 2002.

Bigler, David L., and Will Bagley, eds. *Army of Israel: Mormon Battalion Narratives.* Spokane, WA: Arthur H. Clark, 2000.

Brooks, Juanita. *The Mountain Meadows Massacre.* Norman: University of Oklahoma Press, 1950, rev., 1962, 1970.

Campbell, Eugene E. *Establishing Zion: The Mormon Church in the American West, 1847–1869.* Salt Lake City, UT: Signature Books, 1988.

Daynes, Kathryn M. *More Wives Than One: The Transformation of the Mormon Marriage System, 1830–1910.* Urbana: University of Illinois Press, 2001.

Esplin, Ronald K. "'A Place Prepared': Joseph, Brigham, and the Quest for Promised Refuge in the West." *Journal of Mormon History* 9 (1982): 85–111.

Furniss, Norman F. *The Mormon Conflict, 1850–1859.* New Haven, CT: Yale University Press, 1960; repr. 1977.

Hafen, Leroy R., and Ann W. Hafen. *Handcarts to Zion: The Story of a Unique Western Migration, 1856–1860.* Lincoln: University of Nebraska Press, 1992.

Hill, Marvin S. *Quest for Refuge: The Mormon Flight from American Pluralism.* Salt Lake City, UT: Signature Books, 1989.

Larson, Gustive O. "The Mormon Reformation." *Utah Historical Quarterly* 26 (January 1958): 45–63.

MacKinnon, William P., ed. *At Sword's Point: A Documentary History of the Utah War.* 2 vols. Norman, OK: Arthur H. Clark, 2008, and forthcoming.

Mulder, William. *Homeward to Zion: The Mormon Migration from Scandinavia.* Minneapolis: University of Minnesota Press, 1957.

Orton, Chad M. "The Martin Handcart Company at the Sweetwater: Another Look." *BYU Studies* 45, no. 3 (2006): 5–37.

Peterson, John Alton. *Utah's Black Hawk War.* Salt Lake City: University of Utah Press, 1998.

Poll, Richard D., Thomas G. Alexander, Eugene E. Campbell, and David E. Miller. *Utah's History.* Logan: Utah State University Press, 1989.

Quinn, D. Michael. *The Mormon Hierarchy: Extensions of Power.* Salt Lake City, UT: Signature Books in association with Smith Research Associates, 1997.

Stegner, Wallace. *The Gathering of Zion: The Story of the Mormon Trail.* Lincoln and London: University of Nebraska Press, 1981.

Taylor, P.A.M. *Expectations Westward: The Mormons and the Emigration of Their British Converts in the Nineteenth Century.* London: Oliver and Boyd, 1965.

Verdoia, Ken, and Richard Firmage. *Utah: The Struggle for Statehood,* produced by KUED for PBS, 1996.

Walker, Ronald W., Richard E. Turley Jr., and Glen M. Leonard. *Massacre at Mountain Meadows.* New York: Oxford University Press, 2008.

Conflict: 1869–1890

The completion of the transcontinental railroad was a watershed event in Mormon history, both symbolic and real. While it may be tempting to view the meeting of the rails at Promontory, Utah, on May 10, 1869, as merely a national event that happened in Utah, it in fact held far-reaching implications for the Mormon people living there. The railroad spelled a permanent end to Mormon isolation, the very thing that had attracted the Latter-day Saints to the barren expanses of the Great Basin more than 20 years earlier. The railroad also symbolized the long arm of federal power in the post–Civil War era.

The North, as a result of its victory in the Civil War, won the right to define what it meant to be an American. That definition was largely filtered through a northern, white, Republican, Protestant worldview, a view that ironically abolished slavery and granted civil rights and suffrage to African Americans while it simultaneously began eroding those same privileges for Mormons. From the end of the Civil War to 1890, the federal government passed a series of increasingly stringent bills designed to eradicate plural marriage and to end Mormon political dominance of Utah Territory. The Mormons resisted economically, socially, and politically, claiming that the Constitution protected their religious freedom. They shortly learned, however, that religious freedom had stark limits in the American West. By 1890, the Latter-day Saints capitulated and began to conform to mainstream definitions of what it meant to be an American. That year, in an effort to preserve temple worship, a more fundamental aspect of the Mormon worldview, they started the process of abandoning polygamy, laying the groundwork for Utah's statehood six years later.

To the nation, the railroad symbolized the triumph of people over nature, industrial progress, civilization, manifest destiny, and the unification of east and west just four years after the end of the Civil War, which had severed the Union, north against south. To the Mormons, however, the railroad represented a mixed bag. Brigham Young welcomed the railroad and the economic opportunities it embodied but also feared the effects that outside forces would have upon his efforts to build a religious kingdom. Young's bifurcated response signaled his willingness to both embrace change and to fight against it. Underneath it all was Young's broader goal of protecting and preserving the Mormon people from the same type of harassment that had earlier driven them from the United States as it existed at the time. Young purchased stock in the Union Pacific and signed labor contracts with it and the Central Pacific to provide Mormon workers to lay track at the same time that he enacted a variety of economic reforms designed to stem the tide of external influences and to shore up the self-sufficiency of his religious kingdom.

The Mormons had petitioned the federal government for a rail line to Salt Lake City as early as 1852, and they continued to lobby for a route that would connect the Mormon capital city to the outside world. The railroad represented a more cost effective method of bringing converts to Zion, and it facilitated trade. When it became evident that the railroad would bypass Salt Lake City to the north, Brigham Young offered land in Ogden free of charge to the Union and Central Pacific companies if they would locate their stations there, rather than at Corinne, the "gentile capital of Utah." The railroads readily agreed, and Young set to work connecting Salt Lake City to Ogden. By the beginning of 1870, the Mormons had built a line linking the two cities and then continued stretching steel rails to other important points throughout the Territory.

Even still, Brigham Young worried over the effects that such an easy link to the outside world would have upon his flock. The arrival of the railroad, along with improved technology and increased investment in Utah mines, led to a significant jump in the value of gold, silver, lead, and copper production, from just over $56,000 in 1865 to almost $1.5 million by 1870. To Young, this wealth and the lifestyle that it represented loomed as potential threats to Mormon agrarian values. He worried about the social and economic stratification that mining tended to breed, as well as its inherent cycle of boom and bust. He was building a permanent religious kingdom based upon ideals that honored community concern over individual wants. The fluid and raucous lifestyle at mining camps tended to favor the reverse. In response, Young threatened, warned, and cajoled Mormons and urged them to avoid losing sight of their heavenly pursuits in exchange for the allure of earthly riches. Nevertheless, when opportunity presented itself, Young attempted to control mineral strikes for the good of the kingdom and the benefit of all Latter-day Saints. Erastus Snow, a Mormon apostle, explained the distinction this way: "If the mines must be worked, it is better for the saints to work them than for others to do

ZCMI

Mormon values of self-reliance and economic independence found expression in many cooperative endeavors during the 19th century: Mormons preferred gathering in Mormon villages to being scattered among other people; new colonies in the west were planned with an eye to being self-supporting from the start; and communities joined to dig irrigation canals, raise public buildings, produce iron, build cotton mills, and accomplish other major tasks too great for individual effort alone.

Economic independence received new emphasis in 1868 when the pending completion of the transcontinental railroad raised the specter of Mormon cash flowing out of the Territory as fast as trains could bring outside goods in. Communities throughout the region were encouraged to form cooperative stores, furnishing a market for locally produced goods and establishing an easy marker for group identity; loyal Mormons would patronize their brethren through the cooperative stores, while those less loyal purchased from outsiders.

Zion's Cooperative Mercantile Institution (ZCMI), located in Salt Lake City, was Mormondom's flagship cooperative store and is recognized as the west's first department store. ZCMI and its branches were familiar components of the western Mormon landscape until 2002, when the name was changed by the national company that had purchased ZCMI in 1999.

it, but we have all the time prayed that the Lord would shut up the mines. It is better for us to live in peace and good order, and to raise wheat, corn, potatoes and fruit, than to suffer the evils of a mining life" (Journal History, June 5, 1870, 6).

Young's general prohibition against mining, however, caused tension among some of his followers that quickly led to a rift. William S. Godbe headed a group of like-minded business and cultural leaders in their challenge to Young's vision. Godbe questioned why Mormons should relegate themselves to agricultural pursuits while outside capitalists enjoyed the profits from Utah's mineral wealth. The Godbeites, as they came to be called, argued that Mormons should be free to pursue secular and economic avenues of their choosing. The movement also adopted a spiritualist bent as Godbe searched for answers through séances. Events came to a head in October 1869, when Godbe's news voice, the *Utah Magazine,* ran an article titled "The True Development of the Territory," which argued that mining would bring the Mormons greater financial success than strictly adhering to agriculture. The LDS hierarchy excommunicated Godbe for such open defiance. Other Godbeites were also excommunicated, some at their own request. They founded their own church and continued to disseminate their views in print. Their news voice eventually morphed into the *Salt Lake Tribune,* the leading opposition newspaper in 19th-century Utah.

In July 1870, several leading Godbeites joined a variety of peoples of other faiths to meet at Corinne, Utah, to hold a political convention. They called their new organization the Liberal Party and announced their intention to challenge Mormon theocratic abuses in the Territory and to support a republican form of government. In response, the Mormons organized themselves politically as the People's Party. This formation of politics along religious lines symbolized the growing strength of the non-Mormon population in Utah Territory, as well as the growing chasm between Mormons and non-Mormons. This religious divide grew to dominate not just politics but most aspects of late 19th-century Utah life.

Forces outside Utah Territory also came to bear upon the Mormons and soon posed significant threats to their way of life. With the Civil War over and slavery abolished, the Mormons quickly learned of the growing strength of the Republican Party's fervor to eradicate polygamy, the other relic of barbarism. The first attempt to do so came early in 1869, although through somewhat unconventional means. James M. Ashley, chairman of the U.S. House Committee on Territories, introduced a bill into the U.S. House designed to solve the "Mormon Question" by wiping Utah Territory from the map. Ashley planned to reduce Utah to a mere 22,000 square miles and then divide up the remaining land and its Mormon occupants among Utah's neighboring state (Nevada) and territories. When those neighboring entities were strong enough to absorb the main body of Mormons at Salt Lake City, he would finish the job by eradicating Utah altogether. Ashley believed that this would sufficiently dilute the Mormon vote among surrounding "gentile" populations and thereby end Mormon political dominance of the Great Basin. Ashley also viewed the bill as a signal to the Mormon community that Congress would not consent to statehood for Utah so long as Mormons remained in power. The bill died without coming to a vote, but for the Mormons it was a small portent of the protracted legal and political battles to come.

In 1870, Representative Shelby M. Cullom of Illinois sponsored the Cullom Bill, a mishmash of legislation that included 34 sections, each of which was aimed at ending polygamy and Mormon political control of Utah Territory. Among other things, the bill included provisions that would have prevented those who believed in plural marriage from serving on juries in polygamy trials; defined cohabitation and adultery as crimes alongside bigamy and polygamy; exempted crimes related to polygamy from the statute of limitations; excluded polygamists from voting, being naturalized, or holding public office; and authorized the president of the United States to enforce the bill's provisions with military force if necessary. The Cullom Bill died in the Senate, partly because some members of Congress believed that, if given time, the railroad would serve as an agent of civilization to bring an end to the Mormon problem. Others similarly viewed the Godbeite dissent with hopeful eyes, believing that the internal schism was a promising sign of liberalizing influences already at play among the Mormons. When those predictions did not come true, Congress passed legislation piecemeal over the next two decades that included most of the provisions of the failed Cullom Bill.

Mormon women played significant roles in this growing political firestorm. The prevailing national attitude was that Mormon women were held captive to the tyranny of polygamy and that, given the choice, they would abandon it. By the end of 1868, such ideas found favor with at least one "radical Republican" in the U.S. House. George W. Julian of Indiana introduced legislation designed to grant women's suffrage in the territories, but, when that stalled, he narrowed his focus to Utah. He argued that suffrage there would allow Mormon women to free themselves from polygamy. His bill died in committee but gave an indication of how out of touch some national leaders were with prevailing sentiments of Mormon women and men on the subject of suffrage.

On January 13, 1870, more than 3,000 Mormon women gathered at the Old Tabernacle in Salt Lake City to express themselves politically. The meeting largely grew out of a desire among Mormon women to formally protest the proposed Cullom Bill, then being debated in Congress. More than a protest, however, the meeting and its groundswell of follow-up assemblages throughout the Territory provided Mormon women an opportunity to publicly assert their support for the LDS Church, plural marriage, freedom of religion, and, by their very action, political voice.

At the same time that Mormon women across the Territory responded to the Cullom Bill, men in the Utah territorial legislature demonstrated their support for women's suffrage. These men had little fear that Mormon women would use the vote to abandon plural marriage or Mormonism. In fact, their motivation in part was to demonstrate to outside observers how committed Mormon women were to their faith and their marriages. Utah's suffrage bill passed the territorial legislature in 1870 without a dissenting vote. Utah became the second territory, behind Wyoming, to grant women the right to vote. Much to the dismay of the opponents of polygamy, Mormon women tended to vote to shore up LDS political control and to support polygamy. As historian Kathryn L. MacKay notes, "Mormon women themselves felt powerful. They did not want to be rescued from polygamy. They treated polygamy as a feminist cause, as an institution which had the capacity to liberate women and help them develop independence" (MacKay, "Women in Politics" 372).

To those ends, several Mormon women became active in the national women's suffrage campaign, while others, such as Ellis Reynolds Shipp and Martha Hughes Cannon, became physicians. Emmeline B. Wells served as editor from 1877 to 1914 of the *Woman's Exponent,* at the time the longest-running suffrage publication in the nation. Wells argued in favor of national women's suffrage and supported polygamy, an innovation that she stated "makes woman more the companion and much less the subordinate than any other form of marriage" (Mead, *How the Vote*

Was Won 33). In 1872, Utah also admitted two lawyers, Phoebe W. Couzins and Georgie Snow, to the bar, well in advance of many other states and territories. Nineteenth-century Mormon women, in many regards, pushed feminism along, rather than stood in its way.

When the liberalizing forces of women's suffrage, the railroad, and the Godbeites failed to lead to an erosion of polygamy or Mormon political power, Congress turned to new legislation as an answer. The Poland Act (1874) was the first such bill to make it into law following the Civil War. It was designed to help facilitate convictions for polygamy under the Morrill Act (1862) by stripping power from the hands of territorial probate judges in civil and criminal cases and placing it under federal control. Local probate judges were thereafter limited to matters of guardianship, estates, and divorce, while federal judges would begin to preside over polygamy cases. The Poland Act further placed some power in the hands of federal officials for partial selection of jury pools and allowed for appeal of polygamous convictions to the Supreme Court.

The bill came hot on the heels of a sensationalized divorce case in Brigham Young's own household. In 1873, Ann Eliza Young left both Mormonism and her husband and sued for divorce. In the wake of the very public split, she also undertook a speaking tour that eventually took her, in the spring of 1874, to Washington, D.C., where she spoke in front of President Ulysses S. Grant, his wife, and several congressmen. She detailed jealousies, violence, and a marriage system in which, she alleged, Mormon women were held captive. Ann Eliza's exposé no doubt influenced the passage of the Poland Act that summer, which in turn paved the way for a polygamous test case to wind its way to the U.S. Supreme Court.

Before those events played out, however, Brigham Young would put into play a variety of actions designed to shore up his kingdom against perceived eroding influences. Prior to the completion of the transcontinental railroad, he reorganized the Relief Society for women and the School of the Prophets for men and founded the Zion's Cooperative Mercantile Institution (ZCMI), an early version of the department store, with branches throughout the Territory. Young then instructed Mormons to patronize only ZCMI and was thereby successful in driving some "gentile" businesses out of Utah. His most far-reaching economic reform, however, did not come until 1874, when he launched a last-ditch effort at self-sufficiency known as the United Order. The nationwide depression that began in 1873 hit most Utah communities hard; Brigham Young hoped to better insulate Mormons from the sometimes cruel market forces.

The United Order had its roots in earlier Mormon communitarianism but manifested itself in Utah in a variety of forms. Mormons at Brigham City had much earlier formed a range of business cooperatives of which Brigham Young became enamored, especially as that community seemed to weather the national depression in good order. Mormons in the southwestern part of the Territory, however, did not fare so well. It was there, at St. George, that Young chose to launch a United Order revival that would serve as a model for most United Orders formed that year. At St. George, Mormons who participated maintained possession of their homes and personal property but deeded their businesses and farms to the order. Similar orders were formed in more than 200 communities throughout the Territory. The most extreme example was that at Orderville, Utah, where participants gave personal and real property over to the order, ate at a communal dining hall, functioned under an organized division of labor, and otherwise lived as an extended family unit. The Orderville order enjoyed significant initial success, with communal assets tripling in the first four years alone. The cooperative there survived, albeit in watered-down form, until 1900.

Most orders, however, lasted less than a year before succumbing to both internal and external pressures. The experience at Hebron, Utah, was perhaps most typical. Hebron residents organized themselves communally in March 1874 following the pattern established at St. George. Local LDS authorities appointed Thomas S. Terry superintendent and manager of farming for the community and named Bishop George Crosby president. The day after organizing, all residents met in the school-house to receive their work instructions. Terry then sent some people to plow, some to repair fences, and others to perform a variety of maintenance duties. Each day, residents followed the same pattern.

Before long, however, contention and jealousy crept into the order over perceived favoritisms in work assignments and distribution of material goods. As a result, less than four months after the order began, Terry resigned his office and withdrew from the Order. Before long, others withdrew as well, and within a year the order had all but disappeared at Hebron.

As with the United Order effort, Brigham Young met the challenges of his later years with increased resolve. In 1877, the year he died, he traveled to southern Utah to dedicate the St. George temple, the Mormons' first completed temple west of the Mississippi. The construction of the temple was a significant accomplishment, especially for the impoverished southern Utah Saints. Even still, Young used the occasion to sound a familiar theme. He preached against seeking worldly riches, especially the lifestyles represented at two nearby mining camps, Pioche, Nevada, and Silver Reef, Utah. "[G]o to work and let these holes in the ground alone, and let the Gentiles alone, who would destroy us if they had the power," Young admonished. "You will go to hell, lots of you, unless you repent" (Young, "Remarks" 18:305).

Just a few weeks before Young left to return to Salt Lake City, federal officials took John D. Lee to Mountain Meadows and executed him by firing squad. Lee was an influential participant in the 1857 massacre at the meadows. He endured two trials and was the only Mormon convicted for the atrocity. The first trial, in 1875, ended in a hung jury, with the eight Mormon jurors voting for acquittal and the others for conviction. At the second trial, an all-Mormon jury found Lee guilty of murder, and the judge sentenced him to die.

On his return trip to Salt Lake City, Young received a 25-man escort through Beaver County, the site of the Lee trials. Rumors of threats against Young's life at the hands of Lee's sons concerned the returning entourage. One southern Utah newspaper even suggested that Rachel Lee, one of Lee's widows, was intent upon harming Young. Despite such rumors, Young returned to the Mormon capital without facing violence, although he did face criticism and concern from some Mormons over the Lee trials and the massacre. Young died August 29, 1877, in Salt Lake City, of what attending doctors called "cholera morbus." His passing marked the end of an important era in Mormonism and would usher in one of the Church's more turbulent legal decades.

Brigham Young did not live to see the outcome of the constitutional challenge over polygamy that he helped to initiate. George Reynolds, Young's secretary and husband to two wives, allowed himself to be indicted for polygamy in 1874 and thereby became the defendant in a test case, *United States v. Reynolds.* The Supreme

Hundreds of Mormon men served prison sentences in the 1880s rather than abandon their plural families as demanded by federal law. (Courtesy of the Church History Library, The Church of Jesus Christ of Latter-day Saints.)

Court finally ruled on the case in 1879 and, in doing so, narrowly interpreted constitutional freedom of religion to protect only belief, not practice. It was a stunning blow to the Mormons, who had long believed that polygamy would be protected under the Constitution as a religious principle. The *Reynolds* decision reverberated throughout Utah Territory, especially as Congress acted in its wake to crush polygamy and its sponsoring institution.

It fell to Young's successor, John Taylor, to decide how to handle the Church's stinging legal defeat. Taylor was president of the Quorum of the Twelve Apostles and the person with the most seniority in that quorum at the time of Young's passing. As a result of the precedent established at Joseph Smith's death, succession passed to the quorum, with Taylor at its head. Like Brigham Young, Taylor waited three years before reorganizing the First Presidency with himself at the helm and George Q. Cannon and Joseph F. Smith as counselors. Economically, Taylor proved less committed to communalism than Young and more open to capitalism and business. He made positive statements about mining, and Church leaders invested in silver and gold mines in the 1880s and 1890s.

This economic opening would not, however, shield the Mormons from a federal crackdown on polygamy. It was Taylor who responded to this threat with a policy of civil disobedience. Taylor argued that when the laws of God came into conflict with the laws of the land, he would follow the laws of God. In the wake of the *Reynolds* decision, he announced his intentions to uphold plural marriage and take the consequences.

The consequences grew increasingly bitter for Mormons, especially after Congress passed the Edmunds Act in 1882. This law made it easier to convict polygamists by lowering the standard of proof. No longer would lawyers have to provide evidence of illegal marriage, a difficult task given the secret nature of plural marriages; they would simply have to prove "unlawful cohabitation." The act also disqualified polygamists from voting, serving on juries, and holding public office and appointed a five-person federal commission to oversee elections in Utah. The Utah Commission, as it was called, instituted a test oath that required anyone wishing to vote in the Territory to swear to his or her nonpolygamous status. Before the Supreme Court struck down the test oath as unconstitutional, the Utah Commission had effectively barred more than 12,000 Mormons from the polls. The non-Mormon population in the Territory was overjoyed. Following the passage of the Edmunds Act, the front page of one mining newspaper announced, "Passed! The 'Twin-Relic' Doomed by the Voice of the Nation. Polygamy to the Rear and America to the Front." Another day, it gloated, "The funeral of polygamy will soon begin. No postponement on account of the weather" (*Silver Reef Miner,* March 15, 17, 24, 1882).

The first Latter-day Saint prosecuted under the new law was Rudger Clawson, who was convicted for both polygamy and unlawful cohabitation. Judge Charles S.

Zane ordered him to pay an $800 fine and to serve four years in prison, but President Grover Cleveland pardoned Clawson after he had served three years. By 1893, the courts had handed down more than 1,000 sentences for unlawful cohabitation and another 31 for polygamy.

In the wake of this crackdown, Mormons went into hiding on what came to be called "the underground" in an effort to avoid federal marshals. Men scuttled from home to home in secrecy. Some men moved their multiple wives to different towns, states, and even countries in an effort to protect against the charge of unlawful cohabitation. Polygamists' wives often headed independent households, seeing their husbands only sporadically. Annie Clark Tanner recalled in poignant detail her wedding night following a secret marriage to Joseph Marion Tanner as his second wife in 1883. She returned home to her family while Joseph left with his first wife. She later wrote, "As I sat down to a glass of bread and milk the thought came to me. 'Well, this is my wedding supper.' In those few minutes I recalled the elaborate marriage festivals which had taken place in our own family, of the banquets I had helped to prepare and the many lovely brides among my friends. I even began to compare their wedding gowns. I was conscious of the obscurity of my own first evening after marriage. 'What a contrast,' I said to myself. 'No one will ever congratulate *me*'" (Tanner, *A Mormon Mother* 66). Especially after she became pregnant, Annie had to conceal her marital status and gave birth on the Mormon underground. Some Mormon men went on missions to avoid prosecution, while some women went into exile in foreign countries to protect their husbands. Needless to say, the Edmunds Act and its enforcement severely disrupted family life among Mormon polygamists.

As a countermove, John Taylor instigated Mormon colonization efforts in both Canada and Mexico. Even though both countries outlawed polygamy, neither of them actively enforced their laws. Beginning in 1884, Taylor instructed LDS leaders in Arizona to seek refuge from federal marshals in Mexico if necessary. The following year, Taylor himself visited the northern Mexico state of Chihuahua and spurred the colonization effort along. Within a decade, more than 3,000 Mormons had moved to Mexico and founded three primary settlements: Colonia Juarez, Colonia Dublan, and Colonia Diaz. Taylor also instructed Mormons to move to Canada as a place of "asylum and justice." In 1886, an advance party selected Cardston, Alberta, as a gathering spot for Mormons, and, just nine years later, the Canadian settlements became the site of the first LDS stake organized outside the United States.

Despite these countermeasures, Taylor himself was personally affected by the federal raids. A reward poster offered $300 for information leading to Taylor's arrest. He delivered his last public sermon on February 1, 1885, and then went into hiding. He continued to direct the LDS Church by writing letters from the underground, but his final years were spent being shuttled from place to place in an elaborate network of safe houses that shielded him from the law. He died July 25, 1887, in hiding, at Kaysville, Utah.

It would fall to Taylor's successor, Wilford Woodruff, to deal with the Church's most serious legal challenge to polygamy. In 1887, Congress passed the Edmunds-Tucker Act, a far-reaching piece of legislation designed to grind the LDS Church to dust. Among other things, it dissolved the Church as a legal entity and prevented it from holding any property in excess of $50,000 not used exclusively for religious purposes. It disbanded the territorial militia, dissolved the Perpetual Emigrating Fund Company, abolished women's suffrage in Utah, and required prospective voters, officeholders, and jurors to sign an oath attesting to their support of anti-polygamy laws.

As the Edmunds-Tucker Act went into effect over the next three years, Mormons' temporal and political strength waned considerably. George Q. Cannon, a member of the First Presidency, spent time in prison, and LDS property went into receivership. The Supreme Court, in May 1890, upheld the legality of Edmunds-Tucker and even left the door open for the future confiscation of property used exclusively for religious purposes, including Mormon temples. Temple worship for Mormons represents the highest manifestation of their devotion to their God. When, in late 1890, it became clear to Woodruff that the federal government was intent on confiscating the Logan, St. George, and Manti temples, he was forced to confront the dilemma. As Woodruff later explained, the choice boiled down to polygamy or the temples. In response, he claimed to receive spiritual promptings, or a "revelation," to abandon polygamy in order to preserve a more fundamental aspect of LDS theology embodied in temple worship. Accordingly, on September 24, 1890, he issued as a press release a document that came to be called the Woodruff Manifesto. In it, Woodruff declared his intention to submit to the laws of the land and to use his influence with the body of Saints to do likewise. It was another watershed moment in Mormon history. Although polygamy did not end overnight, the Manifesto began the slow process of its demise as well as laid the groundwork for Utah's admission into the Union by January 1896.

Despite increasing political and social threats at home, Mormons continued to send missionaries, two by two, with their distinctive bowler hats and "grips," to serve as missionaries throughout the United States and Europe. (Courtesy of the Church History Library, The Church of Jesus Christ of Latter-day Saints.)

In the end, the Mormons in the late 19th century provided fertile testing ground for American values. Following the Civil War and the eradication of slavery, the Republican Party turned its attention toward the West and polygamy. In doing so, it worked out, in sometimes heavy-handed ways, a definition of what it meant to be an American. That definition considered plural marriage immoral and saw theocracy as un-American, and it forced the Mormons to comply before Utah could be admitted as a state. As historian Todd M. Kerstetter sees it, the conflict did not end until the Mormons fully realized that "the Constitution is a Protestant document and the United States a Protestant nation" (Kerstetter, *God's Country* 80). It was a difficult lesson to learn, but perhaps a valuable one. The eradication of polygamy and the tempering of the Mormon theocratic millenarian vision, in the long run, served the Mormons well. These steps not only paved the way for statehood and broader mainstream acceptance but laid the groundwork for the LDS Church's future growth and vitality.

—*W. Paul Reeve*

See also: Colonization; Manifesto; Mormonism and Economics; Mormonism and Secular Government; Mormonism and Women; Mountain Meadows Massacre; Polygamy; Taylor, John; Temples; *United States v. Reynolds*; Woodruff, Wilford; Young, Brigham.

References

Journal History of the Church of Jesus Christ of Latter-day Saints (chronology of typed entries and newspaper clippings, 1830 to the Present). Family and Church History Department, Church of Jesus Christ of Latter-day Saints, Salt Lake City, UT.

Kerstetter, Todd M. *God's Country, Uncle Sam's Land: Faith and Conflict in the American West.* Urbana: University of Illinois Press, 2006.

Lyman, Edward Leo. *Political Deliverance: The Mormon Quest for Utah Statehood.* Urbana: University of Illinois Press, 1986.

MacKay, Kathryn L. "Women in Politics: Power in the Public Sphere." In *Women in Utah History: Paradigm or Paradox?* Ed. Patricia Lyn Scott and Linda Thatcher. Logan: Utah State University Press, 2005.

Mead, Rebecca J. *How the Vote Was Won: Woman Suffrage in the Western United States, 1868–1914.* New York: New York University Press, 2004.

Reeve, W. Paul. *Making Space on the Western Frontier: Mormons, Miners, and Southern Paiutes.* Urbana: University of Illinois Press, 2006.

Silver Reef Miner. Silver Reef, Utah, 1882.

Tanner, Annie Clark. *A Mormon Mother.* Salt Lake City, UT: University of Utah Library Tanner Trust Fund, 1991.

Walker, Ronald W. *Wayward Saints: The Godbeites and Brigham Young.* Urbana: University of Illinois Press, 1998.

Young, Brigham. "Remarks by President Brigham Young," January 1, 1877. *Journal of Discourses,* vol. 18. London: LDS Booksellers Depot, 1877.

Transition: 1890–1941

Approval, in October 1890, of President Wilford Woodruff's Manifesto was the first of a series of accommodations that eventually brought the LDS Church into the mainstream of American society. During the final third of the 19th century, the people of Utah had organized political parties on religious lines. Virtually all Mormons belonged to the People's Party, and members of other religions or no religion at all supported the Liberal Party. Following some efforts at offering fusion tickets, in June 1891 the Church leadership agreed to disband the People's Party and to encourage members to support the two national parties. Members then began to cooperate with non-Mormon politicians to organize and promote the Republican and Democratic parties. By December 1893, the Liberal Party had lost so many members that those remaining disbanded the organization.

The attempt to divide into the two national parties proved divisive. Since Republicans had been the major sponsors of the anti-Mormon legislation of the late 19th century, most Mormons flocked to the Democratic Party. The Church leadership believed that if that condition persisted, the split between Mormons and non-Mormons would reappear under the banners of the national parties. As a result, they actively discouraged Democratic general authorities like Moses Thatcher, Heber J. Grant, and B. H. Roberts from recruiting, while they urged Republicans like John Henry Smith and Francis M. Lyman to recruit vigorously. As Mormon women divided into national parties, general and local Church leaders urged Democratic members of the Relief Society general presidency, including Zina D. H. Young, Jane Richards, and Bathsheba W. Smith, and Salt Lake stake leaders, not to recruit as actively for their party. At the same time, Republican women like Emmeline B. Wells and Susa Young Gates worked to strengthen the ranks of the GOP.

Among the male leaders, Moses Thatcher suffered most because he refused to sign a document called the Political Manifesto. The document would have required him as a general authority to secure permission from the First Presidency and the Quorum of the Twelve Apostles to campaign actively for the U.S. Senate, a position for which he appeared to be the front-runner. Following his refusal to sign the document, the Twelve Apostles

Whether for broadcasting sermons by church leaders or musical programs by the Mormon Tabernacle Choir, the Church has been an enthusiastic adopter of new communications technologies from early in the 20th century. (Courtesy of the Church History Library, The Church of Jesus Christ of Latter-day Saints.)

dropped him from the quorum in April 1896, and he saved his Church membership only by recanting in a trial before the Salt Lake Stake presidency and the High Council.

B.H. Roberts, though initially declining to support such restrictions, eventually capitulated. Moreover, after securing permission, he ran successfully as a Democrat for Utah's congressional seat in 1898. Roberts was, however, a polygamist, and the House of Representatives refused to seat him. Utahns elected William H. King, a Mormon attorney and stake high councilman, to Roberts's seat. King lost in his bid for reelection in 1900 to George Sutherland, a non-Mormon Republican of Mormon parentage. In a turnabout, King defeated Sutherland for one of Utah's U.S. Senate seats in 1916.

Mormonism's and Utah's most important battle over the place of Latter-day Saints in American life took place following Reed Smoot's election to the Senate by the Utah legislature in 1903. At the time, legislatures, rather than the public at large, elected senators. Smoot, a member of the Quorum of the Twelve Apostles and a Republican, presented himself in Congress, and, unlike Roberts, the Senate seated him. After his election, a group of anti-Mormon ministers, businesspeople, and politicians lodged a protest. Although the protest contained a number of charges, the anti-Mormon group alleged principally that the LDS Church was a subversive organization and that, because of Smoot's oath as an apostle, he could not legitimately swear to uphold the Constitution of the United States. The hearings, which lasted from 1904 through 1907, constituted what is most likely the most thorough congressional examination of the current affairs of a religious organization in the history of the United States.

If the Senate had refused to seat Smoot before the protest, he would most likely not have been permitted to serve. In the votes to retain his seat, Smoot lost a majority of votes both in the Senate Committee on Privileges and Elections and in the full Senate. Since, however, the Constitution stipulated that two-thirds of the Senate must agree to the expulsion of a sitting member, Smoot retained his seat. He continued to serve until 1933, when Elbert D. Thomas, an active Latter-day Saint and an active New Deal supporter, defeated him.

The investigation accompanying Smoot's effort to retain his Senate seat led to the discovery of a number of embarrassing revelations. A number of general and local Church leaders had themselves entered into new plural marriages, and some had performed such marriages for others. Moreover, most of those members and leaders who had married polygamously before the Manifesto had continued to maintain those relationships. Beyond this, in several cases local leaders had used ecclesiastical pressure in business and political dealings.

In an attempt to come to terms with the fallout from these revelations, the Church leadership took a number of actions. At the April 1904 general conference, several weeks after he returned from testifying in the Smoot hearings, Church president Joseph F. Smith presented a second Manifesto to the general conference. It promised Church discipline, threatening the membership of those who entered new plural marriages. Although a number of general authorities had performed polygamous marriages after 1890, the leadership confined the discipline to those who entered or performed them after 1904. As a result, the Quorum of the Twelve Apostles dropped John W. Taylor and Matthias F. Cowley from the quorum. In trials before the quorum, Taylor was excommunicated, and Cowley was forbidden to exercise his priesthood.

As evidence of additional polygamous sealings after the second Manifesto mounted and the general authorities learned that a number of stake leaders had performed the ordinances, a committee of the Twelve chaired by quorum president Francis M. Lyman convened a series of Church courts. These led to the excommunication of a number of local officials. After these trials, the Church began to excommunicate any members who had entered into new plural marriages.

At the same time, a number of local officials who opposed President Woodruff's Manifesto began to organize splinter groups that continued to practice plural marriage. Although many of these groups live relatively peaceful—though illegal—lives, some organizations, like those associated with the LeBaron and Lafferty families, committed murders in support of their causes.

President Heber J. Grant during the 1920s and Grant and his counselor, J. Reuben Clark, in the 1930s were particularly vigorous in seeking out and excommunicating those who refused to observe the Church's teaching that marriage constituted a union of one man and one woman. Clark also unleashed a verbal attack on fundamentalists who insisted falsely that the Church leadership still continued to sanction new plural marriages.

Since the percentage of members in polygamy had declined dramatically after 1880, such matters did not affect many in the Church. In a careful study of plural marriage in Manti, Utah, Kathryn Daynes found that the percentage of men, women, and children in polygamous families and of widows of polygamists had declined from 25.1 percent in 1880 to 7.1 percent in 1900.

Further evidence of the decline became available in 1902. In that year, the First Presidency secured reports from all of the stake presidents in the United States on the number of polygamous families living within their boundaries. These statistics did not include widows of polygamists as Daynes's figures did. Nor did they include polygamists who lived outside the United States or whose families lived there. Since the Church had one stake each in Canada and Mexico, the statistics excluded a number of polygamous families. Nevertheless, the stake presidents' reports revealed that 897 polygamous families lived in the United States. At the time, 249,927 members lived in the Church's stakes. In 1900, the average family size in the

United States was 5.5 people. If we assume that the two stakes outside the United States had 1,000 members each, we can conclude that perhaps 2 percent of the Church membership lived in polygamous families at the turn of the 20th century.

At any rate, even if Daynes's figure of 7 percent for Manti represented a more accurate picture of the overall number of families living in polygamy by including widows who had lived in polygamous families, by the early 20th century the number of polygamists had declined considerably. Clearly, contrary to anti-Mormon propaganda, by the early 20th century few members lived in polygamous families, and most had accepted the general Western pattern of a family consisting of a man, a woman, and their children.

If the tendency of a quarter of the Church membership to live in polygamous families had ended, the measures of activity of Church members had also changed. In the 19th century, the Church leadership expected members to migrate to the intermountain West. The Church leadership then expected the migrants to respond to calls to settle throughout the region. By the early 20th century, Church members had founded 537 settlements in locations stretching from southern Canada to northern Mexico on the north and south and from western Colorado to southern California on the east and west.

Most Church-sponsored settlements occurred in the 19th century, though some, such as Star Valley, Wyoming, and Delta, Utah, were founded in the early 20th century. Some authorities have considered the settlements in the Uintah Basin following the opening of the Uintah and Ouray Reservation in 1905 as Church-sponsored, but, although a number of Church members settled there, these were actually landrush settlements that resulted from drawings for land sponsored by the federal government.

On the whole, the Mormon settlement process proved remarkably successful. An exhaustive study by Lynn Rosenvall showed that by 1930, only 46 of the 537 settlements, or 8.6 percent, had failed. These were, however, generally small marginal settlements, and they affected only about 5,000 of the 670,000-person membership in 1930. Most of those in failed settlements moved to other Mormon towns. Most of the failures resulted from environmental factors such as floods or insufficient land or other resources. Some settlements in Mexico failed because of the Mexican Revolution of 1912, and the Hawaiian settlement at Skull Valley, Utah, failed in part because of environmental factors and in part because the Church encouraged members to return to Hawaii, where it built a temple.

After the body of the Church moved to Utah, the Church built four temples in the Territory. Between 1919 and 1927, however, the Church dedicated three temples outside Utah. These were in Laie, Hawaii (1919); Cardston, Alberta, Canada (1923); and Mesa, Arizona (1927).

In the years between 1890 and 1940, most members did not attend the temple regularly for vicarious baptism, endowment, and sealing ceremonies. Reed Smoot, for instance, testified that he had participated in temple ceremonies only for his own endowments and for the sealing to his wife. Nevertheless, changes in Church doctrines and practices inaugurated by President Woodruff allowed more frequent attendance, which has become an important aspect of faithful Church membership. Shortly after the opening of the St. George temple, in 1877, Woodruff began performing vicarious ordinances for deceased persons with whom he was not related. Prior to that time, vicarious endowments had been performed only for relatives.

Nevertheless, Woodruff also emphasized the importance of each member's family. In 1894, Woodruff announced the end of the law of adoption, through which members had been sealed to prominent Church leaders. Henceforth, Woodruff said, members should be sealed to their ancestors in an unbroken line as far back as research could take them. To promote the research, in the same year, the Church leaders chartered the Genealogical Society of Utah.

These changes in doctrine and practice facilitated the type of family history and temple work currently practiced by faithful members. The Church leadership encourages members to conduct research on their own ancestral lines. At the same time, members are also encouraged to search out the names of other deceased persons. Members are then encouraged to perform vicarious ordinances for both groups of people.

In the 19th century, although many members attended regular Church services, many did not, and the Church leaders did not account most who failed to attend as slackers. On the other hand, in addition to founding and developing settlements, in the 19th century the Church leadership also expected priesthood holders—all the men in the Church—to respond to calls to serve proselytizing missions throughout the world. Also, though conditions changed over time, the leadership did not expect most members to observe the current interpretation of the Word of Wisdom by abstaining from coffee, tea, tobacco, and alcoholic beverages.

After 1900, however, such practices began to undergo a number of changes, especially those measures that were perceived as constituting full activity. Leaders emphasized the Word of Wisdom, and in 1921 adherence became a requisite for temple attendance. Although the Church continued to call some married men on missions after 1900, more frequently it called young single priesthood holders, rather than those with families.

In addition, Church leaders began to pay more attention to statistics of attendance at Church meetings and to encourage meeting attendance as a sign of worthiness. During the 19th century, the Church held Fast and Testimony during the day on Thursdays. Since most members were self-employed, generally as farmers, they could take the time off to attend. By the 1890s, however, increasingly large numbers of members worked for other people, and they often found it difficult to get the time off on a weekday. Responding to this condition, in 1896 the Church leadership shifted Fast and Testimony meeting to the first Sunday of each month.

Moreover, leaders regularized the meeting times of other Church meetings, which had been held at various times in wards throughout the Church. After experimenting with various configurations of meetings, including holding priesthood meetings during the week, the Church leadership instructed the wards to hold priesthood meeting and Sunday School on Sunday mornings and Sacrament Meeting on Sunday afternoons. Young Men and Young Women Mutual Improvement Association meetings were held on an evening during the week, and the women held Relief Society meeting during the daytime, also during midweek. The women also held Primary meeting for children under age 14 (later under age 12) after school one day during the week.

Moreover, the Church leadership began writing lessons for priesthood quorums and auxiliaries. The Quorums of the Seventy, the YMMIA, and the Primary were the first organizations to have centrally assigned lessons.

These changes had the effect of increasing the percentage of members attending Sacrament Meeting from averages that ranged between 5 and 15 percent at the turn of the 20th century to more than 35 percent by the 1930s. Priesthood and auxiliary meeting attendance also increased.

During the early 20th century, the Church leadership began to exercise greater control over the auxiliaries. The Relief Society, which had been perceived as an organization for women parallel to the priesthood quorums and not as an auxiliary, became an auxiliary under priesthood supervision. The Primary Association, which members perceived as a woman's auxiliary, since the Relief Society had organized and operated it, also became a Church-wide auxiliary. In 1909, the First Presidency assigned apostles Hyrum M. Smith and George F. Richards as advisers to the Primary Association, though the general presidency and board consisted of women. Originally, all children met together in a large class. In 1902, however, the Primary began to use graded instruction, and, during the 1920s the association began to divide children by gender. Girls were trained as homemakers and boys for Scouting and the priesthood. After furnishing a wing of Latter-day Saints Hospital in 1913, during the 1920s the Primary leadership began planning for the institution that became Primary Children's Hospital.

During the late 19th and early 20th centuries, the Young Men's and Young Women's Mutual Improvement Associations were essentially adult education programs. They sponsored reading groups, debating societies, and lectures for their members. In 1904, the four Salt Lake stakes organized a lecture bureau and brought in national figures like Jacob Riis, Hamlin Garland, and Elbert Hubbard.

Increasingly, however, during the early 20th century, the MIA began to emphasize recreational activities. In 1911, the YMMIA inaugurated a program for boys parallel to the Boy Scouts of America. Between 1911 and 1913, the general board considered the question of whether to affiliate with the national organization. In 1913, it did so, and, by 1916, Utah had the highest per capita membership in scouting of any state. To support the program, stakes began building camps. The Ensign Stake of Salt Lake City was the first to open, in 1912.

The YWMIA joined the Camp Fire Girls in 1913 but dropped its membership in 1915 and replaced it with a system of graded classes, beginning with Beehive Girls for 12-year-olds.

In 1914, the Church leadership began a system of training for youth leaders. At first it sponsored a six-week training session at the Church's educational institutions. These were replaced by regular conferences in June of each year.

Athletic programs became a regular feature of the YMMIA. In 1911, the Church sponsored the first annual interstake track meet at Wandamere Park in Salt Lake City. Gradually, basketball replaced the track meets as the favored athletic activity, and the Church eventually sponsored interstake and Church-wide basketball tournaments. During the 1920s, Presiding Bishop Charles W. Nibley purchased Wandamere from the Church and donated it to Salt Lake City as a golf course.

As part of the emphasis on physical fitness for an increasingly urban membership, the Church opened Deseret Gym in downtown Salt Lake City in 1910. B. H. Roberts and others called it a Temple of Health, which paralleled the Temple of the Lord a block away.

As auxiliary organizations expanded and changed their emphasis, the Church leadership urged the payment of tithes and offerings as signs of faith. During the late 19th century, the Church had exercised virtually no budgetary control. In 1899, President Lorenzo Snow appointed a Church auditing committee from the Quorum of the Twelve Apostles. In 1901, the Church leadership opened a new set of books in an attempt to gain better control over income and expenditures.

The decline in value of Church property while the federal government managed it under the Edmunds-Tucker Act, investments made during the 1890s to help promote economic development, and the reluctance of Church members to continue to pay tithes and offerings left the Church in dire financial straits by 1898.

In response, President Lorenzo Snow marketed a series of 6 percent bonds through eastern banks. He and other Church leaders began to preach the importance of the payment of an honest tithe. Members responded, and by January 1907 the Church had completely retired its debt.

The Church itself also moved to a cash basis. In 1907, President Joseph F. Smith called Charles W. Nibley, a prominent businessman, to serve as Presiding Bishop. In 1908, under Nibley's direction, ward bishops began to expect members to pay their tithes and offerings in cash, rather than in kind. Previously, the Church had operated a large number of tithing storehouses where members donated animals, eggs, vegetables, grains, or anything else that they produced as tithing. The Church issued tithing scrip, which circulated as money, and members could use it to purchase goods at the tithing houses. Members could exchange goods at the tithing house, and the Church also sold donated products on the market.

Retiring its debt in 1907 did not relieve the Church of all of its financial problems. In the 19th century, the Church leadership had founded a number of business, cultural, and recreational enterprises to meet the needs of Church members. Some of these, such as Zion's Cooperative Mercantile Institution (ZCMI), Beneficial Life, and Zion's Savings Bank and Trust seem to have functioned profitably. During the 1890s and afterward, the Church founded sugar refineries, which were consolidated as the Utah-Idaho Sugar Company. The Church also operated the Salt Lake Theater, on the corner of State Street and First South in Salt Lake City, and Saltair Resort, on Great Salt Lake, west of Salt Lake City.

Most seriously, the Church under Joseph F. Smith sold a controlling interest in Utah-Idaho Sugar to the American Sugar Refining Company. Also called the Sugar Trust, the company was controlled by Henry Havemeyer, a New York businessman. Church leaders believed that selling an interest in the company offered the only option short of a very nasty fight that they would most likely lose.

Following the First World War, however, a hike in prices for sugar led to an indictment under the Lever Act against Presiding Bishop Charles W. Nibley for profiteering. A decision of the U.S. Supreme Court in 1921, however, invalidated the indictments by declaring the act unconstitutionally vague under the Constitution's Fifth and Sixth Amendments.

During the postwar depression of 1919–1923, prices for sugar, which had skyrocketed shortly after the war, declined dramatically. The company suffered financial losses, which the Church tried to cover by borrowing from eastern bankers. President Heber J. Grant refused to allow the company to seek bankruptcy protection because he feared it would reflect badly on the Church.

At the same time, a number of businesses suffered from outside competition and declining markets. Consolidated Wagon and Machine could not endure under competition from national manufacturers or the decline in the market for horse-drawn conveyances. The Provo Woollen Mills could not compete with larger integrated businesses outside the region. Both companies failed. The Salt Lake Theater suffered from changing theatrical tastes, particularly the tendency of the public to prefer low-class vaudeville performances, and could not compete with motion pictures. In spite of the efforts of Maude May Babcock and others to save the theater, it continued to lose money, and the Church leadership sold the property to the Mountain States Telephone and Telegraph Company in 1928. The Church sold Saltair Beach Company to a local syndicate, reacquired it, then sold it again in 1929 when it could no longer afford to subsidize its operation.

The sale of the Salt Lake Theater and the Saltair Beach Company aroused considerable criticism in spite of the enormous drain on Church revenues from their operation. Similar revenue drains led to a major change in Church educational policy. Between 1875 and 1911, the LDS Church founded 34 institutions variously called colleges, academies, and universities in settlements stretching from Alberta,

Canada, in the north to Chihuahua, Mexico, in the south. Some of these, like Dixie, Weber, and Snow Colleges, offered junior college work. Others, like Brigham Young College, in Logan, Latter-day Saints University, in Salt Lake City, and Brigham Young University, in Provo, offered four-year collegiate degrees. In the 1890s, the Church began to offer weekday classes in religious instruction, called Religion Classes, for children ages 6 through 14. Many of these were held in public school rooms after the school day. In 1912, the Granite Stake in southern Salt Lake County opened the first of what became a series of seminaries for high-school-age youth. In 1926, under the direction of J. Wylie Sessions, the Church opened the first of its institutes of religion, near the University of Idaho in Moscow.

During the 1920s, the Church fell deeper into financial difficulty and struggled to support its business, cultural, and educational institutions. Heber J. Grant recognized that, in effect, the Church members were paying for two educational systems. Members supported the public schools, colleges, and universities through tax revenues while at the same time supporting Church institutions through tithes, offerings, and tuition. Between 1921 and 1923, as the postwar depression deepened, the Church leadership closed most of the academies.

Two institutions, Brigham Young College, in Logan, and Latter-day Saints University, in Salt Lake City, competed directly with tax-supported public institutions in the same cities: the Agricultural College of Utah (later Utah State University) and the University of Utah. The Church closed Brigham Young College in 1926. The Church changed the name of Latter-day Saints University to Latter-day Saints College and then, in 1928, to Latter-day Saints High School. Then, in 1929, it closed the high school, retaining only two departments, renamed McCune School of Music and LDS Business College.

Deciding that it needed to retain one university and several junior colleges, it continued to support Brigham Young University, particularly for its instruction in education. It retained Ricks, Weber, Snow, and Dixie Junior Colleges. Each offered junior college instruction and was expected to serve as a feeder for BYU. The leadership also abolished Religion Classes in 1929, expecting the Primary Association to assume the role of week-day religious instruction for elementary school students.

Then, as the Great Depression deepened after 1929, the leadership recognized that it could no longer afford to offer junior college instruction. Between 1930 and 1932, it succeeded in securing the approval of the Utah state legislature for the state to assume the ownership of Weber, Snow, and Dixie. The Idaho state legislature, however, refused to take over Ricks College, so the Church retained it, eventually expanding it to four-year status and renaming it Brigham Young University-Idaho, in 2001.

Throughout the 1920s, pressed by financial shortages, the Church made a number of decisions about its educational priorities. With the exception of a few select institutions, it left secular education to the state and its subdivisions. Religious education occurred in the Church's auxiliaries and at seminaries for high school students and institutes of religion for college students.

The leadership also moved during the period following 1900 to provide authoritative definitions of some aspects of Church doctrine. In 1909, the First Presidency and the Quorum of the Twelve Apostles issued a statement on the origin of humanity in which they said that Adam was the first man. Most Church leaders probably opposed the theory of organic evolution, but the Church took no official position on the question, and some members with scientific training, like James E. Talmage and John A. Widtsoe, believed in evolution to some degree. In 1916, the First Presidency and the Twelve published a statement on God, Christ, and the Holy Ghost that emphasized the separation of the three personages and defined God and Christ as personages with bodies and the Holy Ghost as a personage of spirit. The Church leadership also de-emphasized the importance of plural marriage by asserting that only 2 to 3 percent of the Church membership had participated and that plural marriage was permissive rather than obligatory for members.

James E. Talmage also wrote authoritative expositions on a number of doctrines, which the Church published as official statements. The 1899 *Articles of Faith* provided an exposition on the Church's basic doctrines as outlined by Joseph Smith in a letter to newspaperman John Wentworth. His *Jesus the Christ,* published in 1915, provided an authoritative exposition of the Church's view of Christ as teacher, redeemer, and Son of God.

By 1929, many of the practices and doctrines that Church members would recognize as standard in the 21st century had been inaugurated. At the time, however, the Church members experienced an economic shock that brought about even more change. Beginning late in 1929, the Great Depression descended on the United States. Moreover, it hit the people of Utah, where most Church members lived at the time, more forcefully than the remainder of the nation. By the winter of 1932–1933, the national unemployment rate had reached 25 percent. Utah's unemployment rate, however, reached 35 percent.

Compassionate service, an extremely important aspect of Church doctrine and practice, became increasingly more difficult. Donations to the Church to assist those in need declined as financial stringency gripped the Church membership. Presiding Bishop Sylvester Q. Cannon and Amy Brown Lyman, General Relief Society First Counselor, worked vigorously to supply the needs of Church members. They cooperated with local governments, and stake presidencies and bishops assisted as much as their resources allowed.

Many of the Church leaders, including Heber J. Grant and J. Reuben Clark, opposed the New Deal and its programs to assist the indigent. With the deaths of the two most prominent New Deal supporters, B. H. Roberts (1933) and Anthony W. Ivins (1934), the Church leadership became increasingly more opposed to the economic measures designed to relieve the Depression's pressure. Cannon and Lyman worked to continue cooperation with New Deal agencies and local governments, but Clark, who replaced Ivins as First Counselor in the First Presidency, undertook a vigorous campaign against the New Deal. Grant allowed him to campaign for anti-New Deal candidates outside Utah.

Following a pattern outlined by Clark, the Church announced what was first called the Church Security Plan and later renamed the Church Welfare Plan, in 1936. Bypassing the Presiding Bishopric, the First Presidency called Harold B. Lee, then a stake president, to head the program, through which the Church expected to care for the economic needs of its own members. The program received considerable national attention, and many observers believed erroneously that the "Church took care of its own." Actually, many Mormons continued to receive employment and assistance from governmental agencies. Nevertheless, the program helped many members by providing food and clothing and by assisting them to find work.

—*Thomas G. Alexander*

See also: Clark, J. Reuben; Colonization; Divergent Churches; Genealogy and Family History; Grant, Heber J.; Local Worship; Manifesto; Mormon Missiology; Mormonism and Economics; Mormonism and Education; Mormonism and Science; Mormonism and Secular Government; Polygamy; Relief Society; Smoot Hearings; Talmage, James E.; Temple Work by Proxy; Temples; Word of Wisdom; Youth Programs.

References

Alexander, Thomas G. *Mormonism in Transition: A History of the Latter-day Saints, 1890–1930,* 2nd ed. Urbana: University of Illinois Press, 1996.

Cannon, Brian Q. " 'What a Power We Will Be in This Land': The LDS Church, the Church Security Program, and the New Deal." *Journal of the West* 43 (Fall 2004): 66–75.

Daynes, Kathryn M. *More Wives Than One: The Transformation of the Mormon Marriage System, 1830–1910.* Urbana: University of Illinois Press, 2001.

Godfrey, Matthew C. *Religion, Politics, and Sugar: The Mormon Church, the Federal Government, and the Utah-Idaho Sugar Company, 1907–1921.* Logan: Utah State University Press, 2007.

Kimball, Richard Ian. *Sports in Zion: Mormon Recreation, 1890–1940.* Urbana: University of Illinois Press, 2003.

Lund, Anthon H. *The Diaries of Anthon H. Lund, 1890–1921.* Ed. John P. Hatch. Salt Lake City, UT: Deseret Book, 2006.

Paulos, Michael Harold, ed. *The Mormon Church on Trial: Transcripts of the Reed Smoot Hearings.* Salt Lake City, UT: Signature Books, 2007.

Quinn, D. Michael. "LDS Church Authority and New Plural Marriages, 1890–1904." *Dialogue: A Journal of Mormon Thought* 18 (Spring 1985): 9–105.

Smoot, Reed. *In the World: The Diaries of Reed Smoot.* Ed. Harvard S. Heath. Salt Lake City, UT: Signature Books, 1997.

Expansion: 1941–Present

On the surface, the Church of Jesus Christ of Latter-day Saints looked little different at the beginning of the 20th and the 21st centuries. Nevertheless, even though the basic doctrines remained the same, there was much that members in 1910 would not recognize were they to observe Mormonism in 2010. Growth drove most of these changes, especially the international dimension of Church membership, which increased dramatically following World War II. Mormonism's response to the challenges of an international membership and its corresponding cultural pluralism, a burgeoning bureaucracy, global missionary efforts, and new humanitarian impulses produced accommodations and adjustments as dramatic as those of earlier decades.

The outbreak of World War II created a significant challenge for LDS leaders as they responded to the needs of an international membership with different political loyalties. In general, the leaders preached peace, spoke against Hitler, and encouraged members to support the governments of their respective countries. Individual Mormons, in turn, faced difficult choices of their own. A German Mormon, Helmuth Hubener (1925–1942), was killed for speaking out against Adolf Hitler, while other Mormons, like Walter Koch, served in the German army and spent time in a Russian prisoner-of-war camp.

As complicated as World War II and the ensuing Cold War were, many Mormons saw in them opportunities to expand the global reach of their faith through missionary work. Mormon service personnel stationed in Japan after the war opened the door for the conversion of many Japanese people in a country where missionaries at the turn of the century had failed. The same was true in Korea and, to a lesser extent, in Vietnam, as Mormon soldiers who fought for the U.S. government still found opportunity to spread a message of peace into these countries. Mormons also participated in U.S. Cold War programs such as Point Four (later renamed USAID), which took Utah State University and Brigham Young University professors to places like Iran, where they made friends with the Shah. Their efforts led to the creation of a LDS mission there that operated for four years before the Iranian revolution shut it down.

The Mormon fondness for remembering historical events was showcased in the 1997 reenactment of the pioneer trek to the Salt Lake Valley. (Courtesy of the Church History Library, The Church of Jesus Christ of Latter-day Saints.)

In the wake of these successes, the Church increased its missionary efforts in a variety of ways. While some mission

White Salamander Letter

In 1985, three bombs rocked Salt Lake City, killing two and injuring a third—Mark Hofmann, a dealer in historical documents. Investigators uncovered a twisted scheme of lies, forgery, and murder plotted by Hofmann himself.

Hofmann had "discovered" a stream of documents shedding negative light on LDS Church origins. The most famous of these, the "Salamander Letter," sharply contradicted foundational LDS history. The letter suggested that Smith was led to the Book of Mormon plates not by an angel but by a magical "white salamander."

To profit by his forgeries, including the Salamander Letter, Hofmann negotiated a complex series of deals involving several bank loans and the sale of a collection of documents Hofmann had not yet forged. Becoming desperate as his scheme unraveled and to deflect attention from himself, Hofmann planted the bombs, one inadvertently exploding in his own car.

Hofmann's sophisticated forgeries fooled many specialists, but innovative detectives discovered the fraud before Hofmann's criminal trial began. To avoid the death penalty, he pled guilty to second-degree murder and theft by deception in 1987. Hofmann's right hand—his forging hand—was later destroyed during an attempted suicide, and, in 1988 a parole board decided Hofmann would spend the rest of his natural life in prison.

presidents immediately after World War II had their missionaries travel "without purse or scrip" as Christ directed His disciples, the Church recognized that the building of chapels and eventually temples would attract members through those physical symbols of the Church's permanence and stability. The Church also adapted uniform lessons and sales techniques to help its missionaries find new members. Church president David O. McKay asked "every member [to be] a missionary" and to invite friends and acquaintances to learn more about the Church. Growth also came as the Church expanded its public relations efforts through pavilions at world's fairs in New York (1964) and Japan (1970). So many Spanish-speaking people were baptized after the New York fair that Church leaders formed a congregation for them in New York City.

The postwar growth of Mormonism was impressive. In 1940, there were only 862,600 Latter-day Saints worldwide. By 1975, that number had expanded to 3.5 million; by 1990, it had swelled to 8 million. The turn of the 21st century saw more than 11 million Mormons. At the 2009 General Conference, in April, Church leaders announced there were 13,508,509 members worldwide. In 1984, sociologist Rodney Stark estimated that, assuming a 30 percent growth rate per decade, there could be 60 million Mormons by 2080; at a rate of 50 percent per decade, there would be 265 million. While Mormonism's growth has slowed, it has still maintained a notable 25 percent rate in the first decade of the 21st century.

Semiannual conferences draw crowds of the Mormon faithful to Salt Lake City's Temple Square. (Courtesy of the Church History Library, The Church of Jesus Christ of Latter-day Saints.)

Most remarkable for the postwar growth is its international component. In 1950, only 7.7 percent of Mormons lived outside North America. By 1960, that number had grown to 10.4 percent, and, by the 21st century, it had mushroomed to more than half of all Church members. Some Pacific Island countries witnessed particularly high levels of LDS membership. One-half of Tongans living in the Tongan islands were Mormon in 2003, the highest percentage of Church membership of any nation in the world. In 2001, there were 4 million members in South America, and all of Latin America (South America, Mexico, and Central America) accounted for 37 percent of the entire Church population. The Church also grew in Africa and Asia. After the end of the Cold War, the Church sent missionaries to Eastern Europe and even built a temple in East Germany before the fall of the Berlin Wall. The major areas with limited growth were mainland China and Muslim countries, where missionary work was not allowed. Even so, Mormons have a presence in Hong Kong, and the Church built a temple there before the island was taken over by the Communist government.

While a few international members continue to immigrate to Utah, the official Church policy since the 1920s has been for members to stay in their countries of origin. To help these members receive saving ordinances, the Church has built temples throughout the world, starting in England, Switzerland, and New Zealand in the 1950s. In the 1990s, it greatly accelerated its rate of temple building globally, and by 2009 there were more than 140 temples either built or under construction throughout the world. Many of these temples also have visitor centers to encourage missionary work.

As part of its effort to reach its international membership, in the 1970s the Church held regional conferences at various venues in global locations and offered talks similar to General Conference and cultural programs to bring the Church to the people. These regional conferences were too expensive and were discontinued, but, in 2008, Mormon leaders started holding regional stake conferences via satellite.

The problem of international growth, however, ran much deeper than maintaining contact with Church membership. It forced Mormon leaders to consider how a Church with strong American ties should deal with other cultures. Should the Mormon Church adjust to meet the needs of its new members, or should converts modify their cultures to more closely conform to American Mormonism? According to historian Jan Shipps, "Notwithstanding the rosy picture of a world filled with Mormons which is projected by the *Church News* and the official *Ensign* [magazine], the power of the LDS gospel to sustain communities of Saints throughout the world without requiring them to adopt particularly American attitudes and stereotyped life styles has not yet been fully proven" (Shipps, "The Mormons" 766).

Anecdotal examples demonstrate some of the concerns. White shirts and ties, the officially encouraged attire for American Mormon men, are not a standard dress for natives in Bolivia and are, in fact, an unnecessary expense. In some parts of Africa, organs are played only in brothels. Church lessons that depict a husband and wife kissing before they leave for work cause children in Japan to ask why they are biting each other. Even something as simple as telling a story about snow can be confusing for Mormons in the South Pacific. To deal with some of these concerns, Church magazines have focused more on doctrines and articles by General Authorities than on lifestyle. But there is still a feeling among some international members that Mormons outside North America have to go through an American socialization process before they are truly considered "no more strangers and foreigners, but fellow citizens with the saints, and of the household of God" (Ephesians 2:19).

Rapid growth and internationalization were not the only difficulties Mormonism faced in its most recent history. At the American Academy of Religion meetings, in 2007, Henry B. Eyring, a member of the LDS First Presidency, was asked what was the greatest challenge facing the Mormon Church. At first Eyring mentioned growth. But when someone else asked about the impact of secularism on the Church, Eyring changed his mind and called dealing with modernity the greatest concern.

Sociologist O. Kendall White argued that, in reaction to modernity, Mormon theologians "have embraced some fundamental doctrines of Protestant neo-orthodoxy," including the "sovereignty of God, the depravity of human nature, and the necessity of salvation by grace" (White, *Mormon Neo-Orthodoxy* 159). While the Mormon Church has adapted to secularization on the institutional level by following corporate patterns, "its efforts at resisting secular society in other respects remain a hallmark" (White, *Mormon Neo-Orthodoxy* 109). For example, Mormons reinforced traditional sexual norms during the sexual revolution of the 1960s. They questioned concerns about population explosion and continued to have large families. Church leaders resisted redefining gender roles. While American women (including Mormon women) entered the work force in increasing numbers, Church president Ezra Taft Benson strenuously encouraged Mormon women to remain at home. In 1995, the First Presidency and the Quorum of the Twelve Apostles issued "The Family: A Proclamation to the World," a document that reinforced the Victorian ideal of the father's role as provider and the mother's role as nurturer of children. It also emphasized the Mormon belief that marriage is between a man and a woman.

Richard L. Evans

For more than 40 years, the mellow voice of Richard L. Evans opened the weekly radio and television broadcasts of the Mormon Tabernacle Choir with the words "Once more we welcome you within these walls, with music and the spoken word, from the Crossroads of the West." His two- to three-minute inspirational messages, which he called "sermonettes," constituted church services for many homebound people and were appreciated by people of many or no faiths.

Born in 1906, Evans became an announcer for KSL radio in 1928; in 1929, he began introducing the numbers performed by the Choir. Drawing from the theme of the music, Evans began sup-

plying simple nondenominational lessons, which soon became as popular as the music itself. He eventually published several volumes of his weekly sermonettes.

Evans was editor of the Church magazine, director of Temple Square, a member of the First Council of the Seventy, and, after 1953, an apostle. His civic service included a term as president of Rotary International.

Evans died in 1971. The familiar words with which he closed each broadcast serve as the man's epitaph: "Again we leave you from within the shadows of the everlasting hills. May peace be with you, this day and always."

In terms of moral and family values, the Mormon Church persistently emphasized Victorian ideals even as much of the secular world around it changed. During the latter part of the 20th century, Mormons continued to extol the virtues of hard work and strong moral convictions so much so that, in some observers' minds, they became "super"-Americans, a sharp contrast to their 19th-century position as perceived outsiders. Sociologists Gordon Shepherd and Gary Shepherd believed that the Church's reinforcement of traditional moral and family values provided "an alternative to the confusing diversity and moral ambiguity of modern secular life" (Shepherd and Shepherd, "Mormonism in Secular Society" 40).

According to historians James B. Allen and Glen M. Leonard, the Church's dealings with social and political concerns were ephemeral when judged against the ever-present challenge of administering a rapidly growing organization, accommodating programs to suit diverse cultures, and pursuing a commitment to further expansion. Yet, all the changes were interrelated. The tremendous growth in membership meant that the Church developed a bureaucracy. The international growth forced the institution to interact with other cultures. Growth meant more visibility, so members and nonmembers became more keenly aware of the Church's stand on social and political issues.

While the Mormon Church has not directly controlled politics, it has, with varying degrees of success, taken public stands on topics Church leaders consider to be moral issues. Usually, leaders have presented a united front, unlike the divided message that they gave regarding the League of Nations. An exception occurred immediately after World War II, when conservative Republican J. Reuben Clark spoke against U.S. involvement in the United Nations, while the more liberal Democrat Hugh B. Brown spoke in favor. Both were counselors to Church president David O. McKay. In reaction to comments that the Church favored the Republican Party, McKay issued a statement that the Church did not take stands on political issues.

Church leaders did, however, comment on what they considered moral issues. During the 1960s civil rights movement, the Church came under attack for its policy that prohibited black men from being ordained to the priesthood and kept black men and women from receiving temple blessings. BYU athletics especially suffered when a few universities refused to play against the school and others allowed players to wear black armbands to protest Church policies. Some universities removed from their teams players who threatened to wear armbands. The Church tried, with limited success, to separate its restrictions on the priesthood from the civil rights movement. When the NAACP threatened to petition at General Conference, the counselors in the First Presidency issued a statement expressing support for equal rights for all people regardless of color. The decision to remove the priesthood restriction came in 1978. By then, the Church's concerns were more internal; for example, it had built a temple in Brazil and was looking for possible Church growth in Africa.

In the last half of the 20th century and at the beginning of the 21st, the Mormon Church expressed positions on other issues, as well. In the 1970s, it spoke out against the Equal Rights Amendment. Initially, the Church did not comment, but, in 1976, the First Presidency issued a statement of opposition. Mormons influenced a negative vote in Utah, Florida, Virginia, and Illinois and impacted states such as Idaho, which rescinded its earlier ratification of the amendment. In 1981, the First Presidency took a stand against the MX, a complex defensive missile system to be housed in the Nevada and Utah desert. In 2008, the Mormon Church asked members to campaign for an amendment to the California state constitution prohibiting homosexual marriages, a move generally applauded by ultraconservatives and detested by liberals, especially gay rights organizations. Before that, members funded anti-gay rights proposals in other states. Mormons also came out strongly against abortion. In Utah, the LDS Church blocked pari-mutuel betting and the sale of liquor by the drink and favored Sunday closing and right-to-work laws in the Utah state legislature. However, in 2008, a popular Mormon Utah governor, John Huntsman Jr., convinced the legislature to modify the state's liquor laws, and the Church did not oppose the change. In 2009, the Church officially endorsed a Salt Lake City ordinance that would protect gays and lesbians from discrimination in housing and employment.

While Church leaders carefully remind members at each U.S. election that they do not support any political party, individual Mormons have been active in U.S.

politics since World War II. During the 1950s, apostle Ezra Taft Benson served as secretary of agriculture in Dwight D. Eisenhower's cabinet. George Romney, a governor of Michigan, made an unsuccessful bid for the Republican presidential nomination in 1968. He became the secretary of housing and urban affairs in President Richard Nixon's cabinet. David M. Kennedy was secretary of the Treasury from 1969 to 1971. In 2008, George Romney's son Mitt Romney also made an unsuccessful bid for the Republican nomination for president. While Mormons are often identified as conservative Republicans and grouped with ultraconservative movements like the John Birch Society and the Eagle Forum, liberal Mormons include Harry Reid, a Mormon convert and senator from Nevada who served as Senate minority leader from 2005 to 2007, and then became majority leader in 2007 when Democrats won control of the Senate in the 2006 midterm election.

The growing Church and its international reach required additional changes, including a burgeoning bureaucracy, an effort to centralize control of curriculum and programs, and changes in welfare and Sunday worship schedules. The centralization of Church programs and curriculum started under Joseph F. Smith but intensified when Harold B. Lee started a correlation program that required all auxiliaries to work with a central committee. This program emphasized the family, and, in 1964, the Church made official a family home evening program that had started locally in 1909 and was recommended to all Church members in 1915. For more than a decade, the Church published manuals for home worship and planned other Church lessons to support these discussions.

The Church hired consulting firms in 1971 and followed their advice that the General Authorities should focus more on policy and transfer day-to-day operations to full-time managing directors. Other programs, such as the Relief Society social services, became a separate Church department; separate magazines published for each auxiliary were consolidated into three English-language magazines and an international magazine in several languages. While more responsibilities were transferred to employees, the Church also expanded its leadership. Assistants to the Quorum of the Twelve Apostles helped with worldwide responsibilities, and regional representatives presided over geographical areas. In 1975, the Church created the First Quorum of the Seventy and gradually added other Quorums of the Seventy over time. At the local level, stake presidents were asked to take on more responsibilities, such as setting apart missionaries.

Changes in finances accompanied bureaucratic changes, especially as the LDS Church grew into what some observers have called one of the richest Churches in the United States. Researching its assets is impossible since it has not published financial statements since 1958, but some business matters are public and reflect changes made because of international growth. For example, in 1975 the Church created a nonprofit organization for its chain of 15 hospitals in the intermountain West because it felt a need to care for the health of its international membership. In

1971, the Church called health and welfare missionaries as part of that effort. While that program did not persist, the Church's humanitarian division did continue to sponsor medical personnel who travel throughout the world.

Church leaders initially established a welfare program during the Great Depression to assist Mormons, and over time it expanded to include all peoples in need throughout the world. Following World War II, Church president George Albert Smith received permission from U.S. president Harry S. Truman to send goods to Europe. Apostle Ezra Taft Benson went overseas to distribute the aid. While the goods went first to Church members in war-torn Europe, those members were encouraged to share with their neighbors. In the early 2000s, Dieter F. Uchtdorf, an apostle and then counselor in the First Presidency and a convert from Germany, explained how his family came in contact with the Church because of this food. Not only did Americans help the impoverished Germans, but Mormons in Holland grew potatoes that they shared with their former enemies.

The Church's welfare efforts have continued to expand. Following a 1962 earthquake in Iran, USU Mormon professors appealed to the Church for help. The Church made arrangements to send clothing through CARE, and the few Mormons in the country distributed the goods. In the 1970s and 1980s, the Church worked through

Church welfare programs met the emergencies of the Depression and war years by organizing the production, preservation, and distribution of food, clothing, and other essential goods. (Courtesy of the Church History Library, The Church of Jesus Christ of Latter-day Saints.)

international humanitarian organizations, including Catholic Relief, to distribute humanitarian aid. The Church then created its own humanitarian program, including Latter-day Saint Charities, organized in 1996, which has responded to suffering and natural disasters throughout the world. In 2009, the Church announced that caring for the poor and needy would join redeeming the dead, proclaiming the gospel, and perfecting the Saints as the fourth element of Mormonism's central Christian objectives.

Church growth and world conditions have also changed LDS meeting patterns and organizations. During the mid-20th century, ward meeting houses were a beehive of activity every day of the week. Children attended Primary after school; teenagers participated in the Young Men and Young Women Mutual Improvement Associations on weekday evenings, and women attended Relief Society on weekday mornings. Men attended priesthood meeting early Sunday morning, followed by Sunday School (including a junior Sunday School for children), and sacrament meeting was held in the evening.

Each ward met in its own building, which also housed genealogical classes, Boy Scout programs, athletic programs for young men, and camping and sports programs for young women. Sometimes for MIA activities and often on other days of the week, teenagers took part in dance, speech, music, and drama programs. Roadshows were especially popular activities in which each ward in a stake produced a short original musical. Each year, the MIA also hosted a Gold and Green Ball, but the highlight for the youth programs was the June conference at which YMMIA and YWMIA gathered to learn the theme and program for the next year. It also included an all-Church dance festival at the University of Utah stadium, along with choirs, drama, and speech workshops.

The all-Church athletic tournaments provide examples of how involved the LDS Church was in recreational activities. The all-Church basketball tournament started in the 1920s and grew until it was eliminated in 1971. Junior and senior teams from throughout the intermountain West competed on a local stake and then at the regional level to win the right to participate in the basketball tournament. The participants were required to follow strict rules of church attendance, Word of Wisdom observance, and sportsmanship. The Church provided lodging and meals. Each year's tournament started with a fireside talk at which General Authorities discussed sportsmanship and the lessons learned from playing sports. The basketball tournament was so successful that in, the 1950s, the Church added a softball and volleyball tournament and sponsored individual sports events in golf, tennis, and even horseshoes. Referred to as spiritualized recreation, the athletic program activated men and families, served as a missionary tool, and promoted character building. The women's program was not as complex as that for men, but women played games and camped to fellowship one another.

Other groups also had special programs that no longer exist in the Church. Relief Society sisters managed their own budgets and furnished their own meeting rooms. To pay for activities, the women held bazaars and rummage sales. Women learned homemaking skills at monthly meetings. Primary girls learned how to embroider, knit, and crochet as part of the arts and crafts movement of the 1950s and 1960s, which also helped them learn their role as women during a time of changing ideas about women's place in society. Women also had a General Relief Society meeting at which the women shared their ideas for the coming year.

Gradually, these programs changed. The athletic programs ended because the Church grew worldwide and not everyone played basketball, softball, and volleyball around the world. There had been some abuses of the sports programs, but the major reason for the change was the Church's shift in focus away from recreation and toward spirituality as its principal concern. In 1957, Thomas O'Dea, a Catholic sociologist who studied Mormons, accurately predicted a time when the Church would focus more on spiritual goals and less on activities that the community could do as well.

A growing Mormon presence throughout the world is marked by a visit by one-time General Relief Society president Elaine Jack with Mormon women in Ghana. (Courtesy of the Church History Library, The Church of Jesus Christ of Latter-day Saints.)

O'Dea also suggested a time when the Mormon Church would no longer focus on Salt Lake City: "The Mormon movement may be on the eve of its Diaspora . . . [a time where] belongingness would no longer be exclusively identified with a specific place" (O'Dea, *The Mormons* 261). Sociologist Armand L. Mauss saw that change in his study *The Angel and the Beehive: The Mormon Struggle for Assimilation*. He concluded that, as the LDS Church grew, "church members might think of Utah as the Rome or Mecca of their faith, but they do not identify with it so strongly as in earlier stages." Instead, members looked at their own temple or their hope for one and focused on the church in their respective areas. As a result, "each cultural community could adapt and embroider the core in accordance with its own needs" (Mauss, *The Angel and the Beehive* 13, 209).

Nevertheless, in the late 20th and early 21st centuries, some of the focus on Salt Lake City returned. The women auxiliaries held smaller training sessions in Salt Lake City at General Conference time. Partially in response to the women's movement, women spoke in the General Conference, and meetings were held for the Young Women in the spring and for the Relief Society in the fall during the week before General Conference.

Some cultural activities also returned. In 2004, the First Presidency sent a letter to all local leaders asking for stake and multistake functions of music, dance, drama, speech, sports, and visual arts. The leaders explained that these would foster unity and opportunities for socializing, especially among the youth. To show how this could be done, the First Presidency asked people to work together to develop programs in connection with temple dedications. On January 10, 2004, for example, 2,000 young people in African costumes performed at the Accra, Ghana, temple dedication. The next month, 600 Church members portrayed Alaska's native culture at the Anchorage temple rededication. The same month, 8,000 local members and 1,200 missionaries performed in the rain for audiences of 60,000 in Sao Paulo, Brazil. New temple dedications continue to have similar cultural events beforehand.

Gradually, the meeting schedule also changed. Recognizing that many women were working and could not attend weekday morning meetings, some wards had an evening or a Sunday morning meeting for these women during the priesthood hour. In 1980, after experimenting with a number of arrangements, the Mormon leaders announced that meetings would be held in a three-hour block on Sundays. The meetings include a 70-minute sacrament meeting, a 40-minute Sunday School, and a 50-minute priesthood or Relief Society meeting. Teenagers met for Sunday School classes and then for meetings of the Young Men and Young Women. At first there were no weekday activities for teens, but later these were reinstated to give weekday contact. Junior Sunday School was replaced by a Sunday Primary, which included age-divided classes and a sharing time for Junior (3–8) and Senior Primary (9–12).

Although the focus of these programs is on Sunday worship, the Church still encourages weekday education. Seminary started in the Salt Lake Valley, and in some districts students received high school credit for participating. That credit disappeared when the ACLU threatened to sue the Logan, Utah, School District. But, in Utah and other western states, students still have released time to take Mormon religious classes. In the 1950s, the Mormon Church introduced an early-morning seminary program in California. Seminary continued to spread, and students throughout the world attend some form of seminary, generally through early-morning or home-study classes.

Following World War II, under the direction of Ernest L. Wilkinson, Brigham Young University expanded to meet the needs of a burgeoning membership. Wilkinson increased the enrollment and encouraged returned missionaries and returning servicemen to enroll. By 1970, Church leaders capped enrollment at 25,000, and BYU has remained at about that level ever since. The Church continued to operate Ricks College and then converted it into a four-year university, now known as BYU-Idaho. The Church College of Hawaii continued to serve the South Pacific as BYU-Hawaii. BYU provided more than education, especially as its athletic program attracted national attention and its music and dance groups performed throughout the world, including in China.

Over the years, Church leaders also created language and ethnic congregations. In the 19th century, Church leaders allowed immigrants to attend special meetings, although they were considered part of a geographical ward. For example, a German-speaking ward in Logan, Utah, included Swiss immigrants. The Swiss Mormons attended German-speaking meetings and also went to the Logan 10th Ward. The German branch was dissolved during World War II and then was restarted when new immigrants moved to the area. Eventually, there was less need for language accommodation, and the branch met once a month and then not at all.

Apostle Spencer W. Kimball felt a special responsibility to immigrants and Native Americans. In the 1950s, he created a Salt Lake Regional Mission and explained that members did not need to go to other countries to convert people. To an already existing Spanish ward (first known as the Mexican ward and then as the Lucero ward), the regional mission added two new Spanish wards. There was also a Japanese branch, a Chinese branch, a Danish ward, and a German ward, to name a few. Whenever Kimball was in town, he visited these wards and was pleased with their success. Kimball was also assigned to work with the Southwest Indian Mission and worked to create Native American wards on the reservations in the southwest United States and in the Northern Plains.

In 1972, Church leaders issued a statement that was interpreted by some members to mean that ethnic wards should be eliminated and that everyone should worship together. When this move resulted in the loss of some members, leaders issued guidelines in 1977 for small congregations, and some language branches were restarted. In the 21st century, there are language and cultural wards through-out the world. In 2007, the Provo, Utah, South Stake, for example, had 10 wards, including two geographically based Spanish wards, as well as deaf and Native American wards. American servicemen stationed around the globe attend special wards that conduct meetings in English. There are wards for English speakers in Japan and for Tongan-language members in New Zealand. Three Tongan-speaking stakes exist in Utah, and similar units based on language or ethnicity and designed to meet the needs of an increasingly diverse Mormon membership can be found around the globe.

At the end of the 21st century's opening decade, the Mormon Church continues to face the challenges that growth, modernity, and internationalization create. Its ex-pansion since the 1940s has led to an increase in its bureaucracy, missionary force, education efforts, financial stability, temple building, and humanitarian assistance worldwide. In a variety of ways, the Church of Jesus Christ of Latter-day Saints is no longer a small sect in Utah that is seen by some observers as strange but a reli-gion with a global reach.

—Jessie L. Embry

See also: Church Organization and Government; Correlation; Local Worship; Mormon Missiology; Mormonism and Education; Mormonism and the Family; Mormonism as a World Religion; Priesthood Revelation of 1978; Temples; Youth Programs.

References

Allen, James B., and Glen M. Leonard. *The Story of the Latter-day Saints.* Salt Lake City, UT: Deseret Book, 1992.

Allen, James B., Jessie L. Embry, and Kahlile B. Mehr. *Hearts Turned to the Fathers: A History of the Genealogical Society of Utah, 1894–1994.* Provo, UT: BYU Studies, Brigham Young University, 1995.

Bradley, Martha Sonntag. *Pedestal and Podiums: Utah Women, Religious Authority, and Equal Rights.* Salt Lake City, UT: Signature Books, 2005.

De Pillis, Mario S. "Viewing Mormonism as Mainline." *Dialogue: A Journal of Mormon Thought* 24 (Winter 1991): 59–68.

Embry, Jessie L. *Black Saints in a White Church: Contemporary African American Mor-mons.* Salt Lake City, UT: Signature Books, 1994.

Embry, Jessie L. *Mormon Wards as Community.* Binghampton, NY: Global, 2001.

Embry, Jessie L. *Spiritual Recreation: Mormon All-Church Athletic Tournaments and Dance Festivals.* E-book, http://www.reddcenter.byu.edu, 2008.

Jacobson, Cardell K., John P. Hoffman, and Tim B. Heaton, eds. *Revisiting Thomas F. O'Dea's* The Mormons*: Contemporary Perspectives.* Salt Lake City: University of Utah Press, 2008.

Mauss, Armand L. *The Angel and the Beehive: The Mormon Struggle with Assimilation.* Urbana: University of Illinois Press, 1994.

O'Dea, Thomas F. *The Mormons.* Chicago: University of Chicago Press, 1957.

Olmstead, Jacob W. "The Mormon Hierarchy and MX." *Journal of Mormon History* 33 (Fall 2007): 1–30.

Shepherd, Gordon, and Gary Shepherd. "Mormonism in Secular Society: Changing Patterns in Official Ecclesiastical Rhetoric." *Review of Religious Research* 26 (September 1984): 28–41.

Shipps, Jan. "The Mormons: Looking Forward and Outward." *Christian Century* (August 16–23, 1978): 761–766.

Stark, Rodney. "The Rise of a New World Faith." *Review of Religious Research* 26 (September 1984): 18–27.

White, O. Kendall, Jr. *Mormon Neo-Orthodoxy: A Crisis Theology.* Salt Lake City, UT: Signature Books, 1987.

Events

Black Hawk War

On April 9, 1865, the same day that Ulysses S. Grant and Robert E. Lee met in Virginia to negotiate an end to the Civil War, other negotiations in Utah Territory between Mormon settlers and Ute Indians went awry. Mormon John Lowry met with several Ute leaders at Manti, in central Utah, to resolve the recent killing of 15 head of cattle. Some of the Utes preferred peace, but two of their party, Black Hawk and Jake Arapeen, were not easily pacified. As the negotiations soured, Arapeen put an arrow to his bow, and in response Lowry pulled him from his horse. The Ute delegation left in anger. Thus began "the longest and most serious Indian-white conflict in Utah history" (Peterson, *Utah's Black Hawk War* 16).

Ute Indians were desperate, starving, and recently decimated by measles and other Euro-American diseases, to which they had no immunity. Utes also fought to resist removal to the Uintah Reservation in northeastern Utah. While the Utes had initially welcomed Mormon settlers to colonize central Utah, the tide of Mormons that crashed in upon them quickly dominated their traditional hunting and gathering locales and drastically altered their way of life. In despair and anger, Black Hawk led the Utes in what would grow into a pan-Indian uprising across Utah Territory, with Navajo and Southern Paiutes conducting incursions of their own. Thousands of Mormon cattle became the target of Indian raids throughout Utah, and invariably settlers and Indians died in the ensuing skirmishes. An estimated 70 whites and perhaps twice as many Native Americans were killed.

Mormons and Indians committed atrocities throughout the war, with both sides sometimes killing men, women, and children. The most tragic incident of the conflict was the Circleville Massacre, at which Mormon settlers, in 1866, killed at least 16 Indians, slitting the throats of some.

Brigham Young's official policy during the war was defensive and included the abandonment of small outlying settlements and the coalescing of settlers at forts for safety. As a result, Mormon colonization in effect retreated during the war, especially as Mormons deserted dozens of settlements and hundreds of ranching outposts for more defensible locales. These defensive tactics notwithstanding, the harsh realities of frontier interaction between Mormons and Indians still led to tit-for-tat raiding and death.

Suffering from ill health, Black Hawk recognized the futility of continued violence and sued for peace. He signed a treaty in 1868, although other Indians continued to struggle against white encroachment until 1872. Following his capitulation, Black Hawk traveled throughout Utah, seeking forgiveness from Mormons. The Mormon response was mixed, with some settlers railing against Black Hawk while others offered compassion and forgiveness. Similar divisions persisted among the Utes, as well. Black Hawk died in 1870.

—*W. Paul Reeve*

See also: Colonization; Mormonism and Native Americans; Mormonism and Race; Mormonism and Violence.

References

Culmsee, Carlton. *Utah's Black Hawk War: Lore and Reminiscences of Participants.* Logan: Utah State University Press/Western Text Society, 1973.

Peterson, John Alton. *Utah's Black Hawk War.* Salt Lake City: University of Utah Press, 1998.

Book of Mormon

The Book of Mormon is a book of scripture used by members of the Church of Jesus Christ of Latter-day Saints (LDS), the Community of Christ (formerly known as the Reorganized Church of Jesus Christ of Latter Day Saints, or RLDS), and all other denominations that look to Joseph Smith (1805–1844) as their founding prophet. Published in Palmyra, New York, in the spring of 1830, it is the foundational text of the LDS Church and is the source of its nickname, the Mormon Church.

Joseph Smith, named according to copyright laws as author and proprietor of the book, claimed to have translated the Book of Mormon from ancient metal plates whose location was revealed to him in 1823 by an angel named Moroni. The narrative begins in Jerusalem in 600 BC with the prophet Lehi, who sailed with his family to the Americas. There they established a civilization that split into two antagonistic groups—those who believed in the "tradition of their fathers" and those who dissented—known respectively as the Nephites and the Lamanites. A tradition of recordkeeping was passed down through successive generations among the Nephites, and these records were compiled and abridged by Mormon, one of the last of the prophets. The narrative covers a thousand-year history of conflict between these groups, as well as a brief history of an earlier group, known as the Jaredites, whose members migrated to the New World at the time of the Tower of Babel. After the Nephites were destroyed by the Lamanites around AD 400, Mormon's son Moroni concluded the record and buried it. It was this same Moroni who appeared to Joseph Smith as an angel in 1823 to reveal the location of the record.

Though much of the narrative covers the pre-Christian era, the Book of Mormon is a Christian book. Prophets as early as 600 BC refer to Jesus Christ by name and prophesy his coming. The culminating event in the book is the appearance of the resurrected Christ to the Nephites shortly after his crucifixion in Jerusalem. A major theme running throughout the book is a self-supporting promise that the Book of Mormon would come forth in the latter days "by way of the Gentile" for the conversion of the descendants of the Lamanites to the Christian faith. As such, it has been used by Mormons as a companion volume to the Bible, being described as "another testament of Jesus Christ" (the official subtitle of the LDS version after 1982). Other major themes include covenants, prophecy, revelation, providence, the latter-day restoration of the House of Israel, and the idea of the Americas as a promised land for believers in Christ.

An estimated 130 million copies of the Book of Mormon have been printed and distributed since it was first published in 1830. (Courtesy of the Church History Museum, The Church of Jesus Christ of Latter-day Saints.)

Joseph Smith declined to explain the details of his method for translating the plates, other than stating that it was done by the "gift and power of God" and through the instrumentality of "interpreters" (later dubbed Urim and Thummim) that were included with the plates. Other early witnesses describe the use of a seerstone placed in a hat as a medium of translation. The text, comprising 588 published pages, was dictated to scribes primarily during a three-month period in the spring of 1829.

Critics were quick to offer alternative explanations. Restorationist preacher Alexander Campbell, implying that Smith was the author, pointed out a similarity between Book of Mormon themes and contemporary religious and theological issues in the American Northeast. Eber D. Howe and Philastus Hurlbut, who opposed the Mormons, suggested that the book had been plagiarized from the stolen manuscript of one Solomon Spaulding. This so-called Spaulding theory was the leading naturalistic explanation during most of the 19th century until comparisons of the two texts seemed to nullify it.

As historian Richard Bushman explained, most scholarly explanations for the Book of Mormon fall into two broad categories he identifies as *composition*—the naturalistic view positing Smith as author and assigning a 19th-century provenance—and *transcription,* the view held by most Mormons that accepts the text as an ancient document translated by Smith via divine revelation. A minority of

Mormons, particularly among the Community of Christ intelligentsia, consider the Book of Mormon a 19th-century production, yet still view it as inspired scripture.

During the second half of the 19th century and throughout the 20th, efforts to defend the Book of Mormon's historicity were undertaken by Church leaders in both the LDS and the RLDS Churches. In the Reorganization, Joseph Smith III organized Zion's Religio-Literary Society in 1893, which included Book of Mormon readings, and amateur archaeological efforts were undertaken to determine Book of Mormon locations. Chief among LDS defenders at the turn of the century was B. H. Roberts, who published several volumes responding to criticisms posed against the book. By the late 20th century, the Community of Christ leadership veered toward a more liberal view of the text; among them Church Secretary Bruce Lindgren, who believed it to be a 19th-century parable witnessing of Jesus, rather than an ancient American history. Defenders of the Book of Mormon's historicity have increasingly become marginalized within the Community of Christ's hierarchy and educational institutions. The official LDS position, on the other hand, has become ever more conservative with regard to historicity. LDS scholar Hugh Nibley was preeminent among the book's defenders, and his legacy has continued with the Neal A. Maxwell Institute, which is dedicated to amassing evidences of historicity through historical, linguistic, literary, and textual scholarship.

While the Book of Mormon was a foundational text to the early Mormon Church, the Bible was the major source in early Mormon preaching. The Book of Mormon seems to have functioned more as a symbol of modern revelation than as a volume of instruction to early Mormon converts, signaling the restoration of the primitive Christian Church and its attendant "gifts of the spirit." Eventually, the content of the book received greater emphasis in Mormon preaching and curriculum, and it continues to play a major role in LDS missionary work as a symbol of restoration and as a tool for conversion. It is an integral part of LDS worship, acting, as Joseph Smith described it, as the "keystone" of Latter-day Saint belief. Within the Community of Christ, the Book of Mormon's canonical status has in all practicality become localized. While the text is still part of the Community of Christ's official canon, African and Haitian members have elected not to use the Book of Mormon. In other geographical areas, Community of Christ members use the Book of Mormon in varying proportions.

The Book of Mormon is currently available in several editions. The most widely distributed is the current, official LDS version, published in 1981 and cross-referenced with the Bible and other standard works in the LDS canon. The Community of Christ published an official edition in 1908 and a modern-language Revised Authorized Version in 1966. University of Illinois Press published a reader's edition in 2003, and Doubleday published a trade edition (with the LDS text) in 2004. As of 2009, the Book of Mormon has been translated into more than 105 languages, and more than 130 million copies have been printed.

—*Stanley J. Thayne and David J. Howlett*

See also: Benson, Ezra Taft; Divergent Churches; Mormon Scripture; Nibley, Hugh; Smith, Joseph Jr.; Witnesses to the Book of Mormon.

References

Givens, Terryl L. *A Very Short Introduction to the Book of Mormon.* New York: Oxford University Press, 2009.

Givens, Terryl L. *By the Hand of Mormon: The American Scripture That Launched a New World Religion.* New York: Oxford University Press, 2002.

Hardy, Grant, ed. *The Book of Mormon: A Reader's Edition.* Urbana: University of Illinois Press, 2003.

Colonization

Brigham Young is widely regarded as one of the greatest colonizers in American history. His colonization efforts in part grew out of his broader ambition to achieve economic self-sufficiency for his people, but they also demonstrate his sweeping vision for building a religious kingdom in physical, not just spiritual, ways. The fact that Young chose the Great Basin for his kingdom building makes his colonization successes all the more remarkable. The semi-arid environment of the intermountain West offers some of the driest desert expanses in America, with Nevada and Utah as the nation's two driest states. It was there and in the broader intermountain West, between southern Canada and northern Mexico and southern California and western Colorado, that Mormon colonizers carved a scattering of more than 500 villages in the 19th and early 20th centuries.

The first stage of Mormon settlement began in 1847 with the establishment of Salt Lake City as its central point and continued until 1857, when it was interrupted by the Utah War. During that time period, Mormon colonizers established more than 100 communities, stretching from Salt Lake City outward in a variety of directions. Eventually, a string of Mormon towns led from the capital city to San Bernardino in California. Young viewed this line of towns as integral to the "gathering" of Saints from international destinations. He initially envisioned Mormon converts sailing from Europe and other locations to the west coast of the United States and from there traveling overland to Salt Lake City, reaching Mormon villages spaced two or three days' travel apart as rest stops for weary wagon travelers. This plan never worked as hoped because of the prohibitive cost of ocean travel around the tip of South America. Nonetheless, the string of Mormon villages that run roughly along present-day Interstate 15, including Las Vegas, Nevada, and San Bernardino, California, stands as evidence of Young's unrealized plan.

Because of the Utah War, Young called in outlying settlements. Following the war, Mormons established a new flurry of more than 100 colonies, this time spreading into Idaho, southeastern Nevada, and Arizona. The final 10 years of

Young's life saw Mormons establish an additional 125 settlements, filling in valleys in Utah and colonizing additional areas of Idaho and Arizona. Following Young's death, his successor, John Taylor, expanded Zion's borders in a variety of directions, including new colonies in the rugged southeastern corner of Utah and in western Wyoming, southeastern Nevada, southeastern Idaho, and south-central Colorado. Mormons also moved beyond the borders of the United States in this final phase of settlement, as they built colonies of refuge (from the federal crackdown on polygamy) in northern Mexico and in Alberta, Canada.

Several of these colonies served more than one function. Young was interested in providing stable villages into which Mormon converts could integrate and provide for themselves. He was also interested in missionary work among Native Americans and in establishing an economically independent kingdom. The Mormon outpost at Las Vegas, for example, began as a mission to the Southern Paiutes but later was involved in an effort to mine lead. Leadership conflict left the post in disarray by the time of the Utah War.

The Iron Mission and the Cotton Mission were the Mormons' two best-known economic colonization efforts. Neither of these succeeded in accomplishing its original aims. Parowan and Cedar City, Utah, formed the core towns of the Iron Mission in the 1850s, as Mormons there attempted to produce iron. Mormon lead-

---

Gathering

"Gathering"—leading believers out of a metaphorical Babylon and into a unified body of the faithful—began early in Mormon history. Converts clustered around Joseph Smith to listen to his teachings and, as differences grew between converts and their neighbors, to live among like-minded believers.

As conditions required, early leaders removed from New York, to Ohio, to Missouri, to Illinois, and, finally, to Utah. With each removal in leadership, members moved to resettle near their leaders. Gathering was not a requirement of fellowship, however; isolated members who communicated with leaders remained members in good standing.

While in Nauvoo, Illinois, the Church received its first significant influx of European converts, some of whom arrived via ships chartered by the Church. Such early programs evolved into a complex network of emigration agents in Europe, New York, and on the frontier to ease the difficulties of gathering. The Perpetual Emigrating Fund, bulk purchase of overland equipment, and relays of wagon trains helped to finance the gathering.

Eventually, Mormon leaders asked converts to remain at home, building the Church in their own lands. In the 21st century, "gathering" focuses on local congregations as places designed to sustain members' faith, rather than gathering to a single physical location.

ers recruited converts from Europe who were skilled in iron works, coal mining, and blacksmithing, encouraging them to immigrate and hoping to use their expertise at the Iron Mission. The mission did succeed in producing some nails, andirons, kitchen utensils, and other products, but it never became economically viable. Settlers thereafter turned to agricultural pursuits and survived.

The story of the Cotton Mission was similar. After test crops demonstrated that cotton could grow in the heat of southwestern Utah, Young sent more than 300 Latter-day Saint families there in 1861. The harsh desert environment as well as the unruly Virgin River conspired against the colonizers, making the Cotton Mission, or Utah's Dixie, as it came to be called, one of the most unpopular places to be sent in 19th-century Utah. Mormons there abandoned their homes and moved elsewhere at rates higher than Mormons in other areas of the Territory. Although communal cotton production proved difficult, Mormons did manage to establish a variety of agricultural communities in the region that capitalized upon the ready markets for fruit, grain, wine, lumber, and other products at Pioche, Nevada, and Silver Reef, Utah, two boom silver mining towns.

Some Mormon settlers formed colonization efforts of their own, independent of Church directive or oversight. In general, centrally planned colonization was over by the end of the 19th century, although a few colonies were planted in the early 20th century.

—*W. Paul Reeve*

See also: Exodus and Settlement: 1845–1869; Mormonism and Economics; Transition: 1890–1941; Ungathered; Utah War.

References

Arrington, Leonard J. *Great Basin Kingdom: An Economic History of the Latter-day Saints, 1830–1900.* Cambridge, MA: Harvard University Press, 1958.

Campbell, Eugene E. *Establishing Zion: The Mormon Church in the American West, 1847–1869.* Salt Lake City, UT: Signature Books, 1988.

Hunter, Milton R. *Brigham Young the Colonizer.* Salt Lake City, UT: Deseret News Press, 1940.

Correlation

Correlation—the unifying and coordinating of programs—reflects the Church's growth. Initially, Church organization consisted only of Joseph Smith and Oliver Cowdery as First and Second Elders. In time, a more complex priesthood organization governed a growing membership.

In the late 19th century, Church quorums and auxiliaries developed rapidly. For example, the Sunday Schools, established in 1849, quickly spread; by the 1860s, teachers adopted the *Juvenile Instructor* as their organ to meet a growing demand for a uniform curriculum. Other auxiliaries for the youth and children of the Church were formed, each organization publishing its own periodical, preparing an independent curriculum, and managing its own financial affairs.

In the early 20th century, the auxiliaries dealing with children and youth began to divide their charges by age, providing centrally written lessons tailored to the needs and interests of each group. The Relief Society added formal courses of study to its historic mission of charity, with the women learning about genealogy, child development, and civic betterment. A parents' class was added to the Sunday School.

In 1907, B. H. Roberts published *The Seventies Course in Theology*, introducing a systematic study of doctrine for use by that quorum. The manual's popularity led Joseph F. Smith to create a committee (called here "Correlation Committee," although its formal name changed repeatedly) to prepare lesson manuals for all priesthood quorums. Four years later, the Correlation Committee was charged with reviewing the curricula of all Church auxiliaries. It devoted its efforts through the first half of the century to coordinating the responsibilities of the auxiliaries.

By the 1960s, the Church needed further consolidation. Instruction manuals produced for different auxiliaries overlapped in content and failed to meet the needs of the international Church: object lessons involving snow sledding were irrelevant to

Church Publications

Mormon periodicals have a longstanding history, with the dual purpose of instructing members and presenting the Mormon side of contested issues to the public.

Early Mormon newspapers included *Evening and Morning Star* (1832–1833, Independence, Missouri); *Messenger and Advocate* (1834–1837, Kirtland, Ohio); *Times and Seasons* (1839–1846, Nauvoo, Illinois); and *Deseret News* (1855–present, Salt Lake City). Newspapers intended primarily as a public defense of Mormonism were published at various times in major American cities.

The important *Millennial Star* (1840–1970, Liverpool, England) carried sermons, letters from missionaries throughout the world, news from Church headquarters, and, during the 19th cen-

tury, instructions for emigrating Saints. Other European missions issued publications with variants of the Star title in local languages.

The Contributor, Juvenile Instructor, Improvement Era, Relief Society Magazine, Young Woman's Journal, and *The Children's Friend* remain important sources of Mormon history and culture for the late 19th and much of the 20th centuries. Especially notable was the *Woman's Exponent,* published by and for Mormon women.

Current publications, issued monthly in English, are *Ensign,* for adults; *New Era,* for youth; and *Friend*, for children. The international magazine *Liahona,* issued from 2 to 12 times annually, appears in languages ranging from Armenian to Fijian to Urdu.

members in the South Pacific; class themes based on American Indian lore did not translate well to members in Europe. Correlation called for curricula to be priesthood directed, scripture based, and otherwise relevant throughout the world. Harold B. Lee coordinated this streamlining effort, restructuring lesson manuals and realigning Church auxiliaries to bring them under the direct supervision of priesthood leaders.

In 1971, the Church employed two business consulting firms to analyze internal operations. Their recommendations included lightening the administrative load of senior Church leaders, allowing them to focus on policies and spiritual matters. Professional educators and writers took direct charge of developing all Church curricula. The Correlation Committee eliminated overlap and ensured that publications conformed to doctrine.

Under the supervision of the First Presidency and the Quorum of the Twelve Apostles, the Correlation department continues to develop Church publications, including new instruction manuals and the four Church magazines. While efforts have proven effective at unifying Church instruction and encouraging simplicity of programs and materials, some members have complained of a "watering-down" effect, noting that, while oversight decreases speculation, it also diminishes innovation. Others recognize an increase in the quality and scholarship of Church manuals. As the Church continues its growth, the Correlation Committee continues to prepare materials suitable for a remarkably diverse audience.

—*Blair Dee Hodges*

See also: Church Organization and Government; Lee, Harold B.; Relief Society; Roberts, B. H.; Smith, Joseph F.; Youth Programs.

References
Kimball, Edward L. *Lengthen Your Stride: The Presidency of Spencer W. Kimball.* Salt Lake City, UT: Deseret Book, 2005.

Prince, Gregory M., and Wm. Robert Wright. *David O. McKay and the Rise of Modern Mormonism.* Salt Lake City: University of Utah Press, 2005.

Exodus from Nauvoo

The Mormon exodus from Nauvoo in 1846 to the Salt Lake Valley included elements of both a planned, prophesied, and carefully orchestrated migration and a violent and forced expulsion. It was a massive transplanting of an entire religious society from the Midwest to a place of isolation in the Great Basin.

Joseph Smith and other Mormon leaders had earlier connected the future destiny of the faith with the American Far West, and, following Smith's murder, Brigham Young began preparations for a move. In September 1845, anti-Mormon vigilantes began burning homes of Mormons at outlying farms and made calls for a total Mormon removal. Brigham Young revealed that the Saints were already preparing to leave Illinois beginning in late spring 1846, when there would be grass on the prairie for cattle and the rivers would be free of ice. With pressure from outsiders, however, Mormon efforts intensified over the coming months. Mormons readied more than 1,500 wagons by November, and close to 2,000 more were under construction.

Mormon leaders prepared for the exodus by reading John C. Fremont's report of his western explorations, as well as Lansford Hastings's *Emigrants' Guide to Oregon and California.* As a result, the Mormons were among the best-prepared people on the overland trail in terms of their foreknowledge of the West. In fact, some leaders saw the move to the West as fulfillment of prophecies, both modern and ancient, that the Saints would establish Zion in the tops of the mountains.

At the same time that Mormons planned for the move, they frantically worked to complete the Nauvoo temple in order to receive a promised "endowment," a sacred religious ritual that Smith initiated before his death. More than 5,600 Saints received the ritual before the exodus. Mormons completed and dedicated their temple and then promptly abandoned it.

Although they had planned to depart in April, Mormon leaders moved the date forward to avoid repercussions from charges that they were sheltering a counterfeiting operation and in response to rumors that federal troops might interfere with their plans. The exodus thus officially began on February 4, 1846, when many leaders and their families crossed the Mississippi on flatboats and skiffs. By February 24, the river froze, thereby facilitating a more rapid departure.

Almost 12,000 Mormons had evacuated Nauvoo by May and were spread out in various camps across Iowa. More than 600 sick or poor Saints remained behind, however. Residents of Hancock County continued to harass and plunder these remaining Mormons and engaged them in violent skirmishes. By September, the Mormons abandoned Nauvoo. When news of the plight of this poor camp of Saints reached Mormon leaders, they responded by sending tents, provisions, and wagons. In an event that the Mormons perceived as providential, flocks of exhausted quail settled among the destitute group, providing welcome relief, as it were, from heaven. After spending the rest of 1846 in various makeshift camps in Iowa and Nebraska, a vanguard company of Mormons reached the Salt Lake Valley in July 1847.

—*W. Paul Reeve*

See also: Exodus and Settlement: 1845–1869; Mormon Battalion; Pioneering; Temples.

References

Christian, Lewis Clark. "Mormon Foreknowledge of the West." *BYU Studies* 21 (Fall 1981): 403–415.

Esplin, Ronald K. "'A Place Prepared': Joseph, Brigham, and the Quest for Promised Refuge in the West." *Journal of Mormon History* 9 (1982): 85–111.

First Vision

The First Vision is the founding theophany of Mormonism, its genesis miracle. In it, Joseph Smith claimed to receive the first of many heavenly visitations, this one from God the Father and his Son, Jesus Christ.

Smith left multiple different accounts of the vision, each of which emphasizes different points. In sum, he wrote that he was caught up in what historians would later call the Second Great Awakening, an intense excitement over religion that permeated upstate New York, where Smith lived. This excitement caused him concern over the state of his own soul and incited him to ponder the state of religion in general, with its competing notions of salvation. After reading in the Bible (James 1:5), he felt prompted to seek wisdom from God. As he later recorded, in the spring of 1820, at the age of 14, he sought solace in a nearby grove of trees and uttered his first spoken prayer. In response, he claimed that a light descended upon him above the brightness of the sun, and in it two personages appeared, "whose brightness and glory defy all description." He recalled, "One of them spake unto me calling me by name and said (pointing to the other) "This is my beloved Son, Hear him" (Jessee, "Early Accounts" 290).

Smith reported that Jesus Christ delivered a message of personal forgiveness to him. Smith also recounted later that Jesus instructed him not to join any of the Churches then competing for adherents and told him that, at a future time, "the fullness of the gospel" would be made known to him. This founding miracle, followed by a series of heavenly visitations, became the basis for the eventual establishment, in 1830, of the Church of

The centrality of the First Vision to Mormonism is reflected in the way the story has been adapted and represented in folk art around the world. This batik was created by an artist in Sierra Leone. (Courtesy of the Church History Museum, The Church of Jesus Christ of Latter-day Saints.)

Christ, later renamed the Church of Jesus Christ of Latter-day Saints, with Smith as its prophet.

In Mormon theology, the First Vision assumed growing significance over time and became a doctrinal touchstone in the 20th century. Mormons use it to substantiate their belief in three distinct members of the Godhead, in that God the Father and Jesus Christ appeared simultaneously to Smith as discrete corporeal beings, with the Holy Ghost as a separate personage of spirit. Mormons also suggest that the First Vision ushered in a new dispensation of God's direct interaction with humankind and that He is a personal, merciful, forgiving God who knows individuals by name and answers their prayers.

—*W. Paul Reeve*

See also: Mormonism as Restoration; Smith, Joseph Jr.

References

Allen, James B. "The Significance of Joseph Smith's 'First Vision' in Mormon Thought." *Dialogue: A Journal of Mormon Thought* 1 (Autumn 1966): 29–45.

Jessee, Dean C. "The Early Accounts of Joseph Smith's First Vision." *BYU Studies* 9 (Spring 1969): 275–294.

Handcart Migration

Even though the Mormon handcart migration included only 10 immigrant companies spread over a five-year period (1856–1860), its impact on Mormon culture and collective memory persists into the 21st century. For Mormons, handcarts have grown into an iconic symbol of pioneering, suffering, privation, perseverance against great odds, and, ultimately, the compelling power of faith and spirit of sacrifice.

Handcarts were two-wheeled devices with beds large enough for only a few material possessions. Long handles protruded from the cart, which the immigrants, lacking cattle or oxen to do the job, pulled by hand. Mormon leaders settled upon the handcart idea in 1855 as a more cost-efficient means than overland wagons for bringing poor converts from Europe to Utah.

In 1856, five handcart companies made the 1,300-mile journey from the railroad terminus in Iowa City to Salt Lake City. The first three companies arrived safely in the Salt Lake Valley with little difficulty. The fourth and fifth companies, under the direction of James G. Willie and Edward Martin, respectively, did not fare so well. Both companies left late in the season and were subsequently pinned down by an early severe blizzard in Wyoming. Low on food and without adequate shelter and clothing, members of both companies began to die. In Salt Lake City,

Nineteenth-century Mormon folk artist Dan Weggeland painted this image of the Mormon handcart trek. (Courtesy of the Church History Museum, The Church of Jesus Christ of Latter-day Saints.)

Brigham Young received word of the immigrants' plight and sent rescue parties to their aid. In total, more than 200 members of the Willie and Martin companies died. Others lost extremities to frostbite and otherwise suffered from cold and starvation.

Of the estimated 70,000 Mormon immigrants to travel to Utah before the completion of the transcontinental railroad, in 1869, fewer than 3,000 walked with handcarts. In total, around 250 died along the trail, the majority of them with the Willie and Martin companies.

Willie and Martin company stories and that of their rescue have grown over time to form a significant aspect of Mormon collective identity, even though handcarts were the least typical form of travel to Utah. Handcart pioneers are celebrated in sculpture, art, verse, song, parades, sermons, books, logos, film, folklore, and reenactments. In many ways, the handcart migration in general and the Willie and Martin tragedies specifically stand in for all forms of Mormon overland travel. Mormon youth groups go on scripted "treks" replete with handcart pulls over rough terrain and steep inclines designed to connect them to the Mormon past and the physical privations and fortitude bound up in faith. Even Mormons in international locations with no biological connection to the 19th-century pioneers sometimes participate in handcart reenactments. Such events serve to solidify group identity and solidarity and to connect and reconnect 21st-century Latter-day Saints to each other and to a constructed version of sacred history.

—*W. Paul Reeve*

See also: Immigration; Pioneering; Ungathered.

References

Eliason, Eric A. "Pioneers and Recapitulation of Mormon Popular Historical Expression." In *Usable Pasts: Traditions and Group Expressions in North America.* Ed. Tad Tuleja. Logan: Utah State University Press, 1997.

Hafen, Leroy R., and Ann W. Hafen. *Handcarts to Zion: The Story of a Unique Western Migration, 1856–1860.* Lincoln: University of Nebraska Press, 1992.

Orton, Chad M. "The Martin Handcart Company at the Sweetwater: Another Look." *BYU Studies* 45, no. 3 (2006): 5–37.

Haun's Mill Massacre

On October 30, 1838, more than 200 members of the Missouri State Militia attacked a small band of Mormon settlers at Haun's Mill, a Mormon outpost along Shoal Creek, in Caldwell County. It was the most brutal massacre in the broader Missouri War, especially as the militia fired mercilessly at Mormons fleeing for shelter and crying for peace. The massacre left 17 Mormons dead or mortally wounded and another 12 to 15 wounded.

Five days prior to the massacre Jacob Haun met with Joseph Smith at Far West, Missouri, amid growing concerns about mob violence. Smith allegedly told Haun to bring the settlers at his mill into Far West for mutual protection. Haun, however, returned to his mill and reported only that Smith had instructed the settlers to stay and protect the mill.

That same day, Missouri vigilantes rode into Haun's Mill and demanded that the Mormons surrender their arms. Some Mormons complied and then entered into peace negotiations with the vigilantes. Similar occurrences took place over the following days and seem to have been a part of the vigilantes' plan to minimize resistance when they did attack.

On the day of the massacre, as the militia rode into Haun's Mill, Mormon David Evans "swung his hat and cried for peace" (Baugh, "Joseph Young's Affidavit"

A lone millstone served as an early-20th-century marker of this site of deadly violence against the Mormons. (Courtesy of the Church History Library, The Church of Jesus Christ of Latter-day Saints.)

192). The leader of the militia answered his gesture with gunfire, and the slaughter began. Many Mormons sought shelter in the blacksmith shop, a poor choice given the gaping holes between the wooden slats that formed its walls. The militiamen simply poked their guns through and fired at point-blank range. The elderly Thomas McBride was wounded after attempting to escape from the blacksmith shop. Militiaman Jacob S. Rogers later found McBride still alive and cut him to pieces with a corn cutter. Another militiaman later boasted of stealing the boots of one victim before he was dead. Three young boys—Sardius Smith, 10, Charles Merrick, 9, and Alma Smith, 6—hid behind the bellows in the blacksmith shop, trembling with fear. Upon discovering them, militiamen blew off the upper part of Sardius's head; mortally wounded Charles in three places, leading to his death four weeks later; and wounded Alma in the hip. As justification for shooting the boys, one militiaman reportedly exclaimed, "Nits will make lice," and explained that if they had lived, they would have become Mormons (*History of Caldwell* 149). Fearing the militia's return, Mormons placed several of the bodies in a common grave down a dry well and covered them with dirt.

A year later, in a redress petition to the federal government, Amanda Smith, who lost a husband and a son at Haun's Mill, pointed to the paradox at the heart of their deaths. They were killed, she said, "For our religion, where, in a boasted land of liberty, 'Deny your faith or die,' was the cry." In an effort to quantify her losses, she concluded, "Whole damages are more than the State of Missouri is worth" (Amanda Smith quoted in Smith, *History* 3:323–325).

—*W. Paul Reeve*

See also: Development: 1831–1844; Missouri War; Mormonism and Violence.

References

Baugh, Alexander L. "Joseph Young's Affidavit of the Massacre at Haun's Mill." *BYU Studies* 38, no. 1 (1999): 188–202.

Blair, Alma R. "The Haun's Mill Massacre." *BYU Studies* 13 (Autumn 1972): 62–67.

History of Caldwell and Livingston Counties, Missouri, Written and Compiled from the Most Authentic Official and Private Sources, Including a History of Their Townships, Towns and Villages. St. Louis, MO: National Historical, 1886.

Smith, Joseph Jr. *History of the Church.* Ed. B. H. Roberts. Salt Lake City, UT: Deseret Book, 1973.

Immigration

Between the first overseas mission in 1837 and 1962, when the Church stopped keeping immigration records, tens of thousands of Mormon missionaries and converts sailed across oceans in search of Zion. Approximately 100,000 immigrants came from Ireland and the United Kingdom, about 27,000 from Scandinavia, and a few thousand more from continental Europe, Australia, and the South Pacific.

Most European Mormon immigrants departed from Liverpool, England, the headquarters of the British Mission. Though most Scandinavian and continental Saints also went through Liverpool, their journey as part of a Mormon immigration company began earlier with intermediate staging in such cities as Copenhagen, Hamburg, Hull, and Grimsby. Until 1855, Saints usually disembarked at New Orleans and rode riverboats to Iowa. Thereafter, semitropical diseases, the Civil War, and declining rail prices made New York the primary destination, but competition for the best rail rates sometimes drew Mormons to Philadelphia and Norfolk.

Mormon immigration distinguished itself by organization and cooperation, with Church officials coordinating all stages of the trip, from immigration savings accounts to rail passage after arrival in the United States. The Saints usually traveled in groups, most often on ships chartered by Church officials, which enabled them to negotiate lower prices, provide one another mutual support, and ensure a more wholesome atmosphere onboard. Mormons had long-term shipping relationships with the Wilson, Morris, and Guion Lines.

Onboard, the travelers organized themselves into a ward (congregation) to provide security and order, maintain sanitation, resolve difficulties, and conduct religious services. Sea travel in the 19th century was perilous and often uncomfortable, and more than a few Mormons died en route. However, cooperation, organization, long-term relationships with shipping companies, and "institutional memory" enabled Mormon immigration companies to travel, overall, more safely, cleanly, and comfortably than other immigrants. Mormon travelers in the Pacific followed similar patterns on a much smaller scale.

As the 19th century progressed, immigrants moved more quickly and in smaller groups. Throughout the Mormon gathering, steamships carried Saints across the North Sea to England. By the end of the 1860s, steamers replaced trans-Atlantic sailing ships and reduced the duration of the trip from five to two weeks. By the early 1890s, when objections to Mormon immigration by some Americans and decreased Mormon immigration overall led Church leaders to stop chartering voyages, Church agents had supervised approximately 550 transoceanic voyages. As the ease of travel increased, immigrants in the 20th century tended to make individual arrangements.

The *Brooklyn* in 1846 made the longest of the Mormon immigration voyages, at 24,000 miles, from New York, around South America, to Hawaii, and then to

Emigration Agents

Because of its emphasis on gathering converts to a central community, the 19th-century Church was responsible for more immigration to and within the United States than any other single entity. The Church rapidly developed systems to streamline the process.

Key to smooth emigration was the positioning of agents in Liverpool (to handle emigration from all European countries), in New York City (to transfer emigrants from ship to train), and on the frontier (to help travelers embark on the overland trail). Agents were often mission presidents or other high Church officials; sometimes, as with William C. Staines, who served for many years in New York City, agents were called from lay ranks because of their exceptional ability and dedication.

Agents negotiated for favorable rates on ships and trains; the volume of business was so great that a threat to move immigration to another city or rail line was often enough to ensure improved rates. Agents chose routes, helped emigrants deal with bureaucracy, found employment and lodging for emigrants temporarily unable to continue the journey, and arranged for the purchase of wagons, handcarts, cattle, and foodstuffs.

Few agents are well known in Mormon history, yet the value of their assistance is incalculable.

California. In 1855, the *Julia Ann,* carrying Saints from Australia, grounded on a reef near the Society Islands, and five of the Mormons drowned.

Immigration by sea played a major role in the early Church and the development of its culture and continued to be an important part of the Mormon experience until after World War II. More recently, stories from Mormon sea immigration have promoted values such as cooperation and organization in Mormon culture.

—Edward H. Jeter

See also: Handcart Migration; Pioneering; Ungathered.

References

Devitry-Smith, John. "The Wreck of the Julia Ann," *BYU Studies* 29, no. 2 (Spring 1989): 5–29.

Sonne, Conway B. *Saints on the Seas: A Maritime History of Mormon Migration 1830–1890.* Salt Lake City: University of Utah Press, 1983.

Kirtland Pentecost

During the winter of 1835–1836, the Latter-day Saints in Kirtland, Ohio, labored to construct their temple as stipulated by Joseph Smith's revelation and in anticipation of a promised endowment of power. The temple was dedicated on Sunday, March 27, 1836. Mormons recorded great outpourings of otherworldly manifestations during the events surrounding the dedication. For them it was their own Pentecost, like that recorded in New Testament scripture.

The service included the reading of psalms, preaching, and singing, after which Smith read the later-canonized dedicatory prayer. Following the prayer, the Saints accepted the dedication and then participated in the Sacrament of the Lord's Supper. Many Saints bore witness of the truthfulness of the restored gospel. Others claimed to have seen angels.

On March 29 and 30, the priesthood hierarchy gathered in the temple and administered feet washings and blessings, retrospectively referred to as part of the "Kirtland Endowment." After the execution of these rituals, the priesthood blessed one another and cursed their enemies. They ate bread and wine and preached through the night. Joseph recorded in his diary:

The first Mormon temple was built at Kirtland, Ohio; it stands today, the property of the Community of Christ. (Courtesy of the Church History Library, The Church of Jesus Christ of Latter-day Saints.)

The brethren continued exhorting, prophesying, and speaking in tongues until 5 o clock in the morning—the Saviour made his appearance to some, while angels minestered unto others, and it was a penticost and enduement indeed, long to be remembered for the sound shall go forth from this place into all the world, and the occurrences of this day shall be handed down upon the pages of sacred history to all generations, as the day of Pentecost. (Jessee et al., *Joseph Smith Papers* 215–216)

Erastus Snow recorded:

[T]he Lords anointed assembled in the Lord house . . . they continued there meeting from morning untill evening & from evening untill morning & the angels of the Lord appeared unto them & cloven tongues like fire sat upon many of them & they prophecied and spake with other tongues as the spirit gave them uterance. & in the evening they eat the Passover & feasted upon bread & wine untill they were filled and after these things were over the deciples went from house to house breaking bread & eating it with joyful hearts being fill with the spirit of prophecy & the sick were heald & Devels were cast out. (Snow, Autobiography 30)

Some disaffected members later claimed not to have had or witnessed any charismatic wonders. There were even accusations that some of the exultation was the result of drunkenness. One former Mormon, however, wrote, "The sacrament was . . . administered, in which they partook of the bread and wine freely, and a report went abroad that some of them got drunk: as to that every man must answer for himself. A similar report, the reader will recollect, went out concerning the disciples, at Jerusalem, on the day of Pentecost" (Corrill, *Brief History* 23).

—*Jonathan A. Stapley*

See also: Mormonism as Restoration; Temples.

References

Corrill, John. *A Brief History of the Church of Christ of Latter Day Saints.* St. Louis, MO: John Corrill, 1839.

Jessee, Dean C., Mark Ashurst-McGee, and Richard L. Jensen. *The Joseph Smith Papers: Journals.* Vol. 1: *1832–1839.* Salt Lake City, UT: Church Historian's Press, 2008.

Snow, Erastus. Autobiography/Journal. Holograph. LDS Church Archives.

Manifesto

For Mormons, 1890 marked an important watershed in their history. It signaled the divide between a polygamous past and a monogamous present. It is the year that Church president Wilford Woodruff issued what came to be known as the Manifesto, renouncing polygamy. Issued in the wake of the federal government's effort to begin confiscating LDS temples, Woodruff made it clear that the dilemma he faced was between two important elements of Mormon religious life, polygamy and temples. He claimed that spiritual manifestations prompted him to abandon polygamy in order to preserve the more fundamental tenets of LDS theology bound up in temple worship.

The Manifesto was first issued as a press release on September 24, 1890. Woodruff in part declared, "Inasmuch as laws have been enacted by Congress forbidding plural marriages, which laws have been pronounced constitutional by the court of last resort, I hereby declare my intention to submit to those laws, and to use my influence with the members of the Church over which I preside to have them do likewise" (Official Declaration 1, Doctrine and Covenants 291–292). The Manifesto was then presented to the Mormon faithful at a general conference about two weeks later, where those gathered sustained it by vote.

The Manifesto, did not, of course, put an immediate end to polygamy. Reaction was mixed among Mormons and led the Church into a period of ambiguity during which some adherents clung tenaciously to "the principle" of plural marriage. Some Mormons argued that Woodruff had simply bowed to political pressure and was therefore a fallen prophet. Others expressed relief that the tension between the federal government and the Mormons was coming to an end. Perhaps the reaction of one plural wife, Annie Clark Tanner, was typical: "With the long years of sacrifice just back of me, I was easily convinced that it was from the Lord—quite as much as other revelations. . . . Perhaps it had required even more concentration, prayer, and serious thought to produce it. Certainly it was as far-reaching in effect as any other revelation in Church history—perhaps even more" (Tanner, *A Mormon Mother* 129).

Post-Manifesto plural marriages continued in Mexico and Canada and some even clandestinely in the United States. In 1904, Church president Joseph F. Smith issued what historians refer to as the "Second Manifesto," which proclaimed excommunication as the penalty for Mormons who took additional plural wives. After 1910, the Church actively excommunicated Mormons who entered into plural marriage, a policy continued in the 21st century. Some who were excommunicated began their own Churches based upon the continuation of polygamy.

—*W. Paul Reeve*

See also: Divergent Churches; Mormonism and the Family; Polygamy; Temples; Woodruff, Wilford.

References

Hardy, B. Carmon. *Solemn Covenant: The Mormon Polygamous Passage.* Urbana: University of Illinois Press, 1992.

Official Declaration 1. The Doctrine and Covenants of the Church of Jesus Christ of Latter-day Saints. Salt Lake City, UT: The Church of Jesus Christ of Latter-day Saints, 1981.

Tanner, Annie Clark. *A Mormon Mother.* Salt Lake City: University of Utah Library Tanner Trust Fund, 1991.

Martyrdom of Joseph and Hyrum Smith

On June 27, 1844, in the Carthage, Illinois, jailhouse, the lives of Joseph Smith Jr. and his brother Hyrum came to a violent end. The Smith brothers were in prison awaiting trial for treason, having surrendered to local authorities three days earlier. The initial charge was rioting; however, when bail for the rioting charge was quickly posted, the brothers were charged with treason and, consequently, imprisoned without bail. Thus, they were forced to remain in Carthage despite the fact that local hostility toward them was at a boiling point and numerous threats had been made on their lives. On the fateful afternoon, at shortly after 5:00 P.M., the prison guards offered virtually no resistance as a mob of more than 200 men stormed the jail. In the jailhouse with the prisoners were their friends John Taylor and Willard Richards. Taylor was severely wounded in the attack, but Richards escaped with minor injuries. Both Smith brothers were shot and killed.

Hostility toward the Mormons and toward the Smith brothers, in particular, had been escalating for a number of weeks. Dissident Mormons fomented the fury by traveling throughout the area representing Joseph Smith as an immoral charlatan. One particular group of Mormon dissenters acquired a printing press in June 1844 and began publishing the *Nauvoo Expositor,* a periodical whose first issue accused Smith of building a personal harem under the guise of religious doctrine. The Nauvoo City Council, with Joseph Smith as mayor, declared the *Expositor* a public nuisance and ordered its press destroyed.

The subsequent destruction of the press provided the basis for the rioting charge that was later levied against the Smiths.

Non-Mormon hostility toward the Mormons had been mounting before the destruction of the press. Many locals expressed concern over rumors that the Mormons were practicing polygamy; however, economic and political factors appear to be the primary source of non-Mormon animosity. A number of influential residents of Hancock County (the county in which the Mormon city of Nauvoo was located) felt threatened by

Joseph Smith and his brother Hyrum were shot to death by a mob storming this jail in Carthage, Illinois, in 1844. (Courtesy of the Church History Library, The Church of Jesus Christ of Latter-day Saints.)

the prosperity and growth of the Mormons. In response, they organized an anti-Mormon political party and garnered public support through periodicals such as the *Warsaw Signal*. When informed of the destruction of the *Expositor,* several powerful anti-Mormons, who viewed this act as an overt disregard for the law, openly called for the extermination of Mormon leaders and organized a group of more than 3,000 to attack Nauvoo. As a defensive measure, Joseph Smith declared martial law in Nauvoo and called out the city's militia, actions that later brought charges of treason against the Smiths.

Hoping to save Nauvoo from imminent attack, Joseph and Hyrum Smith surrendered to authorities in Carthage, where, three days later, they were shot and killed. Although there were more than 200 men in the Carthage mob, only five were tried for the murder of the Smith brothers. All were found innocent, the court ruling that the defendants had acted in accordance with the moral sensibilities of the community.

—Debra J. Marsh

See also: Development: 1831–1844; Mormonism and Violence; Smith, Hyrum; Smith, Joseph Jr.

References

Marsh, Debra J. "Respectable Assassins: A Collective Biography and Socio-economic Study of the Carthage Mob." Master's thesis, University of Utah, 2009.

Oaks, Dallin H., and Marvin S. Hill. *Carthage Conspiracy.* Urbana and Chicago: University of Illinois Press, 1979.

Missouri War

The summer and fall of 1838 saw the outbreak of the Mormon War in Missouri, the most violent encounter in Mormon history prior to the exodus to Utah. The causes of the conflict were multivalent. First, non-Mormons were worried about the influx of thousands of Mormon immigrants and the resultant concentration of Mormon political and economic power. Second, non-Mormons often viewed the Latter-day Saints through the lens of fanaticism, seeing the new religious group as irrational, unrepublican, and, like Native Americans and African Americans in antebellum America, unworthy of citizenship. Third, in June, the Mormons formed the Danites, an ultraloyalist vigilante group organized to stop dissent and oppose external persecution, which further aroused suspicions among non-Mormons about Latter-day Saint fanaticism. Fourth, remembering their violent expulsion in 1833 from Jackson County, Missouri, the Latter-day Saints declared their intentions to resist any future persecutions. These factors combined in an explosive fashion just prior to the August 1838 election.

On August 6, 1838, violence broke out at the polls among Mormons and non-Mormons in Gallatin, Daviess County. No one was killed, but inflated rumors led armed Mormons to confront the anti-Mormons, resulting in further rumors of Mormon aggression. Meanwhile, anti-Mormon vigilantes harassed Mormon settlers in DeWitt, Carroll County, expelling them from the county on October 10. Hearing that vigilantes from Carroll and other counties were marching to Daviess County to drive out the Latter-day Saints there, Mormon vigilantes pre-empted the Missourians by expelling all non-Mormon inhabitants from the county (including non-combatants), taking their goods as war appropriations and burning dwellings that could be used by the non-Mormon vigilantes.

On October 25, Mormon forces met non-Mormon vigilantes at Crooked River, near the Caldwell and Ray County border, seeking to liberate three captured Mormon scouts. Although the Latter-day Saints routed the Missourians, three members of the Mormon company, including apostle David W. Patten, were killed, while one Missourian was killed. Rumors of a massacre by the Mormons led Missouri governor Lilburn W. Boggs to issue an order authorizing the militia to exterminate the Mormons or drive them from the state. While a large militia force marched to Far West, rogue Missouri militiamen attacked the Mormon settlement of Haun's Mill, apparently to avenge earlier Mormon depredations in Daviess County; the militia killed 17 Mormon men and boys. On November 1, word of the massacre

Extermination Order

Mormons began migrating to the northwestern counties of Missouri in 1831. Religious, political, and social differences between the Mormon newcomers and established settlers led to escalating conflicts, resulting in bloodshed and widespread destruction of property on both sides. These events are sometimes called the "Mormon War" in Missouri history or the "Missouri persecutions" among Mormons.

Receiving word of yet another clash between Missourians and Mormons, Governor Lilburn W. Boggs ordered units of the state militia to quell a supposed Mormon uprising in Ray County, declaring that Mormons were in "open and avowed defiance of the laws" and had "made war upon the people of this State." The Mormons "must be treated as enemies, and must be exterminated or driven from the State if necessary for the public peace." This October 27, 1838, "Extermination Order" resulted in the imprisonment of Mormon leaders and the wintertime expulsion from Missouri of thousands of Mormons under appalling and life-threatening conditions. The refugees trekked eastward, many of the survivors finding shelter among the charitable citizens of Quincy, Illinois.

Missouri governor Christopher S. Bond rescinded the Extermination Order on June 25, 1976. In the 21st century, more than 60,000 Latter-day Saints live in Missouri.

reached Joseph Smith, convincing him to submit to the governor's militia force at Far West. During November, Smith and other Mormon leaders were charged with treason against Missouri, and the main body of the Latter-day Saints left the state for Illinois. Incarcerated during the winter of 1838–1839 in Liberty Jail, in Clay County, Smith and his fellow prisoners escaped in April 1839, apparently with the connivance of their guards, who were transferring the prisoners to Boone County on a change of venue. This effectively ended the conflict, although Missouri officials made unsuccessful attempts during the 1840s to extradite Smith and these leaders to Missouri for trial.

—*David W. Grua*

See also: Development: 1831–1844; Haun's Mill Massacre; Mormonism and Violence.

References

Baugh, Alexander L. *A Call to Arms: The 1838 Mormon Defense of Northern Missouri.* Provo, UT: Joseph Fielding Smith Institute for Latter-day Saint History and *BYU Studies,* 2000.

LeSueur, Stephen C. *The 1838 Mormon War in Missouri.* Columbia: University of Missouri Press, 1987.

LeSueur, Stephen C. "The Danites Reconsidered: Were They Vigilantes or Just the Mormons' Version of the Elks Club?" *John Whitmer Historical Association Journal* 14 (1994): 35–51.

Mormon Battalion

The Mormon Battalion was a volunteer army unit of around 500 men. This unit, commanded by U.S. Army officers and otherwise consisting exclusively of Mormons, served from July 1846 to July 1847. During their enlistment, Battalion members marched about 1,900 miles from Council Bluffs, Iowa, to San Diego, California.

Earlier in 1846, Brigham Young wrote a letter to Elder Jesse C. Little, a Mormon missionary in New England, instructing him to secure a contract for the creation of an army to protect U.S. interests in the West. Young wished to demonstrate the Mormons' loyalty to the U.S. government and to earn much-needed cash to fund their migration to the Rocky Mountains. Before Little arrived in Washington, D.C., however, war broke out with Mexico. After meeting with Little, President James Polk agreed to enlist 500 men.

Accordingly, Captain James Allen arrived at Mormon encampments at Mount Pisgah, Iowa, on July 1, 1846, to enlist 500 volunteers. Because the Mormons were then fleeing the United States after being driven from their homes in Illinois, it took Brigham Young's influence to persuade men to join. After three weeks, the Battalion left for Leavenworth, Kansas, for outfitting and training. The muster included more than 30 women—20 to work as laundresses—and more than 50 children.

Those who enlisted were given a uniform allowance and wages eventually totaling more than $71,000. Under the direction of Church officials, much of this money was used to buy food and supplies to support the rest of the Mormon migration.

The Battalion's first commander, the recently promoted Lieutenant Colonel James Allen, died shortly after leaving Leavenworth. He was replaced temporarily by Lieutenant Andrew Jackson Smith. The Mormons, however, resented Smith's strict adherence to military discipline. Once they reached Santa Fe, Lieutenant Colonel Philip St. George Cooke arrived to take permanent command. Cooke proved to be well suited to leading the Mormons. Cooke sent a detachment of the sick, most of the women, and all of the children to Pueblo, Colorado, where they would spend the winter. Four of the women, wives of the officers, were allowed to stay.

On the journey from Santa Fe to San Diego, the Battalion fought only one battle, with wild bulls, near the San Pedro River in what would become Arizona. But they came close to fighting with Mexican troops outside Tucson on December 16, 1846. Inexplicably, the Mexican detachment temporarily left Tucson without firing a shot. Later that month, the Mormons also happened upon the aftermath of the Temecula Massacre. Their presence allowed the surviving Luiseno Indians to bury their dead unmolested.

After arriving in San Diego, California, on January 29, 1847, the Mormon Battalion occupied southern California. When their service ended, on July 16, 1847, about 80 men re-enlisted for an additional six months. Only 22 Mormons in the Battalion died, all from natural causes. Battalion members built roads and dug wells, and a few were part of the discovery of gold at Sutter's Mill before they made their way to Utah or back to Iowa.

—Bruce A. Crow

See also: Exodus from Nauvoo; Mormonism and Secular Government.

References

Bigler, David L., and Will Bagley. *Army of Israel: Mormon Battalion Narratives.* Spokane, WA: Arthur H. Clark, 2000.

Ricketts, Norma B. *The Mormon Battalion: U.S. Army of the West, 1846–1847.* Logan: Utah State University Press, 1996.

Mountain Meadows Massacre

In September 1857, dozens of local militiamen in southern Utah, aided by Paiute Indians, massacred some 120 California-bound emigrants in a highland valley called

This monument, on the site of the massacre, pays respectful tribute to the approximately 120 men, women, and children who were murdered there in 1857. (Courtesy of the Church History Library, The Church of Jesus Christ of Latter-day Saints.)

the Mountain Meadows. This horrific crime, which came to be known as the Mountain Meadows Massacre, is arguably the worst incident in Latter-day Saint history and one of the greatest tragedies in the history of the American West.

Any attempt to comprehend the massacre requires understanding the conditions of the time. In 1857, an army of roughly 1,500 U.S. troops was marching toward Utah Territory to suppress what some saw as a rebellion there. At the same time, thousands of overland emigrants were also traveling west—most of them headed for California. Brigham Young, the territorial governor and Church president, and other Utah leaders preached with strong rhetoric against the enemy they perceived in the approaching army and sought the assistance of Indians in resisting the troops. Young and his advisers also instructed the Latter-day Saints in the Territory to prepare for possible war by saving ammunition and grain.

These wartime policies led to conflicts between Latter-day Saint settlers who were saving their resources and emigrants who were frustrated in their attempts to replenish supplies as they passed through the Territory. During a heated exchange that occurred in the southern Utah town of Cedar City, one emigrant man in a train made up mostly of Arkansans reportedly said something that led local people to claim he had helped kill Joseph Smith Jr., the Church's founding prophet, 13 years earlier. Other emigrant men in the train purportedly threatened to join the incoming federal troops against the Mormons. None of the identified victims of the massacre are known to have been among Smith's killers, however, and none would survive to tell his side of the story.

Whatever the emigrant men said, Alexander Fancher, captain of the wagon company, rebuked them on the spot, but, in the charged environment of 1857, Cedar City's leaders took the travelers at their word. The town marshal tried to arrest some of the emigrants on charges of public intoxication and profanity but was forced to back down. Yet the agitated Cedar City leaders were not willing to let the matter go. Angry and fearful after a long history of what they viewed as religious persecution and now facing the prospect of war, they overreacted, convincing themselves that the emigrants were their enemies.

Isaac Haight, the mayor of Cedar City, a Church leader, and a major in the militia, sent an express dispatch to William Dame, the district militia commander and the local Church leader in nearby Parowan. The letter sought permission to use the militia to arrest the emigrants seen as offenders by the Utahns. After convening a council to discuss the matter, Dame denied the request. Still intent on chastening the emigrants, however, Cedar City authorities formulated a new plan. If they could not formally muster the militia, they would try persuading local Paiute Indians to give the Arkansas company "a *brush*," attacking it in a canyon below Mountain Meadows, shooting some of its men, and stealing its cattle (Bishop, *Mormonism Unveiled* 219).

Needing someone to lead the attack, Haight chose John D. Lee, a militia major and a federally funded "Indian farmer" in the settlement of Fort Harmony. Lee and Haight had a long discussion in which Lee told Haight he believed the Indians might "kill all the party, women and children, as well as the men," if incited to attack (Bishop, *Mormonism Unveiled* 220). The two men agreed to move ahead with the attack, planning to lay the blame for it at the feet of the Indians. On the slippery slope that often leads to group violence, one bad decision led to another, until finally the men were willing to sanction the complete destruction of the emigrants.

The generally peaceful Paiutes were reluctant when told of the plan. But Cedar City's leaders promised them plunder and assistance, convincing them that the emigrants were aligned with "enemy" troops who would kill Indians along with Mormon settlers.

On Sunday, September 6, Haight presented the plan to a council of local leaders. It was met with stunned resistance by some. When council members asked who had authorized the plans, Haight and his supporters acknowledged that they had acted independently. The council decided to send an express rider to Salt Lake City with a letter to Brigham Young asking what should be done before taking action against the emigrants.

But the next day, shortly before the express rider left with the letter, Lee led a premature attack on the emigrant camp at Mountain Meadows, rather than waiting for the company to reach the canyon below. The assault killed several emigrants, and the remainder fought off their attackers, forcing a retreat. The emigrants quickly pulled their wagons into a tight circle, holing up inside the defensive corral. They also repelled two other attacks in what became a five-day siege.

Not all the emigrants were in camp during the initial assault. Two men were away gathering stray cattle. Early in the siege, two Cedar City Mormons discovered them a few miles outside the corral. The Cedar City men killed one of the emigrants, but the other escaped on horseback to the wagon corral, bringing with him news that his companion's killers were white men, not Indians.

The conspirators knew that if the surviving emigrants were freed and continued on to California, word would spread that Mormons had been involved in the attacks. An army was already approaching the Territory, and southern Utah leaders believed that if news of their role in the assault got out, it would result in retaliatory military action that would threaten their lives and the lives of their people.

On September 9, Haight and his associate Elias Morris again sought Dame's permission to call out the militia. Dame held another council meeting in Parowan, and it was decided that men should be sent to help the beleaguered emigrants continue on their way in peace. Haight later lamented, "I would give a world if I had it, if we had abided by the deci[s]ion of the council" (Jenson, Notes).

Instead, when the meeting ended, Haight got Dame alone, sharing with him information he had apparently not shared with the council: the corralled emigrants knew that white men had been involved in the initial attacks. Haight also led Dame to believe that most of the emigrants had already died. This information caused Dame to rethink his earlier decision. Tragically, he gave in, and, when the conversation ended, Haight left feeling he had permission to use the militia against the emigrants.

Arriving back in Cedar City, Haight called out militia members to join others already waiting near the emigrant corral at the Mountain Meadows.

On Friday, September 11, Lee entered the emigrant wagon fort under a white flag and convinced the besieged emigrants to accept desperate terms. He said the militia would safely escort them back to Cedar City but that they must leave their possessions behind and give up their weapons, signaling their peaceful intentions to the Indians. The suspicious emigrants debated what to do but in the end accepted the terms, seeing no better alternative.

Pursuant to these terms, the emigrants put some of the youngest children and the wounded into two wagons, which left the wagon corral first, followed by women and children on foot. The men and older boys filed out last, with armed militiamen at their sides. The procession marched for a mile or so until, at a prearranged signal, militiamen turned and fired on the emigrant men and boys, while Indians rushed as directed from their hiding place to pursue the women and children. Militiamen with the two front-running wagons began murdering the wounded. Only 17 children, considered "too young to tell tales," were spared (*San Francisco Daily Evening Bulletin,* "Lee's Last Confession" 7). Although some of the perpetrators, consistent with the original plan, tried to fix the blame for the massacre on Paiutes, participant Nephi Johnson later said that his fellow white militiamen did most of the killing.

Brigham Young's express message of reply to Haight, dated September 10, arrived in Cedar City two days after the massacre. "In regard to emigration trains passing through our settlements," Young wrote, "we must not interfere with them untill they are first notified to keep away. You must not meddle with them. The Indians we expect will do as they please but you should try and preserve good feelings with them. There are no other trains going south that I know of. If those who are there will leave let them go in peace. While we should be on the alert, on hand and always ready we should also possess ourselves in patience, preserving ourselves and property ever remembering that God rules" (Young, 1857, 3:827–828).

When Haight read Young's reply, he sobbed like a child and could manage only to say, "Too late, too late" (Haslam, Letter 13).

In 1859, government officials retrieved the 17 spared children from the Utah families who had adopted them and returned them to family members in Arkansas. The massacre snuffed out some 120 lives and immeasurably affected the lives of the surviving children and other relatives of the victims. More than a century and a half later, the massacre remains a deeply painful subject for their descendants.

Although Brigham Young and other Church leaders in Salt Lake City learned of the massacre soon after it happened, their understanding of the full details of the terrible crime came incrementally over time. In 1859, they removed Isaac Haight and other massacre participants from their positions of authority in the Church. In 1870, they excommunicated Haight and John D. Lee.

In 1874, a territorial grand jury indicted nine men for their roles in the massacre. Most of these men were eventually arrested, though only Lee was tried, convicted, and executed for the crime. Another indicted man turned state's evidence, and others spent years running from the law. Meanwhile, the Paiutes suffered unjustly as others, including the white perpetrators, blamed them for the crime.

Since 1857, the Mountain Meadows Massacre has continued to cause pain and controversy. Descendants and other relatives of the emigrants and the perpetrators have joined efforts to memorialize the victims. These efforts have had the support of Latter-day Saint leaders, officials of the state of Utah, and other parties. Members of these groups continue to work toward healing and reconciliation.

—Richard E. Turley Jr.

See also: Conflict: 1869–1890; Exodus and Settlement: 1845–1869; Mormonism and Violence; Utah War; Young, Brigham.

References

Bagley, Will. *Blood of the Prophets: Brigham Young and the Massacre at Mountain Meadows.* Norman: University of Oklahoma Press, 2002.

Bigler, David L., and Will Bagley, eds. *Innocent Blood: Essential Narratives of the Mountain Meadows Massacre.* Norman, OK: Arthur H. Clark, 2008.

Bishop, W. W., ed. *Mormonism Unveiled; or the Life and Confessions of the Late Mormon Bishop, John D. Lee; (Written by Himself).* St. Louis, MO: Bryan, Brand, 1877.

Brooks, Juanita. *The Mountain Meadows Massacre,* 2nd ed. Norman: University of Oklahoma Press, 1991.

Haslam, James H. 1884. Interview by S. A. Kenner, reported by J. Rogerson. December 4. Typescript. Transcripts and Notes of John D. Lee Trials, Church History Library, The Church of Jesus Christ of Latter-day Saints, Salt Lake City, UT.

Jenson, Andrew. 1892. Notes of discussion with William Barton. January. Mountain Meadows file, Jenson Collection, Church History Library, The Church of Jesus Christ of Latter-day Saints, Salt Lake City, UT.

Novak, Shannon A. *House of Mourning: A Biocultural History of the Mountain Meadows Massacre.* Salt Lake City: University of Utah Press, 2008.

San Francisco Daily Evening Bulletin Supplement. "Lee's Last Confession." March 24, 1877.

Turley, Richard E., Jr., and Ronald W. Walker, eds. *Mountain Meadows Massacre Documents.* Provo, UT: Brigham Young University Press, 2009.

Walker, Ronald W., Richard E. Turley Jr., and Glen M. Leonard. *Massacre at Mountain Meadows: An American Tragedy.* New York: Oxford University Press, 2008.

Young, Brigham. Letter to Isaac C. Haight. September 10, 1857. Letterpress Copybook 3:827–828. Brigham Young Office Files, Church History Library, The Church of Jesus Christ of Latter-day Saints, Salt Lake City, UT.

Nauvoo Legion

The Mormon military unit known as the Nauvoo Legion was of a divided nature. Lawfully organized under the 1840 charter granted to Nauvoo, it was a regular unit of the Illinois militia, subject to the governor's call in the event of public emergency. Concurrently, it was a Mormon defensive unit subject to the mayor of Nauvoo. Mormons viewed the Legion as a line of defense against the mob action they had faced in Missouri; their neighbors viewed the Legion as an offensive threat, a precursor to possible rebellion.

The Legion's chief activities were drilling, parading, and staging sham battles, all typical of 19th-century militias throughout the United States. However, when Mayor Joseph Smith Jr. declared martial law in June 1844, the Legion was called into defensive action, serving until the Nauvoo charter was revoked at the end of 1844.

The Nauvoo Legion was reformed in the Great Basin as Utah's territorial militia and saw action in several conflicts between white settlers and Indians. When Brigham Young forbade U.S. troops to enter Utah Territory in 1857, Legion action helped to force the Utah Expedition into winter quarters at Fort Bridger. The Legion also saw brief duty during the Civil War, guarding overland mail and telegraph lines.

In 1870, Utah's non-Mormon governor, professing doubts as to the loyalty of the Legion, outlawed its gathering, even to march in parades. The Legion was disbanded in 1887 upon passage of the Edmunds-Tucker Act, leaving Utah without a militia until the organization, in 1894, of the National Guard.

—Ardis E. Parshall

See also: Mormonism and Secular Government; Utah War.

Reference

MacKinnon, William P., ed. *At Sword's Point: A Documentary History of the Utah War.* 2 vols. Norman, OK: Arthur H. Clark, 2008, and forthcoming.

Organization of the Church

On April 6, 1830, a small crowd of 40 to 60 people gathered at Fayette, New York, in the home of Peter Whitmer Sr. to form a Church.

Following prayer, Joseph Smith Jr. asked those present if they would accept Oliver Cowdery and him as their teachers and if they were willing to organize. Those gathered expressed unanimous approval, following which Smith ordained Cowdery an elder and then Cowdery did the same for Smith. For legal purposes, six attendees were entered as founding members.

Twentieth-century restoration of the Peter Whitmer cabin in Fayette, New York, site of the April 1830 organization of the Church of Jesus Christ of Latter-day Saints. (Courtesy of the Church History Library, The Church of Jesus Christ of Latter-day Saints.)

Smith and Cowdery then blessed and passed bread and wine as the sacrament of the Lord's Supper. The two leaders also laid hands upon the heads of many of those gathered and bestowed the Holy Ghost. Members of the little congregation praised the Lord, prophesied, and otherwise rejoiced in the feelings of the spirit. Smith received a new revelation and ordained men to priesthood offices. Some were baptized as members of the new Church.

The name of the new organization was originally the Church of Christ, but it was changed in 1834 to The Church of the Latter Day Saints. In 1838, Smith announced a revelation designating the name of the Church as the Church of Jesus Christ of Latter-day Saints, the name by which it continues to be known. Outsiders sometimes called adherents of the new faith "Mormons" for their belief in the Book of Mormon and have similarly nicknamed the organization the "Mormon Church." Members are also referred to as LDS, Latter-day Saints, or Saints.

—*W. Paul Reeve*

See also: Book of Mormon; Church Organization and Government; Mormonism as Restoration.

Reference

Bushman, Richard Lyman. *Joseph Smith and the Beginnings of Mormonism.* Urbana: University of Illinois Press, 1987.

Pioneering

The Mormon pioneering movement began in 1847 and lasted through 1868. Throughout those 22 years, more than 250 companies and 70,000 people answered the call to "come to Zion." The most commonly held images are of people riding and walking beside Conestoga-style covered wagons or pushing and pulling handcarts filled with all their belongings. But companies were also organized to bring food, supplies, and equipment. A few pioneers even came west to California by ship, the *Brooklyn* being the most famous, and then went on to the Great Basin.

The first pioneer companies arrived in the spring of 1847. These companies consisted of hand-picked individuals who were given specific tasks to ensure the success of later pioneers. They planted crops and built roads, ferries, and shelter to prepare the way for the thousands who were expected to follow. Brigham Young arrived in the Great Basin on July 24, 1847, an event now commemorated as Pioneer Day in Utah.

Proven leaders were selected to captain each immigrant company. Companies were organized into groups of 100 and subdivided into groups of 50 and 10. Some companies were created as early as the fall of 1845 in Nauvoo, Illinois, to prepare

"Come, Come Ye Saints"

Written by William Clayton on April 15, 1846, as his pioneer company struggled through the mud of Iowa, this poem, set to an English folk tune, quickly became the anthem of the westward-bound Mormons. Its text urged the weary to "gird up your loins, fresh courage take" and reassured the fearful that "none shall come to hurt or make afraid" in the promised land of the West. Succeeding generations have treasured this link to pioneer heritage, making this perhaps the best-known and most beloved of Mormon hymns.

Come, come, ye Saints, no toil nor labor fear;
But with joy, wend your way.

Though hard to you this journey may appear,
Grace shall be as your day.
Tis better far for us to strive
Our useless cares from us to drive;
Do this, and joy your hearts will swell—
All is well! All is well! . . .
And should we die before our journey's
    through,
Happy day! All is well!
We then are free from toil and sorrow, too;
With the just we shall dwell!
But if our lives are spared again
To see the Saints their rest obtain,
Oh, how we'll make this chorus swell—
    All is well! All is well!

Source: George Careless et al., *The Latter-day Saints' Psalmody.* Salt Lake City, UT: Deseret News Co., 1889, 327.

for the expected move west. These companies combined resources to purchase food, supplies, livestock, and raw materials. They cooperated to build wagons and much-needed equipment. In subsequent years, companies were organized in other cities in the Midwest, such as Iowa City, Iowa.

Gathering to "Zion" was considered as much a communal responsibility as an individual one. Those who were able to get their own families to the Great Basin were sent back to bring others who were without the means to come on their own. In 1849, a Perpetual Emigrating Fund (PEF) was established to assist poor Mormons who could not afford to leave their temporary homes in Iowa. It was later expanded to bring converts from Europe, as well. The fund was started with donations and Church support, and those who benefited from it were to later pay back their loans, thereby replenishing the fund and providing for the immigration of additional converts. Even though it was never a financial success, the PEF did succeed in gathering many Mormons to Utah.

As PEF funds diminished, Mormon leaders devised more efficient means to bring Saints to Zion. One such effort was the use of handcarts, instead of wagons. Ten handcart companies migrated between 1856 and 1860. Only two of them, the Martin and Willie Companies, encountered severe problems. Trapped by early snows, many emigrants perished before rescue parties arrived from Utah. "Out and Back" migrations replaced the handcarts in 1861, with Mormons from Utah traveling "out" to meet the immigrants at the rail terminus and bringing them "back" to the Great Basin in wagons.

Regardless of how the pioneers traveled, most of them experienced the same overland trail, even if not in the same company. This created a shared, unifying, faith-building experience. Pioneers were driven by persecution; experienced hunger, thirst, and fatigue; and yet found time to sing, dance, and pray together. Many died, though not in greater numbers than those who survived the travel to Oregon or California.

The pioneering period came to a close with the completion of the transcontinental railroad, on May 10, 1869.

—*Bruce A. Crow*

See also: Exodus and Settlement: 1845–1869; Exodus from Nauvoo; Handcart Migration; Immigration; Ungathered.

References

Hartley, William G. "Brigham Young's Overland Trails Revolution: The Creation of the 'Down-and-Back' Wagon-Train System, 1860–61." *Journal of Mormon History* 28 (Spring 2002): 1–30.

Slaughter, William W., and Michael Landon. *Trail of Hope: The Story of the Mormon Trail.* Salt Lake City, UT: Shadow Mountain, 1997.

Priesthood Revelation of 1978

David O. McKay was the first LDS Church president to seriously consider rescinding the restriction preventing blacks from holding the priesthood. He softened the restriction by identifying it as a "policy," not a "doctrine," which conceptually provided for the possibility of reversal. He also tied the restriction to African lineage rather than to black skin color, which allowed blacks in areas such as the Pacific Basin who did not have known African ancestry to receive the priesthood. However, he agreed with predecessors that any change in the Church's position required revelation.

Spencer W. Kimball became president in 1973. He sustained the restriction, also believing that only revelation could reverse it. Long an advocate against racial prejudice, Kimball found himself preoccupied by the ban.

Spending countless hours in prayer, Kimball became sure that a change in policy was the "will of the Lord." Details of how Kimball arrived at this assurance are unclear, but words like "impression," "inspiration," and "clear in Spencer's mind" have been used by historians and Kimball himself to describe the revelation's reception. Though personally convinced, Kimball felt that unity among the Quorum of the Twelve Apostles and the First Presidency would be necessary before he could

The 1978 revelation opened the way for all worthy men, regardless of race, to officiate in priesthood ordinances. (Courtesy of The Church of Jesus Christ of Latter-day Saints.)

release a public announcement. He disclosed his thoughts to his counselors in the First Presidency, who offered their support. Sensing some resistance, Kimball spoke with members of the Twelve individually and urged continued fasting and prayer on the issue.

Finally, on June 1, 1978, Kimball, his two counselors, and the Quorum of the Twelve met to consider the issue. Kimball disclosed his previous feelings about lifting the ban and invited the 10 apostles present to express their views. Each apostle provided a favorable assessment, after which Kimball offered to lead them in prayer seeking a spiritual confirmation.

Those present later struggled to describe the "marvelous experience" they enjoyed during that prayer. Participants described feelings of unity that were ineffable and said that the Holy Ghost descended on those present, rendering them unable to speak because of the depth of their emotion, with some weeping. Each participant expressed a personal confirmation of the rightness of the decision to rescind the restriction.

On June 7, the First Presidency and the Quorum of the Twelve agreed upon a formal statement extending the priesthood to all worthy males. On June 8, the statement received unanimous approval in a special meeting of all the General Authorities and was released to the public to a highly enthusiastic reception. Subsequently, Church members have often referred to June 8, 1978, as "the long promised day" that brought the Church into compliance with its scriptural mandate to take the gospel to the entire world. The text of the statement was accepted by Church members on August 30, 1978, and is canonized in the Doctrine and Covenants as Official Declaration 2.

—Jared Tamez

See also: Kimball, Spencer W.; McKay, David O.; Mormonism and Blacks; Mormonism and Race.

References

Kimball, Edward L. "Spencer W. Kimball and the Revelation on Priesthood." *BYU Studies* 47, no. 2 (2008): 5–78.

Prince, Gregory A. and Wm. Robert Wright. *David O. McKay and the Rise of Modern Mormonism.* Salt Lake City: University of Utah Press, 2005.

Reformation

During the first years of Mormon settlement in the Rocky Mountains, matters of survival—growing crops; building homes, fences, and irrigation canals; caring for the thousands who arrived with each new season—overwhelmingly occupied the attention of settlers. By 1856, leaders felt a need for Church members to focus again on spiritual matters and to recommit themselves to religious life. The period of recommital that began in September 1856 is remembered as the Reformation.

Jedediah M. Grant, first counselor to Brigham Young, launched the Reformation during a tour of settlements north of Salt Lake City. His series of fiery sermons called upon the people to repent of their laxness in observing the commandments and to be baptized again as a sign of their commitment to the gospel. Grant's revivalist enthusiasm spread rapidly. "Home missionaries," Church elders called to preach in every congregation, carried the Reformation to places not personally visited by Grant or other Church leaders.

A "catechism," or list of questions for evaluating one's spiritual worthiness, was developed, inquiring into behavior ranging from adultery to gossip to the frequency of bathing. In some settlements, the catechism was used for self-evaluation; in others, members were questioned privately or even publicly about intensely personal matters. Individuals were encouraged to confess their sins, make restitution, and improve their behavior. Forgiveness was extended to those who sincerely repented and abandoned past sins.

Reformation speakers also encouraged recommitment to neglected Mormon practices. Attendance at Church meetings increased, as did the payment of tithing. A marked increase in plural marriages occurred during the months of the Reformation, as well.

There is evidence that Church leaders used the emotional and spiritual severity of the Reformation to encourage those with waning devotion to Mormonism to leave Utah Territory. Not only did Brigham Young report favorably to colleagues in California and England that many "lukewarm" Mormons were planning to leave in the spring of 1857, but also his sermons during that winter were laced with references to "blood atonement," the idea that some sins were so grievous that forgiveness could be gained only through the shedding of one's blood. Whether such sermons were merely rhetorical, as most Mormon historians claim, or were directives for the murder of backsliders, as some anti-Mormon historians claim, there is no doubt that such sermons contributed to a climate of fear among those who were alienated from the Church.

The Reformation was carried to Mormon congregations outside the Great Basin, particularly to England. Few if any of the excesses of the Reformation in Utah were experienced abroad. There, the Reformation took the form of renewed calls for emigration and in the pruning of many hundreds of names of nonparticipating members from the record books.

The fervor of the Reformation dissipated after the winter of 1856–1857, both because the intense spirit of revival burned itself out and because the Church was faced in the summer of 1857 with the approach of a federal army and preparations for the looming Utah War.

—*Ardis E. Parshall*

See also: Exodus and Settlement: 1845–1869; Mormonism and Violence; Utah War.

References

Larson, Gustive O. "The Mormon Reformation." *Utah Historical Quarterly* 26 (January 1958): 45–63.

Peterson, Paul H. "The Mormon Reformation of 1856–1857: The Rhetoric and the Reality." *Journal of Mormon History* 15 (1989): 59–87.

Relief Society

One of the largest and oldest women's organizations in the world, the Relief Society was founded in 1842 in Nauvoo, Illinois, to support the building of the Nauvoo temple by sewing shirts for workers. A constitution and by-laws were written by Eliza R. Snow and given to Joseph Smith for review. He acknowledged the by-laws but said the Lord had something more important for the women and that he would organize them as an auxiliary of the Church.

The Female Relief Society met for the first time on March 17, 1842, with Emma Smith as president, Sarah Cleveland and Elizabeth Ann Whitney as counselors, and Eliza R. Snow as secretary. The Relief Society took as its purpose "the relief of the poor, the destitute, the widow and the orphan, and . . . the exercise of all benevolent purposes" (Smith, *History* 4:567–568).

By July 1843, the Relief Society had almost 1,200 members. The women donated money, goods, and services for the poor. Within each ward, women visited homes to solicit donations and to assess needs. The Relief Society also became a source of social and religious strength for its members. The Nauvoo organization last met in March 1844 and did not hold meetings as the Church moved west.

In Salt Lake City, in January 1854, some members of the original Relief Society organized an Indian Relief Society to clothe Native Americans. The organization soon divided into individual societies within each ward, but most of these groups stopped meeting during the Utah War of 1857–1858.

In December 1866, Brigham Young appointed Eliza R. Snow to reorganize the Relief Society throughout the Church. As Snow traveled from ward to ward, she consulted her original minute book of the Nauvoo Relief Society for procedure and purpose. The revived Relief Society had three guiding principles: caring for the poor, caring for the Church, and promoting economic self-sufficiency. The women continued visiting members to solicit donations and to care for the poor, sick, and elderly. They blessed the sick, taught each other, stored wheat against a time of need, and set up cooperative stores. They helped send women to medical school in the eastern United States and trained nurses and midwives who provided decades of service to their communities.

The Relief Society, now claiming millions of female members worldwide, was organized by a handful of Mormon women in a room above a general store in 1842. (Courtesy of the Church History Museum, The Church of Jesus Christ of Latter-day Saints.)

The *Woman's Exponent,* published from 1872 to 1913, with Emmeline Wells as editor during most of its run, served as the unofficial voice of the Relief Society. It covered politics, women's rights, suffrage, education, and home topics. Its masthead read, "The Rights of the Women of Zion, and the Rights of the Women of All Nations."

The Relief Society strongly supported the suffrage movement and world peace movements. It was a charter member of the National Council of Women.

At the beginning of the 20th century, the Relief Society trained women in public speaking, home and family education, and social reform. Members also raised funds to build temples. In 1913, the Relief Society adopted its motto, "Charity Never Faileth." In 1914, the *Relief Society Magazine* replaced *The Woman's Exponent,* publishing articles on a variety of subjects, poems, short stories, and weekly lessons for local Relief Societies covering theology, culture, and practical subjects.

During World War I, the Relief Society assisted relief efforts, often working with the Red Cross. Near the end of the war, the U.S. government bought 200,000 bushels of Relief Society wheat.

During the Great Depression, the Church streamlined its welfare program. Along with helping bishops provide for charitable needs, the Relief Society continued to educate the women of the Church and to provide opportunities for musical training. Women formed more than 2,700 Singing Mothers groups around the world, and the Society operated an employment bureau and adoption agency.

During World War II, the Relief Society again mobilized relief efforts, worked with the Red Cross, and organized conser-

After the move to Utah, Relief Society women built halls, like this one in Beaver, to meet their needs. (Courtesy of the Church History Library, The Church of Jesus Christ of Latter-day Saints.)

vation and home production efforts. The Relief Society canceled the grand centennial celebration of its founding because of the war, so the occasion was marked only by small observances and the planting of 874 trees in units around the world.

Many projects occupied the postwar Relief Society. Members delivered almost 10,000 quilts and other supplies to war-torn Europe and Japan, and the Society raised more than half a million dollars to build a new office building. Additional projects included strengthening Relief Society units outside the United States, social service activities, and a continued emphasis on education among its members. Relief Society units regularly raised funds by holding bazaars with homemade quilts and other crafts for sale. The Relief Society strengthened its ties with the National Council of Women, especially when Relief Society president Belle Spafford served a term as NCW president.

By the 1970s, Church expansion throughout the world led to a new drive for simpler lessons, with the priority given to strengthening women and their families. Fund-raising and the payment of dues ceased, and all costs were handled through the

Church budget. The *Relief Society Magazine* ceased publication at the end of 1970. Relief Society leaders took a stance against the Equal Rights Amendment in the United States because of its lack of protection of women's privacy and other issues. In 1978, the Relief Society turned over its remaining wheat (more than 220,000 bushels) and its wheat fund (approximately $750,000) to the General Church Welfare Committee.

As the Church moved into the 1980s, the Young Women and Primary (the youth and child auxiliaries) established a closer working relationship with the Relief Society, with officers of all three organizations sharing space in the Relief Society building. The Relief Society emphasized literacy programs within and without the Church, with the president of the Relief Society serving as a board member of the Church Educational System.

In the 21st century, the Relief Society claims the following purposes: strengthening each member and her home and family; visiting teaching; providing gospel instruction; and improving members' welfare. The Relief Society continues to lead or participate in worldwide efforts to aid refugees, provide health missionaries, and respond in times of crisis or natural disaster.

—*Amy Tanner Thiriot*

See also: Church Organization and Government; Lyman, Amy Brown; Mormonism and Women; Smith, Barbara Bradshaw; Smith, Emma Hale; Snow, Eliza R.; Spafford, Belle Smith; Wells, Emmeline B.

References

Derr, Jill Mulvay, Janath Russell Cannon, and Maureen Ursenbach Beecher. *Women of Covenant: The Story of Relief Society.* Salt Lake City, UT: Deseret Book, 1992.

Peterson, Janet, and LaRene Gaunt. *Elect Ladies.* Salt Lake City, UT: Deseret Book, 1990.

Smith, Joseph Jr. *History of the Church of Jesus Christ of Latter-day Saints.* 6 vols. Ed. B.H. Roberts. Salt Lake City, UT: The Church of Jesus Christ of Latter-day Saints, 1973.

Seagulls and Crickets

The "Miracle of the Gulls" refers to three weeks in June 1848, when flocks of seagulls ate the crickets that were ravaging the Mormons' first crop in Utah.

In late May, what are now known as "Mormon crickets"—actually a type of katydid—began attacking crops in enormous migratory bands that reminded pioneers of the biblical eighth plague of locusts. More than 4,000 Mormons desperately needed to save their harvest, since they had little reserve food and no way to receive help; in addition, a late frost had killed many plants, and scarce rain had stunted what crops were left.

Although the historical foundation of the event has been questioned, Mormons retain an unshakable folk memory of the rescue of their ancestors' crops through the "miracle of the gulls." (Courtesy of the Church History Museum, The Church of Jesus Christ of Latter-day Saints.)

In June, large numbers of seagulls—California gulls from the Great Salt Lake—began eating the crickets. Observers reported that, every day for three weeks, the gulls would gorge, drink some water, regurgitate, and then eat more. By that fall, some commentators credited the gulls with saving the crop, claiming that the regurgitation was against instinct and thus evidence of a higher power's influence. Others, however, reported no help from gulls, and later studies showed that the birds eat the bugs every year and regurgitate only the indigestible exoskeletons. Whether or not God inspired the event, historical records are clear that, at least in some areas, seagulls made the harvest better than it would have been.

Over time, the "Miracle of the Gulls" entrenched itself in Utah and Mormon cultures. In 1913, Mormons dedicated the "Seagull Monument" at Temple Square, and in 1955 the California Gull became the state bird.

—*Edward H. Jeter*

See also: Exodus and Settlement: 1845–1869.

References

Hartley, William G. "Mormons, Crickets, and Gulls: A New Look at an Old Story." *Utah Historical Quarterly* 38 (Summer 1970): 224–239.

Madsen, David B., and Brigham D. Madsen. "One Man's Meat Is Another Man's Poison: A Revisionist View of the Seagull 'Miracle.'" *Nevada Historical Quarterly* 30 (1987): 165–181.

Smoot Hearings

On January 21, 1903, the Utah legislature elected Reed Smoot to the U.S. Senate. Five days later, 19 Utah businessmen and clergy protested to the president of the United States and Senate leaders, demanding that Smoot be denied his seat. The initial complaint, issued under the auspices of the Salt Lake Ministerial Association, was soon joined by other protests from Utah and across the nation. Millions signed petitions demanding that the Senate prevent the seating of Smoot. Reform groups, led by the Woman's Christian Temperance Union, and numerous religious organizations were especially active in the anti-Smoot agitation.

Smoot's election aroused such controversy because he was an apostle in the Church of Jesus Christ of Latter-day Saints. The protestors charged that Smoot and the Church he represented were guilty of a number of crimes, including the continued practice of plural marriage long after its ostensible end in 1890. Additional principal charges involved an anti-American oath allegedly taken by Smoot and other Mormons and an indictment of Mormon economic and political power in the west. Although Smoot was permitted to take his seat, the Senate's Committee on Privileges and Elections initiated an extensive investigation into the apostle's worthiness to remain in Congress.

Hearings on Smoot's case began in March 1904 and continued until June 1906, generating nearly 3,500 pages of testimony and supporting documentation. The first and most dramatic witness to testify was the president of the Mormon Church, Joseph F. Smith. Smith denied any knowledge of continuing plural marriage but surprised many listeners by his admission that he had willfully violated the laws of the Church and the state by continuing to cohabit with his plural wives. Smith sidestepped loaded questions about what Mormon revelations might require the faithful to do by testifying that he had "never pretended to nor do I profess to have received revelations. I have never said I had a revelation except so far as God has shown to me that so-called Mormonism is God's divine truth; that is all" (*Proceedings* 1:99). Smith successfully deflected his Senate interrogators but found a criminal fine waiting for him in Utah along with a host of confused and embittered parishioners.

The hearings provided their own revelations. A number of witnesses testified to their participation in polygamy contracted after 1890 and implicated high Church officials, including some of Smoot's fellow apostles. One Utah minister, John Leilich, averred that Smoot himself practiced polygamy. The ease with which this latter charge was disproved tended to obscure other evidence incriminating the Mormon leadership. In April 1904, Joseph F. Smith renewed the Church's vow of monogamy and promised to repudiate new plural marriages. To placate the protestors, two apostles most conspicuously involved in polygamy, John W. Taylor and Matthias F. Cowley, resigned their ecclesiastical positions in 1905.

Perhaps the most sensational charge against Smoot and his co-religionists was the anti-American oath allegedly taken in Mormon temples. According to the Protestants, Mormons vowed to take vengeance against the United States for the murder of their founding prophet, Joseph Smith. Additionally, devout Mormons pledged to obey the commands of the Church even when they were in conflict with the laws of the nation. Despite damning testimony detailing the anti-American oath, the protestors failed to prove that Mormons had exacted vengeance against the government. Although they refused to discuss the specifics of Mormon temple ceremonies, loyal Mormons, including Richard Young, a high-ranking veteran of the Spanish-American War, denied the charges and thus destroyed the credibility of that portion of the Protestants' claims.

Smoot's opponents depicted the Mormon Church as omnipotent in the Rocky Mountain region. Under the direction of the hierarchy, the Mormon Church allegedly controlled the economic and political lives of all within its shadow. The protestors attempted to show that Mormon leaders chose candidates for elections, dictated how ballots were cast, and authored the laws enacted by the state legislature. Frustrated Utah politicians testified that the Church had engineered their defeat. Former Mormon dissidents B. H. Roberts and Moses Thatcher denied that their Church was involved in politics and retracted earlier charges of ecclesiastical involvement. Some national leaders believed that the Mormon Church exercised political control over its members but shrewdly sought to capitalize on this authority, rather than punish it.

At the end of the hearings, in June 1906, Smoot's status remained uncertain. A majority of the Committee on Privileges and Elections voted to remove Smoot from the Senate. Yet, a majority of Senators rejected that advice and voted, in February 1907, to allow Smoot to retain his seat. Most of Smoot's fellow Republicans, including Nelson Aldrich and Albert Beveridge, voted for the apostle, while the minority counted insurgent Republican Robert La Follette among them. Instrumental in Smoot's victory was President Theodore Roosevelt. The president had initially opposed the presence of a Mormon apostle in the Senate, but, hoping to win electoral support from the Mormon Church, Roosevelt became a firm ally.

The Smoot hearings resulted in a pyrrhic victory for the Mormon Church. Although Smoot retained his seat and won powerful allies for his beleaguered Church, he also brought it great enmity. Many within and outside the Church were shocked by the continuing practice of polygamy and the apparent connivance of the hierarchy. The invidious attention generated by the Smoot hearings helped usher in the end of Mormon polygamy. The hearings also assisted in solidifying an alliance between the Mormon Church and the Republican Party, in large part because of the pivotal role of Roosevelt. Because Smoot retained his seat in the Senate, unlike George Q. Cannon and B. H. Roberts, who had been expelled from Congress, the apostle-senator helped pave the way for the Mormon Church to enter the American mainstream. As a result of the hearings, Smoot and his Church surrendered much of their 19th-century distinctiveness but found wide acceptance and respectability during his tenure in the Senate.

—Jonathan H. Moyer

See also: Manifesto; Mormonism and Secular Government; Polygamy; Smith, Joseph F.

References

Flake, Kathleen. *The Politics of Religious Identity: The Seating of Reed Smoot, Mormon Apostle.* Chapel Hill: University of North Carolina Press, 2004.

Moyer, Jonathan H. "Dancing with the Devil: The Making of the Mormon-Republican Pact." PhD dissertation, University of Utah, 2009.

Proceedings before the Committee on Privileges and Elections of the United States Senate in the Matter of the Protests against the Right of Hon. Reed Smoot, a Senator from the State of Utah, to Hold His Seat. 4 vols. Washington, DC: Government Printing Office, 1904–1906.

Temple Work by Proxy

Within temples, Mormons participate in various rituals centered upon reverence for and worship of Jesus Christ. Temple rituals are performed for both the living and the dead. Even before the Nauvoo, Illinois, temple was finished, Joseph Smith introduced the concept of universal salvation through baptisms for the dead, a ritual that Mormons believe answers the dilemma of Christian exclusivity. In their view, those individuals who might have lived without ever hearing the name Jesus Christ or receiving baptism through Mormon priesthood authority are not damned by the happenstance of the time and place of their birth but through proxy baptisms are afforded equal opportunity for salvation. Mormons believe that deceased persons are given the choice in the afterlife to either accept or reject the vicarious work done in their behalf. The first baptisms for the dead occurred in 1840 in the Mississippi River, with living proxies being immersed on behalf of deceased individuals. This ritual was later moved into temple baptismal fonts, where it continues in the 21st century.

Mormons also receive other saving rituals for themselves first and then for deceased individuals upon return visits to temples. Joseph Smith introduced the initiatory or washing and anointing at Kirtland, Ohio, in 1836. It served as a preparatory ritual designed to help the initiate leave the sins and cares of the world behind. Smith commenced the endowment ceremony in 1842, a ritualization of the biblical creation narrative that anchors Mormons in sacred time and space, placing them in a covenant relationship with God and promising them a return to His presence if they are faithful to Christian principles. Mormons also perform marriages or "sealings" in temples wherein Mormon couples believe they are married

Fonts like this one in the Salt Lake temple are used to perform baptisms for those who died without an opportunity to perform that ordinance themselves in life. (Courtesy of the Church History Library, The Church of Jesus Christ of Latter-day Saints.)

not only for mortal time but for eternity. In addition to saving rituals, Mormons attend temples to meditate, seek solace, and commune with God.

—*W. Paul Reeve*

See also: Genealogy and Family History; Local Worship; Temples.

Reference
Packer, Boyd K. *The Holy Temple.* Salt Lake City, UT: Bookcraft, 1980.

Temples

For Mormons, temples represent the highest manifestation of their devotion to their God. Within temples, Mormons participate in various rituals centered upon reverence for and worship of Jesus Christ. Temple rituals are performed for both the living and the dead and include proxy baptisms for deceased persons; washings and anointings, a preparatory ritual designed to help the initiate leave the sins and cares of the world behind; an endowment ceremony, which ritualizes the biblical creation narrative; and marriages or "sealings" wherein Mormon couples believe they are married not only for mortal time but for eternity.

Temples assumed a central and growing importance for Mormons from the Ohio period on. The Kirtland, Ohio, temple, completed in 1836, little resembled the

Mormon temples, like this one in Hong Kong, are built throughout the world. All temples are open for touring by the public before they are dedicated to the sacred ritual of the Church. (Courtesy of the Church History Library, The Church of Jesus Christ of Latter-day Saints.)

later temples in both purpose and structure. It was the site for a variety of reported heavenly manifestations and what Mormons described as restorations of ancient priesthood powers and keys. Joseph Smith introduced the washing and anointing ritual at Kirtland, the only significant carryover into later temple worship.

It was the Nauvoo, Illinois, temple, completed in 1846, that adopted the form and function of temple worship that would continue into the 21st century. Even before the Nauvoo temple was finished, Smith introduced the concept of universal salvation through baptisms for the dead. Smith also introduced the endowment ceremony and sealings at Nauvoo.

In Utah, as Mormons colonized the Great Basin, they constructed chapels for Sunday worship and preaching, while simultaneously building temples. They thereby formalized a distinction in

Temple Square

This 10-acre block in downtown Salt Lake City is the emotional heart of Mormonism. It is the site of the iconic Salt Lake temple, dedicated in 1893 after 40 years of labor. The distinctive Tabernacle, with its elongated dome roof, stone pillars, hand-grained interior woodwork, and magnificent pipe organ, is home to the Mormon Tabernacle Choir. The Assembly Hall is a jewel of pioneer architecture. Millions of tourists annually are hosted in two visitors' centers and tour the handsomely landscaped grounds dotted with monuments to people and events in Mormon history. Temple Square is lit each Christmas with millions of tiny lights. All Utah land surveys begin at the southeast corner of Temple Square, and Salt Lake City's distinctive street grid measures addresses by their distance from the Square.

Prominent buildings formerly on this site include the Endowment House, the site of most 19th-century plural marriages, which was torn down as a sign that the Church was abandoning polygamy; a museum, replaced by the Museum of Church History and Art one block west; an astronomical observatory; and an earlier pitched-roof Tabernacle, which itself was successor to an open-air Bowery.

The public is welcome everywhere within Temple Square, except within the temple itself.

Mormon worship: The larger and more elaborate temples are closed on Sundays but open weekdays to faithful Latter-day Saints who meet certain standards. The much more numerous chapels, used for Sunday worship and weekday activities, are open to all comers, including people of other faiths or of no faith.

The Salt Lake City temple, completed in 1893, took 40 years to construct and stands as an iconic symbol of Mormonism in the heart of its capital city. Temple construction in the 20th century followed the pattern of Mormon growth, with the first temple constructed outside the continental United States, in Laie, Hawaii, in 1919, followed by others in a variety of international locations. With the advent of smaller, less expensive temples in the 1990s, the rate of construction exploded, much of which reflected the increasingly global nature of Mormonism. More than 150 temples were either planned or in operation worldwide in 2010.

—*W. Paul Reeve*

See also: Genealogy and Family History; Kirtland Pentecost; Local Worship; Temple Work by Proxy.

References

Cowan, Richard O. *Temples to Dot the Earth.* Salt Lake City, UT: Bookcraft, 1989.

Talmage, James E. *The House of the Lord: A Study of Holy Sanctuaries Ancient and Modern.* Salt Lake City, UT: Deseret Book, 1974.

Ungathered

One of the distinguishing features of 19th-century Mormonism was the doctrine and practice of gathering, in which all converts to the faith were invited to gather to the ecclesiastical center of the Church in order to help build a Zion community. Historians of Mormonism have thus traditionally narrated the Mormon story in the 19th century as the movement of one ever-growing group from one cultural center to another. Consequently, Mormon history is often told in episodic periods defined as much by place as by people. It is common, for example, to read about the Kirtland, Nauvoo, and Utah periods of the Latter-day Saint past. However, since the formal inception of Mormonism in 1830 to the present, there have existed large numbers of Latter-day Saints who chose for various reasons not to gather with the rest of their co-religionists in Ohio, Missouri, Illinois, or Utah.

These "un-gathered" Saints generally formed small branches and Sunday Schools and maintained contact with Church leaders indirectly through visits from traveling missionaries and subscriptions to Church periodicals. Some of the larger peripheral congregations in early Mormonism were located in Philadelphia, New York City, Boston, and St. Louis. Other large branches were formed in England,

While the spotlight has always been on Mormons who joined the main body of the Church in Utah or its earlier headquarters, the 1909 Northcutts Cove, Tennessee, chapel and congregation typifies the thousands of Mormons who built the Church in their own neighborhoods. (Courtesy of the Church History Library, The Church of Jesus Christ of Latter-day Saints.)

as well. In these locations, local members were ordained to the priesthood and thus possessed authority to govern the affairs of the local congregation. In some of the smaller branches and congregations, however, members were almost entirely dependent on sporadic visits from traveling elders to conduct Church business and perform sacramental ordinances. This was especially true of those Mormons in peripheral regions following the exodus to Utah. Many Latter-day Saint converts in the American South who did not migrate to Utah, for instance, were organized into Sunday Schools and, less frequently, branches, but often no persons were ordained to the priesthood, and the faithful thus relied upon the elders to baptize prospective converts, administer the sacrament, and otherwise perform ordinances and conduct worship meetings whenever they visited the small outlying groups.

Some outlying congregations located in communities with universities were either created or reinforced by the arrival of Mormon students from Utah and Idaho pursuing graduate studies in the late 19th century. But these students rarely became permanent congregants in peripheral regions, instead opting to return to the intermountain West to help strengthen and improve the Mormon stronghold with their newly acquired educational skills and specialized training. At the turn of the 20th century, Church leaders began de-emphasizing the gathering and, throughout the century, increasingly encouraged converts to remain in their home communities. Additionally, a large outmigration of Mormons occurred in the mid-20th century in which scholars and professionals left Utah in search of employment and educational opportunities in various large cities throughout the United States. International congregations also continued to grow and flourish throughout the 20th century, as a result of increased proselytizing efforts and the construction of numerous meetinghouses and temples throughout the world. By the 1990s, more Mormons lived outside the United States than in it, and by 2010 fewer than 12 percent of all Mormons lived in Utah.

—*Christopher C. Jones*

See also: Church Organization and Government; Colonization; Expansion: 1941–Present; Mormonism as a World Religion; Transition: 1890–1941.

References

Fleming, Stephen J. "Discord in the City of Brotherly Love: The Story of Early Mormonism in Philadelphia." *Mormon Historical Studies* 5, no. 1 (Spring 2004): 3–27.

Fleming, Stephen J. "An Examination of the Success of Early Mormonism in the Delaware Valley." M.A. thesis, California State University, Stanislaus, 2003.

Johnson, G. Wesley, and Marian Ashby Johnson. "On the Trail of the Twentieth-Century Mormon Outmigration." *BYU Studies* 46, no. 1 (2007): 41–83.

Simpson, Thomas W. "Mormons Study 'Abroad': Latter-day Saints in American Higher Education, 1870–1940." PhD dissertation, University of Virginia, 2005.

United States v. Reynolds

In 1879, the U.S. Supreme Court decided *United States v. Reynolds,* 98 U.S. 145 (1879). The case held that the Morrill Anti-Bigamy Act (1862), which criminalized polygamy, did not violate the Free Exercise Clause of the First Amendment. According to the Court, the Constitution protected religious beliefs but not religious actions. It rejected the Mormon defendant's argument that the First Amendment protected religious conduct like polygamy so long as it was not *malum in se.* Crimes like murder are *malum in se* because they are inherently wrong, unlike other crimes (such as driving on the wrong side of the road) that are wrong only because they are prohibited.

Initially, federal prosecutors in Utah could not convict Mormons for polygamy because Mormon juries believed that the Morrill Act was unconstitutional. In 1872, Congress increased non-Mormon control of the Utah courts, and Church leaders agreed to provide a Mormon defendant to test the constitutionality of antipolygamy laws. George Reynolds, secretary to the First Presidency, was chosen and convicted, although not before the initial agreement between prosecutors and the Church fell apart. After the Court ruled for the prosecutors, Congress passed further legislation to punish polygamy, resulting in the massive antipolygamy raids of the 1880s.

Reynolds was the first time the Court ever interpreted the Free Exercise Clause. While the belief-action distinction has been criticized, the case is still followed and was essentially reaffirmed by the Court in *Employment Division v. Smith,* 494 U.S. 872 (1990).

—*Nathan B. Oman*

See also: Conflict: 1869–1890; Mormonism and Secular Government; Polygamy.

References

Gordon, Sarah Barringer. *The Mormon Question: Polygamy and Constitutional Conflict in Nineteenth-Century America.* Chapel Hill: University of North Carolina Press, 2002.

Van Orden, Bruce A. *Prisoner for Conscience' Sake: The Life of George Reynolds.* Salt Lake City, UT: Deseret Book, 1992.

Utah War

Sometimes wrongly dubbed "Johnston's Army," this armed confrontation pitted Brigham Young and his territorial militia (Nauvoo Legion) against James Buchanan and the U.S. Army. Rooted in decades of Mormon persecution, poor communications and insensitivity on both sides, and conflicting philosophies of governance, it was the nation's most extensive military undertaking between the Mexican and Civil Wars. Even without large-scale pitched battles, there were enough killings to belie the persistent myth of a "bloodless" conflict. It ended with Mormon acceptance of a new governor, the entrance of the army into Salt Lake Valley, and a presidential pardon for Utah's population.

The nonmilitary phase of this struggle began soon after Mormon arrival in Utah, with disputes arising over almost every territorial-federal interface, especially the quality of federal appointees to territorial offices. The new Republican Party's introduction of Mormon polygamy into the 1856 national presidential campaign aggravated these conflicts, as did the public's perception that Utah was a violent territory led by a disloyal governor. In early 1857, the new Buchanan administration decided to replace Young and to provide his successor with a military escort to enforce federal law. The result was the creation, in May, of the U.S. Army's 2,500-man "Utah Expedition," commanded by Brevet Brigadier General William S. Harney and the July appointment of Alfred Cumming as Utah's new governor.

Buchanan failed to communicate these changes to Young and cut postal service to Salt Lake City from Missouri. When Young became aware of these activities unofficially, he took the position that he had been loyal; Utah had been ill served by unacceptable federal appointees; he would remain governor; and the Utah Expedition was an armed mob bent on persecution—one to be resisted. Accordingly, Young proclaimed martial law, sealed Utah's borders, mobilized the Nauvoo Legion, recalled missionaries, pulled in distant Mormon colonies, and stimulated local manufacture of arms and munitions. In southern Utah, a Nauvoo Legion unit and Indian auxiliaries committed the war's worst atrocity at Mountain Meadows in September 1857. The Legion also fortified canyons and executed a scorched-earth policy east of Salt Lake Valley, burning grass needed by army animals and torching Fort Supply and Fort Bridger, as well as 75 unguarded federal supply wagons. In mid-October, Young authorized the use of lethal force if the army moved west of Fort Bridger.

What followed was a nightmarish time for the army as it crawled west in deteriorating weather while awaiting a new commander, Colonel Albert Sidney Johnston. With brutal weather killing thousands of his animals, Johnston reluctantly

Thomas L. Kane

Born to a politically prominent Philadelphia family, Thomas L. Kane (1822–1883), a social reformer, became the most ardent 19th-century defender of the Mormons' religious rights. A Democrat and a romantic humanitarian, Kane (who also agitated against slavery and served as a Civil War officer) saw the downtrodden Latter-day Saints as the ideal object of his reforming energies. In 1846, he convinced President James Polk to commission a battalion of Mormons for the U.S. War with Mexico, which helped fund the Saints' westward exodus. In influential pamphlets and the press, Kane portrayed the Saints as members of a persecuted religious minority, rather than as dangerous fanatics. During the Utah War of 1857–1858, Kane, though physically slight and often sickly, obtained the unofficial blessing of President James Buchanan to undertake an arduous winter journey to Utah to mediate the conflict between the Mormons and the federal army. At the army camp in Wyoming, Kane convinced the newly appointed governor, Alfred Cumming, to travel without the army to Utah. Kane then successfully brokered a peace between the Mormons and the nation. He remained the Saints' principal political adviser and defender until his death, forming a close bond with Brigham Young and exerting enormous influence on Mormon history.

concluded that he could not force the snow-clogged, heavily defended passes into Salt Lake Valley. Accordingly, his command settled into Fort Bridger's charred remains in late November for a winter on short rations. Facing unexpected Mormon resistance and massive desertion, Johnston sent east for reinforcements while ordering detachments south to New Mexico and north to Oregon for provisions and remounts.

As 1858 opened, both sides regrouped. Young created a 2,000-man "Standing Army" to supplement the Nauvoo Legion. Washington prepared to reinforce Johnston by enlarging the army and by sending a second brigade into Utah from the Pacific Coast. Simultaneously, Thomas L. Kane traveled to Utah from the Atlantic Coast as an unofficial mediator to prevent more bloodshed. In February, Kane found Young friendly but distrustful of the army's intentions, and, as he traveled east to Fort Bridger in March to negotiate with Cumming and Johnston, Young launched the "Move South." Under this plan, 30,000 people abandoned Utah's northern settlements and trekked south to Provo, where they marked time as refugees with an uncertain destination. In April, under military pressure from all directions and with Kane counseling moderation, Young relinquished his governmental roles. In June, unknown to Kane, two official representatives from Buchanan arrived with a mass presidential pardon in exchange for Mormon acceptance of Cumming and federal authority. Young accepted these arrangements. On June 26, 1858, the Utah Expedition marched unopposed through a Salt Lake City deserted and ready for the torch. It then established Camp Floyd in Cedar Valley to the south, Mormon refugees returned home, and the active phase of the Utah War ended. Nonetheless, animosities lingered for decades, delaying statehood. When the Civil War began, in 1861, the army auctioned off its matériel, blew up its ammunition, and marched east to confront the greatest rebellion of them all.

—*William P. MacKinnon*

See also: Exodus and Settlement: 1845–1869; Mormonism and Violence; Mountain Meadows Massacre; Nauvoo Legion; Young, Brigham.

References

Furniss, Norman F. *The Mormon Conflict, 1850–1859.* New Haven, CT: Yale University Press, 1960; repr. 1977.

MacKinnon, William P., ed. *At Sword's Point: A Documentary History of the Utah War.* 2 vols. Norman, OK: Arthur H. Clark, 2008, and forthcoming.

Word of Wisdom

Joseph Smith reported a revelation in February 1833 that came to be known as the Word of Wisdom, a code of health that both proscribes and prescribes certain foods for consumption. As Smith originally described it, the Word of Wisdom was "given for a principle with a promise," but emphasis and interpretation have led to growing importance ascribed to this "principle" over time (Smith, *History* 1:327–329).

Perhaps best understood within the broader context of Jacksonian America and its growing clamor for temperance and health reform, Smith's revelation echoed the concerns of his day. The Word of Wisdom advised against "wine" and "strong drink," except for the sacrament of the Lord's Supper. It further admonished against tobacco, except for medicinal purposes, and "hot drinks," which was later clarified to denote tea and coffee. It recommended that meat be used "sparingly" but suggested that grain and "fruit of the vine" were "ordained for the use of man." Smith's revelation ended with a promise to those who observe the health code that they will be rewarded with good health, wisdom, and "treasures of knowledge" (Smith, *History* 1:327–329).

Emphasis on different aspects of the Word of Wisdom varied over time as Church leaders and circumstances varied. Brigham Young himself struggled to overcome a tobacco habit and recognized the difficulty that quitting presented. He therefore preached a more stringent adherence to the Word of Wisdom among the rising generation of Mormons while encouraging moderation for the older generation. It was during the 1920s, with a nationwide prohibition against alcohol and a limited prohibition against cigarettes in 14 states (including Utah), that Church president

Heber J. Grant began to make Word of Wisdom compliance a prerequisite for holding positions of responsibility in the Church's lay leadership and for temple worship.

Historian Thomas G. Alexander argues that adherence to the Word of Wisdom replaced polygamy as an important element in distinguishing Latter-day Saints from other Christian denominations in the 20th century. As implemented in the 21st century, the Word of Wisdom requires abstinence from tobacco, coffee, tea, alcohol, and harmful drugs for baptism into the faith and for temple attendance among the faithful.

—*W. Paul Reeve*

See also: Grant, Heber J.; Transition: 1890–1941.

References

Alexander, Thomas G. *Mormonism in Transition: A History of the Latter-day Saints, 1890–1930.* Urbana and Chicago: University of Illinois Press, 1986.

Peterson, Paul H., and Ronald W. Walker. "Brigham Young's Word of Wisdom Legacy." *BYU Studies* 42, nos. 3 & 4 (2003): 29–64.

Smith, Joseph Jr. *History of the Church of Jesus Christ of Latter-day Saints.* 6 vols. Ed. B.H. Roberts. Salt Lake City, UT: The Church of Jesus Christ of Latter-day Saints, 1973.

Youth Programs

The Church's concern for its youth and for the inculcation of Mormon values has been expressed in the establishment of auxiliary and recreational programs, schools and other educationally based programs, and the printing of a number of youth-focused publications.

Among the earliest youth-focused programs was a Sunday School established in Nauvoo in June 1844. There, Joseph Smith instructed Stephen Goddard to take charge of teaching the gospel to the children. The school was discontinued after Smith's death but was reestablished in Utah on December 9, 1849, by Richard Ballantyne. In 1867, the Deseret Sunday School Union was organized to coordinate the efforts of Sunday Schools throughout the Church. Church leaders viewed Sunday School as essential to counteract worldly influences upon youth by teaching them scripturally based values. The Sunday School has since been an important auxiliary, often functioning as the only organized worship in areas of low Church membership.

Also significant was the development of Mutual Improvement Associations for Mormon adolescents. The Junior Retrenchment Society, later renamed the Young Women's Mutual Improvement Association, was organized in 1869 to counteract

Mormons adopted the Boy Scout program for its youth program early in the 20th century; a comparable program, called Beehive Girls, was developed for girls of similar age. (Courtesy of the Church History Library, The Church of Jesus Christ of Latter-day Saints.)

outside fashions popular among young women, styles that became available following the completion of the transcontinental railroad. Elmina Shepard Taylor became its first president. Encouraged by the success of the young women's program, Brigham Young asked Junius F. Wells to create a similar program for the young men in 1875. The aim of the Young Men's Mutual Improvement Association was to establish an individual testimony within each youth and to provide gospel learning. These auxiliaries continue as the Young Men and Young Women programs, which guide youth who have advanced beyond the age of Primary. They serve more than 1 million youth. (Primary is an auxiliary organization founded in 1878 by Aurelia Spencer Rogers for children up to age 12.)

In connection with the Mutual Improvement Associations, the Church developed a large-scale recreational program in the early 20th century. The program encouraged participation in activities, such as scouting, basketball, and outdoor events, and often included Church-wide competitions. These programs were modeled on many of the practices and philosophies of the Protestant YMCA and served to counterbalance undesirable activities associated with the urbanization of Mormonism. While some aspects of the program, such as Church-wide tournaments, are now defunct, important facets of the program continue.

The Church also supported the establishment of a worldwide educational system. From 1875 to 1933, the Church established and maintained as many as 40 private schools, called academies, throughout the intermountain West. By the mid-1930s, the majority of these academies were transferred to state control due to economic uncertainty, though the Church continues to maintain a few of these schools. The academies were replaced by a worldwide system of seminaries and institutes, which provide religious instruction to Mormon youth in non-Mormon schools. The Church Educational System serves more than 700,000 Mormon youth.

In addition to these other efforts, the Church established a number of magazines over the years, including *The Juvenile Instructor, The Contributor, The Young Woman's Journal, The Improvement Era,* and the present *New Era,* to provide LDS youth with devotional literature meant to inculcate Mormon values.

—*Brett D. Dowdle*

See also: Local Worship; Mormonism and Education; Parmley, LaVern Watts; Rogers, Aurelia Spencer; Taylor, Elmina Shepard; Transition: 1890–1941.

References

Gates, Susa Young. *History of the Young Ladies' Mutual Improvement Association of the Church of Jesus Christ of Latter-day Saints from November 1869 to June 1910.* Salt Lake City, UT: General Board of the Y.L.M.I.A., 1911.

Kimball, Richard Ian. *Sports in Zion: Mormon Recreation, 1890–1940.* Urbana: University of Illinois Press 2003.

Zion's Camp

In May and June 1834, approximately 200 Mormon men, accompanied by a few women and children, marched 900 miles from Kirtland, Ohio, to Jackson County, Missouri. This mission, known as Zion's Camp, had as its goal to assist Mormons recently driven out of Jackson County to return to their homes and then to protect the Mormon settlers from further disturbances.

Zion's Camp was a military expedition, and the marchers, well armed with both firearms and knives, practiced military maneuvers en route. Their approach and intent became known to the non-Mormon residents of Jackson County, who prepared to meet them with force; one attempted attack on Zion's Camp by a superior force of Missourians was thwarted by a severe hailstorm, interpreted as providential by the Mormon marchers.

With insufficient manpower to achieve their goals militarily and without the co-operation of Missouri's governor, who had at first promised to provide state troops to escort Mormon settlers back to their lands, Zion's Camp disbanded at the end of June, seemingly having accomplished nothing but the delivery of much-needed money and supplies to the Mormons who had fled Jackson County.

The significance of Zion's Camp is found by later generations in the leadership of those who answered Joseph Smith's call for participants and who were the Prophet's intimate associates during this physically and emotionally demanding event: two future Church presidents, 9 of the first 12 apostles, and all 70 of the first Quorum of the Seventy were members of Zion's Camp.

—*Ardis E. Parshall*

See also: Development: 1831–1844.

Reference

Crawley, Peter, and Richard L. Anderson. "The Political and Social Realities of Zion's Camp." *BYU Studies* 14 (1974): 406–420.

People

Arrington, Leonard James

Leonard James Arrington (1917–1999) was the most important LDS historian of the second half of the 20th century and the first non-General Authority to serve as official LDS Church Historian.

Arrington was born on July 2, 1917, on a sugar beet farm near Twin Falls, Idaho, to Noah Wesley Arrington and Edna Grace Corn Arrington. He had planned to major in agriculture at the University of Idaho but changed his mind when he learned he would have to take chemistry and instead enrolled in agricultural economics. After graduation, he continued his studies at the University of North Carolina, Chapel Hill. He was drafted into the U.S. Army in March 1943 and, a month later, on April 24, married Grace Fort. The following July, he was sent to North Africa, and the next year he was in Italy. He returned home in December 1945. In July 1946, he began teaching economics at Utah State Agriculture College (later Utah State University), while also completing his doctoral studies at North Carolina (he graduated in 1952). His dissertation on 19th-century Mormon economic history was published in revised form by Harvard University Press in 1958 (and reprinted in 1993 by the University of Utah Press and again in 2005 by the University of Illinois Press) as *Great Basin Kingdom: An Economic History of the Latter-day Saints, 1830–1890*.

Over the course of Arrington's research, he changed his field of academic interest from economics to history, and *Great Basin Kingdom* may be said to mark the beginnings of the so-called New Mormon History. In the book's preface, Arrington stated: "The true essence of God's will, if such it be, cannot be apprehended without an understanding of the conditions surrounding the prophetic vision, and the symbolism and verbiage in which it is couched. Surely God does not reveal His will except to those prepared by intellectual and social experience and by spiritual insight and imagination, to grasp and convey it. A naturalistic discussion of 'the people and the times' and of the mind and experience of Latter-day prophets is therefore a perfectly valid aspect of religious history, and, indeed, makes more plausible the truths they attempt to convey" (Arrington, *Great Basin Kingdom* xxiv).

Arrington was convinced that the best historical narratives treated all relevant elements, including, where appropriate, the secular and the religious, of past events. He believed that such comprehensive approaches helped to provide the foundation of truth upon which faith was most solidly built. He explained, of his own religious belief: "I was never preoccupied with the question of the historicity of Joseph

Smith's first vision—though I find the evidence overwhelming that it did occur—or of the many reported epiphanies in Mormon, Christian, or Hebrew history. I am prepared to accept them as historical or as metaphorical, as symbolic or as precisely what happened. That they convey religious truth is the essential issue, and of this I have never had any doubt" (Arrington, "Myth, Symbol, and Truth" 307).

During the academic year 1958–1959, Arrington took his wife and three children (James [b. 1948], Carl [b. 1951], and Susan [b. 1954]) to Italy, where he was Fulbright Professor of American Economics at the University of Genoa. From 1966 to 1967, he was a visiting professor of history at the University of California, Los Angeles. Also during the 1960s, he helped to found both the *Western Historical Quarterly* and the Mormon History Association, serving as its first president. Additionally, he was president of the Western History Association, the Agriculture History Association, and the Pacific Coast Branch of the American Historical Association. In 1970, he was one of a committee of historians to advise the LDS First Presidency regarding the possible reorganization of the Church Historian's Office. Less than two years later, in 1972, he agreed to serve as the new Church Historian and at the same time was appointed to the Lemuel Redd Chair in Western History at Brigham Young University, in Provo, Utah, and named director of the school's Charles Redd Center for Western Studies. On April 6, 1972, Arrington was formally sustained by LDS members worldwide as the new official Church Historian. This was the first—and only—time to date that the position has been held by a professionally trained historian and not by an LDS Church General Authority.

During the next decade, Arrington and the historians working under his direction as members of the Church History Division published scores of books and hundreds of articles on LDS history. Arrington's own publications include *David Eccles: Pioneer Western Industrialist* (1975); *Building the City of God: Community and Cooperation among the Mormons* (co-author, 1976); *The Mormon Experience: A History of the Latter-day Saints* (co-author, 1979); and *Brigham Young: American Moses* (1985, winner of the Evans Prize). In addition, Arrington championed greater public access to the Church's vast archival holdings, a change in policy that had actually begun prior to Arrington's appointment. Some of Arrington's colleagues later referred to this period of scholarly inquiry and openness as a "Camelot." However, not all of Arrington's policies sat well with some General Authorities, who believed that, in Church-sponsored LDS history, explicitly faith-promoting explanations should prevail. In 1975, some of Arrington's managerial responsibilities were curtailed, and his position was renamed Director of the History Division. Two years later, a new Managing Director of the Historical Department was named. These changes effectively released Arrington as Church Historian, though he was not officially notified of the change until 1982, when the History Division was disbanded and most of its employees were transferred to Brigham Young University as members of the newly created Joseph Fielding Smith Institute for Church History, with Arrington as director. Also in 1982, Arrington's wife, Grace, died. A year and a half later, he married Harriet Ann Horne, and in 1984 he underwent a sextuple heart bypass operation. On July 2, 1987, he officially retired from Brigham Young University. He continued to write and publish, mostly commissioned works, and, with his wife, to travel. In 1996, he received the Utah Governor's Award in Humanities. He published his memoirs, *Adventures of a Church Historian,* in 1998 and by the end of the year arranged to donate his papers, including his voluminous diary, to Utah State University as the Leonard J. Arrington Historical Archives. He died the next year, on February 11, 1999.

—*Gary James Bergera*

See also: Church Organization and Government.

References

Arrington, Leonard J. *Adventures of a Church Historian.* Urbana: University of Illinois Press, 1998.

Arrington, Leonard J. *Great Basin Kingdom: An Economic History of the Latter-day Saints, 1830–1890.* Salt Lake City: University of Utah Press, 1993.

Arrington, Leonard J. "Myth, Symbol, and Truth." In *Faithful History: Essays on Writing Mormon History.* Ed. George D. Smith. Salt Lake City, UT: Signature Books, 1992.

Bitton, Davis. "Ten Years in Camelot: A Personal Memoir." *Dialogue: A Journal of Mormon Thought* 16 (Autumn 1983): 9–33.

Bennion, Lowell L.

Known as "Mormonism's Saint," Lowell Lindsay Bennion (1908–1996) was possibly the most influential LDS teacher, counselor, and humanitarian of the late 20th century. Bennion described his three-pronged career as covering the sanctuary of the institute, the halls of ivy, and the real world. His selfless dedication earned him the labels "Utah's Mother Teresa," "Mormonism's Gandhi," and "the conscience of a community."

Bennion was born July 26, 1908, in Forest Dale, a suburb of Salt Lake City, to Milton Bennion, dean of education and a vice president at the University of Utah, and Cora Lindsay Bennion, Utah's Mother of the Year in 1952.

In 1928, after graduating from the University of Utah and a few months before his departure for a Swiss German LDS proselytizing mission, Bennion married Lela Merle Colton. Two and a half years later, she joined her husband in Europe, where he entered a PhD program at the University of Erlangen in Bavaria, just ahead of Hitler's rise to power. Bennion subsequently transferred to Vienna and then to Strasbourg, in France. He researched his dissertation subject in German, defended it in French, and wrote it in English. It was published as *Max Weber's Methodology,* the first book-length study of Weber in English. This could have landed him at a top university, but the young couple, having lost their firstborn child to infection, longed to return to Utah.

Back in Utah, Bennion eventually received a call from LDS apostle John A. Widtsoe, representing the Church Education System (CES). This led him into the most satisfying years of his career as teacher and counselor of LDS young men and women. He founded the LDS Institute of Religion at the University of Utah, where he taught for 27 years (1935–1962). Institute classes covered philosophy of life, world religions, missionary training, and courtship and marriage, as well as Mormon scripture. Bennion moved the Institute into a building large enough for varied classes and activities, including his invention, fireside chats, inspirational talks centered upon spiritual themes. In 1937, responding to student requests, Bennion founded a co-ed fraternity for LDS students, Lambda Delta Sigma, which is distinct for its emphasis on service and leadership.

In 1953, administrative changes brought the entire CES under the leadership of Ernest L. Wilkinson, then president of Brigham Young University. Wilkinson, a conservative Washington, D.C., lawyer, ruled with a heavy hand, a fact that eventually forced Bennion from his dream job at the Institute of Religion in 1962.

Bennion moved to the University of Utah proper, where he became full professor of sociology while also serving as associate dean of students. He also finally received an honorary doctorate. He immersed himself in student affairs and designed a student code based upon due process, which recognized students as adults. In his decade there, he met with troubled students and was instrumental in calming the unrest of the 1970s. He also reached out to the community in significant ways. He transformed the Salt Lake City Community Services Council from an "umbrella" charitable clearinghouse to a hands-on volunteer organization. He founded Utah's first food bank and its first homeless shelter and established the Teton Valley Boys Ranch for the purpose of "teaching city boys how to work."

After Bennion's retirement, in 1988, a variety of honors came to him. The state legislature passed a resolution praising him, and the Caring Institute of Washington, D.C., chose him as one of the 100 "most caring people in the world." The honor that meant the most was the creation of the Lowell Bennion Community Services Center at the University of Utah. Funded by substantial anonymous gifts, it sponsored service learning professors and majors, allowing students the opportunity to carry on Bennion's legacy. Even as he grew old, Bennion ignored advice to rest on his many awards. He was driven by his motto from the Bhagavad-Gita, "To action alone hast a right, not to its fruits" (Bradford, *Lowell Bennion* x). There was much to be done for minorities, the homeless, the hungry, the aged, even the youth of Utah.

He continued to serve in religious capacities as well. In June 1980, LDS leaders called Bennion as the bishop of the East Mill Creek Twelfth Ward. At 72, he believed he was too old for such a calling, but his counselor, Kent Murdock, called his three-year term "a lovely rejuvenation of the ward" (Bradford, *Lowell Bennion*

301). He focused his energy upon creating Christ-centered worship and a service-centered people.

Bennion died of Parkinson's disease, on February 22, 1996.

—Mary Lythgoe Bradford

See also: Mormonism and Education.

References

Bennion, Lowell L. *How Can I Help? Final Selections from the Legendary Writer.* Salt Lake City, UT: Aspen, 1996.

Bradford, Mary Lythgoe. *Lowell Bennion: Teacher, Counselor, Humanitarian.* Salt Lake City, UT: Dialogue, 1995.

England, Eugene. *The Best of Lowell Bennion: Selected Writings, 1928–1988.* Salt Lake City, UT: Deseret Book, 1988.

Benson, Ezra Taft

Ezra Taft Benson (1899–1994) served as 13th president of the Church, from 1985 to 1994. Because of his service as U.S. President Dwight D. Eisenhower's secretary of agriculture and because of his well-publicized opposition to communism, no previous Church president had come to his office with as much national notoriety as did Benson.

He was born on August 4, 1899, to a third-generation Mormon family, in Whitney, Idaho. His great-grandfather and namesake had been a Church apostle during Brigham Young's era. "T" or "Taft," as he was known as a young man, grew up in a farming family, and he chose agriculture as his life's vocation.

When Benson was 12 years old, his father accepted a call to serve a full-time Church mission for two years in the midwestern United States. George Benson sold part of his land to pay for the mission and then left the rest of the farm in the care of his wife and his not-yet-teenage son. This experience became a touchstone of faith for the Benson family. Ezra and all of his 10 younger siblings would eventually follow their father's example of missionary service, and, not surprisingly, the expansion of Church missionary work would figure prominently in Benson's presidency. (During his nine years as Church president, the number of full-time missionaries rose from fewer than 30,000 to nearly 50,000.) Benson's own missionary opportunity came in 1921, when he interrupted his college studies and spent two years in Great Britain. He married his college sweetheart, Flora Amussen, in 1926, after she returned from a Church mission of her own to Hawaii. They would become the parents of two sons and four daughters.

While Flora served her mission, Ezra finished his bachelor's degree at Brigham Young University in animal husbandry and marketing. He was awarded a scholarship for graduate study at Iowa State, and the Bensons spent the first year of their marriage in Ames, Iowa, where Ezra earned a master's degree in agricultural economics.

His advanced training and passion for farm innovation soon led him away from the family homestead in Whitney and to important leadership positions in agriculture. His extensive experience and reputation made him Dwight D. Eisenhower's choice for secretary of agriculture, even though the two had never met. Because Benson had been called as a full-time Church apostle in 1943, he became the "first clergyman in [a] century" to serve in a cabinet post (Dew, *Ezra Taft Benson* 256). One consequence of his appointment was immediate: President Eisenhower agreed with Secretary Benson's suggestion that weekly cabinet meetings open with prayer.

Benson's tumultuous eight years in office can be succinctly summarized by the political philosophy that both allies and enemies saw in him: "he's in the habit of deciding everything on principle" (Dew, *Ezra Taft Benson* 259). He was opposed to excessive government price supports and surpluses, and he traveled the country actively preaching a conservative message against "the dangers of big government" (Dew, *Ezra Taft Benson* 262).

When Benson came to his cabinet post, he was no stranger to demanding travel schedules or to administrative complexities. His Church service had already given him a taste of both. Assigned by the Church's First Presidency, the relatively new apostle left his family in early 1946 and spent 10 months traversing war-torn Europe. In the face of what could have been overwhelming devastation and desperation, Benson directed the distribution of tons of relief supplies sent by the Church and oversaw the reconstitution of disrupted local church units and missionary activities. This herculean tour of duty became a watershed moment in the history of the Church in Europe. Benson returned to Europe in 1964 to preside over Church affairs on that continent for another year and a half.

His time in Europe and his service in the Eisenhower administration also honed his political views. He became increasingly outspoken about the threat posed by communism. Benson's strong feelings were evident, for example, in his urging that Eisenhower respond to the Soviet repression of Hungarian dissidents in 1956. He even crafted the initial drafts of the statement that Eisenhower eventually read to condemn the violence there.

In later sermons and speeches, Benson strenuously decried communism as an insidious and potentially worldwide menace to religious and intellectual freedom. While the LDS Church under David O. McKay had officially denounced communism, some of Benson's colleagues in the Church hierarchy became increasingly uncomfortable with the forcefulness of his rhetoric and his visible association with the John Birch Society in its early years (though Benson followed the instructions of McKay about preserving the Church's political neutrality and never joined the Society). Because some of Benson's comments could have given the impression that the

Church supported the Society and espoused its ultraconservative views, McKay and later Church president Spencer W. Kimball issued follow-up statements in order to reaffirm that the Church did not endorse candidates, parties, or political groups. In an era of increasing media coverage and information dissemination, these leaders stressed the importance of circumspection, since personal opinions could easily be interpreted as Church pronouncements.

Perhaps tempered by that recognition, when Benson became Church president, in late 1985, he gave no hint of his previous political involvement. Instead, the preeminent focus of his ministry was the Book of Mormon. In nearly every sermon, Benson encouraged Church members to redouble their efforts to study and teach from the Book of Mormon. Importantly, the renewed focus on this uniquely Latter-day Saint scripture had significant doctrinal implications for contemporary Mormonism. Observers noted that fundamental Christian doctrines such as the fall of humanity and grace, always principal tenets of the faith, received increased attention in Latter-day Saint writing and teaching. While some were critical of what they perceived as a cultural turn to "neo-orthodoxy," others pointed to the determinative Church-wide impact of Benson's emphasis on the Book of Mormon, a text that is replete with Christian themes. It is for these themes that Benson is best remembered.

—*J. B. Haws*

See also: Book of Mormon; Kimball, Spencer W.; McKay, David O.; Mormonism and Secular Government.

References

Dew, Sheri L. *Ezra Taft Benson: A Biography.* Salt Lake City, UT: Deseret Book, 1987.

Hartley, William G. "Ezra Taft Benson." In *The Presidents of the Church.* Ed. Leonard J. Arrington, 421–450. Salt Lake City, UT: Deseret Book, 1986.

Brooks, Juanita

Juanita Brooks's (1898–1989) fame as a historian rests upon her account of the Mountain Meadows Massacre, which would remain the definitive history of that bloody event throughout the second half of the 20th century. Following a childhood in Bunkerville, Nevada, she spent most of her adult years in nearby St. George, the principal town in a desert region known as Utah's Dixie. In 1919, Juanita Leavitt married a young farmer, Ernest Pulsipher, by whom she had a son. Her prospect of becoming a farm wife ended abruptly with Ernest's premature death from cancer, in 1921. After acquiring a bachelor's degree from Brigham Young University under the most penurious of circumstances, she accepted a position teaching English at Dixie Junior College in St. George. Offered a scholarship for the school year 1928–1929, she left her son with her parents and took an MA degree in English at Columbia University. Upon her return to Dixie College, she was appointed dean of women.

Her life took another major turn in 1933 when she married county sheriff Will Brooks, a widower with four children, by whom she bore a daughter and three sons. Her temporarily stifled professional ambition soon found release in her appointment as stake Relief Society president. Designated a coordinator of local federal work projects, she put a team of women to work cataloguing and transcribing handwritten pioneer diaries. Already aware that she dwelled in a region rich in pioneer diaries, Brooks soon excelled at locating them and persuading their owners to allow typescripts to be made of them. Thanks to her work with pioneer diaries, Brooks began a long-term friendship—chiefly conducted by letters—with Dale Morgan, a Salt Lake WPA official and a Mormon historian who in effect tutored Brooks in historiography, providing encouragement and training that she could have acquired nowhere else.

Among the pioneer documents Brooks collected were firsthand accounts of the Mountain Meadows Massacre. Keenly sensitive to the undercurrents of blame and suppression that still circulated in her native Dixie region, Brooks undertook—with Morgan's encouragement—to write a detailed account of the affair and of the subsequent singling out for blame of John D. Lee, the only one of a half dozen responsible local leaders to be executed for his part in the massacre. Although non-Mormons greeted her book, *The Mountain Meadows Massacre* (1950), with respect, her fellow Latter-day Saints generally regarded it as an unfortunate—and unnecessary—stirring of a subject best allowed to die. A faithful Church member, Brooks sought a vindication that did not come until 1962—and then only indirectly—when Church leaders posthumously restored Church membership to John D. Lee. The vindication Brooks sought was an admission by the leaders of the Church that the blame for the massacre was not to be restricted to its actual perpetrators but was to be spread widely by reference not only to the mobs that drove the Mormons from Missouri and Illinois and an invading U.S. Army but also to Brigham Young and other Church leaders from Salt Lake City, who had issued impassioned and confusing instructions. Unquestionably, Brooks had an extraordinary fascination with Lee, with whom she dealt in two other major works. In 1955, in collaboration with Robert Glass Cleland, she published Lee's major diaries as *A Mormon Chronicle: The Diaries of John D. Lee—1848–1876,* and, in 1962 she published a biography, *John D. Lee: Zealot—Pioneer Builder—Scapegoat.*

Brooks also became a sought-after public speaker about the massacre and the scapegoating of Lee, not only in Utah but in nearby states. She became, in effect, a minstrel, telling and retelling the gripping saga to groups of many sorts and sizes. Without intending it, she became a symbol to liberal Mormons, who saw a model for faithful dissent in her insistence that the Church confront the realities of its history. Always busy, Brooks served throughout most of her productive years as housewife, mother, community activist, and (following her husband's retirement) instructor at Dixie College. Nonetheless, she produced a respectable number of books, articles, reviews, and sketches. The best of these include, in addition to the aforementioned works, the following: *Dudley Leavitt: Pioneer to Southern Utah* (1942), a biography of her grandfather; *Emma Lee* (1975), a biography of a plural wife of John D. Lee; and *On the Mormon Frontier: The Diary of Hosea Stout—1844–1861* (1964), which Brooks edited during a three-year residence in Salt Lake City. Her autobiography, *Quicksand and Cactus: A Memoir of the Southern Mormon Frontier* (1982), was assembled from previously written fragments by an editor following her decline into Alzheimer's disease.

—*Levi S. Peterson*

See also: Mormonism and Women; Mountain Meadows Massacre; Utah War.

Reference

Peterson, Levi S. *Juanita Brooks: Mormon Woman Historian.* Salt Lake City: University of Utah Press, 1988.

Cannon, George Q.

George Quayle Cannon (1827–1901) served in the First Presidencies of Brigham Young, John Taylor, Wilford Woodruff, and Lorenzo Snow. His tenure in the LDS hierarchy spanned much of the Church's territorial period (1847–1896), and, because of his political acumen, he may be called the father of Utah statehood.

Cannon was born on January 11, 1827, to George Cannon and Ann Quayle Cannon, in Liverpool, England. His aunt, Leonora Cannon, had married John Taylor, and both were subsequently baptized into the LDS Church in 1836. Four years later, Taylor, now as LDS apostle, was a missionary in Liverpool and baptized all of the members of the George Cannon family. In 1842, the Cannon family immigrated to LDS Church headquarters in Nauvoo, Illinois. Cannon's mother died on route; his father remarried in 1843 and died the following year.

In Nauvoo, Cannon lived with John and Leonora Taylor and worked as a printer's apprentice. Following Joseph Smith's death, in 1844, Cannon immigrated with the Taylors to Winter Quarters (in present-day Nebraska) and later to the Great Salt Lake Valley, in October 1847. Beginning in 1849, at age 22, he served a Church mission to California and to the Sandwich Islands (Hawaii). After his return to Utah, he was called to preside over the Church's California and Oregon missions. In California, he published the first edition of the Book of Mormon in Hawaiian and founded the LDS-oriented *Western Standard* newspaper. In September 1858, he was called as president of the Church's Eastern States Mission and helped direct LDS immigration west. On April 26, 1860, he was ordained an LDS apostle, replacing apostle Parley P. Pratt, who had been murdered in Arkansas. He was called to the Church's European Mission but, after a few months, learned that he had been elected as one of Utah's two representatives to Congress. He spent what time remained of 1862's congressional session in Washington, D.C., then returned to England as mission president.

Back in Utah in 1864, Cannon was named private secretary to LDS Church president Brigham Young, and in 1866 he founded the *Juvenile Instructor,* which he owned and published until his death. In 1867, he was named general superintendent of the Deseret Sunday School Union. Later that same year, he was named president and editor of the semiweekly *Deseret News* and helped to oversee its transition to a daily newspaper under the banner *Deseret Evening News.* In 1872, he was elected Utah's delegate (nonvoting) to Congress. For the next 10 years, he both championed and helped to protect Utah's political and economic interests nationally. On April 8, 1873, Cannon was sustained as one of Young's counselors. (Cannon was not named a First or Second Counselor, simply an additional counselor in the First Presidency.) Upon Young's death, on August 29, 1877, Cannon returned to the Quorum of the Twelve Apostles.

Three years later, with the appointment of his uncle John Taylor as Young's successor as Church president, Cannon was sustained as Taylor's First Counselor on October 10, 1880. In 1882, with the passage of the Edmunds Act, a measure intended to combat the LDS Church's practice of plural marriage, Cannon's congressional

Sam Brannan and the Ship *Brooklyn*

On February 4, 1846, as the Mormons began wending their way out of Nauvoo and taking up the march that would eventually end in the Salt Lake Valley, 226 Mormons, with 12 non-Mormon friends, under the leadership of Samuel Brannan, sailed out of New York harbor aboard the ship *Brooklyn* on their own pilgrimage to the West.

The *Brooklyn* carried her passengers south, rounding Cape Horn at the bottom of the world and touching at Hawaii before it reached Yerba Buena, now San Francisco, on July 3, 1846. The passengers suffered from seasickness, storms, close confinement, intense cold in the south and severe heat at the equator. They buried 10 of their number at sea and celebrated the birth of a boy named Atlantic and a girl named Pacific, born just before and just after passing Cape Horn.

The *Brooklyn* passengers were the first shipload of American emigrants to arrive in California. Although they preferred the lushness of California to the deserts of Utah, most eventually made their way to Utah. Some became prominent in early California history. Some, like Brannan himself, failing to convince the main body of Saints to settle in California, eventually disassociated from the Church.

seat was vacated. In 1885, Cannon, a polygamist, lived on the "Mormon Underground" to avoid arrest for "unlawful cohabitation." At Taylor's death, on July 25, 1888, Cannon was released from the First Presidency, and the following September he surrendered to federal law officials. He eventually served nearly six months in the Utah penitentiary. With the appointment of Taylor's successor, Wilford Woodruff, as Church president, Cannon was again named First Counselor, on April 7, 1889. Following Woodruff's death, he was reappointed as First Counselor to the new Church president, Lorenzo Snow, on September 13, 1898. Less than three years later, Cannon, age 74, died on April 12, 1901, in Monterey, California.

Cannon's extensive political and business interests and acquaintances benefited the Church, but they also concerned some Church members, including several of his colleagues in the Quorum of the Twelve Apostles. Some occasionally worried that Cannon too freely associated with men of the world and too easily mixed his own interests with those of the Church, not always to the Church's advantage. Cannon helped to spearhead the Church's use of financial payments to secure favorable press coverage and to gain access to political influence. His actions were sometimes divisive, but his political savvy helped to facilitate Utah statehood. In addition, he was not only a practicing polygamist—he had five wives and fathered 32 children—but a vocal, pragmatic proponent of a principle he regarded as divinely mandated. Following the Wilford Woodruff Manifesto (1890), which ostensibly banned plural marriage, he helped to implement a secret but short-lived system whereby worthy men could sometimes be married to additional wives outside the reach of U.S. law.

—*Gary James Bergera*

See also: Conflict: 1869–1890; Manifesto; Mormon Missiology; Polygamy.

References

Bitton, Davis. *George Q. Cannon: A Biography.* Salt Lake City, UT: Deseret Book, 1999.

Ekins, Roger Robin. *Defending Zion: George Q. Cannon and the California Mormon Newspaper Wars of 1856–1857.* Spokane, WA: Arthur H. Clark, 2002.

Landon, Michael N., ed. *The Journals of George Q. Cannon.* Vol. 1: *To California in '49.* Salt Lake City, UT: Deseret Book/Historical Department of the Church of Jesus Christ of Latter-day Saints, 1999.

Cannon, Martha Hughes

Dr. Martha Maria Hughes Cannon (1857–1932) is in many ways a symbol of the opportunities and independence some 19th-century Mormon women enjoyed. Cannon led a full life in a variety of roles. Most notably, she was a physician, state senator, national women's suffragist, feminist, public health advocate, mother, and plural wife.

Cannon was born July 1, 1857, the second of three daughters, to Peter and Elizabeth Evans Hughes, in northern Wales, United Kingdom. Her family converted to Mormonism and immigrated to the United States in 1860, eventually arriving in Salt Lake City.

From an early age, Cannon expressed interest in studying medicine, a notion her family encouraged and LDS Church officials would later endorse. She lived frugally and saved her money while working as a schoolteacher and typesetter. After she graduated with a degree in chemistry from University of Deseret, LDS Church president John Taylor blessed her and "set her apart" for medical studies. In 1878, she entered the University of Michigan medical school, where she washed dishes and made beds at a boarding house to cover her expenses. Eventually, Cannon entered the University of Pennsylvania's Auxiliary School of Medicine and in 1882 was the only woman in a class of 75 to graduate with a bachelor of science degree. She also enrolled in the National School of Elocution and Oratory to improve her speaking skills and earned a bachelor of oratory degree.

Following school, she returned to Utah and opened a private practice, but she was soon called to be resident physician of the LDS Church's Deseret Hospital in Salt Lake City. It was while working at the hospital that she met Angus Munn Cannon, a member of the hospital board 23 years her senior. Martha fell in love, and on October 6, 1884, she became the fourth of Angus's six plural wives. They would have three children together.

After the birth of her first child, Cannon largely put her medical career on hold and went into voluntary exile to prevent her husband's arrest under federal antipolygamy laws. She spent time in England, France, and Switzerland but longed for home on occasion. In one letter to her husband, she wrote, "you could never realize my present situation unless you were suddenly banished seven thousand miles from the scenes of your former activity, your identity lost, afraid to audibly whisper your own name and limited to *one* correspondent" (Lieber, "'The Goose Hangs High'" 45). She would spend time away from Utah again when her second child was born.

After government prosecution of polygamy ended, Cannon began a vigorous and active public life, both in medicine and in politics. She built a training school for nurses and centered her practice on treating women and children. In 1893, she spoke at a national women's suffrage meeting in Chicago held in conjunction with the Columbian National Exposition. Three years later, she fully entered the political arena as one of five Democrats running for the Utah State Senate in her district. Cannon's political bid gained particular attention not only because she was a woman but because her husband, Angus, was running for the same seat. When the votes were counted, Martha received more than 4,000 more votes than her husband. She became the first woman state senator in U.S. history.

She served two terms as a senator and championed public health initiatives, including the introduction of bills providing for the education of deaf, dumb, and blind children and for the creation of the State Board of Health. When she left the Senate, Governor Heber Wells appointed her as a member of the newly created health board, where she helped shape its purpose and direction.

Cannon continued to agitate for national women's suffrage. In 1898, she traveled to Washington, D.C., where she spoke at a convention commemorating the Seneca Falls declaration of women's rights issued 50 years earlier. She also spoke before a congressional committee, urging its members to grant women the right to vote.

Cannon spent her later years in Los Angeles, where she worked at the Graves Clinic and in the orthopedic department of the General Hospital. She died at the age of 75, on July 10, 1932. Her life embodied in every regard the progressive attitude that some 19th-century Mormon women took toward their place in society, politics, and the home.

—*W. Paul Reeve*

See also: Mormonism and Women; Polygamy.

References

Lieber, Constance L. "'The Goose Hangs High': Excerpts from the Letters of Martha Hughes Cannon." *Utah Historical Quarterly* 48 (Winter 1980): 37–48.

Lieber, Constance L., and John Sillito, eds. *Letters from Exile: The Correspondence of Martha Hughes Cannon and Angus M. Cannon, 1886–1888.* Salt Lake City, UT: Signature Books, 1989.

Clark, J. Reuben Jr.

Joshua Reuben Clark Jr. (1871–1961) served in the First Presidencies of LDS Church presidents Heber J. Grant, George Albert Smith, and David O. McKay. During his 28 years in the Church's highest-governing quorum, Clark emerged as a doctrinal purist and scriptural literalist.

He was born on September 1, 1871, in Grantsville, Salt Lake Valley, Utah, to Joshua Reuben Clark and Mary Louisa Woolley Clark. He graduated in 1898 from the University of Utah, where he was student body president, editor of the student newspaper, and class valedictorian.

Clark married Luacine Annetta Savage on September 14, 1898. They raised three daughters and one son. Until 1903, Clark taught school and was an educational administrator. In 1903, the Clarks moved to New York City, where Clark studied law at Columbia University. He graduated in 1906 and that same year was appointed assistant solicitor for the U.S. State Department. In addition, from 1906 to 1908, he taught law at George Washington University, and, from 1910 to 1913, he was solicitor for the State Department. He also opened private law offices in New York City, Washington, D.C., and Salt Lake City.

During World War I, Clark was a major in the Judge Advocate General Officers' Reserve Corps and helped to write some of the original regulations for the Selective Service. He also served in the U.S. Attorney General's Office, and was awarded the Distinguished Service Medal. In 1928, Clark was named undersecretary of state by President Calvin Coolidge. During this time, he wrote the "Clark Memorandum on the Monroe Doctrine," in which he rejected the notion that the United States could intervene without cause in Latin American affairs. On October 3, 1930, Clark was appointed U.S. ambassador to Mexico, serving until 1933.

In April 1933, Clark was called to Heber J. Grant's First Presidency, and on April 6 he was sustained as Second Counselor. At the time, Clark was not an LDS Church General Authority and had never before "presided" even at a local level. The next year, on October 6, 1934, he was sustained as First Counselor to Grant; on October 11, he was ordained an apostle and made a member of the Quorum of the Twelve Apostles. At Grant's death, on May 14, 1945, Clark was released from the First Presidency and joined the Quorum of the Twelve Apostles. During the previous 12 years, he had been a vocal critic of President Franklin D. Roosevelt's New Deal programs and had opposed American participation in World War II. Nevertheless, with George Albert Smith's succession as Church president, Clark was again called to the First Presidency and was sustained as Smith's First Counselor on May 21, 1945. After Smith's death, on April 4, 1951, Clark was named Second, not First, Counselor, to new Church president David O. McKay. The change—viewed as a demotion by some—was a shock. Clark's response was that it did not matter where one served, only how well. Following the death of McKay's First Counselor, Clark was named First Counselor, on June 12, 1958. Clark died in Salt Lake City on October 6, 1961. He was 90.

Of Clark's influence on the LDS Church, biographer D. Michael Quinn writes: "Among the long-lasting contributions that Reuben originally proposed were the centrally directed Church Welfare Plan, reorganization of Church finances, establishment of Assistants to the Quorum of the Twelve Apostles, 'simplification' of the relationship between the Church's auxiliaries and its priesthood leadership, establishment of regional priesthood leadership, closed-circuit media broadcasts of general conferences to outlying wards and stakes, simultaneous translation of general conferences into the languages of non-English speakers, construction of multiward buildings, and the administrative anticipation of the conferral of priesthood on men of black African descent by establishment of 'preparatory' priesthood groups and branches. Although resistant to social change, President Clark was in the vanguard of LDS administrative innovation" (Quinn, *Elder Statesman* 427–428).

Clark was a forceful public speaker. In one of his best-known, most influential speeches, "The Chartered Course of the Church in Education" (1938), he stated: "No teacher who does not have a real testimony of the truth of the gospel as revealed to and believed by the Latter-day Saints . . . has any place in the church school system. . . . Any Latter-day Saint psychologist, chemist, physicist, geologist, archaeologist, or any other scientist [who attempts] to explain away, or misinterpret, or evade, or elude, or most of all to repudiate or deny the great fundamental doctrines of the church . . . can have no place in the church schools or in the character building and spiritual growth of our youth" (Bergera and Priddis, *Brigham Young University* 61).

—*Gary James Bergera*

See also: Correlation; Grant, Heber J.; McKay, David O.; Mormonism and Blacks; Mormonism and Economics; Mormonism and Secular Government; Smith, George Albert.

References

Bergera, Gary James, and Ronald Priddis. *Brigham Young University: A House of Faith.* Salt Lake City, UT: Signature Books, 1985.

Fox, Frank W. *J. Reuben Clark: The Public Years.* Provo, UT: Brigham Young University Press, 1980.

Quinn, D. Michael. *Elder Statesman: A Biography of J. Reuben Clark.* Salt Lake City, UT: Signature Books, 2002. Expanded from *J. Reuben Clark: The Church Years.* Provo, UT: Brigham Young University Press, 1983.

Grant, Heber J.

Heber J. Grant (1856–1945), a prominent businessman, served as seventh president of the Church, a position he held for more than 26 years, second only to Brigham Young in tenure. He presided over a public relations campaign that saw the Church emerge from isolation and move toward acceptance. He led the Church during the difficult years of the Great Depression and World War II, a time in which his business acumen proved beneficial. Under his leadership, adherence to the Church's health code became a requirement for temple worship.

Grant was born to Jedediah M. Grant and his seventh wife, Rachel Ridgeway Ivins Grant, November 22, 1856, and into the heart of Mormon prominence. His father's house stood comfortably on Main Street in Salt Lake City close to the homes of other leading Mormons, including that of Brigham Young. In addition, his father served as counselor in the Church's governing first presidency and as mayor of Salt Lake City. Grant, however, would never know his father. He died of "lung disease" only nine days after Heber's birth. His mother struggled to provide for her family.

Perhaps it was out of his impoverished youth that Heber's business acumen emerged. As a teenager, he took work at an insurance and finance company and by the age of 19 had bought the insurance company. He opened another insurance company and purchased the Ogden Vinegar Works. In his early 20s, he was making 10 times more than a typical Utah wage earner. Flush with business success, in

1877 he took Lucy Stringham to wife. In 1884, he married two additional women, Hulda Augusta Winters and Emily Harris Wells, making him the last Church president to be a polygamist.

In 1880, Grant was called to serve as the president of the Tooele, Utah, Stake, a Church administrative unit roughly equivalent to a Catholic diocese. It was a tremendous load for young Grant, not yet 24 years old. His business ventures floundered, his Vinegar Works burned and was ironically underinsured, and his first wife suffered from ill health that led to her death more than a decade later. The stress of it all caused health concerns for Grant, too.

Less than two years later, his Church responsibilities grew to a full-time occupation. In October 1882, he was called to fill a vacancy in the Quorum of the Twelve Apostles, a position he would hold for more than 30 years, before becoming Church president. As an apostle, he found that the Church leaned heavily upon his business experience to deal with its deepening financial crisis. The Edmunds-Tucker Act (1887) allowed federal receivers to confiscate Church property valued at more than $50,000 and to thereby control significant portions of the Church's marketable assets. The nationwide depression in 1893 only exacerbated the problem. Grant traveled to New York City and negotiated loans from leading banks that saved the Church from financial ruin. His personal fortune, however, suffered during this time and never fully rebounded.

In 1918, Grant became the president of the Church and set out to improve its public image. He spoke at civic affairs across the country and was well received. He cultivated relationships with four U.S. presidents, from Harding to Roosevelt, as well as a variety of influential politicians and news editors. He promoted the Mormon Tabernacle Choir and U.S. Senator and Mormon apostle Reed Smoot as salutary symbols of Mormonism. He also aided production of two Hollywood movies favorable to the Mormons, *Union Pacific* and *Brigham Young,* and was featured on the cover of *Time* magazine. His efforts set the Church on a new trajectory toward acceptance and growth.

During the nationwide prohibition of alcoholic beverages and the temporary prohibition of cigarettes in 14 states, Grant moved toward a more stringent implementation of the Word of Wisdom, a health code for Latter-day Saints that admonished against alcohol, tobacco, coffee, and tea. By 1921, observance became a requirement for temple worship.

His next challenge was the Great Depression. Grant's own experience growing up in poverty endeared him to his Mormon flock and led him to direct the founding of the Church Welfare Program in an effort to ameliorate suffering. Here his business experience again came to the aid of the Church. Grant cut back on construction projects, trimmed expenses, and conserved resources. He ensured that the Church remained financially viable even as the Mormon people suffered from the devastating effects of the depression.

Utah was fourth in the nation in terms of the number of people on relief, mostly because of the severe effects of the depression on agriculture and mining, the two mainstays of Utah's economy. In response, in 1936, Grant approved the Church Welfare Program, designed to help those in need to help themselves. As a measure of his commitment, he donated his own dry farm to the welfare program. With memories of his own mother in mind, Grant helped widows in need. Upon learning of one widow's plight, he made her house payments and included enough extra money for a Christmas present.

Grant also responded to the horrors of World War II. At the beginning of the war, the First Presidency issued a statement under his direction that proclaimed that "the Church is and must be against war. . . . It cannot regard war as a righteous means of settling international disputes" ("Message" 348–349). It marked evidence of Grant's growing pacifism.

Grant's pace slowed markedly in his later years, especially as a series of strokes in 1940 took their toll. He died at Salt Lake City on May 14, 1945.

—*W. Paul Reeve*

See also: Mormonism and Economics; Non-Mormon Views of Mormonism; Word of Wisdom.

References

Alexander, Thomas G. *Mormonism in Transition: A History of the Latter-day Saints, 1890–1930.* Urbana: University of Illinois Press, 1986.

"Message of First Presidency." *Improvement Era* 45 (May 1942): 348–349.

Walker, Ronald W. "Crisis in Zion: Heber J. Grant and the Panic of 1893." *Arizona and the West* 21 (Autumn 1979): 257–278.

Walker, Ronald W. "Heber J. Grant." In *The Presidents of the Church.* Ed. Leonard J. Arrington. Salt Lake City, UT: Deseret Book, 1986.

Hinckley, Gordon B.

Gordon Bitner Hinckley (1910–2008) was the 15th president of the Church. While not the longest-serving member of the LDS hierarchy (David O. McKay's tenure spanned nearly 64 years, Hinckley's almost 50), he governed as the oldest sitting Church president. He was a career Church employee whose public relations acumen and charisma helped to usher the LDS Church into the 21st century.

Hinckley was born on June 23, 1910, in Salt Lake City, Utah, to Bryant Stringham Hinckley and Ada Bitner Hinckley. At age two, he battled pertussis and later developed asthma and several allergies, including hay fever. (Because of this, he was barred from entering the U.S. Navy in 1941.) He attended Salt Lake City public schools and graduated from the University of Utah with a degree in English in 1932.

The Church expanded rapidly in Africa during the administration of Gordon B. Hinckley. A Mormon batik artist of Sierra Leone adapted his ancient art to the symbols of his new religion. (Courtesy of the Church History Museum, The Church of Jesus Christ of Latter-day Saints.)

As he approached graduation, Hinckley confronted what his biographer has described as "questions" regarding "life, the world, and even the Church" (Dew, *Go Forward with Faith* 46, 47). "It [i.e., the Great Depression] was a time of terrible discouragement," Hinckley later said, "and I'm frank to say that I felt some of that myself. I began to question some things, including, perhaps in a slight measure, the faith of my parents and some of those things. That isn't unusual for university students, but the atmosphere was particularly acute at that time. But I'm grateful to say that through all of that, the testimony which had come to me as a boy remained with me and became as a bulwark to which I could cling through those very difficult years" (Bergera, "'The Challenges of Those Days'" 41–42).

Hinckley briefly entertained the idea of touring the South Pacific with a friend for a year but then decided to pursue graduate studies in journalism at Columbia University in New York City. Instead, he received a surprise LDS mission call to the London-based British Mission, where he served from 1933 to 1935. After his mission, he was invited by LDS Church president Heber J. Grant to work for the Church full time as secretary to the newly established Radio, Publicity, and Mission Literature Committee (later the Church Public Communications Department). For the next 20 years, Hinckley helped to direct all official LDS public relations activities. On April 29, 1937, he married Marjorie Pay in the Salt Lake temple; they raised five children. (Pay died on April 6, 2004.) Also in 1937, Hinckley was appointed to the Church's Sunday School General Board (he was released in 1946). Beginning in 1951, Hinckley served for seven years as executive secretary of the Church's General Missionary Committee. He was part of a committee that helped to adapt the Church's temple endowment ceremony for use in languages other than English; the result was a film version of a portion of the endowment. At the time of his calling as an Assistant to the Quorum of the Twelve Apostles on April 6, 1958, he was president of the East Millcreek (Salt Lake City) Stake. Three and a half years later, on October 5, 1961, he was called to the Quorum of the Twelve Apostles. As a member of the Twelve, he helped to supervise Church activities in Asia, Europe, and South America. His assignments included temples, missionary work, welfare services, priesthood, and the military. He helped to draft several official First Presidency declarations, including statements on liquor by the drink (1968), blacks and the priesthood (1969), the Equal Rights Amendment (1978), and the MX missile system (1981). He chaired the executive committee for the commemoration of the Church's 150th anniversary, in 1980.

On July 23, 1981, Hinckley joined Church president Spencer W. Kimball's First Presidency as an additional counselor. (Kimball's First and Second Counselors were infirm, but Kimball chose not to release either.) Later the next year, following the death of First Counselor N. Eldon Tanner, Hinckley was named Second Counselor to Kimball on December 2, 1982. During the last years of Kimball's presidency, Hinckley guided the Church as de facto president. When Ezra Taft Benson was appointed Church president following Kimball's death, Hinckley was named First Counselor on November 10, 1985. With Benson's decline in health during the early 1990s, Hinckley again managed the daily routine of the Church. Following Benson's death, in 1994, Hinckley was retained on June 5, 1994, as First Counselor by the new Church president, Howard W. Hunter (and was also named president of the Quorum of the Twelve Apostles). At Hunter's death, in 1995, Hinckley was ordained and set apart as Church president on March 12, 1995. He dedicated more LDS temples worldwide than any other LDS official. He was the first sitting Church president to visit Spain, where he broke ground for a temple in Madrid in 1996, and to tour Africa, where he visited Nigeria, Ghana, Kenya, Zimbabwe, and South Africa. Under his direction, the Church issued two important proclamations to the world on the family (1995) and on Jesus Christ (2000).

Hinckley chaired the executive committees of the Board of Trustees of the Church Board of Education and of LDS-owned Brigham Young University (Provo, Utah). He received the Distinguished Citizen Award (from Southern Utah University), the Distinguished Alumni Award (University of Utah), and honorary doctorates from Westminster College (Salt Lake City), Utah State University (Logan), University of Utah, Brigham Young University, and Southern Utah University. He received Scouting's national Silver Buffalo Award and was honored by the National Conference (formerly the National Conference of Christians and Jews) for his work in fostering greater tolerance and intercultural understanding. In 2004, he was awarded the U.S. Presidential Medal of Freedom, the country's highest civilian award. During his presidency, he gave numerous interviews to major American and world news media, including the *New York Times,* the *Los Angeles Times,* the CBS *60 Minutes* television news program, and *Larry King Live* on CNN cable television. In early 2006, cancerous tumors were removed from his large intestine. In 2007, he presided at the dedication of the Gordon B. Hinckley Alumni and Visitors Center at BYU and at the re-dedication of the Salt Lake Mormon Tabernacle. Early the next year, on January 27, 2008, he died in his Salt Lake City home.

Hinckley was a moderate, ecumenical theologian. His public comments revealed a man of great faith and optimism, concern for the human condition, and a champion of the intellect. "I have seen a good deal of this earth," he noted. "I have seen its rot and smelled its filth. . . . And yet I am an optimist" (Hinckley, 1997, 410). "We have a lot of gloomy people in the Church," he admitted, "because they do not understand, I guess, that this is the gospel of happiness" (Hinckley, *Teachings of Gordon B. Hinckley* 256). Yet, he also sometimes lamented: "How very heavy is the burden of human suffering, the suffering that comes of war, of so-called ethnic cleansing, of conflict in the name of religion, of foolish ideas of racial superiority, of intolerance, bigotry, and egotism" (Hinckley, *Teachings of Gordon B. Hinckley* 665). He was especially frank in his views on war. "War I hate with all its mocking panoply," he said. "It is a grim and living testimony that Satan, the father of lies, the enemy of God, lives. War is earth's greatest cause of human misery. It is the destroyer of life, the promoter of hate, the waster of treasure. It is man's costliest folly, his most tragic misadventure" (Hinckley, *Teachings of Gordon B. Hinckley* 683). Of education, which he termed "an endless process," he counseled: "The Lord wants you to educate your minds and hands, whatever your chosen field. Whether it be repairing refrigerators, or the work of a skilled surgeon, you must train yourselves" (Hinckley, "A Prophet's Counsel" 7). He was equally adamant regarding critical thinking: "Fundamental to our theology is belief in individual freedom of inquiry, thought, and expression" (Hinckley, "Keep the Faith" 5).

—*Gary James Bergera*

See also: Church Organization and Government; Mormonism and Education; Mormonism and Other Faiths; Mormonism and the Family; Temple Work by Proxy; Temples.

References
Bergera, Gary James. "'The Challenges of Those Days': President Gordon B. Hinckley and the Will to Believe." *Sunstone* (May 2005): 38–45.

Dew, Sheri L. *Go Forward with Faith: The Biography of Gordon B. Hinckley.* Salt Lake City, UT: Deseret Book, 1996.

Hinckley, Gordon B. "Keep the Faith." *Ensign* 15 (September 1985): 5.

Hinckley, Gordon B. "A Prophet's Counsel and Prayer for Youth." *Ensign* 31 (January 2001): 7.

Hinckley, Gordon B. *Teachings of Gordon B. Hinckley.* Salt Lake City, UT: Deseret Book, 1997.

Hunter, Howard W.

Howard William Hunter (1907–1995) became the 14th president of the Church on June 5, 1994. His tenure as president, just eight months and 26 days, was the shortest in Church history. He emphasized temple worship and qualification for temple attendance as great symbols of Mormon religious life. Hunter's life experiences and route to positions of influence within the LDS hierarchy followed an atypical course. His life was also marked by ill health, for both him and his first wife, Claire Jeffs; it was perhaps the hard-won fruits of those physical struggles that led many to describe his leadership style and personal demeanor as gentle and compassionate.

Born on November 17, 1907, in Boise, Idaho, to Nellie Marie Rasmussen and John William "Will" Hunter, Howard, the first of two children, would become the first Church president born in the 20th century. Hunter's father was raised an Episcopalian, but, at the time of his marriage to Nellie, he was not affiliated with any denomination; he would later convert to the LDS Church. Will did not oppose attendance by his wife and children at LDS worship services, and, when his work schedule allowed, he would join them. However, he preferred that his children wait to be baptized until they were mature enough to choose their faith for themselves. As a result, Howard and his sister, Dorothy, were not baptized at the customary age for Mormons of eight. At the age of 12, when his Mormon friends were ordained deacons and began passing the sacrament to congregants, Howard, not yet baptized, felt left out. His pleadings with his father eventually won out, and Howard and Dorothy were baptized at the age of 12 and 10, respectively.

Hunter worked his way through high school in a variety of jobs. Hunter's most ambitious project, however, also brought him the most satisfaction. After winning a marimba in a contest, he learned to play it and then went on to learn the drums, saxophone, clarinet, trumpet, piano, and violin, although the clarinet was his favorite. In 1924, while still in high school, Hunter organized his own group, Hunter's Croonaders, and began playing at dances throughout the Boise region. After high school, he secured a contract for his band to play aboard a passenger liner for a cruise to the Orient. Upon his return, he hitchhiked to California to visit a former band member and ended up making California his new home.

It was in California that Hunter met Clara May (Claire) Jeffs. After three years of courtship, Hunter opted to get married rather than serve a mission for the Church. The couple married in 1931. Hunter came to the conclusion that his band did not offer the type of lifestyle that he intended for his future family, and so he gave up professional music. He eventually enrolled at Southwestern Law School, where he graduated cum laude in 1939. He went on to practice corporate and business law and to serve on the boards of more than two dozen companies.

Ecclesiastically, he was called as bishop of his local congregation and then president of the Pasadena, California, Stake. He was serving in the later capacity when he was unexpectedly called as an apostle in October 1959. He recalled that Church president David O. McKay told him, "The Lord has spoken. You are called to be one of his special witnesses, and tomorrow you will be sustained as a member of the Council of the Twelve" (Knowles, *Howard W. Hunter* 144). He thereafter left his law practice and spent the rest of his life in Church service.

As an apostle, and later as Church president, Hunter traveled the globe as a representative for the Church. Perhaps his greatest accomplishment during his apostolic ministry was securing land on the Mount of Olives for the construction of the Brigham Young University Jerusalem Center for Near Eastern Studies. Hunter's friendship with Jerusalem mayor Teddy Kollek proved influential in cutting through red tape as well as in overcoming Jewish and Palestinian opposition to the planned center. Hunter dedicated the building in May 1989.

Hunter's greatest challenges came as a result of health problems for himself and his family. Howard and Claire's first son, Howard William Hunter Jr., died after six months. Howard later recalled, "We were grief-stricken and numb as we left the hospital into the night" (Knowles, *Howard W. Hunter* 88). Two additional sons, Richard and John, would survive their parents into adulthood and follow their father's path as lawyers. Hunter's beloved wife, Claire, however, suffered a variety of health setbacks, including a collapsed lung, adult-onset diabetes, and strokes. Throughout her illnesses Howard took vigilant care of his wife, even as he maintained a demanding schedule for the Church. She died October 9, 1983. He later married Inis Bernice Egan, in 1990.

Hunter himself experienced his share of health problems—a heart attack, major back surgery, a bleeding ulcer, and a gall-bladder operation—through which he came to know the frailties of mortality. Hunter additionally broke three ribs after falling backward while delivering a Church conference sermon. As a consequence, he knew of what he spoke when he reminded Mormons, in 1987, that "suffering can make saints of people as they learn patience, long-suffering, and self-mastery" (Knowles, *Howard W. Hunter* 264).

During his brief stint as Church president, he admonished Latter-day Saints to make Mormon temple worship a symbol of their devotion to Jesus Christ. He also invited "all members of the Church to live with ever more attention to the life and example of the Lord Jesus Christ, especially the love and hope and compassion He displayed" (Holzapfel and Slaughter, *Prophets of the Latter Days* 191). He died March 3, 1995, at the age of 87.

—*W. Paul Reeve*

See also: Temples.

References

Holzapfel, Richard Neitzel, and William W. Slaughter. *Prophets of the Latter Days*. Salt Lake City, UT: Deseret Book, 2003.

Knowles, Eleanor. *Howard W. Hunter*. Salt Lake City, UT: Deseret Book, 1994.

Kimball, Spencer W.

Spencer W. Kimball (1895–1985) served as the 12th president of the Church. Presiding from 1973 to 1985, Kimball led an administration that represents one of the most important to 20th-century Mormonism. Kimball initiated an increase in missionary activity abroad and made essential bureaucratic changes that facilitated a burgeoning worldwide membership. Indeed, as a result of Kimball's progressive leadership, the Church began to conceive of itself as an international organization. The First Presidency, under Kimball's guidance, also boldly asserted the Church's political power by issuing important public statements opposing the Equal Rights Amendment in 1976 and efforts to deploy the MX missile in the Great Basin in 1981. Kimball is perhaps most remembered for the 1978 policy change that ended the restriction that kept black male members from holding the priesthood. Kimball endeared himself to the Church membership through a rigorous work ethic, embodied in his personal motto, "Do it!" and through his devotion to and personal interaction with the membership.

The sixth child of Andrew Kimball and Olive Woolley, Spencer Woolley Kimball was born on March 28, 1895, in Salt Lake City, Utah. In 1898, Andrew Kimball accepted a call to serve as president of the St. Joseph Stake, which comprised several Mormon settlements along the Gila River in southeastern Arizona. The Kimball family established a farm in Thatcher, Arizona. As a youth, Spencer did farm chores, played the piano, and excelled in high school athletics and scholastics. Following graduation, in 1914, he served a two-year mission in the Central States Mission. Upon his return, Kimball enrolled at the University of Arizona with the intention of becoming a teacher. After his first semester, he began courting his future wife, Camilla Eyring. Kimball married Camilla in November 1917. Together, the couple had four children.

Following his marriage, Kimball began employment as chief teller of a local bank in Stafford, Arizona. After his father's death, in 1924, Kimball was appointed a counselor in the St. Joseph Stake presidency. Kimball's service in the Church limited his ability to continue his education. To better provide for his family, Kimball partnered with Joseph Greenhalgh to launch the Kimball-Greenhalgh Agency, a development company that dealt in insurance, bonds, and real estate. The men's scrupulous leadership helped the company weather the Great Depression.

In 1938, the St. Joseph Stake split, and Kimball was called to preside over the new Mount Graham Stake. The flooding of the Gila River, in September 1941, brought tragedy to the members under his care in Duncan, Arizona. Through an innovative application of the LDS Welfare Program, Kimball helped provide aid to those in need. Kimball's actions impressed Church leadership, and in 1943 he received a called to join the Quorum of the Twelve Apostles.

A majority of Kimball's apostolic efforts involved working with Native Americans and the members in Latin America. Appointed chairman of the Lamanite Committee, in 1946, Kimball traveled widely among reservations and worked tirelessly to uplift Native Americans. He also helped establish the Indian Student Placement Program, which provided education for thousands of young Native Americans. Kimball also toured Latin America extensively. These travels provided him with a unique appreciation for the difficulties of blacks and those of mixed ancestry in the Church. Later, as a member of the Missionary Committee, he emphasized the importance of South America and believed the membership would benefit from the construction of a temple. Kimball presided over many milestones in the growth of the Church in Latin America, including the dedication of Central America for preaching the gospel and the creation, in 1966, of the Sao Paulo, Brazil, Stake—the first stake organized in South America.

As an ecclesiastical authority, Kimball also counseled members who violated the Church's chastity code. In 1969, he published *The Miracle of Forgiveness,* a hallmark in LDS literature, providing insight into overcoming transgression, especially sexual sin.

During his 13 years as an apostle, Kimball experienced a series of health problems. Numerous heart troubles culminated with open-heart surgery in April 1972. Repeated bouts with throat cancer necessitated the removal of most his vocal cords. Miraculously, Kimball retained some ability to speak—albeit through a raspy whisper. Because of his seemingly fragile health, when Harold B. Lee died, on December 26, 1973, making Kimball, at age 78, the next in line for the presidency, many believed his administration would be brief.

Though Kimball predicted no deviation from previous LDS policy under his leadership, his 12 years as president were marked by important changes that paced international growth and guided the Church through the tumultuous years of the 1970s and early 1980s. Kimball emphasized missionary work, and the number of missionaries increased dramatically under his direction. By presenting itself as an apolitical institution to foreign governments, the Church made significant inroads in countries previously closed to LDS proselytizing. Kimball also facilitated growth by taking steps to decentralize and expand the Mormon leadership. Alterations included the activation of the First Quorum of the Seventy, the creation of area presidencies, the authorization of stake presidents to ordain bishops and patriarchs, and the introduction of emeritus status and temporary General Authorities. Kimball also expanded the Church's international presence by constructing a number of smaller temples outside the United States. In all, his administration oversaw the dedication or rededication of 26 temples.

Kimball's administration also strengthened the role of minority groups within the Church. Kimball called a number of non-Caucasians to serve in the Church's general leadership, including George P. Lee, a Navajo. On June 9, 1978, Kimball announced a revelation allowing all worthy male members to be ordained to the priesthood. The policy change ushered in an era of growth, especially in Brazil and Africa.

Under Kimball's leadership, the First Presidency released several encyclicals with significant political implications. Believing the Equal Rights Amendment detrimental to the family, the Church released a statement opposing the bill in 1976. Despite claims that Church leaders sought to restrain women in the Church, Kimball supported women's education and recognized that economic necessity required some women to work outside the home. Kimball also instituted the first general women's meetings of the Church in 1978. At the height of the Cold War, Kimball also voiced his concern that the United States was relying too heavily upon weapons to secure peace. Accordingly, the First Presidency issued a statement opposing the construction of the MX missile system in the Great Basin in 1981.

Despite continual health problems, Kimball maintained a rigorous work load into the late 1970s. A stroke, two additional subdural hematomas, and a host of other ailments significantly limited Kimball's strength. His failing health, as well as the faltering health of his counselors, necessitated the calling of apostle Gordon B. Hinckley as a third counselor in the First Presidency in July 1981. Kimball made his last public appearance in April 1982 and died on November 5, 1985, at age 90. His example inspired members to "lengthen their stride" through greater devotion to the work of the Lord. While setting the Church on a path toward greater spirituality, Kimball provided dynamic leadership that also paved the way for exponential international growth in the late 20th century.

—*Jacob W. Olmstead*

See also: Mormon Missiology; Mormonism and Blacks; Mormonism and Native Americans; Mormonism and Race; Mormonism and Women; Priesthood Revelation of 1978; Temples.

References
Kimball, Edward L. *Lengthen Your Stride: The Presidency of Spencer W. Kimball.* Salt Lake City, UT: Deseret Book, 2005.

Kimball, Edward L., and Andrew E. Kimball Jr. *Spencer W. Kimball: Twelfth President of the Church of Jesus Christ of Latter-day Saints.* Salt Lake City, UT: Bookcraft, 1977.

Olmstead, Jacob W. "The Mormon Hierarchy and the MX." *Journal of Mormon History* 33 (Fall 2007): 1–30.

Lee, Harold B.

Less than a month after Harold B. Lee's (1899–1973) unexpected death, apostle Boyd K. Packer used a telling metaphor to suggest what this 11th president of the Church had meant in the shaping of modern Mormonism: "Imagine a group of people who are going on a journey through a territory that is dangerous and unplotted. They have a large bus for transportation, and they are making preparations. They find among them a master mechanic. He is appointed to get their vehicle ready, with all of us to help. He insists that it be stripped down completely, every part taken from the other part and inspected carefully, cleaned, renewed, repaired, and some of them replaced" (Goates, *Harold B. Lee* 608). In the minds of many observers, Harold B. Lee was just such a master mechanic, overseeing the organizational overhaul of an increasingly global Church.

Harold B. Lee was born in Clifton, Idaho, in 1899, into a farming family. Early on, he proved to be a precocious learner and leader. He started school a year early because the schoolmaster noticed that the young boy already knew the alphabet. At age 17, after completing training at the Albion (Idaho) State Normal School (and passing the certification exams for 15 subjects), he was appointed principal and teacher of the one-room Silver Star School. After four years of supervising and teaching at local schools, his father (who was also the area's Church bishop) recommended Harold for missionary service. He was called to the Western States Mission, where he distinguished himself as president of the Church region known then as the Denver Conference, with ecclesiastical responsibility for both full-time missionaries and local Church members in eastern Colorado.

After completing his two-year mission, in 1922, he moved to Salt Lake City to further his schooling and to renew his acquaintance with a former fellow missionary, Fern Lucinda Tanner. The two were married in November 1923. They had two daughters, Maurine and Helen. Fern Lee died in 1962. Elder Lee then married Freda Joan Jensen in 1963; she died in 1981.

After five years of teaching school in Salt Lake, Harold switched careers in 1928 to become a salesman for Foundation Press. He left that position when he was appointed to fill a vacant seat on the Salt Lake City Commission in 1932. He was reelected to the post in 1933 and oversaw the city's Department of Streets and Public Works until he entered full-time Church employment in 1936 to head the new welfare program.

His growing prominence in the community paralleled his expanding responsibilities in Church assignments. After several years of involvement with youth and adult Sunday School and daily seminary programs, he was called as president of the Church's Pioneer Stake in 1930. Harold B. Lee was 31 years old, the youngest of the Church's 104 stake presidents.

The Pioneer Stake covered much of the hard-hit west side of depression-era Salt Lake City, and more than half of his 7,300 stake members relied on relief aid. In the early years of the Great Depression, Church general authorities encouraged local initiative in dealing with the economic crisis, and President Lee and his Pioneer Stake associates proved to be especially innovative, setting up crop harvesting cooperatives and Church building projects. The success of these efforts impressed the three members of the Church's First Presidency, who for some time had been contemplating the organization of a unified, Church-wide response to the desperation of the depression. On April 20, 1935, Church president Heber J. Grant met with Harold B. Lee and invited him to direct the creation of the new Church Security Plan (later called the Church Welfare Program), which was officially announced in April 1936.

Perhaps no other Church endeavor has generated as much early and consistent positive media attention for Mormons as has the Church's welfare effort. Harold traveled extensively throughout the United States to oversee the implementation of the Security Plan. A network of commodity storehouses, canneries, Church farms, and volunteer labor was the result. His intimate involvement with the design and execution of the program only intensified when he was called as one of the Church's Twelve Apostles, in 1941.

Significantly, Elder Lee stressed that no new organization was necessary for the success of the welfare program; what *was* needed was a renewed emphasis on the importance of the Church's lay priesthood leadership structure. This would be a running theme in Elder Lee's work as an apostle, especially when, in 1960, he chaired a committee charged by Church president David O. McKay with correlating the various curricula and activities of Church auxiliaries. Up to that point, the age-specific auxiliaries largely had operated independently, produced their own curriculum materials, conducted their own local training meetings, and, in Church leaders' eyes, duplicated other auxiliaries' efforts. Under the auspices of Elder Lee's new All-Church Coordinating Council, Church committees produced curriculum materials for all of the auxiliaries in order to reduce redundancy and improve the uniformity of doctrinal instruction. The supervisory role of priesthood officers was reinforced. New Church magazines, new stake and ward council meetings, a new level of Church leadership (Regional Representatives), and the modern variants of the home teaching and family home evening programs all grew out of the correlation project. Because this centralizing and streamlining effort coincided with the Church's international expansion, one biographer suggested that "some historians may well argue that President Harold B. Lee's most significant lifetime work for the Church . . . was [this] reorganization" (Goates, *Harold B. Lee* 363).

Harold B. Lee served as the first counselor to his predecessor, President Joseph Fielding Smith, from 1970 until President Smith's death in July 1972. President Lee's 17 months as Church president came to an end when he passed away from sudden heart failure on December 26, 1973. The brevity of his tenure belies his impact. The Church of Jesus Christ of Latter-day Saints still bears the imprint of the processes and programs set in motion during Harold B. Lee's three decades of leadership in the highest circles of the Church's hierarchy.

—*J. B. Haws*

See also: Correlation; Mormonism and Economics.

References

Cowan, Richard O. *The Latter-day Saint Century,* rev. ed. Salt Lake City, UT: Bookcraft, 1999.

Goates, L. Brent. *Harold B. Lee: Prophet and Seer.* Salt Lake City, UT: Bookcraft, 1985.

Rudd, Glen L. *Pure Religion: The Story of Church Welfare since 1930.* Salt Lake City, UT: The Church of Jesus Christ of Latter-day Saints, 1995.

Lyman, Amy Brown

Social worker and Relief Society leader Amy Brown Lyman (1872–1959) was born in Pleasant Grove, Utah, the youngest daughter of pioneer John Brown's three polygamous families. She was taught to revere education and trained as a teacher at Brigham Young Academy, where her talents led her onto the faculty before she moved to teach in the Salt Lake City schools. Her career ended with her 1896 marriage to educator and civil engineer Richard R. Lyman, son of apostle Francis M. Lyman. In 1902, she accompanied him to Cornell University for graduate study, but a summer session at the University of Chicago en route brought her to Jane Addams's Hull House, where she was exposed to modern social work, a life-changing experience. After Richard completed his studies, the Lymans returned to Salt Lake, he to his faculty position at the University of Utah, she to the life of wife and club woman.

That changed in 1909 with her call to the Relief Society general board. The Society was then struggling against declining membership as its activities, legacies of the territorial period, were seen as irrelevant to women of the time. Part of a cohort of young board members, Lyman helped create the *Relief Society Magazine* and a widely popular curriculum of theology, literature, genealogy, home economics, and social work. In 1913, she became general secretary, essentially a full-time position, and was charged by President Joseph F. Smith with modernizing business and charitable practices. She soon helped steer the Society toward activism in public health. In 1916, she joined the Salt Lake Charity Organization Society to help coordinate municipal relief efforts and then became vice chair of the Church's Social Advisory Committee, which organized programs to prevent juvenile vice and delinquency. World War I brought new opportunities: participation in Red Cross work to aid servicemen and their families led her to study social work method and practice with the Denver Public Charities. Church leaders subsequently charged Lyman to use these techniques to establish a social service department in the Relief Society offices. Lyman developed close ties to leaders in the field through her association with local and national social work organizations and used these links to gain first-rate training for her small staff. A series of summer schools and social service institutes extended her efforts to thousands of rank-and-file women, enabling them to better administer aid in their communities. A highpoint of her activities came in the 1920s, when, under President Clarissa Williams, she marshaled this veritable army of paraprofessionals in support of the Federal Maternity and Infancy Act of 1921, which provided grants to states for educational work in health and nutrition. Consequently, Utah saw significant declines in infant and maternal mortality. She also led the Society in a successful lobbying campaign to win funding for a state school for the mentally retarded.

A change of administrations diminished her influence in the 1930s. Nevertheless, she utilized resources at the social service department to address, in cooperation with public agencies, the crisis of the Great Depression. As the Church Welfare Plan was developing, in 1936, Lyman was unable to assist as she was presiding with her husband over the European Mission. After their return to Utah, she was called as Relief Society president, in January 1940. Lyman's administration was greeted with great anticipation, but circumstances prevented her from carrying out plans for renewed community activism: J. Reuben Clark, Counselor in the First Presidency, was calling for reduced programs to allow women more family time, while wartime travel restrictions soon limited activities. A devastating blow came four years into her presidency when Richard, then an apostle, was excommunicated for adultery. This led to her release in April 1945. Despite such impediments, before that time Lyman brought the Society's support for the welfare plan up to its highest level, and the organization made significant contributions to war-related activities.

Lyman was a woman of great energy, intelligence, and ability. A nationally known figure among organized women and social workers, she was a strong advocate for women's equality in the workplace, community affairs, and politics. A demanding administrator, she nevertheless earned the loyalty and affection of her staff through her fairness, sympathetic manner, and efforts to build them up personally and professionally. As a Church leader, she was the best-known and most widely admired woman of her time. A dynamic speaker, she served as an inspiring reminder of the Relief Society's potential to strengthen Mormon women and benefit their communities.

—*David R. Hall*

See also: Relief Society.

References

Hefner, Loretta L. "Amy Brown Lyman: Raising the Quality of Life for All." In *Sister Saints.* Ed Vicky Burgess-Olson, 95–113. Provo, UT: Brigham Young University Press, 1978.

Lyman, Amy Brown. *In Retrospect: Autobiography of Amy Brown Lyman.* Salt Lake City, UT: General Board of Relief Society, 1945.

McConkie, Bruce R.

Bruce Redd McConkie (1915–1985) served almost 40 years as a general authority, the last 13 as an apostle. He is representative of 20th-century Mormon leaders in his lifelong service and oft-expressed testimony of the divinity of Jesus Christ; he exerted a disproportionate influence on popular Mormon thought and public discourse through his published writings, especially *Mormon Doctrine.*

McConkie was born July 29, 1915, and was raised chiefly in Monticello, Utah, and in Salt Lake City. He graduated from the University of Utah in 1937, his law studies having been interrupted by a mission to the eastern United States from 1934 to 1936. Following military service in World War II, principally in Salt Lake City with Army Intelligence, McConkie worked briefly as a newspaper reporter. In 1946, he became a member of the First Council of the Seventy, where he served for the next 26 years. He was president of the Southern Australia Mission in 1961–1964, and was ordained as an apostle in 1972.

McConkie approached the study of religion with the same analytical mind that attracted him to law school and military intelligence. Recognizing a lack of systematic explication of the complex doctrines of Mormonism, McConkie determined to produce such a work; the result was published in 1958 as *Mormon Doctrine.*

The book was an immediate success among the general Mormon public, reflecting, perhaps, a long-felt need for such a compact reference work. Aspects of the book, however, disturbed many readers, including McConkie's fellow general authorities. At the request of Church president David O. McKay, an apostolic committee examined the book and reported problems, including McConkie's description of non-Mormon groups in unnecessarily inflammatory terms (e.g., McConkie identified the Catholic Church as "the great and abominable church of the devil" [McConkie, *Mormon Doctrine* 129], although the Book of Mormon in which that phrase is found does not apply the label to any formal organization) and seemingly authoritative statements on controversial, officially unresolved questions (e.g., McConkie denounced the theory of organic evolution as in conflict with the teachings of the Church, although the official Church position is that God has not revealed the exact mechanism by which He created the Earth and put life here). Also of concern was the authoritative manner in which personal opinion was set forth as revealed doctrine (a later study of McConkie's publications disclosed that the single most cited authority for statements in his works was earlier writings by McConkie himself). Not noted in the report but since condemned was McConkie's entry on "Negroes," which presented as doctrine various speculations (now repudiated) used to justify withholding priesthood from African American men.

In response to concerns over the content of *Mormon Doctrine,* Church officials instituted a policy requiring that all manuscripts written by general authorities be reviewed prior to publication. McConkie rewrote some, but not all, of the controversial articles prior to *Mormon Doctrine*'s 1966 re-publication.

McConkie was a powerful public speaker. Among his best-remembered addresses is one given to a gathering of Church Education System personnel immediately following the 1978 extension of priesthood to worthy male members regardless of race: "Forget everything that I have said . . . in days past that is contrary to the present revelation. We spoke with a limited understanding and without the light and knowledge that now has come into the world. It doesn't make a particle of difference what anybody ever said about the Negro matter before the first day of June 1978. It is a new day and a new arrangement, and the Lord has now given the revelation that sheds light out into the world on this subject" (McConkie, "All Are Alike unto God"). During the late 1970s and early 1980s, McConkie published a six-volume study of the messiahship of Jesus Christ. This intense focus on Christ is mirrored in an address delivered in April 1985, which his listeners recognized as the final testimony of a dying apostle: "The most powerful testimony I can bear, is of the atoning sacrifice of the Lord Jesus Christ. His atonement is the most transcendent event that ever has or ever will occur from Creation's dawn through all the ages of a never-ending eternity. . . . I am one of his witnesses, and in a coming day I shall feel the nail marks in his hands and in his feet. . . . But I shall not know any better then than I know now that he is God's Almighty Son, that he is our Savior and Redeemer, and that salvation comes in and through his atoning blood and in no other way" (McConkie, "The Purifying Power of Gethsemane" 9).

McConkie died April 19, 1985.

—Ardis E. Parshall

See also: Mormonism and Blacks; Mormonism and Race; Mormonism and Science; Priesthood Revelation of 1978.

References

McConkie, Bruce R. "All Are Alike unto God." Address. Second Annual CES Symposium, Salt Lake City, August 1978. http://www.zionsbest.co/alike.html (August 4 2009).

McConkie, Bruce R. *Mormon Doctrine.* Salt Lake City, UT: Bookcraft, 1958.

McConkie, Bruce R. "The Purifying Power of Gethsemane." *Ensign* (May 1985): 9–10.

McConkie, Joseph Fielding. *The Bruce R. McConkie Story: Reflections of a Son.* Salt Lake City, UT: Deseret Book, 2003.

McConkie, Mark L., ed. *Sermons & Writings of Bruce R. McConkie.* Salt Lake City, UT: Bookcraft, 1998.

McKay, David O.

David Oman McKay (1873–1970) served as president of the Church from 1951 to 1970, the third-longest tenure of any LDS Church president. His administration was one of transition on two broad fronts: modernism and internationalism.

At the time McKay became president, the public image of Mormonism had changed little since the time of Brigham Young (1801–1877): the bearded polygamist. Young and each of his successors wore full beards and were either polygamists or, in the case of George Albert Smith (1870–1951), McKay's immediate predecessor, the son of a polygamist. McKay was a vivid contrast on several accounts: he was a monogamist with no polygamy in his ancestry; he was clean-shaven; he dressed distinctively, often wearing double-breasted white suits instead of the dark suits universally worn by his colleagues; and he was the first college graduate to serve as president. These attributes combined to make him the icon of Mormonism. Indeed, to this day, many who lived during his presidency say, "He looked like a prophet," a description seldom if ever accorded to other presidents before or since.

His modernism was demonstrated particularly well in two arenas: broadcasting and education. A keen observer of the electronic media since the 1930s, when commercial radio came of age, he greatly expanded the Church's use of those media. In 1953, he became the first televised Church president. In 1960, he recruited Arch L. Madsen, a veteran broadcaster then serving as an industry lobbyist in Washington, D.C., to shore up the Church's flagging broadcasting properties. Together, they established a broadcasting empire, Bonneville International, whose television and radio properties not only assisted in disseminating the Church's message but also generated sufficient revenue to produce the award-winning "Homefront" series of public service programming.

An educator by profession, having served as principal of the Weber Academy (predecessor of Weber State University, in Ogden, Utah), he gave constant emphasis to the importance of education, encouraging the youth of the Church to gain as much higher education as possible. He and Ernest L. Wilkinson, president of Brigham Young University, teamed to transform BYU from a small, bucolic college into the largest private university in the United States.

Though his efforts to modernize the Church were impressive, perhaps the most important accomplishment of his presidency was the transformation of the Church from a provincial, Great Basin-centered organization into one that was urbane and international. This achievement required bold initiatives on several fronts.

McKay had unprecedented overseas experience prior to becoming president. He served as a missionary in Scotland (1897–1899), circumnavigated the globe on assignment to visit the Church's foreign missions (1920–1921), and served as president of the European Mission (1923–1924). As a result, he understood the factors that had combined to keep the

David O. McKay, church president in the 1950s and 1960s, successfully bridged the church's pioneer past and its modern worldwide development. (Courtesy of the Church History Library, The Church of Jesus Christ of Latter-day Saints.)

Church a weak and ephemeral presence in foreign countries: poor public image; dilapidated meeting places, nearly all of which were rented and generally located in undesirable neighborhoods; a policy dating to the 1830s that encouraged all foreign converts to immigrate to Utah; and a missionary force that represented only a small fraction of its potential.

By using positive images of the Church in the media—the Mormon Tabernacle Choir; the high domestic and international profile of Ezra Taft Benson, who served simultaneously as a member of the Quorum of the Twelve Apostles and as secretary of agriculture to Dwight D. Eisenhower (1953–1961); and the power of his own persona—he dramatically transformed the public image of the Church.

Taking advantage of surplus tithing revenues that had built up during the war years prior to his presidency, when most domestic building projects were frozen by the war effort, he enlisted the services of Wendell Mendenhall to embark upon an unprecedented construction program. During the first dozen years of his presidency, nearly 2,000 chapels were constructed—significantly more than in the prior 120 years combined. Many were built overseas, replacing the rented halls that so often embarrassed Church members and discouraged potential converts. But perhaps more significant than the chapels were temples in Switzerland, England, and New Zealand. They were the first ever built outside North America (other than Hawaii) and the only ones, either before or since, that were constructed in areas where stakes (dioceses) did not already exist.

The construction of these buildings was a calculated move on the part of McKay, who understood that until he built temples in foreign countries, he could not ask Church members to remain in their native lands and thus deprive themselves of blessings that the temples in North America afforded them. As soon as he announced the decision to construct these temples, he reversed the century-old policy of "gathering" and asked that Church members remain in their native countries and establish a strong and permanent presence worldwide.

McKay's efforts to expand the missionary force and thus accelerate the Church's growth in foreign countries were initially frustrated by draft restrictions coincident with the Korean War. With the end of the war, however, he began to change the culture of the missionary program, eventually tripling the number of full-time missionaries, while at the same time asking that "every member" become a missionary. The results were dramatic. Convert baptisms, which had numbered 17,000 during the first year of his presidency, soared to 115,000 by 1962. A large percentage of the converts were in countries other than the United States, and the combination of new members, new buildings, new temples, an upgraded public image, and a reversal of the policy of gathering led to the creation, in 1958, of the first stake outside North America, in New Zealand—a remarkable statistic, considering the Church was 128 years old. By the time of McKay's death, in 1970, the number of stakes outside North America had risen to 34.

Many crucial issues confronted the Church during David O. McKay's presidency, and, although historians may debate which one was the most significant, there was no question in McKay's mind. Little more than a year prior to his death, he was interviewed by the *New York Times*. In response to the question "What do you regard as the most outstanding accomplishment of your ministry as President of the Church?" he replied, "The making of the Church a world-wide organization." In the early 21st century, more than half the Church's membership and nearly half its temples are outside the United States and Canada.

In spite of these accomplishments, however, the greatness of David O. McKay is not captured in facts and figures. Other Church presidents have served longer, traveled farther, presided over greater growth, built more buildings, defined more doctrines, and instituted more sweeping changes in organization and policy.

Perhaps most important, he adjusted the relationship between Church and member. For a full century, since Brigham Young announced to the world that the rumored practice of plural marriage was more than rumor, Church members had been asked to sacrifice themselves for the good of the institution. McKay reversed that, asserting that the Church was made for the members, not the members for the Church. He emphasized the paramount importance of free agency and individual expression, for he understood that improvement of the parts would inevitably improve the whole. "Let them conform" was replaced by "Let them grow." He willingly discarded institutional uniformity for the higher goal of individual excellence. He pitched a big tent and then told members of all stripes that he welcomed them to join him and build the Church within it. Walter Reuther, the great American labor leader, perhaps summed it up best when, following a meeting with McKay, he remarked to a colleague, "I doubt that another generation will produce a character like that."

—*Gregory A. Prince*

See also: Mormon Missiology; Mormonism and Education; Temples.

References

Gibbons, Francis M. *David O. McKay: Apostle to the World, Prophet of God.* Salt Lake City, UT: Deseret Book, 1986.

McKay, David Lawrence. *My Father, David O. McKay.* Salt Lake City, UT: Deseret Book, 1989.

Prince, Gregory A., and Wm. Robert Wright. *David O. McKay and the Rise of Modern Mormonism.* Salt Lake City: University of Utah Press, 2005.

Monson, Thomas S.

In 2010, Thomas Spencer Monson (1927–) serves the LDS Church as its 16th president, having been ordained to office on February 3, 2008. He is known among

LDS faithful for his testimony, his compassion and understanding, especially toward the poor, widowed, and elderly, and his ecumenical outreach. His sermons and writings often feature accounts highlighting the needs of the Church's disfranchised members, particularly those suffering and grieving. The non-LDS Church-owned *Salt Lake Tribune* once described him as "maybe the most sought-after Church authority for funeral orations" (Rolly, "President Monson" 2B). His approach to management exhibits a pragmatism informed by cautious intellect.

Monson was born on August 21, 1927, in Salt Lake City, Utah, to G. Spencer and Gladys (Condie) Monson. He attended local public schools and joined the U.S. Navy (Reserves) during the closing months of World War II; he did not see combat. In 1948, he graduated cum laude from the University of Utah in business management; later that year, on October 7, he married Frances Beverly Johnson (born October 27, 1927) in the Salt Lake temple. (They raised two sons and one daughter.) Also in 1948, he joined the LDS-owned *Deseret News,* where he was an advertising executive. He later became sales manager of the Deseret News Press and eventually was appointed its general manager. He subsequently chaired the board of directors of Deseret News Publishing Company for 19 years, presided over the Printing Industry of Utah, and served on the board of Printing Industry of America. He also, for a brief time, taught business classes at the University of Utah and later earned an MBA degree from the LDS Church–owned Brigham Young University, in Provo, Utah. In his leisure time during much of his adult life, he raised Birmingham Roller pigeons. He was diagnosed in his 60s with Type II diabetes.

In 1950, at age 22, Monson was called as bishop of the Church's Sixth-Seventh Ward, composed of some 1,080 members, on the southwestern edge of downtown Salt Lake City. "Why I was called as bishop, I can't tell you," he later quipped. "Only the Lord would know that" (Avant, "On Lord's Errand" 4). Five years later, he was called to the presidency of the area's Temple View Stake. From 1959 to 1962, he presided over the Church's Canadian Mission (based in Toronto). The following year, on October 4, 1963, at age 36, he was sustained as a member of the Church's Quorum of the Twelve Apostles and was ordained an apostle on October 10. He was the Church's youngest apostle since 1910. He later chaired the Church's Scriptures Publications Committee, which resulted, beginning in 1981, in new editions of the Church's four Standard Works: Bible, Book of Mormon, Doctrine and Covenants, and Pearl of Great Price.

On November 10, 1985, Monson was called to the Church's governing First Presidency as Second Counselor to Church president Ezra Taft Benson. At 58, he was the youngest member of a First Presidency since 1901. In 2008, following service in two additional First Presidencies, Monson succeeded to the presidency himself. From Monson's birth to his appointment as Church president, LDS membership worldwide grew from some 650,000 to more than 13 million.

In 1968, Monson was assigned to help supervise LDS affairs in Europe and took special interest in the lives of Church members residing in the German Democratic

Republic, or East Germany, where government policies restricted religious expression. On his first visit there, a U.S. official informed him: "If anything happens, we can't get you out" (Avant, "On Lord's Errand" 4). Monson continued to oversee Church interests in East Germany and other Soviet-allied countries, dedicated East Germany for LDS proselytizing activities in 1975, was instrumental in helping to secure official permission from the East German government to build an LDS temple in Freiberg (1982–1985), and, in 1988, helped to secure the entrance into East Germany of LDS proselytizing missionaries. Monson viewed these latter two events as high points in his Church ministry.

In his rhetoric, Monson displays an affable directness that both comforts and admonishes. "If only all children had loving parents, safe homes, and caring friends, what a wonderful world would be theirs," he once lamented. "Unfortunately, all children are not so bounteously blessed. Some children witness their fathers savagely beating their mothers, while others are on the receiving end of such abuse. What cowardice, what depravity, what shame!" (Bergera, *Statements* 59). "God left the world unfinished for man to work his skill upon," he also observed. "God gives to man the challenge of raw materials, not the ease of finished things. He leaves the pictures unpainted and the music unsung and the problems unsolved, that man might know the joys and glories of creation" (Bergera, 2007, 107).

—Gary James Bergera

See also: Expansion: 1941–Present; Mormon Scripture.

References

Avant, Gerry. "On Lord's Errand since His Boyhood." *Church News* (February 9, 2008): 4–5.

Bergera, Gary James, ed. *Statements of the LDS First Presidency: A Topical Compendium.* Salt Lake City, UT: Signature Books, 2007.

Kuehne, Raymond M. "The Freiberg Temple: An Unexpected Legacy of a Communist State and a Faithful People." *Dialogue: A Journal of Mormon Thought* 37 (Summer 2004): 95–131.

Kuehne, Raymond M. "How Missionaries Entered East Germany: The 1988 Monson-Honecker Meeting." *Dialogue: A Journal of Mormon Thought* 39 (Winter 2006): 107–137.

Rolly, Paul. "President Monson Has Always Been Underdog's Friend." *Salt Lake Tribune.* November 17, 1985, 2B.

Nibley, Hugh

Hugh Nibley (1910–2005) was a historian, philologist, Church apologist, and social critic. He was widely known for his articles and books setting the Book of Mormon, Book of Abraham, and LDS temple rituals in an ancient Middle Eastern milieu. He was also an apologist, responding to critics of LDS history, doctrines, and beliefs. Finally, he was a vocal critic of Mormon cultural practices.

Nibley was born March 27, 1910, in Portland, Oregon, to Alexander and Agnes Sloan Nibley. His grandfather, Charles W. Nibley, the Presiding Bishop and member of the First Presidency of the LDS Church, was a wealthy businessman. Nibley's father oversaw his grandfather's sugar company and, later, his real estate business. Nibley spent his early years in Portland and in Medford, Oregon, surrounded by the giant redwood forests and gaining a deep love for nature. Tragically, his grandfather's logging company was instrumental in the great forests' destruction, which Nibley watched, even at an early age, with despair.

In 1921, Nibley's family moved to Los Angeles, where he attended public schools. After high school graduation, he served in the Swiss-German mission. He then attended UCLA, graduating summa cum laude in 1934. In 1938, Nibley received his PhD in history from Berkeley. His dissertation was entitled "The Roman Games as a Survival of an Archaic Year Cult." From 1939 to 1941, Nibley taught at the Claremont consortium of colleges.

In 1941, Nibley enlisted in the U.S. Army, serving in the European theater of World War II. As a member of an Order of Battle Military Intelligence team, he was attached to the 101st Airborne division throughout most of the war. He landed on Utah Beach on D-Day, flew in a glider into Holland during Operation Market Garden, and was at Mourmelon-le-Grand prior to the German offensive at Bastogne. He had a unique position from which to view the war. As a member of an OB Team, responsible for knowing the strength and position of the German army, he had a broad view of the war, but his position with the 101st Airborne division gave him the foot soldier's view. His experiences affected his pessimistic view of war and led to his later protests against the Vietnam War and the Gulf War.

In 1946, Nibley married Phyllis Anne Hawkes Draper and began teaching at the LDS Church–owned Brigham Young University, teaching classes in history, languages, and religion. Nibley established himself as an apologist for the LDS Church when he responded to Fawn Brodie's psychosocial biography of Joseph Smith, *No Man Knows My History,* with his sardonic *No Ma'am, That's Not History* (1946). His book *Myth Makers* (1961) was a defense against criticism of Joseph Smith, and his book *Sounding Brass* (1963) responded to Irving Wallace's *Twenty-Seventh Wife.*

Additionally, he became well known for his almost monthly articles, which appeared for more than three decades in the Church magazines the *Improvement Era* and the *Ensign.* In these articles, he argued for the truth claims of the Book of Mormon and other Mormon scripture by comparing them with historical works of the ancient Middle East. From these articles came the books *Lehi in the Desert and the World of the Jaredites* (1952) and *Since Cumorah* (1967). His *An Approach to the Book of Mormon* was used as a Church manual in 1957. His extensive knowledge of languages allowed him to work with many different texts, often crossing disciplines. His knowledge and characteristic wit made him a popular speaker throughout the intermountain West.

With the discovery of the Joseph Smith Papyri, in 1966, Nibley began a campaign to respond to critics who noted that the papyri contained an ancient Egyptian funerary text, rather than the text of the Book of Abraham, which Joseph Smith claimed to translate from the papyri. Nibley focused on the English text of the Book of Abraham, again comparing it to other ancient texts to argue for its authenticity regardless of its method of transmission.

In the late 1960s, Nibley began to speak out on social issues, against the Vietnam War, for environmental stewardship, and against materialism and greed. His speeches and writings were a stark contrast to the right-ward shift of Mormon culture during this period. With his commitment to the LDS Church well established by his apologetic work, his social criticism sparked debate but never earned him censure.

Nibley officially retired from BYU in 1975 but continued to teach, publish, and give lectures until 1994. He continued writing into his early 90s. Nibley died on February 24, 2005, a month short of his 95th birthday.

—*Boyd Jay Petersen*

See also: Book of Mormon; Mormon Scripture; Mormonism and Education; Mormonism and Science.

References

Nibley, Hugh W. "An Intellectual Autobiography." *Nibley on the Timely and the Timeless,* xix–xxvii. Provo, UT: Brigham Young University Press, 1978.

Nibley, Hugh, and Alex Nibley. *Sergeant Nibley, Ph.D.: Memories of an Unlikely Screaming Eagle* Salt Lake City, UT: Shadow Mountain, 2006.

Petersen, Boyd Jay. *Hugh Nibley: A Consecrated Life.* Salt Lake City, UT: Kofford Books, 2002.

Parmley, LaVern Watts

LaVern Watts Parmley, born on January 1, 1900, worked with children throughout her life, beginning with directing her eight brothers and two sisters in family work projects and continuing with her career as a schoolteacher immediately after her graduation from high school. She was particularly drawn to boys and considered herself a leader of boys. As general president of the Primary Association (the Church's program for children ages 3–11) from 1951 through 1974, Parmley guided the organization through its period of greatest growth and adaptation.

Earlier in the century, and after a protracted struggle between auxiliaries, responsibility for 12- and 13-year-old boys and girls had been transferred from the Primary to the Young Men's and Young Ladies' Mutual Improvement Associations, largely to meet the needs of the Boy Scout program. Scouting posed another challenge to the Primary as Parmley's tenure began by inviting 11-year-old boys to become Scouts. The unparalleled popularity of the Cub Scouting program also tended to draw LDS boys away from Primary into Cub packs sponsored by other Churches.

Parmley won a concession from the national Boy Scout committee to allow women, who made up the vast majority of Primary teachers, to serve as Scout leaders for the 11-year-old boys. She also spearheaded the integration of Scouting principles into the boys' Primary lessons, preparing the boys to become not only deacons but also Second Class Scouts upon graduation from Primary. The Cub Scout program was not incorporated into weekly Primary activities but was adopted as a separate organization within LDS wards, supervised by Primary leadership.

Parmley was invited, in 1967, to serve as a member of the Boy Scout Religious Relations Committee, the first woman ever appointed to serve on a national Scouting committee. She also won the Silver Beaver, Silver Antelope, and Silver Buffalo awards, among other honors, for her service to Scouting.

Church membership, and consequently Primary enrollment, increased dramatically during the 1950s and 1960s, and Parmley pioneered methods of adapting Primary to an international Church, rewriting lessons and choosing new class names that were less tied to traditional western Mormon history and more universally suited to the varied cultures of the world. Her board created new programs—including Lamanite (Indian) Primaries and Primaries for the mentally and physically handicapped—to serve children who had been overlooked in earlier days.

Another concern for the Primary during those years was teacher training and annual conferences that would serve workers who might be lifelong Church members from the western United States or new converts from the far corners of the world. Parmley also superintended the creation of a number of teacher training manuals with an emphasis on teaching children. She oversaw publication of *The Children's Friend* through 1970, when she assisted with transition to the new children's magazine, *The Friend*.

Seeking a song to embody the purposes of Primary, in 1957 Parmley requested

Primary children saved their pennies to build and operate Primary Children's Hospital, one of the world's foremost charitable pediatric medical centers. (Courtesy of the Church History Library, The Church of Jesus Christ of Latter-day Saints.).

that Naomi W. Randall, working with musician Mildred T. Pettit, compose such a theme. The result is now a beloved Mormon hymn, "I Am a Child of God."

As president of the Primary, Parmley also served as the chair of the board of trustees of the Primary Children's Hospital, whose new building was completed under her supervision. One of her chief tasks in that regard was to raise the funds to allow charity treatment for any child of any origin who needed care. Primary children continued to give their birthday pennies to the hospital fund, and Parmley instituted an annual Penny Drive to raise larger sums.

LaVern Watts Parmley passed away in Salt Lake City in 1980.

—*Ardis E. Parshall*

See also: Church Organization and Government; Mormonism and Women; Rogers, Aurelia Spencer; Youth Programs.

References

Madsen, Carol Cornwall, and Susan Staker Oman. *Sisters and Little Saints: One Hundred Years of Primary.* Salt Lake City, UT: Deseret Book, 1979.

Peterson, Janet, and LaRene Gaunt. *The Children's Friends: Primary Presidents and Their Lives of Service.* Salt Lake City, UT: Deseret Book, 1996.

Pratt, Orson and Parley P.

Brothers Parley Parker Pratt (1807–1857) and Orson Pratt (1811–1881) profoundly shaped early Mormon history through their leadership as apostles and their prolific writings elaborating and defending Latter-day Saint theology. Parley and Orson were the third and fourth of five sons born to Jared and Charity Pratt, farmers who moved several times around eastern New York (Parley was born in Burlington and Orson in Hartford) in search of economic opportunity. They found primarily debt and disappointment. As teenagers, the Pratt sons boarded with more prosperous local farmers; Orson never lived at home after age 11. Though they received little formal education, both brothers were intellectually curious and pursued self-education. Devout Christians, Jared and Charity kept a distance from traditional denominations and encouraged religious seeking.

In the late 1820s, Jared Parley moved to Ohio and became associated with Sidney Rigdon and the Campbellites, a religious movement that emphasized the restoration of the purity and practices of the New Testament Church. An encounter with the Book of Mormon in 1830 converted Parley to Mormonism, and he soon baptized Orson. That fall, a revelation to Joseph Smith directed Parley and three others to travel from New York to Missouri and preach to the Native Americans. Along the way, Parley stopped in Kirtland, Ohio, and taught Rigdon, who became a prominent Mormon leader, and many members of his congregation also converted. Their conversions transformed Kirtland into a center of early Mormonism; soon after,

Smith and the other New York Mormons moved there. During the 1830s, Parley and Orson served numerous missions in the eastern and midwestern United States. In 1835, Smith called both as members of the newly formed Quorum of the Twelve Apostles, a position they served in for the remainder of their lives.

As apostles, both Pratts played key roles in the expansion and internationalization of early Mormonism. On a mission to Canada in 1836, Parley taught a Methodist lay preacher named John Taylor, who became the Church's third president. Both participated in the critical mission of the apostles to England in 1840–1841, when thousands joined Mormonism and immigrated to the United States. Orson returned several times to supervise missionary work in the British Isles (1848–1851, 1856–1857, 1864–1867, and 1877). In the 1850s, Parley's two missions to gold rush California and a mission to Chile (the first Mormon mission in Latin America) helped orient the Church toward the Pacific Rim and Latin America. Their constant missions left both brothers and their families in a state of almost perpetual poverty (http://www.ldschurchnews.com/articles/51946/Who-was-Parley-P-Pratt.html).

Upon his return from his first English mission, Orson became disaffected from Smith over the practice of plural marriage in Nauvoo, Illinois, in 1842, and the dispute led to his excommunication. Orson soon reconciled with Smith, who declared his excommunication illegal and directed him to be rebaptized and reinstated as an apostle. Both Pratts came to view polygamy as a religious duty and became leading defenders of the system. In 1852, Brigham Young assigned Orson to publicly announce the doctrine for the first time. Orson subsequently published *The Seer,* a Washington, D.C., newspaper, which offered the nation the first sustained defense of polygamy in 1853–1854. In 1870, Orson famously engaged in a three-day long debate in Salt Lake City with John Philip Newman, a prominent eastern minister, over whether the Bible sanctioned polygamy. In their personal lives, Parley and Orson embraced plural marriage. Parley married 12 wives and fathered 30 children; Orson married 10 women and had 45 children. Their descendants number in the tens of thousands.

The Pratt brothers helped lead the trek to Utah in 1847 and contributed to the subsequent colonization of the intermountain West. Orson traveled with the first company of pioneers, keeping meticulous topographical and scientific records for later companies. On July 21, 1847, Orson (along with a companion) became the first Mormon to enter the Salt Lake Valley. By the time, three days later, that Young pronounced the Valley the "right place," Orson had already dedicated it as a city for the Saints and planted the first field. Parley arrived at the head of a large group of pioneers later that fall. Orson assisted in the surveying of the Salt Lake Valley and later served several terms as speaker of the territorial assembly. In 1849–1850, Parley led a 50-man group to explore and assess the resources of southern Utah, which led to Mormon colonization of that area.

The Pratts exerted a profound influence on Mormon thought through their preaching and writing. Together, they preached thousands of sermons, produced dozens of pamphlets, wrote several books, and edited numerous newspapers. Parley's early

writings established the standards for Mormon apologetics and shaped a generation of writers, including Orson. A romantic, Parley wrote not only doctrinal texts
but also poetry, hymns, and fiction. Orson, meanwhile, was a precise and rigorous
logician and a systematizer of Mormon theology who also wrote scientific and
mathematical texts.

Parley's *Voice of Warning* (1837), a missionary pamphlet, became one of the
most widely read Mormon writings over the next half-century. Following the Mormon expulsion from Missouri in 1838–1839 (during which Parley spent eight months
in jail before Orson helped him escape), Parley shaped Mormon memory and reinforced an early collective identity forged in persecution in his *History of the Late
Persecutions* (1839). In 1840, Parley served as the founding editor of the *Latter-
day Saints' Millennial Star,* the Church's influential British periodical (which Orson
also edited on several occasions). In *Key to the Science of Theology* (1855), Parley
produced Mormonism's first comprehensive theological treatise. His *Autobiography* (1874) remains a classic in Mormon literature.

Orson's first pamphlet, *Interesting Account of Several Remarkable Visions*
(1840), contained the first published account of Joseph Smith's First Vision. During
his later mission to England in 1848–1851, Orson produced a series of 16 pamphlets,
which introduced Mormon doctrines to thousands. His writings demonstrated his
deep interest in mathematics and science. A frequent lecturer on astronomy and
mathematics at the University of Nauvoo and the University of Utah and before
large Mormon meetings, Orson also constructed an astronomical observatory at
Temple Square in Salt Lake City. In his writings, Orson integrated Mormon theology with 19th-century science and philosophy. He particularly emphasized the
notion—taught by Smith and Parley—of the essential materialism of God and spirit
in works such as *Absurdities of Immaterialism* (1849), *Great First Cause* (1851),
and *Key to the Universe* (1877).

Partly as a result of his writings, Orson clashed over doctrinal issues repeatedly
with Brigham Young, who was suspicious of his philosophical tendencies and forced
him to recant some of his teachings. Orson disagreed with several of Young's doctrinal assertions, though he recognized his ecclesiastical authority. (Later Church leaders sustained Orson's views on some of the disputed issues and Young's on others.)
In 1876, Young reshuffled the order of seniority within the Quorum of the Twelve
Apostles to take into account Pratt's 1842 disaffection. As a result, Orson did not
succeed to the Church presidency.

In 1857, while on a mission to the eastern United States, Parley was murdered in
Arkansas by Hector McLean, the estranged husband of Parley's final plural wife,
Eleanor McComb. While the national press celebrated Parley's assassination, the
Mormons mourned him as a martyr. Orson continued his writings and administra-
tive work until his death, in 1881.

—*Matthew J. Grow*

See also: Mormon Missiology; Mormonism and Science.

References

England, Breck. *The Life and Thought of Orson Pratt.* Salt Lake City: University of Utah Press, 1985.

Pratt, Parley Parker. *Autobiography of Parley Parker Pratt.* New York: Russell Brothers, 1874.

Rigdon, Sidney

Born February 19, 1793, near Pittsburgh, Pennsylvania, to a farming family, Sidney Rigdon (1793–1876) became a Baptist minister and a powerful public orator. Working in Pennsylvania and Ohio, Rigdon was acquainted with Alexander Campbell, founder of the Disciples of Christ, and other ministers who were advocating a return to primitive Christianity, especially in the practice of spiritual gifts, and associated with them for a time in the Mahoning Baptist Association.

In 1830, Rigdon hosted an old friend, Parley P. Pratt, as Pratt crossed Ohio on a mission to the West. Pratt gave Rigdon a Book of Mormon, which Rigdon read. He and members of his congregation were soon baptized and formed a branch of the Church in Mentor, Ohio. A month after his conversion, Rigdon met Joseph Smith for the first time; from that point until Smith's death, Rigdon was one of the Prophet's closest friends and supporters.

Rigdon accompanied Smith on missionary journeys, assisted in Smith's revision of the Bible, and, in 1833, was ordained as a counselor to Smith in the First Presidency. He took charge of the Church in Kirtland in 1834 during Smith's absence with Zion's Camp; he helped to arrange the written revelations that became the basis of the Doctrine and Covenants; he preached at the dedication of the Kirtland temple. During the Missouri period, Rigdon's strongly worded denunciation of the Church's enemies provoked renewed persecution, and Rigdon was imprisoned with Smith in the Liberty Jail for three months during the winter of 1838–1839. He aided in building the city of Nauvoo and accompanied Smith on a visit to Washington, D.C., to petition the government for protection. Following accusations that Rigdon was involved in intrigue with Smith's enemies in Nauvoo, Smith dropped Rigdon as a counselor; Rigdon retained his office when Hyrum Smith convinced the Prophet that Rigdon was loyal. When Smith was nominated by the Saints as a presidential candidate, Rigdon was nominated as his vice president; he was in Pittsburgh promoting that candidacy when Smith was murdered.

Immediately following Smith's murder, Rigdon returned to Nauvoo. He proposed that he be named "guardian of the Church," a position for which there was no scriptural or organizational precedent. Rigdon's claim to leadership was based on his being the sole remaining member of the First Presidency. His proposal, along with those of other claimants, was presented to a Church assembly on August 8, 1844; minutes of the meeting record a unanimous rejection of Rigdon in favor of Brigham Young.

Refusing to accept the decision of the Church, Rigdon attempted to gather disciples to form his own Church. He was excommunicated in September 1844 and continued his Church-building efforts in Pennsylvania and, later, in New York, where he associated with an organization called the Children of Zion. He died July 14, 1876, in Friendship, New York. His obituary indicated that

> He has often been interviewed by those intent upon clearing up some of the mysteries and delusions that attended the origin of Mormonism, but invariably without success. On these occasions he would defend the Mormon account of the origin [of] the Book of Mormon, and also the chief doctrines of the early Mormon church, and in many ways exhibit sympathetic interest in its prosperity. . . . In his prime he took an active part in the theological controversies that raged so fiercely . . . yet for many years past he held himself aloof from the church affairs in this vicinity . . . his religious ambitions were buried at the time he was superseded by Young.

Rigdon's name has long been associated with the so-called Spaulding Manuscript, proposed by Doctor Philastus Hurlbut and Eber D. Howe as early as 1834 as the source for the text of the Book of Mormon. About 1812, Solomon Spaulding, a former minister, had written a romance about early inhabitants of the American continent, whose history he said he had discovered written on scrolls buried in a stone box in Ohio. Because of such superficial resemblances to the claimed origins of the Book of Mormon and Rigdon's residence in Spaulding's neighborhood, Hurlbut and Howe claimed that Rigdon had stolen the manuscript and delivered it to Smith, who modified it slightly for publication as the Book of Mormon. The Spaulding manuscript was discovered among Howe's papers in 1884; its publication, bearing not the slightest resemblance to the narrative, style, or religious import of the Book of Mormon, erased the last serious support for the theory that Spaulding—or Rigdon—was the source of the Book of Mormon text.

—Ardis E. Parshall

See also: Book of Mormon; Church Organization and Government; Divergent Churches; Martyrdom of Joseph and Hyrum Smith.

Reference

Van Wagoner, Richard S. *Sidney Rigdon: A Portrait of Religious Excess.* Salt Lake City, UT: Signature Books, 1994.

Roberts, B.H.

Brigham Henry (B. H.) Roberts (1857–1933) was an important late-19th-/early-20th-century LDS historian and theologian. He was born on March 13, 1857, in Warrington, Lancashire County, England, to Benjamin Roberts and Ann Everington Roberts. (Though he was christened Henry, his mother later added Brigham in honor of LDS Church president Brigham Young.) When Ann Roberts immigrated with two younger children to Utah, Roberts, age five, and an older sister remained behind. Four years later, Roberts and his sister secured transport to the United States. According to Roberts, he walked much of the way across the Great Plains to Utah Territory, where he joined his mother in Bountiful, north of Salt Lake City. Roberts's childhood and adolescence continued along a hardscrabble path until he began attending special area-wide classes for young men (the classes were forerunners of the Church's Mutual Improvement Association). He subsequently graduated from high school and from the University of Deseret.

At first employed as a schoolteacher, Roberts married Sarah Louisa Smith in 1878 (fathering seven children) and in 1880 was called as an LDS proselytizing missionary to the Northern States Mission. The next year, he was transferred to the Southern States Mission, serving in Tennessee. In 1883, he returned to Utah, where he herded sheep and taught school. He returned to the Southern States Mission in 1884 as assistant mission president but for much of the time functioned as acting mission president. He helped to retrieve and return to Utah the bodies of the two missionaries murdered in the anti-Mormon Cane Creek Massacre (August 1884). He returned briefly to Utah and married Celia Ann Dibble in October 1884 as his first plural wife (fathering eight children with her).

In response to some financial setbacks, Roberts returned again to Utah in 1886 and for much of the remainder of the year edited the *Salt Lake Herald.* He was arrested for polygamy (unlawful cohabitation), and, while free on bond, accepted a missionary call to England, where he worked much of the time in the office of the LDS Church's official British publication, *The Latter-day Saints' Millennial Star,* until 1888, when he was released and returned to Utah. From late 1888 to late 1889, he edited the Church's *Contributor* magazine while continuing to evade arrest for polygamy. At age 31, he was sustained as one of the First Seven Presidents of the Seventy on October 7, 1888, and was set apart as one of the Church's general authorities by apostle Lorenzo Snow. He surrendered to federal law officials in 1889, was convicted, fined $400, and served several months in the Utah territorial penitentiary. He married Margaret Curtis Shipp in 1891 (several months after the Church's 1890 Manifesto ostensibly prohibited new plural marriages) but fathered no children with her.

Roberts was an active participant in partisan politics and an outspoken advocate of the Democratic Party. In 1893, he was not allowed to attend the dedication of the

Salt Lake City temple until he admitted his error in too vocally championing Democratic candidates; in 1896, he was nearly dropped from his Church office for some unauthorized political activities. His independence of speech and action would continue periodically to test the patience of his Church file leaders. He served as a delegate to the Utah constitutional convention in 1895 and strongly argued against including female suffrage in the state constitution (he was unsuccessful). He was a candidate for U.S. Congress in 1895 but was defeated. He ran again in 1898 and won but subsequently was denied a seat because of his practice of polygamy, which was judged to render him unfit for office. A member of Utah's National Guard unit, he was the first LDS chaplain, as well as one of the oldest U.S. chaplains generally, to serve in World War I (though he did not see any fighting).

Roberts is best remembered as an articulate defender of LDS belief and practice; he was a prolific self-taught theologian and historian. Among his publications are a biography of LDS Church president John Taylor (1892), narrative histories of the LDS Church in Missouri and Illinois (both 1900), and the multivolume *Comprehensive History of the Church* (1909–1915, 1930). He was appointed Assistant LDS Church Historian in 1902 and re-edited for publication Joseph Smith's *History of the Church* in six volumes (1902–1912), as well as an additional volume on Brigham Young (1932). His book-length apologetic works include *The Gospel* (1888, 1893), *Succession in the Presidency* (1894), *New Witness for God* (1895, 1903), *The Mormon Doctrine of Deity* (1903), *Defense of the Faith and the Saints* (1907–1912), and *The Truth, The Way, The Life* (written 1927–1928), which he considered his masterpiece but which, because of some controversial content regarding evolution and pre-existing spirit-intelligences, was published posthumously more than 60 years after his death.

Roberts's commitment both to Mormonism and to intellectual inquiry and freedom of thought is best evidenced in his studies (written 1921–1923) of the ancient historicity of the Book of Mormon. He argued that the Book of Mormon (1830), which the LDS Church treats as official scripture and as a factual history of some of the aboriginal inhabitants of the Americas, could have been written entirely by someone of Church founder Joseph Smith's intellectual prowess and creativity. Roberts believed that the foundational faith claims of the LDS Church were convincing enough to withstand the most critical, probing scrutiny. Whether Roberts himself doubted the Book of Mormon's historical assertions remains open to question. His thought-provoking studies were first published in 1985.

From 1922 to 1927, Roberts served as president of the Church's Eastern States Mission. He died of complications from diabetes in Salt Lake City on September 27, 1933. In surveys conducted decades after his death, Roberts was twice voted the most influential intellectual in LDS Church history. For Roberts, any attempt to "comprehend the things of God" required "striving—intellectual and spiritual." One's goal in life, he insisted, should be the acquisition of "intellectual faith," namely "the faith that is the gift of God, supplemented by earnest endeavor to find through prayerful thought and research a rational ground for faith—for acceptance of truth . . . in which the intellect as well as the heart—the feeling—has a place and is a factor" (Madsen, *The Essential B. H. Roberts* 260–261).

—*Gary James Bergera*

See also: Mormon Missiology; Mormonism and Science; Mormonism and Secular Government.

References

Bergera, Gary James, ed. *The Autobiography of B. H. Roberts.* Salt Lake City, UT: Signature Books, 1990.

Larson, Stan, ed. *The Truth, the Way, the Life: An Elementary Treatise on Theology: The Masterwork of B. H. Roberts.* San Francisco, CA: Smith Research Associates, 1994.

Madsen, Brigham D., ed. *The Essential B. H. Roberts.* Salt Lake City, UT: Signature Books, 1999.

Sillito, John, ed. *History's Apprentice: The Diaries of B. H. Roberts, 1880–1898.* Salt Lake City, UT: Signature Books/Smith Research Associates, 2004.

Rogers, Aurelia Spencer

Aurelia Read Spencer Rogers (1834–1922) created the first Primary Association in the Church, an organization focused upon meeting the spiritual needs of children. She was born October 4, 1834, at Deep River, Connecticut. Her father, Orson Spencer, was a Baptist minister who, after his 1840 conversion to Mormonism, became an influential missionary and the author of early and important missionary tracts.

The Spencer family evacuated from Nauvoo in February 1846, when Aurelia was 11. Her mother died only 30 miles from Nauvoo; when the family reached Winter Quarters, Nebraska, her father left his children in the care of other refugees while he went to preside over the British Mission. Aurelia, by then 12 years old, and her sister Ellen, just one year older, cared for four younger siblings with little supervision and assistance; they immigrated to Utah in 1848 with the Brigham Young Company. At the age of 17, Aurelia married Thomas Rogers, a man with whom she had become acquainted on the overland trek.

Her early devotion to children typified Rogers's life. Mother of 12 children (7 of whom lived past infancy), Rogers became a schoolteacher. The Rogers family was living in Farmington, Utah, in 1878, when Rogers grew concerned over the number of young boys who were growing up without adequate education and employment and especially without training in the gospel and genteel refinements. "Many of them were allowed to be out late at night; and certainly some of the larger ones well deserved the undesirable name of 'hoodlum'" (Rogers, 1898, 205–206). Discussing the situation with Eliza R. Snow, Rogers asked "What will our girls do for good husbands, if this state of things continues? Could there not be an organization for little boys, and have them trained to make better men?" (Rogers, *Life Sketches* 208). Snow conveyed Rogers's concerns to John Taylor, who asked Rogers to devise a program to assist parents in training their sons.

Rogers organized the first Primary Association of the Church in August 1878. She included little girls as well as boys, to mellow the boys' singing and to exercise a gentling influence on the boys. "Obedience, faith in God, prayer, punctuality and good manners were subjects oft repeated; and we always endeavored to impress the children with the fact that home is the place to begin to practice all good things" (Rogers, *Life Sketches* 215–216). Within 10 years, most wards had Primary organizations that met weekly and emphasized singing, poetry, and short lessons. Each ward's Primary leaders devised their own curriculum and traditions, with little input from the organization's general officers.

As part of the Primary work in Farmington, Rogers encouraged the establishment of Children's Fairs, at which Primary children displayed their crafts and the produce of their lessons in farmwork and housework. In 1882, she organized a Primary Martial Band. After having learned simple tunes on their flutes, drums, and triangles, the boys began holding small parades and serenading residents; coins contributed by their listeners paid for more music lessons. Another year, she rented a town lot on which the children raised beans and corn.

Primary became more formalized by the turn of the century, under the leadership of Primary general president Louie B. Felt and her successors. Lessons suitable to different ages were outlined and published in the *Children's Friend,* a magazine that debuted in 1902 and remained in publication until 1970, when it was replaced with the current *Friend.* Reflecting the social work concerns of the era, the Primary established a pediatric ward in Salt Lake City's LDS Hospital.

Rogers's activities were not limited to the care of children. She served as secretary in her ward's Relief Society for 22 years. Along with the other home-manufacturing duties thrust upon women by life on the frontier, she became an expert seamstress; she was still sewing her own clothes at the age of 80, proud of her ability to sew without the necessity of using eyeglasses. She participated in the women's movement of her generation, serving as a delegate to the Woman's Suffrage convention held at Atlanta, Georgia, and as a delegate to the National Council of Women held at Washington, D.C., both in 1895. While in Georgia, Rogers spoke at a Unitarian meeting and answered many questions about Utah and Mormonism; she gave the invocation at one session of the Washington council.

In 1898, Rogers published *Life Sketches of Orson Spencer and Others, and History of Primary Work.* The "others" included Rogers herself, as well as numerous relatives and prominent Mormons. Unknown to Rogers beforehand, Primaries throughout the Church held entertainments on August 11, 1897, the anniversary of the first Primary meeting, to raise funds for the publication of her book.

She died August 19, 1922, in Farmington.

—Ardis E. Parshall

See also: Church Organization and Government; Mormonism and Women; Parmley, La-Vern Watts; Youth Programs.

References

Ashton, Wendell J. *Aurelia Spencer Rogers, Primary Mother.* Salt Lake City, UT: Bookcraft, 1945.

Rogers, Aurelia Spencer. *Life Sketches of Orson Spencer and Others, and History of Primary Work.* Salt Lake City, UT: Geo. Q. Cannon, 1898.

Sessions, Patty Bartlett

Patty Sessions (1795–1892) was born on February 4, 1795, in Bethel, Maine, and she died 97 years later in Utah Territory. While many events in Sessions's life were particularly fantastic, the bulk of what made the period that spanned these two events remarkable was Sessions's quotidian devotion to her faith, family, and finances. In many ways, she represents the unsung 19th-century Mormon woman.

Patty was raised in the primitive countryside, and married David Sessions at age 17. Moving 10 miles away, the young couple lived with David Sessions's parents. David's mother was a local midwife who suffered with rheumatism, and Patty quickly became the primary homemaker. In one instance, when her mother-in-law was unable to attend to an emergency delivery, Patty stepped in, untrained, and saw to the birth of a healthy baby. With the encouragement of a local medical professional, Patty studied and practiced midwifery for the balance of her life, delivering a reported 3,997 babies. Much to her own anguish, however, only three of her seven children were living when she converted to Mormonism.

Patty, a devout Methodist, joined the fledgling Mormon Church in 1834. Leaving the community of their relatives, the Sessionses moved to Missouri in 1837 to gather with the body of the Church, a pilgrimage marred by sickness. They were forced to leave the state under order of extermination soon thereafter, and the formerly prosperous family was financially devastated. After relocating to Nauvoo, Patty became part of a trusted inner circle within the Church and was privy to Joseph Smith's controversial and secret teachings. She even became, with her daughter, one of Smith's polyandrous wives. At age 47, Sessions was much older than Smith, and apparently she was "sealed" to him for ceremonial or dynastic reasons. When her own husband became a polygamist in Nauvoo and again in the Great Basin, she felt deeply dejected but ultimately affirmed the principle.

Despite the challenges associated with living her religion, Patty was committed to Mormonism and was known as a woman of great faith and power. As was common from the late 1830s through to the early 20th century, Patty actively participated in female ritual healing and in expressions of charismatic "gifts of the spirit" (e.g., glossolalia, prophecy). Her diary is illustrative of the chimeric blend of the transcendent and the banal that typified Sessions's life. For example, while in the Omaha Nation, on May 19, 1847, she recorded simply, "visited the sick then put Jedidiah Grants wife to bed then went to sister Levets to meeting 18 sisters met we spoke in toungues interpreted and had a good time" (Smart, 1997, 81).

Sessions served in the Nauvoo temple, administering washings and anointings before the Church left for the Great Basin. She eventually drove her own team to the Salt Lake settlement less than two months after the vanguard company of 1847. Her husband, David, died in 1850, and she married John Parry (1789–1868) in 1851. Parry also became a polygamist, and, as was frequently the case in polygamous relationships, Patty was required to support herself. This level of independence forced Sessions to develop keen business acumen, and she was successful in a variety of affairs. Working as a midwife, Sessions also cultivated gardens and orchards and invested in various local ventures, including the Zion's Cooperative Mercantile Institution (ZCMI). By 1883, she owned stock valued at $16,000, a significant sum for that period.

When Willard Richards, a practicing Thomsonian physician, established the Council of Health, in 1848, Patty Sessions was a charter member and became the most well-known midwife of the period. Having actively participated in the Nauvoo Relief Society, Sessions continued with the organization in Utah, even being elected, in 1854, as the president of the "Indian Relief Societies," an organization to help impoverished Native Americans and an important interim organization before the Relief Society was formally reestablished.

Sessions lived the final three decades of her life as a widow. She eventually moved to Bountiful and used her house as a hotel. In 1883, she established the Patty Sessions Academy as a free school for the community. Through the second half of that decade, Sessions suffered from tremors and deafness and ultimately passed away peacefully at 4:30 A.M. on December 14, 1892.

—*Jonathan A. Stapley*

See also: Mormonism and Women; Polygamy; Smith, Joseph Jr.

References

Compton, Todd. *In Sacred Loneliness: The Plural Wives of Joseph Smith.* Salt Lake City, UT: Signature Books, 1997.

Smart, Donna Toland. *Mormon Midwife: The 1846–1888 Diaries of Patty Bartlett Sessions.* Logan: Utah State University Press, 1997.

Smith, Barbara Bradshaw

Barbara Bradshaw Smith (1922–) was the 10th general president of the all-female Relief Society, serving from 1974 to 1984, and the first Society president born in the 20th century. Smith's tenure as president occurred during a period of intense discussion and debate over the role of women in American and Mormon society, including controversies surrounding the Equal Rights Amendment (ERA). She was born on January 26, 1922, in Salt Lake City, to Dan Delos and Dorothy (Mills) Bradshaw. While in high school, she met Douglas Hill Smith, whom she married two years later, on June 16, 1941, in the Salt Lake temple. They have seven children.

Smith was sustained as Relief Society general president on October 3, 1974 (succeeding Belle Spafford, whose presidency had spanned the previous 29 years). Soon after taking office, Smith began to speak publicly in opposition to the ERA, a proposed addition to the U.S. Constitution reading, in part, "Equality of rights under the law shall not be denied or abridged by the United States or by any State on account of sex." Smith and others in the Church administration believed that the national legislation would result in many, mostly negative unintended consequences, would deprive women of legal rights and protections they already possessed, and did not acknowledge or make allowances for differences existing between the sexes. She was at the forefront of the Church's official opposition to the ERA and lobbied forcefully against its passage. (When not enough states had ratified the ERA by 1982, the proposed amendment effectively died.) Smith also discouraged women from serving in the military and opposed abortion on demand (legalized by the U.S. Supreme Court in 1973).

The LDS Church's coordinated effort to defeat passage of the ERA represented one of a handful of instances in which Church officials have taken a public stand on a topic some observers view as political. The Church typically considers such subjects as moral issues. The protracted debate surrounding the ERA and women's rights generally acted to mobilize members of a generation of Mormon women on both sides of the divisive issue. Of this period in LDS Church history, one historian has written: "Certainly, the Equal Rights Amendment helped the church grow stronger at a personal and institutional level. For the first time in their lives, thousands of Mormon women participated directly in the American political process. . . . for the most part these women enthusiastically participated in the anti-ERA campaign as an expression of their own deeply felt views. . . . Also, for the first time, the Mormon hierarchy planned and successfully administered a multidirectional political campaign in widely scattered states and in hundreds of cities and towns" (Quinn, *The Mormon Hierarchy* 400).

In other areas during her presidency, Smith championed the Relief Society's construction of a Monument to Women, installed in Nauvoo, Illinois (site of the founding of the Relief Society in 1842). She participated in various regional LDS Church conferences around the world. She advocated for increased training for the

Church's health and welfare missionaries and for the wives of newly called LDS mission presidents. She oversaw the transfer to the Church of the Society's wheat and wheat trust funds (totaling more than $2.4 million) in 1978, a program begun nearly a century earlier. She supervised the simplification of the Society's instructional curriculum when the Church adopted a consolidated three-hour Sunday meeting schedule program in 1980. She expanded the role and responsibilities of the counselors to stake Relief Society presidents and of stake Relief Society boards. She encouraged the participation of Society members in their local communities and emphasized the importance of the family and a mother's role. During her presidency, membership in the Relief Society worldwide doubled. According to a history of the Society: "Located in eighty-nine countries and sixteen territories, speaking some eighty languages, the women of the Church numbered over 1.6 million in 1984. . . . All were Relief Society sisters" (Derr et al., *Women of Covenant* 382–383). Smith was formally released as Relief Society president on April 7, 1984.

During the years following her departure from the Relief Society general presidency, Smith continued to serve the LDS Church in various capacities.

—*Gary James Bergera*

See also: Mormonism and Women; Relief Society; Spafford, Belle Smith.

References

Bradley, Martha Sonntag. *Pedestals and Podiums: Utah Women, Religious Authority, and Equal Rights.* Salt Lake City, UT: Signature Books, 2005.

Derr, Jill Mulvay, Janath Russell Cannon, and Maureen Ursenbach Beecher. *Women of Covenant: The Story of Relief Society.* Salt Lake City, UT: Deseret Book, 1992.

Jolley, JoAnn. "Barbara Smith: A Call to Service, a Time to Rejoice." *Ensign* 11 (March 1981): 16–20.

Quinn, D. Michael. *The Mormon Hierarchy: Extensions of Power.* Salt Lake City, UT: Signature Books/Smith Research Associates, 1997.

Smith, Emma Hale

Emma Hale (1804–1877), wife of Joseph Smith Jr. and the first Relief Society president, was born July 10, 1804, to Elizabeth and Isaac Hale. She grew up in Harmony Township, Pennsylvania, near the banks of the Susquehanna River, riding horses and mastering canoeing under the tutelage of her older brothers. She was strong, independent, and tall like her mother. Her chestnut hair shone, as did her intelligence and quick wit.

She first encountered Joseph Smith Jr. as he and his father boarded at her home. When Emma left with Joseph in January 1827, she did not plan on marrying him, but she decided she "prefer[red] to marry him to any other man she knew," and they eloped (Newell and Avery, *Mormon Enigma* 1). With a new husband in tow, Emma fled to Manchester, New York, to avoid the disapproval of her father.

Emma was central not only to the family she made with Joseph but also to his Church. Joseph Knight recorded that Joseph could receive the plates in September 1827 only "if he brot with him the right person." Joseph believed Emma was the "right person," and she accompanied him to the Hill Cumorah to retrieve the gold plates (Jessee, "Joseph Knight's Recollection" 31–32). This began a lifetime of involvement alongside Joseph.

Emma regularly endured privation. She lost her first three children and later lost one adopted son and two more biological children. The Smiths did not always have their own home, and Joseph's frequent absence required Emma often to take charge of the household. Emma consistently looked after friends, boarders, and others in need. In Nauvoo, the sick initially filled the Smith home and spilled out into the yard while Joseph and Emma tended to their distress.

Shortly after Emma's baptism, Joseph received what would be known as "The Elect Lady" revelation (Doctrine and Covenants 25). Election is a function of personal will and choice within LDS theology. The revelation entreated Emma to continue her work as a scribe for Joseph and to be a "comfort" to him but also to take more of a leading role and to "expound scriptures, and to exhort the church." She was also to make a "selection of sacred hymns"; her first hymnal was published in 1836.

Emma played an important role for her family and the Church. While Joseph was in Liberty Jail, Emma left their home and walked with four clinging children across the frozen Mississippi with Joseph's papers and manuscripts tied around her waist. Emma petitioned Thomas Carlin, the Illinois governor, multiple times for Joseph and the Saints. She was the first woman to participate in temple rites and then shared the sacred rites with other women. She was voted the first president of the Relief Society as Joseph organized it. Emma argued that the purpose of the society was "to do something extraordinary!" (Newell and Avery, *Mormon Enigma* 103).

Near the end of Emma's life, she affirmed, "I believe [Joseph] was everything he professed to be" (Newell and Avery, *Mormon Enigma* 25). Her support of Joseph was complete until it came to plural marriage. Aroet Hale later commented, "There never was a more Dutiful woman than Emma Smith . . . till after the Prophet had made publick the revelation of Seelestial marriage. . . . This proved a grate trial to her" (Newell and Avery, *Mormon Enigma* 173). This "grate trial" was "torturous" for Emma (Bushman, 2005, 554). She used her position as Relief Society president to fight against polygamy. Ultimately, she either absolutely ignored or completely repudiated polygamy.

This anguish did not lessen her pain at Joseph's loss. Their love continued despite the clash. Her son remembered his mother weeping over Joseph's body, "Oh, Joseph, Joseph! My husband, my husband! Have they taken you from me at last!" (Bushman, *Joseph Smith* 554).

In the wake of Joseph's death, factional competition for her allegiance erupted among potential successors to Joseph, but Emma's main concern was providing for her family and disentangling Joseph's assets from the Church. Three years later, she married Lewis C. Bidamon. Their letters exhibit a close and loving relationship as they cared for their blended family for 30 years. Emma supported her son Joseph III when he chose to lead the Reorganized Latter-day Saints.

She died on April 30, 1877. Her final words were "Joseph, Joseph, Joseph. Joseph! Yes, yes, I'm coming!" (Newell and Avery, *Mormon Enigma* 304).

—*Janiece Lyn Johnson*

See also: Divergent Churches; Martyrdom of Joseph and Hyrum Smith; Polygamy; Smith, Joseph Jr.

References
Bushman, Richard L. *Joseph Smith: Rough Stone Rolling: A Cultural Biography of Mormonism's Founder.* New York: Knopf, 2005.

Doctrine and Covenants of the Church of Jesus Christ of Latter-day Saints. Salt Lake City, UT: The Church of Jesus Christ of Latter-day Saints, 1981.

Jessee, Dean. "Joseph Knight's Recollection of Early Church History." *BYU Studies* 17, no. 1 (1976): 31–32.

Newell, Linda, and Valeen Avery. *Mormon Enigma: Emma Hale Smith.* New York: Doubleday, 1984.

Smith, George Albert

George Albert Smith (1870–1951) was the eighth president of the Church. He was born on April 4, 1870, in Salt Lake City, to apostle John Henry Smith (son of apostle George A. Smith) and Sarah Farr Smith. He attended Brigham Young Academy, in Provo, Utah, and the University of Deseret (later University of Utah) and married Lucy Emily Woodruff (granddaughter of Church president Wilford Woodruff) on May 25, 1892. They had three children. Together Smith and his wife served an LDS proselytizing mission to the southern United States from 1892 to 1894. Smith was a member of the Republican Party and in 1896 campaigned for William McKinley for U.S. president. He also supported McKinley's successor, Theodore Roosevelt. Smith was a sergeant in the Utah National Guard, worked for ZCMI (a Church-owned department store), and was a surveyor for the Denver and Rio Grande Western Railroad. (Regular exposure to sunlight may have further damaged his already weak eyes.) On October 8, 1903, at age 33, he was called to join the Church's Quorum of the Twelve Apostles. Shortly afterward, he began to suffer recurring bouts of extreme fatigue and depression. He was eventually diagnosed as having systemic lupus erythematosus (or lupus), a chronic, debilitating disease of the immune system.

Smith was an avid supporter of the Boy Scouts and urged its incorporation as an official program of the Church's Young Men's Mutual Improvement Association. In 1931, he served on Scouting's National Advisory Board. The next year, he received Scouting's Silver Beaver Award and in 1934 its Silver Buffalo Award, two of Scouting's highest honors. He was also president of the International Irrigation and Dry Farm Congress in 1918 and served for 16 years as president of the Society for Aid to the Sightless. He enjoyed family history and genealogy. He was founding president of the Utah Pioneer Trails and Landmarks Association (1937) and helped to organize the American Pioneer Trails Association. He was appointed national vice president of the Sons of the American Revolution in 1922. From 1919 to 1921, Smith was president of the Church's European Mission, and he traveled throughout much of England, France, Germany, the Netherlands, Scandinavia, and Switzerland. In 1938, he toured the Church's missions in Hawaii, Fiji, New Zealand, Australia, Tonga, and Samoa.

On July 1, 1943, Smith was sustained as president of the Quorum of the Twelve Apostles. Less than two years later, on May 21, 1945, at age 75, he was named LDS Church president. Four months later, on September 23, 1945, he dedicated the Idaho Falls temple. During 1945–1946, he ordered the shipment of tons of LDS relief aid to Europe's Latter-day Saints and others. In 1947, he chaired the Utah state-sponsored commission to commemorate the centennial of Utah's settlement by the Mormon pioneers, which included completion of the "This Is the Place" monument at the entrance of Emigration Canyon in Salt Lake City. He was the second sitting LDS president to visit Mexico, where he helped to facilitate the return to the Church of some 1,200 dissidents known as members of the Third Convention. He also served as president of many Church businesses, including Beneficial Life Insurance Company, Hotel Utah Company, Utah Home Fire Insurance Company, Utah-Idaho Sugar Company, Utah First National Bank, Zions Savings Bank and Trust, ZCMI, and Zions Securities Corporation. He was president of the Church Board of Education and editor of the Church's official magazines. Smith died on April 4, 1951, his 81st birthday.

Smith was known especially for his compassion, a result perhaps of the poor physical and emotional health he lived with for much of his adult life. His biographer, Merlo J. Pusey, explains:

> He loved people and had a great capacity for understanding them. His friendly spirit brought out a warmth of feeling toward himself and toward the church he represented. Being a natural peacemaker, he was frequently able to reconcile estranged husbands and wives or parents and children, as well as to iron out conflicts with the ward and stake organizations. His formula for dealing with tangled or embittered human relations was always the same: let the love of Christ drive out hatred and distrust; induce men to pray together instead of fighting or spreading malicious gossip; encourage sinners to repent of their wrongdoing;

remember that we are all the children of God. He had an extraordinary capacity to put his arm around disgruntled or erring members and warm them into fellowship again. (Pusey, *Builders of the Kingdom* 227)

Historian D. Michael Quinn recounts a revealing incident involving Smith's response to two gay members of the LDS Church. Smith's reported counsel—that they should "live their lives as decently as they could"—demonstrates the charity for which he was remembered (Quinn, *Same-Sex Dynamics* 372).

Among the several dictums Smith adopted as his personal "creed" are the following: "I would be a friend to the friendless and find joy in ministering to the needs of the poor"; "I would not seek to force people to live up to my ideals, but rather love them into doing the thing that is right"; "I would live with the masses and help to solve their problems that their earth life may be happy"; "I would avoid the publicity of high position and discourage the flattery of thoughtless friends"; "I would not knowingly wound the feelings of any, not even one who may have wronged me, but would seek to do good and make him my friend"; "I would overcome the tendency to selfishness and jealousy and rejoice in the success of all the children of our Heavenly Father"; and "I would not be an enemy to any living soul" (Gibbons, *George Albert Smith* 134–135). Smith characterized himself thus: "That he lacked the prowess of an athlete, that he was too homely to win popular favor, and that his weak eyes prevented him from becoming a scholar, but he could excel in human kindness. So, he made kindness his specialty" (Pusey, *Builders of the Kingdom* 301).

—*Gary James Bergera*

See also: Genealogy and Family History; Mormon Missiology; Youth Programs.

References

Gibbons, Francis M. *George Albert Smith: Kind and Caring Christian, Prophet of God.* Salt Lake City, UT: Deseret Book, 1990.

Pusey, Merlo J. *Builders of the Kingdom: George A. Smith, John Henry Smith, George Albert Smith.* Provo, UT: Brigham Young University Press, 1981.

Quinn, D. Michael. *Same-Sex Dynamics among Nineteenth-Century Americans: A Mormon Example.* Urbana: University of Illinois Press, 1996.

Smith, Hyrum

Hyrum Smith (1800–1844) was the older brother of LDS Church founder Joseph Smith Jr. He was born on February 9, 1800, to Joseph Smith and Lucy Mack Smith, in Tunbridge, Vermont. At 11, he attended Moor's Charity School (affiliated with Dartmouth College). Following the Smith family's relocation to New York, Hyrum joined his brothers in working at a variety of odd jobs to help supplement the family's finances, as well as helping to clear and farm the Smith family's own land. On November 2, 1826, he married Jerusha Barden; they had four daughters and two sons. In 1828 and 1829, he traveled to Harmony, Pennsylvania, to visit his brother Joseph, who was at work dictating the text of what would be published in 1830 as the Book of Mormon. Like the other members of the Smith family, Hyrum believed in his brother's religious claims. He was told in an early revelation that he would be asked to "assist to bring forth" God's work (Doctrine and Covenants 11:9). In June 1829, Hyrum was baptized for a remission of sins in Seneca Lake (near Fayette, New York). Later that same month, he said he saw and touched the golden plates of the Book of Mormon and became one of the book's Eight Witnesses. The next year, on April 6, 1830, he was one of the original six organizers of his brother's Church of Christ (later Church of Jesus Christ of Latter-day Saints). He soon engaged in missionary work, and presided over the Colesville, New York, branch of the young Church.

In 1831, Hyrum and other Church members relocated to Kirtland, Ohio, and he was ordained a high priest. In 1834, he helped to organize and participated in Zion's Camp, a kind of militia sent to aid Church members in Missouri. He helped to build the Kirtland temple and in December 1834 was ordained assistant president of the Church (Joseph was Church president). Two years later, on November 7, 1837, he was named Second Counselor in his brother's First Presidency. (Sidney Rigdon was First Counselor; Oliver Cowdery was associate president.) In October 1838, Hyrum was arrested with other Church leaders on charges of treason. He and others were imprisoned for nearly five months in Liberty Jail, in Missouri, while awaiting trial. On April 16, 1839, he and the others were allowed to escape; they soon rejoined the main body of the Church in Commerce (later Nauvoo), Illinois. On September 14, 1840, he was ordained presiding patriarch to the Church (succeeding his father), and in January 1841 he was appointed assistant Church president (replacing Cowdery, who had been excommunicated in 1838). (Though Hyrum was never explicitly ordained to the apostleship, his appointment as assistant president may have included such authority.) Hyrum pronounced hundreds of patriarchal blessings on Church members, and he occasionally served as acting Church president. He helped to found Nauvoo's Masonic lodge and, with his brother Joseph, helped to administer and received the first temple-related endowment ceremony rituals, in May 1842. He was also a founding member of his brother's politically oriented Council of Fifty in 1844. He was designated as his brother's possible successor but was killed along with Joseph on June 27, 1844, in Carthage Jail, in Illinois, where they had again been charged with treason. He was 44.

Following the death of his wife, Jerusha, in 1837, Hyrum married Mary Fielding, a recent English convert. They had one son and one daughter. Initially, Smith refused to accept his brother Joseph's teachings regarding plural marriage. But when he realized that he could be sealed eternally to his first wife, he abandoned his opposition and became one of the controversial doctrine's strongest supporters, performing scores of plural marriages for his brother's followers. He married at least two known plural wives. One of his sons, Joseph F. Smith, later became 6th president of the LDS Church; a grandson, Joseph Fielding Smith, became the Church's 10th president; and four of the Church's six presiding patriarchs were his direct descendants.

Of Hyrum's contribution to the early LDS Church organization, historian and Smith family descendant Paul M. Edwards writes:

> Hyrum Smith was the first member of the Mormon church. Joseph [Smith] was a prophetic voice, but no more the first Mormon than Christ was the first Christian. Hyrum was a churchman by inclination, a religious man by conviction rather than experience. It was he who . . . recognized that his contribution was to change a culture rather than to share the mystical experiences of his brother. The loving and sustaining sibling, the cool mind, the natural man; he saw the importance of his brother's mystical experience and the impossibility of translating it into anything but secular events with a sacred mantle. . . . To a very large extent Hyrum made the religious experience historical. (Edwards, "The Secular Smiths" 12)

—Gary James Bergera

See also: Book of Mormon; Martyrdom of Joseph and Hyrum Smith; Organization of the Church; Polygamy; Smith Family; Temples; Witnesses to the Book of Mormon; Zion's Camp.

References

Bates, Irene M., and E. Gary Smith. *Lost Legacy: The Mormon Office of Presiding Patriarch.* Urbana: University of Illinois Press, 1996.

Corbett, Pearson H. *Hyrum Smith, Patriarch.* Salt Lake City, UT: Deseret Book, 1962.

Edwards, Paul M. "The Secular Smiths." *Journal of Mormon History* 4 (1977): 12.

O'Driscoll, Jeffrey S. *Hyrum Smith: A Life of Integrity.* Salt Lake City, UT: Deseret Book, 2003.

Smith, Joseph F.

Joseph F. Smith (1838–1918), sixth president of the Church, presided over it from 1901 until his death, in 1918, during one of Mormonism's most significant periods of transition.

Born on November 13, 1838, in Far West, Missouri, the future prophet entered a world rife with tension between Latter-day Saints and their neighbors. His father,

Hyrum Smith, was imprisoned at the time of his birth, and, when he was five years old, his father and his uncle, Joseph Smith, were murdered. His father's death instilled in him the understanding that persecution and sacrifice were central to the Mormon experience, something he was consistently reminded of throughout his life. From his mother, Mary Fielding Smith, he inherited a stubborn temperament and the ability to withstand intense adversity. These traits, combined with the rigors of frontier life and his later experiences as a Church leader, created "a curious combination of frontier toughness, political sophistication, and religious certainty" (Flake, *Politics of American Religious Identity* 58).

At age nine, he drove his mother's team of oxen across the plains to Mormonism's new home in the Salt Lake Valley. His early years in Utah were spent as a herd boy until his mother's death in 1852 left him and his sister orphaned. Two years later, Smith was expelled from school after a physical altercation with the schoolmaster. Though this ended Smith's formal education, it also signaled the beginning of his ecclesiastical career. At the next general conference, he was called on a mission to the Sandwich Islands (Hawaii). In Hawaii, Smith learned the language quickly, was given ecclesiastical responsibility, and returned home four years later prepared for a life of leadership.

Upon his return, he enlisted in the Nauvoo Legion and participated in the Utah War. In April 1859, he married his cousin, Levira Smith, and subsequently married five polygamous wives: Julina Lambson (1866), Sarah Ellen Richards (1868), Edna Lambson (1871), Alice Ann Kimball (1883), and Mary Taylor Schwartz (1884). His marriage to Levira ended in divorce in 1867.

Joseph F. Smith's adult life was preoccupied with Church leadership and political involvement. He served as territorial representative, city council member, and delegate to Utah's constitutional convention. When Mormonism's People's Party disbanded in 1891, Smith united himself with the Republican Party. Meanwhile, his ecclesiastical duties included missions to Europe, Great Britain, and Hawaii. He also accompanied Orson Pratt to the eastern states in 1878 in an effort "to gather up records and data relative to the early history of the Church" (Holzapfel and Shupe, *Joseph F. Smith* 61).

When federal antipolygamy legislation led to raids in Utah, Smith went "underground" and hid from the authorities, spending two years in Hawaii. From 1888 to 1889, Smith went to Washington, D.C., lobbying Congress on behalf of the Church. While his efforts were largely unsuccessful, Wilford Woodruff's Manifesto of 1890 advised Mormons "to refrain from contracting any marriage forbidden by the law of the land" (Kenney, "Joseph F. Smith" 198), which appeased the government, and, in 1891, Smith was granted amnesty by U.S. President Benjamin Harrison.

In 1866, Smith was ordained an apostle by Brigham Young, and in 1867 he was sustained as a member of the Quorum of the Twelve Apostles. From 1880 until

1901, he served as a counselor to John Taylor, Wilford Woodruff, and Lorenzo Snow. Following Snow's death, Joseph F. Smith was set apart as Church president on October 17, 1901. He set out "to end Mormonism's Rocky Mountain isolation," seeking to improve the image of the Church in America and throughout the world (Flake, *Politics of American Religious Identity* 26–27). His efforts signaled perhaps the most significant period of transition in Latter-day Saint history. Smith's presidency was marked by the controversial election of Mormon apostle Reed Smoot to the U.S. Senate and by renewed emphases on the Church's history and theology.

Subpoenaed to testify before Congress as part of the controversy surrounding Smoot's election, Smith was queried regarding the Church's political influence and plural marriages authorized by Church leaders—himself included—since the Manifesto in 1890. In his testimony before Congress, Smith did not deny that he continued to have marital relations with his plural wives but carefully explained that *the Church* had not performed any polygamous marriages since 1890, employing a subtle discursive distinction "between the church and its members" (Flake, *Politics of American Religious Identity* 76). In 1904, Smith issued a second manifesto, prohibiting new plural marriages and authorizing Church discipline for those who disobeyed.

The era witnessed not only the end of polygamy and isolation but also a change in the Church's focus and identity. The year 1905 marked the 100th anniversary of Joseph Smith's birth and offered "the occasion for identifying what about him and his legacy mattered" to the Mormon Church as it started a new century and phase of its existence (Flake, *Politics of American Religious Identity* 110). Smith's presidency saw an increased focus on Joseph Smith's First Vision, the authority received from angelic visitors, and the Book of Mormon, symbolized in visits to Church history sites and the dedication of a monument commemorating Joseph Smith's birth. The emphasis placed on the "ideals of revealed knowledge and restored authority" now constituted the "creative and untouchable core of Latter-day Saint identity and belief" (Flake, *Politics of American Religious Identity* 117).

In line with the revived emphasis on revelation, knowledge, and authority, his presidency issued a number of doctrinal statements. In a vision near the end of his life, in 1918, Smith saw Christ ministering to the spirits in prison and biblical and Mormon prophets assembled in paradise. The vision—canonized in Latter-day Saint scripture in 1976—further explained how the work of redemption was organized among the dead, a comforting notion to a world engrossed in war and threatened by a flu pandemic. More personally, "death had surrounded [Smith] throughout his life"—including the deaths of a son and a daughter-in-law earlier that year—"and the longings these deaths awakened in him could not be soothed in mortality," giving added significance to the vision (Tate, "'Great World of the Spirits of the Dead'" 12, 40). Joseph F. Smith passed away a month later, on November 19, 1918.

—Christopher C. Jones

See also: First Vision; Manifesto; Martyrdom of Joseph and Hyrum Smith; Nauvoo Legion; Polygamy; Pratt, Orson and Parley P.; Smoot Hearings; Utah War.

References

Flake, Kathleen. *The Politics of American Religious Identity: The Seating of Senator Reed Smoot, Mormon Apostle.* Chapel Hill: University of North Carolina Press, 2004.

Holzapfel, Richard Neitzel, and R. Q. Shupe. *Joseph F. Smith: Portrait of a Prophet.* Salt Lake City, UT: Deseret Book, 2000.

Kenney, Scott. "Joseph F. Smith." In *The Presidents of the Church.* Ed. Leonard J. Arrington. Salt Lake City, UT: Deseret Book, 1986.

Tate, George S. "'The Great World of the Spirits of the Dead': Death, the Great War, and the 1918 Influenza Pandemic as Context for Doctrine and Covenants 138." *BYU Studies* 46, no. 1 (2007): 4–40.

Smith, Joseph Fielding

Joseph Fielding Smith (1876–1972) was the 10th president of the Church of Jesus Christ of Latter-day Saints, serving from 1970 to his death, in 1972. He also served 60 years in the Quorum of the Twelve Apostles, and his long career and prolific writings made him a particularly influential conservative force in 20-century Mormon theology and culture.

He was born July 19, 1876, in Salt Lake City, Utah, scion of a particularly distinguished Mormon family. Joseph Fielding was the firstborn son of Joseph F. Smith, an apostle who would later become the sixth president of the Church, and Julina Lambson, the first of his father's six plural wives. He was also grandson of Hyrum Smith, the brother of Church founder Joseph Smith and a prominent Mormon leader in his own right.

Smith was married and widowed three times. He wed his first wife, Emily Louise Shurtliff, in 1898, and they had two children together. Emily died 10 years later, and, within a year, Smith was married again, to Ethel Reynolds. They had nine children before Ethel died, in 1937. He married his last wife, the opera singer Jessie Evans, in 1938, and she nearly matched Smith's own longevity, dying only a year before he himself passed away.

Joseph F. Smith, then president of the Church, called his son to the Quorum of the Twelve Apostles and ordained him an apostle on April 7, 1910. The non-Mormon *Salt Lake Tribune* and other critics raised cries of nepotism; however, the younger Smith had already made a name for himself as a religious thinker. He had been employed in the Church Historian's office since returning from a two-year mission in 1901 and had authored two apologetic pamphlets on controversial issues in Church history—polygamy and the dispute over the succession to Joseph Smith. In addition to his status as an apostle, he would serve as Church Historian from

1921 until he assumed the presidency. In that capacity, he published, in 1922, *Essentials in Church History,* an introductory history of the Church intended for use as a textbook. It has been reprinted more than 20 times and remained in use until the end of the 20th century, surviving several competing works and criticism of its celebratory style. Sixteen years later, he published his edited volume *The Teachings of the Prophet Joseph Smith,* making many of Joseph Smith's sermons and writings available to the general public for the first time.

Smith became known in the Quorum for his expansive knowledge of Church history and scripture, as well as for his tenacious defense of conservative theological positions. As battles over biblical literalism and evolution tore asunder American Christianity in the 1920s, Smith emerged as the Mormon leader most vocal in his defense of a literal reading of the creation account of Genesis. He was convinced that evolution meant lack of faith in a literal Adam and a literal fall and that this would in turn destroy belief in the need for the atonement of Jesus. His use of the work of Protestant fundamentalist writers such as the creationist geologist George McCready Price introduced the arguments of Price's movement into Mormon discourse and placed Smith in conflict with other Mormon leaders more sympathetic to scientific views, such as apostle James E. Talmage and Seventy Brigham H. Roberts. In the early 1930s, he was involved in a series of disputes with these men and others on the issue of evolution and at that point acquiesced with them in a First Presidency directive to cease public airing of the disagreement. However, the 1954 publication of *Man: His Origin and Destiny* revealed that Smith's views had not changed over the intervening 20 years. In that work, he argued forcefully that evolution was incompatible with the fundamental doctrines of Christianity. Smith had become president of the Quorum of the Twelve three years earlier, and the work received wide attention among Mormons.

The prominence of his position combined with his reputation as a theologian and scripturist meant that his decision to begin a column entitled "Answers to Gospel Questions" in the Church periodical *The Improvement Era,* in 1953, was greeted with great popularity. The column ran for 14 years, and Smith's answers were concurrently compiled into five volumes soon frequently used as reference books. Other of his shorter works—articles and speeches—were collected in the three-volume *Doctrines of Salvation,* published between 1954 and 1956. With these works, Smith cemented his reputation as the preeminent religious scholar among the Church's leadership and promoted his conservative theology widely among the membership. This did not consist merely of opposition to evolution; his *Signs of the Times* (1945), for example, offered a reading of biblical prophecy and current events heavily reminiscent of the detailed narrative of the End Times outlined by such fundamentalist thinkers as Cyrus Scofield.

Of course, Smith was not merely a theologian and writer. He was widely praised for directing the withdrawal of missionaries from Europe at the outbreak of World

War II. As Church Historian, he oversaw the reorganization of the Church archives according to modern archival standards, commissioning a vast microfilming program in 1949. He served as chair of both the Missionary Committee and the Board of Education in the 1950s and 1960s and cooperated in the Church-wide reorganization project that came to be known as correlation, an effort that began in the 1960s but that would also characterize his own presidency.

In 1965, Smith entered the First Presidency as a counselor to David O. McKay. Five years later, on January 18, 1970, McKay died, and Smith was ordained as his successor on January 23. His age limited his activity as president, but several fruits of correlation were achieved during his tenure: several Church periodicals were consolidated into the single journal the *Ensign;* the hierarchies of the Sunday School and missionary programs were reorganized; and two new temples were dedicated, in Ogden and Provo, Utah. Smith served as president for two and a half years, dying in Salt Lake City on July 2, 1972.

—Matthew Bowman

See also: Correlation; Mormonism and Science; Roberts, B. H.; Smith, Hyrum; Smith, Joseph F.; Talmage, James E.

References

Sherlock, Richard. "'We Can See No Advantage to a Continuation of the Discussion:' The Roberts/Smith/Talmage Affair." *Dialogue: A Journal of Mormon Thought* 13, no. 3 (1980): 63–78.

Smith, Joseph Fielding. *Doctrines of Salvation.* Salt Lake City, UT: Deseret Book, 1954–1956.

Smith, Joseph Fielding, III. *The Life of Joseph Fielding Smith.* Salt Lake City, UT: Bookcraft, 1972.

Smith, Joseph Jr.

Joseph Smith Jr. (1805–1844) was the founder and the first prophet of Mormonism. Of the scores of independent Churches and sects that trace their origins to Smith, the largest by far is the Church of Jesus Christ of Latter-day Saints, headquartered in Salt Lake City, Utah. Mormons think of Smith as a prophet like unto Moses or Isaiah, sent by God to preach and testify. He was also called a seer and a revelator because he brought forth new scripture, primarily the Book of Mormon and the Doctrine and Covenants. Mormons believe these revelations helped restore the pure Christian Gospel in preparation for Christ's Second Coming.

Smith was the fifth-generation descendant of English Puritans who arrived in America during the Great Migration of the 1630s. His relatives were respected

No photograph of Joseph Smith is known to exist. Mormon artist Sutcliff Maudsley made several drawings, including this one, of Smith in life. (Courtesy of the Church History Museum, The Church of Jesus Christ of Latter-day Saints.)

farmers and merchants, officeholders in their New England towns, not controversial people as Smith later was. By the 1790s, both family lines had broken free of Congregationalism and were seeking popular religion. Smith's maternal line inclined toward Seekerism, which looked for a renewal of spiritual gifts; his fraternal line gravitated toward Universalism, which offered salvation to all. Both movements circumvented the authority of the mainline Churches. Religious independence may have been the most important legacy Smith's progenitors left to him.

Smith did not have an easy childhood. Although his parents, Joseph Sr. and Lucy Mack Smith, who married in 1796, started out well, they lost their Tunbridge, Vermont, farm in 1803 when a business deal went awry. That forced them into tenancy and frequent moves as they looked to feed their 11 children (9 of whom lived to adulthood). Joseph Jr. was born the third son, December 23, 1805, in Sharon, Vermont, making him a key source of labor and leaving little time for educational pursuits. Smith's only "reprieve" came at age six, when typhoid infected his leg, requiring that a portion of his shin bone be removed and hobbling him for three years. In 1816, unseasonable cold forced the Smiths to push West for better prospects. They settled in Palmyra, New York, and eventually bought land but lost it when they overbuilt and could not make the payments.

Palmyra was situated in the Finger Lakes region and was one of a band of towns later famed for religious revivals. By the late 1810s, the Baptists, Presbyterians, and Methodists all competed with Congregationalists for converts. Smith's mother united with the Presbyterians, but, with his father, Smith stayed home. Perplexed by the religious confusion, at 14 he turned to God for help. In the spring of 1820, according to his later account, Smith went to the woods near his home to pray. God and Christ appeared to him, assured him that his sins were forgiven, and promised that if he remained faithful, the "fullness of the gospel" would be revealed to him (Smith, *Papers of Joseph Smith* 1:430). Mormons call this visitation the "First Vision," because it marked the dawning of a new epoch in God's involvement with his children. Smith only rarely mentioned this theophany during his early ministry, in part because of the hostile reactions it initially elicited. Later on, compelled by rumor and slanderous report, Smith filled out the vision in more detail, reframing it in more expansive terms.

The First Vision made no immediate dent in Smith's daily routine. He continued his labor in the family economy and went three years without another heavenly communication. Then, having become entangled in the "vanities of the world," he prayed one night in 1823 to learn whether he was still in favor with God. In response, an angel appeared by Smith's bedside and told him about an ancient record deposited in a hill not far from the Smith home. The record contained the "fullness of the everlasting Gospel," as personally delivered by Christ himself, to the "former inhabitants of this continent" (Smith, *Papers of Joseph Smith* 1:278). The angel, who called himself Moroni, instructed Smith to locate the record and to translate it. Smith went to the hill the next day but was prevented from obtaining the record at that time. The plates had the appearance of gold, and Smith later said he had thoughts of using them for commercial gain. Four years later, after Smith had proven trustworthy, the angel finally delivered up the record.

The story of the angel with a gold book sounds strange to outsiders, but Mormons accept it as their founding miracle, like Moses parting the Red Sea in Judaism or Muhammad's night journey in Islam. Mormons place the Moroni visitations within an ongoing stream of providential history. When important messages need to be conveyed, Mormons point out, God sends an angel, as with Mary or Cornelius in the Bible. Like them, Smith seems to have had total confidence in his visions. At one point he wondered whether Moroni was a "dream," but the thought quickly left him after further interaction (Smith, *Papers of Joseph Smith* 1:8). Smith showed no hesitation anywhere else. If the First Vision could be explained as a conversion experience not unlike those of other religious eccentrics of the era, the Moroni visitations put Smith's life on a new trajectory. By giving him a public task, they secured his place in history.

The task of locating treasure in the ground did not sound bizarre to Smith; it would have reminded him of one of his avocations. In 1822, Smith found a small stone in a well, which he proceeded to use to search for lost or buried treasure. Carrying forward a tradition that stretches back through Renaissance alchemy, poor rural New Englanders like the Smiths believed that riches could be obtained through supernatural means. Smith's associates seem to have believed that he possessed a special gift for "seeing in a stone," and quite naturally Joseph Sr., always down on his luck financially, enlisted Joseph Jr. to use his abilities in the family's behalf. One of these digs took Smith to Harmony, Pennsylvania, where he met an eligible young woman named Emma Hale, whom he married on January 18, 1827. Although later stung by the doctrine of plural marriage, Emma believed Smith's revelations and stayed with him to the end. Together they had eight children (only four of whom lived past infancy) and adopted two more.

Smith obtained the plates from the hill on September 22, 1827. For the next three years, his life revolved around getting them translated. The angel told him that he was not allowed to show the plates to anyone, not even Emma. Smith's earnest and winning way allowed him to convince a small circle of his sincerity. These included his immediate family and a handful of others who not only believed in visions and angels but who anxiously awaited their return. Many of Mormonism's early converts were people who, finding the existing Churches barren, sought a restoration of ancient Christianity, with its charisma and gifts.

One of these early believers was Martin Harris, a prosperous Palmyra farmer. Harris followed Smith to Pennsylvania and, between April and June 1828, transcribed 116 manuscript pages of the Book of Mormon while Smith dictated from behind a curtain. Then tragedy struck. With Smith's reluctant permission, Harris borrowed the 116 pages and, while trying to satisfy his skeptical wife, had them stolen from his possession. Distraught, Smith lost the power to translate for a season. Harris's turn as scribe was over. The translation started again when Oliver Cowdery, an itinerant school teacher, appeared in Palmyra. He met Smith in Harmony in April 1829 and, with Cowdery serving as scribe, the two men completed the translation in just three months, finishing up in Fayette, New York. Backing from Harris financed the printing of 5,000 copies of the Book of Mormon in Palmyra in March 1830.

Smith did not claim mastery over ancient languages the way conventional translators do. The Book of Mormon was written in an unknown script called "reformed Egyptian." To help Smith render the English, the angel provided a set of ancient spectacles called the Urim and Thummim, which consisted of two crystals set in silver bows. Smith may have used the spectacles in his work with Harris, but, during Cowdery's stint, he apparently used his seerstone only, the curtain down, the plates not even on the table. This process was observed by a dozen or so people, and none of them expressed skepticism. They thought Smith too ignorant to have been able to dictate the book without divine help. Smith's own explanation was always the same. He translated, he said, "by the gift and power of God" (Smith, *Papers of Joseph Smith* 1:128, 431, 450).

Initially Smith carried the burden of being the only witness to the existence of the plates. That changed in the summer of 1829. A passage in the Book of Mormon spoke of three additional witnesses, and Harris, Cowdery, and another believer named David Whitmer lobbied to fill the role. The three testified that an angel appeared to them in broad daylight and showed them the plates leaf by leaf; they also heard a voice command them to testify of what they saw. Later, eight others were allowed to handle the plates. The statements of these two groups of witnesses, found today in the front of every copy of the Book of Mormon, are important to Mormons, for they constitute "proof" that Smith was telling the truth. Although the plates are not available today for independent confirmation (Smith said he returned them to the angel after the job of translation was over), devout Mormons do not murmur. Religion requires faith, they say, and Jesus extolled believing over seeing (John 20:28).

After the publication of the Book of Mormon, Smith turned to organizing a Church. He was not a seasoned preacher at this early stage; he is not known to have preached a sermon before he organized the Church of Christ, in April 1830. The main attraction was the return of primitive Christianity, not eloquent preaching. The original Church structure was extremely simple. Smith was designated "first elder," and Cowdery was "second elder." Deacons, teachers, and priests were added later on.

Smith led this new Church through revelation. Beginning in 1828, Smith started writing down words as they came to him, and these documents provided the basis for his actions and decisions. Early Mormons called them "commandments." Written in the voice of God, these commandments ranged from mundane instructions on building a store to ethereal descriptions of the heavens. They carried great weight among believers, and Smith greatly prized them himself. In 1833, he proudly published a collection of the revelations, the Book of Commandments, and two years later expanded it into the Doctrine and Covenants.

Smith's claim to revelation was not in itself unique; others claimed that God had spoken again. But the expansiveness of Smith's revelations, more than anything, roused anger and suspicion on all sides, leading eventually to his death. The sheer audacity of the Book of Mormon had already provoked intense persecution. Smith's later revelations did not just call people to make minor adjustments in their spiritual lives, as conventional sermons did. They called for sweeping change: moving from homes and cities, economic redistribution, and even, in a few instances, subversion of civil law. Smith's followers thrilled at the thought of God speaking again, through a prophet, as in olden times. For outsiders, the thought was terrifying. Smith's power seemed limitless.

Perhaps the largest of these revelatory plans, equally thrilling and terrifying, was the call to build Zion. For Smith, Zion was not just a metaphor or a state of mind. It was an actual city. In the fall of 1830, Smith deployed missionaries to western Missouri, on the boundary of the United States, where they were to locate a site for the city of Zion. In July 1831, Smith traveled to Independence, Missouri, and put down stakes for a city there. Smith's "Plat of the City of Zion" (1833) called for a city of between 15,000 and 20,000 people, organized around three central public squares containing 24 temples. It was an ambitious undertaking for anyone, let alone for a man not yet 30. In Zion the Mormons were to live in harmony and love, protected from storms of wickedness, while they awaited Christ's imminent return.

While Smith sought to establish Zion in Missouri, he built up a second Church center in Kirtland, Ohio. In 1831, Smith received a revelation for the New York Mormons to move to Kirtland, where Smith lived for the next six years. The process of "gathering" had begun, and, by 1835, about 900 Mormons were living in Kirtland (constituting about half the town's population), while another 200 lived nearby.

In Kirtland, Smith enthusiastically moved forward his vision of the ideal society. The Mormons practiced economic communalism, in which people deeded their property to the bishop for redistribution according to need, thus caring for the poor. Smith's day-to-day business until about 1833 included a retranslation of the Bible. He opened a store, a bank, and a newspaper. He started the School of the Prophets, which helped train missionaries, who fanned out across the United States and in 1837 arrived in Great Britain. Yearning to read the Bible in the original, Smith organized a school for Hebrew study. Earlier angelic visitors had restored priesthood, and in Kirtland Smith elaborated its ecclesiology, organizing all adult males into priesthood quorums. The zenith of the Ohio years was the completion of the Kirtland temple, begun in 1833. A Pentecost rained down upon the Mormons at the dedicatory services in March 1836. Three angelic messengers appeared to Smith and Cowdery, giving them power to gather Israel and seal families into eternal units.

This total society incited opposition from within and without. Smith's followers proved unwilling to accept complete economic consecration, persuading him to introduce private ownership. In 1832, Smith was dragged from his bed in the dark of night, tarred, feathered, and beaten by a mob. The following year, armed mobs drove the Mormons out of Independence, effectively ending the Zion dream in Missouri. The setback stunned Smith, who had supposed the way would be opened. By 1837, dissension had infected Kirtland. During that year's nationwide economic downturn, the Mormon bank failed, and angry creditors proclaimed Smith fallen. Unable to pay off the outstanding notes, Smith escaped with his life in January 1838, with Kirtland in flames.

Everywhere Smith went, the cycle of optimism, opprobrium, and violence followed. Like Catholic ghettos, Mormon cities aroused the ire of Protestants who feared domination in local government. At Smith's next stop, Far West, Missouri, it happened again, beginning with an election-day scuffle in nearby Daviess County in August 1838. Tempers escalated, and Mormons flew into battle against local citizen militias. Smith did not lead the charge, but he did sanction violent engagements. Two Missourians were killed, and 17 Mormons were later massacred in a barn at Haun's Mill. "The Mormon War" was Smith's great sorrow. In November 1838, Smith was arrested on trumped-up charges of treason and languished in a cold Missouri jail for the next six months.

While Smith was incarcerated, his followers relocated to Illinois. In April 1839, sympathetic guards allowed Smith to escape, and, rejoining his people, he purchased land on the banks of the Mississippi, at a town called Commerce. Renamed Nauvoo, it soon became the center of the Mormon world, with converts streaming in from across the globe. "Nauvoo the beautiful," as Smith called it, was Smith's home for the last five years of his life.

At Nauvoo, Smith's resilience was made manifest. "He possessed the most indomitable perseverance," Smith's non-Mormon attorney once said (McConkie, *Remembering Joseph* 29). Rather than abandon the Zion project, Smith started up once again, gathering Mormons as before. With the help of John Bennett, an adventurer-convert, Smith turned Nauvoo into a Mormon stronghold. They pushed through a generous charter with a city militia and—important for Smith's safety—a municipal court with power to issue writs of habeas corpus. They organized a university and a system of schools, and Smith began work on a hotel and another temple. By 1844, Nauvoo had more than 12,000 residents, rivaling Chicago's claim to be the largest city in Illinois.

The meteoric rise of Nauvoo allowed Smith many opportunities to mingle with the people he loved. A handsome man with light auburn hair, a prominent nose, and very little beard, he stood 6'1" and weighed more than 200 pounds. Naturally fraternal and gregarious, Smith took time out to play ball with the children, skate on the ice, and wrestle with his friends. He and Emma held large socials with dancing and fine feasts. By the Nauvoo years, he had developed into a voluble preacher with a folksy, jocular, occasionally bombastic style. Parley P. Pratt recalled: "I have even known him to retain a congregation of willing and anxious listeners for many hours together, in the midst of cold or sunshine, rain or wind, while they were laughing at one moment and weeping the next" (McConkie, *Remembering Joseph* 33). His followers affectionately called him "Brother Joseph"—or, sometimes, simply, "the Prophet."

In Nauvoo, the Prophet unleashed himself in a torrent of doctrinal innovation. Earlier, during his prison confinement, he had received profound doctrine on the nature of human suffering. Smith had always taught a basic Christian gospel of faith and repentance, but now he added more idiosyncratic teachings on the uncreated nature of human intelligence, premortal existence, the embodiment of God, and baptism for the dead. In 1842, he published a translation of the Book of Abraham, which included ruminations on cosmology. He introduced the endowment, a dramatic Creation ritual with Masonic overtones. Three months before his death, in his famed King Follett sermon, Smith taught that God had a history. God "once was a man like us, and the Father was once on an earth like us" (Smith, *Words of Joseph Smith* 344). Such doctrines startled even his most trusted hearers and divided his followers. After Smith's death, Mormons who accepted the radical Nauvoo doctrines moved West with Brigham Young; those who clung to the more basic Christian message of the earlier years stayed behind.

The most controversial of these doctrines was, of course, plural marriage. Smith never wrote down his reasons for introducing such a charged and potentially damaging teaching, other than to suggest that its practice among Old Testament patriarchs justified its return, in order to raise up righteous "seed" unto the Lord. Others later recalled Smith speaking of an "angel with a drawn sword" who commanded him to move forward. Smith married his first plural wife in Kirtland; in 1841, he started up again, eventually marrying more than 30 women, 10 of whom were already married to other men. The mixed evidence of sexuality in these marriages, along with an other-worldly dynastic component, has led historians to suggest that Smith did not intend to start a harem like Solomon of old. The three to five cases of alleged paternity are all inconclusive (Bushman, *Joseph Smith* 436–445). For Smith and his followers, plural marriage had a pretext of believability because it fit within the larger nexus of already restored Old Testament practices: temples, prophets, Zion, and the gathering of Israel.

After introducing plural marriage to a small circle of trusted followers, Smith found that his life began to unravel. The practice could not be contained. Bennett started his own illicit version, and, when Smith publicly exposed him, Bennett lashed out in a damning exposé whose salacious charges circulated widely. Meanwhile, in trying to defend Nauvoo from the vulnerabilities of previous Mormon communities, Smith had accumulated temporal power, generating new critics. He was already head of the municipal court and the militia; after Bennett's defection, Smith took over the mayoralty, too. In early 1844, Smith announced his candidacy for the presidency of the United States, and the semisecretive Council of Fifty voted him "king" in the Kingdom of God. All this was more monarchialism than frontier democrats could bear.

The end came when Nauvoo apostates opened a rival newspaper "seeking to explode the vicious principles of Joseph Smith." After long deliberation, Smith and the Nauvoo city council found the paper libelous and ordered it closed. The shop was burned and the press scattered, enraging citizens across the county. Mobs gathered, and Smith countered by putting Nauvoo under martial law. After initial hesitation, Smith backed down and turned himself in to authorities. The original charge was riot, and an earlier charge of adultery was still outstanding. While Smith was detained in the county jail in Carthage, Illinois, on the muggy afternoon of June 27, 1844, an angry mob stormed the building and shot and killed Smith and his brother Hyrum. Five men were eventually brought to trial for the crime, but all were acquitted by the non-Mormon jury.

Although still controversial today, Smith's capacity for religion-making has been extolled in recent years. In 2001, a team of scholars began an ambitious project with the goal of publishing all of Smith's papers in some 30 volumes of carefully annotated text. To mark the occasion of the bicentennial of Smith's birth, the Library of Congress held a 2005 symposium that gathered scholars and religious dignitaries from across the globe to Washington, D.C. An outcast and a pariah in his own lifetime, Smith is now widely regarded as one of America's most successful religious innovators.

—Jed Woodworth

See also: Book of Mormon; Divergent Churches; First Vision; Haun's Mill Massacre; Kirtland Pentecost; Martyrdom of Joseph and Hyrum Smith; Missouri War; Mormon Scripture; Mormonism as Restoration; Organization of the Church; Polygamy; Smith, Emma Hale; Smith Family; Witnesses to the Book of Mormon.

References

Brodie, Fawn M. *No Man Knows My History.* New York: Knopf, 1945.

Bushman, Richard Lyman. *Joseph Smith: Rough Stone Rolling: A Cultural Biography of Mormonism's Founder.* New York: Knopf, 2005.

McConkie, Mark L. Comp. *Remembering Joseph: Personal Reflections of Those Who Knew the Prophet Joseph Smith.* Salt Lake City, UT: Deseret Book, 2003.

Smith, Joseph. *The Papers of Joseph Smith.* 2 vols. Ed. Dean C. Jessee. Salt Lake City, UT: Deseret Book, 1989.

Smith, Joseph. *Personal Writings of Joseph Smith.* Ed. and comp. Dean C. Jessee. Salt Lake City, UT: Deseret Book and Provo, UT: Brigham Young University Press, 2002.

Smith, Joseph. *The Words of Joseph Smith: The Contemporary Accounts of Nauvoo Discourses of the Prophet Joseph.* Comp. and ed. Andrew F. Ehat and Lyndon W. Cook. Provo, UT: Religious Studies Center, Brigham Young University, 1981.

Vogel, Dan. *Joseph Smith: The Making of a Prophet.* Salt Lake City, UT: Signature Books, 2004.

Smith Family

Joseph Smith Sr. (born July 12, 1771, at Topsfield, Essex County, Massachusetts) and Lucy Mack Smith (born July 8, 1775, at Gilsum, New Hampshire) were married at Tunbridge, Orange County, Vermont, on January 24, 1796. (Lucy dated her own birth as the revolutionary year of 1776, but town records place it a year earlier.) Both were the descendants of longtime New England families but, perhaps more significant, sprang from families that not only took religion seriously but also gave greater weight to a relationship with God than to a relationship with an institutional Church. Lucy's mother was a pious Christian, but her father was not converted until he had a vision late in life. Joseph's father and Joseph himself explored the "new" ideas of deism, Unitarianism, and the anti-Christianity of Thomas Paine. In addition to following conventional religious beliefs, including relying on authoritative statements and scriptural study and seeking divine guidance through prayer, both Joseph and Lucy also participated in a culture of folk magic and quasi-biblical beliefs that included ascribing power to magical talismans and objects, seeking enlightenment in dreams, and accepting the reality of usually unseen presences, both demonic and holy.

This family background of seeking coincided with a series of economic reversals and ill-fated mercantile ventures. They disrupted the hard-working but relatively secure future the young couple envisioned when they married, in which farming, storekeeping, and possibly schoolteaching would provide an adequate income in their home state of Vermont. Instead, Joseph and Lucy were forced into a series of moves from their own property, a gift from Joseph's father, to rented farms within Vermont, New Hampshire, and finally New York. They had 11 children, an unnamed first child who died at or near birth, Alvin (1798), Hyrum (1800), Sophronia (1803), Joseph Jr. (1805), Samuel Harrison (1808), Ephraim (1810, died in infancy), William (1811), Katharine (1813), Don Carlos (1816), and Lucy (1821).

In addition to the children who died at or near birth, nearly all of the children suffered when a typhoid epidemic swept their New Hampshire neighborhood, a prolonged siege of illness that was a heavy blow to the family finances. Sophronia was given up for dead but revived when her parents united in prayer, pleading for her life. Joseph Jr. was afflicted by a secondary infection that attacked the bone in his leg, necessitating a series of rarely performed and agonizing operations, which saved both his life and his leg but left him with a limp.

Although parental deaths, abandonment, remarriages, and the orphaning or fostering of children were common in 19th-century families, the Smith family seems to have been not only emotionally stable but also surprisingly resilient and united. The move to Palmyra, New York, during the fall and winter of 1816–1817, when the couple had been married for 21 years, was another forced move caused by three growing seasons so unnaturally cold (caused by volcanic dust in the atmosphere) that crops would not mature. Palmyra brought a season of respite. They regrouped financially, arranged to purchase land, cleared it of timber in preparation for farming, tapped scores of sugar maples, engaged in small-scale craft (coopering, oilcloth painting), and peddled refreshments at town gatherings such as militia musters. They also participated with their neighbors in the religious revivals, preaching, and debate of the time. Lucy, who had been baptized as an unaffiliated Christian as a young married woman, formally joined the Presbyterian Church with three of the children (Hyrum, Sophronia, and Samuel).

Signs of the family's unity—whether motivated by the voluntary affiliation of affection or by their quasi-shunning of a community that perceived them as marginal—include (1) their living and working together; (2) their day employment working for others in the near neighborhood (except for Alvin's leaving home to earn a year's payment on their land); (3) their united presence at Alvin's deathbed in 1823 and their subsequent grief; and (4) most notable, their willing acceptance and support of Joseph Jr.'s religious odyssey, apparently beginning with his personal conversion in a revelatory experience, his production of a new scripture (the Book of Mormon), his founding of a new Church, which he described as a restoration of

Christ's primitive Church, buttressed by restorations of various priesthoods and authoritative keys, and the subsequent 14 years of removal through three states (from New York to Ohio, Missouri, and Illinois), where Joseph and Hyrum were killed in prison on June 27, 1844. Joseph Sr. became patriarch, pronouncing blessings in the style of the aged Jacob (Gen. 49) on the members of Joseph's Church. Brothers Hyrum, William, Samuel, and Don Carlos were ardent missionaries.

Hyrum's devotion was particularly unwavering. In addition to numerous missions, he willingly undertook any responsibility Joseph assigned him, including apostle, assistant president, and, after Joseph Sr.'s death, on September 14, 1840, Church patriarch. He also refused to leave Joseph's side, crossed the Missouri River to escape arrest in June 1844 but returned with Joseph when his younger brother changed his mind, and died with him in 1844. Even William, the only brother to live past 1844 and the least zealous missionary of the group, recalled no instances of resistance or disbelief on the family's part to Joseph's early claims of revelation and interaction with heavenly messengers during the production of the Book of Mormon or the many moves and persistent poverty caused by their new religion.

Furthermore, although a typical marriage pattern for the 19th century would have had Joseph's three sisters leaving the core unit of the family when they married to move into their husbands' orbit, their husbands in fact became part of Joseph Jr.'s movement—though, granted, not among its most stalwart or highly rewarded members. Although Mother Lucy comments personally and briefly on only four daughters-in-law (Jerusha Barden, Emma Hale, Mary Bailey, and Agnes Coolbrith), she speaks of them in ways that betoken acceptance and affection. This ability to maintain a strong clan feeling and to integrate new members into it is impressive.

Even after all the children were married and forming families of their own, they remained near (within the same town or, at the greatest distance, in a neighboring county) the parental unit of Joseph Sr. and Lucy, who lived near Joseph and Emma. After Joseph Sr.'s death, Lucy was frequently a member of Joseph and Emma's household. After the murders of Joseph and Hyrum, followed within the month by the death of Samuel (of unspecified causes), Lucy followed the pattern of most 19th-century widows, living with and being cared for by her children and grandchildren, except for a few months when she lived in a small house with a granddaughter as company and helper. She had obviously hoped that William would become more of a supportive son, but he was erratic, feuding with the Twelve, bouncing from one branch of the movement to another, and never adopting either a stable profession or, until late in life, a permanent residence. As a widow, Lucy departed from the predictable pattern, however, in ending her days not with one of her three daughters, all of whom survived her, but with her daughter-in-law Emma and her second husband. She had the great satisfaction of seeing her family memoir published in England in 1854 by Orson Pratt, although she failed to realize any monetary benefit from it. She died on the family farm outside Nauvoo on May 14, 1856, attended by her grandson Joseph III.

—Lavina Fielding Anderson

See also: Book of Mormon; Smith, Emma Hale; Smith, Hyrum; Smith, Joseph Jr.

References

Smith, Lucy. *Lucy's Book: A Critical Edition of Lucy Mack Smith's Family Memoir.* Ed. Lavina Fielding Anderson. Salt Lake City, UT: Signature Books, 1992.

Walker, Kyle R., ed. *United by Faith: The Joseph Sr. and Lucy Mack Smith Family.* American Fork, UT: BYU Studies/Covenant Communications, 2006.

Snow, Eliza R.

Hailed as the "mother of this people," Eliza Roxcy Snow (1804–1887) stands as an influential Latter-day Saint figure. She was born in Massachusetts and raised in Ohio and followed the Saints to Ohio, Missouri, Illinois, Nebraska, and Utah. Her poetry chronicled the history and theology of her people and commemorated individuals, events, and ideas. Called the "Elect Lady," she worked valiantly for women, empowering them in their religious and public roles, including their work for the Relief Society, the Deseret Hospital, the 1876 centennial territorial fair, and movements to support cooperatives, home manufacture, silk production, and plural marriage. Her temple service earned her the titles "prophetess" and "priestess."

Snow was born January 21, 1804, in Becket, Berkshire County, Massachusetts, the second of Oliver and Rosetta Pettibone Snow's seven children. At the age of two, she moved with her family to the Ohio Western Reserve, where she grew up in Mantua, Portage County. Oliver Snow farmed and served as justice of the peace and county commissioner, utilizing Eliza as his secretary. Rosetta Snow taught her daughters domestic skills; Eliza later supported herself with prize-winning needlework. Her family remained influential, and in Utah she interacted closely with her older sister Leonora Snow Morley and her younger brother Lorenzo Snow, who served as Church President.

Mormonism became Snow's life cause. Her family encouraged religious exploration, joining the reformed Baptists, then the Disciples of Christ or Campbellites. They welcomed ministers and missionaries to their home, including Sidney Rigdon and Joseph Smith in the winter of 1830–1831, when Rosetta and Leonora converted. Eliza studied for five years before being baptized, in April 1835. "It is no trifling thing to be a Saint," she wrote. "My heart is fix'd" (Beecher, *Personal Writings* 61). She donated her inheritance to the Kirtland temple fund and taught the Smith family school. With her family, she experienced extreme persecution in Missouri, then moved to Nauvoo, Illinois. There she became the plural wife of Joseph

Smith. Although his death initially devastated her, Snow remained devoted to him and his cause, calling him the "crown of my life" (Snow, "Past and Present" 37). She was later married for time to Brigham Young. Her Nauvoo diary and trail journals and her correspondence, sermons, editorials, and poetry record her religious convictions.

Hailed as Zion's Poetess, Snow wrote verses that captured the essence of Mormon culture and history in more than 500 poems. The Snow family strongly supported education—Eliza sometimes wrote school assignments in verse, and she taught school in Kirtland and Nauvoo. She published several poems in Ohio newspapers. After Snow became a Latter-day Saint, her classical style transitioned to capture evolving religious theology and practice. Her grand epics situated the LDS Church in its historical setting, and she penned personal messages celebrating births and weddings and mourning deaths. Snow wrote several hymns and didactic poems for children. Her poems describe crossing the plains and travels to Europe and the Holy Land in 1872–1873. She published two volumes of *Poems, Religious, Historical, and Political* (1856, 1877).

Snow's work for women stemmed from her participation in the Nauvoo Female Relief Society. As secretary, she recorded the words of Joseph Smith. She carried the minutes across the plains, using them to reorganize local groups throughout Utah. "To me it was quite a mission, and I took much pleasure in its performance" (Beecher, *Personal Writings* 35). She influenced the organization of the children's Primary Association and the Young Ladies' Retrenchment Society. She developed policy and procedure, demonstrated leadership, and expounded doctrine with authority and insight: "We stand in a different position from the ladies of the world; we have made a covenant with God, we understand his order" (Snow, "Miss E. R. Snow's Address" 578). She taught women about redemption, from the curse of Eve through eternal marriage, access to the priesthood, and accountability in building the Kingdom. "Do you know of any place on the face of the earth, where woman has more liberty, and where she enjoys such high and glorious privileges as she does here, as a Latter-day Saint?" (Snow, "Great Indignation Meeting").

Snow died December 5, 1887, in Salt Lake City at age 83. Her funeral, a state occasion, included a procession of women and words of mighty praise. She was buried in Brigham Young's family cemetery in Salt Lake City. For years following her death, her birthday was celebrated by women around the world, and her words and hymns continue to be used. Although she had no children, she was fondly considered a Mother in Israel. "To be able to perform the many duties, and labors of love required of me, is certainly worthy of a higher tribute of gratitude to God, the Giver of all good, than I am capable of expressing" (Beecher, *Personal Writings* 42).

—*Jennifer Reeder*

See also: Mormonism and Women; Polygamy; Relief Society.

References

Beecher, Maureen Ursenbach, ed. *The Personal Writings of Eliza Roxcy Snow.* Logan: Utah State University Press, 2000.

Snow, Eliza R. "Great Indignation Meeting." *Deseret News Weekly,* January 19, 1870.

Snow, Eliza R. "Miss E. R. Snow's Address to the Female Relief Societies of Weber County." *Latter-day Saints' Millennial Star* 33 (September 12, 1871): 578.

Snow, Eliza R. "Past and Present." *Woman's Exponent* 15 (August 1, 1886): 37.

Snow, Lorenzo

In addition to serving as the fifth president of the Church, from 1898 to 1901, Lorenzo Snow (1814–1901) was a student, missionary, mystic, vegetarian, teacher, polygamist, father, apostle, legislator, world traveler, city planner, cooperative leader, utopian, federal prisoner, temple president, financier, and prophet. As Church president, he saved the organization from financial ruin and set it on a path of temporal security.

Lorenzo Snow, the fifth of seven children and the oldest son of Oliver and Rosetta Snow, was born April 3, 1814, in Mantua, Portage County, Ohio. By the time of his birth, his parents had established themselves as a leading family in the young community. Their prosperity afforded young Lorenzo time to concentrate on his studies, which eventually took him to Oberlin College. While he was there, his sister convinced him to move to Kirtland, Ohio, to study Hebrew with Joseph Smith's "school of the prophets." In June 1836, he joined the Church of Jesus Christ of Latter-day Saints.

The defining moment of his life came several weeks after his baptism, when he concluded that he had not received a spiritual witness of the truthfulness of the "Latter-day work." He walked a short distance from his house and started to pray, when he "heard a sound, just above my head, like the rustling of silken robes, and immediately the Spirit of God descended upon me, completely enveloping my whole person, filling me, from the crown of my head to the soles of my feet, and O, the joy and happiness I felt!" (Smith, *Biography* 8). Soon after this experience, he left on the first of several proselytizing missions. As a missionary in England from 1840 to 1843, he delivered a specially printed copy of the Book of Mormon to Queen Victoria.

During his years in England, Lorenzo's older sister, Eliza, became a plural wife of Joseph Smith. Uncertain how to break the news to her recently returned brother, she asked her husband to do it. Up to this point, Lorenzo Snow had believed that his life's calling was to be a missionary, not a husband and father. But he took to "celestial marriage" as completely as he had to missionary work, marrying his first two wives at the same time, in 1845. Eventually, he wedded nine women and fathered 42 children.

In 1849, Lorenzo Snow joined the main body of Saints in Salt Lake City. That year, Brigham Young selected him to fill a vacancy in the Quorum of the Twelve Apostles and sent him to Europe to establish the Italian mission. There he miraculously healed a deathly ill boy. Latter-day Saints believed Snow was a healer, even requesting him to bless handkerchiefs and religious clothing. In 1891, he purportedly raised a young girl from the dead. She recalled, "I heard Apostle Snow administer to me, telling me that I must come back, as I had some work to do on the earth yet. I was loath to leave the heavenly place, but told my friends that I must leave them" (Romney, *Life of Lorenzo Snow* 409). Years earlier, during a mission to Hawaii, Lorenzo Snow was on the receiving end of a miracle when he was revived after reportedly drowning.

In 1853, Brigham Young sent Snow to preside over Box Elder, the northernmost Mormon settlement at the time. An outstanding feature of the community was the cooperative, organized in 1863, which began as a mercantile store and grew to include more than 40 departments that met most community needs. Lorenzo Snow was proud of his experiment. On a return trip from Palestine, he visited the French president and cabinet ministers, who seemed intrigued by his suit, made of wool woven at the cooperative's woolen mill and sewn by its tailors.

Lorenzo Snow opposed the taking of animal life. He argued for a more strict interpretation of the Word of Wisdom, the LDS law of health, which stated that meat should be eaten sparingly, preferably only in time of necessity. Snow's change of heart occurred while he was hunting in 1838, when he realized the "nature of my pursuit—that of amusing myself by giving pain and death to harmless, innocent creatures that perhaps had as much right to life and enjoyment as myself" (Romney, *Life of Lorenzo Snow* 35).

In 1886, Lorenzo Snow spent 11 months in a federal prison in Salt Lake City for violation of the Edmunds Act, which outlawed polygamy. In 1893, he moved from Brigham City to Salt Lake, where he presided over the recently completed temple. Shortly before the death of Church president Wilford Woodruff, Snow entered the temple and pled in prayer for the preservation of the ailing leader's life beyond his own but pledged that he would accept God's will. He later indicated that, on that occasion, Jesus Christ had appeared and instructed him regarding the reorganization of the Church's leadership.

In September 1898, Lorenzo Snow inherited a Church on the verge of bankruptcy. He determined that his mission as president was to place the Church on a solid financial footing. To meet the demands of several fiscal emergencies, he issued Church bonds, which went on sale January 1, 1899. That summer, he developed a program that stressed the expectation that every Latter-day Saint would pay a full tithing. As a result, the Church was debt-free by early 1907.

The ministry of Lorenzo Snow is best summarized in his own words delivered January 1, 1901, as a "Greeting to the World." He admonished world leaders to "Disband your armies; turn your weapons of strife into implements of industry; take the yoke from the necks of people; arbitrate your disputes; meet in royal congress and plan for union instead of conquest, for the banishment of poverty, for the uplifting of the masses, and for the health, wealth, enlightenment and happiness of all tribes and peoples and nations" (Romney, *Life of Lorenzo Snow* 478).

Lorenzo Snow died from the effects of pneumonia on October 10, 1901, at the Beehive House in Salt Lake City. His body was interred days later in the Brigham City cemetery.

—Alan L. Morrell

See also: Mormon Missiology; Mormonism and Economics; Polygamy; Word of Wisdom.

References

Bennion, Lowell C., Alan L. Morrell, and Thomas Carter. *Polygamy in Lorenzo Snow's Brigham City: An Architectural Tour.* Salt Lake City: University of Utah, 2005.

Romney, Thomas C. *The Life of Lorenzo Snow, Fifth President of the Church of Jesus Christ of Latter-day Saints.* Salt Lake City, UT: Deseret News Press, 1955.

Smith, Eliza R. Snow. *Biography and Family Record of Lorenzo Snow.* Salt Lake City, UT: Deseret News Co., 1884.

Spafford, Belle Smith

Belle Smith Spafford (1895–1982) served for nearly three decades as the ninth general president of the Relief Society from 1945 to 1974, the longest term of any Relief Society president in Church history. During her tenure, membership grew from a localized 100,000 sisters, to nearly 1 million women worldwide. Her capable leadership provided the vision and skill needed to assist in elevating the status of women during a time of rapid and widespread social change.

Marion Isabelle Sims Smith, known during her life simply as Belle, was born to Hester Sims and John Gibson Smith on October 8, 1895, in Salt Lake City, Utah. She was the seventh and youngest child born to her parents; her father died seven months prior to her birth. Raised by her mother and her maternal Scottish grandmother, Belle graduated from LDS High School in Salt Lake City and in 1914 received a two-year degree at the University of Utah. She also studied at Brigham Young University Training School, where she taught classes in remedial work for handicapped children. At BYU, she met her future husband, Willis Earl Spafford. They married on March 23, 1921, in the Salt Lake City temple and became the parents of two children, Mary and Earl. As a lifelong student, she set aside personal daily study time and would later institute a weekly "scholar night" to mentor her grandchildren individually.

As a young mother, Spafford was called to be a counselor in her ward Relief Society presidency and later to serve on the stake Relief Society Board. While reluctant at first, she soon caught the vision provided by the organization's compassionate service during the depression years. By 1935, she was called to the Relief Society General Board, where she was assigned as editor of the *Relief Society Magazine.* During her eight years as editor, the magazine doubled its circulation. In 1942, she became a counselor to Amy Brown Lyman, and, in April 1945, she was called by President J. Reuben Clark Jr. to be the ninth general president of the Relief Society. One of her first tasks was to provide aid to victims of World War II.

A hallmark of the Spafford administration was the raising of $500,000 from Relief Society members within one year to complete the construction of a long-awaited Relief Society Building. In her dedicatory remarks, in 1956, she suggested that the new structure represented "the spirit and character of Latter-day Saint womanhood in its strength, its beauty, and its usefulness" (Spafford, *Women* 476). She also directed and established numerous welfare and social programs to benefit women and children, such as adoption services for unwed mothers and programs to prevent abuse and to provide foster care. She strengthened educational and leadership training and promoted cultural programs such as "Singing Mothers" Relief Society choirs in the 1960s.

Known as a leader with great wisdom coupled with a keen sense of humor, Spafford focused her teachings on safeguarding the role of mothers in the home, compassionate service, reverence for priesthood authority, and the need for Relief Society in the lives of women worldwide.

Encouraged by President George Albert Smith to "make your influence felt," Spafford expanded her leadership outside the Church (Hangren, "Guide" 84). She served for 28 years as a member, delegate, and leader in the National and International Councils of Women. In October 1968, Spafford was unanimously voted president of the National Council of Women, a position she held for two years, while simultaneously serving as Relief Society president. During her tenure at NCW, she delicately balanced her religious convictions, including Church policy, with the common interests of the national organization.

Spafford received numerous regional and national honors as a result of her civic and Church responsibilities, including her service as the first female member of the board of trustees of the Church school system. She died on February 2, 1982, after a lingering illness. At her funeral, Elder Boyd K. Packer stated that, "when all of the tomorrows have passed, Belle S. Spafford will stand as one of the greatest women of this dispensation" (Peterson, *Faith* 178).

—*Michele A. Welch*

See also: Lyman, Amy Brown; Mormonism and Women; Relief Society.

References

Hangen, Tona J. "Guide to a Generation: Belle Spafford's Latter-day Saint Leadership." In *New Scholarship on Latter-Day Saint Women in the Twentieth Century.* Ed. Carol Cornwall Madsen and Cherry B. Silver, 81–97. Provo, UT: Brigham Young University, 2005.

Peterson, Janet, and LaRene Gaunt. *Faith, Hope, and Charity.* American Fork, UT: Covenant Communications, 2008.

Spafford, Belle S. *Women in Today's World.* Salt Lake City, UT: Deseret Book, 1971.

Talmage, James E.

James Edward Talmage (1862–1933) was a member of the Quorum of the Twelve Apostles from 1911 to his death, in 1933. He was a leading Mormon intellectual in a period rich with them, distinguished as a scientist and a religious thinker, and author of several classic works of devotion and theology.

He was born September 21, 1862 in Hungerford, Berkshire, England, first son and second child of James Joyce Talmage and Susannah Preater Talmage. The family joined the Church of Jesus Christ of Latter-day Saints in 1873 and in 1876 moved to Provo, Utah, where James entered Brigham Young Academy. His interest was in the sciences; he was influenced by Mormon educator Karl Maeser's enthusiasm for reconciling that subject with faith and through his life argued that science revealed the hand of God as Creator. From 1882 to 1884, he studied at Lehigh University and Johns Hopkins University, graduating from the former. He received a PhD from Illinois Wesleyan University in 1896, the first Mormon to achieve that degree. After teaching science for several years at Brigham Young Academy, he moved, in 1888, to Salt Lake City. There he taught geology at Latter-day Saints College and at the University of Utah, where he was president from 1894 to 1897.

In 1888, Talmage married Mary Booth in the Manti, Utah, temple. They would have eight children together.

On December 8, 1911, he was ordained an apostle and joined the Quorum of the Twelve Apostles. He was already well known among Mormons, for over the previous two decades he had written several influential works of theology. *Articles of Faith* (1899) is the most significant of these. It had been composed several years before as lectures for a theology course at Latter-day Saint College. Using as a framework the 13 statements Joseph Smith presented as the essentials of Mormonism, Talmage explored the basics of Mormon theology. In 1898, the First Presidency gave its official imprimatur to the lectures' publication as a book, which Mormons since have understood as authoritative. In particular, Talmage clarified ambiguities in Mormon conceptions of the Trinity, affirming the personhood of the Holy Spirit as an independent member of a three-person trinity.

In the years following his ordination, Talmage's pen was twice again commissioned by the First Presidency. His 1912 *House of the Lord* discussed worship and presented photographs of the Salt Lake City temple's interior in order to trump an anticipated exposé. In 1915, he published his best-known work, *Jesus the Christ,* a biography that, like *Articles of Faith,* began life as a series of lectures. Talmage was unable to pursue the adaptation for almost 10 years, until he was granted the privacy of a room in the Salt Lake City temple in which to complete it. Like his earlier work, particularly 1907's *The Great Apostasy, Jesus the Christ* demonstrated Talmage's willingness to use European biblical scholarship. It also solidified the trinitarianism of *Articles of Faith*. Talmage identifies the premortal Christ as the Jehovah of the Old Testament—a doctrine then nascent in Mormon thought. The book's influence was confirmed when, in 1916, the First Presidency confirmed his trinitarianism as official doctrine.

Talmage was an intellectual leader in the Quorum. He was involved in the production of revised editions of scripture and the standardization of temple rituals. He also became a national spokesman for the Church. In 1904, he testified at congressional hearings on the seating of apostle Reed Smoot as a senator, and in 1915 he represented the Church at the World Congress of Religions. He authored a newspaper column and a series of radio addresses. His prominence as a religious leader combined with his scientific training meant that it was natural that many Mormons would turn to him as an authority when controversy over evolution erupted in the 1920s.

Talmage strove to chart a middle way between the biblical literalism of his fellow apostle Joseph Fielding Smith and leaders more sympathetic to Darwin, such as the Seventy Brigham H. Roberts. Though Talmage stated his belief in the Genesis account of divinely designed life, he acknowledged, in a 1931 speech, "The Earth and Man," that geology reflected an Earth "countless generations" old. He sought to distinguish between what he called "Adamic man" and the rest of creation, the latter subject to natural cycles of time, the former destined for a "true evolution"—eternal progression toward divinity (Talmage, "The Earth and Man").

Two years later, on July 27, 1933, Talmage died at age 70 at his home in Salt Lake City. He is buried in the Salt Lake City cemetery.

—*Matthew Bowman*

See also: Mormonism and Education; Mormonism and Science; Roberts, B. H.; Smith, Joseph Fielding.

References

Harris, James, ed. *The Essential James E. Talmage.* Salt Lake City, UT: Signature Books, 1997.

Talmage, James E. *Articles of Faith.* Salt Lake City, UT: Deseret News Press, 1899.

Talmage, James E. "The Earth and Man." *Deseret News,* November 21, 1931.

Talmage, James E. *Jesus the Christ.* Salt Lake City, UT: Deseret News Press, 1915.

Taylor, Elmina Shepherd

Elmina (also Mina) Shepherd Taylor (1830–1904) was the first president of the LDS Church's Young Women's Mutual Improvement Association, serving from 1880 to 1904. She was born in Middlefield, New York, on September 12, 1830, to David S. and Rozella Bailey Shepherd. She attended public schools, then left home, in 1854.

While teaching in Haverstraw, New York, in 1856, she was baptized a member of the LDS Church on July 5. "I fought against my convictions," she recalled, "for I well knew how it would grieve my dear parents . . . and I also thought I should lose my [teaching] situation. . . . However, I could not silence my convictions, and . . . I went forth and was baptized" (Crocheron, *Representative Women* 49). The next month, on August 31, 1856, she married George Hamilton Taylor. Not quite three years later, she and her husband immigrated by ox team to the Salt Lake Valley, arriving on September 16, 1859. They resided in Salt Lake City's 14th Ward, where she was called as secretary of the ward's Relief Society in 1867 and as president of its Young Ladies' Mutual Improvement Association in 1874. She was also appointed to the presidency of the multiward Salt Lake Stake Relief Society in 1879, a position she held for 16 years.

On June 19, 1880, during a conference of the Church's women's organizations in Salt Lake City, Taylor was called to serve as the first Church-wide general president of the Young Ladies' Mutual Improvement Association. She subsequently joined the National Council of Women, serving as ex officio vice president beginning in 1891 and attending several of its annual conventions. She also presided at meetings of the Young Ladies' Mutual Improvement Association held in conjunction with the 1893 Chicago Fair. She bore seven children, four of whom survived to adulthood. She died on December 6, 1904. Her funeral was held in the Salt Lake Assembly Hall; the ushers and choir were members of the Young Ladies' Association. Joseph F. Smith, president of the LDS Church, eulogized: "She was one of the few in the world who had the light within her. . . . She was a strong character, . . . tempered and softened by the . . . spirit of kindness, of love, of mercy, and of charity" ("Death of Elmina S. Taylor," 221).

The Young Ladies' Mutual Improvement Association had its beginnings in the Young Ladies Department of the Cooperative Retrenchment Association, first organized by LDS Church President Brigham Young for his daughters beginning in November 1869. Its mission, according to Young, was to "spend more time in moral, mental and spiritual cultivation, and less upon fashion and the vanities of the world" (*Woman's Exponent* 59). Eliza R. Snow, the general president of the Church's all-female Relief Society, supervised the various local Retrenchment Associations; Emma Young Emprey, age 23, was named founding Retrenchment Association president.

By 1871, the now-renamed Young Ladies' Retrenchment Association encouraged weekly meetings, public speaking, moderate exercise programs, clean living, modest dress habits, and discussions of gospel and current events. Some two years after the organization of the Young Men's Mutual Improvement Association, in 1875, Retrenchment changed its name to Young Ladies' National Mutual Improvement Association. (In 1904, the word "National" was dropped in deference to the Church's international focus.)

Initially, the Young Ladies' Association operated strictly locally; the first stake-wide, multiward governing board was not created until 1878, in the Salt Lake Stake. According to historian Carol Cornwall Madsen: "The Retrenchment Association was unique among Church organizations. As an ad hoc auxiliary, it was attached to no ecclesiastical unit, had no geographic boundaries (its meetings were open to all LDS women), and functioned under no specific line of ecclesiastical authority. . . . Members of the congregation (sometimes numbering two hundred) expressed religious sentiments or spoke impromptu on themes suggested by the presiding officers" (Madsen, "Retrenchment Association" 1224).

When Elmina Taylor was named as the first general president of the various ward and stake associations, in 1880, the Young Ladies' Association emphasized religious study, charitable service, and personal development. General, stake, and ward association boards followed; activities held monthly in conjunction with local Young Men's Associations were encouraged; and association-oriented periodicals and lesson manuals, including the *Young Woman's Journal* (1889, edited by Susa Young Gates), soon began to appear. The association's first annual Church-wide conference convened in June 1888 and featured instruction in physical exercise, public speaking, music, and lesson planning and presentation. Following Taylor's presidency, the association changed its name to Young Women's Mutual Improvement Association and eventually simply to Young Women, the name by which it is known in the 21st century.

—*Gary James Bergera*

See also: Local Worship; Youth Programs.

References

Crocheron, Augusta Joyce. *Representative Women of Deseret.* Salt Lake City, UT: J.C. Graham, 1884.

"Death of Elmina S. Taylor." *Improvement Era* 8 (January 1905): 218–222.

Madsen, Carol Cornwall. "Retrenchment Association." In *Encyclopedia of Mormonism,* vol. 3. Ed. Daniel H. Ludlow, 1223–1224. New York: Macmillan, 1992.

Woman's Exponent 11 (September 15, 1882): 59.

Taylor, John

John Taylor (1808–1887), third president of the Church, was born November 1, 1808, at Milnthorpe, Westmoreland, England. Drawn early to religion, Taylor became a Methodist preacher at 17; in 1832, he immigrated to Canada because of his conviction that God wanted him to preach the gospel in America. Still seeking a people who practiced primitive Christianity more nearly than any he then knew, Taylor investigated Mormonism and became a convert in 1836.

Taylor moved to Far West, Missouri, in 1837; the following year, he was ordained to the Quorum of the Twelve Apostles. He served his first mission in 1839, becoming the first to preach the restored gospel in Ireland and on the Isle of Man.

Rejoining the body of the Church in Nauvoo, Taylor filled many roles: city councilman, colonel in the militia, and editor of the *Times and Seasons* (a Church publication) and the *Nauvoo Neighbor* (a city newspaper).

Taylor accompanied Joseph and Hyrum Smith when they were jailed at Carthage. When the Smith brothers were murdered, on June 27, 1844, Taylor was himself severely wounded by several balls, which he carried in his body for the rest of his life. His account of the martyrdom reflects his poetic skill: "Henceforward their names will be classed among the martyrs of religion; and the reader in every nation will be reminded that the Book of Mormon, and this book of Doctrine and Covenants of the church, cost the best blood of the nineteenth century to bring them forth for the salvation of a ruined world. . . . They lived for glory; they died for glory; and glory is their eternal reward" (Doctrine and Covenants 135).

Taylor evacuated from Nauvoo in 1846; from Winter Quarters he was sent on another brief mission to Great Britain, and, when he returned, in 1847, he led a company of emigrants to Utah, following close behind the vanguard company of Brigham Young.

Taylor returned to Europe in 1849–1851, opening missionary work in France and supervising the translation of the Book of Mormon into French and German. He established the first non-English newspapers published in the interest of Mormonism, *L'Etoile de Deseret* (French) and *Zions Panier* (German). While in France, he engaged in a memorable debate with clergymen, the text of which was published and used extensively as missionary literature.

Stationed in New York City in 1855–1857, Taylor served several important functions. He edited the newspaper *The Mormon* to represent LDS interests and to influence public opinion. He presided over the eastern ecclesiastical organization. He served as agent for the purchase of goods needed in the West. He assisted with political missions in Washington, D.C., including Utah's statehood bid, in 1856. As the Church's emigration agent, Taylor greeted shiploads of Mormon emigrants and helped them through the legal maze at Castle Garden, the immigration reception center in New York City. He negotiated rates and routes on the railroads and arranged to transfer emigrants and their luggage from shipboard to train. When emigrants were financially unprepared to continue their journey, he assisted them in finding housing and employment.

Among Taylor's duties was implementation of the first handcart emigration, in 1856. In the months prior to dispatching the first company, he investigated routes, handcart specifications, and locations for resupplying the emigrants. Perhaps more than any other leader, he recognized the difficulties and dangers of the plan: "We would not recommend [it] to those who have means to carry them in a more comfortable manner . . . but we think we discover in it barely a means of transit for thousands of limited means" who otherwise would wait years to emigrate (Taylor, "Hand Carts" 2).

In addition to his ecclesiastical duties through the 1860s and 1870s, Taylor served in the territorial legislature and as superintendent of schools. He directed the Church as president of the Quorum of the Twelve Apostles after Young's death and was sustained as its president in 1880. One of his first acts as president was to forgive debts to the Perpetual Emigrating Fund.

Taylor's ministry was marked by unswerving commitment to his God and to the well-being of the Church; his personal motto was "The Kingdom of God or Nothing." An unfortunate impression exists that Taylor was a combative opponent of Brigham Young, an impression created largely by the unsupported allegations of a biographer-descendant. To the contrary, whatever differences in style and temperament existed between the two men, Taylor's words and actions reflect constant support for Young as his leader and a wholehearted effort to fulfill obligations assigned to him by Young. Taylor's writings and sermons, both as apostle and as prophet, reflect a scholarly mind, a sensitivity to spiritual impressions, and a desire to serve.

Taylor presided over the Church during the most repressive period of its history. Polygamous husbands were disfranchised; missionaries were slain with impunity; U.S. policy opposed overseas proselyting and the emigration of converts; homes and even the sanctuary of the Endowment House were raided by federal marshals in the search for men with plural families. Convicted of "unlawful cohabitation," men were fined and imprisoned, some sent to penitentiaries as far away as Detroit.

Despite his voluntary separation from his several plural wives (he lived in Salt Lake City with his sister Agnes as housekeeper), Taylor was subject to arrest. To avoid that eventuality and the disruption it would cause to the Church, he went into hiding. From the date of his last public address, on February 1, 1884, until his death, Taylor moved frequently from safehouse to safehouse, guarded by trusted men who carried communications between Taylor and others. Unable to appear at the annual conferences of the Church, Taylor advised the Saints through printed epistles to remain faithful to their covenants and to trust in God come what may. He died, "on the underground," in Kaysville, Utah, on July 25, 1887.

—*Ardis E. Parshall*

See also: Handcart Migration; Immigration; Martyrdom of Joseph and Hyrum Smith; Mormon Missiology; Polygamy.

References

Doctrine and Covenants of the Church of Jesus Christ of Latter-day Saints. Salt Lake City, UT: The Church of Jesus Christ of Latter-day Saints, 1981.

Roberts, B. H. *Life of John Taylor.* Salt Lake City, UT: Bookcraft, 1963.

Taylor, John. "Hand Carts for the Plains." *The Mormon* (New York City), December 1, 1855, 2.

Wells, Emmeline B.

Emmeline Blanche Woodward Harris Whitney Wells (1828–1910) was the fifth general president of the Relief Society. An articulate defender of the Mormon faith in written and spoken word, she served for 37 years as editor of the *Woman's Exponent,* a feminist semimonthly periodical. She published her poetry in a compilation entitled *Musings and Memories* and published many short stories in the *Exponent* under the pen name Blanche Beechwood. As a leader in the suffrage movement, she spoke out against legislation that denied women the right to vote and lobbied extensively as a staunch public supporter of polygamy.

Emmeline Blanche Woodward was born February 29, 1828, in Petersham, Massachusetts. After her father's death, her mother moved the family to Salem, Massachusetts, where Emmeline received an exceptional education for the time. She was baptized a member of the Mormon Church on her 14th birthday and thereafter began teaching school. At age 15, she married James Harvey Harris and left with him to join the Saints in Nauvoo, Illinois. Soon after their arrival, in 1844, her newborn son, Eugene Henri, died, and her husband left to find work. For support, she began teaching school, and later, when her husband didn't return, she became the plural wife of Newel K. Whitney. In the fall of 1848, the Whitney family arrived in Salt Lake City, where her daughters Isabel and Melvina were born.

When Whitney died, in 1850, Emmeline returned to teaching school, and, two years later, she married prominent Church and civic leader Daniel H. Wells as his seventh plural wife. Together they had three daughters, Emma, Elizabeth Ann, and Louisa. Emmeline and her five daughters resided independently from Wells's main family in a small adobe home where she supported herself for most of her remaining years.

Wells's public service began at the enlistment of Church president Brigham Young in 1876 to direct a grain-saving mission. Through the *Woman's Exponent,* she asked women in the Church to glean leftover wheat from their fields and ditch banks to donate to the Relief Society. The wheat project was extremely successful and helped to relieve suffering across the world and especially during World War I. President Woodrow Wilson expressed his gratitude for her efforts in a personal visit in 1919.

Wells continued her 45 years of public service in 1879 at a national suffrage convention in Washington, D.C., and was thereafter intensely involved in the State and National Women's Suffrage Association and the National and International Councils of Women. She relentlessly fought against antipolygamy legislation such as the Edmunds-Tucker Act (1887) and wrote strong editorials to represent the Mormon woman's view to the nation regarding woman's suffrage. She asserted that women "have stamina enough to stand boldly forth in defense of right. . . . It matters little what name they give us, so long as our motives are pure, and our actions are honorable" (Beachwood [Wells], "Our Daughters" 131). She confidently lobbied at many conventions and congressional hearings and before three U.S. presidents. In 1899, she was invited to speak at the International Council of Women in London as representative of the United States. Her powerful voice in public debate, as well as her personal friendships with national suffragist leaders, promoted understanding and enabled her to serve as a liaison between Mormons and non-Mormons.

In 1910, at the age of 82, Emmeline B. Wells was elected as the general president of the Relief Society after serving 22 years as secretary. During her 11-year presidency, she continued to support causes that elevated the status of women and children, raised funds for temples, and taught regarding the noble role of womanhood. In her declining years, she focused her attention on the religious work of her Mormon sisters until a month prior to her death, on April 25, 1921, at the age of 93. At her large funeral in the Salt Lake Tabernacle, flags flew at half-staff to honor her. On February 29, 1928, to commemorate her birth 100 years earlier, a marble bust was placed in the rotunda of the Utah State Capitol with the inscription "A Fine Soul Who Served Us."

—Michele A. Welch

See also: Mormonism and Women; Polygamy; Relief Society.

References

Beechwood, Blanche [Emmeline B. Wells]. *Woman's Exponent* 2 (February 1, 1874): 131.

Madsen, Carol Cornwall. *An Advocate for Women: The Public Life of Emmeline B. Wells 1870–1920.* Provo, UT: Brigham Young University Press, 2006.

Scott, Patricia Lyn, and Linda Thatcher, eds. *Women in Utah History: Paradigm or Paradox?* Logan: Utah State University Press, 2005.

Witnesses to the Book of Mormon

In September 1827, Joseph Smith claimed to have received from an angel a book of ancient scripture written on gold plates from which he would translate the Book of Mormon. However, Smith stated that he was not allowed to show this record to anyone during the translating period and further reported that, after he had finished the translation, in summer 1829, the same angel retrieved the plates from him. This left the validity of the plates' existence in doubt, for only Smith had personally seen them. Believers in Smith's account relied completely on faith. Perhaps in anticipation of later accusations calling Smith a fraud who had fabricated a story about golden plates, Smith allowed 11 men to become official "witnesses."

Several months before the completion of the plates' translation, Martin Harris visited Smith in Harmony, Pennsylvania, and asked him to inquire of the Lord if he could see the gold plates. In response, Smith reported a revelation that stated that, "in addition to [Joseph's] testimony," three others would have the privilege of viewing the sacred record; if Harris humbled himself, he would be among these three witnesses (Book of Commandments, 10–13). Three months later, Smith, now in Fayette, New York, claimed another revelation that named Oliver Cowdery and David Whitmer as witnesses along with Harris. It also stipulated that they would be granted a view of the gold plates, the breastplate, the sword of Laban, the Urim and Thummim, and the Liahona, all artifacts mentioned in the Book of Mormon. The revelation told them that once they saw these artifacts, the three witnesses were to bear testimony to the world concerning them (Doctrine and Covenants Section 17).

Several days after this instruction, the three chosen witnesses, along with Smith, retired to the woods outside the Whitmers' home to pray. When at first nothing seemed to occur, Martin Harris withdrew himself, feeling that he was the reason for the failure. Those remaining then reported being visited by an angel who showed them the plates and "turned over the leaves one by one" in front of them. They also heard a voice from the heavens confirming the divine translation and commanding them to bear record of it to others. David Whitmer later claimed that there was also a table upon which were laid the other items promised in the revelation. When the vision concluded, Smith left Cowdery and Whitmer to find Harris. Once he located him, Smith and Harris both prayed, and Harris reported that he was granted the same vision.

Joseph Smith's mother, Lucy Mack Smith, remembered the young prophet returning from these events ecstatically relieved. She would later write that he "threw himself down beside me, and exclaimed, 'Father, mother, you do not know how happy I am; the Lord has now caused the plates to be shown to three more besides myself . . . for now they know for themselves, that I do not go about to deceive the people, and I feel as if I was relieved of a burden which was almost too heavy for me to bear'" (Smith, *Lucy's Book* 453). Smith's lone testimony of the plates had been ridiculed by naysayers. Now he felt that critics would have to take into account these additional testimonies.

Shortly after these events, a separate and somewhat different witness experience was reportedly granted to other followers. A few days after the previous experience, Joseph, along with members of the Whitmer family, traveled to the Palmyra, New York, area in order to finalize printing arrangements for the Book of Mormon. While there, Joseph took his father, two of his brothers (Hyrum and Samuel), four members of the Whitmer family (Christian, Jacob, Peter Jr., and John), and Hiram Page (who had married into the Whitmer family) into the woods outside his parents' home. There, without implying the supernatural elements claimed at the first witness experience, these eight witnesses were able to casually examine the record. Many would later testify in private as well as public settings about this experience by discussing the size, weight, color, structure, and texture of the gold plates.

The first chance these observers had to bear record came later that night. Lucy Mack Smith reminisced that, "the ensuing evening, we held a meeting, in which all the witnesses bore testimony" to what they had experienced (Smith, *Lucy's Book* 457). Their testimonies were later recorded and printed on the last pages of the Book of Mormon (these are found in the front matter of recent editions). The testimonies were addressed "unto all nations, kindreds, tongues, and people, unto whom this work shall come" and bore record to what they had seen and felt. In their affirmation, the three witnesses wrote that they had experienced an angel showing them the plates and had heard the voice of God, while the eight witnesses testified that they had merely seen, handled, and hefted the ancient record (Book of Mormon, 1986). Besides the significance of their written testimonies, these witnesses, particularly the three witnesses, held important positions in the early Church. For instance, Martin Harris, David Whitmer, and Oliver Cowdery were commissioned to locate, call, and ordain the original 12 apostles.

Even though many of the eight witnesses and each of the three witnesses would eventually leave the Church, none of them renounced his statements concerning the Book of Mormon. For example, shortly before David Whitmer passed away, he reaffirmed his previous claims: "I have never at any time denied that testimony or any part thereof which has so long been published with that book [the Book of Mormon], as one of the three witnesses. . . . I do again affirm the truth of all my statements as then made and published. He that hath an ear to hear let him hear; it was no delusion!" (Cook, *David Whitmer Interviews* 202). Mormons then and now view these testimonies as important voices validating the reality of the plates.

Early critics questioned these accounts by doubting the reliability of the witnesses. They pointed to the fact that not only were all witnesses members of the Smith or Whitmer families but that they were all believers in the new religion and therefore had personal agendas. A common critique was that a true testimony could come only from an unbiased observer. Later critics, however, have questioned not the witnesses' credibility but rather the experiences themselves. They argue that the eight witnesses' claims are as "supernatural" as the three witnesses' experience and that therefore they should all be regarded as spiritual encounters, rather than rational evidence.

Besides the official testimonies, there were several other "unofficial" incidents wherein additional individuals reported experiences with the plates. Emma Smith, Joseph's wife, would later claim that she had had close contact with the plates while cleaning the house during the translation. She explained that she once felt them while they lay covered on the translating table: "They seemed to be pliable like thick paper, and would rustle with a metallic sound when the edges were moved by the thumb" (Bushman, *Joseph Smith* 70). Joseph's brother William later recalled that he was able to hold the plates the first night Joseph returned home with them, while they were covered in a cloth: "They were not quite as large as this Bible. Could tell whether they were round or square. Could raise the leaves this way [raising a few leaves of the Bible before him]" (Smith, *Lucy's Book* 20). It is also purported that Mary Whitmer, mother of the Whitmers who were witnesses, was visited by an angel who showed her the plates because of her willingness to allow the Book of Mormon translation to take place in her home.

For believers, these testimonies combined to form a clear assertion of the reality of the plates. From those who claimed supernatural events, to those who detailed personal encounters, to those who described plates under a cloth sheet, the witnesses collectively substantiated Smith's claim that he possessed physical plates containing sacred writings of an ancient civilization.

—*Benjamin E. Park*

See also: Book of Mormon; Mormon Scripture.

References

Anderson, Richard L. "Attempts to Redefine the Experience of the Eight Witnesses." *Journal of Book of Mormon Studies* 14, no. 1 (2005): 18–31.

Anderson, Richard L. *Investigating the Book of Mormon Witnesses.* Salt Lake City, UT: Deseret Book, 1981.

Book of Commandments. Zion, MO: W.W. Phelps, 1833.

Book of Mormon. Salt Lake City, UT: The Church of Jesus Christ of Latter-day Saints, 1986.

Bushman, Richard L. *Joseph Smith: Rough Stone Rolling: A Cultural Biography of Mormonism's Founder.* New York: Knopf, 2005.

Cook, Lyndon W. *David Whitmer Interviews: A Restoration Witness.* Orem, UT: Grandin, 1991.

Doctrine and Covenants of the Church of Jesus Christ of Latter-day Saints. Salt Lake City, UT: The Church of Jesus Christ of Latter-day Saints, 1981.

Smith, Lucy. *Lucy's Book: A Critical Edition of Lucy Mack Smith's Family Memoir.* Ed. Lavina Fielding Anderson. Salt Lake City, UT: Signature Books, 2001.

Woodruff, Wilford

Wilford Woodruff (March 1, 1807–September 2, 1898) was the fourth president of the Church, a prophet, a community leader, and an agriculturalist. He was born in Farmington (now Avon), Connecticut, the son of Aphek Woodruff, a miller and farmer, and Bulah Thompson. His mother died when he was a year old, and Aphek then married Azubah Hart. Educated at the Farmington Academy, Woodruff grew up in a family of local leaders and pillars of the Congregational Church. Woodruff's father, some of his immediate family, and one uncle left Congregationalism.

Woodruff and some of the dissenters became seekers, searching for a modern form of primitive Christianity.

Woodruff continued his religious quest while operating mills and farming in Connecticut and New York until his conversion to the LDS Church in 1833. At the time of his conversion, controversy had grown in western Missouri between Mormon migrants and the old settlers. Disputes arose over Mormon religious beliefs and practices, over economic exclusiveness, and over LDS attitudes toward slavery and free blacks. Dissension between the two groups led to violent opposition to the Mormons and to their expulsion from Jackson County by the southern majority by force of arms. In early 1834, Joseph Smith called for volunteers to form an expedition, called Zion's Camp, to help restore the homes and businesses of the Missouri Mormons. Woodruff joined the failed expedition and afterward served proselytizing missions to Tennessee and Kentucky and to Maine.

Called in 1838 to the Quorum of the Twelve Apostles, Woodruff spent the remainder of his life as a missionary, community leader, and Church official. On a mission with others of the Twelve to England in 1839–1841, Woodruff converted hundreds of people. Returning to the United States, he served as a missionary and as business manager for a Nauvoo, Illinois, newspaper.

Sent with other Church leaders to campaign for Joseph Smith in the 1844 presidential race, Woodruff and others in the Twelve learned of the Mormon prophet's murder while in New England. Returning to Nauvoo, the Twelve, under the leadership of Brigham Young, assumed the presidency of the majority of Latter-day Saints. Following a bloody civil war, the Twelve led the Mormons to Utah beginning in 1846–1847.

As a religious leader, horticulturalist, rancher, educator, and politician, Woodruff settled in Salt Lake City, where he assisted in building communities and in governing the LDS Church. Serving as Church Historian, he collected documents and established archives for Mormon records. Deeply spiritual, he received numerous revelations that provided guidance for the members. Operating farms and ranches, he promoted education and scientific and cultural societies. Serving as president of the Deseret Agricultural and Manufacturing Society (1862–1877), he sponsored the importation of animals, seeds, plants, and machinery from the United States and Europe to develop the economy.

First married to Phebe Whittemore Carter (four of their children survived infancy), in 1837, Woodruff was subsequently married polygamously to Mary Ann Jackson (married in 1846, one child survived infancy, divorced), Sarah Elinore Brown (married in 1846, no children, divorced), Mary Carolyn Barton (married in 1846, no children, divorced), Mary Giles Meeks Webster (married 1852, no children), Emma Smith (married 1853, six children survived infancy), Sarah Brown (married 1853, six children survived infancy), Sarah Delight Stocking (married 1857, five children survived infancy), and Eudora Lovina Young (married 1877, no children survived infancy, divorced). The divorces from Mary Ann and Eudora resulted from incompatibility, and those from Sarah Elinore and Mary Carolyn resulted from his belief that they had been unfaithful to him.

As a Church leader, he worked loyally with the First Presidency and others in the Twelve while introducing modifications that reiterated the need for love, family solidarity, and harmony. In the Mormon Reformation of 1856–1857, where harsh teachings and elaborate catechisms called members to task for straying from Church teachings, he served to mitigate some of the blunt preaching of other Church leaders by emphasizing the need for love and concern. He served as president of the St. George temple (dedicated 1877), the first completed in Utah. In that role, he received revelations that promoted, for the first time, vicarious temple ordinances for deceased men and women not related to Mormons—particularly national and international political, literary, and scientific leaders.

The 1860 victory of the Republican Party resulted in a series of laws attacking the LDS Church. Passed in 1862, 1874, 1882, and 1887, these laws prescribed fines and imprisonment for polygamy, brought the Utah territorial courts under closer federal oversight, and resulted in the confiscation of property belonging to the Church. Because of the campaign to imprison Mormons who had married polygamously, Woodruff and others hid from U.S. marshals during part of the 1880s.

Leading the Church as president of the Council of the Twelve Apostles, the Church's second governing body, after the death of John Taylor and the consequent dissolution of the First Presidency in 1887, Woodruff was called to serve as president of the LDS Church in 1889. Following the imprisonment for practicing polygamy of more than 1,000 Latter-day Saint men and a number of women and the confiscation of much of the Church's property, Woodruff received a revelation directing the abandonment of plural marriage, which he presented to the Church leaders and membership in September and October 1890.

Throughout his presidency, he worked for accommodation with the remainder of American society. Before he became Church president, the Mormons and others in Utah had separated into the People's (Mormon) and the Liberal (non-Mormon) parties. In 1891, Woodruff divided the Church membership into national political parties. In addition, he encouraged Church members to renounce offensive doctrines and to develop productive relationships with national and local business and political leaders. He died in San Francisco while visiting a non-Mormon friend.

Arguably the third most important LDS leader after Joseph Smith and Brigham Young, Woodruff was a transitional figure. At first helping to build the LDS community on a millennialist basis (expecting Christ to return soon to Earth to reign for 1,000 years), after he became president of the Church he promoted accommodations that enabled the LDS Church to become one of the largest American Churches in the 20th century. Deeply spiritual, he was also well educated, intelligent, and personable. Establishing relationships with leaders outside the LDS community, he facilitated changes in Mormonism to retain the essential spiritual aspects of LDS life while accommodating on other matters. In doing so, he strengthened Mormonism as a distinctive religious tradition within Christianity.

—Thomas G. Alexander

See also: Manifesto; Mormonism and Blacks; Polygamy; Transition: 1890–1941; Zion's Camp.

References

Alexander, Thomas G. *Things in Heaven and Earth: The Life and Times of Wilford Woodruff, a Mormon Prophet.* Salt Lake City, UT: Signature Books, 1991.

Gibbons, Francis M. *Wilford Woodruff: Wondrous Worker, Prophet of God.* Salt Lake City, UT: Deseret Book, 1988.

Wilford Woodruff's Journal, 1833–1898. Typescript ed. Ed. Scott G. Kenney. 9 vols. Midvale, UT: Signature Books, 1983–1885.

Young, Brigham

Brigham Young (1801–1877) was the second president of the Church. Born in the Vermont backcountry to impoverished parents, Young grew up in central and western New York as the area emerged from frontier conditions. Brigham's mother, Nabby Howe Young, died when he was 14. Moving to Auburn, New York, after his father's remarriage, Young spent his early adulthood working at an assortment of trades and odd jobs, becoming a talented carpenter, joiner, and painter.

Spiritually restless, Young followed the example of his father and several siblings and in the early 1820s joined the Reformed Methodist Church, a Wesleyan offshoot dedicated to spiritual healing, lay leadership, and perfectionism. Though a sincere convert, within several years Young grew disenchanted with evangelical Protestantism and was consumed with depression and doubts about his salvation.

Brigham Young, Mormonism's "Moses," at about the time he led the pioneer company to the Salt Lake Valley. (Courtesy of the Church History Library, The Church of Jesus Christ of Latter-day Saints.)

Along with his wife, Miriam Works, Young joined several other family members converging on the outskirts of Rochester. There he and other family members encountered the Book of Mormon. After two years of reflection and visits with several elders, the Young family converted en masse, including Miriam, who died of tuberculosis in September 1832.

Immediately after his baptism, Young became an itinerant Mormon preacher, and he also experienced the charismatic gift of speaking in tongues. He displayed the latter practice during a trip to Kirtland that began a lifelong allegiance to the prophet Joseph Smith Jr. Shortly thereafter, Young married Mary Ann Angell, with whom he cultivated a companionate and warm marriage, often through romantic and winsome letters he wrote during his frequent travels.

In 1834, Young accompanied Smith on the Zion's Camp excursion to Missouri, which marked the beginning of Young's rise to prominence in Smith's eyes. Young sharply defended the prophet against his critics, and Smith rewarded his loyalty by selecting him as an inaugural member of the Quorum of the Twelve Apostles.

After several years of missionary service, Young fled Kirtland late in 1837 when the Ohio Stake of the Church imploded amid infighting and dissension. Having taken refuge in Missouri, Young, as the senior member of the Twelve, became the interim leader of the Church during its forced exodus to Illinois. Late in 1839, Young left Illinois to take charge of the Church's British Mission, cementing his reputation as a skillful organizer while also promoting the spiritual gifts of tongues, healing, and prophecy among converts.

Upon his return, Young found himself buffeted by Nauvoo's mounting theological and political storms. Quickly receptive to Joseph Smith's doctrine of plural marriage, Young first proposed unsuccessfully to a British immigrant, then was sealed to Lucy Ann Decker Seeley, a 20-year-old mother of two children who was estranged from her husband. In November 1843, he married two additional women on the same date, including Augusta Adams Cobb, whose subsequent divorce from her husband created notoriety for Young and the Church. Inured to criticism from his many years as a missionary, Young never displayed any concern for how outsiders viewed his family. Mary Ann Young proved supportive of Young's additional wives, but over time her relationship with Young gradually lost its prior intimacy.

Smith's murder created a confusing power vacuum in the Church and left several candidates eager to fill it, including Smith's longtime counselor in the Church presidency Sidney Rigdon. At an August meeting of the Church, some in the audience claimed they heard and saw the martyred Smith when Young claimed that the "keys of the kingdom are with" the Quorum of the Twelve (Arrington, *Brigham Young* 115). Moreover, Young's fealty to Smith's later teachings and his ability to promote the construction of the temple and its rituals put him and the Twelve in a much better position to assume leadership of the Church than Rigdon. Three years later, Young persuaded his fellow apostles—several recalcitrant members, including Orson Pratt, received a severe browbeating—to permit him to form a new Church presidency.

Before leaving Nauvoo, Young oversaw the completion of the temple amid rising anti-Mormon pressure in Illinois. Joseph Smith had insisted that temple ordinances were necessary to secure eternal life and exaltation and to bind couples with their ancestors and children in eternity. By overseeing a flurry of endowments and sealings, Young cemented his role as spiritual leader of the Church.

After establishing temporary refuges on the plains, Young led an advance party to the Salt Lake Basin in the spring of 1847, reaching the Valley of the Great Salt Lake in July. The initial exodus and subsequent emigrations furthered a key aspect of Young's presidency, his emphasis on making Saints and forging a distinctive Mormon identity. For Young, people became Saints not in the waters of baptism but through trials, tribulations, and "living their religion," which meant sacrifice, obedience, and morality. "I want hard times," he insisted, "so that every person that does not wish to stay, for the sake of his religion, will leave." In their new mountain home, Young's followers found those hard times abundantly, suffering from famine, rumors of war, difficulty creating harmonious plural families, and a long struggle to carve viable communities out of inhospitable portions of the American West. "This is a good place to make Saints," Young concluded (Arrington, *Brigham Young* 167). While Young demanded more than some of his followers could stomach, thousands flocked to and abided by his leadership, attracted by his stewardship of Smith's theological and ritual legacy (symbolized by temple building), his fervent belief in and preaching of the gospel, and the close connection he maintained with the Saints. Young undertook regular preaching tours to visit with the people, and, like an Old Testament judge, he advised and counseled his followers on disputes, marriages, and business.

"With us," Young maintained, "it is the Kingdom of God, or nothing" (Young, "Present and Former Persecutions" 5:342). At the heart of Young's presidency was his drive to build up the Kingdom of God upon Earth, "not in the starry heavens" (Young, "Love for the Things of God" 10:329). Ensconced in the Rocky Mountains and temporarily granted a large measure of autonomy by the federal government, Young pursued this vision relentlessly. The initial pioneer trek brought the Saints into Mexican territory, but one year later their mountain refuge had become American territory through the Treaty of Guadalupe Hidalgo. Congress rejected the Saints' petition for the proposed state of Deseret but created a still large Utah Territory in 1850, appointing Young territorial governor and superintendent of Indian affairs. By dispatching trusted and capable leaders and new emigrants, Young created a far-flung network of settlements from southern California to Idaho and started a variety of personal and Church enterprises that shaped Utah's economic development.

Young served four years as governor, then several more as acting governor, until President James Buchanan declared the Utah Territory in rebellion and sent

Beehive

The beehive is ubiquitous in Utah and Mormon culture. It appears on state highway signs, on the state flag, as an architectural decoration, and on jewelry. It is cast into the doorknobs of the Salt Lake temple, was stamped on gold coins minted in Utah in the 1850s, and until 2000 appeared on the seal of Brigham Young University. Since 1914, the Mormon youth program has used "Beehive Girls" as the class designation for young teens. Innumerable folk art pieces bear the symbol of the beehive. Utah's nickname is the "Beehive State."

Ironically, the honeybee is not native to the state, and the first generation of Mormon settlers struggled to import bees and to establish domestic honey production. The beehive was adopted as a symbol of industry and cooperative labor, ideals essential to the successful settlement of the Great Basin. The beehive was made the official symbol of the State of Deseret in 1848 and of the State of Utah in 1896.

Despite its wide acceptance as a symbol of secular government and commercial enterprise, in 2006 the beehive was criticized and ultimately rejected as the design for Utah's commemorative quarter because of its dual use as a Mormon symbol.

an army to forcibly install a non-Mormon governor. The 1857–1858 Utah War provided the sternest test of Young's leadership, a test that produced mixed results. Young's bellicose rhetoric emboldened Saints in southwestern Utah to perpetrate the duplicitous and vicious murder of 120 pioneers at Mountain Meadows, though no evidence suggests that Young ordered the massacre. While preparing a military defense and contemplating relocating the Saints yet again, Young ordered the inhabitants of northern Utah (including Salt Lake City) to "move south" and to prepare to burn their improvements. Coupled with the army's embarrassing failure to reach the Mormon capital before being trapped in early-winter snows, Young's threat to leave behind a deserted and scorched capital encouraged the Buchanan administration to offer amnesty and substantial autonomy in return for Young's acceptance of the new governor. Young brought his Church close to the brink of open warfare with the United States, but he pulled back from that brink and compromised under the most favorable circumstances possible.

In addition to his ecclesiastical, economic, and political responsibilities, Young faced the daunting task of providing for and managing an expanding and unwieldy family. He married more than 40 additional women in the first few years after Smith's death. In Utah, Young created privileged living circumstances for Mary Ann Angell and Lucy Decker Seeley and provided space for additional wives and children in the "Lion House," a working farm outside the city, and at two residences in St. George, which Young used as a winter destination late in life. With

16 wives, Young fathered children—nearly 60 in all—until 1870, when he was 68 years of age. As was the case in many polygamous families, these arrangements suited some wives and rankled others who became dissatisfied through jealousy or feelings of neglect.

Young's leadership belies simple characterization. While sometimes seeking to hedge his distinctive people off from the outer world, he also insisted that talented young adults (including several of his own children, men and women) travel East for their education, to gain the best possible training and also to better understand the country. While denouncing modern fashions and certain novels, he also promoted culture, encouraging the founding of the Salt Lake Theater and importing pianos for his own family's use. Young complained that his puritanical parents had forbidden dancing and violin music. By contrast, he attended balls and dances and never separated religion from mirth and pleasure. Thoroughly a 19th-century patriarch, Young nevertheless permitted the reorganization of the Relief Society, supported the publication of the *Woman's Exponent,* and respected female leaders like Eliza Snow and Emmeline Wells. These paradoxes, cultivated by Brigham Young, continue to shape Latter-day Saint culture.

In the end, Young failed to create an autonomous Kingdom of God upon Earth, as the Church could not exist in isolation from wider economic and political pressures. Young's promotion of "United Order" enterprises and communitarian experiments largely failed, though they forged a legacy of self-sufficiency, cooperation, and industriousness among his people. Even Young's stalwart defense of plural marriage, under severe pressure from the federal government by the end of his presidency, was abandoned within a generation of his death. Young himself endured a long and contentious divorce case at the hands of a discontented wife, Ann Eliza Webb; he spent a night in jail and then five months under house arrest when he was held in contempt of court for refusing to pay alimony. Mormon leaders did not abandon Young's vision of a temporal Kingdom of God, but, by the time of Young's death, the fulfillment of that vision seemed far less possible.

These many setbacks, however, should not obscure the decisive role Young played in the survival and growth of the Church. As an organizer and colonizer, he shepherded thousands of Saints to a region of the country largely untouched by white settlement. He expanded the Church's missions to foreign lands and enabled tens of thousands of emigrants to reach Utah.

Known primarily as a colonizer, politician, and economic leader, Young also guided the Church spiritually. Some of Young's controversial teachings, such as the exclusion of African Americans from the priesthood, ultimately were reversed and became a source of embarrassment to the Church. Others, such as his identification of Adam as "the only God with whom we have to do," never became official Church doctrine (Young, "Self-Government" 1:50). Nevertheless, Young shaped

Orrin Porter Rockwell

With his piercing gaze, flowing locks, unerring aim with weapons, and reputation as a relentless tracker and killer of his enemies, Orrin Porter Rockwell is a larger-than-life figure in Mormon folklore.

Born in 1813 and living in childhood near the family of Joseph Smith, Rockwell idolized Smith and was loyal to him throughout life. He followed the Church through its wanderings; in 1842 (as the Church moved on to Illinois), Rockwell was jailed in Missouri for eight months on a charge of the attempted murder of Governor Lilburn Boggs.

Rockwell's faith was simple and pragmatic, based more on personal devotion to Smith than on sophisticated doctrine. He claimed Smith had told him to let his hair grow as Samson's; Rockwell cut his hair only once thereafter, to make a wig for a sister-in-law of Smith's who had lost her hair to illness.

There is no question that Rockwell killed multiple men, both in his roles as deputy sheriff in Utah and in his rumored role as "avenging angel" or "Danite." Nevertheless, he is unlikely to have been responsible for more than a fraction of the deaths attributed to him in legend.

He died peacefully in 1878, under indictment for murder.

the development of Mormon theology and religious practice. Young further developed Joseph Smith's doctrines of human spiritual preexistence, eternal progression, and the corporeality of God. He ordered the construction of an Endowment House in Salt Lake City so that proxy baptisms and endowments could proceed under makeshift circumstances. Simultaneously, he pressed his followers to complete temples so that the Saints could fully pursue work for the dead and the welding of the generations. Young's promotion of temple work in Nauvoo and Utah ensured the central role of those ordinances in Latter-day Saint spirituality. Fittingly, he dedicated the St. George temple eight months before his death. A pragmatic prophet who referred to himself as a "Yankee guesser" (Arrington, *Brigham Young* 253), Young also grew into his role as the Church's "prophet, seer, and revelator."

—John G. Turner

See also: Colonization; Conflict: 1869–1890; Divergent Churches; Exodus and Settlement: 1845–1869; Genealogy and Family History; Mormonism and Blacks; Mormonism and Economics; Mountain Meadows Massacre; Polygamy; Temple Work by Proxy; Temples; Utah War; Zion's Camp.

References

Arrington, Leonard J. *Brigham Young: American Moses.* New York: Knopf, 1985.

Bringhurst, Newell G. *Brigham Young and the Expanding American Frontier.* Boston, MA: Little, Brown, 1986.

Young, Brigham. "Love for the Things of God." June 22–29, 1864. *Journal of Discourses,* vol. 10. London: LDS Booksellers Depot, 1865.

Young, Brigham. "Present and Former Persecutions of the Saints." October 18, 1857. *Journal of Discourses,* vol. 5. London: LDS Booksellers Depot, 1858.

Young, Brigham. "Self-Government." April 9, 1852. *Journal of Discourses,* vol. 1. London: LDS Booksellers Depot, 1854.

Issues

Church Organization and Government

The LDS Church is organized geographically and governed hierarchically by an all-male, mostly lay priesthood. The Church's basic congregational units are branches and wards (similar to parishes). Branches, the smallest, are generally composed of fewer than 300 Church members; wards have between 300 and 800 members. Groups of branches make up districts; groups of districts, missions. Groups of 5 to 12 wards (sometimes including branches) make up stakes (similar to dioceses); groups of stakes (and missions), areas. When the number of Church members in branches grows beyond 300, wards and stakes are organized. Wards and stakes (typically 2,000–7,000 members) are the ideal self-operating ecclesiastical units of the LDS Church.

Church members meet weekly on Sundays for three hours in branch and ward meetinghouses to worship, partake of the sacrament (bread and water), receive religious instruction, and socialize. Members also participate in Church-related auxiliary activities, including the Relief Society (for women), the Young Men and Young Women organizations (for adolescents), and the Primary (for children). The task of meeting the needs of the Church's local membership is typically undertaken by the members themselves. Most members are invited to serve in specific capacities in branches, wards, and stakes. Such "callings" often include administrative, teaching, and/or service-related duties. The assignments may change from time to time.

Presiding over the affairs of the Church's branches and wards are branch presidents and ward bishops (each of whom has two counselors). Presiding over the Church's districts, missions, and stakes are district presidents, mission presidents, and stake presidents (again each with two counselors). Thus are branch presidencies, ward bishoprics, and district, mission, and stake presidencies. Bishops typically serve for about five years, stake presidents for about nine years (though there are exceptions). In addition, stake presidencies are aided by, and preside over, 12-member stake high councils. Groups of two to six stakes form welfare-oriented regions, presided over by regional representatives. Ten to 40 regions form areas, the largest geographic divisions of the Church. Areas are presided over by area presidencies (a president and two counselors). The members of area presidencies are called Area Authority Seventies. They form Quorums of the Seventy according to geographic locations and report to the seven-member Presidency of the Seventy. The Presidency of the Seventy reports to the Quorum of the Twelve Apostles. The Quorum of the Twelve reports, in turn, to the First Presidency (the Church president and two counselors). The First Presidency is the supreme governing body of the Church; the Quorum of the Twelve is the second-highest governing body. Together, they "are responsible for establishing and approving all Church policies and procedures" (Bergera, *Statements* 349).

Most of the men filling Church-wide governing offices are typically appointed for five years. The exceptions are the members of the First Quorum of the Seventy (appointed until about age 70 but sometimes beyond), the members of the Quorum of the Twelve Apostles (appointed for life), and the members of the First Presidency (appointed for life). Local, stake, and regional Church appointments are part time, voluntary, and unpaid. Before serving, Church leaders are publicly presented—either locally or Church-wide—to Church members for their approval. Such a manifestation by members, known as "common consent," is not a vote per se but an expression of support. "The law of common consent is a basic principle that allows Church members to exercise their free agency" (Bergera, *Statements* 89).

All of the Church's presiding officers—local, regional, area, and general—are adult men who hold the priesthood. The priesthood is the "authority to act in God's name"; it is "the eternal power and authority of God. Through the priesthood God created and governs the heavens and the earth" (Bergera, *Statements* 345, 346). As administered in the LDS Church, the priesthood is divided between the Aaronic, or preparatory, Priesthood (for males ages 12–18) and the Melchizedek Priesthood (for males 19 and older). The Aaronic Priesthood is composed of the offices of deacon (ages 12–13), teacher (14–15), priest (16–18), and bishop (one per ward)—though the men called as bishops receive the Melchizedek Priesthood. The Melchizedek Priesthood is composed of the offices of elder, high priest, patriarch (one per stake), Seventy, and apostle (the highest priesthood office in the Church). The latter two—Seventy and apostle—are general Church-wide governing offices. Each of the other offices—except bishop and patriarch—function locally within branches, wards, districts, missions, and stakes—as priesthood quorums; the various local quorum members meet together separately on Sundays in priesthood quorum meetings.

The Church's worldwide governing officers—known collectively as General Authorities—are the members of the First and Second Quorums of the Seventy, the seven men who make up the Presidency of the Seventy, the Presiding Bishopric (the Presiding Bishop and two counselors), the Quorum of the Twelve Apostles, and the First Presidency. The General Authorities are full-time paid employees of the Church; their salaries and living allowances come from the Church's investments and not from Church members' voluntary tithing contributions (10 percent of one's income). Also presiding in the Church are the general presidencies of the Primary, Relief Society, Sunday School, Young Men, and Young Women, each of which reports either to one of the first two Quorums of the Seventy or to the Quorum of the Twelve Apostles and then to the First Presidency. The priesthood is available only to worthy men; women who preside do so under the authorization and supervision of local, stake, area, and general presiding priesthood officers.

At the head of the Church is the president. He is the only person authorized by God to use, or to permit others to use, the priesthood and to receive, as needed, revelation for the entire Church. (Other leaders are encouraged to receive revelation for their specific assignments.) The Church president's authority is absolute and plenary: "the final authority, both temporal and spiritual, in all matters, whatsoever—legislative, executive, and judicial—is vested in the President of the Church" (Bergera, *Statements* 162–163). But, while he may govern the Church unilaterally, the president usually seeks to preside by consensus. The president, along with his counselors and all members of the Quorum of the Twelve Apostles, are annually sustained by LDS Church members worldwide as "prophets, seers, and revelators." At the death of the sitting Church president, the most senior apostle (as determined by length of membership in the Quorum of the Twelve) traditionally becomes the new Church president.

The 15 members of the First Presidency and Quorum of the Twelve are revered by Latter-day Saints as living witnesses of Jesus Christ. Their mission broadly is to preach the gospel, perfect the Saints, care for the poor and needy, and redeem the dead through vicarious ordinances performed in LDS temples. Church policy is made by the First Presidency, overseen by the Quorum of the Twelve, and carried out by the Presidency of the Seventy, by members of the first two Quorums of the Seventy, and by the Presiding Bishopric. The members of the Twelve are divided into four executive committees responsible for the following operations: Correlation, Missionary, Priesthood, and Temple and Family History. The Presidency of the Seventy directs the day-to-day activities of Correlation, Missionary, Priesthood, Curriculum, Temple, and Family History. The Presiding Bishopric, which reports directly to the First Presidency, oversees Welfare Services, Physical Facilities, Materials Management, Information Systems, Finance and Records, Investments, LDS Foundation, and Security. Also reporting directly to the First Presidency are the Auditing Department, Budget Office, Personnel Department, the advisers to the Mormon Tabernacle Choir and Mormon Youth Symphony, and the Church's temple presidents.

The duties, responsibilities, and relationships among the Church's various priesthood leaders and quorums are outlined in *Church Handbook of Instructions: Book 1. Stake Presidencies and Bishoprics* and in *Church Handbook of Instructions: Book 2. Priesthood and Auxiliary Leaders.* Both handbooks are published periodically by the Church; the former has limited distribution, whereas the latter is distributed more widely. The Church's current leadership is profiled in the most recent edition of *Deseret Morning News Church Almanac* (published annually).

When the LDS Church was organized as the Church of Christ, on April 6, 1830, Church founder Joseph Smith and associate Oliver Cowdery presided as First and Second Elders, and Church members relied on Smith's revelations to answer questions of organization and governance. During the Church's first two years, local congregation (branch) affairs were administered by deacons, teachers, priests, and elders. In 1831, the office of bishop was established. At first, one bishop presided

LDS Church Hierarchy—Ecclesiastical and Temporal Organization

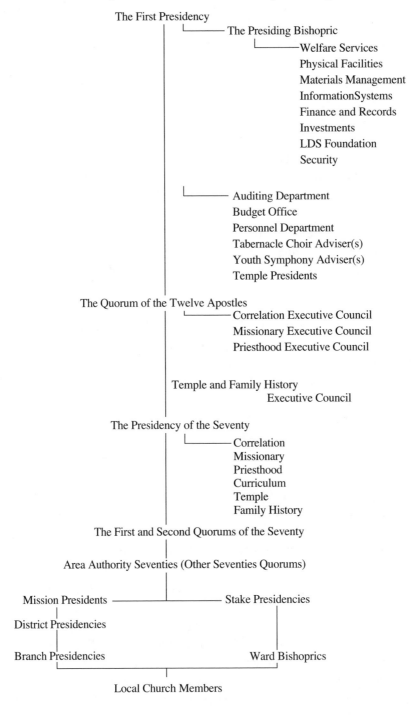

over the Church's Ohio congregations, another over its Missouri congregations. Eight years later, in Nauvoo, Illinois, local bishops began presiding over wards and reporting to regional bishops. Also in 1831, the priesthood office of high priest was established, and Joseph Smith was appointed presiding high priest—or president— over the entire Church. The next year, Smith called counselors to form a First Presidency. (Though the president is always aided by First and Second Counselors, he may at his discretion call additional or assistant counselors.) In 1834, the first two Church stakes were organized (in Ohio and Missouri). Stakes, led by stake presidencies and high councils, governed the affairs of the branches within the stake's boundaries. High councils settled disagreements and tried stake members for behavioral and doctrinal infractions. In either late 1833 or late 1834, Smith appointed his father as the first presiding Patriarch to the Church. (Smith also established, in 1834, the office of assistant Church president. Only two men have ever filled this position, however, and, after Smith's death in 1844, the office was effectively retired.)

In 1835, the Quorum of the Twelve Apostles and the Quorum of the Seventy were established. The members of the Twelve formed a traveling high council and presided over the affairs of the Church outside its organized stakes. The Seventy assisted the Twelve in proselytizing activities. The Seventy were presided over by seven presidents, called the First Council of the Seventy. Following a proselytizing mission to England in 1839–1841, the Quorum of the Twelve was authorized, under the First Presidency, to begin presiding over the affairs of stakes. Also in 1841, Joseph Smith created the office of Trustee-in-Trust—usually the Church president—to administer Church properties. The next year, Smith organized the all-female Relief Society, initially to aid the Church's poor. In 1847, following Smith's death, the first Presiding Bishop was called. In 1856, the Presiding Bishop received two counselors, and the Presiding Bishopric was created. A century later, a small group of men called as Assistants to the Twelve (eventually their number reached 38) served the Church from 1941 to 1976. (They were replaced when the First Quorum of the Seventy was reactivated in 1975–1976.) In 1979, the office of presiding Patriarch to the Church was retired (though the office of stake patriarch was retained).

At various times in his life, Joseph Smith proposed different possible successors as Church president, as well as different possible methods of presidential succession. At Smith's death, in June 1844, the question of presidential succession remained unsettled. Within weeks, a majority of Church members agreed with the reasons advanced by the Quorum of the Twelve for an apostolic presidency. Following the Saints' trek westward in 1846–1847, the Twelve's longest-serving (or most senior) member, Brigham Young, asserted the need for a new First Presidency. He persuaded the other members of the Quorum of the Twelve, some of whom were initially unreceptive to his arguments, to support his proposal. In December 1847, Young was sustained as Church president by the Church-at-large and called two apostles as counselors in his new First Presidency. Since that time, the most senior member of the Twelve has always been named as the new Church president (though in the 19th century this sometimes occurred up to several years after the previous president's death, during which time the Church was governed by the Twelve Apostles as a quorum). The question of presidential succession in the event the most senior member of the Twelve is *non compos mentis* has never been addressed publicly, though the Twelve would probably preside as a quorum.

During the Utah territorial period (1847–1896), the reach of the Church's priesthood leadership was extensive and pervasive. Members of the Quorum of the Twelve often lived in and helped to oversee various areas of LDS settlement throughout the intermountain West. Locally, bishops and stake presidents saw to the distribution and development of land and other natural resources; the construction of roads, dams, and waterways; and the operation of various commercial and economic enterprises. Bishops and the Presiding Bishopric managed the contribution and reallocation of Church members' tithing (mostly in-kind donations) to support the Church's public projects and to provide relief to the Church's poor. The First Presidency and the Presiding Bishopric helped to direct the Church's immigration, colonization, and settlement activities. Local Church courts often arbitrated both ecclesiastical and civil cases involving Church members (and occasionally nonmembers), including land disputes, criminal offenses, and probate matters. In the 1860s and 1870s, various Church-related auxiliary organizations began to surface locally and then were adopted by the Church generally. These included Sunday schools, Retrenchment and Mutual Improvement Associations (forerunners of the Young Men and Young Women organizations), and the Primary. The Relief Society was also revitalized Church-wide beginning in 1867.

Shortly before his death, in 1877, Brigham Young undertook a reconsideration of the relationship among, and the function of, the Church's wards, stakes, and priesthood quorums. Members of the Quorum of the Twelve no longer held local Church callings, new quorums for elders and members of the Aaronic Priesthood were organized, the number of adolescent males affiliated with the Aaronic Priesthood increased, a bishop's ward-related assignments grew, stakes received additional responsibilities, quarterly stake conferences were established, and Church-wide reporting procedures were implemented and standardized. The First Presidency also remained involved in the economic and political affairs of the Church's members. Following a period of economic cooperation and united orders (communitarian-oriented local organizations) during the 1860s and 1870s, the First Presidency established a general Board of Trade, as well as companion organizations at the stake level, to safeguard the Church's business interests. During the 1880s, Young's successor as Church president, John Taylor, championed the role of the Seventy as stake callings. Stakewide boards were formed for the Primary, Relief Society, Sunday School, and Young Men's and Young Women's Mutual Improvement Associations. With Utah statehood, in 1896, Church courts (later called disciplinary councils) dealt exclusively with infractions of Church policy and practice among Church members.

In the early 1920s, Zions Securities Corporation and the Corporation of the President were established to manage, respectively, the Church's income-producing and charitable properties.

During the first two decades of the 20th century, the Church began ordering deacon, teacher, and priest quorums by age of members; inaugurated weekly priesthood meetings; and emphasized monthly ward teaching visits to the homes of Church members and their families. Beginning in the 1920s, the Quorum of the Twelve assumed responsibility for the Melchizedek Priesthood Churchwide, while the Presiding Bishopric directed the Aaronic Priesthood and Young Men's Mutual Improvement Association. Previously the Melchizedek and Aaronic Priesthoods had tended to function more or less autonomously on the ward and stake levels. The Church published the first handbook for Melchizedek Priesthood holders in 1928. Beginning in the 1960s, during the administration of Church president David O. McKay, the Church embarked upon an ambitious program designed to correlate all of its activities and programs under a carefully ordered priesthood-structured organizational hierarchy. The intent was to simplify, streamline, and coordinate the Church's increasing demands on the limited resources of its members. The uniting of the Church's programs under the supervision of its General Authorities also represented, however, a loss of some autonomy and independence for the Church's auxiliary organizations, especially those administered by women.

In 1961, the members of the First Council of the Seventy were ordained high priests. In 1967 and 1972, the Church began calling regional representatives and mission representatives of the Twelve (the two callings were combined into one in 1974). In 1975, the First Quorum of the Seventy was re-established; later, the office of Seventy was made strictly a Church-wide—not a stake—appointment. (As of 2008, there were eight Quorums of the Seventy, each authorized to contain up to 70 members.) In 1984, in a move to further decentralize Church government, area presidencies were called to preside over the Church's various geographical divisions. Also in the 1980s, the Church moved to consolidate its financial operations; ward and stake buildings were financed completely from the Church's general tithing funds, instead of locally, as were, beginning in 1990, Church-related activities in Canada and the United States. Commenting upon his decades of experience in LDS Church government, Church president Gordon B. Hinckley said, in 2003:

> The Church will not dictate to any man, but it will counsel, it will persuade, it will urge, and it will expect loyalty from those who profess membership therein. . . . I have now served in the general councils of this Church for 45 years. I have served as an Assistant to the Twelve, as a member of the Twelve, as a counselor in the First Presidency, and now for eight years as President . . . although I have sat in literally thousands of meetings where Church policies and programs have been discussed, I have never been in one where the guidance of the Lord was not sought nor where the there was any desire on the part of anyone present

to advocate or do anything which would be injurious or coercive to anyone. (Hinckley, *Discourses* 174–175)

—*Gary James Bergera*

See also: Correlation; Divergent Churches; Local Worship; Mormonism and Economics; Organization of the Church; Relief Society; Youth Programs.

References

Allen, James B., and Glen M. Leonard. *The Story of the Latter-day Saints.* Salt Lake City, UT: Deseret Book, 1976, 1986.

Bergera, Gary James, ed. *Statements of the LDS First Presidency: A Topical Compendium.* Salt Lake City, UT: Signature Books, 2007.

Hinckley, Gordon B. *Discourses of President Gordon B. Hinckley.* Vol. 2: *2000–2004.* Salt Lake City, UT: Deseret Book, 2005.

Quinn, D. Michael. *The Mormon Hierarchy: Extensions of Power.* Salt Lake City, UT: Signature Books in association with Smith Research Associates, 1997.

Quinn, D. Michael. *The Mormon Hierarchy: Origins of Power.* Salt Lake City, UT: Signature Books, 1994.

Divergent Churches

Few religious movements have become as divided in such a short amount of time as has the Latter Day Saint movement. Even while its founder was still alive, the Church was beset with constant dissension and defection. Following the death of Joseph Smith, the Latter-day Saints sought direction from a number of would-be leaders. The largest group of Latter-day Saints traveled west to Utah Territory with Brigham Young, while others followed competing leaders to Pennsylvania, Texas, California, and Michigan. Many of the faithful remained in the Midwest, eager to carry on the work of the original Church without immediately aligning with any leader. The major branches of the Latter Day Saint movement outside the Salt Lake City–based Church of Jesus Christ of Latter-day Saints are discussed here.

In understanding the process of schism within Mormonism, two common threads are crucial. The first is the concept of authority. Joseph Smith Jr. taught the necessity of proper priesthood authority in order to preach the gospel and perform sacred ordinances. He did not recognize such authority in any existing Churches but claimed divine guidance, angelic ministrations, and instruction in restoring the necessary keys to unlock the doors to inspiration and truth. His example led some of his followers to claim similar experiences. Such experiences divided some followers and united others.

Second, the concept of continuing revelation has led to the development of doctrinal differences among believers. This concept can also put them at odds with their own founding prophet. While some groups claimed new revelation, most groups profess to derive their beliefs from Joseph Smith himself. Because of the evolving nature of Smith's theology, beliefs that are very different and even contradictory can all be traced to him during various periods of his ministry. For instance, groups that espouse trinitarianism, modalism, and henotheism all found support in the teachings of Joseph Smith. The Latter Day Saint movement thereby provided fertile ground for schism and dissension.

Strangite Tradition

Church of Jesus Christ of Latter Day Saints (Strang)

James J. Strang was a recent convert to the Church when he claimed to receive a letter from Joseph Smith Jr. designating him to be Smith's successor as "Prophet, Seer, and Revelator." At the very hour of Smith's death, Strang claimed that he was visited by angels and ordained to his new office. In 1848, Strang moved his flock to Beaver Island, in Lake Michigan. It is estimated that, at one time, his followers numbered 12,000. Like Smith, Strang discovered a set of metallic records that he was inspired to translate. This new work, the Book of the Law of the Lord, was considered to be scripture by his followers.

Perhaps one of the most well-known events in Strang's religious career was his coronation as king, in 1850. This controversial action led to charges of treason, but the publicity surrounding it helped Strang make a successful bid for the Michigan state legislature. Upon his death at the hands of dissenters, the majority of Strang's followers joined what would become the Community of Christ. Several extant groups claim a belief in Strang and his teachings, with the largest body located in Voree, Wisconsin.

Cutlerite Tradition

Church of Jesus Christ (Cutler)

Alpheus Cutler was a close associate of Joseph Smith and claimed the right and responsibility to reorganize the Church after Smith's murder. Cutler's claim to authority was that he was a member of what he called the Seven High Priest Apostles. According to this tradition, Joseph Smith set apart seven men who could reorganize and lead the Church after his death. Cutler taught that he was the last of the seven alive who had not followed another leader.

In 1852, Cutler and about 30 families settled in Iowa at a place they named Manti. The following year, Cutler received a sign that led him to reorganize the Saints as the True Church of Jesus Christ. After Cutler's death, in 1864, his followers moved their colony to Clitherall, Minnesota. In 1928, a portion of the group relocated to Independence, Missouri, and established headquarters there. In the 21st century the Church has an estimated 12 members.

Reorganized Church Tradition

Community of Christ (Formerly Reorganized Church of Jesus Christ of Latter Day Saints)

Jason Briggs, a Latter Day Saint from Wisconsin who had been a follower of both James J. Strang and Joseph Smith's brother, William, claimed, in 1851, to have had a revelation insisting that believers should look to a descendant of Joseph Smith as their slain prophet's successor. Briggs's revelation was widely circulated in the Midwest and found fertile ground in the hearts of many. Those who agreed with Briggs met together in conference in 1852 at Beloit, Wisconsin, and formed the New Organization of the Church of Jesus Christ of Latter Day Saints. While the Prophet's eldest son, Joseph Smith III, was initially too young and then too reluctant to lead the New Organization, he did agree to head the Church at its conference in 1860 at Amboy, Illinois.

During the next few decades, the energies of the Church were spent in bringing together the scattered Saints who did not follow Brigham Young. Temporary headquarters were set up at various locations, including Lamoni, Iowa, and Plano, Illinois. In the early 1890s, the Church was engaged in a series of litigations with the Church of Christ (Temple Lot) over certain plots of land in Independence, Missouri, which both groups believed to be the place dedicated in 1831 by Joseph Smith Jr. to be the center of Christ's millennial kingdom. Ultimately, the Temple Lot Church kept title to the property, and its ownership remained a painful and divisive issue for both Churches.

Just before the death of Joseph III, the Church began moving its operations to Independence. In 1915, Frederick Madison Smith succeeded his father as prophet and president of the Church. Under the leadership of Frederick, the Church struggled with tremendous internal strife as he began a policy known as Supreme Directional Control. Unlike Joseph III, Frederick saw his position as not only spiritual leader but also CEO of the Church's temporal operations. This policy resulted in a showdown between Frederick and other leaders. The Church lost thousands of members during this struggle, many of whom transferred to the Church of Christ (Temple Lot).

Frederick M. Smith's presidency was not without certain accomplishment, however. Under his leadership, the Church began construction in 1926 on a large auditorium that would both serve as a meeting place for conferences and contain offices for Church officials. Although halted by the Great Depression, construction was eventually completed in 1962. Frederick died in 1946 and was succeeded by his brother Israel A. Smith.

Upon Israel's death, in 1958, W. Wallace Smith, another son of Joseph III, led the Church. Under his tenure, the Church began a process of internationalization and growth in many parts of the world. His presidency marked a liberalizing trend within Church leadership, with many in top Church positions taking courses at theologically moderate seminaries. He made the unprecedented move, in 1978, of resigning his position and appointing his son, Wallace B. Smith, as his successor. Under his leadership, the Church made some of its most significant, if not traumatic, changes.

In 1984, Wallace B. Smith offered inspired counsel to the Church membership that called for two major changes, both of which came at great cost. First, he announced that a temple was to be built in Independence. It was completed in 1994 and both serves as center for Church leadership offices and houses the Church's Temple School, library, and archives. Second, the Church's priesthood would now be open to all worthy persons, regardless of gender. This change convinced many members that the Church was headed in a liberalizing direction and caused traditionalists to dissociate themselves from it. As his father had done before him, Wallace B. Smith designated a successor before resigning. However, for the first time in the Church's history, the prophet-president would be from outside the lineage of Joseph Smith Jr. In 1996, W. Grant McMurray became the Church's leader.

Under McMurray's leadership, the Church continued its journey toward the mainstream. In 1998, he called two women into the Church's Quorum of Twelve Apostles, and in 2001 he led the Church in changing its name to Community of Christ. McMurray resigned as Prophet-President in 2004 without naming a successor. The Church met in conference in 2005 and approved Stephen M. Veazey as its new Prophet-President.

In the 21st century, the Church has more than 200,000 members in more than 50 countries. It operates Graceland University in Lamoni, Iowa, and Community of Christ Seminary in Independence, Missouri.

RLDS Restorationists

Beginning with the presidency of W. Wallace Smith, in 1958, many members of the Reorganized Church of Jesus Christ of Latter Day Saints (now Community of Christ) became concerned with what they perceived as liberalizing tendencies in the Church hierarchy, especially open communion and the ordination of women to the priesthood. In response, many more traditional members aligned themselves with "independent restoration branches." Most such independent branches view themselves as retaining a historical relationship with the Reorganized Church, while not being officially associated with the legal institution.

Several umbrella organizations have been created to join these independent branches in common purposes. The Conference of Restoration Elders was established in 1993 and the Joint Conference of Restoration Branches was established in 2006 as ways for restorationist elders and branches to work together in common evangelism and educational efforts.

Other traditionalists were not as hopeful about the institutional Church's ability to correct its course and acted to form their own Churches. One successful group is the Remnant Church of Jesus Christ of Latter Day Saints, led by Frederick N. Larsen, a descendant of Joseph Smith Jr.

Rigdon/Bickerton Tradition

Church of Christ (Rigdon)

Shortly after the death of Joseph Smith, Sidney Rigdon returned to the Church's headquarters at Nauvoo from a mission in Pennsylvania and presented himself as guardian and "protector" of the Church. His claim was based on the fact that, as counselor to Smith, Rigdon was the last remaining member of the Church's First Presidency. The majority of the Saints in Nauvoo rejected Rigdon's offer, and he returned to the Pittsburgh area, where he reorganized the Church as the Church of Christ. Rigdon gained a following and attempted to institute a communitarian colony called the Adventure Farm, but by 1847 most of his followers had deserted him.

Church of Jesus Christ (Bickerton)

One of the followers of Sidney Rigdon, William Bickerton reorganized the Church at Green Oak, Pennsylvania, in 1862 and called it the Church of Jesus Christ. In 1875, Bickerton led a group of about 40 families to found the colony of Zion Valley at what would later become St. John, Kansas. Also in 1909, the Church established a community in Comanche County, Kansas, called the Colony. Like the Zion Valley community, the Colony was not successful and was dissolved in 1917. The majority of the Church remained in Pennsylvania and is now headquartered at Monongahela. It reports a membership of close to 15,000 in many countries; about 3,000 of its members live in the United States.

Hedrickite Tradition

Church of Christ (Temple Lot)

After the vacuum of leadership left by the death of Joseph Smith Jr., a group of loosely affiliated congregations came together under the leadership of Granville Hedrick. These local branches, known collectively as the Woodford County Saints, included Bloomington, Crow Creek, Half Moon Prairie, and Eagle Creek, all in Illinois, and Vermillion, in Indiana. At first, the organization used the name Church of Jesus Christ (of Latter Day Saints) to identify itself, but it soon reverted to the original 1830 name of Church of Christ. Slowly, Church members settled around Jackson County, Missouri, which they believed had been consecrated by Joseph

Smith Jr. as the center of God's coming kingdom on Earth. The Church continues to hold title to this property.

The Church of Christ remained a small group of fewer than 200 members until the 1920s, when it grew rapidly through transfers from the RLDS Church. In 2009, the Church reported having between 8,000 and 9,000 members, with about 1,000 residing in the United States.

Church of Christ (Fetting)

A great excitement entered the Church of Christ in 1927 when recently ordained apostle Otto Fetting claimed to have been visited by a heavenly messenger who encouraged the small Church to make haste constructing its long-awaited temple, which would serve as the center of Christ's millennial reign. Fetting continued to receive instruction from the messenger until a rift arose between him and certain leaders in the Church over the doctrine of rebaptism. Fetting left the Church in 1929 to establish his own Church of Christ. He died four years later, having received 30 messages from John the Baptist. Two remaining groups hold to Fetting's messages; both are headquartered in Independence, Missouri.

Elijah Message Churches (Draves)

William August Draves, originally a member of the Church of Jesus Christ of Latter-day Saints, joined the Church of Christ (Temple Lot) but became a believer in Fetting's messages and left with him in 1929. Draves was an active elder in the Fetting church at Nucla, Colorado. He claimed to begin receiving visits from a Messenger on October 4, 1937. Understandably, these claims caused division within the Church. Many members were happy to believe that the Messenger had returned, while others felt the young elder was stepping beyond his bounds.

The smoldering tension erupted at the June 1943 General Assembly. After the meeting, Draves and several followers filed suit against the Fetting church for possession of Church properties. The suit was decided against Draves, and he and his followers formed a new Church the following year, using the name Church of Christ Established Anew. This new Church became known as the Church of Christ with the Elijah Message. Several Churches accept the 90 messages received through Draves; these have a combined membership of between approximately 5,000 and 7,000.

Schell City Missouri Groups (Nerren/Gayman)

After the death of Otto Fetting, Thomas B. Nerren claimed to receive visits from the Messenger. Nerren was a leader in the Denver branch of Fetting's Church, and he and those sympathetic to his claims broke with Fetting's followers to form their own Church in 1938. Nerren received a revelation in 1940 that the faithful should begin gathering in Missouri in preparation for the last days. Although Nerren remained in Colorado, many of his followers moved to a piece of property known as Halley's Bluff, near Schell City, Missouri.

A division arose in the Church of Christ at Halley's Bluff in the early 1970s when a group of members, led by Dan Gayman, began espousing racist ideas. A court battle ensued, and Gayman's group lost to the faction led by his brother, Duane Gayman. Duane's followers formed the Church of Christ at Zion's Retreat, and Dan's group became the Church of Israel. Both groups are relatively small, although Dan's teaching and writings have been influential in the broader American Christian Identity movement.

Fundamentalist Groups

Adherents of Mormon Fundamentalism believe that the Church of Jesus Christ of Latter-day Saints has strayed drastically from the teachings of the Church's first three presidents, Joseph Smith Jr., Brigham Young, and John Taylor. Among the doctrines that they claim the institutional Church has rejected are plural marriage, blood atonement, the Adam-God doctrine, and the belief that blacks are cursed of God.

Most Fundamentalists trace their origin to a meeting held on September 27, 1886, at which they claim that LDS Church president John Taylor ordained a select group of men to continue the principle of plural marriage in the face of growing opposition to the practice. Among the five men set apart at the meeting for this unique calling were John W. Woolley and his son Lorin C. Woolley.

Four years later, then Church president Wilford Woodruff issued a document known as the Manifesto, which officially condemned polygamy. Joseph F. Smith issued a second Manifesto in 1904, and, thereafter, members found to be practicing plural marriage were excommunicated from the Church. In response to this change in the Church's official stance, the men who claimed authority from the 1886 meeting began operating separately from the institutional Church, with John W. Woolley being the primary leader of the "Priesthood Council." Upon his father's death, in 1928, Lorin C. Woolley became the last remaining member of the group ordained by Taylor. He reinstituted the Priesthood Council and ordained six other men before his death, in 1934.

Fundamentalist Church of Jesus Christ of Latter Day Saints (Barlow/Jeffs)

John Y. Barlow, as senior member of Lorin C. Woolley's Council, together with LeRoy Johnson, established a colony for polygamous families at Short Creek on the Utah-Arizona border in 1935. This action caused a split in the Priesthood Council, with Joseph W. Musser leading a faction that eventually became the Apostolic United Brethren. The same year, the Short Creek settlement was raided, and most of the men were jailed. The community was raided again in 1944 and in 1953.

The United Effort Plan, established in 1942, centralized the structure and administration of the Short Creek members. In 1963, the settlement at Short Creek was legally divided into two bordering communities, Colorado City, Arizona, and Hilldale, Utah. Upon Johnson's death, in 1987, the mantle of leadership fell to Rulon Jeffs. Jeffs led the Church to incorporate as the Fundamentalist Church of Jesus Christ of Latter Day Saints, in 1991, and he continued to lead it until his death, in 2002. The loss of Rulon Jeffs left the Church in a highly tumultuous state, especially as his son, Warren, took control.

Under the direction of Warren Jeffs, many members of the Church began moving to Church-owned property near Eldorado, Texas. Jeffs predicted that the end of the world would occur on January 1, 2005, and members relocated to the new land, believing that they would be under divine protection. Jeffs adjusted the date to April 6, 2005, when the January date passed with no apocalypse. In 2008, Texas authorities raided the FLDS compound after allegations of abuse surfaced and took its children into protective custody. The children were later returned.

In 2005, former FLDS members accused Warren Jeffs of sexual misconduct with minors. In 2006, after appearing on the FBI's Most Wanted List, Jeffs was apprehended near Las Vegas. He was tried and convicted in September 2007 of two counts of accomplice to rape. Although, in 2009, the leadership and future of the FLDS Church remained in question, Jeffs retained the devotion of some followers from his prison cell. FLDS membership totals between 8,000 and 10,000 adherents.

Centennial Park Group (Hammon/Timpson)

In opposition to the authoritarian rule of LeRoy Johnson, Marion Hammon led like-minded believers, in 1984, to form the "Second Ward" at a community they established and named Centennial Park. Hammon died in 1988, leaving Del Timpson as its senior leader. His son, John Timpson, assumed leadership when his father died, in 1998. An estimated 1,500 members of this group live in the Centennial Park community, and approximately 200 more live in the Salt Lake City area.

Nielson-Naylor Group

Led by Ivan Nielson and Frank Naylor, this group separated from the Centennial Park community in 1990. There are about 300 members, mostly in the Salt Lake City area.

Bountiful Canada Group

A large group of FLDS members in a community near Creston, British Columbia, split from the Church in 2002 in protest against the leadership of Warren Jeffs. The group, led by Winston Blackmore, numbers more than 400 members.

Apostolic United Brethren (Musser/Allred)

Disagreeing with the Short Creek Settlement plan, Joseph W. Musser dissented from the Priesthood Council leadership of John Y. Barlow and instituted his own Council in 1952. Musser's death, in 1954, left Dr. Rulon C. Allred as senior apostle on the Council. Allred served in that capacity until he was assassinated by representatives of a rival faction in 1977. For the next two decades, Allred's son, Owen, led this group. J. LaMoine Jenson assumed leadership in 2005. The Apostolic United Brethren, with headquarters at Bluffdale, Utah, has approximately 7,500 members. Other membership clusters are located at Rocky Ridge and Cedar City, in Utah; at Pinesdale, Montana; and at Ozumba, Mexico.

Davis County Cooperative Society (The Kingstons)

Concerned about survival during the Great Depression, Charles Kingston, in 1935, led his family and a handful of others to form an economic cooperative in Davis County, Utah. The Cooperative has more than 1,200 members and an impressive and diverse business empire. It has also been the target of public scrutiny due to allegations of child abuse and incest, resulting in several convictions against high-ranking leaders. Since 1987, Paul Elden Kingston has led the group.

Church of the Firstborn (The LeBarons)

One group that claims authority outside the Taylor/Woolly tradition is the Church of the Firstborn, founded by Alma Dayer LeBaron. LeBaron traced his authority through Benjamin F. Johnson, a close associate of Joseph Smith Jr. LeBaron led a small group to Colonia Juarez, Mexico, in 1924. A LDS settlement already existed at Colonia Juarez, and LeBaron gained some converts there. After great contention with local LDS leaders, the LeBarons moved and established the Church of the Firstborn at a new location, called Colonia LeBaron. A second colony was also established in Baja California.

The Church of the Firstborn has a reputation for division and violence. Alma LeBaron's son Joel, head of the Church, was murdered in 1972 by a faction that disagreed with his teachings and leadership. Joel's brothers—Ross, Floren, and Ervil—also led factions. In 1977, Ervil and several members of his group were imprisoned for the murder of Rulon Allred, leader of the Apostolic United Brethren. An estimated 300 members live at Colonia LeBaron.

True and Living Church of Jesus Christ of Saints of the Last Days (Harmston)

Another Mormon Fundamentalist group outside the Taylor/Woolley line is the True and Living Church of Jesus Christ of Saints of the Last Days headquartered in Manti, Utah. The TLC Church, as it is also known, began as a prayer and study group under the direction of James D. Harmston, then a member of the LDS Church. Harmston claimed an experience in which he was given special priesthood authority at the hands of Enoch, Noah, Abraham, and Moses. The TLC Church was formed four years later. Many of the members left the Church after Jesus Christ failed to appear in March 2000, as Harmston had prophesied. There are still approximately 100 to 300 members.

Independent Fundamentalists

The majority of those holding to the beliefs of Fundamentalism are not directly connected to any of the groups mentioned. Generally, these independent polygamists view their families as autonomous patriarchies, with senior male family members providing spiritual guidance. Some estimates place their number at more than 15,000.

—*Jason Smith*

See also: Church Organization and Government; Manifesto; Polygamy; Rigdon, Sidney.

References

Bringhurst, Newell G., and John C. Hamer, eds. *Scattering of the Saints: Schism within Mormonism.* Independence, MO: John Whitmer Books, 2007.

Hales, Brian C. *Modern Polygamy and Mormon Fundamentalism: The Generations after the Manifesto.* Draper, UT: Kofford Books, 2006.

Launius, Roger D., and Linda Thatcher, eds. *Differing Visions: Dissenters in Mormon History.* Urbana: University of Illinois Press, 1994.

Genealogy and Family History

Mormon involvement in genealogical research was foreshadowed in 1823 when Joseph Smith reported receiving an angelic visitation from Moroni, an ancient prophet. Among other instructions, Moroni quoted a variation of the Old Testament verses of Malachi 4:5–6, remembered by Smith as "Behold, I will reveal unto you the Priesthood, by the hand of Elijah the prophet, before the coming of the great and dreadful day of the Lord. And he shall plant in the hearts of the children the promises made to the fathers, and the hearts of the children shall turn to their fathers. If it were not so, the whole earth would be utterly wasted at his coming" (Pearl of Great Price, Joseph Smith,

The Mormon effort to preserve the world's genealogical records by microfilming began in the 1930s, as soon as the technology was available. Microfilming and digital scanning continue today. (Courtesy of the Church History Library, The Church of Jesus Christ of Latter-day Saints.)

History 1:38–39). According to Mormon teaching, the ancient prophet Elijah appeared to Smith and others in the Kirtland temple on April 3, 1836, and, as part of the restoration of the ancient gospel, delivered the priesthood keys, or authorities, to Smith, in fulfillment of Malachi's prophecy.

Understanding of these restored keys came gradually. In January 1836, before Elijah's visit, Smith had puzzled over a vision in which he had seen his older brother, a man who had died without baptism, in the presence of God. He recorded that the Lord said to him that "All who have died without a knowledge of the Gospel, who would have received it if they had been permitted to tarry, shall be heirs of the celestial kingdom of God" (Smith, *History* 2:380). By August 15, 1840, Smith had worked out a partial solution to the conundrum of that revelation, seemingly contradicting the biblical injunction that "except a man be born of water and of the Spirit, he cannot enter into the kingdom of God" (John 3:5) when he preached the funeral sermon for Seymour Brunson in Nauvoo, Illinois. He declared, "The Saints have the privilege of being baptized for those of their relatives who are dead, whom they believe would have embraced the Gospel, if they had been privileged with hearing it" (Smith, *History* 4:231). That privilege was immediately sought by widow Jane Neyman, who was baptized in the Mississippi River for her deceased son, Cyrus.

This teaching was eagerly embraced by Church members, with a reaction typified by Brigham Young: "It made me glad . . . that I could go forth and officiate for my fathers, for my mothers, and for my ancestors, of the earliest generation, who have not had the privilege of helping themselves; that they can yet arise to the state of glory and exaltation as we that live have a privilege of rising to ourselves" (Young, "Speech" 120). The enthusiasm with which the Saints responded to the doctrine, however, and the haphazard way in which it was carried out caused Smith to seek further revelation. On January 19, 1841, he announced that baptism for the dead was an ordinance that belonged to the holy temple, not to the streams and rivers of the everyday world, and called for a temple with a baptismal font to be built at Nauvoo. On October 14, 1841, Smith declared that "there shall be no more baptisms for the dead, until the ordinance can be attended to in the Lord's House" (Smith, *History* 4:426). So anxious were the Saints to continue the work of baptisms for their deceased relatives that a temporary font in the unfinished basement of the Nauvoo temple was dedicated on November 8, and baptisms resumed.

In 1842, Smith further refined the practice of baptism for the dead and expanded his understanding of its importance. He taught that a recorder must witness each baptism to ensure its proper performance, and, inaugurating the Mormon practice of keeping detailed genealogical and ordinance records, he declared the Lord's call to "let all the records be had in order, that they may be put in the archives of my holy temple, to be held in remembrance from generation to generation" (Doctrine and Covenants 127:9). Extending baptismal rites to the dead not only benefited the dead, he taught, but was critical to the salvation of the living: "Let me assure you

Family History Library

The Family History Library in Salt Lake City is the largest genealogical library in the world, with a constantly growing collection housed on five floors and in off-site storage. Open to the public at no charge, the library is visited by nearly 2,000 patrons, Mormon and non-Mormon, each day. Unnumbered others visit the library's familysearch.org Web site and use thousands of smaller Family History Centers throughout the world. These centers, also open to the general public, have access to most materials from the main library. No proselyting is permitted in the library or its satellite centers.

The library's collections began with records gathered by the Utah Genealogical Society, founded in 1894. This investment reflects the enormous commitment of the Church and its members to identify deceased ancestors and provide proxy ordinances for them in Mormon temples. The Church began microfilming the world's genealogical records in 1938, a program that continues today, supplemented by newer technologies, preserving such records and making them more conveniently available to researchers.

In recent years, the Church has embarked on a program to produce indexed digital images of its vast holdings for eventual placement on the Internet, making the library's resources freely available to family historians everywhere.

that these are principles in relation to the dead and the living that cannot be lightly passed over, as pertaining to our salvation. For their salvation is necessary and essential to our salvation" (Doctrine and Covenants 128:15).

The summer of 1842 saw further doctrinal developments that would eventually lead to the modern Church's emphasis on genealogical research. Smith began to present the "endowment" ordinance (a rite involving the symbolic representation of the purposes of mortal life and the making of sacred covenants between human beings and God); as an ordinance necessary to salvation, the endowment would eventually be extended to the dead, just as was baptism, by having a living person perform the ordinance in behalf of a deceased relative.

Finally, in July 1843, the concept of "sealings" was added to Smith's teachings of ordinances necessary to the living and to the dead. Husbands and wives could be sealed by priesthood authority, extending their marital relationship through eternity. Children could also be sealed to parents, with those parents sealed to their own parents, and so on back generation by generation to Adam and Eve, until the entire human family was linked in an endless network of eternal family ties. Any person who failed to provide the ordinances of salvation to his dead kindred would eventually find himself outside this network, outside the family of God, and outside the greatest blessings of eternity.

In one of his last public sermons before his death, Smith connected the Old Testament prophecy quoted to him by Moroni in 1823 to man's obligation to extend rites of salvation to the dead:

> What promises are made in relation to the subject of the salvation of the dead? . . . The greatest responsibility in this world that God has laid upon us is to seek after our dead. The apostle says, "They without us cannot be made perfect"; for it is necessary that the sealing power should be in our hands to seal our children and our dead. . . . It is necessary that those who are going before and those who come after us should have salvation in common with us; and thus hath God made it obligatory upon man. Hence, God said, "I will send you Elijah the prophet before the coming of the great and dreadful day of the Lord: he shall turn the heart of the fathers to the children, and the heart of the children to their fathers, lest I come and smite the earth with a curse." (Smith, *History* 6:313)

In the aftermath of Smith's murder, the Mormons were forced to leave Nauvoo and seek a new home in the Rocky Mountains. They hastened to complete the temple to receive their endowments and sealings before leaving. Once established in Utah Territory, the Mormons began to build new temples. The first would not be completed until 1877, however; in the 30-year interim, the Endowment House, a temporary building used chiefly for temple rites for the living, was erected at Salt Lake City. Some baptisms for the dead were performed in the Endowment House, but very little attention was given to the work for the dead until the dedication of the St. George temple in 1877.

Although temple rites for the dead were generally postponed until they could be performed in a dedicated temple, many Church members began researching their ancestry in preparation for the day when temple work could resume. This research was conducted under difficult circumstances. While some Saints serving as missionaries in the regions from which their ancestors had come had access to parish registers and public records, most did not. Research was limited to correspondence with distant family, with the custodians of public records, and with a growing number of genealogists in New England and elsewhere who publicized their work on one family name or another. There were no professional standards of evidence, no system for recordkeeping; each family preserved what data it gathered in family Bibles, in carefully saved correspondence, or in diaries and other personal records. The archived diaries of 19th-century Mormon families of all ranks and origins include listings of parents, children, and birth dates, indicating a widespread recognition of the importance of genealogical records.

Interest in genealogical research increased following the dedication of the first temples, and Mormons began seeking more efficient ways of collecting and preserving their records. Missionaries, especially those in Great Britain, sometimes established good relationships with local recordkeepers, enabling them to obtain significant amounts of information for Church members at home. Led by John Nicholson, one group of Latter-day Saints organized a private genealogical bureau in 1888 to coordinate research among Mormons of Scottish descent. Benjamin F. Cummings, who had devoted a considerable portion of his two missions in the eastern United States to gathering genealogical records for himself and friends at home, may be considered the first professionally trained genealogist among the Latter-day Saints; in 1892, he toured government offices and records repositories throughout the eastern states to learn what records were available and how each organization gathered and preserved such records.

During the Church's conference in April 1894, President Wilford Woodruff

The Church's Family History Library welcomes all visitors, whether Mormon or not, to research their genealogy in the main library at Salt Lake City or in thousands of Family History Centers around the world. This mid-century library has been replaced by a state-of-the-art building. (Courtesy of the Church History Library, The Church of Jesus Christ of Latter-day Saints.)

announced a major reinterpretation of salvation for the dead. Prior to this date, Mormons had sealed themselves to their parents and grandparents only if those parents had been members of the LDS Church. Because the purpose of the sealing, they reasoned, was to secure one's place in a chain of worthy progenitors leading back to Adam and thence to God, and because one could not be certain that his ancestors were among those who, in the words of Joseph Smith's 1836 revelation, "would have received [the restored gospel] if they had been permitted to tarry," sealing oneself to such an ancestor was risky—if the ancestor did *not* accept the restored gospel, the family chain would be broken, leaving descendants outside the family of God. After Smith's death, the custom developed to seal oneself not to parents, whose eternal status was ambiguous, but to Church leaders, generally apostles or Church presidents, whose status was considered secure. Such sealings to Church leaders were called "adoptions."

But Woodruff announced that such adoptions were improper, the result of an incomplete understanding of the nature of temple sealings. Such adoptions, he said, unrighteously deprived good people of their posterity. A more mature understanding called for each person to be sealed to his natural parents, with those parents sealed to *their* natural parents, regardless of any ancestor's presumed worthiness or unworthiness. "Let every man be adopted to his father," Woodruff declared.

When a man receives the endowment, adopt him to his father; not to Wilford Woodruff, nor to any other man outside the lineage of his fathers. That is the will of God to this people. . . . What business have I to take away the rights of the lineage of any man? What right has any man to do this? No; I say let every man be adopted to his father; and then you will do exactly what God said when he declared He would send Elijah the prophet in the last days. . . . We want the Latter-day Saints from this time to trace their genealogies as far as they can, and to be sealed to their fathers and mothers. Have children sealed to their parents, and run this chain through as far as you can get it." [Likewise, women were to be sealed to their deceased husbands, regardless of Church membership:] "Why deprive a woman of being sealed to her husband because he never heard the Gospel? What do any of us know with regard to him? Will he not hear the Gospel and embrace it in the spirit world? . . . There will be very few, if any, who will not accept the Gospel. (Woodruff, "The Law of Adoption" 148–150)

The result of this announcement was a desire among many Saints to engage in more extended genealogical research than had previously been undertaken. Only seven months later, on November 1, 1894, the First Presidency announced the organization of the Genealogical Society of Utah, with the goals of establishing a genealogical library, gathering records to facilitate temple ordinances, and teaching Latter-day Saints the principles of accurate genealogical work. Although the Society's primary purpose was to assist Church members in carrying out their religious duties, from the beginning the Society served non-Mormons as well as Mormons, all of whom were responding, the Society felt, to the proddings of what had become known as "the spirit of Elijah."

The Genealogical Society, now known as the Family History Department of the Church, established its first library in 1894 in a room of the Church Historian's Office. As its collections grew and patronage increased, the library outgrew its first makeshift home and several others; since 1985, the Family History Library has been housed in a dedicated five-story building in downtown Salt Lake City, the largest genealogical library in the world, equipped with a constantly expanding collection of books, journals, microfilmed records, and digital tools. Supplementing the parent library, thousands of Family History Centers have been established around the world, chiefly in LDS meeting houses, where microfilm copies of Family History Library materials are shipped as requested by local patrons. Family History Centers welcome all comers, regardless of Church affiliation, and, by direction of the Church, no proselytizing activity is permitted in such centers.

In 1938, the Genealogical Society embarked on a project not only to obtain published genealogies but also to microfilm primary sources held by governments, Churches, and archives of all descriptions. This effort was given added emphasis following World War II, when agencies throughout the world recognized the value of microfilmed records as security against the destruction of war and natural disaster. The microfilming and digital imaging of the world's genealogical records has

Granite Mountain Records Vault

Located in a canyon 20 miles southeast of Salt Lake City, the Granite Mountain Records Vault tunnels 600 feet through solid rock, 700 feet beneath the surface of the mountain. Natural conditions of the vault provide optimal temperature and humidity conditions for the storage of printed and microfilmed records; reflecting the political fears prevalent during its construction between 1958 and 1963, massive doors are designed to protect the vault's contents from the effects of a nuclear blast.

The vault is the permanent storage facility for the millions of rolls of microfilm, printed records, and digital media collected by the Church as a part of its emphasis on genealogy and temple work.

Microfilm processing laboratories and associated facilities are included within the complex.

Although the vault's primary reason for being is to protect records gathered by the Church, other organizations rent space for their essential documents. Following the September 11, 2001, attack on the World Trade Center and other sites, some companies were able to resume business following retrieval of their records from the vault; vault personnel fielded forlorn calls from other devastated businesses hoping that their companies might also have stored their records there.

The vault is no longer open for public tours.

continued at an ever-increasing pace since that time. To preserve records thus gathered, the Church began construction, in 1958, of a secure storage facility in tunnels drilled deep into solid rock 700 feet beneath the surface of a granite mountain near Salt Lake City. The Granite Mountain Records Vault not only provides a storage site safe from most forms of natural and man-made disaster but also, because of the steady underground temperature and humidity level, helps to preserve records from the decay of time.

The Genealogical Society pioneered the use of electronic technology for the storage and management of genealogical records. Following early experimentation with punch cards and other mechanical data manipulation systems, the Church entered the computer age in 1961. In 1984, the Church released Personal Ancestral File (PAF), a program for home computers that allows genealogists to organize and display their research and to exchange records easily with other researchers. FamilySearch, a compilation of linked pedigrees, temple ordinances, the catalog of the Family History Library, and other databases became available on compact disks at the Family History Library in 1986; an online version of FamilySearch was launched in 1999 and quickly became one of the Internet's most popular destinations. New releases of these products and the development of others—including a multiyear project inaugurated in 2007 to scan and index tens of millions of images of primary genealogical documents for Internet release—keep the Family History Department at the forefront of computer-aided genealogy.

With the universal longing to know one's roots and the sustained popularity of genealogical research among much of the world's population, programs such as the Family History Center system, FamilySearch, and efforts to make available indexed genealogical records of many types have been a source of favorable publicity for the Church. Governments and private agencies that have made their records available for microfilming have enjoyed easier access to their own records and the security of safe off-site storage in case of local catastrophe. Innumerable people enjoy free use of Mormon facilities to further their own research. In gestures of good will, the Church has researched and presented family histories to statesmen, celebrities, and humanitarians worldwide.

On the other hand, misunderstanding of the purposes underlying Mormon genealogical efforts has sometimes resulted in negative publicity. Despite occasional assertions to the contrary, Mormons do not count deceased persons who have been baptized by proxy in their membership statistics. No deceased person has been "turned into a Mormon" against his will by proxy baptism; rather, Church doctrine is that no proxy ordinance is valid unless the spirit of the deceased accepts the ordinance offered in his or her behalf. The Church makes every effort to prevent data on living persons from appearing publicly in its records; unless death data are available, the names of persons born within the past 110 years are blocked from display in the Church's public databases. Cultural concerns of some groups have been addressed; agreements have been reached with Jewish groups not to perform temple ordinances for victims of the Holocaust unless such persons are ancestors of Church members; similarly, temple work for persons born in traditionally Muslim countries is not permitted unless Church members submit evidence of a family relationship to such persons. The Church repeatedly asks its members not to request ordinances for famous historical personages or the ancestors of modern celebrities unless those people are also ancestors of the Church member; from time to time, violations of this standard by individual members have created embarrassment for the Church.

From first to last, however, from Moroni's 1823 visit to Joseph Smith down to the latest class offered to visitors at the Family History Library, the "spirit of Elijah" has guided all Mormon involvement with genealogical work: "He shall plant in the hearts of the children the promises made to the fathers, and the hearts of the children shall turn to their fathers."

—*Ardis E. Parshall*

See also: Smith, Joseph Jr.; Temple Work by Proxy; Temples; Woodruff, Wilford; Young, Brigham.

References

Allen, James B., Jessie L. Embry, and Kahlile B. Mehr. *Hearts Turned to the Fathers: A History of the Genealogical Society of Utah, 1894–1994.* Provo, UT: Brigham Young University, 1995.

Irving, Gordon. "The Law of Adoption: One Phase of the Development of the Mormon Concept of Salvation, 1830–1900." *BYU Studies* 14 (Spring 1974): 291–314.

Smith, Joseph, Jr. *History of the Church of Jesus Christ of Latter-day Saints.* 6 vols. Ed. B.H. Roberts. Salt Lake City, UT: The Church of Jesus Christ of Latter-day Saints, 1973.

Woodruff, Wilford. "The Law of Adoption." *Utah Genealogical and Historical Magazine* 13 (October 1922): 145–152.

Young, Brigham. "Speech Delivered by President B. Young, in the City of Joseph, April 6, 1845." *Millennial Star,* 1 October 1845, 119–123.

Local Worship

Latter-day Saints define worship as the sustained effort to return to the presence of God the Father through the mediation of Jesus Christ. Worship can take on ritual or ceremonial forms, as in the case of temple worship or weekly communion (known in LDS parlance as the *Sacrament*), but it can also connote an overall attitude or consciousness—with thoughts and feelings directed toward God and Jesus Christ. In this sense, everyday life can be infused with worshipful context. Nevertheless, there are important, patterned, regular, formal elements to LDS worship; an examination of these practices, the institutions within which they are inscribed and regulated, and their historical development follows.

Sunday Worship

Every week, in chapels and meetinghouses around the world, Latter-day Saints gather together to worship God in the name of Jesus Christ. The principal worship service is Sacrament Meeting. Latter-day Saints together partake of bread and water in remembrance of the body and blood of Jesus Christ. A local bishop, the nominal head of the LDS congregation or "ward," presides over the Sacrament Meeting and the administration of the emblems of the Lord's Supper. To create an ambiance of worship and reverence in the meetings, ward members sing hymns, give talks and sermons, pray, and bear public testimony.

A Mormon infant is blessed by her father and family friends before the local congregation. (Courtesy of The Church of Jesus Christ of Latter-day Saints.)

The actual ordinance of the Sacrament begins with the collective singing of a hymn, during which members of the lay, all male priesthood (in most cases "priests," usually young men ages 16 to 19) prepare the emblems by breaking the bread. Following the singing, sacrament prayers are offered, according to a prescribed pattern with pre-scripted wording, by the same men who prepared the emblems. The prayers, pronounced separately but almost identically for the bread and water, supplicate God the Father, in the name of Jesus Christ, to bless the emblems to the spiritual well-being of those who eat and drink, articulate a willingness on the part of all participants to take upon themselves the name of Jesus Christ, to hold him in remembrance, and to strictly keep his commandments, in return for which they ask that God bless them with the continued presence of the Holy Spirit. The bread and water are passed to all, usually by deacons (the entry-level office of the LDS priesthood, conferred upon most young men at age 12). During the passing and partaking portion of the ordinance, silence prevails. The ordinance typically lasts 10 to 15 minutes and takes place early in the Sacrament Meetings. The remainder of the meeting usually includes talks and musical performances by ward members, as well as congregational singing and a benediction.

The Sacrament Meetings run one hour 10 minutes, after which ward members begin Sunday School. Children (to age 12) attend Primary, a locally directed program with specially designed curriculum and activities, including a play Nursery for toddlers ages 18 months to three years. Adolescents ages 12–19 attend Sunday School in small classes with coeval peers, male and female. Adults attend larger Sunday School classes where they study LDS scriptures on an annually rotating, four-year cycle (one year for each major book in the LDS canon). Sunday School typically lasts 40 minutes. For the third portion of the block, children remain in gender-integrated classes, while adolescents and adults separate along sex-specific lines—youth into the Young Men and Young Women organizations, adults into Relief Society (women) and various priesthood quorums. At the close of the three-hour block, ward members return home but are encouraged to continue to cultivate a worshipful spirit in observance of the Sabbath.

On the first Sunday of every month, LDS Sacrament Meetings are conducted on a somewhat different basis. Singing, prayer, and the ordinance of the Sacrament remain central fixtures, but, in place of prepared talks and sermons by previous assignment, ward members are encouraged to stand extemporaneously and bear testimony. These short public speech events often include descriptions of personal conversion to the LDS Church, recounting of spiritually uplifting personal experiences, occasional mild exhortation, but most often declarations that the speaker "knows" one or many of the fundamental claims of Mormonism to be true—for example, that Joseph Smith was (or the current Church president is) a true prophet, that the Book of Mormon is an authentic scriptural record, that the fullness of Christ's gospel has been restored to Earth, that Jesus is the Christ, or simply that "the Church is true." These Sundays are set aside as days of fasting. Participants typically go without food or drink for two meals, and those who bear testimonies do so within the context of a personal fast. Participants also donate the money they would have spent on the forgone meals (and often a more generous amount) as fast offerings to the bishop for the benefit of the poor.

On a fairly regular basis, Latter-day Saints participate in larger conferences in place of their usual Sunday worship services. Such conferences are held semiannually at the level of a stake—an intermediate unit of organization between the Church headquarters and local wards (similar to a Catholic diocese). A stake can be composed of anywhere from 5 to 12 separate wards, with individual stake

Mormons meet as congregations at least weekly, with services conducted by lay leaders. (Courtesy of the Church History Library, The Church of Jesus Christ of Latter-day Saints.)

membership at or around 3,000. Stakes have the formal authorization to administer all Church programs within their boundaries, and stake presidents monitor and oversee the work of ward bishops. At the semiannual conferences, all stake members are asked to attend a single two-hour meeting. For logistical reasons, the ordinance of the Sacrament is not performed at the typically very large gatherings. Attendees are informed of important changes in local leadership and administration and listen to talks from stake leadership as well as local members.

Also semiannually, Mormons gather for the Church General Conference, which takes place in and is transmitted via satellite from Church headquarters, in Salt Lake City, Utah. The Church's central governing bodies—the First Presidency and the Quorum of the Twelve Apostles, as well as the general presidencies of auxiliary organizations such as the Primary, Young Men and Young Women, and Relief Society, and the Quorums of the Seventies—address the Saints collectively. The conference lasts two full days and is composed of five separate two-hour sessions—two general sessions on Saturday morning and afternoon, one session Saturday evening (for male priesthood holders only), and two general sessions Sunday morning and afternoon. Church members unable to attend the Conference in Utah can gather in their local chapels or stake centers or even watch or listen at home via television, radio, or the Internet.

Domestic Worship

Worship in the home figures centrally in Mormon life. LDS Church members are encouraged to pray daily—morning and evening as well as before meals, individually and as families. Daily individual and family scripture study is also strongly promoted. Additionally, one evening is set aside (usually Mondays) for Family Home Evening—a time for family interaction and activities, spiritual focus, and parental instruction. LDS families are admonished to keep their homes clean and orderly as a means for creating a spiritually enriching atmosphere and as a refuge from the potentially harmful influences of the world.

Another important component of this domestic side of LDS worship is the Home and Visiting Teaching programs. Under the direction of the local Elders Quorum, each household has two priesthood holders assigned to visit on a monthly basis. Home teachers typically visit their families in pairs and are usually assigned to between two and five families. They are encouraged to get to know their families well and to develop close relationships. They are expected to share a brief devotional message during each visit. They are to seek opportunities to offer more substantive service to help their families. Finally, home teaching is an effective communication system, as home teachers are expected to report on the welfare of their assigned families to local priesthood leadership. Visiting teaching, under the direction of the ward Relief Society, functions similarly. Women are paired up and assigned specific families in the ward that they are expected to visit monthly. They offer service, share spiritually uplifting messages, render support, and report on the well-being of the families to which they are assigned. During the week, LDS youth (ages 12–19) participate in regular activities under the direction of the local Young Men and Young Women organizations.

An important key to the nature of local worship in Mormonism is the lack of a professionally trained, paid clergy. All of the leadership, administrative, clerical, teaching, and service responsibilities by which the Church is run at the stake and ward levels are filled by lay members who are called to serve but do so on a voluntary basis. Bishops and stake presidents, along with their counselors and clerks, the Stake High Council, and the presidencies of the local priesthood quorums, relief societies, youth organizations, and primaries are all drawn from the ranks of the laity, without monetary compensation. A person might serve as a bishop or Relief Society president for a period and subsequently as a ward organist or teacher in the Primary. All LDS Church members who seek full participation in the life of the Church are expected to serve in some capacity.

Historical Developments

Mormonism's official organization and the recognition of its status as a church came on April 6, 1830. In the home of Peter Whitmer, a small group of Joseph Smith's closest associates and believers in his visions and revelations gathered for a Sacrament Meeting. Smith administered the Lord's Supper, and those present participated in song and prayer. The informal setting for this foundational meeting was not just a matter of necessity; it would serve as a prototype for Sunday worship services during the LDS Church's formative years. During his lifetime, Smith never constructed a chapel or meetinghouse, that is, a building set aside primarily for Sacrament Meetings and other aspects of Sunday worship. He was fascinated by organizing urban and rural space and dedicated much of his own effort and the efforts of his followers to the construction of sacred buildings, especially temples. The construction of temples was inscribed within the larger process of planning and building cities for the gathering of LDS converts. Smith planned or began construction on temples in Kirtland, Jackson County, Far West, Adam-ondi-Ahman, and Nauvoo, although only the Kirtland and Nauvoo temples were completed. Temples were public buildings that were also set off as sacred space. But weekly worship services and Sacrament meetings were usually conducted in the homes of local Church members or, weather permitting, in open air.

City planning merged with ecclesiastical organization in the concept of "ward." Mormons today understand "ward" as the functional equivalent of a congregation or parish. The term itself comes from municipal political organization, and its uptake into the fabric of Mormonism dates to the Nauvoo period. At Nauvoo, Smith organized his city into wards and appointed a bishop to preside over each. The bishop's primary duties were the processing of tithes (offerings made by the local Saints) and to assist immigrant converts and aid the poor. Bishops did not conduct weekly worship services, which were usually held outdoors on a city-wide basis.

After expulsion from Nauvoo, at Winter Quarters the Saints were divided into 22 wards, and bishops were appointed to care for the needy, manage tithes and offerings, and look after the temporal affairs of the westward-trekking Mormons. After the Saints' arrival in the Salt Lake Valley, Brigham Young divided the valley into wards and appointed bishops. Initially, Sunday worship services were held in the Bowery, a public building at the fledgling city's center. With the influx of immigrant converts and the growth of the population, individual wards began to construct their own meetinghouses for Sacrament services. Young's plans for settling the Saints included the establishment of small agricultural villages dispersed across the territory. These Mormon villages were organized individually into wards, in the process fusing the religious congregation and the civic political, economic, and social community. Indeed, one of the primary goals for settling immigrant Mormons in the small, communitarian villages was socialization—forging the polyglot mass of converts from throughout the United States and Western Europe into a unified, orderly, productive community.

Fast meetings became a regular fixture of Mormon worship during the early territorial period. Originating in Kirtland during the pentecostal outpouring that accompanied the dedication of the temple in 1836, the Thursday fast meetings largely disappeared in Missouri and Illinois. The winter of 1855–1856 in Utah brought intense famine. Mormon leaders felt that fidelity to the systems of economic cooperation that had been implemented throughout the Territory was crucial to their independence as a kingdom. Fast day and its accompanying testimony meeting were reinstituted alongside the practice of donating fast offerings to the local bishop to be used for the benefit of the poor and needy. When the famine abated, Church leaders were convinced that fast offerings were instrumental in the process, and they decided to continue the practice indefinitely.

The year 1856 also marked a period known among historians of Mormonism as the "Mormon Reformation." Under the direction of apostle Jedediah Grant, Mormon leaders began to impose their authority on the lives of Latter-day Saints throughout the Territory with a thoroughness not felt since the height of Smith's power just before his death, in 1844. During the 1856 campaign, the Church's central authority consolidated its control over local administration in an effort to "wake the Saints up," ranging from directives about personal hygiene and orderly streets and communities to the encouragement of rebaptisms, visions, healings, and speaking in tongues. The aims and successes of the Reformation, along with the overlapping civil and spiritual jurisdiction of bishops, demonstrate the fusion of temporal and ecclesiastical affairs in 19th-century Mormondom.

During this time, several of the elements common to contemporary LDS worship either did not exist or were not incorporated into Sunday services. As noted earlier, fast meetings were held monthly on Thursdays. Sunday Schools were organized in the various settlements but were managed independent of ward leadership. Relief Societies became a regular fixture of ward organization only in the late 1860s, and the relationship between Relief Society leadership and the ward bishops was ambiguous. In larger settlements, wards functioned as subunits of city government—as welfare areas, school boundaries, and home teaching (known then as "ward teaching") and voting districts. Other prominent LDS programs and activities—the Schools of the Prophets, cooperative mercantile organizations, community prayer circle groups, and United Order projects—have since largely disappeared from Mormon religious and social life.

Privatization, Routinization, and Correlation

In the late 1870s wards and stakes were further institutionalized under the consolidated authority of LDS central governing quorums. Administrative reforms regulated the size of wards and stakes, ensuring that units would be divided when they became unmanageably large due to immigration. Church officials instructed bishops to ordain more young men to the Aaronic Priesthood, a position traditionally reserved for adult males. The Primary Association was founded and implemented centrifugally throughout the Church. Existing auxiliary organizations, the Young Men's and Young Ladies' Mutual Improvement Associations as well as the Relief Society, were regularized with central governing bodies and general presidencies. Increasingly, individual wards were treated as on-the-ground delivery systems for activities, policies, instructional curricula, and missionary and welfare programs directed from the central Church. Following the 1890 Manifesto, institutionalization and centralization proceeded more rapidly. Printed directives from LDS headquarters were no longer confined to instructions for financial regulation but increasingly dealt with explicitly ecclesiastical, instructional, and administrative matters. In 1896, leaders incorporated Thursday fast meetings into Sunday worship services.

This process of institutionalization, begun at the turn of the 20th century and accelerated since, took place alongside the retreat of Mormonism from the public domain of politics and economics and its move into the private, more traditionally religious sphere of weekly worship and interiorized personal spirituality. To a degree, the Church compensated for this redefined status through cooperative efforts with groups like the Boy Scouts of America and through the implementation and increased attention to athletic and cultural programs. Most LDS chapels constructed in the past century include a large basketball floor in a giant room designated a "cultural hall." Most meetinghouses also include ward libraries and facilities for doing family history and genealogical research. The cession of political and economic power accompanied the consolidation and bureaucratization of central ecclesiastical control. The changes also facilitated a new emphasis on the participation of all ward members in the implementation of programs and policies. Each worthy Latter-day Saint was now expected to shoulder a portion of ecclesiastical leadership and administration, whether as bishop, teacher, pianist, or clerk or in any other capacity.

Other significant developments on the path of transforming the 19th-century Mormon village into the present-day ward include the development and implementation of the Church Welfare program during the Great Depression of the 1930s; the expansion of the home teaching program, in 1963; the development of a Church Correlation program in the late 1960s and early 1970s that displaced local control over the administration of auxiliaries and regularized and standardized Church publications and curricula during a period of rapid international postwar growth; the subsuming of the General Relief Society, concomitant with the development of Correlation, under the direction of the priesthood in 1968; the institution of Family Home Evening, first in 1915 and then, with a renewed emphasis, in 1970; the 1978 revelation extending access to priesthood ordination and temple worship to all Church members, regardless of racial, ethnic, or genealogical background; the formal discontinuation of the private prayer circles outside the temple in 1978; the centralization of ward and stake budgets and financial allocation, in 1990; and the consolidation of the block meeting schedule, in the early 1980s.

Conclusion

Today, Mormons can travel to locations throughout the world and, in a local ward (or "branch," a smaller, less independent equivalent as a unit of collective worship), find a group of strangers with whom they share a profound sense of unity, trust, acceptance, and commitment. The historical changes in the modes of local LDS worship sketched here raise important questions regarding the contemporary and future status of worship. Have the changes that accompanied Mormonism's accommodation to its host society enabled the preservation of an element of the ward's continuity with the Mormon village? Is the Mormon ward still a community, or has it devolved into a more typically Protestant congregation? In an era of increased emphasis on the primacy of the nuclear family, is the ward declining in significance as a center of LDS worship, and, to the degree that it is, what are the consequences for the Mormon village legacy of collective identity and community? These and similar questions, along with their answers, will figure centrally in the LDS Church's international growth and stability and in determining its status as a world religion.

—*Bradley H. Kramer*

See also: Church Organization and Government; Correlation; Kirtland Pentecost; Manifesto; Mormonism and Economics; Organization of the Church; Priesthood Revelation of 1978; Reformation; Relief Society; Rogers, Aurelia Spencer; Temples; Youth Programs.

References

Alder, Douglas D. "The Mormon Ward: Congregation or Community?" *Journal of Mormon History* 5 (1978): 61–78.

Bushman, Claudia. *Contemporary Mormonism: Latter-day Saints in Modern America.* Westport, CT: Praeger, 2006.

Shipps, Jan, Cheryll L. May, and Dean L. May. "Sugar House Ward: A Latter-day Saint Congregation." In *American Congregations.* Vol. 1: *Portraits of Twelve Religious Communities.* Ed. James P. Wind and James W. Lewis, 293–348. Chicago: University of Chicago Press, 1994.

Mormon Missiology

In June 1829, Joseph Smith dictated several revelations that instituted missionary work as one of the prime tenets of his soon-to-be-established Church:

And now, behold, I say unto you, that the thing which will be of the most worth unto you will be to declare repentance unto this people, that you may bring souls unto me, that you may rest with them in the kingdom of my Father. (Doctrine and Covenants 15:6 & 16:6)

Wherefore, you are called to cry repentance unto this people. And if it so be that you should labor all your days in crying repentance unto this people, and bring, save it be one soul unto me, how great shall be your joy with him in the kingdom of my Father! And now, if your joy will be great with one soul that you have brought unto me into the kingdom of my Father, how great will be your joy if you should bring many souls unto me! (Doctrine and Covenants 18:14–16)

In June 1830, after the establishment of the Church, Samuel H. Smith, brother of the Prophet, packed copies of the recently published Book of Mormon and traveled across New York as the first missionary of the Church. Missionaries during this time followed a pattern similar to that of the itinerant Methodist preachers, though without a formalized circuit. Missionaries often traveled without purse or scrip and sometimes suffered great deprivations. Often, men were called to proselytize soon after converting. Fortunately, many of these early missionaries kept records of their efforts.

After forming the Quorum of the Twelve Apostles, in 1835, Joseph Smith stated:

They are the Twelve Apostles, who are called to the office of Traveling High Council . . . and they are to travel and preach among the Gentiles, until the Lord shall command them to go to the Jews. They are to hold the keys of this ministry, to unlock the door of the kingdom of heaven unto all nations, and to preach the Gospel to every creature. This is the power, authority and virtue of their apostleship. (Kirtland High Council Minutes, February 27, 1835)

From this point until the death of Joseph Smith, in 1844, the apostles concerned themselves primarily with the activities in the missions, though they grew in administrative authority in the early 1840s. In 1837, apostles Heber C. Kimball and Orson Hyde opened the British mission, the first outside North America, and many of the Twelve followed in 1839. This missionary effort resulted in a great number of conversions, and for many years there were more Mormons in the United Kingdom than in the United States.

After the Nauvoo exodus and the Saints' relocation to the Great Basin in the late 1840s, the Church renewed its missionary efforts, sending elders across the world, with the bulk of them going to Europe and the Pacific Islands. By the end of the century, the Church had sent missionaries to such remote (by the standards of the day) locations as South Africa, Siam (present-day Thailand), Turkey, and India.

Concurrent with the U.S. government's antipolygamy campaign in the 1880s, the U.S. Department of State encouraged foreign governments to discourage Mormon

Missionaries, like these in England in 1910, attempt to deliver religious writings and to engage residents in religious discussion. (Courtesy of the Church History Library, The Church of Jesus Christ of Latter-day Saints.)

efforts to make converts. This action contributed to difficulties for missionaries and converts alike, with missionaries being barred from service in many countries throughout the world. This effect persisted even after the Church and the federal government reconciled in the 1890s.

During World War I, most of the Church's missionary activities were halted, and by the end of the war missionaries were denied entry into many countries where they had traditionally labored. Apostle and U.S. senator Reed Smoot worked to procure visas for missionaries, and in 1921 he traveled through Europe with apostle John Widtsoe on a diplomatic mission to open doors for the Mormons. While some progress was made, it was not until after World War II that missionaries had open access to most Western countries.

Other significant changes in missionary access include the opening of missions in sub-Saharan Africa after the 1978 revelation extending the priesthood to all worthy males and the opening of missions in former communist countries during the political changes of 1989–1991. In the early 21st century, full-time proselytizing missionaries still do not work among a significant portion of the world's population. There are no such missionaries in India, China, or most countries with significant Islamic populations.

Missionary Program Development

Starting at the turn of the 20th century, mission presidents began to publish manuals of instruction for their missionaries. These manuals included advice, doctrinal expositions, mission guidelines, and outlines for priesthood ordinances. In 1935, fresh off his own mission and cognizant of the needs in the mission field, the 25-year-old Gordon B. Hinckley accepted an assignment to run the newly created Radio, Publicity, and Mission Literature Committee of the Church. In 1937, this new department released the first edition of *The Missionary's Hand Book*. This book marked the beginning of a centralized focus on a worldwide missionary effort, as well as the inclusion of multimedia presentation elements. Drawing on several publications in circulation at the time, the handbook was published under the copyright of President Heber J. Grant and remained in general usage for more than a decade.

After World War II, Richard Lloyd Anderson, a veteran and missionary in the northwestern United States, developed a system for teaching the gospel that resulted in a large increase in the number of converts. In 1952, the Church released *A Systematic Program for Teaching the Gospel,* which incorporated many aspects of this "Anderson Plan." This book was a manual for proselytizing and for teaching individuals in preparation for their induction into the Church. This program involved a series of six topical lessons, which were outlined in conversation form and were to be followed with all new converts, much like a catechism. This program was supplanted by the similar *A Uniform System for Teaching Investigators* in 1961.

During the 1950s, Church president David O. McKay reorganized the worldwide missionary effort with more General Authority responsibility over geographic regions. McKay popularized the phrase "every member a missionary" and placed highly successful businessmen in key positions in the missionary hierarchy. In 1959, the minimum age for missionary service was reduced from 21 to 19 for men and from 23 to 21 for women. These changes in teaching and organization, coupled with a building program designed to enhance the public image of the Church, resulted in dramatic increases in convert baptisms.

One of these major changes in missionary teaching was a focus on quick conversions. While previous programs insisted on months of preparation and study, some leaders believed in extending baptismal invitations during the first meetings with potential converts and having baptismal services within weeks or even days. These new emphases, as well as increased pressure for missionaries to teach and baptize, resulted in a quadrupling of the number of convert baptisms over four years, from 1959 to 1962. These gains were not, however, unalloyed. Reacting to institutional pressure, many missionaries baptized people, including children without parental consent, who were not fully cognizant of what commitments baptism entailed. The results were extremely low convert activity rates and disastrous public relations. By 1963, systematic changes were made in order to curb abuses, and the Church experienced significant real growth during the decade.

Church president Spencer W. Kimball further expanded the Church's missionary activities by focusing on missionary preparation and training and also by reinforcing a worldwide perspective in the ministry. In 1976, Kimball dedicated a new Language Training Mission for missionaries with foreign-language assignments. The facility was enlarged in 1978 and renamed the Missionary Training Center, where all missionaries, including those with English-language assignments, went to receive training in scripture, teaching methodology, and, where applicable, foreign languages.

Another of Kimball's major concerns was the development of potential missionaries. He preached fervently that "[e]very boy *ought* to go on a mission. There may be some who can't, but they *ought* to go on a mission. Every boy, and many girls, and many couples." Kimball's famous "Lengthen our stride" mantra was first applied to missionary work, highlighting his worldwide vision:

> Certainly [Jesus'] sheep were not limited to the thousands about him and with whom he rubbed shoulders each day. A universal family! A universal command!
>
> My brethren, I wonder if we are doing all we can. Are we complacent in our approach to teaching all the world? We have been proselyting now 144 years. Are we prepared to lengthen our stride? To enlarge our vision? (Kimball, "When the World Will Be Converted" 3)

Kimball's emphasis resulted in an increased percentage of eligible individuals serving missions. While 24 percent of eligible males served when Kimball took office, during his administration the figure reached as high as 30 percent. Additionally, the number of potential missionaries increased, leading to a significant rise in the total missionary force. The number of missionaries hailing from outside the United States and Canada rose from 975 to 8,628 during Kimball's administration.

In 1982, the Church shortened missionary service for men from 24 months to 18 months in an effort to make service more economically and socially feasible. Because the number of missionaries did not increase and missionaries faced the disadvantage of having less time to acquire language proficiency, service terms were returned to 24 months in 1985.

In 1986, missionaries began using *A Uniform System for Teaching the Gospel,* a series of presentations to be learned and delivered to potential converts, complete with flip charts. Additionally, missionaries were to study the *Missionary Guide,* a program of instruction based on studies in organizational behavior. Missionary companionships were instructed to study the program daily and to engage in role-play training exercises designed to reinforce the principles of "The Commitment Pattern."

Apostle M. Russell Ballard announced, in October 2002, that the Church was "raising the bar" on missionary standards. Prospective missionaries would be disqualified from service if they had not lived the standards of the Church in their youth. Two years after the change in policy, the global missionary force dropped from close to 62,000 persons to about 51,000. This drop likely contributed to the decline in the number of worldwide converts from approximately 300,000 to 241,000 during the same time period. Changing demographics may also account for some of the decrease in number of missionaries.

The Church announced, in October 2004, the arrival of *Preach My Gospel,* a new program for finding and teaching investigators. Perhaps most notable in this new program was the shift from requiring fixed presentations to allowing individual preparation of lesson plans. Members, missionaries and converts are currently encouraged to study *Preach My Gospel.*

Missionary Training and Preparation

For most of the 19th century, missionaries were generally established men. For example, in 1897, C.T. Nelson was 37 years old and was married with four children when he received a call from the president of the Church to fulfill a mission to Scandinavia. Nelson wrote that many "Relatives Friends bouth Mormons and Gentiles" were generous in their financial contributions in support of his mission. He also sold property and water rights to finance his mission (Nelson, Papers 3–4). At this same time, leaders such as George Q. Cannon and Joseph F. Smith started to renew their focus on missionary preaching "without purse or scrip," encouraging the Church to follow the example of the early missionaries. This emphasis lasted for less than a decade, though some missions applied the principle regionally as late as the 1950s.

The Church also sought to send younger missionaries. Recognizing a disparity between the seasoned men typically sent and the more inexperienced youth, in 1899, the First Presidency authorized the First Seven Presidents of the Seventies to select potential missionaries from the local Quorums of the Seventies and to send them to one of three schools for a year of education in preparation for their service. Smith acknowledged the benefit for these one-year courses set up at various schools, but he conceded that adding another year onto an already two-year mission commitment was asking for more sacrifice than many Mormons were willing to make. He subsequently announced the creation of a correspondence course, in which all prospective missionaries were to engage.

Starting in 1925, a Mission Home in Salt Lake City provided a central location where missionaries could gather and receive instruction. Generally, a missionary would stay for several days, be set apart as a missionary by a General Authority, and participate in temple rituals before leaving for his or her assigned region of service.

Historically, missionaries went directly to foreign-language areas with no language preparation. From the early 1950s, BYU president Ernest Wilkinson lobbied for a center that combined language training with the services of the Mission Home. In 1961, the Church began a pilot program for 24 Spanish-language-speaking missionaries in Provo. In 1963, the program was standardized, and the administration dedicated facilities to the new Language Training Mission, or LTM. Missionaries were able to use the BYU facilities and even attended sporting events.

Concurrent with President Kimball's vision, in 1974 the Church broke ground on the Provo Missionary Training Center (MTC), which was completed in 1976 and is still in use. All missionaries, including those with English-language assignments, stay at the MTC to receive several weeks of rigorous training in language, pedagogy, and gospel topics. In 1977, an MTC was opened in Sao Paulo, Brazil, and, by 1990, 13 MTCs operated in Europe, Asia, and Latin American. In 2009, there were 17 MTCs operational worldwide.

Sister Missionaries

Despite a sense in the 1830s that elders should leave family behind to preach the word of God itinerantly and statements from members of the hierarchy such as the Kirtland High Council "that it is not advisable for any Elder to take [his] wife with him on a mission to preach," some men, including prominent leaders in the Church, did travel with their wives. Phoebe and Wilford Woodruff, who served in Maine, are one such example.

The practice of missionary wives joining their husbands became more common with time, and, by the 1850s, missionary wives were a somewhat regular, though far from universal, part of mission life. Louisa Barnes Pratt, who accompanied her husband to Tahiti, wrote in her journal that, before leaving:

No less distinctive in their modern dress, Mormon elders and sisters continue to search for people open to discussing faith and religion. (Courtesy of the Church History Library, The Church of Jesus Christ of Latter-day Saints.)

We made a call at President Young's . . . and [he] blessed me. He said I was called, set apart, and ordained, to go to the Islands of the sea, to aid my husband in teaching the people. . . . That no evil should befall me on the journey, that I should lack nothing. I should have power to rebuke the destroyer from my house. . . . All of which he sealed upon my head in the name of the Lord. (Pratt, *History of Louisa Barnes Pratt* 108–109)

Louisa worked in the Society Islands teaching school for native children as well as her own, attending meetings, and administering healing rituals to the locals (all common practices for 19th-century Mormon women). It appears that, while Brigham Young did bless Louisa before she embarked and that such blessings were not anomalous during the rest of the century, the Church leadership did not officially recognize these women as missionaries or record them as such in

Church documents. However, in 1898, George Q. Cannon announced a change in policy that signaled the calling of women as missionaries.

Shortly after this announcement, Harriet Nye, wife of the California mission president, was set apart as a missionary. Amanda Inez Knight and Lucy Jane Brimhall, two friends in their early 20s, were subsequently set apart as full-time proselytizing missionaries, the first single women to be so called. They served in Britain, where they engaged in the regular missionary practices of "tracting," home visiting, street preaching, and teaching.

Female missionaries quickly became a successful part of the Church's proselytizing effort, representing 15 to 20 percent of the total missionary force for most of the century. In 1915, the First Presidency issued a call "for lady missionaries of maturity":

> We are greatly in need of lady missionaries . . . and would be pleased to receive from you the names of sisters who are physically and financially able to perform missions, and whom you can recommend.
>
> Care should be exercised in selecting lady missionaries. They should be good, steady, representative women, not too young, with a good education and knowledge of the Gospel, and who have had experience in the auxiliary organizations of the Church. (Clark, *Messages* 4:335)

The First Presidency made a shorter but similar plea in 1922. However, during World War II, women represented as many as 48 percent of all missionaries, and the Church sought to curtail their missionary activity (with the exception of those skilled as stenographers, teachers, and wives of men beyond draft age who could accompany husbands in field). Since World War II, women have served in missions throughout the world as regularly called and set-apart ministers of the Gospel.

Missionaries in the 21st Century

Single men between the ages of 19 and 25 and women over 21 who desire to serve a mission may contact their bishop or branch president in order to file the requisite paperwork to be considered for missionary service. Candidates must be living according to Church standards, including obedience to the Law of Chastity, and be physically, mentally, and emotionally capable of missionary service. After a series of interviews with local leadership, the missionary application is sent to Church headquarters, where an assignment is made.

Missionaries start their missions with several weeks of training at a Missionary Training Center, after which they are sent to their assigned geographic region, called a mission. Each mission is presided over by a mission president, who typically has two missionary assistants who serve in a rotating capacity with the other missionaries to help in training and motivation. Missions are typically subdivided into large regions called zones and further into subregions called districts, with missionary leaders in charge of the work in these areas. Missionaries are to always be with their "companions," one of whom is typically a "senior" to the other.

Missionaries have set rules and schedules, which include rising early, daily individual and companionship study, and regular proselytizing. Men serve a total of 24 months, and women serve 18 months. Missionaries are not paid for their service and are responsible, often with the help of family, for supporting themselves as they labor.

—*Jonathan A. Stapley*

See also: Church Organization and Government; Mormonism and Men; Mormonism and Other Faiths; Mormonism and Women; Non-Mormon Views of Mormonism.

References
Clark, James R. Ed. *Messages of the First Presidency of the Church of Jesus Christ of Latter-day Saints, 1901–1915*. Vol. 4. Salt Lake City, UT: Bookcraft, 1975.

Doctrine and Covenants of the Church of Jesus Christ of Latter-day Saints. Salt Lake City, UT: The Church of Jesus Christ of Latter-day Saints, 1981.

Kimball, Spencer W. "When the World Will Be Converted." *Ensign* 4 (October 1974): 3.

Kirtland Council Minute Book. Manuscript. LDS Church Archives.

Nelson, Christian Theodore. Papers, 1897–1901, 3–4. LDS Church Archives.

Payne, Tally S. "'Our Wise and Prudent Women': Twentieth-Century Trends in Female Missionary Service." In *New Scholarship on Latter-day Saint Women in the Twentieth Century*. Ed. Carol Cornwall Madsen and Cherry B. Silver. Provo, UT: Joseph Fielding Smith Institute for Latter-day Saint History, 2005.

Pratt, Louisa Barnes. *The History of Louisa Barnes Pratt: Being the Autobiography of a Mormon Missionary Widow and Pioneer*. Ed. S. George Ellsworth. Logan: Utah State University Press, 1998.

Thomas, John C. "Apostolic Diplomacy: The 1923 European Mission of Senator Reed Smoot and Professor John A. Widtsoe." *Journal of Mormon History* 28 (Spring 2002): 130.

Mormon Scripture

A unique answer to the question "What is scripture?" is one of the hallmarks of the Church of Jesus Christ of Latter-day Saints. While Mormons include the Bible in their canon, they also add the Book of Mormon, the Doctrine and Covenants, and the Pearl of Great Price. Additionally, several documents have the status of parascripture within the Church. Acceptance of additional scripture is one of the main differences between Latter-day Saints and other Christians.

According to LDS belief, the Book of Mormon is the record of several ancient groups that lived in the Americas; it begins with the story of one family leaving Jerusalem for the Americas shortly before the destruction of Jerusalem and the Babylonian captivity. In the New World, the sons of this family divided into warring factions, and a large portion of the Book of Mormon is devoted to recounting those wars.

The climax of the book is the visit of the resurrected Jesus Christ to the Americas. His teachings are recounted and are similar to those found in the New Testament. After a brief period of peacefulness following his visit, the wars resume, and the Christians are annihilated in the fourth century. The final survivor of the genocide buried the written record in a

Mormon practice encourages study of the Bible and Book of Mormon in the home. Early home lessons are expanded by Sunday school (youth), seminary (high school), and institute (college) training in the scriptures. (Courtesy of The Church of Jesus Christ of Latter-day Saints.)

hillside, where it remained for 1,400 years until that same writer and editor, now a resurrected being and known as the angel Moroni (who is familiar to many non-Mormons as the gold trumpeter on the spires of Mormon temples), appeared to Joseph Smith and guided him through the retrieval of the plates from their entombment and the subsequent translation of the record into the English language. Thus, in 1830, the Book of Mormon was published in English. In a statement well known to Latter-day Saints the world over, Joseph Smith said that "the Book of Mormon was the most correct of any book on earth, and the keystone of our religion" (Smith, *History* 4:461).

Mark Twain called the Book of Mormon "chloroform in print," and even some faithful Latter-day Saints will admit to struggling to read through "the war chapters." Mormons, nonetheless, read it to build and strengthen faith, to seek answers, and to draw closer to Jesus Christ. Many Book of Mormon teachings parallel those in the Bible ("For salvation cometh to none such except it be through repentance and faith on the Lord Jesus Christ" [Mosiah 3:12]), but some are distinct ("It is solemn mockery before God, that ye should baptize little children" [Moroni 8:9]).

Critics dismiss the Book of Mormon for a variety of reasons. One is that the Book of Mormon quotes at length from the Book of Isaiah, which, according to most scholars, was written after the time the first Book of Mormon prophet, Lehi, was supposed to have left Jerusalem. Mormons respond by arguing against such a late date for the writing of Isaiah. Critics also claim that more than 4,000 changes have been made

Articles of Faith

An important letter written on March 1, 1842, by Joseph Smith, commonly called the "Wentworth Letter" (it was addressed to John Wentworth, editor of the *Chicago Democrat* in answer to his earlier query), concludes with 13 statements of basic religious belief. These statements have come to be known as the "Articles of Faith" and function as a convenient summary of belief for a Church that rejects formal creeds. They do not express all key Mormon doctrines but were selected to address the most common misconceptions about Mormon belief at the time they were written.

These statements concern (1) the Godhead; (2) individual responsibility for sin; (3) Christ's atonement; (4) the necessity of faith, repentance, baptism, and the gift of the Holy Ghost; (5) the source of priestly authority; (6) Church organization; (7) spiritual gifts; (8) the scriptural canon; (9) revelation; (10) the gathering of Israel and the millennial reign of Christ; (11) freedom of conscience; (12) submission to civil authority; and (13) characteristics of Christian discipleship.

The Articles of Faith were first published in Nauvoo, Illinois, in 1842, were reprinted extensively in missionary materials, and were accepted into the Mormon canon as a part of the Pearl of Great Price in 1880.

to the Book of Mormon text and find this inconsistent with the idea that it is "the most correct" book; Mormon apologists respond that the overwhelming majority of changes concern grammar and are insignificant. Critics have also pointed to anachronisms in the Book of Mormon (such as references to synagogues, advanced metallurgy, and horses), which most Mormon scholars believe to be simply artifacts of translation. LDS scholars instead point to evidence for the book's antiquity, including the presence of ancient Hebrew poetic forms that would have been unknown to Joseph Smith.

The Book of Mormon is central to the Church's substantial missionary effort. In the 21st century, more than 50,000 full-time missionaries encourage their contacts to read the Book of Mormon, and they regard it as the primary means of conversion to the gospel. Several verses from the Book of Mormon, often referred to as Moroni's Promise, encourage readers to pray about what they have read and promise that if they do so sincerely, they will come to know for themselves that the book is what it purports to be (Moroni 10:3–5).

The Doctrine and Covenants is a compilation of revelations, almost all of which were given to Joseph Smith. Exceptions include one addressed to Wilford Woodruff (ending the practice of polygamy in 1890), one to Joseph F. Smith (dated 1918, concerning the status of those who die without baptism), and—the latest entry—one addressed to Spencer W. Kimball (a 1978 revelation ending the ban on men of African descent receiving the priesthood). Unlike all other book of scripture, the Doctrine and Covenants consists almost entirely of direct exhortation, with few to no parables, historical narrative, or poetry. Much of the counsel is pragmatic and addressed to specific individuals; consider, for example, these verses addressed to Thomas Marsh, who was at that time a new elder in the Church:

> Thomas, my son, blessed are you because of your faith in my work. Behold, you have had many afflictions because of your family; nevertheless, I will bless you and your family, yea, your little ones; and the day cometh that they will believe and know the truth and be one with you in my church. Lift up your heart and rejoice, for the hour of your mission is come; and your tongue shall be loosed, and you shall declare glad tidings of great joy unto this generation. (Doctrine and Covenants 31:1–3)

The Doctrine and Covenants is considered by Mormons to be an "open canon," and it is therefore possible that new material could be added in the future.

The LDS canon also includes the Pearl of Great Price, a short book consisting of a variety of material. Its first section is called Selections from the Book of Moses and is a long segment of a translation of Genesis made by Joseph Smith. Similarly, the third item in the Pearl of Great Price, called Joseph Smith-Matthew, is Joseph Smith's translation of the 24th chapter of the Gospel of Matthew. The second section, the Book of Abraham, has a complicated and controversial history. Joseph Smith purchased papyri in 1835 from a traveling mummy show and proceeded to translate the papyri; the result was the Book of Abraham. For years, the papyri were assumed to have been lost and subsequently destroyed. But, in the 1960s, portions were found in New York's Metropolitan Museum of Art. Egyptologists quickly determined that the text was a common funerary scroll that had nothing to do with Abraham and was, in fact, written centuries after his lifetime. LDS scholars point out that only fragments of the papyri have been found and apparently are not the fragments Joseph Smith translated. They note that it is also possible that, much as Joseph Smith's translation of the Bible involved not an ancient text but rather inspired pondering of the existing text, a similar process may have been at work with the Book of Abraham. The book itself consists of events from the life of Abraham and includes three drawings, called facsimiles.

Also included in the Pearl of Great Price is a document called Joseph Smith—History, which briefly recounts Smith's early life, his inaugural vision, his reception of the gold plates from which the Book of Mormon was translated, and his reception of the priesthood from John the Baptist. Perhaps its most famous (and, among Mormons, beloved) segment is Smith's description of Mormonism's founding miracle:

> When the light rested upon me I saw two Personages, whose brightness and glory defy all description, standing above me in the air. One of them spake unto

The Book of Mormon is currently available (in whole or in part) in 106 languages, including Arabic, shown here. (Courtesy of the Church History Museum, The Church of Jesus Christ of Latter-day Saints.)

me, calling me by name and said, pointing to the other—This is My Beloved Son. Hear Him! My object in going to inquire of the Lord was to know which of all the sects was right, that I might know which to join. No sooner, therefore, did I get possession of myself, so as to be able to speak, than I asked the Personages who stood above me in the light, which of all the sects was right (for at this time it had never entered into my heart that all were wrong)—and which I should join. I was answered that I must join none of them, for they were all wrong; and the Personage who addressed me said that all their creeds were an abomination in his sight; that those professors were all corrupt; that: "they draw near to me with their lips, but their hearts are far from me, they teach for doctrines the commandments of men, having a form of godliness, but they deny the power thereof." (Joseph Smith—History 1:17–19)

This story became foundational to Mormonism; commonly called The First Vision, it would become the bedrock experience upon which faith in the Mormon restoration message is developed. LDS parents teach the story to their children to show that God answers prayers, that the heavens were once again opened after a long apostasy, and that Joseph Smith was called to be a prophet. LDS missionaries share it with the people that they teach in order to emphasize those points, as well as the teaching that the LDS Church is the one, true Church on Earth. Critics point out that Joseph Smith wrote four accounts of the First Vision during his lifetime and that the details differ substantially; LDS apologists find the parallel to the four gospels refutation enough. Rank-and-file members may be only dimly aware of the controversy and consider the account of the First Vision one of the most beloved of all scripture stories.

The final entry in the Pearl of Great Price, known as the Articles of Faith, had its origins in an explanatory letter sent by Joseph Smith to a newspaper editor in 1842. Like the Book of Mormon, the Articles of Faith range from statements that would be acceptable to virtually all Christians ("We believe in God, the Eternal Father, and in His Son, Jesus Christ, and in the Holy Ghost" [Articles of Faith 1]) to those that cover uniquely Mormon ideas ("We believe the Bible to be the word of God as far as it is translated correctly; we also believe the Book of Mormon to be the word of God" [Articles of Faith 8]).

The LDS Church also considers the Old and New Testaments of the Bible to be scripture, with the King James Version as its official English version. While other Christians have moved away from the KJV in record numbers, the Church has maintained its commitment to the KJV into the 21st century. Additionally, the Bible published by the Church contains (in its footnotes and endnotes) selected excerpts from the Joseph Smith Translation (or JST), which consists of changes and additions made by Smith as he studied the Bible. LDS scholars consider the JST to contain four types of material: corrections to the text that restore its original wording, additions to the text that were not originally included, material added to harmonize the text with other scriptural accounts, and inspired commentary on the text. Historically, the status of the JST in the Church was slightly suspect since the original manuscripts were in the possession of what was then called the Reorganized Church of Jesus Christ of Latter Day Saints, but subsequent opportunities to examine those manuscripts by LDS scholars have improved confidence in the reliability of the manuscript. Until 1981, most members of the Church did not have easy access to the JST. But, in that year, a new LDS edition of the scriptures was printed and included excerpts from the JST. Since that time, the role and importance of the JST have increased significantly.

The LDS canon, therefore, comprises the Book of Mormon, which is granted an elevated status as "the most correct book"; the Old Testament; the New Testament; the Doctrine and Covenants; and the Pearl of Great Price. In addition to the canon, there exists in the LDS Church something that might be called parascripture (although LDS do not use that term), which consists of texts given a level of authority approaching that of the scriptures. While it is difficult to define the exact contours of this body of literature, contenders for inclusion would likely include:

1. The written record from the Church's semi-annual conference, which is published in a magazine format that most Church members receive and which consists of talks given by Church leaders
2. The Family, A Proclamation to the World (1995), a statement of LDS beliefs regarding the importance of and the ideal operation of the family
3. Other verbal statements or writings from the current prophet

Again, these documents do not have the status of scripture but enjoy a similar status.

The work of translating scriptures into various languages has followed the growth and development of the Church. By the beginning of the 21st century, the Book of Mormon had been translated in its entirety into 81 languages, with selections translated into an additional 27 languages.

The approach to the scriptures taken by the average Latter-day Saint focuses on the devotional application of the text and not on the issues that concern biblical scholars. In other words, the trappings of academic biblical studies (familiarity with original languages, literary conventions, historical setting, and critical problems) are simply not on the radar of most LDS—they read the text, take it more or less at its literal face value, and then draw lessons from it that they seek to apply to their daily activities. While a small cadre of Church members is conversant with the larger world of academic biblical studies, this group's influence on how the average Church member (or Church leader) approaches the text is extremely limited.

Scriptures are central to the faith and worship of the Latter-day Saints. The Church advocates that members study scripture daily, as individuals and as families, and, while precise compliance rates are not known (and perhaps not as high as Church leaders would like), it can be assumed that LDS children will receive some instruction in the scriptures in their homes. They will also learn of the stories from across the canon in their Sunday School classes. LDS high school students attend a daily hour-long religious education class that focuses on the scriptures, and a similar class is offered during college years.

Scriptures are also used in Sunday worship services. Sunday School attendance is expected of adults; each major book of scripture (Old Testament, New Testament, Book of Mormon, and Doctrine and Covenants) is studied on a four-year rotating basis. Since there is no paid clergy, Sunday sermons (called, simply, "talks") and lessons are offered by Church members in rotation; they use the scriptures in preparing these assignments. In other words, daily contact with the scriptures across the life span is standard for Latter-day Saints.

—Julie Marie Smith

See also: Book of Mormon; First Vision; Local Worship; Mormon Missiology.

References

Barlow, Philip L. *Mormons and the Bible: The Place of the Latter-day Saints in American Religion.* New York: Oxford University Press, 1991.

Book of Mormon. Salt Lake City, UT: The Church of Jesus Christ of Latter-day Saints, 1981.

Doctrine and Covenants of the Church of Jesus Christ of Latter-day Saints. Salt Lake City, UT: The Church of Jesus Christ of Latter-day Saints, 1981.

Givens, Terryl L. *By the Hand of Mormon: The American Scripture That Launched a New World Religion.* New York: Oxford University Press, 2003.

Pearl of Great Price. Salt Lake City, UT: The Church of Jesus Christ of Latter-day Saints, 1981.

Smith, Joseph. *History of the Church.* Ed. B. H. Roberts. Salt Lake City, UT: Deseret Book, 1973.

Mormonism and Blacks

In 1832, the year after the Nat Turner Rebellion and two years after the Church of Jesus Christ of Latter-day Saints was organized, Elijah Abel, a man of African descent (possibly once enslaved), was baptized a Mormon. According to early LDS convert Eunice Kinney, Abel was ordained in 1836 to the Melchizedek priesthood by the Church's founder, Joseph Smith Jr. Other sources make it clear that Smith approved of Abel's later ordination to the priesthood office of a Seventy and of his calling as a missionary.

During the early years of Mormonism, white converts faced great hostility in their second gathering place—Independence, Missouri—some of it generated by the perception that Mormons were inviting slaves to leave their masters and join them. (An article written by Mormon W. W. Phelps stating that "so long as we have no special rule in the Church as to people of color, let prudence guide" [Phelps, "Free People of Color," 218] had been interpreted as just such an invitation and had been answered violently.) Some Mormons in later years saw the difficulties in Missouri as the most important precursor of the later priesthood restriction and perhaps the rationale behind it.

Nonetheless, African Americans did convert to the LDS faith (albeit in small numbers) from its earliest days on. Besides Elijah Abel, free-born Jane Manning James and eight of her family members joined the Saints in Nauvoo after an arduous, on-foot journey from Wilton, Connecticut, where they had been baptized. Abel and James did not meet until they were in Utah, but they were known to their fellow Mormons. Early Church members were aware that Jane had lived with the Smith family, and she claimed to have "handled" the Urim and Thummim (the mysterious instruments used by Smith to translate the Book of Mormon). And, though Abel's ordination to the priesthood would later be questioned, the early Saints were aware that he had been ordained.

Smith, echoing the common perception of 19th-century Protestants, believed that blacks were the "seed of Cain," but he ran an abolitionist presidential campaign in 1844 that called on the nation to "break off the shackles from the poor black man" (Smith, *General Smith's Views*). Smith's campaign was cut short by his assassination, and Brigham Young replaced him as the most prominent Mormon leader.

No record of any policy or doctrine restricting blacks from ordination in the priesthood exists for the years prior to Smith's death, in 1844. In fact, it is clear that Young himself was not aware of any restriction in 1847 when he remarked that "we have a fine elder, an African, in Lowell, Massachusetts" (Young, Minutes); he was referring to Walker Lewis, who had also been ordained to the Melchizedek priesthood.

The race issue itself seems to have been of less importance to Young than the daunting task of heading the Mormon migration, the Latter-day Saints' move, on foot or in covered wagons, from the plains of Iowa to the Rocky Mountains. The vanguard company of pioneers, arriving in Utah on July 24, 1847, included three "colored servants": Green Flake, Oscar Crosby, and Hark Lay. Some of Flake's descendants claim that it was he who drove the wagon in which Young lay ill, and that Young was speaking to him when he said, "This is the right place; drive on."

Soon, many southern converts would also make their way to Utah, bringing their slaves with them as ambulatory wealth. By 1849, Utah included nearly 100 African Americans, most of them enslaved. Several of these enslaved persons would find prominence outside Utah. The most famous was Bridget (Biddy) Smith Mason, who came west with Mormon converts Robert and Rebecca Smith and subsequently accompanied them to California. There, she and 13 other slaves were dramatically emancipated by Judge Benjamin Hayes when Robert Smith was preparing to take his family and slaves to Texas. (Texas allowed slavery. In the California Compromise, California had become a free state and Utah a slave-holding territory.) After being emancipated, Mason became one of the wealthiest women in California, a renowned philanthropist, and a founding member of the First African Methodist Episcopal Church in Los Angeles.

In Utah, by 1852, Young instituted a far-reaching priesthood restriction that denied those of African descent any portion of the LDS priesthood or participation in the highest ordinances performed in the Mormon temples. Young's language suggested that he was speaking without precedent: "If there never was a prophet, or apostle of Jesus Christ spoke it before, I tell you, this people that are commonly called negroes . . . cannot bear rule in the priesthood" (Young, Speech).

Two years after Young's death, Abel (clearly questioning the priesthood restriction) brought a petition to the new Church president, John Taylor, requesting the highest temple ordinance, the Endowment. (He had received initiatory ordinances while Smith was still alive but had moved to Cincinnati by the time the Endowment was introduced in Nauvoo, Illinois.)

Regardless of what Young had stated, Taylor was apparently uncertain of what the policy was or should be, and he summoned Abraham O. Smoot and Zebedee Coltrin, two men who reported memories of Smith's setting a restriction. The meeting took place on May 31, 1879. Taylor's secretary, John Nuttall, took careful notes.

Smoot's words were not surprising. He claimed that, as a missionary in the south, he had been told not to ordain any slave to the priesthood. Inasmuch as it was an understood policy that no slave should be baptized without the master's consent, such a claim seemed obviously true. However, Smoot's words referred only to slaves and did not fully answer the question of whether those of African descent (all of whom had been emancipated by the Civil War) could be ordained to the priesthood.

Coltrin detailed a more specific memory, claiming that Smith had declared directly, "The Spirit of the Lord saith the Negro had no right nor cannot hold the priesthood." Coltrin went on to suggest that Abel had been "dropped from the quorum"

(Stephens, "Life and Contributions of Zebedee Coltrin" 54) as soon as his race was discovered. This claim was later contradicted by the man who would become the sixth president of the Church, Joseph F. Smith. Not only did Smith counter Coltrin's words, but he produced two certificates verifying Abel's status as an ordained Seventy in the Melchizedek priesthood. Further claims by Coltrin also proved to be faulty, suggesting that his memory was not dependable.

Jane James was certainly aware of the controversy. On Christmas day, 1884, the day Abel died, Jane went to Taylor's home to "hold some conversation." Two days later, she dictated a letter to Taylor, pointing out that "God promised Abraham that in his seed all the nations of the earth should be blessed. As this is the fullness of all dispensations—is there no blessing for me?" (Wolfinger, "A Test of Faith" 170). She went on to request the very things Abel had requested: the highest ordinances of the temple.

Neither James nor Abel was allowed the ordinances they requested, though James was permitted to perform proxy baptisms for her deceased relatives in the Salt Lake temple (a common Mormon practice). Five months after James died, Joseph F. Smith changed his position on Abel's priesthood and, echoing Coltrin, stated that Abel's priesthood was "null and void" (Smith, Council Minutes).

During these years, there were very few blacks in Mormon settlements (Utah and Idaho), but there were some. Green Flake, a loyal Mormon, moved to Idaho but visited Utah to be honored as a pioneer during the Jubilee celebration of 1897. Though his two children, Abraham and Lucinda, did not remain active Latter-day Saints, several of his grandchildren did. Samuel Chambers, converted while still in bondage in 1844, journeyed to Utah after emancipation, bringing his wife, Amanda, and son, Peter, as well as his sister and her husband, Susan and Ned Leggroan. Descendants of these and other black pioneers intermarried, some remaining in the Church, some leaving.

For the most part, the priesthood restriction, now widely accepted in the Church, was not a controversial issue, given the segregated nature of most religions of 19th-century America. Although the Mormon Church had never officially segregated its congregations, it counted so few blacks in its ranks that most members never dealt with issues of race directly. Nevertheless, most in the Church were familiar with the priesthood restriction and the purported reasons for its existence. Part of the restriction's rationale hinged on the common idea that blacks were cursed as the seed of Cain and Canaan, but another part, distinctly Mormon, was based on the concept of a pre-mortal life in which spirits (soon to become embodied on Earth) fought a great war over the principle of free agency and the need for a Savior. This concept gave rise to speculations formulated in the mid-1800s by Mormon leaders Orson Spenser and Orson Hyde. They suggested it was "highly probable" that those born into African lineages were "not valiant" in the pre-mortal war and were thus being punished by coming to Earth through a "cursed" lineage (Pratt, "The Pre-Existence of Man,"

Elijah Abel was a black man ordained to the priesthood, by Joseph Smith Jr. in 1836. Although Mormon attitudes toward blacks hardened later in the century, Abel remained a faithful and exemplary Latter-day Saint. (Courtesy of the Church History Library, The Church of Jesus Christ of Latter-day Saints.)

134–135; Hyde, *Speech of Elder Orson Hyde,* 30). Their opinions were repeated often enough that they became part of the institutional memory of Mormonism and were not challenged for many years.

Because of the priesthood restriction and a general uncertainty about the position of blacks in the LDS Church, Mormon missionaries rarely taught those of African descent. When a large group of Nigerians formed their own Latter-day Saint congregation in the 1950s and requested missionaries and manuals, President David O. McKay recognized the problem of having black congregations in which no one could hold the priesthood—an essential element of LDS leadership. He sent officials to see what could be done for the Nigerians, but the Biafran war interrupted any resolution of the problem.

Even in the United States, missionaries were discouraged from proselytizing African Americans. By the 1930s, almost all the descendants of Jane James and of Elijah Abel—and of any other black Mormon pioneer—had left the Church in favor of all-black congregations. When the civil rights movement gained national momentum, in the 1950s, few Mormons remembered the history of and the controversy surrounding Abel's priesthood or Jane James's petitions for temple ordinances. The restriction was understood and thought to be a doctrine instigated by Joseph Smith Jr. from the Church's inception.

Though most American Churches had separate black and white congregations, the LDS Church did not. And, although most Churches had de facto priesthood restrictions (they rarely permitted a man of African descent to preside over a white congregation), the Mormon Church allowed all men—except blacks—to hold priesthood offices. In the heat of the civil rights movement, the policy became conspicuous and much publicized, resulting in boycotts of the Church's Brigham Young University and protests at athletic events in which BYU was participating. The most devastating protest involved the "Wyoming 14"—14 football players from Wyoming University who planned to wear black armbands to protest the Mormon "priesthood doctrine" when the two teams met on October 18, 1969. All 14 were released from the Wyoming team the day before the game, but their

The Church has been fully organized in many parts of Africa, with local leadership and established congregations. (Courtesy of The Church of Jesus Christ of Latter-day Saints.)

supporters soon reached far beyond Wyoming, and black bands could be seen at almost any athletic event involving Brigham Young University players. Not only did BYU face athletic boycotts and protests, but scheduled artists, including Herb Albert and the Tijuana Brass, also refused to do concerts at BYU because of the race issue. The LDS Church's policy and reputation became media fodder. Ironically, the very Church that had once been persecuted for allegedly inviting slaves to leave their masters and become Mormons was now seen as the quintessential example of institutionalized racism.

It should be noted that there were African American Mormons during these turbulent years. Although there were only about 300 black Mormons worldwide during the 1950s and 1960s, the few who remained active (several who converted as adults and others who were descendants of black pioneers) were often invited to be speakers at LDS meetings. Monroe Fleming, who had married a great granddaughter of Jane Manning James, was a particularly popular speaker and often addressed outgoing Mormon missionaries at meetings in the Hotel Utah, where he and his wife both worked.

In 1971, three African American Mormon men, Ruffin Bridgeforth, Darius Gray, and Eugene Orr, approached the president of the Church, Joseph Fielding Smith, seeking a way to keep their families involved and perhaps to re-activate the descendants of the black pioneers. Beginning on June 8, 1971, three "Junior Apostles,"

Gordon B. Hinckley, Thomas S. Monson, and Boyd K. Packer, met twice monthly with these men to discuss their options. The result was the organization of the Genesis Branch (now commonly referred to as the Genesis Group), on October 19, 1971. It served as a gathering place for black Mormons, although it was not a substitute for their regular meetings. It did not give them the priesthood.

Meanwhile, scholars were re-examining Church history with regard to race. Through intellectual inquiry and historical research, the Abel controversy surfaced yet again, and Dr. Lester Bush published his seminal article "Mormonism's Negro Doctrine" in *Dialogue: A Journal of Mormon Thought.* Although most Mormons held to the idea that the restriction had been put into place from the earliest days of the Church by revelation, others began considering the possibility that it was not a part of the nascent Church under Joseph Smith Jr. and perhaps reflected the time during which it was framed rather than the will of God.

The issue had been a festering one for McKay, who did what he could to allow Fijians, Filipino Negritos, and many of mixed race, to receive the priesthood. There was even a failed attempt led by apostle Hugh B. Brown, in 1969, to overturn the policy. Most of the leadership—and particularly Harold B. Lee, who would later become president of the Church—believed that the policy could be removed only by revelation.

When Lee died unexpectedly, in 1973, after only 18 months at the Church's helm, Spencer W. Kimball became president. During his first press conference as the Church president, he was asked about the priesthood issue and responded: "The day might come when they [blacks] would be given the priesthood, but that day has not come yet. Should the day come, it will be a matter of revelation. But we believe in revelation" (Kimball, *Lengthen Your Stride* 7–8). On June 1, 1978, he met with 10 of the 12 LDS apostles in the temple to discuss the issue and to pray together about it. All of those present described it as a day of Pentecost and claimed that revelation revoking the priesthood restriction was indeed received. The result was new LDS scripture, now known as Official Declaration 2 in the Doctrine and Covenants, that made the priesthood available to "all worthy males" regardless of race or ethnicity. The public announcement of the policy change was made on June 8, 1978, which was referred to as "the long promised day."

Since then, Mormon missionaries have gone without restraint into Africa and other nations with large African-based populations. A black man, Helvecio Martins from Brazil, was made a Church General Authority in 1990, and LDS temples were soon erected in areas populated predominately by blacks, including Nigeria and Ghana. Since LDS doctrine teaches that a living person can perform temple ordinances on behalf of a deceased person, Jane James and Elijah Abel both received their long-awaited endowments by proxy soon after the change of policy in 1978.

The LDS Genesis Group continues to meet, and in 1999 it dedicated a monument to Jane Manning James. The dedication was attended by apostle David B.

Haight, whose ancestors had been in James's pioneer company. In 2002, aided by the Missouri Mormon Frontier Foundation, the Genesis Group also dedicated a monument to Abel, the dedicatory speech, acknowledging that Abel was indeed a "black man" and a priesthood holder, was offered by apostle M. Russell Ballard.

The next year, marking the 25th anniversary of the lifting of the priesthood restriction, the Genesis Group hosted Mormon convert Gladys Knight and her Saints Unified Voices Choir to celebrate "the long promised day" with a concert in the tabernacle on Temple Square. This Genesis meeting included more than 5,000 celebrants.

Though the Church has never formally repudiated the teachings and folklore that accompanied the priesthood restriction, Hinckley asked a bold rhetorical question in April 2006, in a talk condemning racism: "How can any man holding the Melchizedek Priesthood arrogantly assume that he is eligible for the priesthood whereas another who lives a righteous life but whose skin is of a different color is ineligible?" (Hinckley, "The Need for Greater Kindness" 85).

Vestiges of the past teachings still exist on some LDS bookshelves, and public perception of Mormons still reveals a view that Mormons are racists, but the Church continues to make strides in overcoming this perception. It has made genealogical finds accessible for African Americans (most notably the Freedman Bank Records project, headed by Marjorie Taylor and Darius Gray) and helped host the Afro-American Historical and Genealogical Society in Salt Lake City in October 2006.

In 2004, Pastor Cecil "Chip" Murray, then pastor of the AME Church, which Biddy Smith Mason helped to found in Los Angeles, visited Salt Lake City and met with LDS Church leaders, including Hinckley. According to Murray, Hinckley made a point of publicly apologizing to him for the Church's "past discrimination." No publicity attended that meeting, and the LDS record does not officially contain any apology for its past teachings. Nonetheless, missionary work continues to be successful throughout countries with large African populations, though the success is considerably less among African Americans, who often join the Church and then cease activity when confronted by past leaders' statements about race.

At present, the LDS Church is still grappling with the lingering effects of its past racialist policies, but it continues to make strides in rehabilitating its image. In 2002, African American student Robert Foster was elected BYU's student body president and helped develop activities celebrating Black History Month and Martin Luther King Day. The Church now has wards and branches in the inner cities of all metropolitan areas of the United States. Though it has only one black in its highest leadership positions (Martins died in 2005; Joseph Wafula Sitati became a member of the First Quorum of the Seventy in April 2009), it does have black bishops, black stake presidents, and black temple workers and will certainly continue its efforts to overcome lingering prejudices and misconceptions, within and outside the Church.

—Margaret Blair Young and Darius Aidan Gray

See also: Mormonism and Race; Priesthood Revelation of 1978; Temple Work by Proxy; Temples.

References

Bringhurst, Newell G. *Saints, Slaves, and Blacks: The Changing Place of Black People within Mormonism.* Westport, CT: Greenwood Press, 1981.

Bush, Lester E., Jr. "Mormonism's Negro Doctrine: An Historical Overview." *Dialogue* 8 (Spring 1973): 11–68.

Hinckley, Gordon B. "The Need for Greater Kindness." *Ensign* (May 2006): 58.

Hyde, Orson. *Speech of Elder Orson Hyde, Delivered Before the High Priest's Quorum in Nauvoo, April 27th, 1845.* City of Joseph, IL: John Taylor, 1845.

Kimball, Edward L. *Lengthen Your Stride: The Presidency of Spencer W. Kimball.* Salt Lake City, UT: Deseret Book, 2005.

Phelps, William W. "Free People of Color." *The Evening and the Morning Star* Vol. 2, No. 14 (July 1833): 218.

Pratt, Orson. "The Pre-Existence of Man." *The Seer* Vol. 1, No. 9 (September 1853): 134–135.

Prince, Gregory A., and Wm. Robert Wright. *David O. McKay and the Rise of Modern Mormonism.* Salt Lake City: University of Utah Press, 2005

Smith, Joseph F. Council Minutes, August 26, 1908. Reprinted in *Neither White Nor Black.* Ed. Lester Bush and Armand Mauss, 140. Midvale, UT: Signature Press, 1984.

Smith, Joseph Jr. *General Smith's Views,* February 7, 1844, available at http://josephsmith.net/josephsmith/v/index.jsp?vgnextoid=6c8fd2efbece4010VgnVCM1000004d82620aRCRD&exhibit=f91808961ece401008961ece401059340c0a____.

Stephens, Calvin R. "The Life and Contributions of Zebedee Coltrin." Master's thesis, Brigham Young University, 1974.

Wolfinger, Henry. "A Test of Faith: Jane Elizabeth James and the Origins of the Utah Black Community." In *Social Accommodation in Utah.* Ed. Clark S. Knowlton, 126–172. Salt Lake City, UT: American West Occasional Papers, 1975.

Young, Brigham. Minutes for March 26, 1847. Brigham Young Papers, LDS Church Archives.

Young, Brigham. "Speech to the Joint Session of the Legislative Assembly, January 5, 1852," in *Journals of the Legislative Assembly of the Territory of Utah,* 108–110 (Salt Lake City, 1852).

Mormonism and Economics

Observers are sometimes struck by the economic power of the Church of Jesus Christ of Latter-day Saints. A 1997 *Time* article by David Van Biema titled "Kingdom Come" characterized the Church as a $30 billion empire and noted that if it were a corporation, its estimated annual gross income would rank it towards the middle of the *Fortune* 500. Some might find it odd for a Church to have that kind of wealth, but an examination of the Church's economic history demonstrates that

Silk Culture

Economic independence was a major goal of Mormon life during the 19th century. Hard cash was scarce, and Mormons were urged to produce goods locally and to sustain home businesses, preserving cash for essential projects such as emigration and the importing of vital industrial machinery.

One key to retaining cash was the local production of clothing. Cotton did not grow well in Utah, but mulberry trees (the preferred food of silkworms) thrived, suggesting that silk could replace cotton for many articles. Utah sericulture was carried on in a limited way as early as 1856; beginning in 1867, when Brigham Young offered silkworm eggs and mulberry cuttings freely to all who would attempt to produce silk, the experimental industry became a quasi-religious mission. George D. Watt, Young's versatile clerk and enthusiastic farmer, visited wards throughout Utah, offering instruction on the care of silkworms and the treatment of their cocoons. Such tasks, he said, were particularly suitable for women and children, and silk was an easily exploitable source of wealth for all.

Adopted as a Relief Society project, sericulture was heavily promoted through the 1880s, with beautiful articles of local manufacture exhibited at fairs. As other fabrics became cheaper, home production of silk ceased.

the spiritual and the temporal have always been closely intertwined in Mormon theology. President Brigham Young taught that "in the mind of God there is no such a thing as dividing spiritual from temporal, or temporal from spiritual; for they are one in the Lord" (Young, "Remarks" 11:18).

Early Mormonism is sometimes characterized as an attempt to escape American pluralism and to establish a theocracy in which God's laws directed all aspects of society. Joseph Smith and other early leaders taught that, as in the days of Noah, the Earth had fallen into corruption and would soon be destroyed. The only hope for God's faithful was to "gather to Zion," where they would establish a kingdom in preparation for the return of Jesus Christ. For the Mormons, this communal "gathering" to specified sacred spaces was an economic as well as a religious withdrawal from the world. In contrast to American ideals of individualism and liberty, early Mormons stressed communalism and consecration of property for the good of the whole.

Joseph Smith was young and poor when he started gaining followers. Naturally, concerns about meeting the financial demands of a fledgling Church constantly dogged Smith. He depended upon the donations and sacrifices of family, friends, and adherents to sustain the new movement. Joseph Knight Sr., an early Mormon convert, supplied Smith with provisions so that the translation of the Book of Mormon could proceed without delay. Martin Harris, another early Mormon, mortgaged his farm to help publish the new scripture, and early missionaries went "without purse or scrip" in search of converts. Even in his personal life, Smith often depended upon the generosity of others to provide a home for his family.

Mormon economic and welfare projects cross all borders. Here, Dutch Mormons ship potatoes to starving German Mormons immediately after World War II. (Courtesy of the Church History Library, The Church of Jesus Christ of Latter-day Saints.)

Following the formal organization of the Church, in 1830, Mormons gathered to Ohio and Missouri. At both places, economic communalism of varying degrees shaped the Saints' experiences for the remainder of the decade. In an effort to meet the needs of poor converts who were faithful to the command to gather and to assist in the establishment of new frontier communities, Joseph Smith implemented the law of consecration and stewardship. Under this new system, members gave all of their possessions to the Church. The bishop then returned an inheritance, or stewardship, to individuals or families that would be sufficient for their needs. Excess goods were distributed to the poor or supported Church projects. Each year, "stewards" were to meet with the bishop and offer their surplus to the bishop's storehouse, a clearinghouse for the collection and disbursement of goods. The program was based on the concept of egalitarianism. Statements such as "if ye are not equal in earthly things ye cannot be equal in obtaining heavenly things," "the poor shall be exalted, in that the rich are made low," and "it is not given that one man should possess that which is above another, wherefore the world lieth in sin" peppered the revelations from this period (Doctrine and Covenants 78:6, 104:16, 49:20). Church leaders and members attempted to implement these communal programs at various times and in a variety of ways, but formal endeavors never persisted.

Despite the Saints' attempts at withdrawing from the harsh market forces that produced marked fluctuations in the national economy, the financial turmoil at Kirtland, Ohio, mirrored that of the nation at large, a reality that dramatically influenced events there. In the summer of 1833, the Church undertook one of its more ambitious projects up to that point: the construction of a temple at Kirtland. The two-story structure, made of sandstone and covered with plaster, represented a significant sacrifice for a small community of believers. Even so, during its first years, Kirtland boomed in both population and activity. The value of land in the area increased more than 600 percent over a five-year period. Community leaders borrowed heavily to facilitate the Church's growth, and creditors caught up in the expansion of the U.S. boom were happy to lend. However, the assets of the frontier community were primarily land, which proved difficult to liquidate. As loans came due, Joseph Smith and other leaders attempted to establish a bank to meet the Church's financial needs. When the Ohio legislature refused to charter a new bank, Mormon leaders established a

Cooperative labor projects, whether digging irrigation canals, plowing, or, as in this instance, harvesting cotton and other crops, have been a mainstay of Mormon economic success since the 19th century. (Courtesy of the Church History Library, The Church of Jesus Christ of Latter-day Saints.)

joint stock company and issued "anti-banking" notes instead. Several factors, including the nationwide panic of 1837, resulted in the bank's collapse. Many Church members who had invested in the company called Joseph Smith a fallen prophet. In January 1838, convinced that his life was in danger, Smith fled on horseback to Missouri. Over the subsequent months, most of the Mormons in the Kirtland vicinity followed him there.

Smith found the Church in Missouri also in turmoil. Internal dissent, some of it over the degree of temporal authority the Church should exercise, led several leaders to leave the faith. Before the end of the year, the Missouri militia expelled the Mormons from the state. Illinois residents welcomed the more than 8,000 Mormon refugees, who found themselves with few material possessions at the start of 1839. In temporal terms, the Mormons had little to show for their first decade of efforts. The Church contracted to purchase land on the Illinois peninsula for a total cost of $114,500, to be paid over 20 years. Once again in debt, Smith relied on land sales to repay the loan.

Unlike earlier communitarian attempts, the Nauvoo economy was based primarily on free enterprise and the profit motive, although volunteerism, aid to the poor, and Church-directed public works played important roles. With converts pouring in not only from within the United States and Canada, but also from Europe, the city

Mormon Money

Even where real wealth exists, cash is always scarce on the frontier. To supply cash necessary to economic life in the earliest years of Utah settlement, Mormons produced handwritten and printed scrip to trade among themselves. When members of the Mormon Battalion reached Utah, in 1848, they brought with them quantities of dust from the gold fields of California, and a system of Mormon coinage was born.

In 1849–1850, the Deseret Mint struck coins in $2-1/2, $5, $10, and $20 denominations, using dies forged and engraved in Salt Lake City. These coins carried Mormon designs, among them the All-Seeing Eye, clasped hands, and the motto *Holiness to the Lord,* with *GSLCPG* (Great Salt Lake City, Pure Gold) designating their origin. The first coins were pure gold, but soon a small quantity of silver was added to produce a longer-lasting alloy.

Coins made from Nevada gold were produced in 1852–1853. Impurities resulted in a considerably lowered value, and those coins were recalled and redeemed by the Church.

Most Mormon gold soon found its way to the eastern states to purchase manufactured goods or was turned in as bullion to the U.S. Mint. Cheap souvenir replicas have been produced in recent years.

was a hive of activity. A building boom created jobs, and the city soon became one of the largest in Illinois. However, Nauvoo's character was still that of a religious center, an unmistakable fact symbolized by the construction of the Nauvoo temple. A communal project, it was paid for in tithes of labor, materials, and money. While the future of the city seemed bright, losses and debts from the Ohio and Missouri years still hounded Church leaders.

Following the murder of Joseph and Hyrum Smith, the Saints were yet again expelled from their homes. Brigham Young, recognized by the majority of the Saints as Joseph's successor, concluded that the Church could not remain in Nauvoo or the United States, for that matter. In 1846, most of Young's followers started west in an exodus governed by broad egalitarian principles. Church members covenanted that none who wished to leave would be left behind, regardless of their circumstances. While some Saints had supplies sufficient for the trek, others did not. Pooling of resources and submission to authority made the extraordinary undertaking possible, though not without tremendous costs. An important economic contribution during these difficult times was the recruitment of Mormon volunteers by the U.S. Army for the U.S. War with Mexico. While it removed the support of able-bodied men, it also provided desperately needed money and moved some of the Saints west at government expense. The first company of pioneers entered the Salt Lake Valley in July 1847. Along the trail, they left ferries, crops, supply stations, and a few communities to assist those who would follow. The Saints did not abandon those settlements until Salt Lake City was well established, thus providing resting stations for future emigrants.

While the Mormon pioneers who settled the Great Basin in what would become the state of Utah were a thousand miles from the closest American city, they were not completely isolated from broader market forces. Even still, Brigham Young and other leaders tried to establish Joseph Smith's communitarian vision in a new land where they were the majority and where there was space to expand, a challenge Mormons met with limited success. Church leaders promoted a worldview in which everyday actions, even of an economic nature, were sometimes characterized as aspects of a broader struggle between good and evil. Mormons believed that they were establishing Zion, a place of refuge for the true in heart who sought to escape the confusion, wickedness, and eventual destruction of Babylon.

After the discovery of gold at Sutter's Mill, thousands of California immigrants poured through Mormon communities, exchanging much-needed products and money for supplies. Groups of Mormons scavenged the trail in search of items left behind by '49ers in their dash for the goldfields. Gold from California entered the Utah market, providing a medium of exchange that freed up the economy. "Gentile" or non-Mormon merchants found Mormon customers hungry for items that could not be produced locally, such as tea, coffee, sugar, and the latest fashions from the East. Eventually, western mines and railroad construction created markets for Mormon agricultural products. Most of these interactions with outsiders frustrated Mormon leaders, who wished to create an autonomous, economically self-sufficient people.

Mormon concepts of Zion infused the economic activities that played out in Utah Territory. Leaders encouraged subsistence farming and the growth of home industries while fighting against mining endeavors and outside trade. In Mormon communities, the priesthood, not the market, ideally determined economic activities, though non-Mormons and Church members often contested its power. Community leaders sought to discourage speculation and tried to control land distribution. They established compact communities surrounded by communal farms. From the pulpit, leaders discouraged economic interaction, be it trade or employment, with "Gentiles." In some cases, they monitored Mormons who patronized non-Mormon merchants and sent Church representatives to call the recalcitrant to repentance.

Within a decade of the Mormon arrival in the Great Basin, Mormon communities stretched over several hundred miles from north to south. In these villages, local bishops collected and dispersed tithes and offerings. The Church expected new members to pay a 10 percent levy on the property they possessed upon conversion. After this initial payment, members were expected to donate 1 day out of 10 to Church or community projects as well as a 10th of their increase, payable in kind. Farmers, for example, might pay a 10th of their wheat crop or hay, dairy products, or livestock. Each community had a tithing office where donations were accepted and goods were distributed to the needy or as payment for work on Church projects. Tithes from surrounding communities poured into the General Tithing Office in Salt Lake City, which then funded Church and public works projects. The bishop or clerk

Perpetual Emigrating Fund

As many as 30,000 Saints from Europe and the eastern United States were assisted in their immigration to Utah by a revolving account known as the Perpetual Emigrating Fund.

Established in 1849 and funded through individual contributions, the PEF paid ship and railroad fares and purchased wagons, cattle, and supplies to supplement the savings of Saints who could not raise the full cost of emigration. Ideally, once in the Salt Lake Valley, those who had been assisted would gradually repay what they had used, making the funds available for other emigrants. In reality, many neglected or were unable to repay their debts, and many would-be donors could contribute only cattle, not the cash required by shipping companies. The PEF functioned only as long as new funds could be raised.

The PEF was used on occasion to bring those with special skills needed in Utah—experienced miners, chemists, and mechanics of all kinds. Otherwise, priority was given to those who had been members the longest, those who had made the greatest efforts toward their own emigration, and those with the least ability to cover their own expenses.

The Church declared 1880 to be a Year of Jubilee, and all debts to the PEF were canceled.

entered in-kind donations into record books as dollar amounts, with prices set at Salt Lake City. This made it possible for the rural tithing office to serve as a place of exchange and a bank, in addition to its religious functions. The tithing system proved an ingenious solution to problems inherent in a cash-poor frontier economy.

One of the main responsibilities of the Church was to gather "the elect" from throughout the world into the Great Basin Zion. This required missionary service to bring converts into the Mormon fold and an organized immigration system to bring those converts to Utah. Individual missionaries and their families paid for their years of service away from home. Missionaries also relied upon the generosity or pity of those among whom they served, both member and non-member, to provide lodging and food.

Church leaders encouraged new members, upon conversion, to "gather" to Zion as quickly as possible. To assist the poor who did not have the means to relocate, the Church organized the Perpetual Emigrating Fund (PEF), in 1849. This fund provided loans to converts with the understanding that the loan would be repaid after the immigrants established themselves in Utah. The repaid money was then used to help new converts immigrate in a perpetual cycle. Even though repayment lagged, the fund enabled as many as 30,000 immigrants to join the main body of Saints in the intermountain West.

During the first several decades in Utah, the Church made additional attempts to become economically independent. Brigham Young always extolled locally produced goods and established various ventures to create a self-sufficient economy. In the early 1850s, leaders sent settlers south to establish an iron mission. A decade later, another group was sent farther south to grow cotton. Other efforts included sugar manufacturing, smelting lead, sericulture, and paper manufacture. A cooperative movement started in the 1860s developed into the "United Order" movement, through which communities sought to be completely self-sufficient. United Orders ranged from communal experiments where all was held in common to joint stock companies. The Zions Cooperative Mercantile Institution (ZCMI), a product of these movements, survived into the late 20th century as a department store, but most of the other experiments dissolved within a few years. In total, the United Order movement signaled Brigham Young's last-ditch effort to stem the tide of outside influences.

Young's successor, John Taylor, was less committed to communalism and more open to free enterprise. Even so, Taylor's tenure as president was marked by the federal crackdown on polygamy, a campaign that had a devastating economic impact.

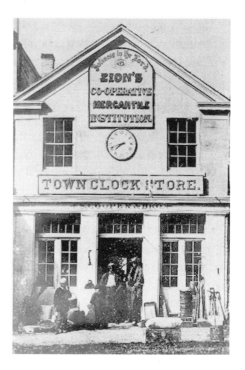

Zions Cooperative Mercantile Institution (ZCMI) and smaller stores like this one, carried symbols like the "all-seeing eye" to let the Mormon faithful know that business was conducted according to approved Mormon methods. (Courtesy of the Church History Library, The Church of Jesus Christ of Latter-day Saints.)

In 1887, Congress passed the Edmunds-Tucker Act, which confiscated Church property (including the PEF) and turned it over to a government receiver. The depression of the 1890s, combined with the effects of the national crusade, took a heavy financial toll on the Church. To make matters worse, many members quit paying tithing while the government controlled Church properties. In the 1890s, the Church gave up and relinquished many of its distinctive practices, including lingering efforts at economic independence.

As a result of the federal crackdown, Lorenzo Snow inherited a Church that was more than $1.250 million in debt when he became its fifth president, in 1898. Snow issued Church bonds worth $1 million that were purchased primarily by Church members to help pay the debt. Then, in 1899, leaders placed an increased emphasis on having members pay a full tithe (10 percent of one's increase) as a means to address the Church's financial struggles. The push worked, and, by 1907, the Church was debt-free.

The Great Depression, however, brought new challenges, especially as Utah's agriculture- and mining-based economy was hit hard. During the 19th and early 20th centuries, local bishops used a portion of donations to support the needy in their wards. The severity of the Great Depression, combined with an increasingly urban membership, pushed Church leadership toward a new program. In 1933, the First Presidency asked stake presidents to survey the resources and needs of their stakes and to look after their members. Learning from the experiences of the stakes, leaders at headquarters launched the Security Plan in 1936, later renamed the Welfare Plan. In 1938, the Church purchased land west of Salt Lake City, upon which it built a large root cellar, cannery, milk-processing plant, grain elevator, and bishop's storehouse, all of which were used to address the needs of the Saints.

Church leaders also tapped into the Mormon practice of fasting, a longstanding aspect of Mormon community outreach. In this practice, Mormons skip two meals one day each month and donate the cost of those meals, or a more generous offering, for the relief of the poor and hungry. In the 1930s, leaders used the donated funds to expand the welfare program, which included purchasing, building, and maintaining farms, canneries, and other food production facilities. The program grew over the years so that, by 1995, the Church operated 100 regional bishops' storehouses stocked with products grown on Church lands and processed at Church plants. A visitor to a bishops' storehouse might be struck by the large variety of items available. Almost the only differences between a commercial grocery store and a bishop's storehouse are the Church labels on the goods and the absence of cash registers. Out of the Church welfare program grew humanitarian and disaster relief initiatives with a global, nondenominational outreach.

The same principles of outreach and uplift continued to animate Mormon concern for the poor into the 21st century, especially those in third-world countries. To respond to the growing demands of a global faith community, President Gordon B. Hinckley announced the Perpetual Education Fund, in 2001. Modeled after the Perpetual Emigrating Fund of the 19th century, the new PEF offers education loans to Latter-day Saints in developing countries to help them secure gainful employment and become self-sufficient. The education loans are then repaid at a low rate of interest, and the money is used to fund education for a new candidate.

Even though in the 20th century Mormons embraced the capitalistic economic philosophies they once had attempted to withdraw from, the pioneer concept of consecration still informs their lives. Community concern still supersedes individual wants as Mormons donate not only their money but their time and talents to shared causes. Tithing strikes a balance between self-interest and paying one's dues to the Lord, and a lay ministry and volunteerism reduce Church expenses. Programs such as humanitarian aid, temple construction, and perpetual education funds provide ways for members to further "consecrate" their surplus.

By the beginning of the 21st century, the LDS Church had built a global kingdom that included Churches and temples, office buildings, universities, seminary and institute programs, real estate, rental properties, farms, canneries, an insurance company, radio stations, a television station, a newspaper, and bookstores. Mormons have always linked the spiritual with the temporal.

—*Alan L. Morrell*

See also: Church Organization and Government; Conflict: 1869–1890; Development: 1831–1844; Lee, Harold B.; Mormon Missiology; Snow, Lorenzo; Transition: 1890–1941.

References

Arrington, Leonard J. *Great Basin Kingdom: An Economic History of the Latter-day Saints, 1830–1900.* Cambridge, MA: Harvard University Press, 1958.

Arrington, Leonard J., Feramorz Y. Fox, and Dean L. May. *Building the City of God: Community and Cooperation among the Mormons.* Salt Lake City, UT: Deseret Book, 1976.

Biema, David Van. "Mormons, Inc.: The Secrets of America's Most Prosperous Religion." *Time* 150 (August 4, 1997): 50–59.

Doctrine and Covenants of the Church of Jesus Christ of Latter-day Saints. Salt Lake City, UT: The Church of Jesus Christ of Latter-day Saints, 1981.

Young, Brigham. "Remarks by President Brigham Young," December 11, 1864. *Journal of Discourses,* vol. 11. London: LDS Booksellers Depot, 1867.

Mormonism and Education

Mormon scripture contains many verses commending learning and education. "Seek ye out of the best books words of wisdom," says one (Doctrine and Covenants 88:118). "It is impossible to be saved in ignorance," says another (Doctrine and Covenants 131:6). Mormon doctrines like theosis and divine embodiment sacralized learning and created a potent motivation for its pursuit. But the Mormon scriptures contained no blueprint for action, no concrete educational program. As Mormons negotiated the elusive, ever-changing boundary between Church and world, they generated—and adapted—their educational institutions accordingly.

Localism (1830–1869)

The Mormons' earliest attempts at educational centralization had an aspirational, though truncated, feel, the casualties of a people always on the run. The School of the Prophets, which followed New Light Presbyterians in training preachers outside a college setting, lasted just three winters in Ohio. Joseph Smith's "plat of the City of Zion" included schools alongside temples, but the Saints' forcible removal from Missouri prevented either from being built. The "University of the City of Nauvoo," the Mormon booster college founded in 1841, was little more than a paper dream when the Saints were forced to flee the United States for good. Indeed, memories of carefree schooldays are mostly absent from the autobiographies of Mormon children and youth who lived through these difficult times. Stories of the mob fill them, instead.

In addition to its 19th-century academies and 20th-century universities, the Church has sponsored schools in many parts of the world (here, Patzicia, Guatemala) where public schooling is unavailable. (Courtesy of the Church History Library, The Church of Jesus Christ of Latter-day Saints.)

Along the trek west, Brigham Young hit upon an idea that would have permanence in the Great Basin. He instructed bishops to make sure each of their wards had a school. "We want every branch of science taught in this place [Utah] that is taught in the world," he said (Clark, "Church and State Relationships" 102). Although he made similar statements over the next three decades, he never told bishops how to carry out the charge. That was for locals to decide. These ward schools, which often doubled as meetinghouses, tended to reflect the personalities who founded, built, and worked in them.

Mormon bishops functioned more as interested parties than overseers. They were like the pastors in colonial New England who made sure parents taught their children to read. The law provided the framework for action. In 1852, the Utah legislature passed a common-school law that remained throughout the territorial period. It called for each county to be divided into school districts, which were to be governed by three trustees, elected by district residents, who assessed taxes for buildings and fuel. A local board of three members was to examine teachers. Later laws added the offices of territorial (1854) and county (1860) superintendent of common schools.

The Mormons imported all of this legal apparatus from the East, including the insistence on local control for the schools' maintenance. Territorial appropriation did not appear until 1874, when 262 schools already enrolled 17,900 children.

Although the claim was often made by outside polemicists, there is little evidence to suggest these schools taught the Mormon religion. Isolated and impoverished, Utah had a scarcity of textbooks, prompting teachers to cobble together whatever they could find. The students learned the rudiments from the same textbooks found in the states. On occasion, teachers turned to the books everyone owned, the Book of Mormon and the Bible. But this was the exception, not the rule. Tattered McGuffey readers and Spencerian copybooks were passed from neighbor to neighbor in Utah as elsewhere.

Tax-assisted schools made up one of many forms of schooling in pioneer Utah. Competition was welcomed, not discouraged. Private schools of countless variety, rivals to the district system, sprang up voluntarily in this protocapitalist Mormon Zion. Poverty made many such ventures short lived. Teachers could take only so many potatoes and beets in tuition payment. The most ambitious educational enterprise, the University of Deseret (later the University of Utah), founded in Salt Lake City in 1850, closed after two years, the victim of an empty treasury. With a frontier still to tame, the absence of a trained clergy within Mormonism made higher education an expendable luxury for the time being.

During its pioneer period, Mormonism was perpetuated more by experience than by formal schooling or books. Many Mormons could afford neither Church organs like the *Deseret News* and the *Journal of Discourses* nor the writings of Orson and Parley Pratt, two of Mormonism's ablest defenders. The young only spottily attended the long, often ponderous sermons delivered weekly by untrained laymen in the local wards. More crucial were the examples of parents and family and acts requiring sacrifice and courage of all ages—caring for the sick and the poor, missionary service, and the very process of gathering to Zion.

Centralization (1869–1912)

After the Transcontinental Railroad ended Utah's isolation from the states, localism gave way to a new era of centralization. The district schools continued, patronized by Mormons and non-Mormons alike. But, alongside them appeared a new institution, the Mormon academy, which introduced explicitly religious instruction into the curricula.

Historians have rightly emphasized the role of religious competition in the onset of these academies. By the mid-1870s, Presbyterians, Methodists, Episcopalians, and Catholics all had schools in Utah. Mormon leaders naturally fretted over wolves plucking their flocks. But the move into secondary education was part of a larger cultural transformation in which the railroad created new markets for skilled labor

Deseret Alphabet

In common with other 19th-century reformers, the Mormons experimented with phonetic spelling to encourage literacy and ease the transition to English by converts from many lands. The Mormon system, called the Deseret Alphabet, was devised in 1852, chiefly by Pitman stenographer George D. Watt, and relied on non-Roman characters to form a one-to-one correspondence between sound and symbol. The alphabet was heavily promoted by Brigham Young, with primary readers, the Book of Mormon, and occasional newspaper articles available to learners.

The Deseret Alphabet was a failure: those literate in standard English had little incentive to use Deseret; those newly literate in Deseret had virtually no reading material; the characters did not lend themselves to smooth writing; and variations in pronunciation among a population gathered from throughout the world prevented standardized spelling. A handful of the faithful wrote letters and diaries in Deseret, and its characters appeared on a few gravestones and Mormon-minted coins, but all attempts to promote Deseret ceased with Brigham Young's death, in 1877.

Non-Mormon writers asserted that Deseret was an attempt to control Mormon reading or to conceal secrets from outsiders; widespread publication of the "key" and constant importation of standard English printed material discount such theories.

and Utah's restless and exploding population arose to fill the need. As youth left the farms for brighter prospects, academies functioned as the high schools Utah did not have.

Although chronically underfunded, the academies enjoyed central backing. The oldest, Brigham Young Academy of Provo (BYA), founded by Young in 1875, provided the model for all the others. Under the able leadership of Karl Maeser, a German convert and polymath, the coeducational BYA produced hundreds of upright teachers and leaders, convincing Church leaders the experiment had to be replicated elsewhere. When the oppressive Edmunds-Tucker Act stripped the office of territorial superintendent from Mormon hands, Church president Wilford Woodruff feared that Mormon teachers would be shut out of the public schools. He called on every stake to found its own academy, under Maeser's supervision. Between 1875 and 1912, more than 40 Mormon schools were founded in seven states and territories in the United States, Mexico, and Canada.

The academies fit within a larger trend toward centralized instruction during the period. John Jaques's *Catechism for Children* (1877), which drilled on the Mormon basics, received official and widespread commendation. The main Sabbath-day institutions for teaching the Mormon young all started out as local initiatives but were incorporated into the Church's program in anticipation of, or in reaction to, the new cultural pluralism: Sunday Schools (1866), mutual improvement societies (1875, 1880), and Primaries (1880). Each of these organizations, still in operation, published its own print magazines. Mormonism had to be kept in front of wandering eyes. As religion diminished in public life, Mormonism expanded its private reach.

The Mormon academies served many important functions. Their curricula, increasingly supervised by a central board of overseers, sought to reconcile science and religion, unifying truth for a generation of Mormons. They also generated a hunger for further study: Mormon intellectuals like James E. Talmage and John Widtsoe used their early academy training as springboards for admission into prestigious eastern universities. Academies also inserted Mormonism into national credentialing and status-seeking patterns. BYA, which began awarding degrees in 1893, became BYU in 1903. Perhaps most important, academies represented a new faith in the power of centralized weekday education to create good Mormons. In a modern, pluralistic world, Sunday education was not enough; the Church must shoulder responsibility for more.

Assimilation (1912–1951)

The demise of plural marriage and the Mormon temporal kingdom hastened a half-century of Mormon assimilation of national values and mores. One casualty was the academies. The multiplication of free public high schools, present in Utah since 1891, effectively felled all rivals. The reach of Mormon academies peaked in 1905, with just over 50 percent of all Utah's students enrolled. By 1910, public school enrollment had surpassed academy enrollment for good. Costly and obsolescent, the academies were either closed or sold off to the state. Only the largest Mormon colleges remained.

The withdrawal from weekday education did not put an end to weekday religious instruction, however. In 1890, the Mormons started holding daily "religion classes" for children of grade-school age. Slow to catch on at first, the movement gained traction in the early 1900s, and, in 1912, the concept was extended to high school students. "Seminary," as it was called, became one of Mormonism's most entrenched and far-reaching institutions. Like Catholic catechism, it created a rite of adolescent passage. It also introduced a new mid-level class of Church employees to the books, the paid clergy Mormonism did not have. By 1928, 70 seminaries enrolled 11,500 students—at just one-eighth the cost of an academy education.

The persistence of weekday religious instruction seems like a gesture to the past, a refusal to engage fully in the modern world. That critique is only partially true. Seminary was modeled on a conservative Protestant program in the states, in which students received credit toward high school graduation for nonsectarian religious instruction taken during "released time" from regular classes. Mormons now became embedded in the public schools, with seminary buildings erected nearby. (In cases where released time was unavailable, seminary was held before school hours in churches.) To pass muster with the public school boards, seminary curricula downplayed doctrinal peculiarities and emphasized the ethical and literary features of the

Brigham Young University

Longest lived of the 19th-century Mormon academies was Brigham Young Academy, founded in 1875, in Provo, Utah. Plagued by debt, destroyed by fire, hard pressed to provide even an elementary education in its early years, BYA survived in part because of the extraordinary gifts of its second president, Karl G. Maeser. Maeser, highly educated in the German system, required academic rigor of his students while following the mandates of Brigham Young "not to teach even the alphabet or the multiplication tables without the Spirit of God" and of John Taylor "that no infidels will go forth from this school."

BYA became Brigham Young University in 1903. The university now offers undergraduate, master's, and doctoral degrees and hosts professional schools of law and management. With the Provo campus as its flagship institution, the BYU system now includes BYU-Idaho (Rexburg; originally Ricks College), BYU-Hawaii (Laie; originally the Church College of Hawaii), and several distance learning programs, most notably at its Jerusalem Center.

BYU students, both LDS and those of other or no faiths, abide by an honor code requiring honesty in academics, respect for law, consideration for others, and adherence to Mormon moral standards, including abstinence from alcohol, tobacco, and extramarital sexual relations.

Bible, instead. This was only one instance of reconciliation with the larger world. The Church also incorporated sports and Boy Scouts and the arts into its regular educational program. Eventually, the Mormons became Scouting's largest supporter nationwide.

The impulse to assimilate appeared on the collegiate level, as well. Franklin S. Harris, president of BYU between 1921 and 1945, built a large library and reorganized and expanded instruction along modern scientific lines. National accreditation followed. Beginning in 1926, the Church expanded its religion instruction on the university level by founding "institutes of religion" in buildings erected adjacent to state campuses in the West. Like Jewish Hillel and Catholic Newman Centers, Mormon institutes served as oases of learning, association, and service. Deseret Clubs, founded on college campuses after 1932, provided an alternative to fraternities and sororities. The Church even started a loan fund for students who wished to pursue graduate study in the East. The business was brisk, and, by the 1940s, observers noted that Utah was the most frequent birthplace for people listed in *American Men of Science.*

The central educational tension in the period was the oscillation between assimilation and retrenchment. In 1911, three BYU professors resigned under pressure rather than modify the religious instruction they had modernized along Darwinian lines. The dismissals ushered in a new period of Mormon neo-orthodoxy. Talmage's *Jesus the Christ* (1915), which relied on conservative Protestant scholarship, found many adoring readers, while the liberal speculations in B. H. Roberts's masterwork

"The Truth, the Way, and the Life" forced it to go unpublished. After a syncretic turn in the 1930s, the pendulum swung back to orthodoxy again. In 1942, at the urging of the powerful J. Reuben Clark, Mormon apostles started interviewing prospective teachers and a committee began reviewing all textbooks, a process that continues into the 21st century.

Unification (1951–1970)

By the early 1950s, the Church educational program had grown large and unwieldy. The institutes enrolled 4,200 students on 18 college campuses. The seminaries taught 32,000 students and employed 170 full time. The Church ran two colleges, an academy, a school of music, and a university, all with their own boards functioning semi-autonomously. In 1954, the Church added the Indian Placement Program, in which LDS foster families housed Native Americans who wanted the advantages of off-reservation public schools. Rapid Church growth and the expansion of educational opportunity after World War II meant that there would be no slowdown or shrinkage in the Mormon educational system. Escalating costs—total operating budgets had climbed to $7.5 million by 1953—suggested the need for unification.

The growth of BYU was by far the biggest spur in this reorganization. Under its pugnacious new president, Ernest Wilkinson, a former trial lawyer, BYU rapidly enlarged virtually every phase of its operations. Wilkinson wanted nothing less than to make BYU "the greatest educational institution in the world" (Wilkinson, *Brigham Young University* 2:539). For him, that meant everything had to be big. During his 20-year tenure (1951–1971), Wilkinson quadrupled the faculty and grew the student body to 25,000, making BYU the largest private university in the country (later surpassed by New York University). The rapidity of this expansion astounded everyone; by 1963, total Mormon educational budgets had ballooned to $20 million, a full quarter of the Church's income.

The Unified Church School System (UCSS), created in 1953, brought seminaries, institutes, colleges, and university under one administration. Wilkinson served as chancellor, helping him funnel students to BYU. The boards of the individual institutions continued day-to-day oversight, but an enlarged General Church Board of Education now directed the overall aims. The move brought the salaries and benefits of seminary and institute teachers closer in line with those at BYU and standardized religious instruction throughout the realm. The loose model for UCSS was the pyramidic University of California system, which used a large base (schools) to supply institutions (colleges, universities) of increasing prestige. Wilkinson's master plan involved a constellation of LDS junior colleges orbiting around BYU, the Mormon Berkeley. He got as far as purchasing seven or eight large tracts for projected sites in places like Phoenix, Arizona; Portland, Oregon; and Anaheim, California. Then the scheme, deemed too expensive, stalled. Institutes continued to be built, instead.

The UCSS was the most extravagant of several ambitious attempts at the grand system during these years. Hugh Nibley, a BYU professor of ancient history and languages, found Mormonism everywhere, unifying world cultural history into a collection of aboriginal revelations and inferior derivatives. In his encyclopedic *Mormon Doctrine* (1958), the attorney-turned-Mormon-general-authority Bruce R. McConkie gave doctrinaire pronouncements on virtually every theological issue, even those about which the authorities had not agreed. By putting a neo-humanist (and thus respectable) Mormonism into dialogue with the likes of Plato and Augustine, Sterling McMurrin's *Theological Foundations of the Mormon Religion* (1965) sought to solve some of philosophy's oldest and most perplexing problems. McMurrin's service as U.S. Commissioner of Education during the Kennedy administration represents the zenith of Mormonism's unity with the nation at large.

By the end of the 1960s, Mormon educational unity had splintered. All-Church athletic events came to an end. Curriculum divorced itself from particularistic work like Nibley's and retreated into insular, anonymous committee reports that sought more to indoctrinate than to illuminate. As with the nation at large, cultural politics created new fissures and divisions. Long admired for its disciplined students, BYU now attracted hostility from those who decried Mormonism's policy of withholding priesthood from black men. The days of the grand system over, Wilkinson's position of chancellor was eliminated. The UCSS, still overseen by a single board, divided into separate administrative entities and changed its name to the more modest "Church Educational System" (CES).

Liberation (1970–2009)

Global Mormonism raised concerns about educational equity. In 1955, the Church founded a college in Hawaii; a college opened in New Zealand three years later. That ended the era of Mormon college founding. After 1970, the Church aggressively sought to bring the same basic program found in the United States to congregations across the world. Under Church correlation, official magazines and CES instructional material were simplified and translated into dozens of languages, fit for exportation on a global scale. By 1985, seminaries and institutes were enrolling 347,000 in 73 countries; by 1999, total enrollment had reached 645,000, 45 percent residing outside the United States.

Mormon education in the states, meanwhile, broke out in new ways. The Church's official magazines faced new competition from independent voices like *Dialogue, Sunstone,* and *Exponent II.* Signature Books, BYU Press, and FARMS arose to challenge a market long dominated by the Church-owned Deseret Book and its ideological sister, Bookcraft. The new scholarship enjoyed a fresh artistic and creative sensibility, embodied by the Church Historical Department (CHD), which professionalized in 1972 under the direction of Leonard Arrington. CHD produced hundreds of useful articles and monographs. Many of their interpretations found their way—unattributed—into the CES manual *Church History in the Fulness of Times* (1989). Under the editorship of former CHD archivist Dean Jessee, the publication of Joseph Smith's papers proceeded, expanding in 2001 to include official Church support. The project promised to put a more realistic Smith in the hands of scholars and laymen alike.

Liberation from authority of all kinds dominated the era. In the 1970s, BYU fought—and amicably settled—a suit brought by the federal government challenging its gender-segregated housing and its dress and grooming code. Mormon feminists later contested restrictions on speech at BYU, and several unaffiliated intellectuals exposed power abuses in the ecclesiastical realm (for which they were summarily excommunicated). In the 1990s, three outspoken junior BYU professors failed to make tenure. Several others either forcibly or voluntarily resigned. Bad press and censure from the American Association of University Professors predictably followed, and observers wondered aloud whether BYU's reaccreditation was in jeopardy.

BYU administrators insisted that a religious institution had to have the right to define itself; a one-size-fits-all approach to free speech could not be applied. Hoping to massage national perceptions, conservative-to-moderate Mormon academics published *Expressions of Faith* (1996), a collection of testimonials trying to show that not all Mormon intellectuals were disgruntled. Although speech restrictions continued at BYU, most faculty did not seem perturbed. At the height of controversy, a survey conducted in 1994 by UCLA researchers found that 85 percent of BYU professors rated their jobs as satisfactory or higher; 83 percent felt their jobs were secure. These numbers were significantly higher than national averages. BYU was eventually reaccredited, and the culture wars soon faded from view. Follow-up studies found that 9 in 10 BYU professors said they "have more freedom at BYU to teach" than elsewhere—the freedom to discuss spiritual truths important to them. But a sizable minority (23%) reported not feeling free to "discuss and advocate controversial and unpopular ideas." In an age of expanding liberation, faculty felt themselves pulled both ways.

Wealth liberated many middle-class Mormons to pursue special forms of education. BYU opened a Jerusalem Center on five acres on the slope of the Mount of Olives, surely one of the largest coups in Mormonism's history. After 1976, "Especially for Youth" (EFY), a costly Mormon version of Bible camp, became a life-changing week in the lives of many Mormon teenagers. By 2000, EFY enrolled almost 37,000 students in 22 locations across the country; in 2006, the program expanded to venues in England, Germany, and Scandinavia. The adult equivalent, BYU Education Week, brought thousands of Mormons to Provo every August in their RVs. All told, Continuing Education enrollments totaled some 457,000 in the year 2000 alone, up 20 percent from 1980. The myriad opportunities for learning within Mormonism may help explain why Mormon religiosity tends to increase with educational attainment, a reversal of the trend found in other Churches.

By the 2000s the Church's expanding educational system was following a curve toward atomization and individualization. Church president Gordon B. Hinckley's gender-inclusive counsel to "get all the education you can" transcended dogma and program. Individuals were free to decide. Education Week lectures could now be seen online and on the Church's satellite network, BYUTV, which democratized learning for shut-ins and the less prosperous. Likewise, the Internet brought a new clientele to BYU Independent Study, which became the leading distance educator in the nation. The Perpetual Education Fund (PEF), created in 2001, followed microlending successes elsewhere by granting Mormons living in third-world regions small loans for educational purposes, in the expectation that the new training would lift people from poverty and liberate them to live happier, more fulfilling lives.

—*Jed Woodworth*

See also: Correlation; McConkie, Bruce R.; Mormonism and Native Americans; Mormonism and Science; Nibley, Hugh; Roberts, B. H.; Talmage, James E.; Youth Programs.

References

Bergera, Gary James, and Ronald Priddis. *Brigham Young University: A House of Faith.* Salt Lake City, UT: Signature Books, 1985.

Buchanan, Frederick S. "Education among the Mormons: Brigham Young and the Schools of Utah." *History of Education Quarterly* 22 (Winter 1982): 435–459.

Clark, James R. "Church and State Relationships in Education in Utah." Ed.D. dissertation, Utah State University, 1958.

Doctrine and Covenants of the Church of Jesus Christ of Latter-day Saints. Salt Lake City, UT: The Church of Jesus Christ of Latter-day Saints, 1981.

Kimball, Richard Ian. *Sports in Zion: Mormon Recreation, 1890–1940.* Urbana: University of Illinois Press, 2003.

Waterman, Bryan, and Brian Kagel. *The Lord's University: Freedom and Authority at BYU.* Salt Lake City, UT: Signature Books, 1998.

Wilkinson, Ernest L., ed. *Brigham Young University: The First One Hundred Years.* 4 vols. Provo, UT: Brigham Young University Press, 1975–1976.

Mormonism and Men

Mormonism is frequently described as patriarchal, especially because only men are ordained to its priesthood and because its entire organizational structure is male governed, both centrally and locally. Even in the home, Church leaders have declared that, "by divine design," men "are to preside over their families" (The First Presidency, "The Family" 102). Particularly in the 19th century, at the height of polygamous marriages among Mormons, outside observers repeatedly described Mormon men as lecherous and lascivious patriarchs who ruled with iron fists over enslaved harems of women. The irony of such descriptions is that, rather than give men

Quorum work projects, such as work on this 1948 welfare farm, foster brotherhood and provide Mormon men with an outlet for unselfish service. (Courtesy of the Church History Library, The Church of Jesus Christ of Latter-day Saints.)

license for such behavior, Mormonism and the exercise of its priesthood demanded the opposite. Mormon leaders articulated ideal male characteristics that focused men's attention away from the worldly pursuits that permeated American culture at the time of Mormonism's founding and directed their attention toward home, family, and Church responsibilities. Even in the 20th and 21st centuries, as Mormons more fully embraced capitalism and Mormon men rose to prominent business and political positions, Mormonism continued to emphasize that men were first responsible to home, spouse, and family. Men were reminded that they were to preside over their homes, not with an iron fist but "in love and righteousness," not traditionally powerful or masculine attributes (The First Presidency, "The Family" 102).

From the inception of the Church, family was a major focus and the restoration of ancient priesthood authority a central tenet. These two forces combined to shape male authority in unique ways. Joseph Smith Jr. was a connected and devoted family man. Both his mother and his father played major roles in the formation of his thought and doctrine. Smith's father experienced several financial reversals, which caused his family difficulties and a hardscrabble existence. At least some of Mormonism's early converts came from similar economic circumstances. Smith's father never owned his own land and therefore had nothing tangible to bequeath his sons. Historian Richard Lyman Bushman argues, however, that Mormon priesthood lifted men in such difficult economic circumstances out of the temporal realm and into the sacred. It gave them an opportunity to grant their posterity spiritual rewards, blessings akin to those bestowed by father Abraham. As Bushman put it, "In restoring priesthood Joseph restored fatherhood" (Bushman, "The Inner Joseph Smith" 76). The Mormon priesthood gave Smith's financially strapped father not worldly success but rather spiritual authority and titles of import. Smith appointed his father Patriarch to the Church and gave him an honored place in its leadership. In this office, the elder Smith gave blessings that pronounced spiritual and eternal inheritances that promised to outstrip any worldly accumulation to which one might aspire. This same priesthood power was then distributed widely to all worthy men, who could, in turn, pronounce blessings upon their own families. Whatever Mormon men lacked in physical or financial wealth, priesthood compensated for in allowing them to pronounce gifts of the spirit upon their posterity. Mormon priesthood also granted ordinary men titles of consequence—deacon, teacher, priest, elder, high priest, and bishop—and not just to the few but to every male. It was at once democratic and hierarchical.

In every way, Mormon men were instructed to use this authority not for personal aggrandizement but for the greater good. An early Church periodical, *The Elders' Journal,* published in August 1838, set a high standard:

> It is the place of the man to stand at the head of his family and be lord of his own house, not to rule over his wife as a tyrant, neither as one who is fearful or jealous that his wife will get out of her place and prevent him from exercising his authority. It is his duty to be a man of God (for a man of God is a man of wisdom), ready at all times to obtain from the scriptures the revelations and from on high, such instructions as are necessary for the edification and salvation of his household. (*Elders' Journal,* "On the Duty of Husband and Wife," 61)

In 1839, Joseph Smith further articulated the principles that governed priesthood power in the Church and in the home: "No power or influence can or ought to be maintained by virtue of the priesthood," he directed, "only by persuasion, by long-suffering, by gentleness and meekness, and by love unfeigned; by kindness, and pure knowledge, which shall greatly enlarge the soul without hypocrisy, and without guile" (Doctrine and Covenants 121:41–42). Smith called Mormon men away from aggressive confrontational tendencies and instead insisted that gentleness, meekness, and kindness govern their behavior and control their use of priesthood power.

The first duty for Mormon men was to be good fathers and husbands, tasks that became more difficult when, in 1841, Joseph Smith introduced plural marriage to an inner circle of leaders. Brigham Young explained his reaction to the new principle this way: "[When] Joseph revealed the doctrine; I was not desirous of shrinking from any duty, nor of failing in the least to do as I was commanded, but it was the first time in my life that I had desired the grave, and I could hardly get over it for a long time. And when I saw a funeral, I felt to envy the corpse its situation, and to regard that I was not in the coffin" (Young, "Plurality of Wives" 3:266).

Despite this initial reaction, Young committed to Smith's teaching and took plural wives. Like all polygamists, this meant that Young had to decipher how to be a husband to many wives and a father to many children. He eventually had 56 children by 16 wives. His daughter Susa Young Gates, who usually gave him a glowing report concerning his ability as a father and husband, admitted that he had a difficult time paying equal attention to so many wives. He had different levels of success with his numerous children, as well. Some were very committed to their father's Church, while a few were not.

Of course, most polygamous households were not as large as Young's, with the average plural family including only two or three wives. Even one additional wife placed financial burdens upon Mormon men. Most scholars of polygamy view it as a woman's issue, but the introduction of plural wives into a family caused many problems for men. They needed to establish housing for a new wife, whether with the other wives or at a separate residence. An independent house might cost more but also might solve some of the problems that developed when wives lived under the same roof. While Young had the resources to care for his large family, other Mormon men stretched financially to provide for multiple households. Some men were unable to do so without their wives working to help support their families.

In some plural households, wives did not get along and the children vied for their father's attention. If the plural wives were of different ages, had different standards of cleanliness, had different desires for luxuries, or did not have the same commitment to Mormonism, it might spark problems that the husband was expected to mediate.

Men also experienced pressure to enter plural marriage, sometimes against their will. In the 19th century, polygamy was preached as the ideal marriage system for Mormons, and particularly men in leadership positions were expected to set an example. Even so, the vast majority of Mormon households (around 80 percent) opted to remain monogamous, a fact that belies the lecherous patriarch stereotype. Perhaps James Jepson Jr. represented many Mormon men when he wrote about his local church leaders:

President McAllister and Counselor Cannon were very enthusiastic on the principle of polygamy. Whenever they spent an evening in my home, they always insisted that I, being a young man of good health and sufficient means, should feel it my duty to take another wife. I was very reluctant about this, but finally I talked it over with Lucinda [his wife]. She said it was alright with her if I wanted another wife, and that if I would marry someone that was sensible and a real helpmate, she would not object, but she didn't want me to marry any silly little girl.

Still I hesitated. I was perfectly content with my lot just as it was. I loved Lucinda dearly. I had a nice family and we were all happy together. But as the brethren thought I was neglecting my duty, I went before the Lord and asked Him to open the way, if it was His will that I should take a second wife. That if it were not His will, I should be hedged about and prevented from marrying another woman. So when I met a girl that I thought might make a desirable wife, I went to the Lord and told Him that if He thought I should marry her, to open the way; if I should not, that the way be closed. The way was never opened up, and when the Manifesto was signed I felt very much relieved, for in my own heart I really never wanted two wives at one time. (Jepson, "Memories and Experiences" 18)

Even so, some men recognized advantages to having plural wives. Benjamin F. Johnson recalled:

And while I can believe that to some plural marriage was a great cross, yet I cannot say so from my own experience, for although in times that tried men's hearts, I married seven Wives, I was blessed with the gift to love them all; and although providing for so many was attended with great labor, care and anxiety, yet there was sympathy and love as my reward. And there is not one of my children or their mothers that are not dearer to me still than life. (Johnson, "The Benjamin F. Johnson Letter" 16)

Polygamy afforded men other advantages, too. Utah's rural, agricultural economy favored large families with boys who could work the land. Men with plural wives were viewed as leaders who were willing to set the example in their communities. Church authorities tended to perceive them as trustworthy, especially as plural marriage became a symbol of one's commitment to the Church. Polygamy also offered more opportunity for husbands to satisfy their sexual desires within the bonds of marriage.

Despite such advantages, the emphasis on the importance of posterity within Mormonism may have caused feelings of inadequacy and longing in men who could not father children. Church leaders praised large families and confirmed that husbands of plural wives were building a kingdom in heaven. Men without children felt that they were somehow not blessed and maybe not as righteous as their neighbors with large families. The Church travel agent William C. Staines was known for his business abilities and his service to the Church, but even with several wives he was unable to father children. The same was true of William H. Dame, stake president in Iron County, Utah, who had four wives but no children.

Single men experienced similar issues in a culture that so heavily emphasized marriage. Joseph Smith reported a revelation on marriage that put it bluntly: "For behold, I reveal unto you a new and an everlasting covenant [of marriage], and if ye abide not that covenant, then are ye damned; for no one can reject this covenant and be permitted to enter into my glory" (Doctrine and Covenants 132:4). Most unmarried men remained on the fringes of Mormonism or left it altogether, but several made an impact on Mormon history. George John Taylor, son of Church president John Taylor, never married but maintained a position within the Mormon mainstream. He became a proxy father for John Taylor's large family, making sure the children received both secular and spiritual training. He helped his brothers in business and kept the family together, especially as his father spent so much time administering the affairs of the Church. John R. Park, president of the University of Utah, remained single but focused his energies upon his students. He took orphans and other disadvantaged children into his home to help provide a good education for them. Evan Stephens, director of the famous Mormon Tabernacle Choir, also never married; he spent his life writing music, including several enduring Mormon hymns.

In 1890, the Manifesto began the process of ending Church-sanctioned plural marriages but also introduced new dilemmas for men. With no clear guidelines on how to move forward in post-Manifesto Mormonism, men wondered if they should give up their existing plural wives and how they should divide their finances in a new style of marriage. Most husbands followed the example of the hierarchy, staying with their plural wives but not entering into new plural marriages. This crisis and the change in teachings concerning marriage created a Fundamentalist movement, leading to the excommunication of men who chose to continue taking plural wives.

Smith's revelations required additional responsibilities of men, including the duty to spread the gospel. For much of the 19th century, missionary work remained a largely male requirement, and even in the 20th and 21st centuries it was emphasized as an obligation for men but a choice for women. Most early male members took the responsibility seriously and contacted their unconverted family members as well as their neighbors and shared their new religion. Soon, official calls for missionaries and organized mission fields became an important part of the Mormon experience. Men left their wives and families behind on unpaid missionary service, with no unified system for caring for their families while they were gone. Often, mission calls came without much notice, and wives, sons, parents and even neighbors filled in for the breadwinner. In addition to providing for themselves, families often sent help to their missionary relative while he was away. In the 20th century, unmarried young men became the main missionary force for the Church, and today they continue to experience considerable social pressure to serve. Young men are expected to postpone educational opportunities, dating, marriage, and work while they fulfill two-year missionary stints.

Mormon culture also anticipates that its men will be financially successful, although its communal ideals have always tempered and redirected this expectation. In the 19th century, land was a means to security and status, and land ownership was a way to fulfill expectations for men as providers, but Mormonism gave conflicting messages. Smith preached a redistribution of wealth, including land, and asked men to turn over their surplus to the Church to aid the poor and to support Church projects. Young implemented a similar United Order effort in Utah, aimed at establishing an egalitarian society. Following Young's death, Church leaders were more open to capitalism and realized that individual surplus was important to build financial security, to pay for family needs, and to send children to school. Even so, tithing and other offerings focused men's financial attention on communal ideals.

Mormon men must also prepare themselves for unpaid Church leadership. Rotating male lay leaders with no formal training direct local congregations, and some positions, especially that of bishop, demand significant time commitments. In the 19th century, bishops not only supervised the activities of their congregations but also provided for the poor and administered to the spiritual and temporal needs of their congregations. They raised money to carry out Church activities, including building projects, with little aid from central authorities. Bishops further gave theological advice and encouraged the spiritual lives of their congregants. Of necessity, such demanding positions took men away from their families and created tension for them as they attempted to juggle home, work, and church obligations. More recently, the length of a bishop's tenure has been standardized to about five years, and a more complex organizational structure distributes responsibilities more broadly.

Mormon leaders also warn men against overattention to work and worldly successes. In April 1935, apostle David O. McKay offered advice gleaned from James Edward McCulloch's *Home: The Savior of Civilization* (1924) that has grown into a mantra for the Church: "No other success can compensate for failure in the home" (McKay, *Conference Reports* 115–116). As president of the Church, McKay repeated the standard often and established it as an ideal for Mormon men to achieve. Church leaders continue to preach the importance of the family and home and often make men the responsible party for familial success. Men are also warned against spouse and child abuse, sexual infidelity, and pornography. "The natural man," the Book of Mormon reminds them, "is an enemy to God" (Mosiah 3:19).

Mormon men are told to be good husbands, good fathers, good missionaries, good providers, and good leaders, and to do so with kindness, love, and compassion. The Church of Jesus Christ of Latter-day Saints has always expected a great deal of its male members.

—Jeffery O. Johnson and W. Paul Reeve

See also: Church Organization and Government; Local Worship; Manifesto; Mormon Missiology; Mormonism and the Family; Mormonism and Women; Polygamy.

References

Bushman, Richard Lyman. "The Inner Joseph Smith." *Journal of Mormon History* 32 (Spring 2006): 65–81.

Cannon, Elaine Winifred Anderson. *Male, Female and the Lord.* Provo, UT: Brigham Young University, 1970.

Doctrine and Covenants of the Church of Jesus Christ of Latter-day Saints. Salt Lake City, UT: The Church of Jesus Christ of Latter-day Saints, 1981.

Elders' Journal. "On the Duty of Husband and Wife." (Far West, MO) 1, no. 4 (August 1838): 61–62.

Embry, Jessie L. "Burden or Pleasure? A Profile of LDS Polygamous Husbands." *Dialogue: A Journal of Mormon Thought* 20 (Winter 1987): 158–166.

England, Eugene. "On Being Male and Melchizedek." *Dialogue: A Journal of Mormon Thought* 23 (Winter 1990): 64–79.

Hardy, B. Carman. *Doing the Works of Abraham: Mormon Polygamy: Its Origin, Practice, and Demise.* Norman, OK: Arthur H. Clark, 2007.

Jepson, James, Jr. "Memories and Experiences of James Jepson Jr." Ed. Etta Holdaway Spendlove. Typescript, 1944. Utah State Historical Society, Salt Lake City.

Johnson, Benjamin F. "The Benjamin F. Johnson Letter to Elder George S. Gibbs." Dugway, UT: Kraut's Pioneer Press, 1968.

McKay, David O. *Conference Reports* (April 1935): 115–116.

The First Presidency and the Quorum of the Twelve Apostles of the Church of Jesus Christ of Latter-day Saints. "The Family: A Proclamation to the World." *Ensign* 25 (November 1995): 102.

Young, Brigham. "Plurality of Wives." *Journal of Discourses.* London: LDS Book Depot, 1856.

Mormonism and Native Americans

The historical relationship between Mormons and Native Americans was complex and varied over time and space in accordance with changing circumstances and personalities. In general, it is best understood as a tension between two competing forces. On one hand, Mormons believed that American Indians were fallen descendants of ancient Israel ("Lamanites," in Mormon parlance) in need of redemption. On the other hand, Mormons viewed American Indians as an impediment to their mission to build a temporal as well as a spiritual kingdom of God. The practicality of colonizing in the heart of Indian land sometimes caused Mormons to lose sight of their religious ideals and to treat American Indians in deplorable ways. Other times, Mormons interacted with their Native American neighbors with Christian grace.

The Book of Mormon shaped Mormon views toward American Indians in significant ways. Mormons believe this book is a condensed sacred history of a group of religious refugees who fled Jerusalem before its fall, in 600 B.C. These refugees arrived in the Americas, where they eventually split into two competing groups: the generally more righteous Christian Nephites and the apostate Lamanites. In the end, the Nephites descended to a level of depravity greater than that of the Lamanites

Despite a mixed record in meeting the needs of Native Americans, the Church numbers many thousands of Native families among its faithful. (Courtesy of The Church of Jesus Christ of Latter-day Saints.)

and were completely destroyed. The Lamanites survived and became, according to early Mormon belief, the ancestors of the American Indians.

Joseph Smith claimed that the Book of Mormon was preserved and translated for the express purpose of convincing Jew, gentile, and Lamanite—the American Indian—of the reality of Jesus Christ. Even before Smith finished his translation, he declared, "For this very purpose these plates [were] preserved, . . . that the Lamanites might come to the knowledge of their fathers, and that they might know the promises of the Lord and that they may believe the gospel and rely upon the merits of Jesus Christ, and be glorified though faith . . . and . . . repentance" (Doctrine and Covenants 3:16–20). Thus, very early Mormons felt an obligation to convert American Indians to Christianity and to raise them to self-reliance (typically defined as Western civilization).

Within months of the organization of the Church, in 1830, Smith sent missionaries to the American Indians. First placing the Book of Mormon with the Catteraugus Indians in New York, these missionaries headed west to Ohio. They continued on to the frontier outpost of Independence, Missouri, and then crossed into Indian country. After initial success with the Shawnee, Delaware, and Wyandot, the Mormons were summarily ejected from Indian country by angry Protestant missionaries.

Charges of Mormon-Indian conspiracies dogged the Church throughout the 19th century. Mormon missionary activities only exacerbated fears among outsiders that Mormons were allying themselves with American Indians and conniving to kill American citizens. Despite such allegations, concern for converting American Indians became a component of most 19th-century Mormon settlements. In the 20th century, it continued to motivate Mormon educators and reformers.

Despite laws against private intercourse with American Indians, early Mormons continued to proselyte whenever possible. Smith called occasional missionaries to the Indians (including Brigham Young). Sac, Fox, and Potowatami visited the Saints in Nauvoo, where they received both the Book of Mormon and advice from Smith. A few American Indians accepted Church ordinances.

As the Saints moved west under Brigham Young's leadership, Young recognized the need to have staging points along the way. He ignored federal injunctions and approached local American Indians to negotiate private treaties of friendship. Hoping to ensure unmolested travel for Mormon emigrants, he arranged to pay fees for resources at places like Winter Quarters. When young warriors stole cattle from negotiated pasturage, Young went to tribal leaders to resolve the problem, rather than responding with aggression.

The Mormon-Indian experience grew more complex when Mormons settled permanently in Indian country. Although Mormons believed they had a duty to convert and train American Indians, Young was more concerned with the survival and expansion of his people. He was eager to convert American Indians to Mormonism and agrarianism—indeed, one of the first things he did after he arrived in Salt Lake Valley was to rise from his sickbed and visit a group of Indians—but he was also prepared to kill if he had to in order to hold onto the new land he believed God had given his people. The practicality of living among Indians complicated the religious equation, and Young struggled to respond to Indians who attacked settlements.

Mormon leaders continued to exhort frustrated congregants to establish peaceful relations, using the Book of Mormon and the fallen-Israelite theme to do so. In 1855, Orson Pratt admonished Saints: "The Lord has caused us to come here [Utah] for this very purpose, that we might accomplish the redemption of these suffering degraded Israelites. . . . It is a great privilege indeed . . . that we enjoy being associated with them in the accomplishment of so great a work." (Pratt, "Salvation" 8: 178). On other occasions, however, Mormon leaders applied a different Book of Mormon narrative. Gadianton Robbers were a depraved, murderous, and thieving subset of people portrayed in the Book of Mormon. At times, Brigham Young and other leaders described Great Basin tribes as descendants of ancient Gadianton Robbers and warned Mormons to be on guard. These two competing theological themes no doubt further complicated Mormon colonization of Indian lands.

Among Young's first order of business in the Salt Lake Valley was his attempt to develop treaties of friendship and alliance with Indian leaders. This proved tricky, especially because tribes at war with each other expected Young to be their special ally. The Mormon prophet found himself acting as peacekeeper and mediator between tribes as often as between Indians and his own people.

After two years of uneasy peace, Young authorized a limited extermination against stock-raiding Indians, but he quickly recognized that such heavy-handed tactics made enemies, not friends. By 1853, he was preaching the policy for which he became best known: that it was better to feed the Indians than to fight them. Thereafter, he developed a strategy of heavily fortified settlements, a defensive militia, and openhanded conciliation. His counsel was not always followed locally, which inevitably led to problems, but it was an idealistic and forward-thinking approach.

Native leaders sometimes saw religious conversion as a political step in forging Mormon alliances. Some leaders were baptized early and received Mormon priesthood ordinances, and a few bands joined wholesale. This proselyting success was affected by many factors. Most Indians found no conflict in compounding religions—if one was good, two should be better. Personal relationships with a particular missionary were also important, as was how much an Indian leader saw the alliance benefiting himself or his band. And relations varied. Some Mormons fought tirelessly in behalf of their Indian neighbors, even gaining title to land to stave off removal to reservations or demanding redress for wrongs committed against Indians. Other Mormons were not so noble-minded and succumbed to the frontier mentality of fear and dislike of Indians. When this happened, abuse, mistreatment, and atrocities occurred.

Because Young perceived conflict between agrarian settlements and nomadic hunter-gatherers living side by side and because the Church had a moral imperative to befriend, convert, and assimilate American Indians, missionary work and Indian charity were necessary components of pioneer life. As settlements spread onto traditional Indian lands, Indians camped near Mormon settlements and were frequent visitors in towns and at back doors, while Mormons likewise visited Indian camps. Young experimented with ways to incorporate Indians into Mormon society, trying to strike a balance between fraternizing and neighborly conversion. He warned Mormons not to mingle too promiscuously when he discovered Mormon men racing or wrestling in common games with Indian neighbors. Even so, he encouraged active, industrious interaction. Mormons were urged to employ Indians on farms, and specific agricultural missions were sent to some areas, such as southwestern Utah and Idaho. In the 1850s, several short-lived Indian farms were set up with federal aid. Mormons were encouraged to be generous to Indians, and the goods stored in bishops' storehouses were available for distribution to needy Indians. By the 1880s, peace-mission settlements were sent among the Navajo in Arizona and Indians in southeastern Utah.

Finding the Saints in the midst of an active Mexican and Indian slave trade, Young urged Mormons to acquire captured Indian children to foster as their own. Mormons purchased children from slavers, redeemed war captives, and adopted orphans. Destitute Indians traded many of their own or other children into Mormon homes for fostering. Hundreds of such fostered/indentured Indian children were raised by Mormon families, with varying degrees of success.

Such a significant difference existed between the way Mormons treated Indians and the ways other frontier Americans did so that Indians distinguished between Mormon and non-Mormon "tribes." Even non-Mormons recognized this relationship, sometimes accusing Mormons of an unholy alliance when they saw Mormons feeding and interacting with local Indians. By the 1860s, most chiefs trusted Brigham Young enough that they asked his counsel during federal treaty negotiations.

Even so, Mormon settlements were resource-intensive and were spreading over the same land upon which nomadic Indians relied. As a result, Indians were forced to change their culture or beg, steal, or starve. Both groups grew frustrated, and conflict ensued. While many Indians attempted peace, some grew angry or desperate enough to rise up against Mormon settlers. Gosiutes raided in the Tintic War (1850–1851), and some Utes fought in the brief Provo War (1850) and then again in the Walker War (1853–1854). Warring Shoshone and Bannock drove out the peaceful Lemhi mission in 1858. The more serious Black Hawk War (1865–1872) cost millions, emptied a dozen central Utah settlements, and eventually forced most Utes onto an unprepared reservation under Protestant control. The last two conflicts brought cycles of retaliatory atrocities on both sides, as Mormon and Indian bitterness escalated. Meanwhile, Shoshone raids occasionally nipped at Mormon settlements in the north, and settlers grew irritated. Eventually, army troops responded to Mormon complaints and concern about bloodier attacks on the Oregon Trail. The result was the infamous 1863 Bear River Massacre in which troops slaughtered well over 200 Northwestern Shoshone.

By the 20th century, the large tribes had been removed to reservations and isolated from Mormon influence, though other Indians remained on small, titled homesteads or small reserves near Mormon communities. Local bishops and Relief Society groups interacted with Indian members who were no longer numerous or deemed threatening. Farmers often exploited their labor the same as they did that of Mexican migrant workers.

By the mid-20th century, the efforts of three influential Mormons had refocused LDS attention on Indians. The first of these men was a young Mormon attorney, Ernest L. Wilkinson. He was retained in the mid-1930s by the Confederated Ute Tribes of Colorado and Utah in their land-claims case against the federal government. During his 16-year pursuit of this secular claim, Wilkinson became one of the leading authorities on Indian law. He frequently testified in Congress and co-authored and lobbied the bill that created the Indian Claims Commission (ICC). The first claim the ICC heard was the "The Big Ute Case," which Wilkinson won. Wilkinson's Mormon-dominated firm become the premier advocate for Indian claims cases and eventually represented more tribes than any other firm. Although his groundbreaking work was significant, the government also had an ulterior motive: to "pay off" tribes so that it could terminate all future financial obligations to them.

Attitudes in Washington were shifting against Indians. Powerful men in Washington wanted to close the expensive Bureau of Indian Affairs (BIA), while many other well-meaning people believed that the solution to all Indian problems was to "emancipate" them from the "paternalistic wardship" of the BIA. They wanted Indians to take on the freedom, responsibilities, and duties of regular citizenship. Leading this crusade was a freshman senator from Utah and former local Mormon Church leader, Arthur Watkins. While his actions in Washington were not connected to the Church, his convictions were firmly rooted in his religious beliefs that the salvation of the Lamanite/Indian lay in their assimilation into industrious self-sufficiency. He was a kindly, soft-spoken man, but rock-firm in his convictions.

Watkins pushed the termination of nearly a hundred tribes from federal recognition and severed their access to federal aid. History has shown that termination and its sister policy of urban relocation were disastrous. Instead of emancipating Indians, it severed unprepared people too quickly from government programs and mired them more deeply in poverty, caused the loss of their little remaining land, and left them with nowhere to go. Almost as quickly as the two-term senator retired from the Senate, his termination policy quietly expired, and tribes began the slow process of repatriation. Although Watkins and his Mormon idealism received the primary blame for pushing the termination policy, many others supported assimilation as the answer to the so-called Indian Problem.

The third and most significant of the Mormon leaders was Spencer W. Kimball, an apostle in the 1940s, and Church president from 1973 to 1985. Responding to the 1947 request of a Navajo girl and her migrant-worker family for better access to education, Kimball made arrangements for three Indian children to stay with Mormon families and to go to school in Richfield, Utah. Heartened by the success of the experiment, Kimball organized an informal Indian student placement program, which grew to serve nearly six dozen students in four western states by 1952.

Formalized under the Church Social Services program and the Southwest Indian Mission, the program grew rapidly. By the mid-1970s, nearly 3,000 Mormon Indian children were enrolled in the Placement Program. Foster parents who had been vetted by their bishops received Indian children into their homes and fed, clothed, and housed the children at their own expense. Away from the limited opportunities of reservation life, these children received superior educations, as well as intensive acculturative and religious training. Kimball asserted that the Placement Program was "the finest program conceived . . . for the rapid and permanent advancement and progress of the Indian child so long deprived" (Kimball, "Discourse" 1956).

The program received both praise and criticism. Detractors were virulent, calling it cultural genocide, an attempt to eradicate the children's religion and culture. Some accused the Mormon Church of coercion. However, federal investigation found the accusations unfounded and called the program the best educational program of its kind at the time. Graduates of the program were generally proud of their academic achievements, biculturalism, and bilingualism, and many went on to college. Most of the published studies about the program were positive.

Not all experiences were favorable, of course. Participants were often lonely, and prejudice was rampant in predominantly white schools; some recalled being bullied and abused by other students. Children were typically referred to as "Lamanites" rather than Indians, a term that carried inherent pejorative connotations. Lamanites were the wicked antagonists of the Book of Mormon, and therefore some placement children found it distasteful.

Students were sometimes enticed into the program. While this practice was officially frowned upon, overeager missionaries sometimes used Placement to get baptisms or perhaps hoped that, if they could baptize a child, Placement acculturation would complete the conversion. Some Indian parents exploited the Placement Program as a means of getting free foster care or free clothes for their children. Some children hated the program but as adults were grateful for its benefits. While some children moved from family to family, others formed close bonds with their foster families. Graduates of the program often became the nucleus of local church leadership on reservations. Eventually, as public education opportunities and communication improved on reservations, the Placement Program was phased out; by 2000, it had ended.

Meanwhile, Ernest Wilkinson took up the question of college education at Church-owned Brigham Young University (BYU). Church president David O. McKay contacted Wilkinson after the successful completion of his land claims case for the Utes and asked him to assume leadership of BYU. Wilkinson accepted, and among the programs he implemented was a vigorous Indian Education Program, with liberal grants and scholarships for college-age "Lamanites."

During Wilkinson's administration, the university enrolled as many as 600 American Indian students a year. BYU established a Native American Studies program, and special efforts were made to help students graduate, including tutoring and Indian-only classes. The "Tribe of Many Feathers" student club provided socialization, while the school's Program Bureau developed the "Lamanite Generation," a troupe of Indian, Latin American, and Polynesian students who performed traditional dances for audiences around the country and ultimately around the world. Later renamed "Living Legends," the group had as its goal missionary work for the Church and recruitment of native students for BYU.

Though later called the Multicultural Department, BYU's scholarship and grant programs for Indians remained generous. Counselors continued to encourage graduation and worked closely to coordinate off-campus aid for Indians. Meanwhile, the school continued an active high school recruitment program, educational seminars, and a Native American Outreach Program that worked with Indian youth across the country.

In the 21st century, the Mormon Church maintains a number of proselyting missions on American Indian reservations, though conversion rates remain low. The definition of Lamanite has morphed and expanded to include Polynesians and Latin Americans, groups with much higher rates of conversion. As a result, some Mormons see the fulfillment of Book of Mormon promises in Latin America, rather than among North American Indians. Here, too, the Church has backed away from its strict construction of American Indians as Lamanites, suggesting that Book of Mormon peoples were only among their ancestors, not their exclusive progenitors.

—*Sondra Jones*

See also: Black Hawk War; Book of Mormon; Kimball, Spencer W.; Mormonism and Race.

References

Christy, Howard A. "Brigham Young and Mormon Indian Policies: The Formative Period, 1836–1851." *BYU Studies* 18, no. 3 (Spring 1978): 428–452.

Christy, Howard A. "Open Hand and Mailed Fist: Mormon-Indian Relations in Utah, 1847–52." *Utah Historical Quarterly* 46 (1978): 216–235.

Doctrine and Covenants of the Church of Jesus Christ of Latter-day Saints. Salt Lake City, UT: The Church of Jesus Christ of Latter-day Saints, 1981.

Farmer, Jared. *On Zion's Mount: Mormons, Indians, and the American Landscape.* Cambridge, MA: Harvard University Press, 2008.

Jones, Sondra. "Saints or Sinners? The Evolving Perceptions of Mormon-Indian Relations in Utah Historiography." *Utah Historical Quarterly* 72 (Winter 2004): 19–46.

Kimball, Spencer W. "Discourse." *Conference Reports.* Salt Lake City, UT: The Church of Jesus Christ of Latter-day Saints, 1956 (October).

O'Neil, Floyd A., and Stanford J. Layton. "Of Pride and Politics: Brigham Young as Indian Superintendent." *Utah Historical Quarterly* 46 (1978): 236–250.

Pratt, Orson. "Salvation of the House of Israel." *Journal of Discourses.* Liverpool: LDS Book Depot, 1861.

Reeve, W. Paul. *Making Space on the Western Frontier: Mormons, Miners, and Southern Paiutes.* Urbana: University of Illinois Press, 2006.

Mormonism and Other Faiths

Mormonism's founding prophet expressed his feelings about religious liberty in the strongest of terms: "If it has been demonstrated that I have been willing to die for a 'Mormon,' I am bold to declare before Heaven that I am just as ready to die in defending the rights of a Presbyterian, a Baptist, or a good man of any other denomination; for the same principle which would trample upon the rights of the Latter-day Saints would trample upon the rights of the Roman Catholics, or of any other denomination who may be unpopular and too weak to defend themselves" (Smith, *History* 5:498). Joseph Smith's sentiments translated into the Church's 11th Article of Faith and into a broad religious tolerance clause passed by the Nauvoo City Council, which guaranteed "equal privileges" to Christians, "Mohammedans," and "all other religious sects, and denominations" (Bushman, *Joseph Smith* 416).

But, in practice, interfaith encounters involving Latter-day Saints have often fallen short of this ideal of mutual respect and tolerance. Because Latter-day Saints believe in a universal apostasy from true Christianity, Mormon missionaries, from the time of the Church's organization forward, have sought to evangelize all listeners, not just the unchurched. Latter-day Saint claims about exclusive saving truths have frequently antagonized and polarized their religiously minded neighbors. These proselytizing efforts, along with Mormonism's embrace of seemingly radical revelations and additional ancient scripture, elicited early clerical reactions that ranged from critical to adversarial. Still, as Joseph Smith entertained a steady stream of curious preachers and ministers, cordial meetings were the rule—the Mormon prophet even invited some of these visitors to address the Saints. In print, however, virulent anti-Mormon messages, many of which were written by religionists of various faith traditions, fueled the serious persecution that contributed to the Saints' repeated re-locations and, ultimately, Joseph Smith's violent death.

After Brigham Young led Latter-day Saints to the Rocky Mountains, their separa-tion from American society—and its religious pluralism—was short-lived. Mining and mercantile opportunities attracted many newcomers, as did federal appoint-ment to government posts, and religious identity came with them. Jews, Catholics, and Protestants established Utah congregations within two decades of the Mormon pioneers' arrival at the Great Salt Lake. It was not unusual for Mormons to welcome these new groups by making available LDS meetinghouses. Brigham Young used his influence to help the Catholic Church secure title to land for a church. The LDS St. George Tabernacle Choir even surprised Father Lawrence Scanlan, a Roman Catholic, by offering their musical services to sing the Latin mass.

Other encounters in the Utah Territory were far less amicable, however. When word spread nationally of the LDS Church's 1852 public announcement regarding the practice of plural marriage, Church groups led the way in petitioning the fed-eral government to intervene. Historian Jan Shipps termed this four-decade antipo-lygamy crusade "politico-religious" because of the difficulty in separating political motives from religious motives in this opposition to Mormonism (Shipps, *Sojourner* 309). Evangelical Protestant bodies formed the vanguard of this force, using their pulpits to decry polygamy and their congregations to amass signatures of protest. Many of Utah's Protestant Churches in the 19th century were established as "home missions," charged with rescuing misguided Mormons and inoculating new arrivals against future conversion to the LDS faith. Several denominations set up schools to attract LDS youth; the quality of these schools worried Mormon leaders, who sub-sequently responded by throwing their support first behind local LDS academies and then later behind the expansion of the public school system and the outside-of-school supplemental religious education classes that have since come to character-ize the LDS seminary system.

Church president Wilford Woodruff's 1890 Manifesto announcing the end of plural marriage seemed to still, for a time, the religious opposition to the Mormons, but the earlier animosity was reignited in 1903 when LDS apostle Reed Smoot was elected to the U.S. Senate. Upset at what seemed an affront to Church-state sepa-ration, and angered over reports that Mormon leaders still countenanced secret po-lygamous marriages, Protestant leaders across the nation began another petitioning campaign. Pressured by these constituents, senators refused to seat Smoot for more than three years, during which time they conducted lengthy hearings about Latter-day Saint beliefs and practices. Influential in this anti-Smoot resistance were the strong testimonies against the Mormons filed by the Salt Lake Ministerial Associa-tion, which included officials from Presbyterian, Methodist, Congregational, and Episcopal Churches. Though Reed Smoot was eventually admitted to the Senate, religionists continued to denounce Mormonism in national periodicals as barbarous and promiscuous.

For their part, Latter-day Saints often dealt with this persecution by retreating deeper into defensive, insular communities and turning up the rhetorical heat. While Latter-day Saint leaders consistently spoke well of the Christian Reformers, they nevertheless agreed that the work of the Protestant Reformation had not returned Christianity to its pristine state. LDS leaders were often unequivocal in their disdain for Christian institutions that seemed to them incomplete or confused at best and corrupt at worst. Thus, in Mormon parlance, everyone who was not a member of the Church was a "gentile." This us-versus-them mindset created community friction in Missouri, in Ohio, in Illinois, and, finally, in Utah. Outsiders complained about Mormon voting blocs and exclusive trading practices, and they perceived the Latter-day Saint religion to be holier-than-thou in its claims about restored Christianity and antirepublican in its deference to a prophet-president.

The struggle for Utah statehood and the Smoot hearings contributed to a new awareness among Latter-day Saints of their sagging national public image. Mormon participation at the 1893 Chicago World's Fair typified the ups and downs of the period. The Tabernacle Choir sang at the fair, and the Church's First Presidency attended. However, at the simultaneous World Parliament of Religions—an enormous, ecumenical event that lasted two weeks—a belated request for inclusion by LDS officials was initially rejected by the Parliament's organizers because of fears that the Church's presence would be disturbing, ostensibly because of its prior endorsement of polygamy. Parliament officials finally conceded a bit, offering Mormon authority B. H. Roberts a chance to speak in one of the gathering's secondary halls. Roberts refused the offer because he felt the Church was being slighted through its relegation to an ancillary meeting. While the whole episode represents both the lingering doubts about Mormon legitimacy in the minds of many American religionists and Mormons' indignation at being so rebuffed, the Church's efforts in Chicago also speak to a turn-of-the-century shift in Mormons' mindset concerning the importance of public relations. Throughout the 20th century, Latter-day Saints showed that they were motivated to foster good relationships with other American institutions, including (and especially so) other religious bodies.

In 1903, for example, Mormons demonstrated their goodwill toward the Salt Lake Jewish community by helping to finance a second synagogue in the city. Mormons' relations with Jews had always been less rocky than their relations with Protestants because Latter-day Saints believed themselves to be modern Israelites, a belief that generated a sense of affinity with the Jewish people. Joseph Smith retained the services of a Jew, Joshua Seixas, to teach biblical Hebrew to LDS elders in Kirtland. Barely a decade after The Church of Jesus Christ of Latter-day Saints was organized, Mormon apostle Orson Hyde traveled to Palestine and there, in 1841, offered a prayer dedicating the land for the return of the Jews, reflecting the LDS expectation of participating in scriptural prophecies related to the gathering of the House of Israel. Later, in the Mormons' Rocky Mountain heartland, Jewish leaders noted the general absence of anti-Semitism among Latter-day Saints; in 1921, Church president Heber J. Grant strenuously reiterated the incompatibility of Mormonism and anti-Jewish prejudice. Mormon periodicals consistently showed support for the concerns of the Jewish community, and, in 1916, Utahns elected a Jew, Simon Bamberger, governor.

During these same early decades of the 20th century, the Prohibition movement gave Mormons and evangelical Christians a common cause. This new cooperative venture created alliances where only acrimony had once existed. Joint concern over alcohol abuse, especially in an era when Latter-day Saint leaders reinvigorated the Church's Word of Wisdom, tempered these past hostilities.

Public opinion of Mormons in the first half of the 20th century changed more subtly than suddenly, but Mormons saw encouraging signs of improving relationships with the American people and their many Churches. National periodicals lauded the LDS Church's Welfare Plan, instituted during the Great Depression, and in many of those publications Mormons were described as true "Christians" because of this charitable work. The Tabernacle Choir began national broadcasts, first on radio and later on television, in 1929. The choir's *Music and the Spoken Word* weekly program eventually garnered an audience that numbered in the millions, and the essentially nondenominational commentary provided by Richard L. Evans (who would become an apostle in 1953) won a nationwide following.

Interfaith outreach efforts expanded significantly during the presidency of David O. McKay (1951–1970). Several converging factors acted as catalysts in this expansion. President McKay brought to the office an international perspective; as an apostle, in 1921, he had toured the Church's missions as part of a 10-month, around-the-world expedition. Economic displacement during the Great Depression meant that many Mormons left the intermountain West in search of occupational and educational opportunities. Mormon congregations began to appear in cities across America, in places where Latter-day Saints were decidedly in the minority. World War II had exposed thousands of Latter-day Saint servicemen to new cultures and new faiths. In fact, LDS military personnel gave the Church its first permanent presence in Asia, after earlier attempts at missionary work in that region proved mostly unproductive. Thus, the second half of the 20th century began as Mormons made connections with communities outside Utah and even outside the Judeo-Christian tradition. All of this portended a new emphasis on the universality of Mormonism; the defensiveness of the Latter-day Saints seemed to soften accordingly.

McKay's disposition made him especially well suited for leading the Church into these new interpersonal and institutional connections. Biographers note that he encouraged friendships across faith lines through personal example, even accepting a blessing at the hands of Episcopal bishop Arthur W. Moulton and then blessing the Reverend Moulton in return. Under his leadership, the LDS Church donated money toward the remodeling of a Presbyterian church in Ogden, Utah, and toward "Israel bonds," as evidence of "our sympathy with the effort being made to establish the Jews in their homeland" (Prince and Wright, *David O. McKay* 111). McKay and the Church were honored publicly by various Utah clergy and by the national publication of the American Jewish Congress. In an obituary tribute that says as much about Mormonism's new national visibility as it does about the changing climate of interfaith relations, *Time* suggested that McKay "was perhaps the first Mormon president to treat non-Mormons as generously as members of his own faith" (Prince and Wright, *David O. McKay* 107).

McKay took a significant symbolic stand in his response to Catholic protests surrounding the publication of *Mormon Doctrine,* a 1958 book written by LDS general authority Bruce R. McConkie. Several entries in this encyclopedia-style doctrinal treatise linked the Roman Catholic Church with the scriptural "great and abominable church." McKay and his associates—who had not seen the manuscript beforehand—responded quickly to requests for clarification from their injured Catholic friends, and McConkie's book was reprinted only after related entries were amended or dropped. This incident seemed to signal a rapprochement after what had become an increasingly testy Catholic-Mormon relationship in mid-20th-century Utah. Many Mormon leaders at the time understood Catholic initiatives that sought to raise funds for Utah parishes as veiled attempts to bolster missionary resources and to win converts away from Mormonism. On the other hand, Latter-day Saints began new missionary thrusts of their own in predominantly Catholic nations. The two groups' historically harmonious interaction was thus threatened for a time, but the friendship of McKay and Catholic bishop Duane Hunt did much to repair the breach, paving the way for future Mormon-Catholic cooperation in humanitarian work.

Another of McKay's general authority colleagues inspired a significant development in LDS interfaith outreach. Apostle Richard L. Evans so impressed fellow Rotarian Lowell Berry that Berry, a philanthropist who was not a Latter-day Saint, made the initial contribution toward an endowed professorship in Evans's name at Brigham Young University. Truman Madsen became, in 1972, the first occupant of the Richard L. Evans Chair of Christian (later "Religious") Understanding. Over the course of two decades, Madsen spearheaded symposia that invited serious scholarship on parallels between Mormon practice and ancient Jewish and Christian teachings, on Eastern burial rites and Mormon views of the afterlife, and on the concept of the temple in Judaism and in Mormonism. Campus exchanges, lecture series, and publications exposed Latter-day Saints and prominent thinkers and practitioners of numerous world religions to one another's ideas and practices. Madsen's successors in the professorship have only accelerated the ventures he initiated, leading to some remarkable collaborations. Mormon-themed interfaith conferences on comparative topics have convened at Brigham Young University, Yale University, Claremont Graduate University, Fuller Theological Seminary, and, in 2005, to commemorate the bicentennial of Joseph Smith's birth, the Library of Congress. Since 2000, a growing group of Mormon and Evangelical scholars has met semiannually for roundtable discussions, an outgrowth of mutual participation in the Society of Biblical Literature conventions. Several academic and traditionally Evangelical presses have published books derived from these various endeavors, and more than a dozen non-Mormon scholars contributed to the landmark 1992 *Encyclopedia of Mormonism*—Lutheran official and former Harvard dean Krister Stendahl even wrote an entry on baptism for the dead, commenting on the possibility of ancient Christian ties to Mormonism's unique concept of proxy ordinance work.

Not all observers approve of these cooperative ventures. Since the 1970s, vocal complaints have arisen, especially from various camps within evangelical Protestantism, over the appropriateness of labeling Latter-day Saints "Christians." Even though Latter-day Saints have participated with likeminded conservative Christians in the Moral Majority and other coalitions of the Christian Right that opposed the ERA and supported antipornography and defense-of-marriage legislation, theological differences often made these moral and political alliances uncomfortable for some and unconscionable for others. Many critics argue that Mormonism's rejection of the creedal beliefs of traditional Christianity disqualifies the LDS Church as a Christian denomination. Several Protestant Churches classify Mormonism as a non-Christian religion or even as a cult, and the Southern Baptist Convention's 1998 "Crossover, Salt Lake City" campaign to evangelize Mormons (and others) seemed, to some, reminiscent of the Utah Territory's "home missions" of the preceding century. Aiming to mitigate these hostilities and mutual misunderstandings, BYU professor Robert Millet and Utah pastor Greg Johnson have conducted dialogues between Evangelicals and Mormons in dozens of venues nationwide. In that same vein, LDS authorities opened the Salt Lake Tabernacle in 2004 to prominent evangelist Ravi Zacharias; significantly, conciliatory introductory comments at the event were offered by Dr. Richard Mouw, president of Fuller Theological Seminary.

The harshest assaults on Mormon doctrine and practice have often come from disaffected Church members. For example, one such organization produced the *Godmaker* series of films and accompanying books, which premiered in 1982. While various Church groups nationwide screened the initial movie, which asserts that there is an underlying deviance in Mormon beliefs, the National Conference of Christians and Jews (now the National Conference for Community and Justice) and many of its regional affiliates condemned the film as sensational and slanderous. These competing reactions seem to mirror a deep ambivalence in American attitudes toward Mormonism. National surveys surrounding Mitt Romney's 2007–2008 presidential campaign revealed that a sizable minority of those Americans polled regarded Mormons as non-Christians. LDS leaders have responded by emphasizing that, while Mormonism does not align itself with traditional Christianity, a shared faith in the divinity of Jesus Christ should qualify Latter-day Saints for inclusion in the Christian community.

Other recent developments have afforded Mormons additional bridge-building opportunities. Latter-day Saints' participation in underwriting the preservation of green space in Jerusalem (with the Orson Hyde Memorial Gardens), together with a strict promise that the Church would not proselytize in Israel, overcame the initially severe local opposition to the construction of the BYU Jerusalem Center. Opened in 1987, the center quickly became a community gathering spot, with concerts and lectures and forums involving Christians, Jews, Muslims, and others. BYU's Institute for the Study and Preservation of Ancient Religious Texts (ISPART) embarked, in the 1990s, on translation of a series of classic Islamic and Eastern Christian works. ISPART also responded to an invitation, in 1999, to digitize and restore ancient Syriac Christian writings that were housed at the Vatican library. At the 2004 World Parliament of Religions in Barcelona, BYU professor Roger Keller led an interfaith panel that included representatives from Utah's Baha'i, Muslim, and Quaker communities, commenting on their joint experience in fostering dialogue during the 2002 Winter Olympics, in Salt Lake City. Finally, the LDS Church has partnered repeatedly in humanitarian initiatives with organizations like Catholic Relief Services and Islamic Relief Worldwide to distribute supplies in response to global crises.

This marked increase in LDS interfaith outreach activities corresponds to what observers have described as an attitudinal adjustment among Latter-day Saints. Jan Shipps has noted that the designation "gentile" was replaced, in the early years of the 20th century, by "non-Mormon" in LDS rhetoric; even more recently, Church authorities have encouraged Mormons to drop the term "nonmember" in favor of "friend of another faith" or other similarly inclusive descriptors. LDS college students nationwide can enroll in Church-sponsored comparative world religion courses, and the course manual, produced by BYU, partakes of the spirit of Joseph Smith's admonition to "gather all the good and true principles in the world and treasure them up" (Smith, *History* 5:517). Reaffirmation of that sentiment came in 1978, when the members of the Church's governing First Presidency issued a statement expressing their strong feelings that the Christian Reformers and the founders of various world religions were divinely inspired in their work. And, in 1995, President Gordon B. Hinckley set the tone for his administration (1995–2008) when, in his first general conference after being ordained president of the Church, he quoted Joseph Smith's aforementioned statement on religious liberty and then offered his own plea for Latter-day Saints to be better neighbors in an increasingly diverse world.

—*J. B. Haws*

See also: Hinckley, Gordon B.; Manifesto; Martyrdom of Joseph and Hyrum Smith; McConkie, Bruce R.; McKay, David O.; Smoot Hearings; Temple Work by Proxy; Word of Wisdom.

References

Blomberg, Craig L., and Stephen E. Robinson. *How Wide the Divide?: A Mormon and an Evangelical in Conversation.* Downers Grove, IL: InterVarsity Press, 1997.

Bushman, Richard Lyman. *Joseph Smith: Rough Stone Rolling: A Cultural Biography of Mormonism's Founder.* New York: Knopf, 2005.

Glanz, Rudolf. *Jew and Mormon: Historic Group Relations and Religious Outlook.* New York: Waldon Press and Lucius N. Littauer Foundation, 1963.

Prince, Gregory A., and Wm. Robert Wright. *David O. McKay and the Rise of Modern Mormonism.* Salt Lake City: University of Utah Press, 2005.

Shipps, Jan. *Sojourner in the Promised Land: Forty Years among the Mormons.* Urbana: University of Illinois Press, 2000.

Smith, Joseph, Jr. *History of the Church of Jesus Christ of Latter-day Saints,* 2nd ed. 7 vols. Ed. B. H. Roberts. Salt Lake City, UT: Deseret Book, 1973.

Mormonism and Race

In contemporary Mormonism, race plays no part, but racial distinctions were so salient to Mormons during their first 150 years that Professor Colin Kidd included Mormonism among the forms of "racialised religion" in his history of race concepts in Protestantism (Kidd, *Forging of Races* 226–237). Historically, the racial issue for which the Church of Jesus Christ of Latter-day Saints (LDS) was best known was its policy toward people of black African ancestry, who were not eligible for either the priesthood or the temple rituals in the Church until that policy was dropped in 1978. Supporting that policy was a widely accepted (but never canonized) rationale based mainly on popular myths, borrowed from Protestantism, about divine curses on supposed descendants of the biblical figures Cain and Ham. To those myths, imaginative Mormon commentators and early leaders added their own theories about supposed moral failures of certain pre-mortal spirits, which caused those spirits to be born as mortals into the cursed lineage. The founding Mormon prophet Joseph Smith, while generally accepting the common biblical myths about "Negro" origins, did not view those myths as a basis for denying his few black followers access to the priesthood or to the temple. A few

Early baptisms in the Mexican Mission, like this one in 1920, set the stage for explosive growth of the Church in Central and Latin America later in the 20th century. (Courtesy of the Church History Library, The Church of Jesus Christ of Latter-day Saints.)

black men were actually ordained to the priesthood during his lifetime, and he was apparently present in person on at least one of those occasions.

The actual reasons for the traditional Mormon racial policy are not clear from documents contemporaneous with its origin. It seems to have developed gradually after Smith's death, in 1844, but was not officially announced until Brigham Young, Smith's successor, declared it as Church policy in 1852. Since this declaration was made in the opening session of the Utah territorial legislature, which went on to pass legislation permitting slavery in the territory, it seems plausible (though speculative) that Young's purposes were largely political, both *externally* (to facilitate Utah's admission to the Union as a slave state—in accordance with the Compromise of 1850—following California's admission that year as a free state) and *internally* (to permit southern converts to bring their slaves to Utah). Whatever might have been the reasons, each Church president after Young seems to have assumed that the policy had a divine origin and didn't seriously question it until the middle of the 20th century. In fairness, it should be noted that the entire country accepted "Jim Crow" practices during those decades, with few black Americans admitted to medical schools, law schools, or theological seminaries anywhere, so as a practical matter very few black men received priesthood ordinations in any denomination (except, of course, for the predominantly black denominations).

With the emergence of the national civil rights movements of the 1950s and 1960s, the Mormon racial restrictions gained increasing public notice, not only because the other denominations had begun dropping comparable restrictions but also because in the LDS Church the priesthood was usually bestowed upon all lay males, so the black exception was really conspicuous (though the Church had very few black members). The result was a public relations nightmare for the Church, whose leaders nevertheless resisted change under such external pressure, as they sought a divine mandate for change and perhaps also hoped to avoid the appearance of making the change simply for political expediency. When the change finally came, after a divine revelation in 1978, the external political pressure had already eased considerably, but it had been replaced by a growing internal awareness that the Church had recently enjoyed surprising proselyting success among people of color in Latin America, particularly in Brazil, where there were now thousands of new Mormons of mixed race or of African origins who were hoping for the priesthood. Since the policy change in 1978, the Church has continued to convert many black members in the western hemisphere and as many as 200,000 in black Africa itself. Conversion rates among African Americans have been noticeably slower, but for three decades now the Church has sincerely reached out in an effort to reverse its earlier image among black Americans, especially through its family-building programs and its sustained sponsorship of genealogical and family history research.

Important as is the history of Mormon relationships with black people, it cannot be fully understood apart from the larger context of the Mormon racialist heritage more generally. First and foremost is the tradition through which Mormons defined themselves as literal descendants of Ephraim, the Israelite tribe destined to lead the final dispensation of the Christian gospel in preparation for the imminent return of the Messiah Jesus. Though it began in rather simplified form during the life of Joseph Smith, this idea of a chosen, vanguard lineage came to be merged later in the 19th century with the popular European mythologies of British Israelism and Germanic (including Anglo-Saxon) superiority. Such a racialist conception of their origins proved a powerful antidote to the pariah status that had been imposed on the Mormons from the outside, and it contributed to the strong sense of separate ethnicity that sociologist Thomas O'Dea saw in the Mormons even as late as the mid-20th century.

There were at least two other lineages included in the racialist Mormon understanding of the divine plan in world history: the Jews and the aboriginal peoples of the western hemisphere (particularly the "Indians" of North America). As remnants of the Israelite tribe of Judah, the Jews were seen as cousins to the Ephraimite Mormons. Jews were destined to be restored to their ancient Palestine homeland, where they would be converted by the return of the resurrected Messiah to their midst, without benefit of any special proselyting by Mormons. The virtual absence of anti-Semitism among Mormons and Mormons' historic disinclination to proselyte among Jews derive from this construction of Jewish destiny. Finally, the Book of Mormon portrays the American Indians as descendants of both Ephraim and Manasseh and thus as remnant Israelite peoples who had forgotten the God of their ancestors but were destined to be restored to high civilization once again through acceptance of the gospel taught in the Bible and the Book of Mormon. In this belief, 19th-century Mormons baptized hundreds of Indian converts in Utah Territory, few of whom were meaningfully converted and retained. In the mid-20th century, thousands more were enrolled in Mormon churches, schools and colleges, but again not many were retained. In more recent years, the Mormons have turned, with considerably greater success, to proselyting the aboriginal and *mestizo* peoples of Latin America.

The significance once assigned by Mormons to race and lineage has largely disappeared from official Church teaching and discourse, as years of proselyting among the variety of the world's peoples have convinced 21st-century Mormons and their leaders that any and all may become the "children of Abraham" and his God (Gal. 3:7, 29) through acceptance of the gospel.

—*Armand L. Mauss*

See also: Book of Mormon; Mormonism and Blacks; Mormonism and Native Americans; Mormonism and Other Faiths.

References

Braude, Benjamin. *Sex, Slavery, and Racism: The Secret History of Noah and His Sons.* New York: Knopf, 2005.

Bringhurst, Newell G. *Saints, Slaves, and Blacks: The Changing Place of Black People within Mormonism*. Westport, CT: Greenwood, 1981.

Bush, Lester E., Jr., and Armand L. Mauss. *Neither White nor Black: Mormon Scholars Confront the Race Issue in a Universal Church*. Midvale, UT: Signature Books, 1984.

Epperson, Steven. *Mormons and Jews: Early Mormon Theologies of Israel*. Salt Lake City, UT: Signature Books, 1989.

Givens, Terryl L. *By the Hand of Mormon: The American Scripture That Launched a New World Religion*. Oxford, UK: Oxford University Press, 2002.

Goldenberg, David M. *The Curse of Ham: Race and Slavery in Early Judaism, Christianity, and Islam*. Princeton, NJ: Princeton University Press, 2003.

Haynes, Stephen R. *Noah's Curse: The Biblical Justification of American Slavery*. Oxford, UK: Oxford University Press, 2002.

Kidd, Colin. *The Forging of Races: Race and Scripture in the Protestant Atlantic World, 1600–2000*. Cambridge, UK: Cambridge University Press, 2006.

Mauss, Armand L. *All Abraham's Children: Changing Mormon Conceptions of Race and Lineage*. Urbana: University of Illinois Press, 2003.

O'Dea, Thomas F. *The Mormons*. Chicago: University of Chicago Press, 1957.

Mormonism and Science

Mormonism directs the faithful to "seek learning, even by study and also by faith" (Doctrine and Covenants 88:118), and finds no incompatibility between truth that is revealed by God and truth that is discovered by the observation and patient inquiry of thoughtful humanity. Any apparent contradiction between religion and science is due to misunderstanding and the temporary incompleteness of both revelation and human knowledge; ultimately, there will be no conflict.

Mormonism tolerates an element of ambiguity where scientific questions are concerned. For example, latter-day scripture affirms the historical reality of Old Testament figures such as Moses, Noah, and Abraham; some facts of their lives are specifically endorsed by Mormon doctrine, yet individual Mormons may hold various opinions as to other details of Old Testament accounts. Mormonism has no official position on the mechanism by which the Red Sea was parted for the crossing of the Israelites (Exodus 14:21–22) and does not explain the phenomenon described by Joshua as "the sun [standing] still in the midst of heaven" (Joshua 10:12–13), among other scriptural challenges to modern scientific understanding.

Joseph Smith's theology embraced ideas that are usually considered the province of science or that contradict common Christian ideas of scientific issues: "God had materials to organize the world out of chaos. . . . The pure principles of element are principles which never can be destroyed; they may be organized and re-organized, but not destroyed" (Smith, *History* 6:308–309); "Spirit is a substance . . . more pure, elastic and refined matter than the body; . . . it existed before the body, can exist in the body; and will exist separate from the body" (Smith, *History* 4:575); "Kolob [a star] is set nigh unto the throne of God, to govern all those planets which belong to the same order as the [Earth]" (Abraham 3:9); and "Worlds without number have I [God] created" (Moses 1:33). The books of Abraham and Moses—published in the Pearl of Great Price—contain many uniquely Mormon concepts of creation and the organization of the cosmos.

Mormonism claims to embrace all truth, wherever it is found. Mormon scientist Henry Eyring, in his University of Utah classroom, typifies Mormon acceptance of scientific truth. (Courtesy of the Church History Library, The Church of Jesus Christ of Latter-day Saints.)

Related ideas are sometimes mistakenly attributed to Smith. It is claimed by some, for example, that Smith taught that the moon was inhabited by men averaging six feet in height who dressed as Quakers and lived for 1,000 years. This notion cannot be traced to Smith, however. It appeared in the 1881 writings of Oliver B. Huntington (Huntington, "Inhabitants of the Moon" 3:263) as the reminiscence of events nearly 30 years earlier, when Huntington was a child. Despite its frequent citation by critics of Mormonism, this idea is absent from the writings of Smith himself and of his adult contemporaries.

Discussions among Smith and his associates encouraged speculation on scientific subjects and in a few cases provoked serious scientific study among men who, had their lives not been limited by the hardships of the frontier and the needs of a missionary Church, might have been dedicated to scientific study. Apostle Orson Pratt may have been such a man. After the Church was established in Utah, Pratt operated an observatory on the grounds of the Salt Lake temple. The observatory was sponsored by the U.S. Coastal Survey, one of a chain of observatories across the continent; there Pratt took daily solar readings to establish the correct time for the city's clocks. Pratt also kept his three-inch telescope there, scanning the night sky through movable slats in the observatory's roof. The observatory also held the stone shaft marking the intersection of the Salt Lake Base and Meridian, the point established by Pratt from which the Great Basin was surveyed. (A replica stone now stands a short distance away, outside the southeast corner of Temple Square, where it is easily seen by tourists.) In addition to his studies and observations, Pratt taught at the University of Deseret, gave public lectures on scientific topics, and published works on mathematics and cosmology.

Archaeology was another focus for early Mormon scientific interest. Because the Book of Mormon purports to be a literal history of the inhabitants of the New World from ca. 600 BC–421 AD, Mormons have looked to archaeology to demonstrate the historicity of scripture and have tended to interpret archaeological discoveries in the light of scripture. Geographical features in the Palmyra area were tentatively identified with events in the Book of Mormon (the hill where Joseph Smith reported finding the plates from which he translated the Book of Mormon was proposed as the Book of Mormon Cumorah, the site of the great final battle), and, during the 1834 march of Zion's Camp, Smith identified a skeleton unearthed by the expedition as that of Zelph, a Lamanite. The first systematic attempt to identify Book of Mormon settings with archaeological sites was published in 1841 (and excerpted the next year in the Nauvoo newspaper) by Charles Thompson. His *Evidences in Proof of the Book of Mormon* compares artifacts and excavations described by Josiah Priest in his *American Antiquities and Discoveries in the West* (1834) with the Book of Mormon narrative.

Mormon belief in the historicity of the Book of Mormon and the existence of the metal plates from which it was translated has occasionally made Mormonism the target of deliberate hoaxes. The most famous of these occurred in 1843, when six bell-shaped brass plates were presented to Joseph Smith for evaluation. The story told by their owners was that these mysterious engraved plates had been found buried in Kinderhook, Illinois, south of Nauvoo. The Mormon public was greatly interested in the discovery. Although some Mormons claimed that Smith planned to translate the plates (an entry to that effect appears in the diary of Smith's clerk, William Clayton), no translation exists and no definitive evidence has been put forward to show that Smith in fact ever did try to translate the plates, either through prophetic power or through his growing knowledge of ancient languages. The owners of the Kinderhook plates eventually reported their creation of the plates as a deliberate attempt to discredit Smith.

The Church has no official position as to the location of events narrated in the Book of Mormon, other than a general view that the setting was somewhere in the New World. Secondhand accounts attribute to Joseph Smith the claim that Lehi's voyage ended on the coast of Chile (a view accepted and taught by Orson Pratt) or, alternatively, south of the Isthmus of Panama. Neither statement can be conclusively traced to Smith. Church officials have preferred to remain aloof from the discussion, with reminders that "There has never been anything yet set forth that definitely settles that question" (Ivins, *Conference Report* 16).

Such official distancing has not discouraged individuals from attempting to define the geography of the Book of Mormon. Attempts generally take one of two approaches: developing an internal geography based on the relative positions of cities, rivers, and seacoasts mentioned in the narrative or identifying Book of Mormon features with existing features (which, of course, must also take into account the book's internal geography). Proposals have been made to identify the scene of the Book of Mormon as the full continents of North and South America, Central and South America, the Great Lakes region of North America, or other limited geographical regions.

An ambitious project in relation to Book of Mormon archaeology was mounted in 1900. Benjamin Cluff, president of Brigham Young Academy (precursor to Brigham Young University), sought permission from the Church's First Presidency to send a student expedition into Central and South America. The men would study geography, geology, botany, and zoology in an attempt to locate sites and verify the material culture described within the Book of Mormon. Some of the students would remain in South America long enough to learn native languages and record local lore and legend. The First Presidency agreed to the project as a scholarly endeavor sponsored by the school; Cluff, however, recruited his participants and backers by claiming that his was a religious mission call extended by Church authority. The line between the academic and ecclesiastic was further blurred when the participants were blessed by Church apostles and counseled to conduct themselves as missionaries.

On April 17, 15 students, 3 faculty members, and a half dozen volunteers set out on horseback for their trek to South America. The expedition reached Thatcher, Arizona, about six weeks after leaving Provo, having been feted at nine banquets and five dances on the southward trail. There Cluff left his young men with instructions to proselyte as missionaries while he went into Mexico to negotiate with officials for the group's passage through that country. Rather than meeting with Mexican officials, Cluff joined a young woman with whom he had made arrangements to enter a polygamous marriage. Left without supervision and eager to get on with their adventure, the students in Thatcher became restless; when they eventually learned the real reason for their leader's absence, the young men abandoned any pretense of missionary work. Word of the disintegrating expedition reached Church leaders, who advised its discontinuance. Most of the students returned to Provo; a few pushed on to Colombia, where, after one week's stay, all but one returned to the United States. Chester Van Buren, the last member of the expedition, remained in Colombia long enough to collect wildlife specimens for shipment to Provo.

Today, although "Book of Mormon tours" are popular among lay Mormon tourists, few expeditions are undertaken with the specific goal of proving the historicity of the Book of Mormon. Mormon scientists continue to examine artifacts in light of Book of Mormon testimony, and linguistic studies linking literary characteristics of the Book of Mormon with Near Eastern counterparts are especially popular. Many such studies are sponsored by the Neal A. Maxwell Institute for Religious Studies (formerly the Foundation for Ancient Research and Mormon Studies [FARMS]), an organization affiliated with Brigham Young University.

Mormonism did not escape the controversy over organic evolution, the age of the Earth, biblical higher criticism, and related issues that disturbed other Churches in the late 19th and early 20th centuries. These ideas reached the Mormon people slowly, in part because so few Mormons studied at eastern universities until the 1890s. A new emphasis on scholarship was adopted at BYU with the opening years of the 20th century, and professors with advanced degrees were hired, bringing with them ideas that were largely unfamiliar in the intermountain West. A new and livelier approach to modern education swept through the Mormon school: "subjects ranging from communism to eugenics were hotly debated both in and out of class" (Bergera, *Brigham Young University* 135).

As Mormon students, and especially their parents, became aware of the new studies, Church leaders were besieged by inquiries asking whether these scientific theories could be reconciled with scriptural descriptions of creation and the nature of man. The First Presidency requested apostle Orson F. Whitney to draft a statement reflecting the Church's position on these questions. Whitney's draft was reviewed and revised by an apostolic committee, endorsed by the First Presidency and the Quorum of the Twelve Apostles, and published in November 1909. This statement confirmed Mormon belief in both a spiritual and a physical creation, God's organization of Earth, and man's position as the literal offspring of God.

Perhaps because this statement did not address evolution directly, partisan debate within the Church and at BYU continued. By 1911, the question had become so contentious that three BYU professors were fired and Church president Joseph F. Smith issued another statement pleading for Church schools to avoid the theoretical questions of science, explicitly refusing "to say how much of evolution is true, or how much is false" (Evenson, *Mormonism* 49).

In 1930–1931, several Church leaders, notably Joseph Fielding Smith (apostle and the son of the Church president), B. H. Roberts (a Seventy and a philosopher/ historian), and James E. Talmage (apostle, chemist, and geologist) engaged in an extended and often rancorous exchange of views in various Mormon publications, with Smith taking a fundamentalist, anti-evolutionary position and Roberts and Talmage advocating elements of the secular scientific theories. The public argument called forth a memorandum of the First Presidency addressed to all of the Church's general authorities. This memorandum noted the detrimental effect of such disputations on the Church and commanded: "Leave Geology, Biology, Archaeology and Anthropology, no one of which has to do with the salvation of the souls of mankind, to scientific research, while we magnify our calling in the realm of the Church" (Evenson, *Mormonism* 67).

The controversy was renewed briefly in 1954 when Smith, the last survivor of the leaders so prominent in the earlier debates, published *Man, His Origin and Destiny*. This volume ignored the First Presidency's injunction to leave such matters alone; Smith instead declared organic evolution "to be the most pernicious doctrine ever entering the mind of man" and dismissed explanations of the geologic record as "ridiculous" and "rubbish" (Smith, *Man, His Origin and Destiny* 133). When Smith requested that his book be adopted as a textbook for the Church's seminary and institute program, instructors, objecting to Smith's dogmatic positions, took their concerns directly to the First Presidency, which essentially repeated the decision of the earlier leaders: "The Brethren were agreed that inasmuch as this book has not been passed upon by the Church that it should not be used as a study course in the seminaries and institutes. They felt that the matter therein discussed is really not essential to the advancement of the cardinal principles of the Church" (McKay office diary, August 18, 1954).

The question remains today essentially as it has throughout the 20th century: The Church neither condemns nor endorses secular scientific explanations for the development of life and the origin of man, the age of the Earth, and related matters. Since 1992, a packet of materials commonly called the "BYU Evolution Packet," or "Evolution and the Origin of Man," has been distributed to BYU students and is widely available elsewhere. This packet reproduces all of the Church's official statements on these topics and constitutes a handy reference for a debate that continues to flare at irregular intervals.

Less controversial within Mormon history has been the Mormon attitude toward health care. Mormons follow the scriptural injunction to call for the elders to bless the sick; Mormons also make full use of modern medicine. Historically, there was some hesitation to rely on the primitive medical treatments available during the early 19th century; by 1866, as medical and especially surgical care became more reliable, such hesitation all but vanished. Brigham Young encouraged women to study midwifery, and the Relief Society provided training. The Church established and maintained hospitals, including Salt Lake City's LDS Hospital, with its nurses' training facilities, and Primary Children's Hospital, which provides charitable care to children from throughout the world; with the increasing availability of other facilities, the Church sold its hospitals in the 1970s. Mormons accept all treatments generally recognized by the broader culture, including blood transfusions, organ transplants, fertility treatments, birth control, and vaccinations. Some Mormons, placing more than ordinary emphasis on the Word of Wisdom's endorsement of "wholesome herbs" (Doctrine and Covenants 89:10–11), practice various forms of so-called natural medicine, but such practices are not dictated by Church teaching. It is becoming increasingly common for Mormon doctors and dentists to render periodic humanitarian service in remote and needy regions of the world, especially in areas where doctors served previously as missionaries.

As the 21st century opens, the scientific question most debated in relation to Mormonism concerns DNA and the Book of Mormon. Critics have pointed toward recent studies showing a lack of affinity between the DNA of modern Jews and Native Americans, claiming that this disproves the Book of Mormon teaching that an ancient family group left Jerusalem and traveled to the New World. Supporters of the Book of Mormon have countered such claims with their own arguments, attacking the science of their opponents and promoting alternate hypotheses. The debate will no doubt continue for the foreseeable future, generating much heat and little light and swaying few participants from their original positions.

While this essay has focused on scientific topics, it should not be overlooked that Mormonism is fully compatible with applied technology. Mormons value labor and cherish tradition but see no special virtue in shunning technological advancements.

One widely known example of Mormon technology is the odometer (or "road-ometer") built during the 1847 trek across the plains. Charged with recording the mileage of each day's travel, William Clayton wearied of counting the revolutions of a wagon wheel and calculating distance by multiplying the wheel's circumference by the number of revolutions made in each day's travel. Consulting with Orson Pratt to determine precise measurements, Clayton designed a set of cogwheels that recorded the wagon wheel's revolutions mechanically. The device was built from wood by the pioneer company's carpenter and put into use on the morning of May 12, 1847. The odometer was not invented on this occasion, but it is believed that the Mormon odometer was the first used on the Mormon/Oregon Trail.

Other Mormon inventors and innovators include Philo T. Farnsworth, who patented elements of the first electronic television; Jonathan Browning, frontier gunsmith, and his even more innovative son Jonathan Moses Browning, who patented several versions of repeating shotguns and machine guns; H. Tracy Hall, who developed the tetrahedron press and was the first producer of synthetic diamonds; Harvey Fletcher, who invented the electronic hearing aid; and William DeVries, the surgeon who performed the first implantation of an artificial heart into a human patient (Barney Clark, also a Mormon).

A list of Mormon accomplishments in the pure sciences, particularly medicine, physics, chemistry, biochemistry, and nuclear engineering, is beyond the scope of this essay. Studies of the birthplaces of scientists whose biographies appear in *American Men and Women of Science* from 1938 to 1999 purportedly demonstrate that Utah's per capita representation—presumably heavily Mormon—is consistently higher than that of any other state.

While much remains to be received through revelation and learned through investigation, Mormons believe that science and religion will ultimately be fully reconciled. In the words of chemist and apostle John A. Widtsoe, "The religion of the Latter-day Saints is not hostile to any truth, nor to scientific search for truth" (Widtsoe, *Evidences and Reconciliations* 1:129).

—*Ardis E. Parshall*

See also: Book of Mormon; Mormon Scripture; Mormonism and Education; Mormonism and Native Americans; Roberts, B. H.; Smith, Joseph Fielding; Talmage, James E.; Word of Wisdom.

References

Bergera, Gary James, and Ronald Priddis. *Brigham Young University: A House of Faith.* Salt Lake City, UT: Signature Books, 1985.

Doctrine and Covenants of the Church of Jesus Christ of Latter-day Saints. Salt Lake City, UT: The Church of Jesus Christ of Latter-day Saints, 1981.

Evenson, William E., and Duane E. Jeffery. *Mormonism and Evolution: The Authoritative LDS Statements.* Salt Lake City, UT: Greg Kofford Books, 2005.

Huntington, Oliver B. "The Inhabitants of the Moon." *Young Woman's Journal* 3 (March 1892): 263–264.

Ivins, Anthony W. *Conference Report* (April 1929), 16.

McKay, David Oman. David Oman McKay Papers, 1897–1983. Special Collections. J. Willard Marriott Library, University of Utah, Salt Lake City.

Pearl of Great Price. Salt Lake City, UT: The Church of Jesus Christ of Latter-day Saints, 1981.

Smith, Joseph Fielding. *Man, His Origin and Destiny.* Salt Lake City, UT: Deseret Book, 1954.

Smith, Joseph F., John R. Winder, and Anthon H. Lund. "Origin of Man." *Improvement Era* 13, no. 1 (November 1909): 75–81.

Smith, Joseph, Jr. *History of the Church of Jesus Christ of Latter-day Saints,* 2nd ed., rev. 7 vols. Ed. B. H. Roberts. Salt Lake City, UT: Deseret Book, 1973.

Sorenson, John L. *An Ancient American Setting for the Book of Mormon.* Salt Lake City, UT: Deseret Book; Provo, UT: Foundation for Ancient Research and Mormon Studies, 1985.

Widtsoe, John A., *Evidences and Reconciliations.* 3 vols. Salt Lake City, UT: Bookcraft, 1951.

"Words in Season from the First Presidency." *Deseret Evening News,* December 17, 1910, 3.

Mormonism and Secular Government

In the early 1830s, Joseph Smith published a series of revelations commanding Mormons "to gather to Zion" and build up the New Jerusalem to be located in Jackson County, Missouri. These revelations laid the foundation for 19th-century Mormon Church-state relations in two ways. First, by making Zion—a vision of the ideal community to be built in the here and now—a central aspect of the new faith, it gave Mormon theology a necessarily political cast. To be a Mormon was not simply an individual, private affair. It necessarily centered on the creation of a particular kind of community. Second, the theology of Zion and gathering had the practical effect of concentrating the Mormon population in a few key locations. As a result, even though they were always a tiny minority in America as a whole, the Mormons generally wielded significant local political power.

During the 1830s, Mormonism divided geographically between Kirtland, Ohio—headquarters of the Church—and Missouri. Religious animus, fueled by rising Mormon voting power in Jackson County, Missouri, and fiery millenarian rhetoric by Mormon leaders, soon led to a series of violent attacks on Mormon settlements in Missouri. In response, Smith—then based in Ohio—organized "Zion's Camp," a Mormon militia that marched to Jackson County. Ultimately, Zion's Camp proved a military failure, and Smith disbanded it after an abortive confrontation with a Missouri mob. Zion's Camp, however, did reveal the way in which Mormonism's strong communitarian emphasis could blur into political and even military organization.

LDS general authority B. H. Roberts served as chaplain to a largely Mormon battalion in France during World War II, cementing Mormondom's newfound commitment to cooperation with secular government. (Courtesy of the Church History Library, The Church of Jesus Christ of Latter-day Saints.)

The early experience in Ohio and Jackson County also showed the economic implications of Zion. Smith's revelations envisioned an egalitarian economic order based on the redefinition of property rights through a system of consecrations—donations of property to the Church—and stewardships—deeds of property from the Church. In addition to this system of voluntary property redistribution, the Church embarked on publishing and building projects that involved it in extensive economic activity. Such ecclesiastical involvement, however, was not without its social costs. As part of an effort to foster development in Kirtland, Smith and his associates created the Kirtland Safety Society, an unchartered bank that ultimately failed in the Panic of 1837. The resulting acrimony forced Smith to flee to Missouri. There was also frequent litigation by disaffected Mormons exiting the system of consecrations and stewardships.

In 1838, Missouri governor Lilburn Boggs ordered the state militia to expel all Mormons from Missouri or "exterminate" them. A group of Missourians massacred the inhabitants of the small Mormon hamlet of Haun's Mill, and, during the winter of 1838–1839, all of the state's Mormons fled to Illinois.

The Mormon experience in Missouri had an enormous impact on the subsequent development of LDS Church-state relations. After unsuccessfully petitioning the federal government for redress, Mormons became convinced that they could not rely on Washington for protection. They also became convinced that the country harbored powerful elements implacably and violently hostile to Mormonism. The Mormon response was the city of Nauvoo, Illinois. They obtained a city charter from the Illinois legislature that was similar to that of other cities in the state. The Mormons, however, interpreted it to maximize their local autonomy. Smith became mayor and lieutenant general of a state-authorized Mormon militia, the Nauvoo Legion. When officials from Missouri sought to extradite Smith—a move Mormons were convinced would result in his murder—a Nauvoo court released him under an extremely broad reading of the city's charter. In the end, Mormon lawyers would insist that Nauvoo was a virtual city state, bound only by the state constitution and the laws and Constitution of the federal government. Such strong claims of political and legal autonomy were seen by Mormons as their only protection against a hostile world. They made non-Mormons, however, extremely nervous and provided ready ammunition for anti-Mormon polemists. Equally, if not more, disturbing was the Mormon practice of block voting under the formal or informal direction of Church leaders, first for this party and then that, as Smith and others sought to maximize Mormon influence in state politics. To Mormons, such practices were seen as the unity and harmony of Zion in the face of a persecuting world. To outsiders, they looked like un-American priestly meddling.

The Nauvoo period also witnessed a radicalization of Mormon theology that was to have important political implications. Smith began introducing plural marriage to a widening inner circle. He also began teaching in earnest a millenarian vision of the near future in which the governments of the world would fail, to be replaced by a divinely led polity. These theological developments, along with a desire to publicize the plight of the Mormons, led Smith to make a quixotic run for the presidency in the election of 1844. By June of that year, he was dead at the hands of a mob, and two years later the Mormons were entirely driven from Illinois, making their way ultimately to the Great Basin.

Early Utah has often been described as a theocracy, but the term must be used with care to avoid misunderstanding. With the exception of the period of the exodus from Illinois to the Great Basin, when ecclesiastical bodies exercised full civil and criminal jurisdiction, Church and state were not formally integrated. In 1849, the Mormon settlers of "Deseret" petitioned for statehood with a proposed constitution modeled on that of Iowa. The bid was ignored in the furor over the extension of slavery into the territories sparked by the end of the Mexican-American War. Ultimately, Congress created Utah Territory as part of the Compromise of 1850. This provided for a federally appointed governor and judiciary, with a locally elected legislature. Brigham Young, Smith's successor as Mormon leader became the Territory's first governor. As Young's position illustrates, however, despite the absence of any explicitly religious content to Utah's formal government, its "secular" institutions operated within a unique and religiously permeated political culture. Most— although by no means all—locally controlled government offices were held by ecclesiastical leaders. Furthermore, Mormons carried forward the ecclesiastically directed block voting of the Nauvoo period. In practice, this meant that there were few, if any, contested elections and no political party organization.

Mormon relations with the federal government deteriorated during the 1850s. In 1852, the Church began publicly teaching polygamy, and in the election of 1856 the Republican Party burst on to the national scene dedicated—in the words of its founding platform—to the eradication of the "twin relics of barbarism," polygamy and slavery. Of more immediate concern, relations with federally appointed officials broke down entirely. With Mormons in control of both the territorial legislature and the executive, conflict focused on the judiciary. Like many religious groups, Mormons were generally hostile to courts and litigation and were expected to take their lawsuits before Church leaders for resolution. In addition, the Mormon-dominated legislature expanded the jurisdiction of the locally controlled probate courts, in effect creating a parallel, Mormon-staffed territorial judiciary. As a result, federally appointed judges had little to do, which they construed as an attack on their authority. They struck back by denouncing Mormon polygamy as religiously licensed prostitution and wrote hostile letters to Washington. The Mormon legislature retaliated by forcing judges to hold court in remote desert settlements, and ultimately an incensed Mormon mob sacked the office of an outspoken judge, dumping his law books in a local privy. The federal judges fled the territory, reporting to Washington that the Mormons were in a state of open rebellion.

The Buchanan administration responded by sending the U.S. Army. The so-called Utah War of 1857–1858 threatened a military showdown between the Mormons and the United States. Ultimately, however, no pitched battle occurred. Mormon skirmishers delayed the army, forcing it to winter on the high plains of Wyoming. Although several people died in scattered confrontations, the Mormons and the invading federal commander negotiated a settlement. Brigham Young was replaced as territorial governor, and the troops marched through Salt Lake City without incident, taking up residence at a site well beyond the Mormon capital. The conflict did not end, however, before a group of panicked settlers in a remote corner of the territory, acting on the orders of local Mormon military and ecclesiastical leaders, massacred more than 100 men, women, and children of an innocent, California-bound immigrant company. The Utah War and especially the Mountain Meadows Massacre fixed the image of Mormons as lecherous and violent traitors in the American imagination. For their part, the Mormons took the Utah War as a confirmation of the lessons learned in Missouri and Illinois. There were powerful forces bent on the destruction of their community, and, so long as they lacked political and legal autonomy, they were vulnerable to attack.

In 1861, the Union plunged into the Civil War, and "the Mormon Question" was largely forgotten. Lincoln's election, however, began the long ascendancy of the Republican Party, which slowly implemented its pledge to eradicate polygamy. In 1862, Congress criminalized polygamy in the territories, but the law remained a dead letter until the U.S. Supreme Court gave its blessing in the 1879 decision *United States v. Reynolds.* Congress responded with a slew of legislation facilitating the prosecution of polygamists. The result was a period of intense legal attacks in the 1880s that Mormons called "The Raid." In the end, thousands of Mormons were incarcerated, all Mormon women and polygamous Mormon men were disenfranchised, Mormons were entirely excluded from the political process in neighboring Idaho Territory, Church assets were confiscated, much of the economic activity in Mormon country was paralyzed, and, ultimately, Utah was placed under the control of a federally appointed commission modeled on those used in the Reconstruction South.

Beginning with the 1849 discovery of gold in California and accelerating after the Civil War with the coming of the railroad, a small but growing and increasingly influential community of "gentiles"—non-Mormons—planted itself in Utah, attracted mainly by mining. These Americans found the Mormon commonwealth alien and threatening. Polygamy affronted their moral sensibilities, and gentiles found themselves excluded from electoral office. In response, they organized the Liberal Party, which allied itself with local federal appointees and lobbied Washington for harsher legislation against the Mormons. The Latter-day Saints created their own People's Party, which dominated local elections.

The overarching Mormon response to the government crackdown was to seek escape from federal domination through a series of unsuccessful bids for statehood. Their most spectacular failure resulted in the so-called Ghost Government of Deseret. In late 1861, the federally appointed governor vetoed a bill providing for elections as a prelude for petitioning for statehood. The Mormons responded by holding the elections anyway and organizing an independent government for the putative "State of Deseret." The hope was that Congress would recognize statehood as a fait accompli. Washington rejected the ploy, but the "ghost government" continued to function. After each session of the territorial legislature, members would solemnly reconvene as the "Legislature of Deseret," hear a message from "Governor" Young, and then adopt all of the laws just passed by the territorial assembly. Once it became clear even to the die-hard Mormons that this gambit would not succeed, the ghost government was quietly abandoned, in 1870. Other unsuccessful bids for statehood followed. By 1890, Mormon society was at a standstill. The Mormon leadership was either incarcerated or in hiding or had fled beyond federal control to Mormon colonies in Canada and Mexico. The government stood ready to annihilate the Church as a legal entity and a functioning institution, and a last-ditch appeal to the Supreme Court failed. With no avenues of peaceful resistance remaining, Church president Wilford Woodruff issued "The Manifesto," announcing a halt to new plural marriages. This move provided an opening for negotiations with power brokers in Washington that led to statehood for Utah six years later.

The period immediately after the 1890 Manifesto proved a time of complex political transformation. The scope of the Manifesto itself was unclear. Some within the hierarchy regarded it as a smokescreen and continued to perform plural marriages in secret. Others thought that it did not apply to Mormons beyond federal jurisdiction in Canada and Mexico. In addition, there was the thorny question of existing plural marriage. Did the end of polygamy require men to sever relations with wives and children? Answers among Mormons committed to the Manifesto differed. The result was that, in the years after statehood, Mormons were increasingly accused of reneging on their solemn pledge to abandon polygamy.

The continuing influence of the Church in electoral politics also raised controversy. Shortly after the Manifesto, the Church disbanded the People's Party, encouraging members to associate with the two national parties. After decades of GOP

Nineteenth-century hostility between Mormonism and secular government had been largely forgotten by the mid-20th century, when church leaders like David O. McKay became personal friends of secular leaders like Lyndon B. Johnson. (Courtesy of the Church History Library, The Church of Jesus Christ of Latter-day Saints.)

leadership in the antipolygamy crusades, rank-and-file Mormons were overwhelmingly Democrats. As part of the deal for Utah statehood, however, the First Presidency had made pledges to Republican leaders. They thus found themselves in the awkward position of intervening in politics on the side of the Republicans in order to ensure political diversity among Latter-day Saints. The First Presidency's policy also lacked unanimous support among high Church leaders, many of who were partisan Democrats eager to use their standing to advance the fortunes of their party. The First Presidency responded with the so-called Political Manifesto, requiring Church leaders to abstain from partisan activity without Church approval. The policy, however, was not applied evenhandedly, as the First Presidency felt obligated to put a thumb on the scales in favor of the Republicans. The result was a public confrontation between the First Presidency and Democrat Moses Thatcher, a member of the Quorum of the Twelve. The First Presidency dropped Thatcher from the Twelve in response but was widely accused of political double-dealing and meddling.

All of these forces came to a head beginning in 1898, when B. H. Roberts—a Church leader and polygamist—was elected to the U.S. House of Representatives. The result was a national campaign—largely organized through the Protestant churches—to deny Roberts his seat. To admit him to the House, they insisted, would encourage the clandestine practice of polygamy (although Roberts had no involvement in post-Manifesto marriages) and pollute the national councils with an agent of the Mormon hierarchy. It was an ironic charge given that Roberts, an ardent Democrat, had clashed with the First Presidency over the Thatcher case. Ultimately, admitting a polygamist proved too much for Congress, which voted to deny Roberts his seat.

Four years later, a similar outcry greeted Utah's choice of Reed Smoot, an Apostle, as a U.S. senator. Smoot, however, enjoyed advantages Roberts had lacked. Most important, he was a monogamist who had never contracted any plural marriages. He

Reed Smoot

Born in Salt Lake City, in 1862, Reed Smoot grew up in Provo, the son of mayor and Church leader Abraham O. Smoot. He was educated at Brigham Young Academy (now University) and engaged in Utah mining, banking, and railroad endeavors. He became a member of the Church's Quorum of the Twelve Apostles in 1900.

With the backing of Church officials, Smoot was elected as a Republican senator from Utah in 1902. Although Smoot himself was a monogamist, he was immediately challenged on his fitness to hold the position on the grounds of his high rank among a polygamous people. It is probably apocryphal that one senator remarked that he "would rather have a polygamist who didn't polyg than a monogamist who didn't monog." Almost three years of hearings were held before the U.S. Senate seated Smoot.

Smoot served five terms as senator before his reelection defeat in 1932. He is best remembered nationally for his co-sponsorship of the Smoot-Hawley tariff. Less well known is his assistance to international Mormon causes. His political position gave Smoot the power to intervene when American Mormon missionaries were banished from some countries or denied entrance to others.

Smoot died in 1941.

was also a Republican from a Democratic state at a time when the GOP controlled Congress, and he enjoyed the full backing of the First Presidency. The Senate conducted a four-year investigation of Mormon affairs. The old accusations of post-Manifesto polygamy and political meddling were given a full airing, and ultimately Church president Joseph F. Smith appeared for several days of grilling by the senators. They extracted a pledge that the Church had abandoned polygamy and interference in partisan politics. Smith dropped one supporter of post-Manifesto polygamy from the Quorum of the Twelve and excommunicated another. In 1904, the Church issued the so-called Second Manifesto, unequivocally renouncing polygamy, and began aggressively excommunicating any who advocated or performed new plural marriages. Reed Smoot retained his seat and served in the Senate into the 1930s.

In retrospect, the Smoot hearings marked the end of the bitter battles of the 19th century. Thereafter, the Mormons increasingly behaved as an ordinary religious denomination, rather than as a separate nationality or a millennial proto-state. To be sure, the Church took public stands on political issues, but for much of the 20th century these efforts met with mixed success at best. Hence, Church president Heber J. Grant proved unable to keep Utah from voting for FDR or the repeal of Prohibition, despite his opposition to both. Typical of the new era were J. Reuben Clark, a successful international lawyer who served as U.S. ambassador to Mexico in the 1930s, and Ezra Taft Benson, a farm lobbyist who became Eisenhower's Secretary of Agriculture. Both men were high Church leaders—Clark was called into the First Presidency while serving as ambassador, and Benson was already a member of the Quorum of the Twelve when he was appointed—but neither man acted as the agent of a Mormon political policy the way that earlier Church-leaders-cum-politicians had.

The second half of the century marked a further political retrenchment. The direct involvement of a general authority as a candidate for office or a high political appointee became all but unthinkable. Politically prominent Mormons such as George Romney (governor of Michigan), Mitt Romney (governor of Massachusetts), David Kennedy (secretary of the Treasury), Harry Reid (Senate majority leader), or Rex Lee (U.S. solicitor general) participated in politics on the same terms as other citizens, albeit subject to some lingering suspicion about their religion. At the same time, the Church became far more effective on the increasingly limited range of issues where it involved itself. Officially, the modern Church denied any involvement with "politics," insisting that it spoke out only on "moral" issues. In practice, this meant opposition to gambling in western states with large Mormon populations, support for Utah's restrictive liquor laws, and opposition to laws seen as hostile to traditional families, most spectacularly in its organized efforts against the Equal Rights Amendment in the late 1970s and support for various state initiatives against same-sex marriage in the 1990s and in California in 2008.

A final factor in the evolution of Mormon Church-state relations in the 20th century was the massive international expansion of the Church. In the early 1830s, Mormon missionaries began venturing beyond the United States, and, ultimately, tens of thousands of European converts "gathered to Zion" America. The 20th century marked an end of the literal gathering to Zion. The result was a growing population of Latter-day Saints overseas. Concern for these non-American Mormon communities increasingly began to drive institutional attitudes toward politics. This trend can be seen in the muted response of Church leaders to Nazism and World War II, which was motivated in large part by the existence of a relatively large Mormon community in Germany. After World War II, Mormon communities began blossoming under a wide variety of political systems, especially in the developing world. The Church responded by emphasizing a political minimalism based on "good citizenship" and political neutrality, an important message in regions like Latin America with a strong anticlerical tradition or where political suspicion of America runs high. Even so, during the 1980s, Shining Path guerrillas bombed Mormon churches in Peru, and the Sandinista regime in Nicaragua sought to suppress Mormonism, forcing Latter-day Saints to meet in secret in one another's homes. At the close of the century, the Church, despite having more members outside of the United States than within it, struggled internationally to shed its image as a purely American Church or—worse yet—as a subtle tool of American foreign policy.

—*Nathan B. Oman*

See also: Benson, Ezra Taft; Clark, J. Reuben Jr.; Haun's Mill Massacre; Manifesto; Martyrdom of Joseph and Hyrum Smith; Missouri War; Mountain Meadows Massacre; Nauvoo Legion; Polygamy; Smoot Hearings; *United States v. Reynolds*; Utah War; Zion's Camp.

References

Firmage, Edwin Brown, and Richard Collin Mangrum. *Zion in the Courts: A Legal History of the Church of Jesus Christ of Latter-day Saints, 1830–1900.* Urbana: University of Illinois Press, 1988.

Flake, Kathleen. *The Politics of American Religious Identity: The Seating of Senator Reed Smoot, Mormon Apostle.* Chapel Hill: North Carolina University Press, 2004.

Gordon, Sarah Barringer. *The Mormon Question: Polygamy and Constitutional Conflict in Nineteenth Century America.* Chapel Hill: North Carolina University Press, 2002.

Hansen, Klaus J. *The Quest for Empire: The Political Kingdom of God and the Council of Fifty in Mormon History.* East Lansing: Michigan State University Press, 1970.

Lyman, Edward Leo. *Political Deliverance: The Mormon Quest for Utah Statehood.* Urbana: University of Illinois Press, 1986.

Mormonism and the Family

From the beginnings of Mormonism to the 21st century, the family unit has been at the core of the Mormon experience. Mormons believe that the family is the fundamental unit of the LDS Church, as well as of secular society. As the historian Lawrence Foster sees it, "Mormonism is not simply concerned *with* the family; it is *about* the family. The church is conceived as the family writ large, with both the strengths and weaknesses that such an emphasis entails" (Foster, "Between Heaven and Earth" 2). The dramatic transformation over time of what constituted the ideal Mormon family, from monogamy to polygamy and back to monogamy, is a central aspect of the historical Mormon story. Because of the traditional family's centrality, the Church has struggled to create a space equally hospitable to homosexuals and to single people of all varieties.

Mitigating some of these challenges and broader than them all is Joseph Smith's doctrine of the "eternal" nature of families and familial relationships. The worldview that Smith introduced to his followers focused upon family relationships and claimed the biblical power to bind in heaven whatever was bound on Earth. Smith called it the "sealing power," which he promised would weld earthly marriage and family relationships not just for time but for eternity. The highest glory in the afterlife was reserved for couples so sealed. Smith further offered his adherents the possibility to reach beyond the grave when he recovered the biblical practice of proxy baptisms for the dead. This offered living Mormons the opportunity to be vicariously baptized in behalf of deceased ancestors and later to be sealed by proxy to

Mormon families typically gather weekly for Family Home Evening, an hour of formal gospel study and family togetherness. (Courtesy of The Church of Jesus Christ of Latter-day Saints.)

them in one long family chain stretching into the eternities. In its broadest sense, Smith's vision of eternal relationships offered the possibility of universal salvation for the entire human family, past, present, and future, not just for those who happened to be born at the right time and place.

Mormon teachings further replicate familial associations in the relationship between humans and God. Mormons believe that they are the literal spirit children of a Father and Mother in Heaven. As such, they view the entire human family as God's spirit children on an earthly sojourn, learning to make good choices so that they might return to live with their heavenly—and earthly—parents again following mortality. The most common expression of this belief is found in the popular Mormon hymn "O, My Father," written by Eliza R. Snow:

> In the heav'ns are parents single?
> No! the tho't makes reason stare!
> Truth is reason; truth eternal
> Tells me I've a mother there.

Mormons also repeat this relationship at the level of local worship, where they refer to each other as "sister" or "brother," a frequent reminder of their position as siblings in God's broad family.

"O, My Father"

This favorite hymn by Eliza R. Snow expresses Mormon belief in a personal God who is the literal Father of the souls of mankind. In a poetic summary of eternal human progression, its author speaks of premortal life in the presence of God, living by faith in mortality, and the longing to return to God after death. The hymn is especially notable as one of the few expressions of the widely held but little-discussed Mormon belief in a heavenly Mother, a female counterpart to God the Father. Then already widely known, the hymn was sung at the dedication of the Salt Lake temple, in 1893.

I had learned to call thee Father,
Thru thy Spirit from on high,

But, until the key of knowledge
Was restored, I knew not why.
In the heav'ns are parents single?
No, the thought makes reason stare!
Truth is reason; truth eternal
Tells me I've a mother there.
When I leave this frail existence,
When I lay this mortal by,
Father, Mother, may I meet you
In your royal courts on high?
Then, at length, when I've completed
All you sent me forth to do,
With your mutual approbation
Let me come and dwell with you.

Source: George Careless et al., *The Latter-day Saints' Psalmody.* Salt Lake City, UT: Deseret News Co., 1889, 233.

With all of the emphasis on the family unit in Mormonism, it is somewhat ironic that in the 19th century Joseph Smith introduced one of America's most radical departures from prevailing Protestant family norms and thereby ensured that the Mormon Church would endure considerable scorn at the hands of the Protestant majority. Historians have attempted to explain Smith's introduction of polygamy in a variety of ways, from insatiable sexual desire to a search for lost patriarchy and from an attempt to create social cohesion to the restitution of biblical polygamy. The historian Richard Lyman Bushman, however, places Smith's introduction of polygamy within the larger context of Jacksonian America and the attendant upheaval that death, westward migration, and market forces wrought upon family ties. As Bushman sees it, Smith "had a passion for family. He did not lust for wives so much as for kin." In that regard, the introduction of priesthood sealings, even into plurality, "were a theological solution to a social problem: how to bind families together in a mobile society" (Bushman, "The Inner Joseph Smith" 77, 80).

Even though polygamy was preached as the ideal familial organization in 19th-century Mormonism, the majority of Mormons lived in monogamous relationships. After officially abandoning polygamy in 1890 and then slowly transitioning away from it in the late 19th and early 20th centuries, Mormons began to champion the monogamous nuclear family as their ideal.

Throughout this transition, Mormons maintained positive attitudes toward sex as long as it was expressed within the marriage relationship. In response to the charge outsiders made against polygamy—that it was an excuse for men to satisfy the lusts of the flesh—some Mormon leaders stressed that sexual relationships were for procreative purposes, while others suggested that sex also strengthened the bonds of marriage. Also, in response to the broader Victorian-era ideal of sexual continence during pregnancy and lactation, Mormons argued that polygamy offered an outlet for male sexual expression within marriage, especially if one wife was pregnant or nursing. Even so, Mormons rejected the notion of original sin and the idea that sexuality was a result of sin. Joseph Smith taught that all spirit is matter and, by extension, eliminated the belief that sex was a "corruption of the flesh against the sublimity of the spirit" (Hansen, "Changing Perspectives" 35). As 20th-century Mormons asserted a monogamist ideal, some leaders continued to link sex only to procreation, while others tended to focus upon the negative consequences of premarital and extramarital sex to the exclusion of positive messages about marital sex. More recent sermons address this oversight and focus upon physical intimacy as a beautiful way of expressing love, loyalty, unity, and joy within the bonds of marriage.

Mormon views about contraception have also changed over time. In the 19th century, polygamy was seen as a means of raising a righteous posterity to the Lord and of providing earthly bodies for the spirit children of God awaiting their earthly sojourn, a process that artificially preventing conception would only hinder. That view persisted for monogamy in the 20th century, prompting some leaders to condemn birth control as unnatural. A 1969 First Presidency statement, however, was more moderate in its expression of regret that some Mormons were taking steps to curtail the birth of children, but it still advised couples to take the health of the mother into account and to seek inspiration. In 1995, the First Presidency and the Quorum of the Twelve Apostles reaffirmed the Church's longstanding view that "God's commandment for His children to multiply and replenish the earth remains in force" (The First Presidency, "The Family" 102). Even so, 21st-century guidance centers upon a concern for the physical and emotional health of the mother and recommends that matters of family planning be worked out between married couples and the Lord, thereby placing "individual decisions above ecclesiastical review" (Bush, "Ethical Issues" 189). Not surprisingly, Mormons tend to have higher fertility rates than the broader American population, and more religious Mormons generally have larger families than their less religiously committed counterparts.

The LDS Church honors the sanctity of life and therefore considers abortion a serious matter. It opposes elective abortions for personal or social convenience but allows for it in the cases of rape or incest or when the life and health of the mother or fetus might be in jeopardy. Even so, it cautions individuals in those circumstances to consult their ecclesiastical leaders and to seek confirmation of their decision through prayer.

Single adults (whether never married, widowed, or divorced) and homosexuals can experience feelings of guilt, loneliness, and seclusion in a Church that so thoroughly extols the family. Historically, single men have been held responsible for not taking the initiative to marry, while single women, although encouraged to marry, have been promised that opportunity in the eternities if they remain faithful yet single in mortality. A 1981 survey concluded that about one-third of North American Mormon adults had never married or were widowed, divorced, or separated. Beginning in the 1970s, the Church attempted to reach out more directly to this segment of the Mormon population, forming congregations for single young adults, those ages 18–30, and single adult groups for those over age 31. Socials, service projects, Family Home Evening groups, and a variety of other activities have been organized in local units throughout the Church in an attempt to embrace single adults within the broader concept of the ward family.

Mormon leaders perceive divorce as a serious threat to the sanctity of the family and disapprove of it as a too-common solution to marriage difficulties. The Church nonetheless allows divorce and annulment for civil marriages and the cancellation of sealings in the case of temple marriages. In the 19th century, perhaps in response to charges that Mormon women were held captive against their will in polygamous marriages, women were liberally granted divorces, although Brigham Young was less sympathetic to men who sought to end their marriages. In the contemporary Church, the Mormon ideal of a two-parent family can lead to feelings of shame, isolation, and/or lack of belonging among divorced Mormons even as the Church attempts to be cognizant of their needs.

Homosexual behavior has always been condemned by the Church, although there has been change over time concerning the perceived causes of homosexuality. In the 19th century, Mormon leaders were somewhat ambivalent about homosocial relationships but released people from Church callings or otherwise ecclesiastically disciplined those who were charged with homosexual behavior. The Church become more vocal over homosexuality as the American gay rights movement gained attention in the 1960s and 1970s. In 1969, Spencer W. Kimball, then a Mormon apostle, argued that masturbation caused homosexuality and suggested that it was a condition that could be overcome. LDS therapists advocated heterosexual marriage as a cure.

In the late 20th and 21st centuries, the LDS Church has perceived attempts to legalize same-sex marriage as a threat to the traditional family and has actively opposed them in a variety of U.S. states. In 2006, it also announced support for an amendment to the U.S. Constitution that would in essence affirm the Church's view that only "marriage between a man and a woman is ordained of God" (The First Presidency, "The Family" 102). Church president Gordon B. Hinckley, in 1999, articulated the Church's position in this regard when he said that defending the "sacred institution" of marriage between a man and woman was "clearly within our [the LDS Church's] constitutional prerogatives. Indeed, we are compelled by our doctrine to speak out." He went on, however, to warn Mormons against using the Church's stance against same-sex marriage as justification for "hatred, intolerance, or abuse of those who profess homosexual tendencies." He then said that "our hearts reach out to those who refer to themselves as gays and lesbians. We love and honor them as sons and daughters of God. They are welcome in the Church. It is expected, however, that they follow the same God-given rules of conduct that apply to everyone else, whether single or married" (Hinckley, "Why We Do" 54).

Hinckley's statement characterized the Church's stance toward homosexuality at the beginning of the 21st century. It no longer took a position as to the causes of homosexuality—that is, whether it was a function of nurture or of nature—nor did it advocate heterosexual marriage as a cure. Instead, it drew a distinction between feelings and actions, condemning only homosexual behavior. The response from homosexual Mormons has varied across a wide spectrum, with some choosing to place their faith above their sexuality and live in celibacy. Others attempt opposite-sex marriage, fully disclosing themselves to their spouses, while still others leave the Church and opt for a homosexual lifestyle. Some continue to live conflicted lives as they struggle to reconcile their faith and their sexuality.

Even as the Church attempts to address the concerns of its members who fall outside notions of a traditional family, it continues to emphasize the nuclear family as the ideal. In 1915, it launched a program that came to be called Family Home Evening, through which Monday nights were set aside for Mormons to gather in their families, to sing, pray, learn gospel principles, counsel together, play games, or otherwise enjoy one another's company and strengthen family bonds. Over time, the Church issued various manuals and materials to help support and enhance these family nights.

In response to the perceived erosion of the family unit in the Church and in society, in 1995 the First Presidency and the Quorum of the Twelve Apostles issued "The Family: A Proclamation to the World," a document that reaffirmed that "the family is ordained of God" and that it "is central to the Creator's plan for the eternal destiny of His children." The Proclamation declared that "all human beings—male and female—are created in the image of God" and that "gender is an essential characteristic of individual premortal, mortal, and eternal identity and purpose." It articulated the "solemn responsibility" parents have to love and care for their children and warned that they "will be held accountable before God for the discharge of these obligations." It stated that fathers were to "preside over their families in love and righteousness" and that they were responsible for providing for the temporal well-being of their families. Mothers were "responsible for the nurture of their children," but the statement stipulated that, in performing these duties, mothers and fathers were to "help one another as equal partners." It ended with a warning "that the disintegration of the family will bring upon individuals, communities, and nations the calamities foretold by ancient and modern prophets" (The First Presidency, The Family 102).

The proclamation thus reemphasized the family unit as the core of the Mormon experience even as the Church continued its efforts to be as inclusive as its familial doctrine would allow for those who fell outside that ideal.

—*W. Paul Reeve*

See also: Mormonism and Men; Mormonism and Women; Polygamy; Temple Work by Proxy.

References

Bush, Lester E. "Ethical Issues in Reproductive Medicine: A Mormon Perspective." In *Multiply and Replenish: Mormon Essays on Sex and Family.* Ed. Brent Corcoran, 183–216. Salt Lake City, UT: Signature Books, 1994.

Bushman, Richard L. "The Inner Joseph Smith." *Journal of Mormon History* 32 (Spring 2006): 65–81.

Foster, Lawrence. "Between Heaven and Earth: Mormon Theology of the Family in Comparative Perspective." In *Multiply and Replenish: Mormon Essays on Sex and Family.* Ed. Brent Corcoran, 1–18. Salt Lake City, UT: Signature Books, 1994.

Hansen, Klaus J. "Changing Perspectives on Sexuality and Marriage." In *Multiply and Replenish: Mormon Essays on Sex and Family.* Ed. Brent Corcoran, 19–46. Salt Lake City, UT: Signature Books, 1994.

Hinckley, Gordon B. "Why We Do Some of the Things We Do." *Ensign* 29 (November 1999): 52–54.

O'Donovan, Rocky. "'The Abominable and Detestable Crime against Nature': A Brief History of Homosexuality and Mormonism, 1840–1980." In *Multiply and Replenish: Mormon Essays on Sex and Family.* Ed. Brent Corcoran, 123–170. Salt Lake City, UT: Signature Books, 1994.

The First Presidency and the Quorum of the Twelve Apostles of The Church of Jesus Christ of Latter-day Saints. "The Family: A Proclamation to the World." *Ensign* 25 (November 1995): 102.

Mormonism and Violence

The study of violence by and against Mormons focuses on the founding generation of Mormons and their sojourn in frontier environments during the mid-19th century. During the antebellum period, the first Mormons made a gradual westerly migration to Ohio and Missouri in the 1830s, then to Illinois and Utah Territory in the 1840s. Thus, early Mormonism developed in and was influenced by the American frontier, where governance and social control were imperfectly formed and resort to extralegal violence was common. It is not surprising, then, that extralegal violence occurred during the Mormons' residence in frontier regions of 19th-century America. On some occasions, Mormons were victims of frontier violence, while on others Mormons resorted to violence themselves.

Violence toward Mormons

In the rural and frontier locales where Mormonism developed, there was a string of violent acts directed against Mormons. Beginning in 1832, Mormon leaders were tarred and feathered in Ohio. In 1833, a separate community of Mormons in western Missouri was forcibly expelled and driven to an adjoining county. In 1835, the same community of Mormons was encouraged to remove itself to northwestern Missouri. Meanwhile, in 1837 many in the Mormon community in Ohio felt compelled to withdraw from the area (although internal dissension among Mormons themselves was a significant factor in their withdrawal). Back in frontier Missouri, the "Mormon Wars" erupted in 1838 in northwestern Missouri, leading to the expulsion of the Mormon community from that region over the winter of 1838–1839. The Mormons relocated to western Illinois, but, in 1844, the Mormon founder, Joseph Smith, was assassinated. In 1845–1846, another "Mormon War" resulted in the expulsion of more than 10,000 Mormons from their main gathering place in western Illinois.

There were various sources of antagonism between the original settlers in Missouri and Illinois and their Mormon neighbors. One was the profound differences in their respective religious views, while another, at least in Missouri, was Mormon opposition to slavery, a view contrary to that of many of their Missouri neighbors. But the political dimension was also significant. American acceptance of the principle of majority rule at all levels of government makes the long-term exercise of political power dependent upon maintenance of consistent political majorities. Loss of majority control effectively means diminished political power. There is evidence that the original settlers' distaste for the Mormon newcomers changed to overt action when the increasing Mormon population threatened to win political control. Perhaps unknowingly, the rapid ingathering of Mormons in concentrated numbers inevitably led to conflict with their neighbors.

Although the use of violence against Mormons in antebellum America was deplorable, it was nevertheless consistent with widely accepted values of rural and frontier America. These included a long tradition of expelling religious outsiders; the folk understanding of popular sovereignty as justifying extralegal violence; and the use of such extralegal violence to expel groups that were perceived as undesirable.

The Mormons Resort to Violence

Arising in 1830 in an American context and sharing many American attitudes and values, Mormonism, it is hardly surprising to note, responded to attacks by using violence. Yet the Mormons contributed to their own unpopularity. In western Missouri, Mormons' talk of their status as God's "chosen people," coupled with speculation among some Mormons that God intended to give the lands of their neighbors to them, exacerbated tensions. By 1838, new conflicts led Missouri governor Lilburn Boggs to order that the Mormons be driven from the state or exterminated. Yet, the first to use "extermination" rhetoric was Mormon leader Sidney Rigdon, who, on the eve of a local election, said that if local settlers continued persecuting the Mormons, there would be a "war of extermination" between them.

In 1838, as events spiraled toward civil war in western Missouri, a vigilante group known as the "Danites" made its first appearance among the Mormons. The extent to which Mormon leaders Smith and Rigdon sanctioned the Danite organization is controversial. The most reliable evidence suggests that they initially endorsed it but later withdrew support. This is the only time in which the presence of "Danites" is confirmed, and the organization did not officially exist thereafter. But that did not keep the specter of Danites (the infamous "avenging angels of Mormonism" in pulp fiction) from appearing later in Illinois and frontier Utah, especially when there were cases of extralegal violence.

Unique Mormon Attitudes Contributing to Violence

The first Mormons unquestioningly accepted the prevailing American view of the inalienable rights of men. In common with other Americans, they had a low tolerance for perceived "usurpations" and insisted on vindicating their rights. Similarly, they implicitly accepted the prevailing attitudes of the "culture of honor" that surrounded them. Joseph Smith's tacit acceptance of the values of the culture of honor, his impatience with criticism, and his occasional resort to blows in defense of his personal honor show his unconscious acceptance of these American presuppositions.

However, Smith also developed a unique theological justification for the use of capital punishment. His view of the atonement of Jesus Christ as covering all sins except murder led him to believe that, in order for murderers to receive redemption, they had to atone for their crime with their own lives. This was understood to mean that the murderer's own blood had to be shed. In antebellum America, the two most common forms of capital punishment were execution by hanging or firing squad. Smith favored the latter.

Some of Smith's followers later elaborated on his ideas. In the 1850s, the Mormon bid for statehood and other factors led Brigham Young, as governor of Utah Territory and prophet-president of the Church, to preach "blood atonement" sermons. Young anticipated that Mormon-controlled Utah would be admitted to statehood and that the Mormon polity could then exercise greater control over its own destiny, including capital punishment. Anticipating that the Church would control the civil government, Young advanced his justification for a particular form of capital punishment that included the shedding of blood. Yet Young also used blood atonement discourses as a method of social control. Outsiders viewed Young as a powerful autocrat, but, with his followers scattered across the Great Basin, his effective power was limited. Partly, then, Young's blood atonement speeches served as *ad terrorem* warnings to wayward followers, intended to maintain social control by frightening them into submission.

Of course, Mormonism was not unique in offering a justification for capital punishment. Rather, its uniqueness lay in prescribing particular methods of execution that were understood to conform to the divine will. There is evidence that some saw a deterrent effect in these forms of execution, but, like most Americans, Mormons generally understood capital punishment as retributive.

Mormon Violence against Native Americans

After the Mormons arrived in the Great Basin, in 1847, the first resort to violence was in conflicts with local Native Americans. Here the Mormons acted much like their American neighbors in other states and territories. During 1850–1851, bloody skirmishes ensued, leaving several whites and dozens of Indians dead. Some Mormons committed atrocities against the Utes in this conflict. The same was true of the 1853–1854 Walker War and the Black Hawk War of 1865–1872, although in these latter conflicts Brigham Young adopted a defensive strategy and announced a more humane Indian policy: it was cheaper to feed the Indians than to fight them. Even so, there were atrocities, the Circleville Massacre during the Black Hawk War, in which Mormons killed at least 16 Paiute Indians, including women and children, being the most aggravated case.

Although these conflicts with Native Americans were regrettable and the atrocities deplorable, they do not appear to have resulted from any uniquely Mormon values or attitudes. In their outlook toward the Indians during these conflicts, the Mormons mirrored the attitudes of other Euro-Americans of the time.

"Frontier Justice": Extralegal Violence Aimed at Undesirables or Apostates

To the average person in rural or frontier America, popular sovereignty was simply the notion that all political power resided in the people. If the people's representatives could make law, it was but a small step to the idea that the people could act directly. If the people could legislate, it seemed to follow that the people could also execute the law, interpret the law, and use the law to pass judgment on others. Thus, vigilante violence was characterized by concentrated powers in which regulators or vigilantes assumed the roles of constable, prosecutor, judge, jury, jailer, and, occasionally, executioner. Just how easily many in the young republic could justify extralegal violence reveals the dark underbelly of American notions of democracy and popular sovereignty. Given the prevailing assumptions, violence was surprisingly easy to justify.

John D. Lee, the sole participant at Mountain Meadows to be convicted of the massacre—although far from the only perpetrator—was taken back to the site of the massacre and executed there on March 28, 1877. (Courtesy of the Church History Library, The Church of Jesus Christ of Latter-day Saints.)

Another factor was that, when lawlessness occurred, existing law enforcement institutions were frequently inadequate. Thus, to defend the existing order from attack, otherwise honorable, law-abiding citizens felt compelled to impose "retaliatory justice" through vigilantism. In arguing that the basic law of nature was survival, vigilante leaders insisted that, in life-or-death struggles, the right to self-preservation took precedence over due process of law. During times of crisis, vigilantes came to believe that the antidote to the inadequacies of their courts was the simple, direct, swift, certain, and severe punishments of vigilantism. Thus, in the showdown between suppressing disruptive behavior and observing due process of law, due process often lost.

After the crisis had passed, citizens, including some of the vigilantes themselves, frequently regretted that their regularly constituted institutions were inadequate to prevent lawlessness. But, in times of danger, an urgent sense of necessity and notions of popular sovereignty easily justified the actions of regulators and vigilantes. Quite naturally, then, in times of perceived crisis, some Mormons from the same American milieu resorted to the speed and certainty of extralegal punishment.

What was the extent of Mormon extralegal violence? Discounting polemical sources, there were a small but not insignificant number of murders or maimings that can reasonably be ascribed to the Mormons' resort to vigilantism. While all of them cannot be covered here, the following is a brief description of some of the more notable episodes, many of which were clustered around the tense years of 1857–1858.

In early 1857, unknown assailants ambushed John Tobin and his party in southern Utah. The clear evidence is that Brigham Young directed southern Utah authorities to "pursue, retake & punish" two suspected horse thieves who were then traveling through the region. Pursuant to Young's instructions, southern Utah officials evidently directed subordinates to make the attack. However, the Tobin party was mistaken for the horse thieves; Tobin received a disfiguring wound to his face, and two companions were also injured. It is noteworthy that this apparent case of extralegal violence was aimed at suspected horse thieves, frequent targets of vigilante action in the West.

The next episode, the Parrish-Potter murders in Springville, is illustrative of violence directed toward those who were perceived as undesirables or apostates. In March 1857, when Warren Parrish and two of his sons tried to leave the Mormon village of Springville under cover of night, he and one of his sons were ambushed and killed along with their guide, "Duff" Potter. Two years later, federal judge John Cradlebaugh began legal proceedings against five men, including prominent Church leaders in Springville, but lack of adequate troop protection caused Cradlebaugh to curtail the investigation.

The 1857 massacre at Mountain Meadows was the bloodiest atrocity in the Mormon past, resulting in the death of approximately 120 emigrants, most of whom were women and children. Only 17 small children survived.

Since then, some have argued that the primary impulse behind the massacre was a religiously motivated desire for revenge. But Juanita Brooks's approach was more nuanced. Citing religious, political, and economic factors, she argued that the massacre could only have happened in the emotional environment of war. More recently, the ongoing investigation of American violence is beginning to influence studies of the massacre. In common with some other mass killings, the massacre occurred in a war environment in which southern Utah settlers feared an army invasion. They also felt provoked by the passing Arkansas company and came to view it as a surrogate for the army. Thus, in an atmosphere of rising fears created by the threat of war, fear of invasion and war hysteria, the threat posed by the passing emigrants was misperceived, exaggerated, and over-reported. Local settlers demonized the emigrants and their escalating fears led to an overreaction out of all proportion to the threat. Viewed in this light, the massacre has commonalities with other mass killings resulting from ethnic or religious conflict while the pattern of misperception, exaggeration, over-reporting, and overreaction has much in common with other moral panics.

The war environment of 1857–1858 also contributed directly to the murder of mountaineer Richard Yates. Mormon militiamen captured Yates to obtain his ammunition and powder. Finding that he had already traded it to the army, his Mormon captors viewed him as having "sold out to the Government." Bill Hickman bludgeoned Yates to death while in Hickman's custody.

Shortly after that, five members of the Aiken party were murdered. There is evidence that the Aiken party, traveling through Utah to meet the approaching army, were suspected of spying. Orrin Porter Rockwell and others are accused of killing four party members near Nephi. Bill Hickman confessed to killing a fifth member who was traveling separately near Bountiful some time later. As in the Mountain Meadows Massacre and the Yates killing, the victims were thought to be in league with the oncoming hostile army.

Hickman later confessed to killing Yates and said he had acted on orders of Brigham Young. Young's role in Yates's death is controversial. While some accept Hickman's charges, others see Young's role as more indirect: Young's war policy of forcibly halting the approaching army, combined with his fiery rhetoric and unclear communications to subordinates, contributed to an atmosphere in which atrocities were likely to occur.

The Morrisite conflict of 1862 was another controversial episode. Joseph Morris and several followers were killed near South Weber during a confrontation with a posse intent on arresting them.

Other violent episodes during this period were characterized by an apparently inconsistent application of criminal penalties. In some cases, harsh punishments were applied extralegally. In one example, Warren Snow, the bishop of Manti, castrated a young man, leaving him on a winter night nearly dead. In some of these cases, the offenders received light punishment or none at all, creating an impression that they acted with impunity. Such incidents created an image of lawlessness that was to dog the Mormons into the 21st century.

As more stable forms of governance and social control grew in Utah Territory, the occasional resort to extralegal violence declined, just as it did in other areas of the nation as the frontier retreated. Although the antipolygamy campaign of the 1870s and 1880s brought the Mormon Church to the brink of collapse, Mormons chose to fight their opponents in the courts. They lost most of these legal battles but eventually chose to accept the judgment of the American judiciary. In a process designated the "Americanization" of Utah, the Mormon Church began accepting American political, economic, and judicial institutions. Of course, crime still existed in Utah (as elsewhere), but, with the closing chapter of the frontier era, the period in which some Mormon officials resorted to a rough frontier justice was over.

One mistaken view has been to treat violence among Mormons as sui generis and to argue that all expressions of violence in the frontier period had a uniquely Mormon character. But, given the evidence that Mormons unconsciously absorbed and expressed many political and cultural attitudes of 19th-century America, such simplistic arguments have to be reexamined. While some scholars point to distinctive Mormon discourses about violence as evidence of unique Mormon attitudes and practices, the peculiarities cannot mask the underlying similarities between Mormons and other 19th-century Americans. Given Mormonism's frontier trajectory, Mormons' move into a region where extralegal violence was especially appealing and where violence was used against them in Missouri and Illinois, it is not surprising that in their early years in the West, they occasionally heeded the siren call of vigilantism.

Michael Quinn and others have argued that Mormonism created a "culture of violence" on the Utah frontier. But there were many cultures within the incipient Mormonism of the frontier era. Early visitors to Utah noted the presence of more than 15 ethnicities among the Mormons. Mormons were drawn from the United States, Canada, northwestern Europe, southern Africa, Asia, and Australia. The presence of these distinctive and unassimilated cultures complicates any attempt to make generalizations about an exclusively Mormon strain of violence. As Quinn concluded, "Mormon theocracy created such a unique context for Utah violence that it will always be impossible to determine how many violent deaths occurred for theocratic reasons and how many merely reflected the American West's pattern of violence" (Quinn, *Mormon Hierarchy* 260).

—*Robert H. Briggs*

See also: Black Hawk War; Haun's Mill Massacre; Martyrdom of Joseph and Hyrum Smith; Missouri War; Mormonism and Native Americans; Mountain Meadows Massacre; Reformation; Utah War.

References

Aird, Polly. "'You Nasty Apostates, Clear Out': Reasons for Disaffection in the Late 1850s." *Journal of Mormon History* 30 (Fall 2004): 129–207.

Bigler, David. *Forgotten Kingdom: The Mormon Theocracy in the American West, 1847–1896.* Spokane, WA: Arthur H. Clark, 1998.

Cannon, Kenneth L., II. "'Mountain Common Law': The Extralegal Punishment of Seducers in Early Utah." *Utah Historical Quarterly* 51 (Fall 1983): 308–327.

Hilton, Hope A. *"Wild Bill" Hickman and the Mormon Frontier.* Salt Lake City, UT: Signature Books, 1988.

MacKinnon, William P. *At Sword's Point: A Documentary History of the Utah War to 1858.* 2 vols. Norman: University of Oklahoma Press, 2008.

Parshall, Ardis E. "'Pursue, Retake & Punish': The 1857 Santa Clara Ambush." *Utah Historical Quarterly* 73 (Winter 2005): 64–86.

Quinn, D. Michael. *The Mormon Hierarchy: Extensions of Power.* Salt Lake City, UT: Signature Books, 1997.

Mormonism and Women

In October 2007, General Relief Society president Julie B. Beck gave a general conference talk that reemphasized Mormon women's primary roles as wives and mothers, equated women's nurturing responsibilities with homemaking, and discouraged women from outside activities that might distract them from their primary familial roles. The positive and negative responses that followed Beck's talk on blogs, Web sites, and newspaper editorials highlighted a recurring dilemma for Mormon women. To what extent should Mormon women focus on motherhood to the exclusion of other activities? Or, to what extent should Mormon women expand their activities into the public and professional sphere, as contributors to their communities?

Beck's talk highlighted this ongoing debate regarding the place of Mormon women; indeed, the history of Mormon women might be understood as a negotiation between the primary emphasis on motherhood and the secondary emphasis on nontraditional roles in politics, professions, education, and public reform. At times, these dual roles for women have been fairly well integrated; at other times, they have been seen as contradictory and mutually exclusive. Within this opposing ideological pull, Mormon women have also experienced conflicting definitions about their own identity. On the one hand, a woman's importance in the Church is often interpreted as a one-size-fits-all role or by her relationship to someone else—usually as a supporter or helper to male authority, or as a wife, potential wife, mother, or potential mother, with strict cultural expectations related to her duties in the home. On the other hand, Mormon women have sometimes experienced recognition for their individuality as women who can make unique educational, political, professional, and cultural contributions to their commu-

nities. The history of Mormon women from 1830 forward has shown how women have tried to negotiate these contradictory emphases between traditional and nontraditional pursuits. At times, Mormon women's activities have departed entirely from feminist ideologies, and, at other times, they have aligned closely with feminist goals.

Mormon women have played an integral role in Mormonism since its founding, in 1830. Women converts were drawn to the early Church because of its promise to restore the doctrines and practices of ancient Christianity. Early women converts and members of Joseph Smith's immediate family participated in important activities related to the Church's restoration. From Lucy Mack Smith's support of her young son's revelations to Emma Hale Smith's assistance in the translation

Nineteenth-century Mormon women built halls like this one in Salt Lake City's 14th ward to conduct their welfare work and to hold spiritual gatherings. (Courtesy of The Church of Jesus Christ of Latter-day Saints.)

of the Book of Mormon, women's significant contributions to early Church history are important and undisputed.

The Prophet Joseph Smith encouraged both sexes to exercise spiritual gifts such as speaking in tongues, translation of tongues, and healing by the laying on of hands. Many early women converts felt great empowerment in the exercising and expression of these gifts. From the 1830s through the 1910s, Mormon women actively participated in the blessing of the sick but honored official warnings to not administer using priesthood authority. Instead, women were encouraged to administer by faith only to women and children, and sometimes men, in times of sickness and childbirth. By the early 20th century, the Church began to discourage women from participating in blessings by the laying on of hands, suggesting that these should be performed by male Melchizedek Priesthood holders only. Gradually, this activity declined among women, either through official Church directives or as the women's social sphere of healing died off to a new generation that was unfamiliar and unpracticed in those traditions. In 1946, Elder Joseph Fielding Smith officially outlined the Church policy restricting women from participating in any healing ceremonies, even for expectant mothers. In the 21st century, washing and anointing by women for women is performed only in temples. For Mormon women's equal participation in these healing rites, many historians view the period between 1830 and 1921 as a period of great gendered progress that eventually came to an end. Historians argue that, as priesthood roles became more strictly defined in the early 20th century, women's spiritual and religious roles increasingly eroded.

As the Church grew in its early years, women converts offered many contributions to the Church's success, including seamstress work, cooking, child rearing, and philanthropy. In Nauvoo, these activities continued through women's penny fund-raising, sewing shirts, and providing meals for temple workers. Joseph Smith showed progressive acceptance of women's higher education through the establishment of coeducational institutions in Kirtland and Nauvoo. Even the School of the Prophets, in Kirtland, accepted women, including Sarah Granger Kimball, a later suffragist and one of the originators of the female Relief Society in Nauvoo. The Prophet's acceptance of women's participation in the sacred endowment was also progressive, especially considering women's traditional exclusion from temple rites during biblical times. Members were also introduced to the new doctrine of a Mother in Heaven in 1845, when Eliza R. Snow published her famous verse "O My Father" in the Nauvoo *Times and Seasons*. The idea of a feminine equivalent to God reflected the Church's beliefs in eternal marriage and perpetuation of families. But it also appealed to women as an empowering notion of women's heavenly equality, usually evoked to raise the political, legal, and religious status of women. The idea of a Heavenly Mother later declined in Mormon doctrinal discussions in the 20th century. Controversies in the 1990s over some women praying to Heavenly Mother resulted in the firing of two Brigham Young University faculty members who had publicly advocated that practice in their classes. While Church leaders have warned members about speculation regarding a wife or wives of Heavenly Father, some have considered this discouragement as a reaction against the use of Heavenly Mother as a doctrinal symbol of women's empowerment.

The Mormon women's motto "Charity Never Faileth" finds expression in countless novel ways, including the hand-production of specialized leper bandages for patients in third-world countries. (Courtesy of The Church of Jesus Christ of Latter-day Saints.)

Early Mormon women's activities corresponded with women's evangelical revivalism of the Second Great Awakening. Mormon women, like their counterparts, not only experienced personal conversions but also turned their renewed Christian sensibilities toward reform activities like temperance activism, the abolition movement, and charitable relief for the poor. Indeed, when the Relief Society was organized in Nauvoo, Illinois, on March 17, 1842, it mirrored other organizations of its same type throughout New England and the Midwest that were connected to women's reform idealism and community charitable work.

Some social-religious movements of the 1840s also introduced nonconformist sexual and marital practices that greatly affected women. Although Joseph Smith secretly introduced the plurality of wives to the highest circles of Church leadership during the Nauvoo period (1839–1846), it was not until 1852 that Orson Pratt publicly announced the official practice of polygamy to the membership in Salt Lake City. From 1852 until 1890, polygamous practice defined Mormon women's lives, as well as outsiders' perceptions of the place of Mormon women in the Church. Historical evidence has shown that polygamy was the most significant connecting thread of Mormon doctrine and familial networks in the mid- to late 19th century. Defended both as a requirement for salvation and as an important part of the restoration of doctrines of the ancient Church, polygamy was also justified for its other social benefit: it protected the virtue of women by keeping both men and women from participating in prostitution, unrestricted marital sexuality, and spousal rape. It took care of widows and destitute women, but mostly it provided for the birth and rearing of many spirit children within the covenants of Church membership and celestial marriage. Because of their practice of polygamy, Mormon women were often stereotyped by critics of the Church as oppressed and submissive brood mares or seen as subject to the disregard of neglectful husbands. The stories of some polygamous wives like Annie Clark Tanner upheld this latter perception, but generally the reality was quite different. Certainly, Mormon women did not always enjoy the ideals of companionate marriage that were upheld by Victorian society, but most wives expressed great satisfaction in their marital roles, especially in their devotion to their children and their sister wives. Circumstances of abuse, neglect, and underage marriage unquestionably occurred, but, ironically, polygamy also provided many complex benefits for women. Polygamous wives found some economic independence, educational advancement, and even public leadership in suffrage, charitable, and progressive organizations. Indeed, even women who found dissatisfaction in their own marriages continued to defend the "Principle" as beneficial to society, while also acting as the most vocal leaders for Utah's feminist goals in the suffrage movement and charitable societies. Some high-profile polygamous wives and female leaders, such as Emmeline B. Wells, Zina Young Williams, and Emily S. Richards, participated in national and territorial organizations like the National Woman Suffrage Association, the National Council of Women, and the Utah Territorial Woman Suffrage Association. In fact, these women tirelessly worked for women's social and political reform while also promoting a more positive national image of Mormon women.

Nineteenth-century suffragists at times could not make sense of polygamous women in Utah, who enjoyed voting rights and liberal divorce laws that were not shared by their eastern sisters. Thus, Mormon women represented a cultural paradox: the realities of their marital roles showed a distinct antifeminism, but these women also found themselves at the cutting edge of 19th-century feminist goals in suffrage, social reform, and divorce and child custody laws that favored women. Mormon women's activities also show their success at balancing the duties of marriage and motherhood with their public and professional interests and responsibilities. Indeed, male leaders encouraged women's contributions as doctors, teachers, journalists, suffrage activists, and politicians and even extended official calls to women to pursue these fields. These successful intersections of private and public activities for Mormon women show how any fears about the dangers of women's nondomestic activities were not as present in the late 19th century as they would be in later decades.

Between 1890 and 1930, Mormon women felt the inclination toward progressive reform activism, based upon the same "Civic Housekeeping" impulse shared by their educated, religious, and middle-class American sisters. Mormon women adapted the Relief Society organization to follow similar types of progressive club work practiced by other civic-minded women. In 1893, Utah women organized the Utah Federation of Women's Clubs, including the Salt Lake Council of Women and the Civic Improvement League, that urged Salt Lake City commissioners to adopt City Beautiful reforms for improving public areas. Through these organizations, Mormon women advocated for urban reform, antiprostitution activism, community charity, and disaster relief. Church leadership encouraged women to focus on needy women and children, especially through nursing, midwifery, obstetrics, infant health and nutrition, and milk sanitation and pasteurization. Mormon women's interest in and contributions to hospital work were manifested in the highly successful Deseret Hospital from 1882 to 1894. Again, as Mormon women entered the public sphere in greater numbers for reform work, these activities were not seen as contradictory to their work in the home. In fact, women's Progressive Era reform brought positive public relations to the Church as a whole.

The fruits of Mormon women's Progressive-Era work came to full realization on a national level during World War I, when the U.S. government accepted large donations of the Relief Society's extensive production and storage of wheat. Mormon women also participated in Red Cross work, home canning, rolling gauze bandages, sewing and knitting clothes for soldiers, and preparing home recipes with rationed ingredients. So, while Mormon women continued their work for the war, they also helped to portray the larger Mormon membership as mainstream patriotic Americans. In 1919, the Social Welfare Department of the Relief Society was organized, reflecting the progressive emphasis on sociology, home improvement, agricultural extension programs, and the "Clean Home, Clean Town" campaigns. In the 1920s and 1930s, as the Progressive Era blended into the state and federal welfare programs of the New Deal, the Relief Society continued its advocacy for infant

Mormon women teach classes, administer women's and children's auxiliary organizations, and serve in other essential capacities within the Church structure. (Courtesy of The Church of Jesus Christ of Latter-day Saints.)

and maternal care and social welfare assistance for families. Throughout the reform activism of the 1880s through the 1930s, Mormon women seemed to feel the conflicting pull between the home and their public reform activities to a lesser degree. Indeed, Mormon women's work for health and welfare seemed a natural extension of their domestic roles. Only after World War II would Mormon women again be encouraged to focus on the home and the family to the exclusion of outside activities.

World War II saw Mormon women participating in war work, including volunteerism, rationing, and employment in various war industries in Utah, Idaho, and California. Some Mormon women also joined women's military auxiliaries, with a few in the army's nursing corps. Following the end of the war, as American women were encouraged to give up their industrial jobs to the men coming home from war, Mormon women also experienced a renewed emphasis on traditional roles in the home. However, like their sisters nationwide, Mormon women did not give up professional work entirely; they followed the national employment pattern by responding to demands for women workers in the secretarial, service, and educational professions.

Perhaps as a reaction to the gains women had made in the workforce during the Depression and World War II, this neo-Victorian age brought renewed expectations for women's primary roles as wives and mothers to the exclusion of all other activities outside the home. Mormon women were subject to cultural directives toward earlier marriage and increased numbers of children. These women accepted and promoted the culture of traditional women's roles, even to the point of retreating from their own educational and activist gains of earlier decades. Indeed, one popular 1961 cultural guidebook for women outlined strategies for married women to regain the romantic attention of their husbands by acting submissive, helpless, and dependent on male authority. *Fascinating Womanhood* was actually written by a Mormon woman and became the subject of Relief Society meetings and discussions for many years.

Mormon women's cultural expectations became increasingly tied to doctrinal declarations about women's separate roles, resulting in new Church policies and programs for women. Some of these were considered positive reactions to the pitfalls of the modern consumer economy and postwar materialism. For instance, the Relief Society implemented the new Homemaking curriculum in 1949 to reinvigorate Mormon women's knowledge of the domestic arts in the face of the erosion of home skills. Official declarations against women working outside the home were also issued in response to increasing fears about unsupervised children and juvenile delinquency. The Relief Society welfare program experienced numerous expansions, but this also produced the negative result of turning most Mormon women's charitable efforts away from non-LDS relief organizations like those they had participated in prior to World War II.

Other earlier advances of the Progressive Era also retreated in the 1950s and 1960s. Although larger numbers of Mormon women were able to attend college, these women typically sacrificed the completion of their college degrees in favor of marriage. This resulted in lower percentages of female graduates than male graduates in the same time period and also in greater cultural confusion about the expectations for Mormon women in higher education. Further, in 1951, the Church raised the mission age for young women to 23, specifically to encourage women to marry at younger ages and discourage female missionary service. Finally, the institutional autonomy of the Relief Society itself experienced increasing erosion that culminated in the priesthood correlation movement of the 1960s and early 1970s. Correlation sought to bring all programs and materials of the Church under one umbrella as "auxiliaries" of the priesthood. Many heralded this attempt to coordinate the Church's activities and publications to better address the needs of a growing international Church amid the political upheavals of the 1960s. Still, in the context of the women's movement, some women members saw this action as a reactionary attempt to bring the women's organization more tightly under the control of male leadership.

The 1970s brought greater fractures in the Church over the place of women, especially as the Church's emphasis on traditional roles for women collided with the national women's movements' goals of bringing equality and greater access to women in education, athletics, politics, and the professions. In 1969, a group of Mormon women whose husbands were graduate students at Harvard began meeting to discuss women's issues. Their work has resulted in the flourishing of Mormon women's history as a new professional area of study and publication. It has also introduced the Church membership to the feminist gains achieved by their foremothers. In 1974, the Boston women also founded *Exponent II,* a magazine specifically to help Mormon women and men address their cultural, domestic, professional, and political challenges in the context of increasing feminist awareness.

Second-wave feminism of the 1970s and 1980s brought attention to issues facing Mormon women such as sexual abuse, domestic violence, single motherhood, abortion, birth control, same-sex attraction, patriarchal domination in the home, women's lack of higher education, and women's marginalized roles in Church leadership. In no arena was the conflict over women's roles more apparent than in the debate over the ratification of the Equal Rights Amendment. Like other conservative religious organizations, the LDS Church took an official position against the passage of the amendment. This resulted in tensions within the Church membership as a number of Mormon women chose to publicly support the amendment. These Mormon feminists gained notoriety for their defiance of the Church's position. One ERA supporter, Sonia Johnson, was excommunicated from the Church, while numerous other feminists experienced institutional condemnation or self-exile from their own LDS affiliation. The Church's response to its feminists brought public relations troubles, as the larger national culture perceived the Church as antifeminist and even antiwoman.

Debates about women holding the priesthood also gained greater discussion. Some scholars maintained that women's exclusion from the priesthood was a cultural result of 19th-century patriarchal structure, while Church leaders have continued to insist on the eternal separation of roles for men and women. Women have not been granted priesthood authority, but women's ecclesiastical participation has increased since the 1970s. Now more women speak and pray in Sacrament meeting; general women's auxiliary leaders are called to speak at General Conference; more young women choose to serve full-time missions; and women's contributions in ward councils have expanded significantly.

Perhaps as a reaction to the more liberal gains for women in education and the workplace in the 1970s and 1980s, Mormon women's traditional marital and maternal roles have again received greater emphasis in recent years. Ezra Taft Benson argued in 1985 that women's primary place was in the home and that married women should work outside the home only in cases of financial emergency. In 1995, "The Family: A Proclamation to the World" again reified women's traditional roles as the primary nurturers in their homes, with men as the primary providers. In spite of these directives, the realities of Mormon women's lives show that increasing numbers of women are negotiating their traditional roles in family and nontraditional roles in higher education, the workplace, creative activities, and even public reform efforts. The renewed celebration of stay-at-home motherhood for women is seen as an empowering recognition of women's traditional maternal choices, especially in the face of some radical feminists' strong antimaternity rhetoric and the increasing instability of family relationships.

That women are increasingly being recognized for their diverse roles is seen in more liberal adaptations by husbands and wives as they share influence in both child-rearing and economic contributions to the home. Others have felt empowered by President Gordon B. Hinckley's encouraging young women to pursue higher education to realize their full potential in marriage and the world. Many Church leaders and members still view women's need for education only in terms of nonmarriage or the death of her husband. But this rhetoric is increasingly countered by the recognition that a woman's education should be encouraged as part of her self-identity and personal growth.

Julie Beck's more traditional message for women in October 2007 can be seen in the context of an ongoing conflict between the expectations for Mormon women's traditional and nontraditional roles. Like their ancestor mothers before them, Mormon women will continue to find their own ways of negotiating opportunities for both fulfillment in families through self-confident motherhood and fulfillment in selves through personal, professional, educational, and spiritual contributions to the world.

—*Andrea G. Radke-Moss*

See also: Correlation; Mormonism and Men; Mormonism and the Family; Polygamy; Relief Society; Smith, Emma Hale; Wells, Emmeline B.

References

Beck, Julie B. "Mothers Who Know." *Ensign* (November 2007): 76–78.

Beecher, Maureen Ursenbach, and Lavina Fielding Anderson, eds. *Sisters in Spirit: Mormon Women in Historical and Cultural Perspective.* Urbana: University of Illinois Press, 1987.

Bradley, Martha Sonntag. *Pedestals and Podiums: Utah Women, Religious Authority and Equal Rights.* Salt Lake City, UT: Signature Books, 2005.

Compton, Todd. "'Kingdom of Priests': Priesthood, Temple, and Women in the Old Testament and in the Restoration." *Dialogue: A Journal of Mormon Thought* (Fall 2003): 41–59.

Hanks, Maxine, ed. *Women and Authority: Re-emerging Mormon Feminism.* Salt Lake City, UT: Signature Books, 1992.

Newell, Linda King. "A Gift Given: A Gift Taken: Washing, Anointing, and Blessing the Sick among Mormon Women." *Sunstone* 22, nos. 3–4 (June 1999): 30–43.

Radke, Andrea G. "The Place of Mormon Women: Perceptions, Prozac, Polygamy, Priesthood, Patriarchy, and Peace." Foundation for Apologetic Information and Research, August 2004. www.fairlds.org/ (March 2 2008).

Wilcox, Linda. "The Mormon Concept of a Mother in Heaven." *Sunstone* 22, nos. 3–4 (June 1999): 78–87.

Mormonism as a World Religion

The idea that Mormonism might be a world religion, despite many analytical and empirical problems with the notion, has gained currency in recent years among some Latter-day Saint scholars and their publics. For example, Terryl Givens and Eric Eliason have both published significant volumes whose titles claim that Mormonism is a world religion. Earlier, Brigham Young University's Spencer Palmer used Mormonism as the comparison point for evaluating world religions in his popular text. Although these usages respond to a Latter-day Saint search for authenticity and legitimacy, they raise important analytical concerns.

Anthropologist Walter E. A. van Beek reminds that "[w]hat constitutes a world religion is hard to establish, as in principle it is not an analytic but more of a public relations term" (van Beek, "Mormonism"). Van Beek's position must be taken seriously. Neither Givens nor Palmer makes a serious attempt to justify the consideration that Mormonism is a world religion. Their usage seems either an assertion of legitimacy and importance for the Church of Jesus Christ of Latter-day Saints or an idea that supports Mormonism's claim to unique spiritual sanction. Eliason, on the other hand, does make an argument when he writes that, among contemporary religions, only the Baha'i, Sikh, and Mormon faiths can be considered as candidates for new world religions, on the basis of "their longevity, population, worldwide distribution, and doctrinal uniqueness" (Eliason, *Mormons and Mormonism* 15). As we shall see, this set of issues is complex and not completely clear in supporting the claim Mormonism is a world religion.

The scholarly roots of the notion that Mormonism is a world religion are found in the work of prominent sociologist Rodney Stark. He suggested the idea in a 1984 article as part of his work on the sociology of religious change and growth. One of the most prominent sociologists of religion in the United States, Stark has been instrumental in the development of a market-based approach to the study of religion derived from a rational-choice theoretical perspective. His work has occasionally led him to study Mormonism, among other religious groups.

Mormon missionaries began proselytizing in the South Pacific in the 1840s; these Samoan members of 1932 could easily be third-generation Mormons. (Courtesy of the Church History Library, The Church of Jesus Christ of Latter-day Saints.)

In his seminal 1984 article, Stark compares the impressive growth of Mormonism

A 1988 seminary graduation for high school-age Church members in Ghana suggests how far the Church has come from its roots in an upstate New York farming village. (Courtesy of the Church History Library, The Church of Jesus Christ of Latter-day Saints.)

in many countries of the world to the burst of Islam from the Arabian Peninsula outward to become one of the most significant faiths numerically on Earth. As a sociologist, Stark laments that, since Islam's origins are "shrouded in the fog of unrecorded history," it is not possible to study its origins from his disciplinary stance, just as it is not possible to study the origins of other world religions, since they originated in the remote and undocumented past (Stark, "So Far, So Good" 18). Stark celebrates Mormon growth because it is massive and contemporary and because it provides data for his kind of sociological study, which focuses primarily on explaining growth.

To make his argument, Stark relies on several problematic notions. He labels Mormonism a new religion that he claims is the fastest growing new religion in U.S. history. Stark then argues that Mormonism will continue to grow, especially internationally, and will attain a worldwide numerical presence "comparable to that of Islam, Buddhism, Christianity, Hinduism, and the other dominant world faiths" (Stark, "So Far, So Good" 18).

By arguing that Mormonism is a new religion, in the context of his comparison with Islam, Stark makes it a particular kind of new religion, one that is not Christian in a conventional sense. Stark further does not locate Mormonism within the realm of new forms of Christianity. These new Christian groups are, in the sociological study of new religious movements, generally considered "sects" or "cults," given their tensions with mainstream society and internal organization. Mormon sociologist Armand Mauss's classic work, *The Angel and the Beehive,* exemplifies the study of Mormonism as a sectarian movement that maintains a tension with mainstream society, religious and secular, while also accommodating itself to that society. For Mauss, Mormonism's Christianity is taken for granted. In contrast, Stark makes Mormonism a different kind of religious family, akin to Buddhism, Hinduism, Christianity, and Islam.

This question of whether Mormonism is or is not Christian is ideologically important for the Church of Jesus Christ of Latter-day Saints and has been a matter of debate between it and various Christian denominations. The question relates to divergent theological stances on the nature of Christianity and its relationship to deity, as well as divergent arguments related to historical legitimacy. Besides promoting different notions of God and mankind and of their relationship, Mormonism claims to be a restoration of the lost early Christianity, while mainstream Christian groups claim a direct historical relationship to early Christianity through tradition.

Despite sectarian debates, an academic argument has been made that Mormonism is as divergent from Christianity as Christianity is from Judaism. In her *Mormonism: The Story of a New Religious Tradition,* historian Jan Shipps, perhaps the most well-known proponent of this position, argues: "While it perceives itself as Christian, Mormonism differs from traditional Christianity in much the same fashion that traditional Christianity, in its ultimate emphasis on the individual, came to differ from Judaism" (Shipps, *Mormonism* 148). As we can see, Shipps drew this distinction by comparing the object of religious action, as well as the narratives and practices that were understood to lead to salvation.

Despite its evident impact on future academic work, Shipps's book was not the first to argue that Mormonism formed a new religious tradition distinct from most Christianity. In her preface to the second edition of her classic biography of Joseph Smith, *No Man Knows My History,* Fawn Brodie observed, "It is exciting and enlightening to see a religion born. And Joseph Smith's was no mere dissenting sect. It was a real religious creation, one intended to be to Christianity as Christianity was to Judaism: that is, a reform and a consummation" (Brodie, *No Man Knows My History* xvii).

However, this argument tends to look at Mormonism's empirical relationship with Christianity in isolation. It does not take account of other competing Churches of similar background that are growing strongly in the contemporary world. Catholic scholars, for example, among other scholars, tend to locate the Church of Jesus Christ of Latter-day Saints, along with the Jehovah's Witnesses and, often, the Seventh-day Adventists, as "para-Christian sects" as a means of indicating their difference on canonical issues related to the relationship of their Christology to their theological anthropology in contrast to Christianity (Martin, *Pentecostalism* 39). These Churches are often also called eschatological sects as a means of emphasizing their doctrines of the end times.

Part of the difficulty with the academic argument that Mormonism is a new religion is that there is no established means of building a taxonomy of religious groups or of the kinds of social factors that are important to such categorizations. As a result, the academic arguments tend, at the moment, to proceed in an ad hoc, comparative framework with little discussion as to the nature of difference and similarity in religious classification.

Another difficulty is that when Stark speaks of Mormonism as a new religion in the set that normally includes Christianity, Islam, Buddhism, and Hinduism, he is arguing that a single Church, a single social organization, is equivalent to the other categories, which comprise families of organizations. Christianity, for example, includes Catholicism, Orthodox Churches, Protestants, and so on. Islam includes both Sunni and Shiite, among others. Nevertheless, Stark studies the Church of Jesus Christ of Latter-day Saints, a single religious body, and not the entire restorationist movement, which includes all the different religious forms and bodies that stem from Joseph Smith. As a result, there are two unanswered questions here: Is Mormonism a family of faiths akin to the world religions, or can a single religious body be fruitfully compared to families of multiple bodies and forms, and, whatever the answer to these first questions, is the degree of diversity similar to that found in the religious families known as world religions?

Much of Stark's argument that Mormonism is a world religion depends on the issue of numbers. In this, he builds on the work of the great sociologist Max Weber, who defined world religions as "religiously determined systems of life-regulation which have known how to gather multitudes of confessors around them" (Weber, "Sociology of World Religions: Introduction"). Weber develops his thought by exploring "systems of life-regulation" and religion and does not elaborate an argument on the sociological ways in which "multitudes of confessors" are formed. Nevertheless, Stark's reliance on the growth in membership in the Mormon Church for his argument suggests the necessity of such a consideration.

The work of Douglas J. Davies specifically addressing the idea that Mormonism might be a world religion argues that the ways in which multitudes are organized in relationship to the societies in which they are found may make the difference between whether a group with a large membership is a world religion or a widespread denomination.

Stark, unfortunately, does not consider this issue. Instead, his argument about Mormonism depends simply on how many members there are. Critics have assailed his readings of Mormon numbers. The criticisms include the following points. First, the official membership statistics supplied by the Church of Jesus Christ of Latter-day Saints are not generally considered by sociologists to be an accurate measure of meaningful affiliation and participation. Not only do Latter-day Saints show very high rates of inactivity, but also the number of members reported represents some five times the number of people who claim membership on censuses in various countries. Second, a straight-line projection, which assumes that patterns of growth from the past will continue into the future, does not take into account changes in the social realities that motivate religious growth. Growth rates have, indeed, declined over the past decade, in part because of changing Church practices and changing global conditions. Third, Mormon growth is not even around the world but is heavily concentrated in the Americas. This makes the Latter-day Saints much more an American Church, North and South, than a world religion. Fourth, Stark does not compare Mormon growth with that of other major religious bodies around the world, such as Pentecostals, Seventh-day Adventists, and Jehovah's Witnesses. All three of these groups have shown stronger growth and are more represented around the world than are the Latter-day Saints. Stark's decision not to mention these other denominations suggests that his consideration of numbers, despite Weber, is contingent on his assumption that Mormonism is a new, and therefore different, kind of religious phenomenon, somehow unlike these others. Finally, the massive growth of Mormonism, as well as of these other bodies, and mainstream Christian religions, such as Catholicism, around the world suggests that the second half of the 20th century, with its particular economic and social situation of increasing globalization and American hegemony, may involve a unique congeries of social dynamics and that projections of them into the future, such as Stark's, are relatively vacuous other than for propagandistic purposes.

Anthropologist Douglas J. Davies takes account of these concerns and adds to them in his formal consideration of the concept of world religion and, specifically, Mormonism's qualification as a world religion. Davies describes the development of classical world religions as a historical process.

> Each current world religion expanded, often from a small group, until it assumed a degree of dominance in its society of origin or of particular networks of groups associated with it. From there it moved into other societies until with time, it became a natural part of that new society. Within the new culture of residence the religion contributed to cultural development, while also bearing a strong family resemblance to its original source and to the other societies of destination. The existence of distinctive scriptures, interpretations, and patterns of ritual helped maintain a unifying identity despite cultural difference. Each has also possessed strong ethical bases in commandments or life principles, while distinctive geographical centres, sources that sustain the growing interpretations of tradition and of ritual performance, have also proved invaluable. Behind all these features has existed a cosmology, an extensive mythological account of the nature of the universe, of divine nature and activity, and of the relationship between these and a destiny for human beings that takes them beyond the level of the ordinariness of earthly life. (Davies, *Mormon Culture* 258)

For his discussion, following Weber, Davies emphasizes the development of a theology and an ethic of transcendence that is translocal and potentially universal. As he notes, Mormonism does show this characteristic. However, Davies also emphasizes the sociology of dominance in its society of origin, the expansion and sinking of deep roots in host societies, and the diversification of the religious tradition while maintaining a "family resemblance" to the religion in the place of origin. Davies notes that Mormonism attempts to maintain a centralized religion that controls its form and content in all the places it is found, which makes it very different from the diversified faiths that characterize most religions that are called world religions. Mormons' authoritarian centralization depends on a social process that Knowlton describes as the development of a supranational, global society, involving the evolution of legal and social possibilities for a transnational religious body and communicative technologies that enable control by the center. Because of active use of surveillance and religious power to avoid the growth of diversity and local forms, Mormonism has maintained a historical unity very different from the experience of Catholicism or Islam, among others. As a result, Mormonism experiences a social process very different from that found in world religions whose social process is historically and contemporaneously much more complex.

The lack of sufficient time for diversification, in the case of Mormonism, and the form of social organization that the Church of Jesus Christ of Latter-day Saints takes as a Church that is found in many parts of the world lead Davies to hold that Mormonism is a global denomination, rather than a world religion. As a denomination, it participates in a religiously pluralist society that has taken hold in most places of the world, as well as one in which secularization is an increasingly important force. Both pluralism as an obligatory social form and secularization make it increasingly unlikely that Mormonism can become a world religion, rather than a transnational denomination.

Although there is considerable similarity from one place to another within the LDS Church's congregations, some evidence is appearing that supports the development of distinctive local Mormonisms. This includes the historical differences among regions of Deseret, the Mormon heartland; differences between core and periphery; and differences in different national and regional Mormonisms. In part, this is the result of metropolitan Mormonism fitting into local milieus with their own social and historical dynamics; at the same time, it depends on the time in which Mormonism has been established in various locales.

As a result, Davies writes, "the chief test [for Mormonism's becoming a world religion] will lie in whether it will prove possible for distinctive African, South American, Japanese, or any other regional forms of Mormonism to emerge" (Davies, *Mormon Culture* 258). This requires that scholars of Mormonism dedicate attention to the specific ways in which sameness and difference are constructed in the many contexts in which Mormonism is present, as well as the means through which a universal Mormonism is maintained.

Nevertheless, the question of whether Mormonism is a world religion remains an open one because of the weakness of the concept of world religion. The idea does make strong claims to legitimacy, and we can expect it to continue to be trumpeted by Latter-day Saint thinkers and friends. A benefit of this problematic usage, with its roots in the work of Rodney Stark, is that it requires us to look more deeply at the sociological issues that make world religions different from other religious forms, such as denominations or localized religions. This consideration can help us obtain more precision in comprehending the place of religion generally, and Mormonism specifically, in the world we inhabit.

—David Clark Knowlton

See also: Expansion: 1941–Present.

References

Brodie, Fawn M. *No Man Knows My History: The Life of Joseph Smith.* New York: Knopf, 1945.

Davies, Douglas J. *The Mormon Culture of Salvation: Force, Grace, and Glory.* Burlington, VT: Ashgate, 2000.

Eliason, Eric A., ed. *Mormons and Mormonism: An Introduction to an American World Religion.* Urbana: University of Illinois Press, 2001.

Givens, Terryl L. *By the Hand of Mormon: The American Scripture That Launched a New World Religion.* New York: Oxford University Press, 2003.

Gooren, Henri. "Analyzing LDS Growth in Guatemala: A Report from a Barrio." *Dialogue: A Journal of Mormon Thought* 43 (Summer 2000): 97–115.

Knowlton, David Clark. "Go Ye to All the World: The LDS Church and the Organization of International Society." In *Revisiting the Mormons: Persistent Themes and Contemporary Perspectives.* Ed. Tim Heaton, Cardell Jacobsen, and John Hofman, 389–412. Salt Lake City: University of Utah Press, 2008.

Knowlton, David Clark. "How Many Members Are There Really? Two Censuses and the Meaning of LDS Membership in Chile and Mexico." *Dialogue: A Journal of Mormon Thought* 38 (Summer 2005): 53–78.

Martin, David. *Pentecostalism: The World Their Parish.* Boston: Blackwell, 2002.

Mauss, Armand. *The Angel and the Beehive: The Mormon Struggle with Assimilation.* Urbana: University of Illinois Press, 1994.

Palmer, Spencer J., Roger R. Keller, Dong Sull Choi, and James A. Toronto. *Religions of the World: A Latter-day Saint View,* revised and enlarged. Provo, UT: Brigham Young University Press, 1997.

Phillips, Rick. "Religious Market Share and Mormon Church Activity." *Sociology of Religion* 59 (Summer 1998): 117–130.

Shipps, Jan. *Mormonism: The Story of a New Religious Tradition.* Urbana: University of Illinois Press, 1987.

Stark, Rodney. "The Rise of a New World Faith." *Review of Religious Research* 26, no. 1 (September 1984): 18–27.

Stark, Rodney. "So Far, So Good: A Brief Assessment of Mormon Membership Projections." *Review of Religious Research* 38 (December 1996): 175–178.

Van Beek, Walter E. A. "Mormonism, a Global Counter-Church?" By Common Consent, June 18, 2009. http://bycommonconsent.com/2009/06/18/mormonism-a-global-counter-church-i/ (June 23, 2009).

Weber, Max. "Sociology of World Religions: Introduction." http://evans-experientialism.freewebspace.com/weber.htm (July 22, 2009).

Mormonism as Restoration

Central to the self-understanding of Latter-day Saints is a belief in a restoration, their complexly supernatural answer to the Protestant Reformation. As the narrative of restoration has evolved over the history of the faith, particular aspects have received more emphasis than others. In the best-known narrative of restoration, Christianity fell from the purity of primitive worship in a Great Apostasy (early Latter-day Saints dated the fall to the fifth or sixth century; modern Mormons tend to push the date

Mormonism sees itself as a literal restoration of the church of Jesus Christ. This monument by Mormon artist Avard Fairbanks commemorates the return of John the Baptist to restore priesthood authority to Joseph Smith and Oliver Cowdery. (Courtesy of the Church History Library, The Church of Jesus Christ of Latter-day Saints.)

back to the first generation after the death of Christ's apostles). In this regard, they differed little from their Protestant peers. Reformed Protestants (the heirs of John Calvin) saw the recovery of Christianity from Catholic "superstition" in the chain of reformers that stretched from Luther and Calvin to Jonathan Edwards and the 18th-century First Great Awakening. Latter-day Saints, for their part, argued that no learned theology or careful Bible reading or personal regeneration by Christ's grace could recover primitive Christianity. With certain others labeled "Seekers," "Restorationists," or "Primitivists"—representatives of a disparate movement dating back to the English Puritans and earlier—the Latter-day Saints believed that only a new revelation from heaven could recover what had been lost. For Mormons, restoration meant many things, including reliving biblical history, the return of charismatic gifts, renewed contact with angels, the rediscovery of the pure language of Eden, and a vision for the future of the Americas, the promised land of Native peoples and Latter-day Saints alike.

As the story would ultimately be told, the first act of restoration was the visit of God to Joseph Smith, now termed the First Vision and seen as the restoration of biblical prophecy. Shortly thereafter and throughout his career, Smith indicated that the mysteries of past ages were to be revealed both by prophetic inspiration and by the visitation of angels, just as had been true in the Bible. Starting with Moroni, with his revelations and Book of Mormon plates, Joseph Smith described visits from a host of angels, similar to if more biblical than, the experience of the 18th-century mystical scholar Emanuel Swedenborg. In the early 1830s, Smith revealed that John the Baptist, as a resurrected angel, had laid hands upon him to confer the Aaronic Priesthood and that he had been followed shortly by Peter, James, and John, who ordained Smith and his colleagues to the more potent Melchizedek Priesthood. The pattern of angelic restoration continued in 1836 when Smith reported visits from many angels, the most important of whom was the immortal Old Testament prophet Elijah, who restored and became the patron for Smith's temple rites. Smith's followers emphasized that in these angels they had solved the Protestant dilemma: if Catholicism was illegitimate, so were its offshoots; if the Roman priesthood was legitimate, Protestants had no right to dissent. Refusing to accept the general Protestant argument that salvation and authority did not derive from ecclesiastical hierarchies or episcopal priesthood, the Latter-day Saints announced that they were the only authorized Christians in the world and traced that claim to the very first Christians.

The emphasis on ecclesiastical authority has come to dominate Mormon restoration narratives. Throughout the 20th century, Mormons have centrally preached that they are the sole legitimate representatives of biblical Christianity. While essential to understanding modern Mormonism, this narrative does not fully describe the richness of the early Latter-day Saints' claims. Early national America buzzed with innovations within the broad rubric of Christianity. Against the ecclesiastical tradition, episcopal priesthood, and creedal theologies of European religion, America's new Protestants sought legitimacy elsewhere. Evangelicals sought a return to the pure religion of Christianity, through social revival and personal regeneration, a movement now called the Second Great Awakening. Through an evolving biblicism, common-sense realism, and carefully managed religious experience, these Protestants believed they had recovered God's voice from both Catholicism and the "metaphysical" traditions of high Calvinism. In struggling toward a consensus in the confusing religious world of pluralism, these groups generally believed that denominational differences mattered little.

Pushing from near the mainstream, a group of critics that came to be best represented by Alexander Campbell and his antidenominational "Church of Christ" pressed for a more rigorous restoration. These restorationists rejected denominational accommodation, even if they agreed with common-sense Bible interpretation and personal regeneration as the best means for securing a religion of purity and unity. When these more aggressive critics coalesced into movements, they tended to claim exclusive access to truth. Richard Hughes and Leonard Allen, the best-known historians of antebellum restorationism, have seen this harsh sectarianism as the defining feature of American primitivism, drawing attention to the irony that several voices were proposing the only solution to the Babel of Protestant denominationalism.

Hughes and Allen, while correct regarding the intersections of primitivism and pluralism, underestimate the dramatic religious valences of primitivism. For many Latter-day Saints, the promise of restoration was the promise of living a biblical life, not just in moral precepts but in actual religious continuity with ancient Christianity. In its march from "Church of Christ," in 1830 to "Church of the Latter Day Saints" to "Church of Jesus Christ of Latter-Day Saints" by 1838, Mormons made the same antidenominational claims as Campbell, affirming in the end, though, that they were the latter-day continuation of the primitive Church, the millennial siblings of the "former-day saints." The identity with "former-day saints" reassured, validated, and inspired these "Latter-Day" believers. Through persecutions by Protestant clergy and vigilantes (whom they saw as the modern antitype of ancient pagan anti-Christians) and their identification with the "small and simple" people of the New Testament, Mormons felt increasingly secure in their authority to represent Jesus and the original Christian Church.

The re-opening of the scriptural canon represents another crucial aspect of Mormon restorationism. From their Book of Mormon, to the canonized Book of Commandments and Doctrine and Covenants, to their official newspapers, to their Church records exemplified by Smith's 1842 "Book of the Law of the Lord," the Saints embodied, recovered, and created the scriptural voice of God. Even the Bible was open to restoration, as Smith undertook to recover its lost truths both through creative exegesis of proof-texts and through frank revisions or amplifications—including the lost Prophecy of Enoch and Moses' preamble to the Pentateuch—ultimately collected as the Joseph Smith Translation (or Inspired Version) of the Old and New Testaments.

The Mormon restoration of scriptures, broadly conceived, pointed toward access to great spiritual power. From glossolalia and faith healings to angelic ministrations and prophecy or perhaps even the raising of the dead, the New Testament miracles figured prominently in early Mormonism. In fact, the power of charismata, the dramatic gifts of the spirit, were invoked to legitimate early Mormonism much as priesthood would be in later decades. The early restoration was a story of God's returning presence, what opponents would call enthusiasm. In complex ways, it was also a protest against the common-sense accommodations of Protestants to Enlightenment rationalism.

Angelic visitors grounded the supernaturalism of the restoration. Many early converts emphasized that these visitors from the other world were necessary; some said revelation could come only through angels. For Smith, though, these angels represented a chance to control enthusiasm while allowing God's voice to be heard again.

Much like the Elizabethan magus John Dee (who revealed the language of Enoch), or Emanuel Swedenborg (who discovered a language of angels), or, less mystically, Ralph Waldo Emerson (who used hieroglyphs as a metaphor for Nature), Smith also pursued the restoration of pure human language. In his protracted interactions with a collection of Egyptian funerary papyri, Smith, with the assistance of his amanuensis, William Phelps, declared the recovery of a language of pure meaning in which pictographic glyphs communicated the deep meaning of the objects they described. Much as Swedenborg had, Smith sought in this sacred language the means to communicate purely, to remove all barriers to human interconnectedness. Restoration meant a time when all humanity would speak the same language and through mutual understanding create a perfectly harmonious world.

Restoration referred also to the Israelites, the Jews in Diaspora who, according to Christian millenarian beliefs, would receive Jesus as their Messiah before their triumphant return to Jerusalem. Mormon Israelitism is complex, but in part the Latter-day Saints believed that, at some point in the world's winding-up scenes, they would take control of North America. Like Adam, they would hold dominion over the Earth, which would again be a paradisiacal garden. Mormons extended this restoration to Native Americans, as well. Early Latter-day Saints fully anticipated that Native groups, dispersed by the social violence euphemistically termed "Removal," would be restored to their inheritance of the Americas even as the Earth itself was restored to its primordial purity. The fact that President Andrew Jackson at that time was relocating Native groups to lands west of the Mississippi was to the Saints no surprise. In fact, Smith revealed that his new Jerusalem would be founded on the "borders by the Lamanites"; they expected that their restored Zion would merge into the restored Zion of the gathered American Natives, all ultimately merging into the holy city of the same name that Smith had revealed in the Prophecy of Enoch.

By the end of his life, Smith's restorationism had moved well beyond the Earth and its inhabitants. He had pushed past Adamic or Edenic primitivism into a set of worlds, creations, and universes that united all possible existences into one. Through his temple rites and supporting theology, Smith prepared his followers to meet humanity's first parents and the Council of Gods that superintended every beginning, even as he prepared his followers to create worlds of their own. What other Christians understood as the millennial regeneration of the fallen Earth was to Smith part of an overall astronomical restoration, the Earth's resurrection into a chain of worlds.

Despite substantial shared context and concerns, the Latter-day Saints were not typical of either restorationists or the more radical hermeticists who sought the earliest beginnings in esoteric texts, metaphysical correspondences, and practices many would now designate as magic. Joseph Smith revealed a distinctive merger of threads from both traditions, threads that neither would have recognized as its own. Smith's restorationism was also not primarily a theological or ecclesiastical exercise, though both aspects are present in his religion-making. More than anything, Smith revealed a religious solution to the disunity and uncertainty of human existence in the antebellum world. He saw through the Babel of religious opinions to a pure state, a situation that transcended time and place, without beginning or end.

Over time, the mainline LDS denomination has had to situate itself in opposition to schismatic figures who invoke restoration claims of their own. Smith himself confronted dissident disciples who followed their own paths of restoration. The predominant narrative of restoration as the recovery of a chain of priesthood authority allowed Smith, later in his career, and the mainline Utah Church, after his death, to demonstrate that the Mormon restoration could stand once, for all. The priesthood structure of the Church could thus absorb the substantial energies of Joseph Smith's grand restoration. This explicit transfer of religious enthusiasm into priesthood office has allowed the mainline Church to move beyond schism for more than a century and a half.

City of Zion

In Mormon parlance, "Zion" refers to anywhere the righteous dwell: the ancient city of Enoch, taken to heaven because of its inhabitants' righteousness, was Zion; so are the homes and temples of good people today; so will be the New Jerusalem at the Second Coming of Christ. Characteristics of Zion are peace, cleanliness, and such concern for one's neighbors that there is no selfishness or poverty.

The orderliness of Zion was reflected in the layout of 19th-century cities established by the Latter-day Saints, including Kirtland, Ohio; Independence and Far West, Missouri; Nauvoo, Illinois; and Salt Lake City, Utah, and elsewhere in the Great Basin. Although there were variations in dimensions, all these towns were laid out in grids of square blocks oriented to the compass, with homes in the center and farms ringing the outer limits. Houses, surrounded by gardens, were set back from streets, and house lots alternated their orientation so that houses faced landscapes rather than other houses across streets. Certain downtown blocks were reserved for temples and schools.

With their balance between neighborliness and privacy and their incorporation of green space throughout, Mormon cities embody two biblical images of paradise: the City of Zion and the Garden of Eden.

The narrative of restoration as ecclesiastical legitimacy not only constrained enthusiastic dissidents; it also justified anti-Catholic and anti-Protestant ideologies. It simultaneously unlocked a certain syncretistic openness to "fragments" of truth wherever they might be found. Despite increasing accommodation to the evangelical mainstream through the 20th century, Mormons continued to identify themselves as the Restored (hence exclusively authorized) Church of Christ, with expected strains on interdenominational relationships. After the middle of the 20th century, Church leaders and prominent laypeople have sought to find common ground with other conservative Christian groups. The flagrant anti-Catholicism and anti-Protestantism of the Church's first 150 years are receding, though traces remain in the Book of Mormon and folk-canonical works like Bruce R. McConkie's *Mormon Doctrine* (1958). Despite increasing ecumenical overtures, the LDS Church continues to affirm its belief that it alone enjoys priesthood legitimacy, refusing to recognize sacraments performed by other Christian Churches, to admit outside clergy or laypeople to its temple communion, or to affirm the validity of traditional creeds. In the first decade of the 21st century, Latter-day Saints seem no more likely than the Catholics to eliminate exclusive priesthood from their belief system, although the original scope of Mormon restorationism does provide narrative threads that could open other approaches to this question.

—Samuel Brown

See also: Book of Mormon; Divergent Churches; First Vision; Kirtland Pentecost; Mormon Scripture; Mormonism and Native Americans; Mormonism and Other Faiths.

References

Baugh, Alexander. "Parting the Veil: Joseph Smith's Seventy-six Documented Visionary Experiences." In *Opening the Heavens.* Ed. John Welch, 265–306. Salt Lake City, UT: Deseret Book, 2004.

Brown, Samuel. "Joseph (Smith) in Egypt: Babel, Hieroglyphs, and the Pure Language of Eden." *Church History* 78, no. 1 (March 2009): 26–65.

Hughes, Richard, and Leonard Allen. *Illusions of Innocence: Protestant Primitivism, 1630–1875.* Chicago: University of Chicago Press, 1988.

Prince, Gregory. *Power from On High: The Development of Mormon Priesthood.* Salt Lake City, UT: Signature Books, 1995.

Mormonism's Contested Identity

Almost from the outset, the Church that Joseph Smith organized in 1830 was more than just a religious project. The religion quickly provided the impulse for creating a people apart, a modern incarnation of an Old Testament-type Israel. Because of this, outside observers have long described Mormons as a peculiar people and even as an American ethnic group. Like other minority groups, Latter-day Saints have inspired a wide range of reactions from their neighbors. The audacity of their religious claims and the numeric success of their community-building efforts have meant that few such neighbors have remained neutral in their perception of Mormonism. Government officials, media representatives, dissident and celebrity Mormons, other religious groups, the LDS Church itself in reactive and proactive ways—many hands have tugged at and shaped Latter-day Saints' reputation and public standing over the years. Recurring themes, some as old as the movement itself, seem to bob in and out of sight on the tidal ebbs and flows of Mormonism's contested image.

From its pioneer roots to its 1893 World's Fair appearance to its continuing television broadcasts, the Mormon Tabernacle Choir (pictured here in 1914) has been a popular goodwill ambassador for the Church. (Courtesy of the Church History Library, The Church of Jesus Christ of Latter-day Saints.)

The first anti-Mormon book, for example, came off the presses in 1834, when the fledgling Church was only four years old. E. D. Howe's *Mormonism Unvailed* drew on affidavits collected by one of Joseph Smith's erstwhile but embittered followers, Doctor Philastus Hurlbut, who had conducted interviews in Palmyra, New York, where Smith had lived when he had the founding visions that led him to organize the Church. With remarkable consistency, all of Hurlbut's witnesses emphasized the untrustworthiness, laziness, and craftiness of the entire Smith family. Howe and Hurlbut also suggested that Joseph Smith's purported translation of the ancient records that became the Book of Mormon was nothing more than the rough plagiarizing of a contemporary romantic novel by Solomon Spaulding. The arguments and testimonials presented in *Mormonism Unvailed* would be rehearsed and rehashed in a litany of similarly themed future publications. Thus, Howe's book became a prototype, the opening volley in a protracted struggle over religious ideas that would surround the Church, its prophet, and its people.

For their part, Mormons responded in an effort to shape a more positive public image for themselves. In 1839, Mormon apostle Parley P. Pratt wrote *Late Persecution of the Church of Jesus Christ of Latter-day Saints,* in which he argued that the Missourians created a racialized image of Mormons, "as if we had been some savage tribe, or some colored race of foreigners." Instead, Pratt argued that the Mormons were the true Americans, "who stood firm in the cause of liberty and law" (Pratt, *Late Persecution* 59). At the time of Joseph Smith's death, several hundred Mormon men were in various U.S. cities promoting Smith's candidacy in the upcoming presidential election. While this campaign was motivated by a number of factors, enhanced public awareness of the Mormon position was near the top. This contested Mormon image would continue, especially following the Mormon's open acknowledgement of polygamy.

In 1852, the Church made public the decade-old practice of plural marriage; this announcement, from that point forward, would define outsiders' view of Mormons for decades to come. By 1856, national Republicans railed against the twin relics of barbarism: slavery and polygamy. President Lincoln approached the Mormon problem with benign neglect, but this brief "live and let live" policy ended after the Civil War. Lobbying groups nationwide urged Congress to remove the blight of polygamy from American soil. Increasingly strident legislation followed throughout the 1870s and 1880s, enforced by federal marshals who raided Utah communities looking for polygamists. Temperance unions, ministerial associations, eastern newspapers—all joined the chorus of voices decrying Mormon depravity. Numerous novels revolved around some variation of the theme of Mormon missionaries seducing young women converts into joining their Rocky Mountain harems. Mormons, almost universally, were portrayed as pariahs.

Latter-day Saint women banded together in the *Woman's Exponent* periodical to express their support of polygamous family life, but the weight of public opinion could not be moved so easily. Utah's petition for statehood, long denied because of the polygamy question, found presidential support after the 1890 Manifesto promising to end future plural marriages. But Mormon optimism about new prospects for public respectability met with the hard reality of the Reed Smoot controversy.

Smoot was a Latter-day Saint apostle elected to the U.S. Senate in 1903. The election of one of Mormonism's highest-ranking elders ignited a firestorm of protests. At issue were rumors that the LDS hierarchy continued to sanction clandestine plural marriages. Though Smoot himself was a monogamist, his opponents feared that he was beholden to a theocratic, polygamist organization. Not only did the Saints again suffer in the press, but LDS leaders, including Church president Joseph F. Smith, faced bruising examinations during almost three years of congressional hearings. President Smith issued the so-called Second Manifesto in 1904, condemning those Mormons who continued to solemnize plural marriages, and the Senate ultimately voted to allow Smoot to retain his seat.

This episode marked the first of several 20th-century turning points for the Mormon image. Some LDS officials began to campaign for more active public relations efforts. For example, a Bureau of Information opened on Temple Square in 1902, and within the first year, more than 100,000 tourists passed through the visitors' center. In the next decade, the Mormon Tabernacle Choir toured eastern cities and garnered wide acclaim.

Other developments proved fortuitous for Mormons. President Theodore Roosevelt, who had backed Senator Smoot—and welcomed the Utahn as an ally—wrote favorably about the Saints in *Collier's* magazine in 1911. World War I afforded Latter-day Saint volunteers and boosters an opportunity to fly their patriotic colors. The Prohibition movement gave teetotaling Mormons and evangelical Protestants a common cause, and reports of the LDS Church's alcohol- and tobacco-free lifestyle (based on "the Word of Wisdom" revelation) stamped on Mormons a new—and positive—identifying marker that began to displace the marker of polygamy (Alexander, *Mormonism in Transition* 307). But nothing generated attention and approval like the Mormon response to the Great Depression.

In 1936, the Church organized a network of farms, canneries, warehouses, and thrift stores. Unemployed Church members found jobs on the Church's work projects in exchange for commodities. LDS apostles traveled to New York and Washington to announce the welfare program to government officials and the press corps. The stated ambitions of the Church—to provide a way for members to get off the federal dole—sparked widespread approbation. Praise for Mormons' success coincided with growing concern over New Deal spending; some enthusiastic periodicals even exaggerated the results of the plan to the point that they mistakenly reported that no Mormons received federal aid money. While the Church never made that claim, the notoriety of the welfare program dramatically boosted the public image of Mormons as hardworking, inventive, and self-reliant people. "They take care of their own" became both a new media tagline and a public opinion coup for Latter-day Saints.

By the late 1940s, some officials at Church headquarters began to lobby for the creation of a public affairs department. While the Church had long sought to spread its message through missionary evangelizing, some leaders recognized the need for

Mormon Tabernacle Choir

More than 300 voices strong, the Mormon Tabernacle Choir may be the most familiar, best-loved feature of the modern Church. From its home in the historic Tabernacle on Temple Square, where it is backed by a notable pipe organ, the choir provides music for Church conferences and civic occasions and has presented a weekly program of "Music and the Spoken Word" since 1929, the longest continually broadcast radio (now television) program in history.

The choir has evolved from small choral groups in the pioneer era, through a period as the choir of the Salt Lake Stake, to its current status as a world-class—yet volunteer and unpaid—body of professional-quality singers. The choir performed at the Chicago World's Fair in 1893, sang in the White House in 1911, won a Grammy in 1959 for its recording of "The Battle Hymn of the Republic," performed at the inaugurations of four American presidents, appeared in films, sang at the opening and closing ceremonies of the 2002 Winter Olympics, and was dubbed "America's Choir" by Ronald Reagan. The choir has toured extensively, performing in the world's greatest concert halls and with some of the world's best soloists, choirs, and orchestras.

a different type of office to respond to the increasing number of press inquiries. Finally, in 1957, the First Presidency inaugurated the Church Information Service. The small department employed a handful of staffers essentially on loan from a Salt Lake City advertising agency. Much prodding finally convinced Church apostles to invest in a large-scale pavilion at the New York World's Fair in 1964–1965. The huge project involved a new film, *Man's Search for Happiness,* and a referral system for contacting interested visitors. Of the 6 million guests who toured the pavilion, 1 million requested a follow-up visit from Mormon missionaries. These gratifying results suggested that Latter-day Saints' larger reputation was improving.

The 1968 presidential campaign of Michigan governor George Romney provided further evidence of that upswing. Romney's Mormonism did not raise anything like the opposition that had flared up around Reed Smoot. Instead, most media profiles of Romney depicted his religion as the source of Romney's most notable strengths: integrity, sobriety, family unity. The fact that Romney led in many pre-election polls for much of 1967 speaks to the relative absence of public anxiety over the possibility of a Mormon president. His perceived inexperience in foreign policy, rather than his religious affiliation, seemed to be Romney's undoing.

However, Romney's political run did, for all intents and purposes, introduce the nation to the Mormon position on its black members. While blacks could join the LDS Church, they were restricted from ordination to the priesthood, an opportunity open to other males in the Church when they turned 12. The Church's First Presidency spoke officially in favor of civil rights legislation in 1963 but maintained that the priesthood issue was one that could only be changed by divine revelation.

George Romney and other Mormons endured growing criticism for this position from the NAACP and various media outlets across the nation, but Romney's strong pro-civil rights record mitigated many of the complaints. By 1970, though, dissatisfaction with the priesthood prohibition led to a number of demonstrations at sporting events that involved the Church's Brigham Young University. The violence of the protests generated extensive publicity about the offending Church policy, yet, more often than not, reporters portrayed the priesthood restriction as deriving from an intransigent *institutional* stance rather than the prejudice of Mormon *individuals.* Observers of this media trend have also noted that human interest stories involving "clean-cut Mormons" contrasted so starkly with depictions of the chaotic "counterculture" movement that favorable impressions of Latter-day Saints survived the negative coverage of the priesthood protests (Shipps, *Sojourner* 100).

As Latter-day Saints continued to emphasize that their support of civil equality was independent of its priesthood theology and as the nation's attention shifted from civil rights to other issues, the anti-BYU demonstrations faded in the early 1970s. Sociologist Armand Mauss noted that "when the church finally dropped its traditional racial restrictions in 1978 there had been no significant outside pressure to do so for several years" (Mauss, *The Angel and the Beehive* 117). In the three decades since the revelation, Latter-day Saints have embraced new opportunities afforded by the change, intensifying missionary efforts in Africa and engaging in several cooperative projects with the African American community. Perhaps because of these efforts, and because so many American institutions have likewise struggled with race-related issues—this was not a uniquely Mormon predicament—the priesthood policy has not proven to have a lasting legacy on the contemporary image of Mormonism the way that plural marriage has.

In fact, by the time of the 1978 revelation on the priesthood, the Church was already garnering recognition for its new public relations touchstone: the family. While Mormons had always been depicted as strong proponents of families, primarily because of their doctrine of eternal family ties that transcend death, a 1970s-era media campaign spearheaded by the Church's Public Communications Department (the successor to the Church Information Service) took that association with family values to a new level of public awareness. The campaign was called "Homefront" and centered on short public service messages distributed to radio and television stations. The response was phenomenal, from industry awards to free air time to requests for Church-produced materials for strengthening marriages and family solidarity.

In line with the Church's pro-family stance, Church elders spoke out against abortion and the Equal Rights Amendment, which seemed to threaten statutory protections for traditional families. Church members actively joined the push to defeat the amendment in a number of states, and that political activism did not go unnoticed.

On the one hand, the amendment's supporters opposed the Church's involvement in what they viewed as a purely political issue. On the other hand, the growing conservative Christian electorate faced what was for them an uncomfortable conundrum: how to reconcile Mormonism's positions on social and moral issues, which conservative Christians shared, with their divergent views about the nature of God and the afterlife. Those on both the political left and the political right recognized the remarkable organizing power that was centralized under the Latter-day Saint leadership—and this made many on both sides increasingly uncomfortable. Both sides began asking questions that awakened old fears about the LDS Church's intentions and its resources.

In the 1980s, several books detailed Mormon wealth and political clout, warning that the Church was both ominous and underscrutinized. Church dissidents wrote disparagingly about secret temple ceremonies and oaths that smacked of occult practices. Forger-turned-murderer Mark Hofmann rocked the Mormon historical community with his "discovery" of documents that seemed to challenge the Church's founding narrative and impugn the character of Joseph Smith. All of these threads wove their way into national coverage of Mormons. At the same time, the threat of Mormon proselytizing success worldwide and especially in the United States prompted some denominations to revive their views that Mormonism was a cult, rather than a Christian religion. The Church's very success seemed to destabilize its image.

Instead of retreating into a defensive posture, new Church president Gordon B. Hinckley ushered in an unprecedented period of openness in the mid-1990s. His professional background was in Church communications, making him predisposed to media outreach. He sat for interviews with *60 Minutes*'s Mike Wallace and with Larry King. He traveled more extensively in the United States and abroad than any of his predecessors, and everywhere he went he met with the press. He redoubled the Church's humanitarian aid efforts, and the "Mormon Helping Hands" logo began to appear at disaster sites worldwide. The Church cooperated with charities operated by various religious groups, and President Hinckley likewise urged Church members to cooperate at the local level with neighbors of other faiths. Events like the 1997 wagon train reenactment that celebrated the Mormon pioneer exodus and the 2002 Winter Olympics in Salt Lake City brought in journalists by the hundreds, and the Church Public Affairs Department offered press kits and tours and interviews. This openness seemed to affect the tone of news stories that dealt with Mormons and their relationships with other religious and civic leaders, as well. The number of Mormons in business, in sports, and in government seemed to temper claims of the religion's hidden deviance.

Yet, notwithstanding these apparent positive gains in terms of the public awareness of Mormons, the 2008 presidential campaign of George Romney's son Mitt revealed that a surprisingly large segment of the U.S. population still maintained deep suspicions of the Church and its theology. Many commentators noted how these expressions of hostility surprised Latter-day Saints, who had seen in recent treatments of their Church hopeful signs that the former antagonism had dissipated. Because of a past riddled with episodes of persecution, contemporary Mormons are sensitive—often acutely so—to blots on their faith's public image. Recent polling suggests that many outsiders still associate Mormons with polygamy and that even more people question the appropriateness of labeling the Church "Christian."

Mormons, whether through BYU sports or the Tabernacle Choir or coverage of prominent politicians, have clearly secured a spot in the national cultural consciousness. Never have Mormons been better known, yet that notoriety has invited more intense curiosity and correspondingly complex characterizations of the Saints. Mormons themselves worry about ignorance and misinformation as never before. What remains to be seen is how future forces will color the impressions that Mormonism evokes. What is certain is that the advent of forums like the blogosphere and social networks will enable more voices to join the dialogue about the meaning of "Mormon."

—*J. B. Haws*

See also: Mormonism and Other Faiths; Non-Mormon Views of Mormonism; Smoot Hearings.

References

Alexander, Thomas G. *Mormonism in Transition: A History of the Latter-day Saints, 1890–1930.* Urbana: University of Illinois Press, 1986.

Chen, Chiung Hwang. *Mormon and Asian American Model Minority Discourses in News and Popular Magazines.* Lewiston, NY: The Edwin Mellen Press, 2004.

Fluhman, J. Spencer. "Anti-Mormonism and the Making of Religion in Antebellum America." PhD dissertation, University of Wisconsin-Madison, 2006.

Givens, Terryl L. *The Viper on the Hearth: Mormons, Myths, and the Construction of Heresy.* New York: Oxford University Press, 1997.

Lawrence, Gary C. *How Americans View Mormonism: Seven Steps to Improve Our Image.* Orange, CA: The Parameter Foundation, 2008.

Mauss, Armand L. *The Angel and the Beehive: The Mormon Struggle with Assimilation.* Urbana: University of Illinois Press, 1994.

Pratt, Parley P. *Late Persecution of the Church of Jesus Christ of Latter-day Saints.* New York: J. W. Harrison, 1839.

Shipps, Jan. *Sojourner in the Promised Land: Forty Years among the Mormons.* Urbana: University of Illinois Press, 2000.

Non-Mormon Views of Mormonism

When religious seekers coalesce around a new mystic or prophetic leader who arrives on the scene without ordination or other credentials, outsiders are typically wary and suspicious, quick to ridicule and deride. So it was when a bevy of followers gathered in western New York around Joseph Smith Jr., who declared that he had translated a new scriptural text from golden plates and that he was receiving revelations about the restoration of the ancient priesthoods and the original Church of Jesus Christ. Everyone except the youthful prophet, many members of his family, and a generous handful of supporters simply failed to believe the claim about the work called the Book of Mormon or that the restored Church of Christ had returned to Earth for the first time since a "great apostasy" had occurred at the end of the apostolic age.

The new scripture generated so much contemporary ridicule that advertisements for Smith's "gold bible," a bogus printed imitation of the work, and other examples of scorn survive as part of the written record of the beginnings of Mormonism. Yet, the ecclesiastical organization of this new religious movement as the restored Church of Christ initiated the most intense opposition. The new Church's members (outsiders called them Mormonites) met all sorts of hostility, which they experienced as persecution even though historical analysis suggests that the skeptical response of their New York neighbors was animated more by a competitive spirit aroused by the new Church's assertion that it was the only true Christian Church than by any actual threat posed by members of the group struggling to become a movement.

The situation changed considerably after Smith and his followers left New York. They moved to Kirtland, Ohio, where Smith emphasized the "Gathering," a revelation that instructed new converts to congregate as close to the center as possible. Responding positively, they created what amounted to a self-imposed ghetto that accentuated a second Mormon restoration that was accompanying the restoration of the Church. This additional restoration, the restoration of Israel, involved

- Detecting which Abrahamic tribes were the ancestors of Smith's followers; and
- A modern gathering of the extended Abrahamic family that had disappeared into the Near Eastern "woodwork" when Israel's northern and southern tribes went their separate ways in Old Testament times.

These efforts gave Smith's followers a powerful identity as God's "Chosen People" in the new world. Henceforth, the Saints would regard those not of their number as "gentiles" while non-Mormons likened the Saints to Jews and treated them accordingly.

The non-Mormon shift away from competitiveness to setting the prophet's flock apart and considering them as *other,* people who were somehow foreign, first manifested itself violently in Independence, Missouri, where a band of Saints had established a second "stake in the tent of Zion" in and among old Missouri settlers. Whether the fact that the Prophet set Missouri apart as the land to which Christ would return to initiate the final dispensation of the fullness of times had anything to do with it or not, the Missourians attacked the Saints and drove them from Independence. The Saints were also expelled from their homes in Illinois and finally settled in the isolated expanses of the Great Basin. As a result of their remoteness and separation from the world, the Mormon-gentile relationship changed dramatically.

After the Saints reached the Great Salt Lake Valley, hostile words became as important as actual physical belligerence, at which point what non-Mormons thought of the Mormons and how the members of the two groups acted toward each other when they met became the real story of Mormon-gentile relations. Because the Saints were too far away from the scuffles and skirmishes that created physical combat, that relationship (apart from the Utah War and Mountain Meadows Massacre) became a war of words, rather than deeds. While the principals in the conflict were usually government officials and LDS Church authorities, these confrontations, as well as general observations, were reported by gentile visitors to the Mormons' new Zion in the West.

Many of these reporters were working journalists, but others—Mark Twain is a good example—were simply western travelers who reported what they saw. A great number of other writers were Protestant clergymen whose accounts conveyed their dismay at what appeared to them as a foreign, unchristian belief system that called for a home (i.e., domestic) missionary effort to move these "pagan people" away from their "depraved, unscrupulous, and corrupt" religious leaders and detestable religious system.

Mormons and Mormonism became popular subjects in the 19th and 20th century press, a fact that creates certain challenges for scholarly analysis. How could one effectively analyze outsider attitudes and arrive at conclusions that went beyond mere impressions? Using methods of modern survey research to track the perceptions of and attitudes toward the Saints of those who wrote about the Mormons turned out to be a useful way to summarize gentile thought. A standard schedule of questions was used as the basis for analysis of a carefully selected sample of articles stratified by date and drawn from every one of the articles about Mormons, Latter-day Saints, Mormonism, polygamy, and Utah indexed in *Poole's Index* and the *Reader's Guide* between 1860 and 1960. The analysis not only looked at the relative emphasis given to the religious and secular dimensions of Mormonism in each article but also included a content analysis and a ranking on a series of five-point attitude scales on attitudes toward Mormon theological claims and toward Mormonism as it affected citizenship, family life, and morality as opposed to immorality. The analytic product also included the number of positive and negative references to the Saints relative to the length of each article and an overall ranking of each article as very negative, negative, somewhat negative, neutral, somewhat positive, positive, or very positive. This analytic approach had many virtues, especially when the impact of the articles was weighted according to the source's circulation, for it permitted comparison of perceptions of and attitudes toward the Latter-day Saints across time.

The study was divided into three calendar units: 1860 to 1895; 1896 to 1919; and 1920 through 1960, reflecting changes in Mormons' relationship with the outside world and notably with non-Mormons. Results revealed that, when the data were weighted by circulation, in the first of these units, the overall attitude score never reached neutral, while the article contents indicated that non-Mormons were mesmerized by the practice of what they called polygamy, while the Saints called it plural marriage and regarded it as the "Principle" that established their identity as God's "Chosen People." The political organization of the Mormon kingdom was a close second in non-Mormon perceptions of what was going on in Zion, while the beauty of the kingdom, including its built environment, was a source of gentile wonder.

In the middle chronological period, the summarized article rankings shifted with regard to content. For one thing, in response to the 1890 Manifesto announcing the cessation of the practice of, but not belief in the Principle of plural marriage, less emphasis was placed on polygamy. Because Utah had been accepted into the American union, its political, economic, and social systems received more attention than anything else, especially during the three-year investigation ostensibly of the right of the LDS apostle Reed Smoot to be seated in the U.S. Senate but actually of Mormonism itself. Perhaps that investigation as much as anything else accounts for a data set that discloses that perceptions of and attitudes toward Mormonism never moved out of negative territory, remaining somewhere between fairly and slightly negative for the entire 25-year period.

Note, however, that these were the years in which "muckraking" was the heart of American journalism and that the Saints did not escape the muckraker's attention. Muckraking articles charged that the Mormon Church controlled the entire intermountain area of the western United States and indicted Mormon culture for being closed to all but those who were members of the LDS Church. Notwithstanding such negative attention, these were the early years of true domestic tourism on the part of ordinary Americans, and their reports of the beauty of the region and the welcome they received at Temple Square, in the remainder of Salt Lake City, and in the rest of Utah balanced the many negative accounts enough to keep the summarized rankings for this period from dipping into the purely negative and extremely negative categories.

The results for the third chronological period start at neutral in the 1920s and dip into the slightly negative in the 1930s before starting an upward trend that was broken only when Arizona and Utah law officers conducted a raid on a polygamous community in the Arizona strip then known as Short Creek (but now called Hilldale). Because the legally responsible authorities tore children from their mother's arms and separated couples, placing all the polygamous men in prison, this assault turned out to be such a public relations disaster that the practice of plural marriage itself appeared to be less offensive to monogamists than it once had been.

All the while, the upward movement of attitude rankings toward "extremely positive" not only reflected the Saints who did not practice plural marriage but also those who actually seemed embarrassed by their polygamous past. Somehow the Saints shed their foreign character to become as American as any other citizens of the United States. To some degree, this was due to the extraordinary reaction of Saints to appeals for servicemen to fight World War II. But it also reflected the growing power of Utah's senators and congressmen in the nation's capital; the presence of a Mormon like J. Reuben Clark in the U.S. diplomatic corps; the entry of powerful financiers like Marriner Eccles and businessmen and -women (the Marriott hotel chain, Rose Marie Reid bathing suits) into the nation's business and economic life; and the ever-present Mormon Tabernacle Choir and many other Saints in the nation's musical life and in the movies. In short, the Mormons had arrived.

After 1960, though, basing an analysis of non-Mormon perceptions of and attitudes toward the Latter-day Saints on the print media would no longer suffice. There was simply too much radio and television to depend entirely on periodicals (even though this was the heyday of *Look, Life, Time, Newsweek,* and the *Reader's Digest,* plus *Collier's,* the *Saturday Evening Post,* and too many women's magazines to count) or even on periodicals, books, and newspapers. After World War II, a new professional category, public relations (in Mormon terms, "Public Affairs"), complicated the picture as much as the diversification of the media that would eventually lead to the Internet, making attitude analysis much trickier and more difficult. Even so, it is still possible to survey the Mormon image by wide-ranging observation—or by becoming, as one LDS Apostle called this author, a "Mormon watcher."

With the election of the first Roman Catholic as U.S. president demonstrating the country's religious tolerance, American culture appeared to be thriving as never before at the beginning of the 1960s. Yet, there were signals that all was not well. Instead of the perpetuation of the family "togetherness" of the 1950s intimated by the development of suburbia, divorce became so ever-present that it assumed a social acceptability that it had never had up to that time. The civil rights movement was nearing its zenith, and the nation, having brought the Korean War to a close without victory, was involved in another foreign war, this time in Vietnam. The much vaunted Peace Corps volunteer movement was balanced by a far larger movement into mind-altering drugs and long hair. Hippiedom was making its appearance, especially in San Francisco and other large American cities.

With all that as background, "those amazing Mormons," to use the title of a 1952 article in *Coronet Magazine,* were suddenly "more American than the Americans" (Shipps, *Sojourner* 351). Their positive image, emanating from the periodical press and the Tabernacle Choir singing with the Philadelphia Orchestra and other highly regarded symphonic organizations (often on television) were matched by appealing and/or impressive Mormon personalities on the national scene: people like the Pulitzer Prize–winning author and columnist Jack Anderson, golfer Johnny Miller,

Michigan's governor George Romney, Secretary of Agriculture Ezra Taft Benson, and, shortly to come, Donny and Marie and the rest of the members of the Osmond family, which turned Mormonism into a very upbeat television staple.

During this period, the Saints had what many Americans regarded as a retrograde position on race. But Mormonism's refusal to allow the ordination of black men to the priesthood was not enough to keep the Mormons from serving as a reminder to the country that the whole nation had not gone the way of the much-maligned long-haired, pot-smoking, flag-burning members of the counterculture. The LDS image as neat, modest, virtuous, family-loving, conservative, and patriotic people made attitudes toward and perceptions of the Saints extremely positive, almost too perfect to be believed.

When a person or group becomes a "media darling," a negative subtext soon appears. In this case, at least two critical *60 Minutes* segments questioned the benign picture of the Saints. But the real unconstructive subtext was rooted in a film called the *God Makers* that both ridiculed Mormon doctrine and charged that Mormonism is not Christian. These charges fit directly into the programs of the Evangelical mega-Church and Southern Baptist movements, which were increasing mightily as traditional Protestantism split apart, leaving liberalism to mainline Churches while the many forms of the new Christian Right used opposition to Mormonism as a means of maintaining a modicum of harmony.

Books about the new polygamy, as well as new versions of 19th-century exposés such as *The Mormon Corporate Empire,* by John Hinerman and Anson Shupe, attracted readers suspicious of the shiny new Mormon image. But, for the remainder of the 20th century, the Latter-day Saints generally managed to escape suspicion, except for a year or so when the saga of the forger Mark Hofmann pushed Mormonism generally into public view in a way that reinforced accusations about religious illegitimacy and secular mendacity.

While the Hofmann case placed the Saints in a dark-hued spotlight, the 2002 Winter Olympic Games in Salt Lake City did precisely the opposite. As the Church had so obviously hoped, when the world came to the Mormon center for what was nigh unto a perfect sports event, traditional negative Saintly stereotypes were shattered, leaving non-Mormon suspicion out in the cold. The happy result was Saints who were ready to leave their time-honored persecution complex behind.

Not for long, however, since renewed emphasis on modern plural marriage, this time in Texas, plus the Church's involvement in the fight to pass California's Proposition 8 and Mitt Romney's presidential campaign in 2008 all undercut the perfection of the Mormon image that the Olympic Games had left behind. Among much else, this last revealed that an astonishingly high percentage of non-Mormons would not vote for a Mormon for president under any circumstances. So, here again, are the Saints worried about how many non-Mormons need to be re-educated to understand that:

- Mormonism really is Christian, although a form of Christianity very different from any other present in the world today;
- Latter-day Saints are as likely as a serious member of any other religious group to serve effectively as president of the United States;
- Saints love and respect their gay and lesbian members even as they are opposed to gay and lesbian marriage.

So it is that Mormonism may have to wait until the eternities to communicate fully and happily with their non-Mormon neighbors. Or, at least they will need to wait for the millennium for perceptions of the Saints and attitudes toward them to be the same from the outside as from the inside.

—Jan Shipps

See also: Divergent Churches; Mormonism and Other Faiths; Mormonism's Contested Identity; Smoot Hearings.

Reference

Shipps, Jan. *Sojourner in the Promised Land: Forty Years among the Mormons.* Urbana: University of Illinois Press, 2000.

Polygamy

Polygamy is both the most noted and the most notorious feature of early Mormonism. Less known is how much its practice differed depending on the number of wives, age at marriage, amount of family wealth, the number of children, the geographic area in which the family lived, and the personalities of the husband and wives. Its prevalence also varied over time. The period during which polygamy was practiced by members of the Church of Jesus Christ of Latter-day Saints may be divided into three basic parts: introduction of the "Principle" from about 1833 until 1846; the period when it was openly practiced, from 1847 to about 1884; and its demise, from 1885 until roughly 1910.

The popular media portrayed 19th-century Mormon plural marriage as destructive of morality and productive of degenerate offspring. The Jonathan Heaton family of Mocassin Springs, Arizona, along with many scores of others, disproved those popular canards. (Courtesy of the Church History Library, The Church of Jesus Christ of Latter-day Saints.)

Kathryn Daynes has called the introductory period proto-polygamy because initially polygamous marriages did not have all the attributes associated with marriage (Daynes, *More Wives Than One* 31). The first plural marriages were performed secretly; plural wives did not live with their husbands, at least not openly; and the marriage was not acknowledged by the community. After Joseph Smith's assassination, in 1844, increasing numbers of Mormons entered plural marriage, especially when the Nauvoo Temple was sufficiently completed that the sacred ordinances sealing couples together could be performed there. The marriages were secret but open enough that the Saints suffered persecution for their practice. In fact, the slaying of the Church's founding prophet can be partly attributed to his introduction of polygamy.

Increasingly, however, these marriages took on the customary attributes of marriage, especially after those in plurality left Nauvoo. They acknowledged their marital status and so were reputed to be married. They cohabited—lived in the same house, ate at the same table, attended social events together—and women began taking the husband's surname.

Beginning in the 1880s, the process was reversed, and the waning of polygamy was in many ways a mirror image of its beginnings. In the face of active federal prosecution of polygamists, any apparent acknowledgement of a plural marriage—cohabiting or even associating with more than one wife; being reputed to be a polygamist; a wife's using her husband's name; or an alleged plural wife bearing a child—could get a man arrested, so outward signs of a marriage decreased. After a brief upsurge of new marriages in the mid-1880s, fewer and fewer plural marriages were performed.

Between the beginning and the waning of polygamy, the practice was lived openly, and faithful Mormons viewed it as the highest form of matrimony. During this period, the attributes of the Mormon marriage system were the accentuation of religion and duty, not romantic love; emphasis on relationships to children, rather than the conjugal dyad; and provision of the opportunity to marry to every woman who wanted to. Men who took additional wives were usually wealthier than average, but residents of Utah were generally poorer than other Americans. While the number of wives a husband could marry was not restricted, two-thirds of polygamists had only two wives. Moreover, given the difficulty of living in plurality, divorce was an option, although certainly discouraged.

Plural marriage was never easy to live, but, of the three periods, living it during polygamy's waning days was the most difficult. Difficult as it was for Mormons to put aside their prejudices in favor of monogamy when plural marriage was introduced, it was even more difficult to endure the enforced breakup of marriages in the face of federal prosecutions. In addition, plural families often faced the heart-wrenching requirement that they testify about their relationships in court, testimony that put their husbands and fathers in prison.

In less than a century, Mormons moved from a monogamous marriage system to a polygamous one and back to a monogamous one. The rules and practices that govern the establishment, continuance, and dissolution of marriage define a society. In general, members of a society see their marriage system as natural and others as strange, but marriage systems are peculiar to particular times and places. Many systems of past centuries emphasized marriage as a working partnership of husbands, wives, and children.

About the time of the American Revolution, romantic love received increasing importance as a necessary precursor to marriage. Romantic love emphasized the exclusive bond between the man and the woman and the accompanying intimate emotional relationship through which the partners exclusively revealed their inner selves. This change of emphasis was gradual, and the older relationship retained its potency. In fact, while marriage systems change, they generally do so gradually.

The 19th-century Mormon marriage system differed from this tendency. Historically, it emerged rather abruptly in response to the religious imperative that Joseph Smith believed he was given from God to introduce the practice, and it also died fairly rapidly as a result of congressional legislation in the 1880s and an official pronouncement by Wilford Woodruff, president of the Church in 1890, known as the Manifesto. Polygamy among the Latter-day Saints thus had a religious foundation, and its practice was fostered by individual members' piety. Like other restorationists, Mormons wished to return to the Bible as the source of their religion, but they differed in returning not only to the New Testament but also to the Old. Abraham, one of the great Old Testament prophets and progenitor of the House of Israel, was especially honored, and the blessing of a numerous posterity, Latter-day Saints believed, applied to all righteous people, not just Abraham. They sought to follow Abraham's example by having several wives to produce that posterity. Also important was Elijah, who held the sealing power to bind in heaven that which was bound on Earth. Applied to marriages, the sealing power made eternal the marriages performed by those who held that power, namely Joseph Smith and those whom he authorized.

There certainly would not have been plural marriage without the revelation regarding it that Joseph Smith dictated, and individuals entered the practice because of their belief in and testimony of its divine origin. Many Mormons initially found polygamy repugnant when their prophet introduced the doctrine to them, but having faith in latter-day revelation and often, as they reported, receiving their own spiritual confirmation, a few select Church members followed their leader into the practice. Even so, overcoming their marital traditions was difficult as the new system evolved. Speaking in 1855 of his introduction to the doctrine of plural marriage, Brigham Young said, "It was the first time in my life that I had desired the grave, and I could hardly get over it for a long time. And when I saw a funeral, I felt to envy the corpse its situation, and to regret that I was not in the coffin" (Young, "Plurality of Wives" 3:266).

Women undoubtedly had even more difficulty accepting plural marriage. Lucy Walker was a teenager living in the Joseph and Emma Smith household when Joseph sought an interview with her. He said he had been commanded of God to take another wife, and she was the woman. She was astonished. When she confirmed that she looked upon him as a prophet, he explained plural marriage to her, saying it would benefit her and her whole family. He told her to pray about it, which she did most fervently. She wrote that she received the testimony of plural marriage that she sought. This certainly was an unusual marriage proposal: no honeyed words, no love-making. The foundation of the marriage was religious.

As the Saints left Nauvoo, their plural marriages were lived more openly, although the official Church acknowledgement of polygamy did not come until 1852. The people leaving their homes in Illinois to strike out across the plains formed a society that was undergoing many stresses and strains. It literally was an entire society that left homes and farms, often unsold, and moved to a new location—a place whose attraction was largely its lack of appeal to other settlers. Colonizing anywhere was rarely easy, but in the Great Basin it was particularly difficult, with periodic droughts and plagues of grasshoppers.

Moreover, Mormondom grew rapidly and needed to incorporate many immigrants who came with their own cultures and sometimes own languages. Irish-born Martha Spence was one such immigrant. In 1850, wanting to live with the Saints in Utah, she traveled in Joseph Heywood's wagon, taking care of his consumptive nephew. Her one joy on the journey was meeting with Joseph E. Johnson as he traveled back to Iowa. She rhapsodized that he was "a noble soul," and she felt "warmly interested in his welfare." This contrasted sharply with her "chilled feelings" when she thought of going to Brother Heywood's house to live (Heywood, *Not by Bread Alone* 32). But she went there nonetheless. Salt Lake City offered few places for rent, and she had few housekeeping skills besides sewing.

After a couple of months in his house, Martha's opinion of Heywood had so far improved that she called him "a good man but not interesting" (Heywood, *Not by Bread Alone* 36). But, two months after she shared that opinion with her diary, her already twice-married host approached her with a proposal to become his wife and go to the South Sea Islands with him as a missionary. The idea of becoming a missionary appealed to her, but Joseph's first wife protested. She had a household to run and responsibility for the children, Joseph's second wife, and a preteen orphan. She wanted Martha to remain and help her with those tasks. In these new circumstances, Martha was undecided but finally agreed. After she married Joseph, she felt calm about her decision and wrote that she was satisfied with the husband the Lord had given her. At age 38, Martha confided to a friend that what she most wanted was a home and children and to belong to someone. These goals and religious motivations were her reasons for marrying. Romantic love had little to do with her accepting Joseph's proposal, although she did learn to appreciate his company.

Not surprisingly in a polygamous society, romantic love was downplayed. Apostle Orson Pratt wrote that love was not "such as is often described in novels, which acts irresistibly, forcing all the other powers of the mind into subjection" (Pratt, "Celestial Marriage" 152). In fact, novel reading itself was discouraged. Apostle Charles Rich stated, "When a person is love struck, there is no reason in them. We should never be struck very bad" (Rich, "Discourse" 19:167). No one, wrote Orson Pratt, should marry without some love, but a righteous woman would love a man who works righteousness, and vice versa. If the couple cultivated that love and mutual kindness, their love would grow into a perfect love. This was love, but not the romantic kind.

Religious reasons were the foundation for entering plural marriage, but those women who also had additional reasons were more likely to become plural wives. Daynes's detailed study of Manti, Utah, found two groups of women who disproportionately entered plural marriage: those whose fathers were dead or not in Utah and those who were widowed or divorced. These two groups shared the problem of not having a breadwinner in pioneer Utah. Women could and did work for money, but the jobs women had—sewing, laundry, teaching school—paid little. Marrying a man who could help provide for them added an extra incentive to the religious ones, and women without male breadwinners were more likely to become plural wives. Even so, the majority of single women, even those without fathers in Utah, became monogamous wives, but slightly more than half of women marrying again, whether widowed or divorced, became plural wives. As for men, those occupying higher positions in the Church hierarchy were most likely to become polygamists, but many men with callings lower than bishop also embraced plural living.

New plural marriages also declined over the period of open polygamy. Considerably more polygamous marriages took place in the pioneer period before the railroad arrived, in 1869. In Manti, a community whose marital behavior appears close to the average for towns settled early, almost three-quarters of new plural marriages took place in that early period, and 44 percent were performed in the 1850s, peaking during the Mormon Reformation of 1856–1857. In the wake of agricultural disasters and record immigration, a series of revivals took place, enjoining the Saints to repent of all sins, including their shunning of plural marriage. The high number of new plural marriages suggests that many did indeed repent. New Manti marriages in 1856–1857 were more than 50 percent higher than in the next highest two-year period.

But a number of the newlywed soon repented of these marriages. Within two years, the peak in new plural marriages was followed by a peak in cancellations of sealings, or ecclesiastical divorces. In Manti, 38.5 percent of the Reformation plural marriages ended in divorce. And, of those who were divorced, 70 percent were 17 years of age or younger. Because those who marry young are more likely to divorce, it is not surprising that plural marriages contracted by the young in the fervor of revivals ended in cancellations of the sealings. Many of those who married during the Reformation period were young. As the number of plural marriages increased, fewer women remained in the marriage market, so plural wives were increasingly found among females ages 16, 15, and even 14. At the height of the Reformation, the average marriage age for women fell to its nadir of 16 years (Daynes, *More Wives Than One* 165–166, 107).

Despite the upturn in divorces immediately following the Reformation, polygamous marriages were remarkably stable, at least in comparison to the high rate of divorce in the 21st century, which is just slightly less than 50 percent of all marriages. Studies of two communities found that 16 to 18 percent of Mormon polygamous marriages in the 19th century ended in divorce. To be sure, monogamous marriages were more stable, with only 6 percent of women in such marriages getting a divorce. More men than women experienced a divorce: they were naturally at greater risk because they had more marriages. Between 32 and 35 percent of men in plural marriages received a divorce, still a smaller percentage than today. The risk of divorce notwithstanding, Brigham Young remained a proponent of plural marriages, despite having granted divorces to a fifth of his 56 wives.

By the late 1860s, the number of new plural marriages was overtaken and surpassed permanently by the number of new monogamous marriages. A number of factors accounted for the decline in plural marriages. First, couples marrying in these later years had higher financial expectations than couples that had married earlier. In early Utah, newlyweds set up housekeeping in wagon boxes and one-room cabins. With greater prosperity by the 1870s, however, couples expected considerably better than that. It simply became more costly to marry a wife and even more costly to marry a plural wife as the Mormon economy matured. Second, women had greater employment opportunities as the economy became more diversified. Most women continued to marry, but if they chose not to or married at an older age, they could more easily support themselves as single women than formerly. Third, Utah's economy was shifting from an agricultural to a mercantile-industrial base. A pioneer farm depended upon family labor, and children were indispensable laborers on that farm. As more men became dependent on salaries or wages, children changed from an economic asset to a liability. That was especially so as the length of education for children increased. Instead of being producers, children increasingly became consumers as they spent more time in school. Fourth, Latter-day Saints moving outside Mormon communities found plural marriage especially difficult without the support of fellow Church members and with the opprobrium of their non-Mormon neighbors. Monogamous families were more mobile in a period when Mormons increasingly migrated beyond their Utah strongholds and became small, scattered minorities.

Finally, the prosecutions under the Edmunds and Edmunds-Tucker Acts proved effective in curtailing the growth of plural families. While marriages among Latter-day Saints increasingly became monogamous, many of the plural marriages contracted years before remained intact. Thus, as late as 1880, probably at least one-fifth of LDS men, women, and children still lived in polygamous families.

The prevalence of polygamy has been a vexing question of long standing. Part of the problem results from its considerable variance over both time and place. Not surprisingly, it appears to have been

Mormon men sentenced to prison terms for "unlawful cohabitation" counted it an honor rather than a shame for standing by their plural families. (Courtesy of the Church History Library, The Church of Jesus Christ of Latter-day Saints.)

most prevalent in the late 1850s and early 1860s, in the wake of the Mormon Reformation. More than 40 percent of the Manti population in 1860 lived in plural families, but only 25 percent did so in 1880. In Manti and in three Salt Lake wards, 44 percent of women were polygamous wives as of 1860 (Daynes, *More Wives Than One* 100–101; Cornwall et al., "How Common the Principle?" 148). By 1880, the percentage of Mormons living in plural households varied from a low of about 5 percent in Virgin City (versus 40 percent in 1870) to a high of 65 percent in Orderville (Bennion, "Incidence of Mormon Polygamy" 30, 31).

If the make-up of the Manti and Brigham City populations is a reliable indicator, the national origins of Mormon pioneers did not affect their disposition for plural living. Both towns had a fairly balanced mix of American-, British-, and Scandinavian-born citizens. In 1876, Jens Weibye, a Danish clerk, counted "253 married men in Manti, Utah—136 Americans, English & Germans, 117 Scandinavians . . . where of 40 is Polygamist, half of them Scandinavisk" (Peterson and Bennion, *Sanpete Scenes* 26). Weibye took obvious pride in his people's edging out the non-Scandinavians as polygamists.

Because of Utah's rapid population growth, the absolute numbers in plural families remained stable or possibly increased, even as the percentage of Mormons living in polygamous households generally declined from 1860 to 1880. In any event, the dense network of family relationships created by plural marriages meant that perhaps a majority of Mormons were involved with polygamy either directly or indirectly (Bennion et al., *Polygamy* 26).

Whatever the percentage, polygamy was sufficiently prevalent that Congress passed increasingly stringent legislation to eradicate it. Despite notable failures in the past, federal officials underestimated the efforts necessary to put down polygamy. But the Edmunds Act of 1882 was a huge step in that direction. The most important section of the act was the one stipulating that unlawful cohabitation could carry a sentence of six months in prison and a $300 fine. Prosecutors found it difficult to prove the more serious crimes of polygamy and bigamy; besides, the statute of limitations prevented the prosecution of many plural marriages. Unlawful cohabitation became the workhorse of federal prosecutors in Mormon Country.

Because of the threat of prosecution, marrying after passage of the Edmunds Act multiplied the problems inherent in plural marriages. Annie Clark had been raised in a plural family and believed implicitly in plural marriage. Unlike Lucy Walker and Martha Spence, who had problems accepting the principle, Annie believed that turning down an offer of plural marriage was a serious matter. When her dashing young professor showed interest in her, she wrote that he had a magnetic personality and that her impressions guided her most favorably toward him. She was deterred neither by her sister's unsuccessful plural marriage nor her father's caution that it was easier for a man to win a woman's affections than to keep them in polygamy. That was especially so in the 1880s, when the marriage had to be kept secret.

After her wedding to Marion Tanner, he and his first wife, Jennie, simply dropped 19-year-old Annie off at the train station near her parents' home, and her wedding celebration consisted of eating bread and milk alone. Two weeks later, Marion failed to keep his first appointment to meet her after their marriage. Deeply disappointed, Annie nevertheless called herself "an ardent lover" (Tanner, *A Mormon Mother* 69). Romantic love was a greater motivation for her than for either Lucy Walker or Martha Spence, but it was not an exclusive, possessive love. She expressed no jealousy of the other wives; her strictures were reserved for the thoughtlessness of her husband.

But Annie's trials went beyond that. The marriage had to remain secret, so she continued to be called Miss Clark and had to fend off suitors without being able to tell them the reason. Even more difficult was her life after she became pregnant. She adopted another name—Mrs. Wilson—and ceased living in her father's home. Her first child was born at the height of the prosecutions in 1888, and revealing her husband's identity would have put his liberty in considerable jeopardy. Having already had the heart-wrenching experience of testifying that her father was a polygamist, an act that helped put him behind prison bars, Annie endured the privations of hiding so that her husband could remain free.

Like plural wives in Nauvoo, she did not use her husband's surname, she did not live openly with him, and the marriage was never acknowledged in the 1880s. Within Mormon society it became known only after the fear of prosecution receded, and she and Marion continued to have children through the 1890s. But Marion's forced resignation from his position as president of the Utah Agricultural College because of his polygamous marriages put additional financial pressures on the family, and in 1912 he ceased providing anything toward Annie's support. She had initially been committed to the practice of plural marriage, but the legal, social, and financial pressures caused by the federal prosecutions and the Church's official withdrawal of support for plural marriages took their toll.

Marion Tanner avoided prosecution for his plural marriages, but many were not so fortunate. When William H. Dickson was appointed U.S. district attorney for Utah, he brought a crusading spirit to uphold the law and to put down the "flaunting" of polygamous households and, of course, an intense desire to win his cases. He was tireless in his efforts, and, along with his assistant Charles S. Varian, he was remarkably successful. During his tenure, which ended in 1887, Dickson garnered guilty verdicts in 90 percent or more of his cases.

Church leaders had initially asked that polygamists fight conviction in the courts, but the high percentage of guilty verdicts appears to have dampened their enthusiasm. Some polygamists pled not guilty and went to trial, but by 1887 the large majority simply pled guilty. For most, to be indicted was to serve a prison sentence—unless of course, the man could avoid arrest, which a number of them did. For a few, the evidence was insufficient, and sometimes plural wives perjured themselves to protect their husbands. Such cases, however, were rare. Federal prosecutions were so successful in part because the Mormons were honest—albeit reluctantly—and prosecutors often regarded the polygamists' family members as hostile witnesses.

Lorenzo Snow's 1885–1886 unlawful cohabitation cases were significant ones. Because he was a high-ranking Church leader, federal officials wanted to ensure his conviction. The apostle had tried to conform to the requirements of the law by living only with the last and youngest of his wives, Minnie. He was not alone; many polygamists had altered their living arrangements to conform to what they thought was the law. Not only were there relatively fewer Mormons entering plural marriage, but also the Edmunds Law meant that many already in plural marriage essentially ceased living it. Testimony showed that Lorenzo Snow lived at Minnie's house, although his big house with three of his other wives stood on the same lot. The prosecutor argued that a polygamist could not choose the wife with whom he would cohabit but had to live solely with his first and only legal wife. The prosecutor proved persuasive: he won this case, and a polygamist who tried to conform to the law by living with only one wife was henceforth at considerable risk if she was not his first one.

In addition, the prosecutor segregated Lorenzo Snow's offense of unlawful cohabitation into three indictments, a strategy Dickson had begun using only three months before. Rather than treating unlawful cohabitation as one continuing offense, Dickson divided the time during which cohabitation occurred into shorter periods and secured indictments for each. Instead of being charged with one offense with a maximum of six months' imprisonment and a $300 fine, Lorenzo Snow was convicted of three offenses of unlawful cohabitation and received a sentence of 18 months.

Segregation was successful in increasing the sentences of those convicted of unlawful cohabitation, making the crime a more serious one than even the Edmunds

Act had envisioned. The Church fought back, however, and took the issue to the U.S. Supreme Court. In February 1887, word reached Utah that the High Court had decided in Snow's favor. He was released, as were others, when they finished serving one sentence.

Also released were a number of men suffering deteriorating health because of conditions in the prison. After John Johnson of East Mill Creek died of pneumonia, in 1888, officials tried to ensure that others with life-threatening illnesses were released. They realized that the prison sentences were creating martyrs enough without having some die in prison.

Congress underestimated the tenacity of Mormons who were determined to hold to their beliefs and practices. The struggle was more expensive than it had anticipated; among other things, Congress had to appropriate money for a new prison because the old one was woefully inadequate to hold such a large influx of prisoners. Congress also passed the Edmunds-Tucker Act of 1887, which supplemented previous legislation and directed that all property of the Church worth more than $50,000 be confiscated. When federal officials moved to take over the temples, they struck at the very heart of the Church's mission: its ability to provide the ordinances its doctrines taught were essential for eternal exaltation. In September 1890, Wilford Woodruff issued the Manifesto that marked the beginning of the end of Church support for new plural marriages. By this date, polygamists' attempts to conform to the law had already considerably reduced the number of plural families still cohabiting.

The last phase was extraordinarily painful as plural families were forcibly broken up. Plural wives and their children suffered most. In many families, cohabitation ceased. Many of the marriages remained, however, so these women were married but without the presence of their husband even on a part-time basis. In other cases, the first wife, with older children, made a great sacrifice by divorcing her husband so that he could marry the plural wife and help her raise her younger children. Some plural families managed to survive, such as the Marion Tanner family, but, despite some new plural marriages in the post-Manifesto period, polygamy was increasingly seen as a remnant of the past. In the midst of the Smoot Hearings, in 1904, Joseph F. Smith issued the so-called Second Manifesto in which the Church iterated its withdrawal of support of new plural marriages, and, in the years immediately following, the Church subjected to discipline those who defied this injunction. The few who insisted on performing new plural marriages found themselves subject not only to antipolygamy laws but also to the laws of the Church, under which they were excommunicated. The result was cessation of plural marriage within the Church of Jesus Christ of Latter-day Saints but its continuance within various break-off groups.

Assessments of the impact of polygamy within Mormon society are ongoing, but clearly its effect was pervasive. Plural marriages in the 19th century built extensive and dense family networks. Ties among elites and within communities were cemented not only by deeply held religious beliefs and common goals but also by family relationships. In addition, some converts left their kin behind in the eastern United States or in foreign lands, and plural marriage fostered their rapid assimilation into Mormon society. Moreover, in a relatively poor pioneer society, plural marriages provided for economically disadvantaged women. Commitments to help other family members create the strongest moral obligations, and, by marrying these women, polygamists assumed the responsibility to support them.

Within American society, the legal effort to eliminate plural marriage among the Mormons represents the largest and longest conflict between Church and state in American history, eventually defining the state's superiority over religion in prescribing behavior. The U.S. Supreme Court's decision in the *Reynolds* case, in 1879, to uphold congressional action in prohibiting a religiously sanctioned behavior remains a potent precedent for religious cases. Moreover, as Carmon Hardy indicates, Mormon polygamy was, except for religious celibacy, "perhaps the largest formally prescribed departure from monogamous marriage" to occur within Western Christian society (Hardy, *Doing the Works of Abraham* 144).

By 1900, conditions had changed within Mormon Country. Many members had moved away. Both physically and socially, monogamy was more conducive to that mobility than polygamy. As the cohesive Mormon community gradually eroded even in Utah, the home became increasingly important as the center in which religious values were transmitted from one generation to another. New converts were encouraged to stay in their homelands where plural marriage had never been encouraged.

By 1910, the Mormon marriage system had changed from one emphasizing religious duty as the main reason for marriage to one that valued romantic love. But the purpose of both was to create happy, stable, eternal families. Over the 19th century, Mormon society changed fundamentally—economically, socially, geographically, and demographically—and those changes supported the religious prohibition of polygamy in transforming the marriage system from a polygamous to a monogamous one.

—*Kathryn M. Daynes and Lowell C. "Ben" Bennion*

See also: Conflict: 1869–1890; Manifesto; Mormonism and Men; Mormonism and the Family; Mormonism and Women; Reformation.

References

Bennion, Lowell "Ben." "Incidence of Mormon Polygamy in 1880: 'Dixie' versus Davis Stake." *Journal of Mormon History* 11 (1984): 27–42.

Bennion, Lowell C., Alan L. Morrell, and Thomas Carter. *Polygamy in Lorenzo Snow's Brigham City: An Architectural Tour.* Salt Lake City: College of Architecture and Planning, University of Utah, 2005.

Compton, Todd. *In Sacred Loneliness: The Plural Wives of Joseph Smith.* Salt Lake City, UT: Signature Books, 1997.

Cornwall, Marie, Camela Courtright, and Laga Van Beek. "How Common the Principle? Women as Plural Wives in 1860." *Dialogue: A Journal of Mormon Thought* 26 (Summer 1993): 139–153.

Daynes, Kathryn M. *More Wives Than One: Transformation of the Mormon Marriage System, 1840–1910.* Urbana: University of Illinois Press, 2001.

Embry, Jessie L. *Mormon Polygamous Families: Life in the Principle.* Salt Lake City: University of Utah, 1987.

Foster, Lawrence. *Religion and Sexuality: The American Communal Experiments of the Nineteenth Century.* New York: Oxford University Press, 1981.

Hardy, B. Carmon. *Doing the Works of Abraham: Mormon Polygamy, Its Origin, Practice, and Demise.* Norman, OK: Arthur H. Clark, 2007.

Hardy, B. Carmon. *Solemn Covenant: The Mormon Polygamous Passage.* Urbana: University of Illinois Press, 1992.

Heywood, Martha Spence. *Not by Bread Alone: The Journal of Martha Spence Heywood, 1850–56.* Ed. Juanita Brooks. Salt Lake City: Utah State Historical Society, 1978.

Ivins, Stanley B. "Notes on Mormon Polygamy." *Western Humanities Review* 10 (Summer 1956): 229–239.

Peterson, Gary B., and Lowell C. Bennion. *Sanpete Scenes: A Guide to Utah's Heart.* Eureka, UT: Basin/Plateau Press, 1987.

Pratt, Orson. "Celestial Marriage." *Seer* 1 (October 1853): 152.

Rich, Charles C. "Discourse." *Journal of Discourses.* London: LDS Book Depot, 1878.

Tanner, Annie Clark. *A Mormon Mother.* Salt Lake City: University of Utah Library Tanner Trust Fund, 1991.

Van Wagoner, Richard S. *Mormon Polygamy: A History.* 3rd ed. Salt Lake City, UT: Signature Books, 1992.

Young, Brigham. "Plurality of Wives." *Journal of Discourses.* London: LDS Book Depot, 1856.

CHRONOLOGY

1805
December 23   Joseph Smith is born in Sharon, Windsor, Vermont
1816   Family of Joseph Smith moves from Vermont to western New York
1820
spring   Joseph Smith experiences his "First Vision"
1823
September   Joseph Smith receives five angelic visits from Moroni, an ancient
  21–22   American prophet, and learns of the Book of Mormon for the first time
1827
September 22   Joseph Smith takes possession of the metal plates engraved with the text of the Book of Mormon and begins translating them
1829
May 15   Joseph Smith and Oliver Cowdery receive the Aaronic Priesthood through a visit from John the Baptist; the two baptize each other in the Susquehanna River near Harmony, Pennsylvania
Spring   Joseph Smith and Oliver Cowdery receive the Melchizedek Priesthood through a visit from the ancient apostles Peter, James, and John, near Harmony, Pennsylvania
June   Joseph Smith completes translation of the Book of Mormon; groups of three and eight witnesses examine the plates from which the book was translated and prepare their written testimony
1830
March   An edition of 5,000 copies of the Book of Mormon is printed at Palmyra, New York
April 6   Joseph Smith organizes the Church of Christ (its name changed in 1838 to The Church of Jesus Christ of Latter-day Saints) at Fayette, New York; six men sign the incorporating documents, with perhaps 40 to 60 others in attendance
June 30   Samuel Smith, Joseph Smith's younger brother, begins a canvass of nearby villages, offering the Book of Mormon to interested persons; this is considered the first proselytizing mission in church history
October 17   At Joseph Smith's direction, Parley P. Pratt, Oliver Cowdery, Peter Whitmer Jr., and Ziba Peterson begin a mission to the Indians on

the western frontier; en route, they baptize converts and organize a congregation near Kirtland, Ohio

December 30 Joseph Smith announces a revelation calling Church members in New York and Pennsylvania to move to Kirtland, Ohio

1831

February 4 Edward Partridge is named the first bishop of the Church

June 3–6 A conference is held at Kirtland, Ohio, resulting in the ordination of the Church's first high priests and a call to some members to gather at Jackson County, Missouri

July 20 Although Joseph Smith and most members remain for the time being at Kirtland, Ohio, the town of Independence, Missouri, is designated as the "center place of Zion" and the future site of the New Jerusalem

1832

June Missionaries begin preaching in Upper Canada (Ontario), the first non-U.S. missionary work

June 1 With William W. Phelps as editor, the first issue of the *Evening and Morning Star,* the first Mormon periodical, is published at Independence, Missouri

1833

January 22–23 The "School of the Prophets," an adult school teaching both secular and sacred knowledge, begins operation at Kirtland, Ohio

February 27 The revelation known as the "Word of Wisdom," the Church's code of health, is given at Kirtland, Ohio

March 18 The First Presidency, with President Joseph Smith and counselors Sidney Rigdon and Frederick G. Williams, is formally organized

July 20 The printing office of the *Evening and Morning Star* at Independence, Missouri, is destroyed by mob action; this action disrupts the printing of the Book of Commandments, but two young girls, sisters, preserve the record by snatching as many uncut sheets as they could carry and escaping into a dense cornfield

November Continuing conflict with other settlers forces Saints to flee from Jackson County, Missouri, and to find shelter in Clay and other neighboring counties

December 18 Joseph Smith ordains his father, Joseph Smith Sr., as the first Church patriarch

1834

February 17 The first stake and the first high council in the Church are organized at Kirtland, Ohio

May	About 200 persons, reinforced by volunteers en route, leave Kirtland, Ohio, on the armed expedition known as "Zion's Camp," in an effort to reinstate the Saints on their lands in Jackson County, Missouri
October	Another LDS periodical, the *Messenger and Advocate,* begins publication at Kirtland, Ohio

1835

February 14	The first Quorum of the Twelve Apostles is organized
July 3	Michael H. Chandler, owner and exhibitor of several Egyptian mummies and related artifacts, visits Kirtland; Joseph Smith eventually purchases parts of Chandler's collection, leading to production of the Book of Abraham, included in the Church's fourth book of scripture, the Pearl of Great Price
December	The first Mormon hymnal, compiled by Emma Smith, is published at Kirtland, Ohio

1836

March 27	The temple at Kirtland is dedicated during a week of spiritual manifestations reminiscent of the day of Pentecost; in the following weeks, Joseph Smith and Oliver Cowdery record angelic visitations and other experiences in the temple, which became important to Latter-day Saint theology
June 29	A meeting of non-Mormon citizens of Liberty, Missouri, calls for the expulsion of the Saints from Clay County, Missouri; submitting to the public will, most Mormons evacuate Clay County and settle in Caldwell County

1837	Parley P. Pratt publishes *The Voice of Warning,* considered the first LDS missionary tract
June 13	Heber C. Kimball and five companions leave Kirtland, Ohio, as the first missionaries to England
July 30	The first English converts are baptized in the River Ribble at Preston, England; George D. Watt wins a footrace to be the first baptized there
November	The Kirtland Safety Society, an unchartered bank-like institution founded by Joseph Smith in 1836, fails in the nationwide financial Panic of 1837

1838

January 12	Fearing for his life, Joseph Smith flees Kirtland, Ohio, for Far West, Missouri
April 26	The Church's name is changed to The Church of Jesus Christ of Latter-day Saints

May 19	Joseph Smith identifies Spring Hill, a rural area 25 miles north of Far West, Missouri, as Adam-ondi-Ahman, "the place where Adam shall come to visit his people" before the Second Coming of Christ
August 6	A violent confrontation at the polls at Gallatin, Missouri, marks an escalation of difficulties between the Saints and their neighbors
October 2	A large body of Saints leaving Kirtland, Ohio (ending significant Mormon presence there for generations), arrives at Far West, Missouri
October 27	Lilburn W. Boggs, governor of Missouri, issues the "Extermination Order," a call for the Mormons to leave Missouri or face the possibility of mass murder (the Order would not be formally rescinded until June 25, 1976)
October 30	An attack by the Livingston County militia kills 17 LDS men and boys and wounds 12 to 15 others, at Haun's Mill (Shoal Creek), Missouri
October 31	Joseph Smith and others are arrested by the militia; a court martial orders their execution on November 1; Gen. Alexander W. Doniphan refuses to carry out what he judges to be cold-blooded murder
December 1	Joseph Smith and others are imprisoned at Liberty, Missouri
1839	
January	Led by apostle Brigham Young, the Saints begin a desperate three-month evacuation of Missouri, retreating with great suffering and difficulty to the neighborhood of Quincy, Illinois
April 16	Joseph Smith and his imprisoned companions are permitted to "escape" from Liberty Jail and make their way to Illinois
April 25	Joseph Smith purchases two farms at Commerce, Illinois, and the Saints begin to drain the swampy ground to establish the new community of Nauvoo
Summer	Members of the Quorum of the Twelve Apostles leave Nauvoo at various times to fill missions in England
October 29	Seeking assistance from the federal government to right injustices suffered by the Saints in Missouri, Joseph Smith leaves Nauvoo for Washington D.C.; although appeals are made to Congress and to Martin Van Buren, no action is taken
November	The *Times and Seasons,* a periodical remembered for its first publication of important Mormon documents, is inaugurated at Nauvoo
1840	
May 24	The first issue of a new and long-running LDS periodical, the *Millennial Star,* is published at Manchester, England, edited by Parley P. Pratt

June 6	A group of English Latter-day Saints sails for the United States, opening decades of immigration to Nauvoo (and later Utah) by non-U.S. converts
September 15	Patriarch Joseph Smith Sr. dies at Nauvoo; his son Hyrum Smith becomes his successor in January 1841
December 16	An extraordinarily generous city charter, with a separate charter authorizing a city militia, is granted to Nauvoo by the Illinois legislature

1841

January 19	Joseph Smith announces the construction of a temple in Nauvoo, a revelation that also introduces ordinances, beginning with baptism, by living persons standing as proxies for the dead
October 24	Apostle Orson Hyde dedicates Palestine for the prophesied return of the Jews
November 21	The first baptisms for the dead are performed in the basement of the as-yet uncompleted Nauvoo Temple

1842

March 1	Joseph Smith publishes 13 brief statements of Mormon belief (now called the Articles of Faith) in *Times and Seasons,* prepared in response to a request from John Wentworth, editor of the *Chicago Democrat,* for a statement of Mormon history and belief
March 17	Joseph Smith organizes the Female Relief Society of Nauvoo; Emma Smith is named its president
May 4	The first temple rites beyond baptism for the dead are introduced by Joseph Smith to seven close associates

1843

May 3	The *Nauvoo Neighbor* opens publication at Nauvoo
June 1	Addison Pratt and three companions leave Nauvoo on the first mission to the South Seas, landing at Tubuai (near Tahiti) the following April
July 12	Joseph Smith records a revelation openly discussing plural marriage and incorporating teachings shared privately since as early as 1831

1844

January 29	Joseph Smith is nominated as a candidate for president of the United States
February 20	Joseph Smith discusses the probable western migration of the Church, and the Quorum of the Twelve forms a committee on western exploration
May 11	Joseph Smith organizes the "Council of Fifty," a semisecret body directing political affairs of the Church

June 7	The anti-Mormon *Nauvoo Expositor* is published; on June 10, the press is declared a public nuisance by the city council and is destroyed; on June 11, Joseph Smith and members of the city council are charged with riot for the destruction
June 27	Five days after surrendering to Illinois authorities under a promise of protection from Gov. Thomas Ford, Joseph and Hyrum Smith are murdered in the jail at Carthage, Illinois
August	Various claimants to succeed Joseph Smith make their cases at Nauvoo; Brigham Young, as president of the Quorum of the Twelve Apostles, is sustained by the majority, although smaller groups adhere to other leaders

1845

January	The charters of the City of Nauvoo and its militia are revoked by the Illinois legislature
May	Five men are tried for the murders of Joseph and Hyrum Smith and are acquitted
September	Church leaders announce their decision to remove the Saints to an unspecified location in the Rocky Mountains; a non-Mormon citizens' meeting at Carthage, Illinois, calls for a rapid exodus; following negotiations, the Saints agree to leave early in the spring, and citizens agree to cease hostilities, which have resulted in the destruction by fire of houses and crops of outlying Mormon farms
December	The Nauvoo Temple is so far completed that rituals can be conducted within its walls, and for the next two months approximately 5,000 Saints hurry to participate before they must leave the area

1846

February 4	Mormons begin leaving for the West, long before travel conditions are optimal; 226 Mormons with 12 non-Mormon friends, led by Samuel Brannan, leave New York City aboard the ship *Brooklyn* to sail to California, arriving at Yerba Buena (the future San Francisco) on July 31
April 24	A way-station for emigrating Saints is established at Garden Grove, Iowa, with other temporary settlements established in the following months at Mount Pisgah and Kanesville, Iowa, and Winter Quarters, Nebraska
May 1	The Nauvoo Temple is dedicated
July 13	The Mormon Battalion is formed at Kanesville, Iowa, for service in the U.S. War with Mexico, following Mormon appeals to the federal government for emigration assistance; the Battalion arrives at San Diego on January 27, 1847

September 17	The last Saints are driven from Nauvoo following a cannon bombardment in the "battle of Nauvoo"

1847

April 5	The vanguard company of 143 men, 3 women, and 2 children, under the direction of Brigham Young, leaves Winter Quarters, Nebraska, for the trek west
July 22–24	The vanguard company arrives in the Salt Lake Valley and begins laying out a city, irrigating for late crops, and building shelters; 10 other pioneer companies arrive in the following weeks, and Brigham Young returns to Winter Quarters
December 5	The First Presidency is reorganized, with Brigham Young as president and Heber C. Kimball and Willard Richards as counselors

1848

May	"Mormon crickets" destroy much of the crop in the Salt Lake Valley
October	A general conference is held in the Salt Lake Valley; among other decisions is the announcement of a "perpetual emigrating fund" to assist the poor to emigrate from Europe

1850

March 26	Thomas L. Kane, a non-Mormon Pennsylvania philanthropist, delivers a speech to the Pennsylvania Historical Society detailing the forced Mormon exodus from Nauvoo
June 15	The *Deseret News* issues its first number at Salt Lake City
September 9	The U.S. Congress creates the Territory of Utah and appoints a slate of officers, with Brigham Young as governor

1851

March 24	A colony, 500 strong, leaves Payson, Utah, to settle in San Bernardino, California
May	The first foreign-language (Danish) edition of the Book of Mormon is published
Summer/Fall	The non-Mormon territorial officers appointed by Congress arrive in Utah; by September, nearly all have returned east

1852

August 28–29	After several years of secret practice, the doctrine of plural marriage is publicly announced

1853

February 14	Ground is broken for the Salt Lake Temple

1855

October 4	The *Julia Ann* runs aground, killing five Saints, the only such incident in the history of Mormon overseas mass migration

1856

November   The "Reformation," a several-months'-long drive for recommitment to the gospel, opens in Utah and spreads throughout the Church

November 9   The Willie Handcart Company arrives in the Salt Lake Valley after intense suffering and death on the plains; the Martin Handcart Company arrives on November 30 after, if possible, even more severe suffering

1857

July 24   News that a federal army has left the frontier and is marching toward Utah is announced, marking the beginning of the 1857–1858 Utah War

September 7–11   A series of bloody events culminating in the Mountain Meadows Massacre occurs on the immigrant road through southern Utah

1858

June 26   A federal army under the command of Albert Sidney Johnston marches peacefully through Salt Lake City, marking the formal end of hostilities to the Utah War

1860

September 24   The 10th and last Mormon emigrant handcart company arrives in the Salt Lake Valley; the handcart experiment is henceforth replaced by sending wagon trains from Utah to meet poor emigrants on the frontier and bring them back to Utah

1862

July 8   The first antipolygamy law striking at Mormon marriage practices is signed into law by Abraham Lincoln

1866

January 1   The *Juvenile Instructor* begins publication at Salt Lake City, opening the modern era of Church magazine publication

1867

October 6   The Salt Lake Tabernacle hosts its first general conference, although the building is not formally dedicated until 1875

December 8   The Relief Society, disorganized in the Utah War upheaval, is reinstated, continuing to the present

1869

March 1   ZCMI, the flagship "cooperative" store of the Saints, opens its doors in Salt Lake City

November 28   The forerunner to the modern Young Women program is organized by Brigham Young

1873

April 8   Brigham Young expands the First Presidency by calling an additional five counselors

1874

May 9   The "United Order of Enoch," an experiment in economic coop-
         eration and communal living finding expression in many different
         forms, is first presented to the Saints

1875

May 19   The forerunner to the present Young Men organization of the Church
         is organized in Salt Lake City

1877

April 6 The St. George Temple, the first to be completed in the West, is
         dedicated

August 29 Brigham Young dies in Salt Lake City; the Quorum of the Twelve
         Apostles, under the presidency of John Taylor, assumes responsibil-
         ity for directing the Church

1878

August 25 The Primary organization for children is held for the first time at
         Farmington, Utah

1879

January 6 The U.S. Supreme Court upholds the conviction of George Reyn-
         olds for polygamy, dismissing the last of the Church's hopes for
         defending plural marriage on constitutional grounds

1880

April 6 A Jubilee Year, calling for charity to the poor and the forgiveness
         of debts, including the debts to the Perpetual Emigrating Fund, is
         announced

October 10 The First Presidency is reorganized with John Taylor as president
         and George Q. Cannon and Joseph F. Smith as counselors

1882

March 22 Congress passes the Edmunds Act, with harsh penalties for the prac-
         tice of plural marriage, inaugurating a period known as "The Raid";
         normal life is disrupted by the arrest, prosecution, and imprisonment
         of many leading Mormon men for "unlawful cohabitation," while
         many more go "underground" to avoid arrest

August 18 The Utah Commission, a five-man panel authorized by the Edmunds
         Act to effectively disenfranchise Mormons, arrives in Utah

1884

February 3 A test oath approved by Idaho's governor disenfranchises all Mor-
         mons living in that territory; on March 22, a similar test oath proposed
         by the Utah Commission is annulled by the U.S. Supreme Court

1887

February Congress passes the Edmunds-Tucker Act, disincorporating the
17–18   Church, seizing its assets, and abolishing woman suffrage

July 25	John Taylor dies at Kaysville, Utah

1889

April 7	The First Presidency is reorganized with Wilford Woodruff as president and George Q. Cannon and Joseph F. Smith as counselors
November	The Endowment House at Salt Lake City, site of the majority of plural marriages, is torn down

1890

September 24	The Manifesto calling for an end to the contracting of new plural marriages is issued by Wilford Woodruff; it is approved by the membership of the Church on October 6

1893

January 4	Benjamin Harrison issues a presidential pardon to all polygamists whose marriages were contracted before November 1, 1890, restoring their franchise
April 6	The Salt Lake Temple is dedicated
September 8	The Mormon Tabernacle Choir, competing at the Columbian World's Fair at Chicago, wins second prize in the choral contest
October 25	Grover Cleveland signs a congressional resolution paving the way for the return, in 1896, of a residue of the Church's property escheated to the government by the Edmunds-Tucker Act

1894

April	Wilford Woodruff announces a change in the Church's practice of temple sealings, inaugurating the massive and ongoing LDS commitment to genealogical and family history research; the Genealogical Society of Utah is organized the following November

1896

January 4	Utah becomes a state, with a constitution providing for the perpetual outlawing of plural marriage
November 5	Fast Day, a monthly observance of fasting and testimony meetings, is moved from the first Thursday of each month to the first Sunday of each month

1898

April 1	Inez Knight and Lucy Brimhall are set apart as missionaries, the first "lady missionaries" commissioned on a par with their male counterparts
September 2	Wilford Woodruff dies at San Francisco, California
September 13	The First Presidency is reorganized with Lorenzo Snow as president and George Q. Cannon and Joseph F. Smith as counselors

1899

May 8	At a conference in St. George, Utah, Lorenzo Snow calls for a renewed obedience to the law of tithing, a practice neglected when

donations to the Church were subject to confiscation by the federal government

1900

January 25   The U.S. House of Representatives denies a seat to B. H. Roberts of Utah, on the grounds of his existing plural marriages

1901

October 10   Lorenzo Snow dies at Salt Lake City; on October 17 the First Presidency is reorganized with Joseph F. Smith as president and John R. Winder and Anthon H. Lund as counselors

1902

August 4   The Bureau of Information, forerunner to today's visitors' centers, opens on Temple Square at Salt Lake City

1904

April 5   Renewing the Church's official commitment to end plural marriage, Joseph F. Smith announces a penalty of excommunication against violators

1905

October 28   Apostles John W. Taylor and Matthias F. Cowley are dropped from the Quorum for their continued encouragement of plural marriage

December 23   On the 100th anniversary of Joseph Smith's birth, a monument and "memorial cottage" are dedicated at his Sharon, Vermont, birthplace

1907

January 10   Due to the faithful payment of tithing by Church members, Joseph F. Smith announces that the Church is out of debt for the first time in a generation

February 20   The U.S. Senate seats apostle Reed Smoot, following his three-year battle to assume his elected position

December 14   The Church calls for European members to remain at home and build up the Church in their nations rather than immigrate to Utah, a call that is renewed (and largely ignored) until the 1950s

1909

November   The First Presidency reaffirms LDS belief in God as the literal father of humanity but otherwise officially takes a neutral position on the question of Darwinian evolution and other scientific theories on the origin of man

1912

November 8   Led by Apostle David O. McKay, the Church institutes a "correlation" program to coordinate practices and procedures within the Church, a systematizing that continues to the present

1915

April 27   The "Home Evening" program is started but does not gain wide-spread emphasis until the 1960s

1918

May   The Relief Society sells 205,518 bushels of grain, accumulated by the women in response to an 1876 request by Brigham Young, to the U.S. government

October 3   Joseph F. Smith receives a revelation concerning salvation of the dead, which is canonized in 1979

November 19   Joseph F. Smith dies in Salt Lake City; on November 23 the First Presidency is reorganized with Heber J. Grant as president and Anthon H. Lund and Charles W. Penrose as counselors

1921   In a major re-edition of the Doctrine and Covenants, the Lectures on Faith are dropped and the text is divided into columns, with improved footnotes, headnotes, and index

1922

May   Primary Children's Hospital, financed by the children of the Church and administered largely by women heading the Primary, opens in Salt Lake City

1929

July 15   A Mormon Tabernacle Choir program is broadcast over the radio, beginning a weekly tradition that remains unbroken

1936

April   The Church Security Program (now the Welfare Program) is introduced to address the temporal needs of Church members facing emergencies

1937

July   The Hill Cumorah Pageant, a dramatic and musical performance, is produced at the Hill Cumorah; rewritten several times through the years, the pageant remains a yearly activity

1938

August 14   The first Deseret Industries thrift store, part of the Church Security Program, opens in Salt Lake City

November   The Church begins a massive microfilming project to gather and preserve the world's genealogical records

1941   A central membership record system administered by the Presiding Bishop's Office ends a century-old practice of members carrying individual certificates to transfer membership from one location to another

1942

January 17   The First Presidency requests discontinuance of many auxiliary activities to preserve resources for the duration of World War II; this request is followed by further cutbacks at later dates, including the cancellation of the March 1942 celebration of the Relief Society centennial and the cessation of calls for draft-age missionaries; however, the austerity program is softened to allow for the production of several publications and other aids to Church members in the armed forces

1945

May 14   Heber J. Grant dies in Salt Lake City; on May 21, the First Presidency is reorganized with George Albert Smith as president and J. Reuben Clark and David O. McKay as counselors

November 3   George Albert Smith meets with Harry S. Truman to arrange permission for the Church to begin private welfare shipments to suffering Saints in the former war zones; the first supplies are shipped in January 1946

1946

February 3   Apostle Ezra Taft Benson leaves for Europe to reestablish contact with Church members in former war zones and to administer personally to their welfare needs

1947

July 24   The centennial of the Mormon pioneer arrival in the Salt Lake Valley is observed

November   Church members in former war zones begin providing aid to fellow Saints, commencing with the donation of 75 tons of potatoes raised by Dutch Saints for those in Germany

December 20   George Albert Smith announces a major new initiative to expand missionary work throughout the world

1949

October   General conference is publicly broadcast via television for the first time

1950

September   The first early-morning seminary classes for high school students are held, in California

1951

April   George Albert Smith dies in Salt Lake City; on April 9, the First Presidency is reorganized with David O. McKay as president and Stephen L. Richards and J. Reuben Clark Jr. as counselors

November 25   Apostle Ezra Taft Benson is named Secretary of Agriculture in Dwight D. Eisenhower's administration; he serves for eight years

1961

November   A Language Training Institute is inaugurated at BYU to provide the first formal language training for outgoing missionaries

1965

September   A quota of two missionaries per ward is established to comply with U.S. draft board request

1966

June 22   Underground vaults in Little Cottonwood Canyon near Salt Lake City, intended for the preservation of Church records, are dedicated

1967

November   The Church acquires, by gift of the New York Metropolitan Museum of Art, portions of the Egyptian papyri once owned by Joseph Smith and long thought to have been destroyed in the 1871 Chicago fire

1970

January 18   David O. McKay dies at Salt Lake City; on January 23, the First Presidency is reorganized with Joseph Fielding Smith as president and Harold B. Lee and N. Eldon Tanner as counselors

1971

January   New Church magazines, still in publication, are inaugurated: the *Ensign* for adults, *New Era* for youth, and *Friend* for children

1972

July 2   Joseph Fielding Smith dies at Salt Lake City; on July 7, the First Presidency is reorganized with Harold B. Lee as president and N. Eldon Tanner and Marion G. Romney as counselors

1973

December 26   Harold B. Lee dies at Salt Lake City; on December 30 the First Presidency is reorganized with Spencer W. Kimball as president and N. Eldon Tanner and Marion G. Romney as counselors

1974

September 6   The Church divests itself of 15 hospitals, a move completed on March 21, 1975

July 24   The Church Office Building is dedicated at Salt Lake City

1975

October 3   Spencer W. Kimball announces the organization of the First Quorum of the Seventy; over the next 30 years, additional Quorums are organized and partially staffed, greatly aiding missionary work and the governing of a rapidly expanding worldwide Church

1978

June 9   A letter dated June 8 issued by the First Presidency announces that henceforth all worthy male members, regardless of race, will be ordained to the priesthood; the decision is endorsed as revelation by a sustaining vote of the general conference on September 30

| September | A new Missionary Training Center at Provo, Utah, replaces the mission homes of Salt Lake City; in following years, missionary training centers are opened in several countries worldwide |

1979

| September 29 | A new edition of the King James Bible with extensive study aids created by the Church is published, followed in 1980 by a similar re-edition of the other three books of scripture |

1980

| March 2 | Beginning with units in the U.S. and Canada, the Church adopts a three-hour consolidated block of Sunday meetings; that schedule is now followed worldwide |

1981

| July 23 | Gordon B. Hinckley is called as an additional counselor in the First Presidency |

1982

| October 3 | A subtitle, "another Testament of Jesus Christ," is added to the Book of Mormon title page |

1985

June 29	A temple is dedicated at Freiberg, German Democratic Republic, the first temple built in a communist country
August 2	A new hymn book is published, replacing the one used for 37 years
November 5	Spencer W. Kimball dies at Salt Lake City; on November 10, the First Presidency is reorganized with Ezra Taft Benson as president and Gordon B. Hinckley and Thomas S. Monson as counselors

1987

| September 4 | The International Mission is discontinued, with oversight for lands outside organized missions and stakes passing to respective area presidencies |

1989

| May 16 | The BYU Jerusalem Center for Near Eastern Studies is dedicated |

1994

| May 30 | Ezra Taft Benson dies at Salt Lake City; on June 5, the First Presidency is reorganized with Howard W. Hunter as president and Gordon B. Hinckley and Thomas S. Monson as counselors |

1995

| March 3 | Howard W. Hunter dies at Salt Lake City; on March 12, the First Presidency is reorganized with Gordon B. Hinckley as president and Thomas S. Monson and James E. Faust as counselors |
| September 23 | A "Proclamation to the World on the Family" is issued |

1997

April–July   A commemorative wagon train honoring the Mormon pioneers travels from Council Bluffs, Iowa, and Winter Quarters, Nebraska, to Salt Lake City

October 4   The building of smaller temples in remote parts of the world with relatively small LDS populations is announced

1999

April 4   The reconstruction of the historic Nauvoo Temple is announced

2000

April   A new Conference Center in Salt Lake City is dedicated

September   Non-English speaking Saints became a majority of Church members

2001

March 31   A Perpetual Education Fund, modeled after the 19th-century Perpetual Emigrating Fund, is announced

2005

January 2   Church members are asked to donate "most generously" to efforts to relieve sufferers of the December 26, 2004, tsunami that devastated southern Asia

October 7   Ground is broken for a new Church History Library, to be opened in June 2009

2007

March 31   The renovated Salt Lake Tabernacle reopens

2008

January 27   Gordon B. Hinckley dies at Salt Lake City; the First Presidency is reorganized with Thomas S. Monson as president and Dieter F. Uchtdorf and Henry B. Eyring as counselors

SELECTED BIBLIOGRAPHY

Alexander, Thomas G. "Church and Community: Latter-day Saint Women in the Progressive Era, 1890–1930." In *New Scholarship on Latter-day Saint Women in the Twentieth Century*. Ed. Carol Cornwall Madsen and Cherry B. Silver. Provo, UT: Joseph Fielding Smith Institute for Latter-day Saint History, 2005.

Alexander, Thomas G. *Mormonism in Transition: A History of the Latter-day Saints, 1890–1930*. Urbana: University of Illinois Press, 1986.

Alexander, Thomas G. "The Reconstruction of Mormon Doctrine." *Sunstone* 5:4 (July–August 1980): 24–33.

Alexander, Thomas G. *Things in Heaven and Earth: The Life and Times of Wilford Woodruff, a Mormon Prophet*. Salt Lake City, UT: Signature Books, 1991.

Alexander, Thomas G. *Utah: The Right Place. The Official Centennial History*. Salt Lake City, UT: Gibbs Smith Publisher, 1995.

Alexander, Thomas G. "The Word of Wisdom: From Principle to Requirement." *Dialogue: A Journal of Mormon Thought* 14, no. 3 (1981): 78–88.

Alexander, Thomas G., ed. *Great Basin Kingdom Revisited: Contemporary Perspectives*. Logan: Utah State University Press, 1991.

Alexander, Thomas G., and James B. Allen. *Mormons and Gentiles: A History of Salt Lake City*. Western Urban History Series, vol. 5. Boulder, CO: Pruett, 1984.

Allen, James B. "Everyday Life in Utah's Elementary Schools, 1847–1870." In *Nearly Everything Imaginable: The Everyday Life of Utah's Mormon Pioneers*. Ed. Ronald W. Walker and Doris R. Dant, 358–385. Provo, UT: Brigham Young University Press, 1999.

Allen, James B. "The Significance of Joseph Smith's 'First Vision' In Mormon Thought." *Dialogue: A Journal of Mormon Thought* 1 (Autumn 1966): 29–45.

Allen, James B., and Glen M. Leonard. *The Story of the Latter-day Saints*, rev. and enlarged ed. Salt Lake City, UT: Deseret Book, 1992.

Allen, James B., Ronald K. Esplin, and David J. Whittaker. *Men with a Mission: The Quorum of the Twelve Apostles in the British Isles*. Salt Lake City, UT: Deseret Book, 1992.

Anderson, Edward H. "The Past of Mutual Improvement." *Improvement Era* 1, no. 1 (November 1897): 1–10.

Anderson, Joseph. *Prophets I Have Known*. Salt Lake City, UT: Deseret Book, 1973.

Anderson, Lavina Fielding. *Doves and Serpents: The Activities of Leonard Arrington as Church Historian, 1972–1982*. Salt Lake City, UT, 1982, privately circulated.

Arrington, Leonard J. *Adventures of a Church Historian*. Urbana: University of Illinois Press, 1998.

Arrington, Leonard J. *Brigham Young: American Moses*. New York: Knopf, 1985.

Arrington, Leonard J. "Cooperative Community in the North: Brigham City, Utah." *Utah Historical Quarterly* 33 (1965): 198–217.

Arrington, Leonard J. *Great Basin Kingdom: An Economic History of the Latter-day Saints, 1830–1900.* Cambridge, MA: Harvard University Press, 1958.

Arrington, Leonard J. "Joseph Fielding Smith: Faithful Historian." *Dialogue: A Journal of Mormon Thought* 7, no. 1 (1972): 21–26.

Arrington, Leonard J. "Joseph F. Smith: From Impulsive Young Man to Patriarchal Prophet." *John Whitmer Historical Association Journal* 4 (1984): 30–40.

Arrington, Leonard J. "The Mormon Tithing House: A Frontier Business Institution." *Business History Review* 28 (1954): 24–58.

Arrington, Leonard J., ed. *The Presidents of the Church: Essays on the Lives and Messages of the Prophets.* Salt Lake City, UT: Deseret Book, 1986.

Arrington, Leonard J., and Davis Bitton. *The Mormon Experience: A History of the Latter-day Saints.* New York: Knopf, 1979.

Ashton, Wendell J. "Gordon B. Hinckley of the Quorum of the Twelve." *Improvement Era* 64 (December 1961): 906–907, 978–983.

Backman, Milton V. *The Heavens Resound: History of the Latter-day Saints in Ohio, 1830–1838.* Salt Lake City, UT: Deseret Book, 1983.

Bagley, Will. *Blood of the Prophets: Brigham Young and the Mountain Meadows Massacre.* Norman: University of Oklahoma Press, 2002.

Barlow, Philip L. *Mormons and the Bible: The Place of the Latter-day Saints in American Religion.* New York: Oxford University Press, 1991.

Barney, Kevin L. "The Joseph Smith Translation and Ancient Texts of the Bible." *Dialogue: A Journal of Mormon Thought* 19, no. 3 (Fall 1986): 85–102.

Baugh, Alexander L. *A Call to Arms: The 1838 Mormon Defense of Northern Missouri.* Provo, UT: BYU Studies, 2000.

Baugh, Alexander L. "Joseph Young's Affidavit of the Massacre at Haun's Mill." *BYU Studies* 38, no. 1 (1999): 188–202.

Baugh, Alexander L. "We Took Our Change of Venue to the State of Illinois: The Gallatin Hearing and the Escape of Joseph Smith and the Mormon Prisoners from Missouri, April 1839." *Mormon Historical Studies* 2, no. 1 (Spring 2001): 59–82.

Beadle, J. H. *Life in Utah, or the Mysteries and Crimes of Mormonism: Being an Exposé of the Secret Rites and Ceremonies of the Latter Day Saints.* Philadelphia, PA: National Publishing, 1870.

Bennion, M. Lynn. *Mormonism and Education.* Salt Lake City, UT: The Church of Jesus Christ of Latter-day Saints, 1939.

Berrett, William E. *A Miracle in Weekday Religious Education.* Salt Lake City, UT: Salt Lake Printing Center, 1988.

Bigler, David L. "The Aiken Party Executions and the Utah War, 1857–1858." *Western Historical Quarterly* 38 (Winter 2007): 457–476.

Bigler, David L. *Forgotten Kingdom: The Mormon Theocracy in the American West, 1847–1896.* Spokane, WA: Arthur H. Clark, 1998.

Bigler, David L., and Will Bagley, eds. *Army of Israel: Mormon Battalion Narratives.* Spokane, WA: Arthur H. Clark, 2000.

Bigler, David L., and Will Bagley, eds. *Innocent Blood: Essential Narratives of the Mountain Meadows Massacre.* Norman: University of Oklahoma Press, Arthur H. Clark, 2008.

Bishop, W. W., ed. *Mormonism Unveiled; or the Life and Confessions of the Late Mormon Bishop, John D. Lee; (Written by Himself)*. St. Louis, MO: Bryan, Brand, 1877.

Bitton, Davis. *George Q. Cannon*. Salt Lake City, UT: Deseret Book, 1999.

Bitton, Davis. "H. Roberts at the World Parliament of Religions." *Sunstone* 7 (January–February 1982): 46–51.

Blair, Alma R. "The Haun's Mill Massacre." *BYU Studies* 13 (Autumn 1972): 62–67.

Blanke, Gustav. "God's Base of Operations: Mormon Variations on the American Sense of Mission." *BYU Studies* 20, no. 1 (Fall 1979): 83–92.

Bradford, Mary Lythgoe. "Lowell Bennion and the Raspberry Cure." *This People* (Fall 1996): 70–80.

Britsch, R. Lanier. "Latter-day Saint Education in the Pacific Islands." In *New Views of Mormon History: A Collection of Essays in Honor of Leonard J. Arrington*. Ed. Davis Bitton and Maureen Ursenbach Beecher. Salt Lake City: University of Utah Press, 1987.

Britsch, R. Lanier. *Unto the Islands of the Sea: A History of the Latter-day Saints in the Pacific*. Salt Lake City, UT: Deseret Book, 1986.

Brodie, Fawn M. *No Man Knows My History*. New York: Knopf, 1945.

Brooke, John L. *The Refiner's Fire: The Making of Mormon Cosmology, 1644–1844*. New York: Cambridge University Press, 1994.

Brooks, Juanita. *The Mountain Meadows Massacre*. Norman: University of Oklahoma Press, 1950, rev., 1962, 1970.

Brown, Richard Maxwell. *No Duty to Retreat: Violence and Values in American History and Society*. New York: Oxford University Press, 1991.

Brown, Richard Maxwell. *Strain of Violence: Historical Studies of American Violence and Vigilantism*. New York: Oxford University Press, 1975.

Brown, Richard Maxwell, ed. *American Violence*. Englewood Cliff, NJ: Prentice-Hall, 1970.

Bush, Lester E., Jr. *Health and Medicine among the Latter-day Saints: Science, Sense, and Scripture*. New York: Crossroad, 1993.

Bush, Lester E., Jr. "Mormonism's Negro Doctrine: An Historical Overview." *Dialogue* 8 (Spring 1973): 11–68.

Bush, Lester E., Jr. "The Mormon Tradition." In *Caring and Curing: Health and Medicine in Western Religion Traditions*. Ed. Ronald L. Numbers and Darrell W. Amundsen, 397–420. New York: Macmillan, 1986.

Bush, Lester E., Jr. "The Word of Wisdom in Early Nineteenth-Century Perspective." *Dialogue: A Journal of Mormon Thought* 14, no. 3 (1981): 46–65.

Bush, Lester E., Jr., and Armand L. Mauss, eds. *Neither White nor Black: Mormon Scholars Confront the Race Issue in a Universal Church*. Midvale, UT: Signature Books, 1984.

Bushman, Claudia L., ed. *Mormon Sisters: Women in Early Utah*. Cambridge, MA: Emmeline, 1976.

Bushman, Claudia L., and Richard L. Bushman. *Mormons in America*. New York: Oxford University Press, 1998.

Bushman, Richard L. *Joseph Smith: Rough Stone Rolling: A Cultural Biography of Mormonism's Founder*. New York: Knopf, 2005.

Bushman, Richard Lyman. *Joseph Smith and the Beginnings of Mormonism.* Urbana: University of Illinois Press, 1987.

Bushman, Richard Lyman. *Making Space for the Mormons.* Leonard J. Arrington Mormon History Lecture Series No. 2. Logan: Utah State University Press, 1997.

Bushman, Richard Lyman. *Mormonism: A Very Short Introduction.* New York: Oxford University Press, 2008.

Bushman, Richard Lyman, and Claudia L. Bushman. *Building the Kingdom of God.* New York: Oxford University Press, 2001.

Cadman, William H., et al. *A History of the Church of Jesus Christ of Latter Day Saints.* 2 vols. Monogehela, PA: The Church of Jesus Christ, 2002–2004.

Campbell, Bruce L., and Eugene E. Campbell. "The Mormon Family." In *Ethnic Families in America: Patterns and Variations.* Ed. Charles H. Mindel, Robert W. Habenstein, and Roosevelt Wright, Jr., 456–494. New York: Elsevier Science, 1988.

Campbell, Eugene E. *Establishing Zion: The Mormon Church in the American West, 1847–1869.* Salt Lake City, UT: Signature Books, 1988.

Cannon, Brian Q. "What a Power We Will Be in This Land: The LDS Church, the Church Security Program, and the New Deal." *Journal of the West* 43 (Fall 2004): 66–75.

Carmack, John K. *A Bright Ray of Hope: The Perpetual Education Fund.* Salt Lake City, UT: Deseret Book, 2004.

Christian, Lewis Clark. "Mormon Foreknowledge of the West." *BYU Studies* 21 (Fall 1981): 403–415.

Christy, Howard A. Christy. "Open Hand and Mailed Fist: Mormon-Indian Relations in Utah, 1847–52." *Utah Historical Quarterly* 46 (Summer 1978): 216–235.

Clark, James R. *Messages of the First Presidency.* 6 vols. Salt Lake City, UT: Bookcraft, 1965–1975.

Cohen, Stanley. *Folk Devils and Social Panics.* New Haven, CT: Yale University Press, 1973, rev., 2003.

Compton, Todd. *In Sacred Loneliness: The Plural Wives of Joseph Smith.* Salt Lake City, UT: Signature Books, 1997.

Corcoran, Brent, ed. *Multiply and Replenish: Mormon Essays on Sex and Family.* Salt Lake City, UT: Signature Books, 1994.

Cornwall, Marie, Tim B. Heaton, and Lawrence A. Young, eds. *Contemporary Mormonism: Social Science Perspectives.* Urbana: University of Illinois Press, 1994.

Corrill, John. *A Brief History of the Church of Christ of Latter Day Saints.* St. Louis, MO: John Corrill, 1839.

Cowan, Richard O. *The Church in the Twentieth Century.* Salt Lake City, UT: Bookcraft, 1985.

Cowan, Richard O. *The Latter-day Saint Century.* Salt Lake City, UT: Bookcraft, 1999.

Cowan, Richard O. *Temples to Dot the Earth.* Salt Lake City, UT: Bookcraft, 1989.

Crawley, Peter, and Richard L. Anderson. "The Political and Social Realities of Zion's Camp." *BYU Studies* 14 (1974): 406–420.

Culmsee, Carlton. *Utah's Black Hawk War: Lore and Reminiscences of Participants.* Logan: Utah State University Press/Western Text Society, 1973.

Davies, Douglas J. *An Introduction to Mormonism.* New York: Cambridge University Press, 2003.

Davies, Douglas J. *The Mormon Culture of Salvation: Force, Grace, and Glory.* Burlington, VT: Ashgate, 2000.

Daynes, Kathryn M. *More Wives Than One: The Transformation of the Mormon Marriage System, 1830–1910.* Urbana: University of Illinois Press, 2001.

Derr, Jill Mulvay, Janeth Russell Cannon, and Maureen Ursenbach Beecher. *Women of Covenant: The Story of Relief Society.* Salt Lake City, UT: Deseret Book, 1992.

Devitry-Smith, John. "The Wreck of the Julia Ann." *BYU Studies* 29, no. 2 (Spring 1989): 5–29.

Doctrine and Covenants of the Church of Jesus Christ of Latter-day Saints. Salt Lake City, UT: The Church of Jesus Christ of Latter-day Saints, 1981.

Durham, G. Homer, ed. *The Gospel Kingdom: Selections from the Writings and Discourses of John Taylor.* Salt Lake City, UT: Bookcraft, 1987.

Dwyer, Robert. *The Gentile Comes to Utah: A Study in Religious and Social Conflict, 1862–1890,* rev. 2nd ed. Salt Lake City, UT: Publisher's Press, 1971.

Ehat, Andrew, and Lyndon W. Cook. *The Words of Joseph Smith.* Provo, UT: Grandin, 1993.

Eliason, Eric A. "Pioneers and Recapitulation of Mormon Popular Historical Expression." In *Usable Pasts: Traditions and Group Expressions in North America.* Ed. Tad Tuleja. Logan: Utah State University Press, 1997.

England, Eugene. "The Legacy of Lowell Bennion." *Sunstone* 19 (September 1996): 27–44.

Esplin, Ronald K. "'A Place Prepared': Joseph, Brigham, and the Quest for Promised Refuge in the West." *Journal of Mormon History* 9 (1982): 85–111.

Esplin, Scott C. "Education in Transition: Church and State Relationships in Utah Education, 1888–1933." Ph.D. dissertation, Brigham Young University, 2006.

Eyring, Henry. *Reflections of a Scientist.* Salt Lake City, UT: Deseret Book, 1983.

Farmer, Jared. *On Zion's Mount: Mormons, Indians, and the American Landscape.* Cambridge, MA: Harvard University Press, 2008.

Firmage, Edwin Brown, and R. Collin Mangrum. *Zion in the Courts: A Legal History of the Church of Jesus Christ of Latter-day Saints, 1830–1900.* Urbana: University of Illinois Press, 1988.

Flake, Kathleen. *The Politics of Religious Identity: The Seating of Reed Smoot, Mormon Apostle.* Chapel Hill: University of North Carolina Press, 2004.

Flake, Kathleen. "Translating Time: The Nature and Function of Joseph Smith's Narrative Canon." *Journal of Religion* 87 (October 2007): 497–527.

Flanders, Robert B. *Nauvoo: Kingdom on the Mississippi.* Urbana: University of Illinois Press, 1965.

Fleming, Stephen J. "An Examination of the Success of Early Mormonism in the Delaware Valley." M.A. thesis, California State University, Stanislaus, 2003.

Fleming, Stephen J. "Discord in the City of Brotherly Love: The Story of Early Mormonism in Philadelphia." *Mormon Historical Studies* 5, no. 1 (Spring 2004): 3–27.

Fletcher, Rupert J., and Daisy Whiting Fletcher. *Alpheus Cutler and the Church of Jesus Christ*. Independence, MO: The Church of Jesus Christ, 1974.

Flint, B. C. *An Outline History of the Church of Christ (Temple Lot)*. Independence, MO: Church of Christ Publication Board, 1953.

Fluhman, J. Spencer. "Anti-Mormonism and the Making of Religion in Antebellum America." PhD dissertation, University of Wisconsin-Madison, 2006.

Ford, Clyde. "The Origin of the Word of Wisdom." *Journal of Mormon History* 24 (Fall 1998): 129–154.

Furniss, Norman F. *The Mormon Conflict, 1850–1859*. New Haven, CT: Yale University Press, 1960; repr. 1977.

Galbraith, David B., and Blair G. Van Dyke. "The Jerusalem Center for Near Eastern Studies: Reflections of a Modern Pioneer." *The Religious Educator* 9, no. 1 (2008): 29–53.

Gates, Susa Young. *History of the Young Ladies' Mutual Improvement Association of the Church of Jesus Christ of Latter-day Saints from November 1869 to June 1910*. Salt Lake City, UT: General Board of the Y.L.M.I.A., 1911.

Gayler, George R. "Attempts by the State of Missouri to Extradite Joseph Smith, 1841–1843." *Missouri Historical Review* 58 (October 1963): 21–36.

Gibbons, Francis M. *Dynamic Disciples, Prophets of God: Life Stories of the Presidents of the Church of Jesus Christ of Latter-day Saints*. Salt Lake City, UT: Deseret Book, 1996.

Gibbons, Francis M. *The Expanding Church: Three Decades of Remarkable Growth among the Latter-day Saints, 1970–1999*. Bountiful, UT: Horizon, 1999.

Gibbons, Francis M. *Heber J. Grant: Man of Steel, Prophet of God*. Salt Lake City, UT: Deseret Book, 1979.

Gibbons, Francis M. *Spencer W. Kimball: Resolute Disciple, Prophet of God*. Salt Lake City, UT: Deseret Book, 1995.

Givens, Terryl L. *By the Hand of Mormon: The American Scripture That Launched a New World Religion*. New York: Oxford University Press, 2002.

Givens, Terryl L. *People of Paradox: A History of Mormon Culture*. New York: Oxford University Press, 2007.

Givens, Terryl L. *A Very Short Introduction to the Book of Mormon*. New York: Oxford University Press, 2009.

Godfrey, Kenneth W., Audrey M. Godfrey, and Jill Mulvay Derr, eds. *Women's Voices: An Untold History of the Latter-day Saints, 1830–1900*. Salt Lake City, UT: Deseret Book, 1982.

Godfrey, Matthew C. *Religion, Politics, and Sugar: The Mormon Church, the Federal Government, and the Utah-Idaho Sugar Company, 1907–1921*. Logan: Utah State University Press, 2007.

Gordon, Sarah Barringer. *The Mormon Question: Polygamy and Constitutional Conflict in Nineteenth-Century America*. Chapel Hill: University of North Carolina Press, 2002.

Gottesman, Ronald, and Raymond D. Brown, eds. *Violence in America: An Encyclopedia*. New York: Charles Scribner's Sons, 1999.

Gottfredson, Peter, ed. *History of Indian Depredations in Utah*. Salt Lake City, UT: Skelton, 1919.

Green, Paul R., comp. *Science and Your Faith in God: A Selected Compilation of Writings and Talks by Prominent Latter-day Saint Scientists on the Subject of Science and Religion.* Salt Lake City, UT: Bookcraft, 1958.

Grimsted, David. *American Mobbing, 1828–1861: Toward Civil War.* New York: Oxford University Press, 1998.

Hafen, Leroy R., and Ann W. Hafen. *Handcarts to Zion: The Story of a Unique Western Migration, 1856–1860.* Lincoln: University of Nebraska Press, 1992.

Hansen, Klaus J. *Quest for Empire: The Political Kingdom of God and the Council of Fifty in Mormon History.* Lansing: Michigan State University Press, 1967.

Hardy, B. Carmon. *Doing the Works of Abraham: Mormon Polygamy: Its Origin, Practice, and Demise.* Norman, OK: Arthur H. Clark, 2007.

Hardy, B. Carmon. *Solemn Covenant: The Mormon Polygamous Passage.* Urbana: University of Illinois Press, 1992.

Hardy, Grant, ed. *The Book of Mormon: A Reader's Edition.* Urbana: University of Illinois Press, 2003.

Hartley, William G. "Mormons, Crickets, and Gulls: A New Look at an Old Story." *Utah Historical Quarterly* 38 (Summer 1970): 224–239.

Haslam, James H. 1884. Interview by S. A. Kenner, reported by J. Rogerson. December 4. Typescript. Transcripts and Notes of John D. Lee Trials, Church History Library, The Church of Jesus Christ of Latter-day Saints, Salt Lake City, UT.

Hickman, Bill. J. H. Beadle, ed. *Brigham's Destroying Angel: Being the Life, Confession, and Startling Disclosures of the Notorious Bill Hickman, the Danite Chief of Utah.* Salt Lake City, UT: Shepard, 1904.

Hill, Marvin S. *Quest for Refuge: The Mormon Flight from American Pluralism.* Salt Lake City, UT: Signature Books, 1989.

Hill, Marvin S., C. Keith Rooker, and Larry T. Wimmer. *The Kirtland Economy Revisited: A Market Critique of Sectarian Economics.* Provo, UT: Brigham Young University Press, 1977.

Hinckley, Gordon B. *Discourses of President Gordon B. Hinckley.* Vol. 1: *1995–1999,* and Vol. 2: *2000–2004.* Salt Lake City, UT: Deseret Book, 2005.

Holland, Jeffrey R. "President Gordon B. Hinckley: Stalwart and Brave He Stands." *Ensign* 25 (June 1995): 2–13.

Holland, Jeffrey R. "President Thomas S. Monson: Man of Action, Man of Faith, Always 'on the Lord's Errand.'" *Ensign* 16 (February 1986): 11–17.

Hollon, W. Eugene. *Frontier Violence: Another Look.* New York: Oxford University Press, 1974.

Howard, Richard P. *Restoration Scriptures: A Study of Their Textual Development,* 2nd ed. Independence, MO: Herald Publishing House, 1995.

Hughes, Richard, ed. *The American Quest for the Primitive Church.* Urbana: University of Illinois Press, 1988.

Hunter, J. Michael. "The Kinderhook Plates, the Tucson Artifacts, and Mormon Archaeological Zeal." *Journal of Mormon History* 31, no. 1 (Spring 2005): 31–70.

Hunter, Milton R. *Brigham Young the Colonizer.* Salt Lake City, UT: Deseret News Press, 1940.

Jenson, Andrew. 1892. Notes of discussion with William Barton. January. Mountain Meadows file, Jenson Collection, Church History Library, The Church of Jesus Christ of Latter-day Saints, Salt Lake City, UT.

Jessee, Dean C., Mark Ashurst-McGee, and Richard L. Jensen. *The Joseph Smith Papers: Journals.* Vol. 1: *1832–1839.* Salt Lake City, UT: Church Historian's Press, 2008.

Johnson, G. Wesley, and Marian Ashby Johnson. "On the Trail of the Twentieth-Century Mormon Outmigration." *BYU Studies* 46, no. 1 (2007): 41–83.

Journal History of the Church of Jesus Christ of Latter-day Saints (chronology of typed entries and newspaper clippings, 1830 to the Present). Family and Church History Department, Church of Jesus Christ of Latter-day Saints, Salt Lake City, UT.

Journal of Discourses. 26 vols. London: LDS Booksellers Depot, 1877.

Kerstetter, Todd M. *God's Country, Uncle Sam's Land: Faith and Conflict in the American West.* Urbana: University of Illinois Press, 2006.

Kimball, Edward L. *Lengthen Your Stride: The Presidency of Spencer W. Kimball.* Salt Lake City, UT: Deseret Book, 2005.

Kimball, Edward L. "Spencer W. Kimball and the Revelation on Priesthood." *BYU Studies* 47, no. 2 (2008): 5–78.

Kimball, James L., Jr. "The Nauvoo Charter: A Reinterpretation." *Journal of Illinois State Historical Society* 54 (Spring 1971): 66–78.

Kimball, Richard Ian. *Sports in Zion: Mormon Recreation, 1890–1940.* Urbana: University of Illinois Press, 2003.

Krakauer, Jon. *Under the Banner of Heaven: A Story of Violent Faith.* New York: Doubleday, 2003.

Kunz, Calvin S. "A History of Female Missionary Activity in the Church of Jesus Christ of Latter-day Saints, 1830–1898." M.A. thesis, Brigham Young University, Provo, UT 1976.

Larson, Gustive O. *The "Americanization" of Utah for Statehood.* San Marino, CA: Huntington Library, 1971.

Larson, Gustive O. "The Mormon Reformation." *Utah Historical Quarterly* 26 (January 1958): 45–63.

Launius, Roger D. *Zion's Camp: Expedition to Missouri, 1834.* Independence, MO: Herald Publishing House, 1984.

Leonard, Glen M. *Nauvoo: A Place of Peace, a People of Promise.* Salt Lake City, UT: Deseret Book, 2001.

Leone, Mark P. *Roots of Modern Mormonism.* Cambridge, MA: Harvard University Press, 1979.

LeSueur, Stephen C. "The Danites Reconsidered: Were They Vigilantes or Just the Mormons' Version of the Elks Club?" *John Whitmer Historical Association Journal* 14 (1994): 35–51.

LeSueur, Stephen C. *The 1838 Mormon War in Missouri.* Columbia: University of Missouri Press, 1987.

Logue, Larry M. *A Sermon in the Desert: Belief and Behavior in Early St. George, Utah.* Urbana: University of Illinois Press, 1988.

Lund, Anthon H. *The Diaries of Anthon H. Lund, 1890–1921.* Ed. John P. Hatch. Salt Lake City, UT: Deseret Book, 2006.

Lyman, Edward Leo. "George Q. Cannon's Economic Strategy in the 1890s Depression." *Journal of Mormon History* 29 (Fall 2003): 4–41.

Lyman, Edward Leo. *Political Deliverance: The Mormon Quest for Utah Statehood.* Urbana: University of Illinois Press, 1986.

MacKay, Kathryn L. "Women in Politics: Power in the Public Sphere." In *Women in Utah History: Paradigm or Paradox?* Ed. Patricia Lyn Scott and Linda Thatcher. Logan: Utah State University Press, 2005.

Mackelprang, Romel W. "'They Shall Be One Flesh': Sexuality and Contemporary Mormonism." In *Multiply and Replenish: Mormon Essays on Sex and Family.* Ed. Brent Corcoran, 47–66. Salt Lake City, UT: Signature Books, 1994.

MacKinnon, William P., ed. *At Sword's Point: A Documentary History of the Utah War.* 2 vols. Norman, OK: Arthur H. Clark, 2008 and forthcoming.

Madsen, Brigham D., ed. *Studies of the Book of Mormon.* Urbana: University of Illinois Press, 1985; Salt Lake City, UT: Signature Books, 1992.

Madsen, Carol Cornwall. *An Advocate for Women: The Public Life of Emmeline B. Wells, 1870–1920.* Provo, UT: Brigham Young University Press; Salt Lake City, UT: Deseret Book, 2006.

Madsen, David B., and Brigham D. Madsen. "One Man's Meat Is Another Man's Poison: A Revisionist View of the Seagull Miracle." *Nevada Historical Quarterly* 30 (1987): 165–181.

Marquardt, H. Michael, ed. *Early Patriarchal Blessings of the Church of Jesus Christ of Latter-day Saints.* Salt Lake City, UT: Smith-Pettit Foundation, 2007.

Marquardt, H. Michael, ed. *Joseph Smith's Revelations: Text and Commentary.* Salt Lake City, UT: Signature Books, 1999.

Marsh, Debra J. "Respectable Assassins: A Collective Biography and Socio-economic Study of the Carthage Mob." M.A. thesis, University of Utah, 2009.

Mauss, Armand. *All Abraham's Children: Changing Mormon Conceptions of Race and Lineage.* Urbana: University of Illinois Press, 2003.

Mauss, Armand. *The Angel and the Beehive: The Mormon Struggle with Assimilation.* Urbana: University of Illinois Press, 1994.

Maxwell, Neal A. "President Gordon B. Hinckley: The Spiritual Sculpting of a Righteous Soul." *Ensign* 12 (January 1982): 7–13.

May, Dean L. "A Demographic Portrait of the Mormons, 1830–1980." In *After 150 Years: Latter-day Saints in Sesquicentennial Perspective.* Ed. Thomas G. Alexander, and Jesse L. Embry, 39–69. Provo, UT: Charles Redd Center for Western Studies, 1983.

May, Dean L. "Utah Writ Small: Challenge and Change in Kane County's Past." *Utah Historical Quarterly* 53 (Spring 1985): 170–183.

McCue, Robert J. "Did the Word of Wisdom Become a Commandment in 1851?" *Dialogue: A Journal of Mormon Thought* 14, no. 3 (1981): 66–77.

McMurrin, Sterling. *The Theological Foundations of the Mormon Religion.* Salt Lake City: University of Utah Press, 1959.

Mead, Rebecca J. *How the Vote Was Won: Woman Suffrage in the Western United States, 1868–1914*. New York: New York University Press, 2004.

Menlove, Frances. "Morning Reflections While Standing on One Foot." *Sunstone* (October 2007): 7–9.

Merrill, Milton. "Reed Smoot: Apostle in Politics." Ph.D. dissertation, Columbia University, 1950.

Metcalfe, Brent Lee. *New Approaches to the Book of Mormon: Explorations in Critical Methodology*. Salt Lake City, UT: Signature Books, 1993.

Millet, Robert L. "Joseph Smith and Modern Mormonism: Orthodoxy, Neoorthodoxy, Tension, and Tradition." *BYU Studies* 29, no. 3 (1989): 49–68.

Monnett, John Daniel. "The Mormon Church and Its Private School System in Utah: The Emergence of the Academies, 1880–1892." PhD dissertation, University of Utah, 1984.

Monson, Thomas S. *Faith Rewarded: A Personal Account of Prophetic Promises to the East German Saints*. Salt Lake City, UT: Deseret Book, 1996.

Monson, Thomas S. *On the Lord's Errand: Memoirs of Thomas S. Monson*. Salt Lake City, UT: Privately printed, 1985.

Morgan, Dale. *The State of Deseret*. Logan: Utah State University Press, 1987.

Moyer, Jonathan H. "Dancing with the Devil: The Making of the Mormon-Republican Pact." PhD dissertation, University of Utah, 2009.

Mulder, William. *Homeward to Zion: The Mormon Migration from Scandinavia*. Minneapolis: University of Minnesota Press, 1957.

Neilson, Reid L., and Ronald W. Walker, eds. *Reflections of a Mormon Historian: Leonard J. Arrington on the New Mormon History*. Norman, OK: Arthur H. Clark, 2006.

Newell, Linda King, and Val Tippetts Avery. *Mormon Enigma: Emma Smith, Prophet's Wife, "Elect Lady," Polygamy's Foe, 1804–1879,* 2nd ed. Urbana: University of Illinois Press, 1994.

Newquist, Jerreld L., ed. *Gospel Truth: Discourses and Writings of President George Q. Cannon*. 2 vols. Salt Lake City, UT: Deseret Book, 1974.

Nielson, Reid L., ed. *Global Mormonism in the 21st Century*. Provo, UT: Religious Studies Center, Brigham Young University, 2008.

Nisbett, Richard E., and Dov Cohen. *Culture of Honor: The Psychology of Violence in the American South*. Boulder, CO: Westview Press, 1996.

Novak, Shannon A. *House of Mourning: A Biocultural History of the Mountain Meadows Massacre*. Salt Lake City: University of Utah Press, 2008.

Oaks, Dallin H., and Marvin S. Hill. *Carthage Conspiracy*. Urbana and Chicago: University of Illinois Press, 1979.

O'Dea, Thomas F. *The Mormons*. Chicago: University of Chicago Press, 1957.

Orton, Chad M. "The Martin Handcart Company at the Sweetwater: Another Look." *BYU Studies* 45, no. 3 (2006): 5–37.

Ostling, Richard N., and Joan K. Ostling. *Mormon America: The Power and the Promise*. Rev. edition. New York: HarperOne, 2007.

Packer, Boyd K. *The Holy Temple*. Salt Lake City, UT: Bookcraft, 1980.

Palmer, Spencer J., Roger R. Keller, Dong Sull Choi, and James A. Toronto. *Religions of the World: A Latter-day Saint View,* rev. and enlarged ed. Provo, UT: Brigham Young University Press, 1997.

Parkin, Max H. "Joseph Smith and the United Firm." *BYU Studies* 46, no. 3 (2007): 1–73.

Parry, Donald W., Daniel C. Peterson, and Stephen D. Ricks, eds. *Revelation, Reason, and Faith: Essays in Honor of Truman G. Madsen.* Provo, UT: Foundation for Ancient Research and Mormon Studies, 2002.

Paulos, Michael Harold, ed. *The Mormon Church on Trial: Transcripts of the Reed Smoot Hearings.* Salt Lake City, UT: Signature Books, 2007.

Peterson, Charles S. "Life in a Village Society, 1877–1920." *Utah Historical Quarterly* 49 (Winter 1981): 78–96.

Peterson, Janet, and LaRene Gaunt. *Elect Ladies.* Salt Lake City, UT: Deseret Book, 1990.

Peterson, John Alton. *Utah's Black Hawk War.* Salt Lake City: University of Utah Press, 1998.

Peterson, Paul H. "The Mormon Reformation of 1856–1857: The Rhetoric and the Reality." *Journal of Mormon History* 15 (1989): 59–87.

Peterson, Paul H., and Ronald W. Walker. "Brigham Young's Word of Wisdom Legacy." *BYU Studies* 42, nos. 3 & 4 (2003): 29–64.

Poll, Richard D., Thomas G. Alexander, Eugene E. Campbell, and David E. Miller. *Utah's History.* Logan: Utah State University Press, 1989.

Prince, Gregory A. *Power from On High: The Development of Mormon Priesthood.* Salt Lake City, UT: Signature Books, 1995.

Prince, Gregory A., and Wm. Robert Wright. *David O. McKay and the Rise of Modern Mormonism.* Salt Lake City: University of Utah Press, 2005.

Proceedings before the Committee on Privileges and Elections of the United States Senate in the Matter of the Protests against the Right of Hon. Reed Smoot, a Senator from the State of Utah, to Hold His Seat. 4 vols. Washington, DC: Government Printing Office, 1904–1906.

Quinn, D. Michael. *J. Reuben Clark: The Church Years.* Provo, UT: Brigham Young University Press, 1983.

Quinn, D. Michael. "LDS Church Authority and New Plural Marriages, 1890–1904." *Dialogue: A Journal of Mormon Thought* 18 (Spring 1985): 9–105.

Quinn, D. Michael. "LDS Church Finances from the 1830s to the 1990s." *Sunstone* 19 (1996): 17–29.

Quinn, D. Michael. *The Mormon Hierarchy: Extensions of Power.* Salt Lake City, UT: Signature Books in association with Smith Research Associates, 1997.

Quinn, D. Michael. *The Mormon Hierarchy: Origins of Power.* Salt Lake City, UT: Signature Books, 1994.

Quinn, D. Michael. "Utah's Educational Innovation: LDS Religion Classes, 1890–1929." *Utah Historical Quarterly* 43 (Fall 1975): 379–389.

Reeve, W. Paul. "'As Ugly as Evil' and 'as Wicked as Hell': Gadianton Robbers and the Legend Process among the Mormons." *Journal of Mormon History* 27, no. 2 (Fall 2001): 125–149.

Reeve, W. Paul. *Making Space on the Western Frontier: Mormons, Miners, and Southern Paiutes.* Urbana: University of Illinois Press, 2006.

Reynolds, Noel B. "The Coming Forth of the Book of Mormon in the Twentieth Century." *BYU Studies* 38 (Spring 1999): 7–47.

Ricketts, Norma B. *The Mormon Battalion: U.S. Army of the West, 1846–1847.* Logan: Utah State University Press, 1996.

Roberts, B.H. *A Comprehensive History of the Church of Jesus Christ of Latter-day Saints.* 6 vols. Salt Lake City, UT: The Church of Jesus Christ of Latter-day Saints, 1930.

Robertson, Richard. "Mormon Inc.: Finances and Faith." *Arizona Republic,* June 30–July 3, 1991.

Rudd, Glen L. *Pure Religion: The Story of Church Welfare since 1930.* Salt Lake City, UT: The Church of Jesus Christ of Latter-day Saints, 1995.

Schlindler, Harold. *Orrin Porter Rockwell: Man of God, Son of Thunder.* Salt Lake City: University of Utah Press, 1966.

Sessions, Gene A. *Prophesying upon the Bones: J. Reuben Clark and the Foreign Debt Crisis, 1933–39.* Urbana: University of Illinois Press, 1992.

Sherlock, Richard. "We See No Advantage to a Continuation of the Discussion: The Roberts/Smith/Talmage Affar." *Dialogue: A Journal of Mormon Thought* 13, no. 3 (Fall 1980): 63–78.

Shields, Steven L. *The Latter Day Saint Churches: An Annotated Bibliography.* New York: Garland, 1987.

Shields, Steven L. *Divergent Paths of the Restoration.* Independence, MO: Herald House, 1990.

Shipps, Jan. *Mormonism: The Story of a New Religious Tradition.* Urbana: University of Illinois Press, 1987.

Shipps, Jan. *Sojourner in the Promised Land: Forty Years among the Mormons.* Urbana: University of Illinois Press, 2000.

Shipps, Jan, and John W. Welch. *The Journal of William E. McLellin, 1831–1836.* Urbana: University of Illinois Press, 1994.

Simpson, Thomas W. "Mormons Study Abroad: Latter-day Saints in American Higher Education, 1870–1940." PhD dissertation, University of Virginia, 2005.

Skousen, Royal. "Towards a Critical Text of the Book of Mormon." *BYU Studies* 30, no. 1 (Winter 1990): 41–69.

Slaughter, William W., and Michael Landon. *Trail of Hope: The Story of the Mormon Trail.* Salt Lake City, UT: Shadow Mountain, 1997.

Smith, George Albert. *Sharing the Gospel with Others.* Ed. Preston Nibley. Salt Lake City, UT: Deseret News Press, 1948.

Smith, Joseph Fielding. *Answers to Gospel Questions.* Salt Lake City, UT: Deseret Book, 1957–1966.

Smith, Joseph Fielding. *Essentials in Church History.* Salt Lake City, UT: Deseret News, 1922.

Smith, Joseph Fielding. *Life of Joseph F. Smith: Sixth President of the Church of Jesus Christ of Latter-day Saints.* Salt Lake City, UT: Deseret Book, 1938.

Smith, Joseph Fielding. *Man: His Origin and Destiny.* Salt Lake City, UT: Deseret Book, 1954.

Smith, Joseph, Jr. *History of the Church of Jesus Christ of Latter-day Saints.* 6 vols. Ed. B. H. Roberts. Salt Lake City, UT: The Church of Jesus Christ of Latter-day Saints, 1973.

Smith, Lucy. *Lucy's Book: A Critical Edition of Lucy Mack Smith's Family Memoir.* Ed. Lavina Fielding Anderson. Salt Lake City, UT: Signature Books, 2001.

Smoot, Reed. *In the World: The Diaries of Reed Smoot.* Ed. Harvard S. Heath. Salt Lake City, UT: Signature Books, 1997.

Sonne, Conway B. *Saints on the Seas: A Maritime History of Mormon Migration 1830–1890.* Salt Lake City: University of Utah Press, 1983.

Speek, Vickie Cleverly. *God Has Made Us a Kingdom.* Salt Lake City, UT: Signature Books, 2006.

Stegner, Wallace. *The Gathering of Zion: The Story of the Mormon Trail.* Lincoln and London: University of Nebraska Press, 1981.

Stubbs, Glen R. "A Biography of George Albert Smith, 1870–1951." Ph.D. dissertation, Brigham Young University, 1974.

Talmage, James E. *The Articles of Faith.* Salt Lake City, UT: Deseret News, 1899.

Talmage, James E. *The House of the Lord: A Study of Holy Sanctuaries Ancient and Modern.* Salt Lake City, UT: Deseret Book, 1974.

Tanner, Annie Clark. *A Mormon Mother.* Salt Lake City: University of Utah Library Tanner Trust Fund, 1991.

Taylor, P.A.M. *Expectations Westward: The Mormons and the Emigration of Their British Converts in the Nineteenth Century.* London: Oliver and Boyd, 1965.

Taylor, Samuel Woolley. *Rocky Mountain Empire: The Latter-day Saints Today.* New York: Macmillan, 1978.

Thomas, Darwin L. "Family in the Mormon Experience." In *Families and Religions: Conflict and Change in Modern Society.* Ed. William V. D'Antonio and Joan Aldous, 267–288. Beverly Hills, CA: Sage, 1983.

Thorndike, Edward L. "The Production, Retention and Attraction of Men of Science." *Science* 92 (August 16, 1940): 137–141.

Tullis, F. LaMond. *Mormons in Mexico: The Dynamics of Faith and Culture.* Logan: Utah State University Press, 1987.

Turley, Richard E., Jr., and Ronald W. Walker, eds. *Mountain Meadows Massacre Documents.* Provo, UT: Brigham Young University Press, 2009.

Underwood, Grant. *The Millenarian World of Early Mormonism.* Urbana: University of Illinois Press, 1993.

Van Orden, Bruce A. *Prisoner for Conscience Sake: The Life of George Reynolds.* Salt Lake City, UT: Deseret Book, 1992.

Van Wagoner, Richard S. *Mormon Polygamy: A History.* 3rd ed. Salt Lake City, UT: Signature Books, 1992.

Vogel, Dan. *Joseph Smith: The Making of a Prophet.* Salt Lake City, UT: Signature Books, 2004.

Vogel, Dan. *Religious Seekers and the Advent of Mormonism.* Salt Lake City, UT: Signature Books, 1988.

Vogel, Dan. "The Validity of the Witnesses' Testimonies." In *American Apocrypha.* Ed. Brent Metcalfe and Dan Vogel, 79–121. Salt Lake City, UT: Signature Books, 2002.

Vogel, Dan, ed. *Early Mormon Documents* (Vols. 1–5). Salt Lake City, UT: Signature Books, 1996–2003.

Walker, Ronald W. *Wayward Saints: The Godbeites and Brigham Young.* Urbana: University of Illinois Press, 1998.

Walker, Ronald W., Richard E. Turley Jr., and Glen M. Leonard. *Massacre at Mountain Meadows: An American Tragedy.* New York: Oxford University Press, 2008.

Welch, John W., ed. "The Worlds of Joseph Smith: A Bicentennial Conference at the Library of Congress." *BYU Studies* 44, no. 4 (2005).

Whittaker, David J. "Leonard James Arrington: His Life and Work" and "Bibliography of Leonard James Arrington." *Dialogue: A Journal of Mormon Thought* 11 (Winter 1978): 23–33, 33–47.

Wilkinson, Ernest L., ed. *Brigham Young University: The First One Hundred Years.* 4 vols. Provo, UT: Brigham Young University, 1975–1976.

Williams, Clyde J. *The Teachings of Lorenzo Snow, Fifth President of the Church of Jesus Christ of Latter-day Saints.* Salt Lake City, UT: Bookcraft, 1984.

Williams, P. W. *Houses of God: Region, Religion, and Architecture in the United States.* Urbana: University of Illinois Press, 1997.

Winder, Michael K., *Presidents and Prophets: The Story of America's Presidents and the LDS Church.* American Fork, UT: Covenant Communications, 2007.

Woods, Fred E., and Nicholas J. Evans. "Latter-day Saint Scandinavian Migration through Hull, England, 1852–1894." *BYU Studies* 41 no. 4 (Winter 2002): 75–102.

Yarn, David H., Jr., ed. *J. Reuben Clark: Selected Papers on Religion, Education and Youth; and J. Reuben Clark: Selected Papers on International Affairs.* Provo, UT: Brigham Young University Press, 1984.

ABOUT THE EDITORS

W. PAUL REEVE is an associate professor of history at the University of Utah and associate chair of the history department, where he teaches Utah history and history of the U.S. West. He is on the board of editors of the *Utah Historical Quarterly,* on the University of Utah Press Faculty Advisory Council, and on the governing board of the Mormon History Association. The University of Illinois Press published his first book, *Making Space on the Western Frontier: Mormons, Miners, and Southern Paiutes,* in April 2007. The Mormon History Association awarded *Making Space* the Smith-Pettit Best First Book award in 2008. His research has been supported by a Mayers Research Fellowship at the Huntington Library in San Marino, California, and by a Virgil C. Aldrich Research Fellowship at the Tanner Humanities Center at the University of Utah. He is writing a book, *Religion of a Different Color: Race and the Mormon Struggle for Whiteness,* to be published by Oxford University Press.

ARDIS E. PARSHALL is an award-winning independent historian living in Salt Lake City, Utah. The *Utah Historical Quarterly* published her article, "'Pursue, Retake and Punish': The 1857 Santa Clara Ambush," in 2005, and the Utah State Historical Society subsequently recognized it with the Dale L. Morgan Award for the best scholarly article of the year. Parshall has presented her research at a variety of scholarly conferences, including those of *Sunstone* magazine, the Utah State Historical Society, and the Mormon History Association. She writes a monthly history column for the *Salt Lake Tribune* and runs an award-winning solo history blog, Keepapitchinin.

LIST OF CONTRIBUTORS

Thomas G. Alexander
Brigham Young University, Emeritus

James B. Allen
Brigham Young University, Emeritus

Lavina Fielding Anderson
Salt Lake City, Utah

Lowell C. "Ben" Bennion
Humboldt State University, Emeritus

Gary James Bergera
The Smith-Pettit Foundation

Matthew Bowman
Georgetown University

Mary Lythgoe Bradford
Lansdowne, Virginia

Robert H. Briggs
Fullerton, California

Samuel Brown
University of Utah

Bruce A. Crow
White House, Tennessee

Kathryn M. Daynes
Brigham Young University

Brett D. Dowdle
Brigham Young University

Jessie L. Embry
Charles Redd Center
for Western Studies
Brigham Young University

Darius Aidan Gray
Salt Lake City, Utah

Matthew J. Grow
University of Southern Indiana

David W. Grua
Texas Christian University

David R. Hall
California State University, Fullerton

J. B. Haws
University of Utah

Blair Dee Hodges
University of Utah

David J. Howlett
University of Iowa

Edward H. Jeter
Sam Houston State University

Janiece Lyn Johnson
University of Utah

Jeffery O. Johnson
Salt Lake City, Utah

Christopher C. Jones
College of William and Mary

Sondra Jones
University of Utah

David Clark Knowlton
Utah Valley University

Bradley H. Kramer
University of Michigan

William P. MacKinnon
Santa Barbara, California

Debra J. Marsh
University of Utah

Armand L. Mauss
Washington State University, Emeritus

Alan L. Morrell
LDS Church History Library

Jonathan H. Moyer
University of Utah

Jacob W. Olmstead
Texas Christian University

Nathan B. Oman
College of William and Mary

Benjamin E. Park
University of Edinburgh

Boyd Jay Petersen
Utah Valley University

Levi S. Peterson
Issaquah, Washington

Gregory A. Prince
Potomac, Maryland

Andrea G. Radke-Moss
Brigham Young University-Idaho

Jennifer Reeder
George Mason University

Jan Shipps
Indiana University-Purdue
University, Indianapolis, Emeritus

Jason Smith
Duncan, Oklahoma

Julie Marie Smith
Round Rock, Texas

Jonathan A. Stapley
Bellevue, Washington

Jared Tamez
University of Texas, El Paso

Stephen C. Taysom
Cleveland State University

Stanley J. Thayne
University of North Carolina
at Chapel Hill

Amy Tanner Thiriot
Harleysville, Pennsylvania

Richard E. Turley Jr.
The Church of Jesus Christ
of Latter-day Saints

John G. Turner
University of South Alabama

Michele A. Welch
Utah Valley University

Jed Woodworth
University of Wisconsin-
Madison

Margaret Blair Young
Brigham Young University

INDEX